Pro WCF

Practical Microsoft SOA Implementation

Chris Peiris, Dennis Mulder, Shawn Cicoria, Amit Bahree, Nishith Pathak

Apress®

Pro WCF: Practical Microsoft SOA Implementation

ISBN-13 (pbk): 978-1-59059-702-6

ISBN-10 (pbk): 1-59059-702-8

Printed and bound in the United States of America 9 8 7 6 5 4 3 2

Lead Editor: Jon Hassell
Technical Reviewers: Vincent Bedus, Shawn Cicoria, Sylvain Groulx, Chris Peiris, Dennis Mulder
Editorial Board: Steve Anglin, Ewan Buckingham, Gary Cornell, Jason Gilmore, Jonathan Gennick, Jonathan Hassell, James Huddleston, Chris Mills, Matthew Moodie, Dominic Shakeshaft, Jim Sumser, Keir Thomas, Matt Wade
Project Manager: Denise Santoro Lincoln
Copy Edit Manager: Nicole Flores
Copy Editor: Kim Wimpsett
Assistant Production Director: Kari Brooks-Copony
Production Editor: Kelly Gunther
Compositor: Lynn L'Heureux
Proofreader: Elizabeth Berry
Indexer: Becky Hornyak
Artist: April Milne
Cover Designer: Kurt Krames
Manufacturing Director: Tom Debolski

Distributed to the book trade worldwide by Springer-Verlag New York, Inc., 233 Spring Street, 6th Floor, New York, NY 10013. Phone 1-800-SPRINGER, fax 201-348-4505, e-mail `orders-ny@springer-sbm.com`, or visit `http://www.springeronline.com`.

For information on translations, please contact Apress directly at 2560 Ninth Street, Suite 219, Berkeley, CA 94710. Phone 510-549-5930, fax 510-549-5939, e-mail `info@apress.com`, or visit `http://www.apress.com`.

The source code for this book is available to readers at `http://www.apress.com` in the Source Code/ Download section.

To my wife, Kushanthi, and my son, Keshera—you give me a reason to wake up every day and tackle the world head-on. Thank you also to my father, Christopher; mum, Shantha; and my brother, Gayan. It is your blessings and inspirations that get me through the hard times. Last but not least, a big thanks to Mr. Pinto and Mrs. Alwis who played a big part in my secondary education. You gave me wings to fly. I wouldn't have made it this far without your help.
—Chris Peiris

To my wife, Janneke—without your patience I wouldn't have been able to get my first book out of the door. I know that it wasn't easy to go through the past year with Anouk's birth and Amber's "childhood puberty" (she's a three year old). To my parents and my sister—thanks a lot for the heads-up and the interest you expressed in my writing.
—Dennis Mulder

I can safely say that I would've never been able to navigate through the past 16 years without my wife, Donna. She has been there for me countless times and is always someone who provides me with comfort, understanding, and lots of reality. And to my two little girls, Christine and Lauren, who to me represent what life is all about. I love them all dearly and couldn't make it through many days without knowing that I'll see their smiling faces and have enjoyable conversations that makes me feel like a kid again.
—Shawn Cicoria

To my wife, Meenakshi, without her support, patience, endless review sessions, ideas, and desire for perfection, this book would not have been possible. She provides the rational balance to my mad world.
—Amit Bahree

To my grandfather, Late Mahesh Chandra Pathak, for his blessings and moral values. To my parents, Pankaj and Bina Pathak, for being the best parents, and to my lovely sister, Tanwi, for her immense support and for teaching me to do what I believe in. I also appreciate the help, support, and encouragement from my mentor Mr. J.P. Kukreti and my dear friends (Amit Rawat, Piyush Suyal, Vikal Devlal, Harsh Nigam, and Shweta Bashani).
—Nishith Pathak

Contents at a Glance

PART 4 ■ ■ ■ Appendixes

Contents

PART 3 ■■■ Advanced Topics in WCF

PART 4 ■■■ Appendixes

Foreword

Modern distributed systems are based on the principles of Service-Oriented Architecture (SOA). This type of application architecture is based on loosely coupled and interoperable services. The global acceptance of web services has changed how these application components are defined and built. They're fueled by vendor agreements on standards and proven interoperability. This combination has helped set web services apart from other integration technologies. Windows Communication Foundation (WCF) is Microsoft's unified framework for building reliable, secure, transacted, and interoperable distributed applications. WCF represents a new step in distributed programming for developers using the .NET Framework. If you are planning or currently building systems using any of today's .NET distributed technologies, you should be paying close attention to WCF and the material in this book. It's only a matter of time before all .NET-targeted code related to communications will be written using WCF.

WCF is designed to offer a manageable approach to distributed computing, broad interoperability, and direct support for service orientation. As the name suggests, WCF provides the .NET Framework with a foundation for writing code to communicate across components, applications, and systems. WCF was completely designed with service orientation in mind. It is primarily implemented as a set of classes on top of the .NET Framework common language runtime (CLR). Because it was designed to extend the .NET Framework, WCF enables developers who are building object-oriented applications today to take their existing skills and start developing service-oriented applications.

SOA is an architectural pattern that has many different styles. To support this, WCF provides a layered architecture. At the bottom layer, WCF exposes a channel architecture that provides asynchronous, untyped messages. Built on top of this are protocol facilities for secure, reliable, transacted data exchange and a broad choice of transport and encoding options. While WCF introduces a new development environment for distributed application, it is designed to interoperate with non-WCF-based applications. WCF interoperability has two important aspects: interoperability with other platforms and interoperability with the Microsoft technologies that preceded WCF.

The typed programming model or service model exposed by WCF is designed to ease the development of distributed applications and provide developers with experience in an ASP.NET web service. .NET Remoting and Enterprise Services offer a familiar development experience with WCF. The service model features a straightforward mapping of web service concepts to the types of the .NET Framework CLR. This includes a flexible and extensible mapping of messages to service implementations found in the .NET languages. WCF also provides serialization facilities that enable loose coupling and versioning. At the same time, this provides integration and interoperability with existing .NET technologies such as MSMQ, COM+, and others. The result of this technology unification is greater flexibility and significantly reduced development complexity.

To allow more than just basic communication, WCF implements web service technologies defined by the WS-* specifications. These specifications address several areas, including basic messaging, security, reliability, and transactions, as well as working with a service's metadata.

Support for the WS-* protocols means that web services can easily take advantage of interoperable security, reliability, and transaction support required by businesses today. Developers can now focus on business logic and leave the underlying plumbing to WCF. WCF also provides opportunities for new messaging scenarios with support for additional transports such as TCP and Named Pipes and new channels such as the peer channel. More flexibility is also available around hosting web services. Windows Forms applications, ASP.NET applications, console applications, Windows services, and COM+ services can all easily host web service endpoints on any protocol. WCF also has many options for digitally signing and encrypting messages including support for Kerberos and X.509.

Building distributed systems using SOA is not a new concept. However, WCF represents a new paradigm in how these applications are developed using the .NET Framework 3.0. Each author has practical real-world experience in building and architecting distributed systems for a variety of customers. They also bring a wealth of knowledge and experience in their understanding of WCF and the .NET Framework. In this book they come together to present practical answers in building a good architecture, the options you have for communication, the various security concerns, and so much more.

This book doesn't merely offer genuine insight into solving real enterprise problems using WCF. It also provides extensive examples to make it easier to put these into practice. This book is definitely a great resource for application developers and architects new to SOA or just new to the core concepts of WCF. It is great to see a resource that both answers common questions and provides guidance that gets right to the point from experienced architects and developers. I hope you enjoy reading this book as much as I did and keep it close as you start building your own WCF applications.

Thom Robbins
Director, .NET Platform Marketing
Microsoft Corporation

About the Authors

CHRIS PEIRIS (MVP, MIT, BComp, BBus–Accounting) currently works for Avanade Australia as a solutions architect. Chris is an avid publisher and a thought leader in the application integration space. He is a frequent speaker at professional developer conferences on Microsoft technologies. In fact, he has been awarded the title Microsoft Most Valuable Professional (MVP) for his contributions to .NET technologies by Microsoft. Chris has been designing and architecting Microsoft IT solutions since 1995. He is an expert in developing scalable, high-performance integration solutions for financial institutions, G2G, B2B, and media groups. Chris has written many articles, reviews, and columns for various online publications including 15Seconds, Wrox (Apress), and Developer Exchange (DevX). He has also coauthored several books on web services, UDDI, C#, IIS, Java, and security topics. These include *C# Web Services*, *C# for Java Programmers*, *MCSA/MCSE Managing and Maintaining a Windows Server 2003 Environment*, and *Managing and Maintaining a Windows Server 2003 Environment for an MCSA Certified on Windows 2000*. Chris's current passions include WCF, IBM Message Broker, and EAI. He lives with his family in Conder, Australian Capital Territory, in Australia. He can be reached at `http://www.chrispeiris.com`.

DENNIS MULDER (MCSD, MCDBA) is senior principal consultant and solution manager with Avanade Netherlands and started his career in 1997. Since the beginning, he has dedicated himself to Microsoft technology. When the first betas of Microsoft .NET were released, he knew he made a good choice. As an early adopter of Microsoft technology, he has kept pace in the certification challenges and succeeded in getting several of his certifications in beta stage. Although Dennis has a broad range of experience on the Microsoft platform, in particular in web and database technology, his current focus is on service orientation, enterprise integration, and software factories. As a consultant he is working with enterprise customers to solve their challenges by leveraging the power of the Microsoft platform, usually in the role of architect and/or team lead. Dennis frequently publishes articles in *Microsoft .NET Magazine* (Dutch) and other (online) places. He is also an Ineta speaker and frequently speaks at Dutch Microsoft conferences and user groups. You can reach Dennis through his blog at `http://www.dennismulder.net`.

SHAWN CICORIA (MCT, MCSD, MCDBA) is a financial services industry solutions architect with Avanade (`www.avanade.com`), living with his family in Denville, New Jersey. He has an MBA in finance and information systems and a BA in economics. Shawn is also an MCT training instructor with SetFocus (`http://www.setfocus.com`), located in Parsippany, New Jersey. He has been working in systems for nearly 20 years mostly in financial services. Shawn has worked on many platforms including VMS, Unix variants, and for most of the past decade Microsoft Windows. He has focused on distributed technologies such as COM+, J2EE, and (for the past five years) .NET, SOAP, BizTalk, database technologies, and now .NET 3.0. You can reach him via his blog at `http://www.Cicoria.com`.

AMIT BAHREE is a senior solutions architect with Avanade with a degree in computer science and several years of experience in IT (more than he will admit), developing and designing mission-critical systems. His background is a mixture of product development, embedded systems, and custom solutions across both the public and private sectors. He has experience in a wide range of industry verticals including financial services, healthcare, defense, utilities, and insurance, and he has implemented solutions for many Fortune 100 companies. For Amit, computers are a passion first, a hobby second, and a career third, and he is glad he gets paid to do what he loves. Amit lives in London. You can contact him via his blog at `http://www.desigeek.com`.

NISHITH PATHAK is a budding solutions architect and a .NET purist who has been working on the .NET platform since its early beta days. Nishith was born, raised, and educated in a town called Kotdwara in Uttaranchal, India. Nishith has worked with companies such as Accenture and Avanade as an expert solution developer. His expertise is in delivering enterprise solutions to Fortune 100 companies spanning the globe. He is a contributing author and an avid technical reviewer for multiple electronic and print publications. Over the years, he has also been involved in providing consultancy and training services to corporations. You can contact him at `NisPathak@Hotmail.com` or visit his blog at `http://DotNetPathak.blogspot.com`.

About the Technical Reviewers

VINNY BEDUS currently works for Avanade as an application development capability group leader for the Metro New York (MNY) office. Vinny has been developing websites since 1994 and is currently a senior architect specializing in enterprise application development. He has more than ten years of experience with Microsoft technologies. He has worked with a variety of organizations ranging from Fortune 500 companies to Internet start-ups. He focuses on technologies such as the Microsoft .NET Compact Framework, Microsoft .NET Framework, C#, BizTalk, SQL Server, Visual Basic, XML, and web development. He is proficient on multiple platforms including Windows, Linux, and Solaris.

DENNIS MULDER

SHAWN CICORIA

Acknowledgments

This book is a collection of labor of many talented individuals. However, one person above all—Jon Hassell of Apress—deserves a special mention. I remember attending a Microsoft Early Adopter conference in 2003 and being exposed to a technology code-named Indigo. It was followed by an e-mail I put together (around 2 a.m.) to Jon. And, as they say, the rest is history. I should also extend my gratitude to Denise for her great job as the project manager. Kim and Kelly also come to mind with the copy edits. Thank you all for your contributions.

I also want to extend a special mention to Avanade management for their continuous assistance. We have been encouraged every step of the way by our management teams in Australia, Europe, US East, UK, France, Global (Seattle, Washington), and India. This would not have been possible without their generosity and encouragement.

A special mention also goes to our tech editors—Vincent Bedus and Sylvain Groulx. I also want to mention Chris Bunio (Microsoft) and Carl Ward (Accenture) for their contributions on an ad hoc basis. Your contributions definitely shaped the book content and gave us valuable insight into our target audience. Yumay Chang, Clemens Vasters, and Thom Robbins from Microsoft also come into mind for assisting us with tech reviews and marketing initiatives. Thanks a lot!

Last but not least, my partners in crime—Dennis, Shawn, Amit, Aftab and Nishith: it has been a great pleasure working with you! I should single out Dennis, Shawn, and Amit for taking on extra responsibilities to facilitate our tight deadlines. I am constantly amazed by your wealth of knowledge and thank you for the privilege of sharing your expertise with the wider IT community.

Chris Peiris
Canberra, Australia
November 2006

Thanks a lot to all the people within Avanade who supported my effort by talking about this book in meetings, bars, and other places: Edwin, Pieter, Andre, Mark, Albert, Willem, Matt, Tim, Kyle, Sumit, Karel, Antoine, Gerben, and the others I missed. A big thanks too to the people at Microsoft who tried to help out in busy times: Erik, Yumay, Steve, Clemens, and Thom.

Dennis Mulder
Almere, The Netherlands
November 2006

Introduction

This book explains the Windows Communication Foundation (WCF) from the Service-Oriented Architecture (SOA) perspective. It explains WCF as an evolution of the SOA concept, not as a "message bus" concept built on the next generation of Microsoft products. The book attempts to answer the following main questions:

- What is SOA?
- Why is WCF so important? What does it solve?
- How does WCF implement SOA principles?
- How does interoperability work between WCF and other SOA implementations?

We will provide answers to these questions by concentrating on the following important features of WCF:

- The WCF programming model
- The unified programming model
- The hosting options available for WCF web services
- How to make WCF web services secure
- How to manage these WCF services (and the tools available to manage them)
- How queue management and reliable messaging work in WCF
- How to implement transaction support in WCF
- How a WCF service interacts with COM+ components and how COM+ interacts with WCF service
- How to use data binding with WCF services
- Whether you can interop a WCF service with other (non-Microsoft) SOA offerings

We will also address the business drivers that dictate the need for these WCF feature. In addition, we'll explore the industry best practices in the process of addressing all these features.

Who This Book Is For

This book is targeted toward novice and intermediate readers who are curious about WCF. In this book, we'll do the following:

- Explain the business motives and pain points of the current SOA offerings.
- Explain how you can address these pain points by using WCF.
- Show practical implementations of these scenarios using code examples.

How This Book Is Structured

This book is divided into three parts, with a total of 13 chapters. The following sections describe each part. The book also has three appendixes, where you'll find a description of the sample application (QuickReturns Ltd), a history of Microsoft web service implementations, and WCF installation information.

Part 1: "Introducing Windows Communication Foundation"

This part of the book introduces web service standards and the fundamental components of SOA. We will also discuss how these principles are illustrated in WCF. Once you understand some of these concepts, including the business and technological factors, you can appreciate the simplicity and flexibility of WCF. Chapter 1 will cover the service standards. Then we will introduce WCF in Chapter 2. This is followed by a discussion of the WCF programming model in Chapter 3.

Part 2: "Programming with WCF"

In this part, we'll discuss the WCF technical features in detail. We'll concentrate on the programming aspects of WCF with the assistance of a fictitious QuickReturns Ltd. stock market application in Chapter 4. We'll initially guide you through installing WCF components. Then we'll walk you through creating services and hosting these services with WCF in Chapter 5. We will discuss all the hosting options available in WCF in detail. Finally, in Chapter 6, we'll cover the management options available to manage WCF services to obtain the best return on investment for your application.

Part 3: "Advanced Topics in WCF"

Real-world SOA applications will have many demanding features to implement. These complex real-world web service implementations will address security issues (both client and service), reliable messaging, transactions, COM+ integration, data integration issues, and peer-to-peer communications. An enterprise can achieve the eventual "value proposition" by utilizing these advanced features of WCF. In Chapters 7 through 12, you will concentrate on these topics. In addition, you'll investigate the WCF interoperability options available to seamlessly communicate with non-Microsoft platforms in Chapter 13.

Prerequisites

To get the most out of this book, you should install WCF/the .NET 3.0 Framework. You can download this for free from `http://wcf.netfx3.com/`. We also recommend using Microsoft Visual Studio as the development environment to experiment with the code samples, which you can find in the Source Code/Download section of the Apress website (`http://www.apress.com`).

Contacting the Authors

Most of the authors of this book have dedicated websites or blogs. Therefore, please refer to the "About the Authors" section to find individual contact information.

PART 1

Introducing Windows Communication Foundation

This part of the book introduces web service standards and fundamental components of Service-Oriented Architecture. We will also discuss how these principles are illustrated in Windows Communication Foundation (WCF). Once you have an understanding of some of these concepts, including the business and technological factors, you can appreciate the simplicity and flexibility of WCF. The first chapter will cover the services standards. Then we will introduce WCF in Chapter 2. This is followed by a discussion of the WCF programming model in Chapter 3.

CHAPTER 1

Introducing Service-Oriented Architecture

In today's world, implementing distributed systems that provide business value in a reliable fashion presents many challenges. We take many features for granted when developing nondistributed systems that can become issues when working with disparate distributed systems. Although some of these challenges are obvious (such as a loss of connectivity leading to data being lost or corrupted), for other aspects such as tightly coupled systems the dependencies between the various components of a system make it cost prohibitive to make changes as needed to meet the demands of the business.

Business processes quite often are supported by systems that are running on different platforms and technologies both within and outside the organization. Service-Oriented Architecture (SOA) is a mechanism that enables organizations to facilitate communication between the systems running on multiple platforms. This chapter introduces the fundamental concepts of SOA. The objective of this chapter is to discuss the following:

- What does SOA mean? How do you use messages, which act as the cornerstone for SOA implementations, to facilitate SOA?
- What makes SOA the preferred approach to design complex heterogeneous IT systems? Are web services the same as SOA?
- What are the four tenets of SOA?
- What are the implementation building blocks of SOA?
- How do you utilize all these building blocks to send messages between loosely coupled services?

Note To explain and demonstrate the various areas of Windows Communication Foundation (WCF), in this book we will show how to build an application that is modeled after a fictitious financial trading institution called QuickReturns Ltd. We will build a reference application that will articulate some of the challenges in today's enterprises and show how WCF can help solve some of the challenges. Each chapter will add functionality to this application, and you can download the code from the book's website. This case study will begin in Chapter 3.

What Is Service-Oriented Architecture?

It is not practical to build monolithic systems in current multinational enterprises. These systems often take many years to implement and usually address a narrow set of objectives. Today a business needs to be agile and adapt processes quickly, and SOA is a design principle that can help address this business need. SOA is a collection of *well-defined services*, where each individual service can be modified independently of other services to help respond to the ever-evolving market conditions of a business. Unlike traditional point-to-point architectures, an SOA implementation comprises one or more loosely coupled and interoperable set of application services. Although some of these aspects might be similar to a component-based development (which is based on strict interfaces), the key difference is SOA provides a message-based approach based on open standards. As a result of being based on open standards and using messages that are generic and not representative of any specific platform and programming language, you can achieve a high degree of loose coupling and interoperability across platforms and technologies. Each of these services is autonomous and provides one or more sets of business functions; in addition, since the underlying implementation details are hidden from the consumer, any change to the implementation will not affect the service as long as the contract does not change. This allows systems based on SOA to respond in a quicker and more cost-effective manner for the business.

For a business it is usually cheaper to "consume" an off-the-shelf application service that constitutes the solution instead of writing all the functionality. If a specific module needs to be updated for some reason, the company also benefits from the changes being confined to the specific service.

When coupled with industry-standard frameworks, service-based solutions provide the highly flexible "building blocks" that business systems require to compete in this age. Services encapsulate business processes into independently deliverable software modules. A service alone is just a building block; it is not a business solution but instead is an autonomous business system that is able to accept requests and whose interoperability is governed by various industry standards. These building blocks also provide the basis for increased improvements in quality and reliability and in the decrease of long-term costs for software development and maintenance.

In addition, even though there is a lot of talk about SOA today, point-to-point architectures are not disappearing. Many companies have invested a lot of resources in implementing proprietary solutions that mostly fulfill their business needs. SOA makes it easier to integrate point-to-point systems more easily because one system does not need to know the detailed mechanics of the other system. For those new to SOA, it is a little difficult to grasp this concept initially. This is primarily because SOA implementations target back-end systems. As a result, from a user's perspective, there are few user interface (UI) changes. However, you can also utilize SOA to provide front-end UI implementations. You can achieve this by combining service output XML with XSL to produce target HTML.

The SOA paradigm departs significantly from the OO model, where you are encouraged to encapsulate data. Therefore, an object will hold and protect the data to facilitate a business need. The enterprise will consist of multiple objects that are specialized to handle "specific scenarios" with the data protected within the objects. SOA instructs you to utilize loosely coupled services. The service describes the *contract* to the consuming entities. It does not tightly couple data to the service interface. It is also difficult to implement a single interface across all platforms and languages because of the nature of distributed systems. To fulfill the goals of

SOA, it is essential to implement the interfaces in a generic fashion. As a result, you need to express application-specific semantics in messages. The following are a few constraints for the messages that you need to consider when designing an SOA:

Descriptive: Messages need to be descriptive instead of prescriptive.

Limited structure: For different providers to understand the request, they need to understand the format, structure, and data types being used. This ensures maximum reach to all entities involved and limits the structure of the message. It also encourages you to use simple types, which are platform neutral.

Extensibility: Messages need to be extensible; only this provides the flexibility that allows SOA implementations to be quicker, faster, and cheaper than OO implementations.

Discoverability: Consumers and providers of messages need them to be discoverable so they know what is out there and how to consume the available services.

Disadvantages of Integrating Multiple Applications on Disparate Networks

We'll now discuss some challenges you'll face when you try to integrate multiple applications today. The following are some of the fundamental challenges when integrating multiple applications that reside on disparate physical networks:

Transports: Networks are not reliable and can be slow.

Data formats: The two applications in question are running on different platforms and using different programming languages, which makes interfacing with the various data types an interesting challenge.

Change: You know the applications need to change to keep up with the ever-evolving business requirements. This means any integration solution would need to ensure it could keep up with this change and minimize dependencies between the systems.

In the past, developers used several approaches to try to integrate applications in an enterprise. These approaches included file transfers, shared databases, remote procedure calls (RPC), and messaging. Although each of these approaches might make sense in some context, messages usually are more beneficial. We'll discuss some of the advantages of using messages in the following section.

Advantages of Using Messaging

The following are the advantages of using messages, like you do in SOA:

Cross-platform integration: Messages can be the "universal translator" between various platforms and languages, allowing each platform to work with their respective native data types.

Asynchronous communications: Messages usually allow for a "fire-and-forget" style of communication. This also allows for variable timing because both the sender and receiver can be running flat out and not be constrained by waiting on each other.

Reliable communication: Messages inherently use a "store-and-forward" style for delivery, which allows them to be more reliable than RPC.

Mediation: Messages can act as the mediator when using the Mediator pattern wherein an application that is disconnected needs to comment only to the messaging system and not to all the other applications.

Thread management: Since messages allow for asynchronous communication, this means one application does not have to block for the other to finish. Since this frees up many threads, the application can get to do other work overall, making it more efficient and flexible when managing its own threads.

Remote communication: Messages replace the need for the serialization and deserialization that occurs when one application makes a remote call to another application. Usually since these can be running on different process or even machines, the calls need to be marshaled across the network. The process of serializing an object to transfer over a network is called *marshaling*. Similarly, the process of deserializing an object on the other end is called *unmarshaling*.

End-to-end security: Unlike in the world of RPC, messages can transfer the "complete security context" to the consumer using a combination of headers and tokens. This greatly increases the ability to provide more granular control including authentication and authorization.

Messages are the "cornerstones" of SOA. Messages enable you to create loosely coupled systems that can span multiple operating systems. SOA relies on messages not only to facilitate the business need but also to provide the "context" around the message (that is, the security context, the routing information of the message, whether you need to guarantee the delivery of the message, and so on). Now you'll dive into more SOA details.

Understanding Service-Oriented Architecture

SOA and web services are the buzzwords that promise to solve all integration issues in the enterprise space. Although any kind of implementation can be an SOA implementation, unfortunately many implementations using web services are marketed as SOA implementations, when in reality they are not.

SOA can be simply defined as an architectural concept or style that uses a set of "services" to achieve the desired functionality. A *service* is an autonomous (business) system that accepts one or more requests and returns one or more responses via a set of published and well-defined interfaces. Unlike traditional tightly coupled architectures, SOA implements a set of loosely coupled services that collectively achieve the desired results.

■ **Note** It is important to understand that although SOA might seem abstract, it is a significant shift from the earlier days of procedural and object-oriented languages to a more loosely coupled set of autonomous tasks. SOA is more than a collection of services. It's a methodology encompassing policies, procedures, and best practices that allow the services to be provided and consumed effectively. SOA is not a "product" that can be bought off the shelf; however, many vendors have products that can form the basis of an SOA implementation.

It is important that the services don't get reduced to a set of interfaces because they are the key communication between the provider and the consumer. A *provider* is the entity providing the service, and the *consumer* is the entity consuming the service. In a traditional client-server world, the provider will be a server, and the consumer will be a client. When factoring in services, try to model the flow and process based on recognized business events and existing business processes. You also need to answer a few questions to ensure a clean design for services:

- What services do you need?
- What services are available for you to consume?
- What services will operate together?
- What substitute services are available?
- What dependencies exist between services and other versions of services?

Service orientation as described earlier is about services and messages. Figure 1-1 shows an example of how various service providers, consumers, and a repository coexist to form an SOA implementation. *Service providers* are components that execute some business logic based on predetermined inputs and outputs and expose this functionality through an SOA. A *consumer*, on the other hand, is a set of components interested in using one or more of the services offered by the providers. A *repository* contains a description of the services, where the providers register their services and consumers find what services are provided.

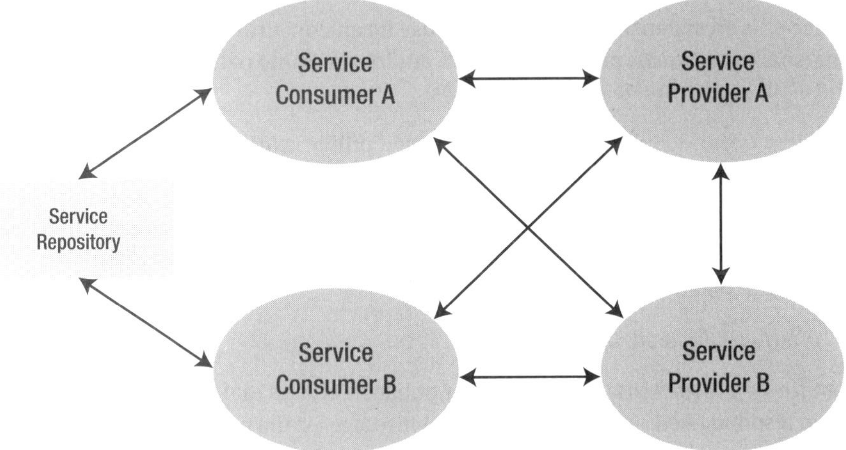

Figure 1-1. *How SOA components interact with each other*

What Is a Service?

The term *services* has been used to describe everything from web services (discussed in detail in the section "Web Services As a Key Enabling Technology for an SOA Implementation" later in the chapter) to business processes and everything in between. You should use services to represent the functions of the business and explicitly define the boundaries of what the business does, which essentially would define what the service can or cannot do. The key is that it is not a technology-driven approach but, rather, is a business-driven approach.

■ **Note** *Loose coupling* means any two entities involved reduce the assumptions they make about each other when they try to exchange information. As the level of assumptions made between two entities goes up (such as the kind of communication protocol used), so does the efficiency between the two entities; for example, the communication between the entities is very efficient. However, at the same time, the two entities are less tolerant to changes or, say, interruptions in the communication, because they are tightly bound or coupled to each other. Local method invocation is an excellent example of tight coupling because there are many assumptions made between the called routine and the calling routine, such as they both need to be in the same process, use the same language, pass the same number of parameters in the agreed data formats, and so on.

Service orientation is a business-driven "modeling strategy" that defines the business functionality in terms of loosely coupled autonomous business systems (or services) that exchange information based on messages. The term *services* is used in many contexts, but in the context of service orientation, a service is based on four fundamental tenets. We'll discuss these four tenets, originally proposed by the WCF team at Microsoft, in the following sections.

Tenet 1: Boundaries Are Explicit

Crossing boundaries is an expensive operation because it can constitute various elements such as data marshaling, security, physical location, and so on. Some of the design principles to keep in mind vis-à-vis the first tenet are as follows:

Know your boundaries: A well-defined and published public interface is the main entry point into the service, and all interactions occur using that.

Services should be easy to consume: It should be easy for other developers to consume the service. Also, the service interface should allow the ability to evolve over time without breaking existing consumers of the service.

Avoid RPC interfaces: Instead, use explicit messages.

Keep the service surface area small: Provide fewer public interfaces that accept a well-defined message, and respond likewise with a well-defined message. As the number of public interfaces grows, it becomes increasingly difficult to consume and maintain the service.

Don't expose implementation details: These should be kept internal; otherwise, it will lead to tight coupling between the consumer and the service.

Tenet 2: Services Are Autonomous

Services are self-contained and act independently in all aspects such as deploying, versioning, and so on. Any assumptions made to the contrary about the service boundaries will most likely cause the boundaries to change themselves. Services need to be isolated and decoupled to accomplish the goal of making them autonomous.

The design principles to keep in mind for the second tenet are as follows:

- Service versioning and deployment are independent of the system in which they are deployed.
- Contracts, once published, should not be changed.
- Adopt a pessimistic approach, and isolate services from failure.

■ **Note** Business Process Execution Language (BPEL) is a business process language that is based on XML and built using web service standards. You can use BPEL to define and manage a long-running business process. BPEL is an orchestration language and is used for abstracting the "collaboration and sequencing" logic from various web services into a formal process definition that is based on XML, Web Services Description Language (WSDL), and XML Schema. BPEL is also known as BPEL4WS or WSBPEL.

Tenet 3: Services Share the Schema and Contract, Not the Class

Services interaction should be using policies, schemas, and behaviors instead of classes, which have traditionally provided most of this functionality. The service contract should contain the message formats (defined using an XML schema), message exchange patterns (MEPs, which are defined in WSDL), any WS-Policy requirements, and any BPEL that may be required. The biggest challenge you face is the stability of the service, once it has been published. It gets difficult to change it then without impacting any of the consumers.

The design principles to keep in mind for the third tenet are as follows:

- Service contracts constituting data, WSDL, and the policy do not change and remain stable.
- Contracts should be as explicit as possible; this will ensure there is no confusion over the intent and use of the service. Additional contracts should be defined for newer versions of the server in the future.
- If breaking service contracts is inescapable, then version the services because this minimizes the ripple to existing consumers of the service.
- Do not expose internal data representation publicly; the public data scheme should be absolute.

Tenet 4: Service Compatibility Is Based on Policy

At times you will not be able to express all the requirements of service interaction via WSDL alone, which is when you can use policies. Policy expressions essentially separate the structural and semantic compatibility. In other words, they separate "what is communicated" and "how/whom a message is communicated." A policy assertion identifies a behavior of a policy entity and provides domain-specific semantics. When designing a service, you need to ensure that policy assertions are as explicit as possible regarding service expectations and semantic compatibilities.

The four tenets of service orientation provide you with a set of fundamental principles when you are designing services. When defining a service, it is always easier to work with well-defined requirements because that allows for a well-defined scope and purpose of a service. This enables a service to encapsulate distinct functionality with a clear-cut context. Sadly, more often than not, requirements are not well defined, which poses more of a problem. It is difficult to define the service that accurately represents its capabilities because one cannot relate the service operations by some logical context.

When defining services from scratch, it is helpful to categorize them according to the set of existing business service models already established within the organization. Because these models already establish some of the context and purpose in their boundary, it makes it easier to design the new services.

In addition, the naming of the service should also influence the naming of the individual operations within the service. As stated earlier, a well-named service will already establish a clear context and meaning of the service, and the individual operations should be rationalized so as not to be confusing or contradict the service. Also, because the context is established, the operations should also try to avoid confusing naming standards. For example, if you have a service that performs stock operations, then one of the operations in that should be GetQuote instead of GetStockQuote, because the context has already been established. Similarly, if you can reuse the service, then avoid naming the operations after some particular task, rather trying to keep the naming as generic as possible.

Naming conventions might not seem important at first, but as your service inventory in the organization grows, so will the potential to reuse and leverage the existing service to achieve integration within the various groups and systems. The effort required to establish a consistent naming convention within an organization pays off quickly. A consistent set of services that cleanly establish the level of clarity between the services enables easier interoperability and reuse.

Unfortunately, no magic bullet can help you standardize on the right level of granularity that will enable service orientation. But, the key point to remember is the service should achieve the right balance to facilitate both current and upcoming data requirements, in essence meeting the business's need to be more agile and responsive to market conditions.

"COMPONENTS" AND "SERVICES"—ARE THEY THE SAME?

It is natural to be confused about the terms *component* and *services* and what they mean. A *component* is a piece of compiled code that can be assembled with other components to build applications. Components can also be easily reused within the same application or across different applications. This helps reduce the cost of developing and maintaining the application once the components mature within an organization. Components are usually associated with the OOP paradigm.

A *service* is implemented by one or more components and is a higher-level aggregation than a component. Component reuse seems to work well in homogeneous environments; service orientation fills the gap by establishing reuse in heterogeneous environments by aggregating one or more components into a service and making them accessible through messages using open standards. These service definitions are deployed with the service, and they govern the communication from the consumers of the service via various contracts and policies, among other things.

SOA also assists in promoting reuse in the enterprise. Services can provide a significant benefit because you can achieve reuse at many levels of abstraction compared to the traditional methods (in other words, object orientation provide only objects as the primary reuse mechanism). SOA can offer reuse at multiple levels, including code, service, and/or functionality. This feature enhances flexibility to design enterprise applications.

WCF makes it easier for developers to create services that adhere to the principle of service orientation. For example, on the inside, you can use OO technology to implement one or more components that constitute a service. On the outside, communication with the service is based on messages. In the end, both of these technologies are complementary to each other and collectively provide the overall SOA architecture.

Although there have been a few attempts to solve the distributed application problem in the enterprise, there has yet to be a more demanding need to be consistent for standardizing. The scope of an SOA approach allows you to incorporate far-reaching systems across a number of platforms and languages. One great example of standardization in an enterprise today is web services, which we will discuss in the next section. Web services expose functionality that can be discovered and consumed in a technology-neutral, standardized format.

Web Services As a Key Enabling Technology for a Service-Oriented Architecture

There has been a lot of discussion about SOA and web services in the past few years. It might seem that web services and services are analogous in the context of SOA. On the surface this might seem accurate, but the reality is far from it. A web service is just *one* kind of implementation of a service. Web services are just a *catalyst* for an SOA implementation. In recent years with the relative ease that allows one to create web services, it has become easier to deliver SOA implementations; the SOA concept is not new, and certain companies (such as IBM) have been delivering it for more than a decade.

Almost everyone talks about web services, but interestingly no definition is universally acceptable. One of the definitions that is accepted by some is as follows: "A web service is a programmable application component accessible via standard web protocols." The key aspects of a web service are as follows:

Standard protocol: Functionality is exposed via interfaces using one of the few standard Internet protocols such as HTTP, SMTP, FTP, and so on. In most cases, this protocol is HTTP.

Service description: Web services need to describe their interfaces in detail so that a client knows how to "consume" the functionality provided by the service. This description is usually provided via an XML document called a *WSDL document*. (WSDL stands for Web Services Description Language.)

Finding services: Users need to know what web services exist and where to find them so the clients can bind to them and use the functionality. One way for users to know what services exist is to connect to a "yellow pages" listing of services. These yellow pages are implemented via Universal Discovery, Description, and Integration (UDDI) repositories. (These can be private or public UDDI nodes.)

■ **Note** A web service is not an object model and is not protocol specific. In other words, it's based on a ubiquitous web protocol (HTTP) and data format (XML). A web service is also not dependent on a specific programming language. You can choose to use any language or platform as long as you can consume and create messages for the web service.

Figure 1-2 shows the basic protocol stack for web services. Interaction with the service will usually follow a top-down fashion—that is, service discovery down to messaging—invoking the methods on the service. If you are new to web services and do not understand the various protocols and standards, don't worry, because we will be describing them later in this chapter.

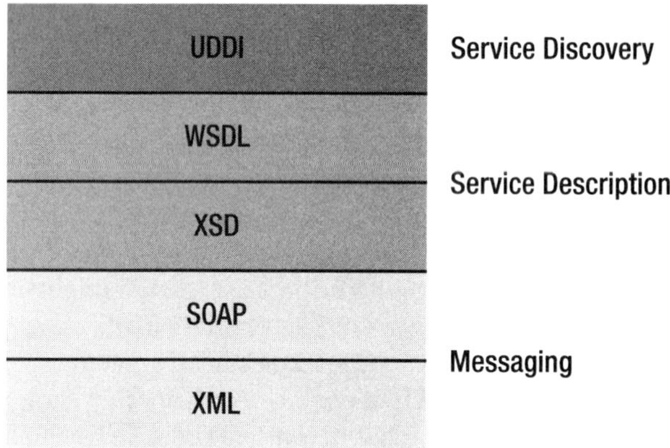

Figure 1-2. *Protocol stack for web services*

To consume a web service, you first find the service and what it offers (you can accomplish this by using UDDI). Once you have found the web service, you need to understand the interface: what the methods are, the parameters accepted, and so on. Traditionally, part of this discovery also entails what the data types are and the schema that the service expects. You can achieve the service description using WSDL and XML Schema Definition (XSD). However, with WCF, the recommendation is to use UDDI purely for publishing Web Services Metadata Exchange (WS-MetadataExchange, or MEX) endpoints and ask the service directly for the WSDL and policies. Lastly, the client needs to invoke the web service from the client via SOAP, which is based on XML.

WCF services also follow the open standards stack. Therefore, this stack not only addresses web services but it also describes the protocol stack for any service. You can argue the terminology *services* originated from *web services*. By definition, services do not need to depend on IIS or web servers to provide hosting environments. WCF enables developers to host services outside IIS. (We'll discuss this topic in detail in Chapter 5.) Therefore, you do not need to restrict the services to originate from a web server. Hence, they do not need to be called *web services*. The protocol stack plays a major role in understanding SOA functionality. Therefore, we'll discuss these protocols one by one. We will start with SOAP.

■ **Note** Web services use metadata to describe what other endpoints need to know to interact with them. This includes WS-Policy (which describes the capabilities, requirements, and general characteristics), WSDL, and XML Schema. To bootstrap communication with web services and retrieve these and other types of lmetadata, you use MEX, which is a specification that defines messages to retrieve metadata and policies associated with an endpoint. This is an industry-standard specification agreed on by most of the leading software companies such as Microsoft, IBM, Sun Microsystems, webMethods, SAP, and so on. The interactions defined by this specification are intended for metadata retrieval only and are not used to retrieve types of data such as states, properties, and so on, that might be associated with the service. For the detailed specification, see `http://msdn.microsoft.com/library/en-us/dnglobspec/html/ws-metadataexchange.pdf`.

Introducing SOAP

Simply put, SOAP is a lightweight communication protocol for web services based on XML. It is used to exchange structured and typed information between systems. SOAP allows you to invoke methods on remote machines without knowing specific details of the platform or software running on those machines. XML is used to represent the data, while the data is structured according to the SOAP schema. The only thing both the consumer and provider need to agree on is this common schema defined by SOAP. Overall, SOAP keeps things as simple as possible and provides minimum functionality. The characteristics of a SOAP message are as follows:

- It is extensible.
- It works across a number of standardized underlying network protocols.
- It is independent of the underlying language or platform or programming model.

■ **Note** SOAP used to stand for Simple Object Access Protocol, but the W3C dropped that name when the focus shifted from object "access" to object "interoperability" via a generalized XML messaging format as part of SOAP 1.2.

SOAP recognizes the following message exchange patterns: one-way, request-response, and so on. Figure 1-3 shows a one-way SOAP message (that is, no response is returned). The SOAP sender will send the message over some communication protocol.

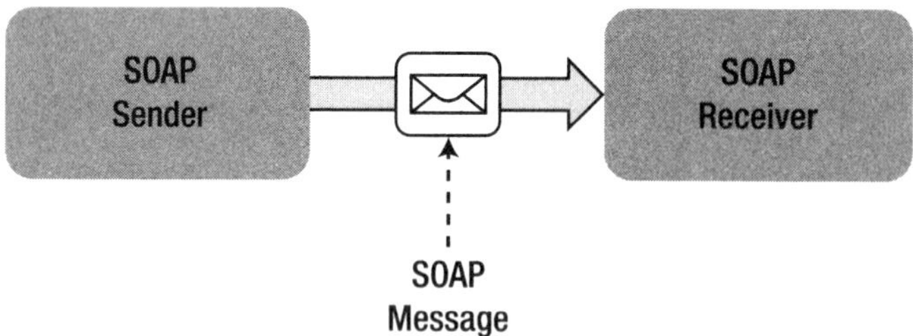

Figure 1-3. *Simple one-way SOAP message*

As Figure 1-3 shows, the SOAP message can be sent over any communication protocol, and the sender and receiver can be written in any programming model or can run on any platform.

Extensible

Extensibility is the key factor for SOAP in addition to the simplicity of design. Extensibility allows various features such as reliability, security, and so on to be "layered" via SOAP extensions. Every vendor defines its own set of extensions providing many feature-rich features on its platform.

Transport

SOAP can use one of the many standard transport protocols (such as TCP, SMTP, FTP, MSMQ, and so on). You need to define standard protocol bindings, which outline the rules for the environment to address interoperability. The SOAP specification provides a flexible framework for defining arbitrary protocol bindings and provides an explicit binding for HTTP because it's so widely used.

■ **Note** Most programmers new to SOAP are confused about the difference between the SOAP specification and the vendor implementations of the SOAP specification. Developers usually use a SOAP toolkit to create and parse SOAP messages instead of handcrafting them. The types of functional calls and supported data types for the parameters vary between each vendor implementation. As a result, a function that works with one toolkit may not work with the other. This is not a limitation of SOAP but rather a limitation of the particular vendor-specific implementation being used.

Programming Model

One of the strengths of SOAP is that it is not tied to RPC but can be used over any programming model. Most developers are surprised to learn that the SOAP model is akin to a traditional messaging model (such as MSMQ) and less to an RPC style, which is how it is used primarily. SOAP allows for a number of MEPs, one of them being the request-response model.

Note MEPs are essentially a set of design patterns for distributed communications. MEPs define the template for exchanging messages between two entities. Some examples of MEPs include RPC, Representational State Transfer (REST), one-way, request-response, and so on. RPC is essentially a protocol that allows one application to execute another application or module on another computer, without the developer having to write any explicit code to accomplish the invocation. REST, on the other hand, is an architectural style that is different from RPC. This uses a simple XML- and HTTP-based interface, but without the abstraction of protocol such as SOAP. Some purists see this as the subset of the "best" architectures of the Web.

SOAP Message

SOAP's building block is the SOAP *message*, which consists of the following four parts:

- A SOAP *envelope* is an XML document that encapsulates the message to be communicated. This is the only part that is required; the rest is optional.
- The second part of the SOAP message is used to define any custom data types that the application is using.
- The third part of the message describes the RPC pattern to be used.
- The last part of the message defines how SOAP binds to HTTP.

A SOAP envelope is the root element of the message. The *envelope* has two sections: the header and the body. The header has metadata about the message that might be needed for some specific processing, such as a date-time stamp when the message was sent or an authentication token. The *body* contains the details of the message or a SOAP fault. Figure 1-4 shows the structure of a SOAP message. A SOAP message can be one of three types, namely, request messages, response messages, and fault messages.

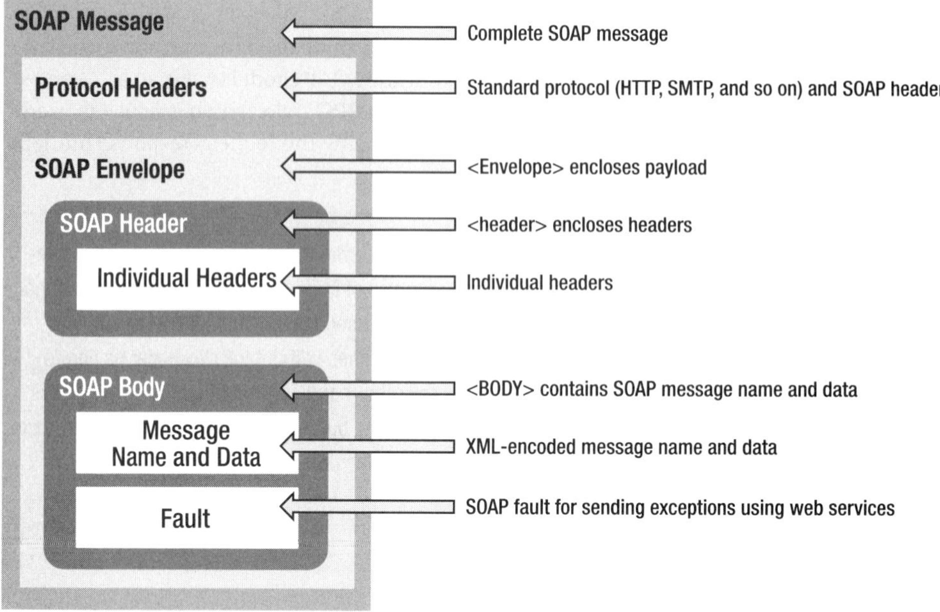

Figure 1-4. *SOAP message structure*

A request-response SOAP message, as Figure 1-5 shows, essentially has two messages: one is the request message sent to the service, and the other is a response message sent back to the client. Although these messages are independent from each other, the request-response pattern provides automatic correlation and synchronization between the messages. This results in "normal" procedure call semantics to the client.

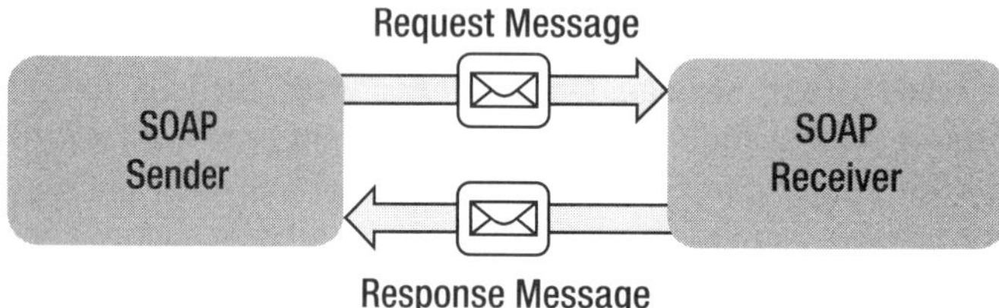

Figure 1-5. *Request-response exchange pattern*

Syntactically a SOAP message is quite simple, but the following are a few rules you need to keep in mind when manually writing SOAP messages:

- Must be encoded in XML
- Must use the SOAP envelope namespace
- Must use the SOAP encoding namespace
- Cannot contain a DTD reference
- Cannot contain XML processing instructions

■ **Note** Contract first or code first? When designing a service contract, you have two approaches; you can either use the contract-first approach or use the code-first approach. The contract-first approach ensures interoperability and for most situations is the recommended approach. This ensures that any consumers of the services conform to the published contract. This is especially important if any third parties are involved who need to conform to a predetermined contract. One of the biggest challenges to the contract-first approach is the lack of tool support, which hurts productivity. If in a given situation productivity has a higher precedence than interoperability, then it might make sense to use the code-first approach. Please refer to Chapter 4 for a more detailed discussion.

SOAP Faults

When an exception needs to be returned by the service, this takes place using a fault element in a SOAP response. A fault element needs to be within the body element of the SOAP message and can appear only once. The fault element must contain a `faultcode` element and a `faultstring` element. The fault message contains the exception details such as error code, description, and so on. Table 1-1 lists the fault codes defined by the specification.

Table 1-1. *SOAP Fault Codes*

Error	Description
`VersionMismatch`	The SOAP receiver saw a namespace associated with the SOAP envelope that it did not recognize.
`MustUnderstand`	The receiver of the message did not understand a required header.
`Client`	The message sent by the client was either not formed correctly or contained incorrect information.
`Server`	An error happened at the server while processing the message.

SOAP Message Format

Two types of SOAP messaging formats or styles exist: document and RPC. Document style indicates the message body contains XML where the format must be agreed upon between the sender and the receiver. The RPC style indicates it is a representation of a method call.

You also have two ways to serialize the data to XML: using literal XML schema definitions and using SOAP encoding rules. In the first option, the schema definition defines the XML format without any ambiguity. These rules are defined in the specification and are sometimes referred to as *Section 5 encoding*. It is more suitable for the RPC-style usage of SOAP, because this option specifies how to serialize most data types including arrays, objects, structures, and so on. On the other hand, in the second option, the various SOAP encoding rules (usually defined via a W3C schema) must be parsed at runtime to determine the proper serialization of the SOAP body. Although the W3C permits the use of both document-literal and RPC-literal formats, Microsoft recommends the former over the latter because the message should not dictate the way it's being processed by the service.

SOAP Implementations by Major Software Vendors

Every major software vendor in the industry has a SOAP stack implemented that covers both the open source market and the commercial market. On the open source front, solutions exist from the likes of Apache Axis implemented in Java/C++ to PocketSoap implemented via COM. Implementations exist for almost all platforms such as Soap::Lite in Perl and PHP Soap in, you guessed it, PHP.

On the commercial side of things, every major software vendor has a stack that is tightly integrated with its other offerings. Microsoft, of course, has the .NET Framework, which tightly integrates with Visual Studio and ASP.NET to provide a seamless experience for a developer. IBM's implementation is its WebSphere web services that allow you to integrate with technologies such as JAX-B, EMF/SDO, and XMLBeans. Oracle's web service is implemented as part of the Oracle Application Server (10g) line. Sun Microsystems has implemented the web services stack via the Web Services Developer Pack (WSDP), and BEA has WebLogic Server.

Note <soaprpc/> lists web service implementations by various vendors at `http://www.soaprpc.com/ws_implementations.html`.

Some vendors do not implement the complete Web Services Interoperability (WS-I) profile stack but do only a subset. Security, for example, has had a lot of interest from most enterprise organizations. Both hardware devices (such as XML Firewall from Reactivity) and software products (such as XML Trust Services from VeriSign) exist that provide many security features and act as catalysts for web services. We'll address some of these implementations in detail in Chapter 13.

With so many implementations covering almost all platforms and runtimes, it is not possible to standardize on the various data types used by the components and how they are represented in memory. A consumer and provider running on different platforms will not be able to exchange any information without standardizing, thus nullifying the promise of web services. To help solve this, the W3C recommends XSD, which provides a platform-independent description language and is used to describe the structure and type of information using a uniform type system.

How do you describe a service to the consuming party? What open standards do you have to "describe" a service to its consumer? You achieve this by implementing WSDL. You'll now learn a bit more about WSDL.

Web Services Description Language: Describing Service Endpoints

If no standards existed, it would have been difficult for web services and in turn SOAs to be so widely accepted. WSDL provides the standardized format for specifying interfaces and allows for integration. Before we get into the details of WSDL, you need to understand the notion of endpoints because they are paramount to WSDL.

What Are Endpoints?

Officially, the W3C defines an endpoint as "an association between a fully specified interface binding and a network address, specified by a URI that may be used to communicate with an instance of a web service." In other words, an *endpoint* is the entity that a client connects to using a specific protocol and data format when consuming a service. This endpoint resides at a well-known location that is accessible to the client. At an abstract level, this is similar to a port, and in some implementations such as BizTalk, this can literally be exposed as a port for others to consume over. When looking from the perspective of endpoints, a service can also be defined as a collection of endpoints.

WSDL

WSDL (pronounced as "whiz-dull") forms the basis of web services and is the format that describes web services. WSDL describes the public interface of a web service including meta-data such as protocol bindings, message formats, and so on. A client wanting to connect to a web service can read the WSDL to determine what contracts are available on the web service. If you recall from earlier in the chapter, one of the key tenets of service orientation is that the services share contracts and schemas, not classes. As a result, when you are creating a service, you need to ensure the contract for that service is well thought out and is something you would not change.

Any custom types used are embedded in the WSDL using XML Schema. WSDL is similar to Interface Description Language (IDL) for web services. The information from the WSDL document is typically interpreted at design time to generate a proxy object. The client uses the proxy object at runtime to send and receive SOAP messages to and from the service.

Note IDL is a standardized language used to describe the interface to a component or routine. IDL is especially useful when calling components on another machine via RPC, which may be running on a different platform or build using a different language and might not share the same "call semantics."

A WSDL document has three parts, namely, definitions, operations, and service bindings, which can be mapped to one of the elements listed in Table 1-2.

Table 1-2. *WSDL Document Structure*

Element	Description
`<portType>`	Operations performed by the web service
`<message>`	Message used by the web service
`<types>`	Data types used by the web service
`<binding>`	Defines a communication endpoint (by means of protocol and address) to access the service
`<Service>`	Aggregates multiple ports (in combination with binding and address into a service)

Definitions

Definitions are expressed in XML and include both data type and message definitions. These definitions are based upon an agreed-on XML vocabulary that in turn should be based on a set of industry-wide vocabulary. If you need to use data type and message definitions between organizations, then an industry-wide vocabulary is recommended.

Note Definitions are not constraints to XML and can be expressed in formats other than XML. As an example, you can use the Object Management Group (OMG) IDL instead of XML. If you use a different definition format, as with XML, both the senders and receivers would need to agree on the format and the vocabulary. However, as per the official W3C WSDL specification, the preference is to use XSD as the canonical type system. Sticking to this would ensure maximum interoperability and platform neutrality.

Operations

Operations describe the actions for the message supported by the web service and can be one of four types, as listed in Table 1-3. In a WSDL document structure, operations are represented using the `<portType>` element, which is the most important element because it defines the operations that can be performed. In context of the OO paradigm, each operation is a method.

Table 1-3. *Operation Types*

Error	Description
One-way	The service endpoint receives a message.
Request-response	The service endpoint receives a message and sends a correlated message.
Solicit-response	The service endpoint sends a message and receives a correlated message.
Notification	The service endpoint sends a message.

Figure 1-6 shows the structure of a WSDL document, which consists of abstract definitions and concrete descriptions. On the left is the abstract definition where the data type's definition is a container for using some type system such as XSD. *Message definitions*, as the name suggests, are the typed definitions of the data being communicated. An *operation* is a description of the action supported by the service and contains one or more data types and message definitions, as shown in Figure 1-6. Port types are a set of operations supported by more than one endpoint. All of these are brought together by the *binding*, which is the concrete protocol and data format specified for a particular port type. A *port* is a single endpoint defined as the combination of the binding and the network address. Most developers do not handcraft the WSDL but instead use the underlying .NET Framework to generate this for them.

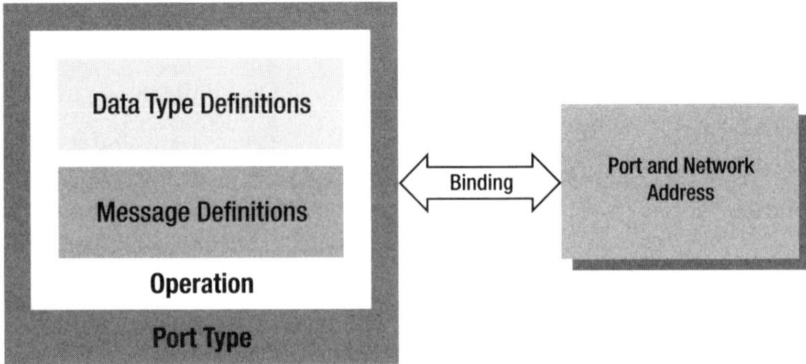

Figure 1-6. *WSDL*

Service Bindings

Service bindings connect port types to a port (that is, the message format and protocol details for each port). A port is defined by associating a network address with a port type. A service can contain multiple ports. This binding is commonly created using SOAP. The binding element has two attributes: a name that can be anything to define the binding and the type, which points to the port for the binding.

Now you are familiar with SOAP and how you describe the services with WSDL. However, how can you discover all the services that are available to you? What open standards are available to dynamically discover services and consume them at runtime? You achieve this by implementing UDDI. You'll now investigate what UDDI is.

Dynamically Discovering Web Services

UDDI is a platform-independent directory protocol for describing services and discovering and integrating business services via the Internet. UDDI is also based on industry-standard protocols such as HTTP, XML, SOAP, and so on, and it describes the details of the services using WSDL and communicates via SOAP. The philosophy behind UDDI is like a traditional "yellow pages" where you can search for a company, search for the services its offers, and even contact the company for more information.

A UDDI entry is nothing but an XML file that details the business and the services it offers. It consists of three parts: the white, yellow, and green pages. The *white pages* contain details of the company and its contact information. The *yellow pages* include industry categories based on standardized taxonomies such as the North America Industry Classification System, and so on. The *green pages* contain the technical details that describe the interface via a WSDL so a consumer has enough information about how to use the service and what is expected. A UDDI directory also includes several ways to search for the services it offers including various filtering options such as geographic location, type of business, specific provider, and so on.

Before UDDI was standardized, there was no universal way to know what services were offered by partners or off-the-shelf options. You also have no way to get standard integration and dependencies between providers. The problems that UDDI solves are as follows:

- UDDI makes it possible to discover the right service that can be used, instead of reinventing the wheel.
- UDDI solves the customer-driven need to remove barriers to allow for the rapid participation in the global Internet economy.
- UDDI describes services and business processes programmatically in a single, open, and secure environment.

■ **Note** UDDI offers more than design-time support. It plays a critical role after the discovery of a service because it allows the client to programmatically query the UDDI infrastructure, which further allows the client applications to be more robust. With a runtime layer between the client and the web service, the clients can be loosely coupled, allowing them to be more flexible to the changes. Microsoft recommends publishing a WS-MEX as part of the entries in the UDDI registry.

Now you are familiar with SOAP, WSDL, and UDDI. However, how do all these technologies work together to send a message from the sender to the receiver in a loosely coupled system? You'll now investigate how to achieve this.

Sending Messages Between Loosely Coupled Systems

To achieve service orientation, you need the ability to send messages from one service to another. In the context of WCF, *service invocation* is a general mechanism for sending messages between an entity that requests a service and another entity that provides the service. It is important to understand that it does not matter where the provider and consumer physically exist; they could be on the same physical machine or spread across the opposite ends of the planet. However, from a service *execution* perspective, it matters, and WCF fills this infrastructure gap.

Service invocation, irrespective of platform and technology, follows a similar pattern. At a high level, the steps involved when a consumer sends a message to a provider are as follows:

1. Find the relevant service that exposes the desired functionality.
2. Find out the type and format of the messages that the service would accept.
3. Understand any specific metadata that might be required as part of the message (for example, for transaction or security).
4. Send the message to the provider with all relevant data and metadata.
5. Process the response message from the service in the appropriate manner (for example, the request might have been successful, or it might have failed because of incorrect data or network failure, and so on).

Because web services are the most popular implementation of service orientation, let's look at an example of how you would use a web service to send messages from one application to another. Invoking a web service "method" is similar to calling a regular method; however, in the first case, the method is executed on a remote machine. As the web service is running on another computer, all the relevant information needed by the web service needs to be passed to the machine hosting the service. This information then is processed, and the result is sent to the client.

The life cycle of an XML web service has eight steps, as shown in Figure 1-7:

1. A client connects to the Internet and finds a directory service to use.
2. The client connects to the directory service in order to run a query.
3. The client runs the relevant query against the directory service to find the web service that offers the desired functionality.
4. The relevant web service vendor is contacted to ensure the service is still valid and is available.
5. The description language of the relevant web service is retrieved and forwarded to the client.
6. The client creates a new instance of an XML web service via the proxy class.
7. The runtime on the client serializes the arguments of the service method into a SOAP message and sends it over the network to the web service.
8. The requested method is executed, which sets the return value including any out parameters.

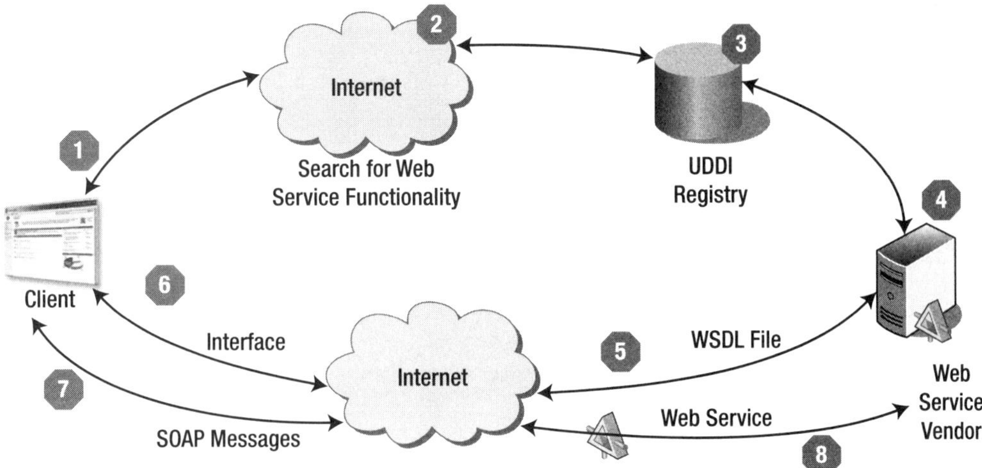

Figure 1-7. *Web service lifetime*

■ **Note** Although we have shown the example of a web service implementation, WCF provides unification across the many distributed computing technologies and provides a common programming model irrespective of the underlying protocol or technology. Also, differences exist in the design time and the runtime of a WCF implementation. At design time, for example, an SOA implementation would usually account for the definition of the service, the different data types it expects in what order, and so on. But many elements are accounted for only at runtime, such as the physical location of the service, network latency and failure, error detection and recovery, and so on. All these attributes are not usually addressed at design time but are picked up by the WCF runtime; the WCF runtime can also change the behaviors of the service during the actual operation. This behavior can also be adjusted based on the demand of the service. For more details, refer to Chapter 2.

Summary

This chapter introduced the concepts of services and SOA. We also described the governing principles for services, in terms of the four tenets. It is important to understand that at the end of the day SOA is not about how to invoke objects remotely or how to write web services; it is all about how to send messages from one application to another in a loosely coupled fashion. Web services are just one of the many, albeit the most popular, ways to send messages between disparate systems. Adopting an SOA approach is important to an enterprise to help it deliver the business agility and IT flexibility needed to be able to succeed in today's marketplace.

The next chapter will introduce you to the new features of WCF, the challenges it helps solve, and the unification of the various distributed technologies. We will also illustrate how WCF addresses SOA concepts to promote WCF as a practical SOA implementation from Microsoft.

CHAPTER 2

Introducing WCF Basics

During the past decade, a lot of research has been done in the field of distributed computing. Microsoft and other leading vendors have come up with various distributed technologies. Each of the technologies reduces the convolution of building rich applications and lowers development costs. The latest from Microsoft is Windows Communication Foundation (WCF), the next-generation uniform way of developing distributed applications by providing a service-oriented programming model.

WCF (formerly known as Indigo) handles the communication infrastructure of Windows Vista and has been extended to Windows XP and Windows 2003 through the .NET Framework 3.0 (formerly known as WinFX). The .NET Framework 3.0 is a managed programming model for Windows (Windows XP, Windows 2003, and Windows Vista) that is designed to replace the Win32 application programming interface (API) in future releases. WCF provides the communication infrastructure that allows you to create diverse ranges of applications through its simplified model. Based on the notion of services, WCF contains the best features of today's distributed technology stack to develop the connected systems.

After completing this chapter, you will have the following knowledge:

- You'll know about existing distributed technologies and their pitfalls.
- You'll know about the key architectural concepts that underpin WCF.
- You'll have seen a high-level overview of WCF's features.
- You'll understand how WCF unifies existing distributed technologies.

Introducing the Microsoft Remote Object Invocation Model

Microsoft started its remote invocation technologies with Distributed Component Object Model (DCOM), which extended Component Object Model (COM). Then, .NET introduced technologies such as .NET Remoting and XML web services. We'll now cover these technologies in bit more detail.

Introducing COM and DCOM

Microsoft developed COM to enable applications to interact with each other and to promote reusability. COM is the set of specifications that, when followed, allows software components to communicate with each other. Each component exposes its functionality through an interface and is uniquely identified by global unique identifiers (GUIDs). The advantage of using COM is that different components developed in different languages can write these software components and interact with each other by using `IUnknown` and other standard COM interfaces. Most of Microsoft's products, including Microsoft Office, SQL Server, and even Windows, are based on COM. Though COM provides the ability to reuse the components locally, it was not designed to work well with remote components.

Few specifications and extensions had been made that were based on COM and that interacted with remote components. However, the need for remote method invocations grew substantially. To solve this concern, Microsoft developed DCOM. This essentially is a combination of COM and the network protocol that allows you to run a COM object on a remote computer. DCOM was a proprietary wire-protocol standard from Microsoft to extend COM so it could work in distributed environments. DCOM provides an opportunity to distribute your component across different locations according to the application requirements. In addition, DCOM provides basic infrastructure support such as reliability, security, location independence, and efficient communication between COM objects that are residing across processes and machines.

■ **Tip** Covering DCOM and COM in more detail is beyond the scope of this book, but if you want to delve into it, we suggest you refer to *Inside COM* (Microsoft Press, 1997) by Dale Rogerson.

The following are the problems with DCOM:

- DCOM and other distributed technologies such as CORBA, RMI, and so on, are based on several assumptions. One of the key assumptions is that one organization will manage all the components in the systems that are interacting with each other. Another is that the location of a component will not vary from one place to the other. This scenario can work fine within an organization, but as you cross organization boundaries, the limitations of DCOM become more significant.

- Microsoft has invested a lot in DCOM to ensure that calling a remote method is as simple as calling the local component by simplifying the low-level network communication requirements. Most of the time this resulted in bad programming practices by programmers, which resulted in increased network traffic and performance bottlenecks.

- DCOM, being based on a proprietary standard, was essentially built taking only the Windows operating systems into account, making it not suited for heterogeneous environments.

- Another issue with DCOM is that its client is tightly coupled with the server, so any changes done on the client mandate a modification on the server.

- DCOM, like other distributed technologies, is based on two-tier architecture and suffers from some of the same flaws of two-tier architecture.

- DCOM came before the computer world experienced the Internet boom. DCOM was never built with the Internet in mind. System administrators need to compromise the security of the firewall in order to use DCOM across firewalls/locations. DCOM is used to communicate through ports that are generally restricted by firewalls because the ports are susceptible to attacks.

Introducing .NET Remoting

Though COM and DCOM are able to provide reusability and a distributed platform, they also suffer from problems of versioning, reference counting, and so on. Microsoft .NET came up with a vision to be more connected than ever. It wanted to deliver software as a "service" and also resolve issues related to COM. The release of .NET was termed as the biggest revolution ever on the Microsoft platform after the introduction of Windows. .NET Remoting is one of the ways to create distributed applications in .NET. Developers now have additional options such as XML web services and service components. Essentially, .NET Remoting takes a lot of lessons from DCOM. It replaces DCOM as the preferred technology for building distributed applications. It addresses problems that have wounded distributed applications for many years (that is, interoperability support, extensibility support, efficient lifetime management, custom hosts, and an easy configuration process).

.NET Remoting delivers on the promises of easy distributed computing by providing a simple, extensible programming model, without compromising flexibility, scalability, and robustness. It comes with a default implementation of components such as channels and protocols, but all of them are pluggable and can be replaced with better options without much code modification. Earlier, processes were used to isolate applications from each other. Each process had its own virtual address space, and the code that ran in one process could not access the code or data of another process. In .NET, one process can now run multiple applications in a separate application domain and thereby avoid cross-process communication in many scenarios. In normal situations, an object cannot access the data outside its application domain. Anything that crosses an application domain is marshaled by the .NET runtime. Not only does .NET Remoting enable communication between application domains, but it also can be extended across processes, machines, and networks. It is flexible in the channels and formatters that can be used and has a wide variety of options to maintain state. Though .NET Remoting provides the best performance and flexibility, it too suffers from some vital pitfalls.

The following are the problems with .NET Remoting:

- .NET Remoting works best when assemblies that define the types that are used to integrate are shared. .NET Remoting works fairly well if there is full control over both ends of the wire. Therefore, it works well in an intranet where you have complete control of the deployment, the versioning, and the testing.

- Practically, .NET Remoting is proprietary to .NET and works seamlessly to exchange data between two .NET applications. It is deeply rooted in the common language runtime (CLR) and relies on the CLR to obtain metadata. This metadata means the client must understand .NET in order to communicate with endpoints exposed by .NET Remoting.

- .NET Remoting requires a big leap between programming at a high level and dropping down into the infrastructure. It's pretty easy to code .NET Remoting with the available components, but if you want to start learning about adding your own transports, the level of complexity increases. .NET Remoting gives you finer-grained control on each architectural component but also requires a deep knowledge of its architecture.
- .NET Remoting suffers from the issues of load balancing because it is not intelligent enough to shift a request from a busy application server to one that is not as busy.

Why Are Web Services the Preferred Option?

Unfortunately, with an existing distributed technology stack, you'll often find a number of limitations, especially with interoperability between platforms. For example, if you try to deploy a COM+ application to converse across a firewall or to converse across smart routers or organizational boundaries, you'll often find some significant differences. Most of the earlier distributed component technologies were by no means built to deal with firewalls and intelligent routers. For instance, if you build an application using Microsoft Enterprise Services (a set of classes provided by Microsoft to be leveraged in enterprise applications), how do you utilize the service from a Java client? Considering that most of the enterprises are working on different technologies and different platforms, interoperability is a major issue. Generally, companies used to buy some complex software and invest a lot of money in building a bridge between the existing components to make them distributed. Other complexities and difficulties soon arose when these custom solutions needed to be extended further. Web services solve these problems by relying on open standards and protocols that are widely accepted.

Web services are not just another way of creating distributed applications. The distinguishing factor of web services from other distributed technologies is that rather than relying on proprietary standards or protocols, web services rely on open web standards (such as SOAP, HTTP, and XML). These open standards are widely recognized and accepted across the industry. Web services have changed how distributed applications are created. The Internet has created a demand for a loosely coupled and interoperable distributed technology. Specifically, prior to web services, most of the distributed technologies relied on the object-oriented paradigm, but the Web has created a need for distributed components that are autonomous and platform independent.

XML web services are designed with interoperability in mind and are easily callable from non-Windows platforms. It is common to confuse web services with .NET Remoting. Web services and .NET Remoting are related, but web services have a more simplified programming model than .NET Remoting. In other words, they both look similar from a high-level architecture level, but they differ in the way they work. For example, they both have different ways of serializing data into messages. .NET Remoting supports RPC-based communication by default, and web services support message-based communication by default. Web services rely on XML Schema for data types, and .NET Remoting relies on the CLR. You can use .NET Remoting to build web services, but the Web Services Description Language (WSDL) generated by .NET Remoting is not widely adopted and might be ignored by some clients. Though you can use either for creating components, .NET Remoting is suitable for creating components to be used by your own application running in the .NET environment, and XML web services create components that can be accessible to any application connected via the Internet. Through web services, Microsoft wants to achieve the best of both worlds—Web development and component-based development. Web services were the first step toward service orientation, which is a set of guiding principles for developing loosely coupled distributed applications. SOA is a vision of services that have well-defined interfaces. These loosely coupled interfaces communicate through messages described by XML Schema Definition (XSD) and through the message patterns described by WSDL. This provides for a great base architecture for building distributed applications. Since a web service and its clients are independent from each other, they need to adhere only to the XSD and WSDL document standards in order to communicate.

The next Microsoft offering to address SOA is WCF. We'll now discuss how WCF complements web services and enhances their value.

What Does WCF Solve?

WCF is not just another way of creating a distributed solution but provides a number of benefits over its predecessors. If you look at the background of WCF, you'll find that work on WCF started with the release of .NET. Microsoft unveiled this technology at the Microsoft Product Developers Conference 2003 in Los Angeles, California. In other words, it has taken years to build and come to market. WCF addresses lots of issues, and Figure 2-1 shows the three main design goals of WCF:

- Unification of existing technologies
- Interoperability across platforms
- Service-oriented development

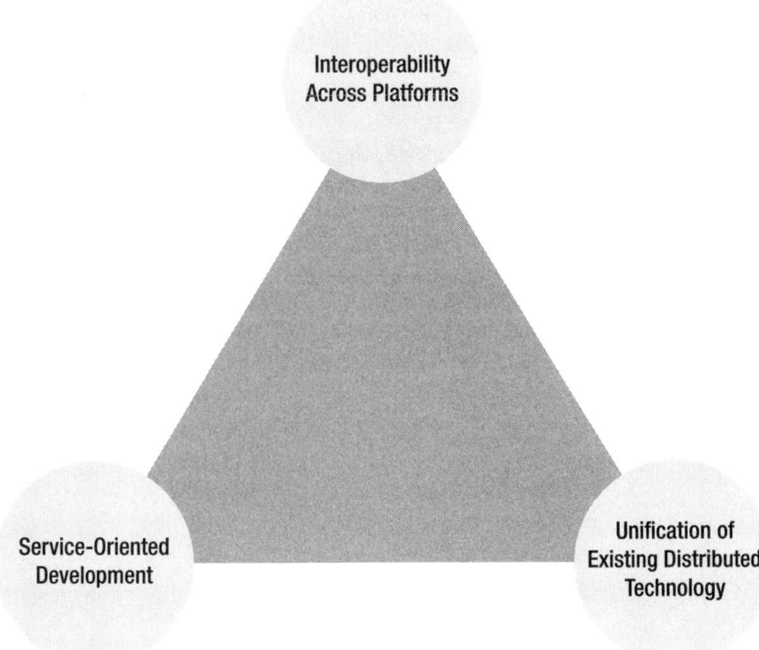

Figure 2-1. *Design goals of WCF*

Unification of Existing Technologies

The current world of enterprise computing has many distributed technologies, each of which has a notion to perform a specific task and have its distinct role in the space. Apart from that, these distributed technologies are based on different programming models. (For example, if you are building an application that happens to communicate over HTTP, you will be required to change your programming model if you want to switch to using TCP. If you are used to building XML web services today, you don't have the ability to support and flow transactions with message queuing enabled without changing your programming model.) This has created problems for developers, who have to keep learning different APIs for different ways of building distributed components.

The constant fight since the 1990s between distributed technologies has led to a debate about which technology is best suited for developing distributed applications in the long term. One of the interesting questions is, why not have just one technology that can be used in all situations? WCF is Microsoft's solution to distributed application development for enterprise applications. It avoids confusion by taking all the capabilities of the existing distributed systems' technology stacks and enables you to use one clean and simple API. In other words, WCF brings the entire existing distributed stack under one roof. All you need to do as a developer is reference the `System.ServiceModel` assembly and import its namespace.

WCF is a set of class libraries that comes with the .NET Framework 3.0. The .NET Framework 3.0 will become a core API with the Windows Vista operating system. You can also install it on a machine running Windows XP (Service Pack 2) as well as Windows Server 2003.

■ **Note** For more information about installing WCF, refer to Appendix C.

If you look at Figure 2-2, you will find that WCF subsumes the best of all the distributed technologies. WCF brings together the efficiency of ASMX, the gift of merely adopting transactions with Enterprise Services just through using attributes, the extensibility and flexibility of .NET Remoting, the supremacy of MSMQ for building queued applications, and WSE's interoperability through WS-*. Microsoft took all these capabilities and built a single, steady infrastructure in the form of WCF.

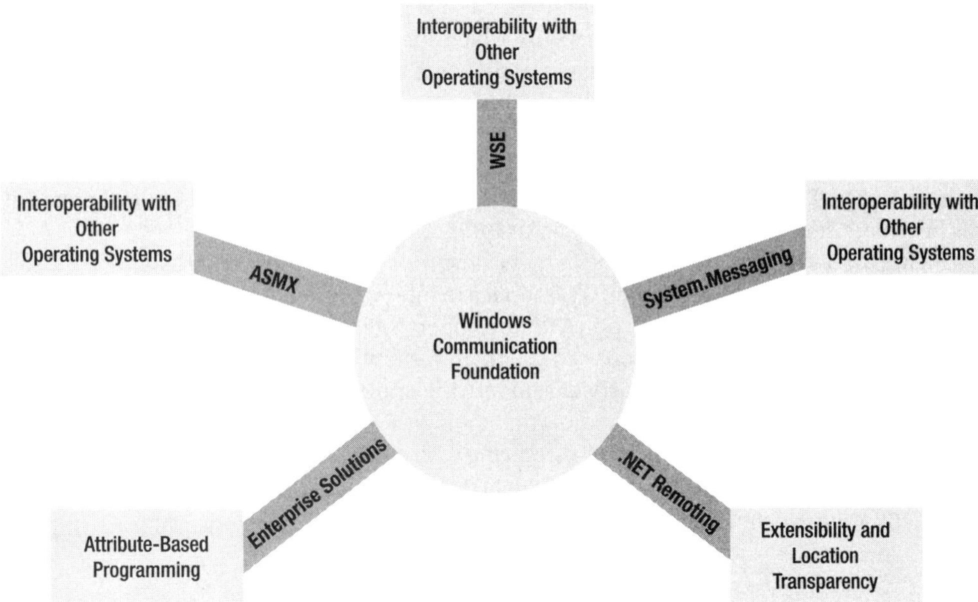

Figure 2-2. *Unification of distributed technologies*

Interoperability Across Platforms

Most of the big software companies are developing software using proprietary protocols that are tightly coupled with a specific platform. This succumbs to the problem of not being interoperable with other software running on different platforms. When you look at any large enterprise in particular, you often notice a number of disparate systems built and bought over periods of time. Often these systems are incompatible with one another. The ability to link the systems becomes a crucial need for a large number of organizations. In addition, newly developed applications need to interoperate with the existing platforms, and the business needs to support applications written in different programming languages with different technologies. Also, companies need seamless interoperability across the organization between "purchased" software from different software vendors.

As you can see, interoperability has been a major issue for all the major software vendors, and they wanted to use a suite of protocols that was widely accepted and adopted. Therefore, leaders in the industry such as Microsoft, IBM, BEA, and Sun formed the Web Services Interoperability (WS-I) organization, which has developed a constant suite of specifications that, if adopted, allows software to seamlessly communicate with other software running on different platforms.

One of the great features of the WS-I specifications is that they are simple, small, modular, and easy to implement. You are free to choose which specification you need to implement. For example, implementing WS-Security does not mandate that you implement transaction specifications. It is broken down into several layers. (For example, there is a specification for sending a digital signature in a SOAP message and a different specification for sending a simple username and password in SOAP.) The core architecture of a web service specification for all this is WSDL. Therefore, WCF speaks the language of the latest web service suite of protocols to achieve seamless interoperability across platforms.

Figure 2-3 shows that the WCF native messaging protocol is SOAP, which as an open standard provides the opportunity for the WCF service to interact with different technologies running on different platforms and non-Windows operating systems. Since services are based on open standards, other applications can use them without requiring that these clients possess detailed knowledge about the service's underlying implementation. This is exciting for software architects, because they can know that their WCF application that runs on a Windows 2003 or Vista web server can do reliable messaging with a Java application running on an IBM mainframe. The technical world will not speak in different languages anymore, and with WCF, diverse and heterogeneous systems can coexist peacefully.

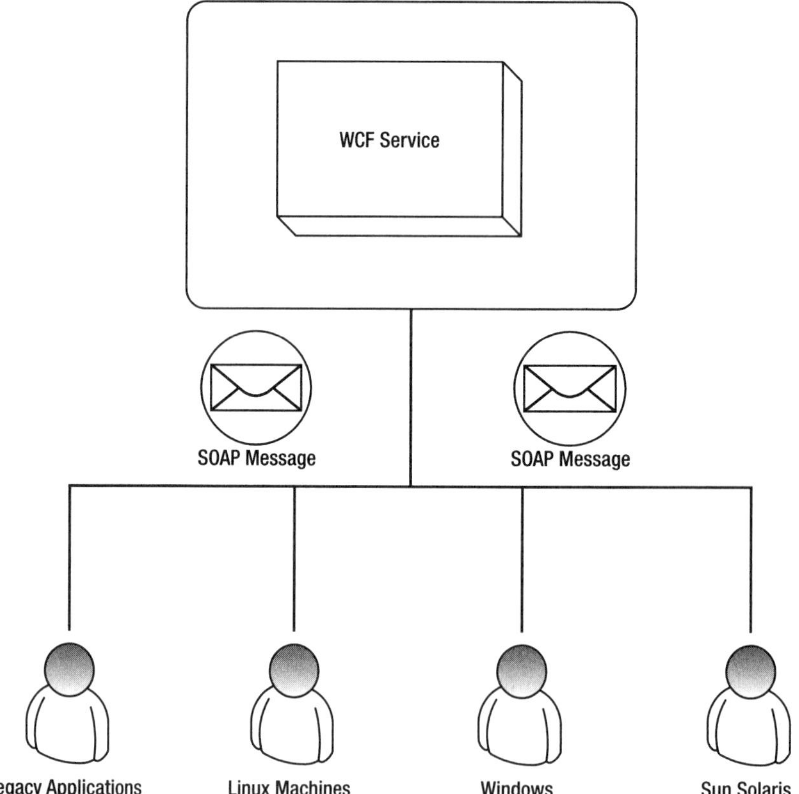

Figure 2-3. *Interoperability with Windows and non-Windows operating systems*

Not only can WCF interact with its counterparts from other vendors, but it also can exist peacefully with its predecessors such as COM+ and Enterprise Services. For developers, this drastically reduces the amount of infrastructure code required to achieve heterogeneous interoperability.

WCF As a Service-Oriented Development Tool

WCF is the first programming model built from the ground up to provide explicit service-oriented application development and ready-to-face-the-future business orientation. Service orientation is not a technology but instead is a design concept. Service orientation uses the best practices for building today's distributed applications. Purists and gurus of distributed applications consider service orientation to be the design guideline for overcoming some of the complicacy existing in designing loosely coupled applications. Service orientation is not a new concept, and it has been around for some years. Some projects have tried to implement the concept of service orientation by tweaking existing distributed technologies; these projects have always demanded a framework that has built-in support for service orientation. Although existing distributed technologies can offer the groundwork for interoperability and integration, a new platform was required—a new infrastructure that makes it much easier to build these distributed technologies. The new distributed technology should also support adequate extensibility so that when fresh technologies and innovative protocols come along, they can be rapidly and effortlessly adopted without having to revamp the entire platform time after time.

Although it may seem surprising, one of the most intriguing parts of designing a service is deciding how it should expose its functionality to the outside world. The level of granularity of the service quite often is one of the most heated topics of debate within an organization. If the service is "finely grained," then the focus is usually on exchanging small amounts of data to complete a specific task. This is usually associated with the more traditional RPC type of communication style. Any additional tasks, if required, are invoked similarly. Since message-based service invocations are expensive, finely grained approaches might not be practical in most situations because the overhead of transmitting and processing many individual messages would not be acceptable. On the other hand, coarse-grained services expose more functionality within the same service invocation, combining many small tasks. This relates to fewer messages transmitted with more data as opposed to many messages with less data. In other words, the service is less chatty. This also relates to less overhead on both ends of the service, enabling a coarse-grained service to scale better.

When designing services, you need to extend yourself beyond the basic object-oriented design principles and use the four tenets of service orientation briefly discussed in Chapter 1 as the guiding principles. Figure 2-4 shows the four tenets of service orientation from Chapter 1. One of the challenges in developing WCF is shifting developers' mind-sets away from thinking about building distributed systems in terms of objects and components and starting to think about building distributed systems as services. WCF offers that foundation for service-oriented applications built on Windows. It will be basic to the SOA efforts of many organizations. WCF provides this platform for building the next generation of distributed applications.

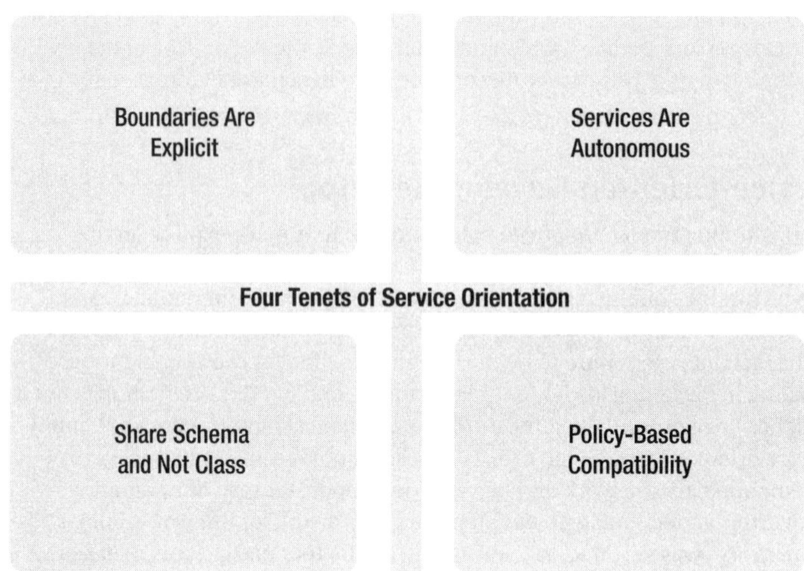

Figure 2-4. *Four tenets of service orientation*

Until now you probably have been creating applications utilizing an object-oriented programming model. Service-oriented architecture (SOA) is a fundamental shift to dealing with the difficulties of building distributed systems. The following are some of the key differences between object-oriented and service-oriented programming:

- Technology and business are changing rapidly, and companies are constantly investing in application development. For years, developers and organizations have struggled to build software based on object-oriented paradigms that adapt at the momentum of business. Design needs to be flexible and time tested. Services of WCF are built in an autonomous way, and by following key principles of SOA, they promise less maintenance cost, allow for change, and are interoperable across platforms.

- Most object-oriented applications target homogeneous environments, and no simple and flexible way exists in object orientation to work in heterogeneous environments because it is tightly coupled with the platform being built. An SOA targets both heterogeneous and homogeneous environments.

- Object-oriented developers share interfaces and classes that give them a comfortable way to program. However, the programming practices are much simpler if the schema is shared rather than the objects. A schema is defined in the XML Schema language, and contracts are defined in WSDL. An SOA application (WCF) allows you to share schemas and not objects.

- In object-oriented architecture, behaviors are implicitly remote, or everything is distributed by default. For instance, we created the following interface:

  ```
  public interface Ihello
  {
  string Hello(string name);
  }
  ```

  This interface can be accessible remotely without any restrictions. Classes are also not left behind, and an access specifier determines the behavior of the class. Classes have the default access specifier. This default and implicit behavior of object orientation proves to be an issue in developing complex applications where thousands of objects are interacting with each other. In WCF, the behavior is explicitly defined remotely by decorating the class with the appropriate attributes. Nothing is visible outside your code, unless you want that facet of your code to be publicly exposed to a service-oriented interface. The concepts of public and private are pointless when identifying methods on a service contract. With WCF, you will need to start writing applications explicitly as being remote. Similar to the `[WebMethods]` attributes of web services, you can decorate the method with the `OperationContract` attribute. Chapter 4 covers more about `OperationContract` and how to create a service.

- Object-oriented programming gives a tight coupling with the underline platform, and services are free to act independently. A service and its clients are independent of each other, and as long as they agree upon the interface, it hardly matters whether they are written in different languages, are using different runtime environments, or are getting executed on different operating systems.

- Most distributed object technologies such as DCOM have a goal to make remote objects look as much as possible like local objects. Microsoft and other companies have gone to extraordinary lengths to ensure that a call to a remote component is as easy as a call to the local component. A call to a remote component involves a lot of work going behind the scenes and is abstracted from the programmer. (For example, Visual Basic 6.0 uses COM in an abstracted manner. How many Visual Basic developers are aware of COM?) Although this approach simplifies development in some ways by providing rapid application development (RAD), it also hides the inescapable differences between local objects and remote objects. Contrary to this, services avoid this problem by making interactions between services and their clients more explicit.

- Most of the technology based on object orientation provides a way to encapsulate code in the classes, which requires an explicit compilation in case of any changes. Service orientation also supports policy-based compatibility through which code that needs to be changed frequently can be put in the configuration-based file. This policy-based configuration can be changed when required. Services encapsulate behavior and information in a way that is immeasurably more flexible and reusable than objects.

Exploring New Features in WCF

To a distributed object veteran, WCF might look like yet another distributed technology. WCF has taken a lot of features from the existing distributed stack but also extends the existing features and defines new boundaries. We'll now discuss some of the new features in WCF.

Developer Productivity

WCF increases a developer's productivity in several ways by simplifying the development of service-oriented applications. Previously, developers were forced to learn different APIs for building distributed components. It cannot be denied that developers who are good at building service components might not be as efficient at building remote components using .NET Remoting. Creating custom solutions that require the functionality of two or more distributed technologies has always raised butterflies in the bellies of developers and architects.

WCF has a simple and unified programming model that has the potential to create applications with diverse requirements. WCF is built from the ground up to support the features of service orientation. One of the best aspects of WCF is that developers using existing technologies will find their favorite features in it, and all developers will benefit from the consistent architecture. The WCF support of the declarative and imperative programming model will make you write less code, which offers the likelihood of fewer errors. An application requiring hundreds to thousands lines of code prior to WCF can now be accomplished in few lines of code.

Attribute-Based Development

WCF is a message-plumbing engine and has a simple, clear, and flexible programming model that sits at the top of this message engine. The programming model provides different ways to leverage the message engine. You can use the classes to directly write code similar to other distributed applications such as DCOM. You also get the opportunity to use configuration files that can be changed at runtime. The simplest and easiest way is WCF's support for the attribute-based programming model. One of the main intentions of the SOA is to separate the application code from the messaging infrastructure. The developer specifies infrastructure requirements declaratively by decorating the service class with custom attributes but does not actually write any infrastructure code.

In simple terms, you can think of an attribute as a simple string or annotation. Attributes are just declarative tags that, when applied to classes, methods, properties, and so on, provide viable information about behavior to the CLR and are the way to add metadata to the runtime. You can view metadata through any of the metadata-reading tools such as ILDASM. Attributes have been part of .NET since its beta releases, but the power of attributes has never been exploded in the wild jargon of the enterprise world. In WCF, attributes are central to the programming model and are treated as first-class citizens. This attribute-based model is not a new concept in WCF but has its roots in Enterprise Services and web services. Microsoft used the attribute-based programming model in Microsoft Transaction Server (MTS). If you have created a web service using .NET, you are already familiar with the `[WebMethods]` attribute. WCF has extended the immense support of declarative programming in the message engine. So, whenever you need transactional support or some security, you just need to decorate the service class with the specific attributes, and the messaging engine will provide you with the necessary infrastructure to achieve your desired result. This offers a real advantage to developers who can now concentrate on the real logic and then decorate the class and methods with the appropriate attribute to get the necessary infrastructure.

Attribute-based programming is simply the best way to get things done with the WCF engine, but you should also not forget the power of the object model of WCF. Depending on your application requirements, you can fulfill different application needs through minor configuration file changes. You can use an extensible API programming model for instances where you need finer-grained control. Actually, most of the attributes in WCF are shortcuts for imperative tasks you can do via APIs. Which method you use depends on your requirements.

Coexisting with Existing Technology

With .NET, Microsoft espouses a vision of how the Internet can make businesses more efficient and deliver services to consumers. WCF takes all the capabilities of the existing technology stacks while not relying upon any of them. WCF is a new investment and relies on the classes that are available in the .NET Framework 3.0. All your existing investments will run side by side with WCF. Applications built with these earlier technologies will continue to work unchanged on systems with WCF installed. It also provides you with an opportunity to communicate with, or even replace, existing Windows communications APIs and technologies, including ASMX, ASP.NET web services, Web Services Enhancements (WSE), Enterprise Services, `System.Messaging`, and .NET Remoting.

■ **Note** WCF has been coded with Managed C#, so existing technology will be able to coexist with WCF because WCF is just another managed-code implementation. The development of WCF started in parallel with .NET 1.*x* and .NET 2.0, and it is therefore being smoothly integrated into the existing technologies in the space. We cover coexistence in later chapters in more detail.

Hosting Services

A class implementing a WCF service is typically compiled into a library, and thus it needs a process to host the services. If you look at earlier distributed technologies, you will find that most of the distributed technologies are bound with only one hosting environment. For example, ASMX web services can be hosted only with `HttpRuntime` on IIS. A COM+ application requires component services as the hosting environment. .NET Remoting is a bit more flexible, with channels and transports being used. This limits the variety of clients that can access your component.

WCF has been made with a vision to allow endpoints to be seamlessly available for any kind of scenario and thereby ready to meet any requirement. A WCF component can be hosted in any kind of environment in .NET 3.0, be it a console application, Windows application, or IIS. To be honest, it hardly matters that the WCF client knows which environment is hosting its services. (Not only does it provide you with a variety of hosting environments, it also supports various activation models.) By hosting the service in IIS, it offers a lot of benefits such as automatic object activation and periodic recycling. Along with providing a lot of benefits, it comes with a tight coupling with HTTP. However, WCF gives you the freedom to self-host a WCF service. (Chapter 5 details the hosting options.) This is the reason for calling the WCF services *services* as opposed to *web services*. The terminologies have changed because you can host services without a web server. Earlier, web services used a default transport protocol such as HTTP. WCF provides different transport mechanisms such as TCP, Custom, UDP, and MSMQ.

■ **Note** Hosting services in normal EXEs requires the code to activate and run the service. They are generally also called *self-hosting*. Self-hosting the services gives you the flexibility to use transports other than HTTP with service development today. Chapter 5 describes hosting environments in more detail.

Migration/Integration with Existing Technology

WCF, being the next-generation way of developing distributed applications, has raised the curiosity level of developers working in existing distributed technologies. This is true because existing applications are likely to be impacted in the near future. There are already a lot of investments in applications built on ASMX, WSE, and `System.EnterpriseServices`. Here are some important questions when thinking about working with WCF:

- Will new applications developed using WCF work with your existing applications? For example, will your new WCF transacted application work with your existing transaction application built on `System.Transactions`?
- Will your existing applications be able to upgrade with WCF?

Fortunately, the answers to these questions are yes and yes! In truth, existing distributed applications cannot be migrated to WCF in a single day. Microsoft has created a durable surface for WCF to interoperate with existing investments. The WCF team consists of the same developers who built the `System.Messaging`, `System.EnterpriseServices`, WSE ASMX, and .NET Remoting technologies. WCF can use WS-* or HTTP bindings to communicate with ASMX pages, as shown in Figure 2-5. In other words, integration with existing systems was on the minds of the WCF team from the beginning.

Microsoft has implemented a set of capabilities within the WCF product suite to enable you to interact with and to reuse COM+ applications without having to fundamentally change your programming experience. Therefore, if you have COM+ applications, WCF lets you essentially write code that can access existing WCF applications as if they were COM+ applications.

This technology is simple to use. The samples that accompany WCF show how to use it. Also, a command-line tool called `COMSVCConfig.exe` (discussed in Chapter 10) lets an existing COM+ application spit out a WCF stub to interoperate with COM+ applications. The stub brokers call back and forth between the stub and COM+ application. MSMQ also integrates well with WCF. If you have an existing MSMQ application and use it to send messages back and forth between systems using queues, then WCF offers an `msmqIntegrationBinding` binding that allows communication with existing MSMQ applications. If you want to use a WCF application to utilize MSMQ on the wire, this binding is available to you so your applications can communicate with MSMQ applications openly.

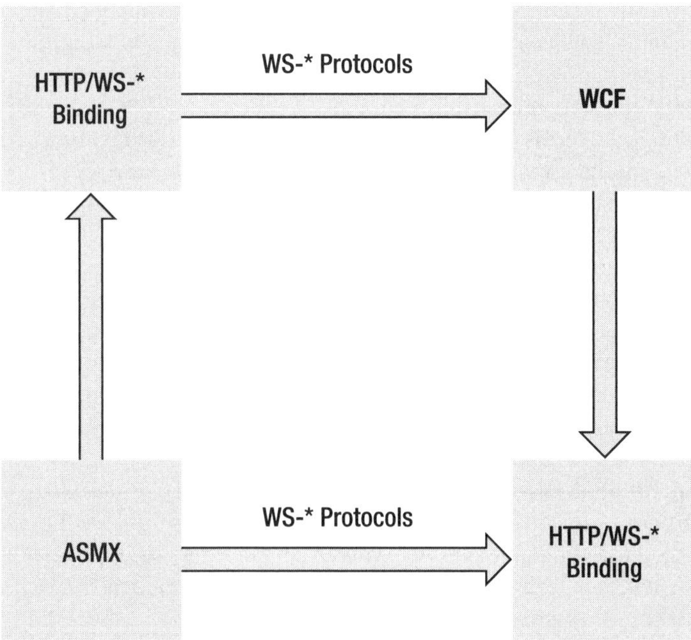

Figure 2-5. *ASMX to WCF connectivity*

■ **Note** You can find more information about integration between WCF and MSMQ in Chapter 8.

A WCF application not only interoperates with applications running on other platforms but also integrates with other distributed programming models that Microsoft has come up with over the past ten years. Microsoft has been providing the upgrade path through the use of wizards, which are the easy way to perform complex tasks. Honestly, these wizards are good in labs and can be used only for upgrading sample and testing applications. Using wizards to upgrade a complex application is ill advised. This time, Microsoft, having learned from past experiences of wizards to migrate applications, is using a more practical approach by providing a bunch of white papers and guidance, samples, demos, and examples illustrating how to port applications from ASMX, Enterprise Services, .NET Remoting, WSE, and MSMQ to WCF and other technologies. These examples also address many of the concerns you'll have when going through the porting process.

Components vs. Services

Reusability is the key to success in a distributed environment. Most of the architecture focuses on the way to maximize the components' usage in an easy and efficient manner. Most components are built on an object-oriented paradigm that also provides reuse in terms of encapsulating the state (data) and behavior (function) in a container called a *class*. We have already discussed the flaws in object-oriented technology in applications that mandate the need of loosely coupled distributed systems. Services compose a distributed system that can loosely couple one another to achieve a particular business goal. These services can later be composed differently to achieve a different business goal.

A lot of confusion exists about the terms *component* and *services*; a *component* is compiled code. It can be assembled to build applications and can also be deployed. Ease of reusability, maintenance, and lower application costs are some of the major factors for initiating component-based development. Most of the time, the term *component* has been associated with object-oriented programming but as per our earlier definition, you can use components to build services. The functionality that gets added on top of the component features is the service definition. This service description gets deployed with the components, and the communication with the service is governed by data contracts and policies.

The term *services* is used widely in various contexts. In service orientation, the term *service* is that which adheres to the four tenets of service orientation, and services are independently versioned, deployed, operated, and secured in a message-oriented fashion. To paraphrase Martin Fowler from his book *Enterprise Integration Patterns: Designing, Building, and Deploying Messaging Solutions* (Addison-Wesley, 2003), interesting applications rarely live in isolation. We discussed some of the challenges we face when trying to integrate applications in a homogeneous environment in Chapter 1. These can range from the tactical issues that a developer may face to the more strategic issues in a corporate environment where the challenges are quite difficult.

For a more detailed understanding of WCF's unified programming model, please refer to Chapter 3. The WCF stack maps almost on a one-to-one basis to all the SOA principles, as shown in Figure 2-6, which covers both the concrete and abstract implementations. WCF simplifies the development of connected systems because it unifies a wide range of distributed systems in a composite and extensible architecture. This architecture can span various transport layers, security systems, messaging patterns, network topologies, and hosting models.

■ **Note** Chapter 3 will explain aspects of the WCF stack from Figure 2-6 such as the service contract, the message contract, the data contract, and so on.

Building an application in terms of a service and not components also provides enormous benefits in terms of the reuse of code, the reuse of service and functionality, and the ability to glue together far more dynamic, far more agile business applications and business services. WCF makes it easy for developers to create services that adhere to the principle of service orientation. If you are an OO person, you will find a few things to be restrictive in SOA. The SOA world is a world of messages and not objects. Few key features (such as the ability to pass an object reference) exist in the current technology stack that are not available in WCF. Actually, the paradigm has shifted now from object oriented to service oriented, and it makes more sense to pass messages between services instead of objects.

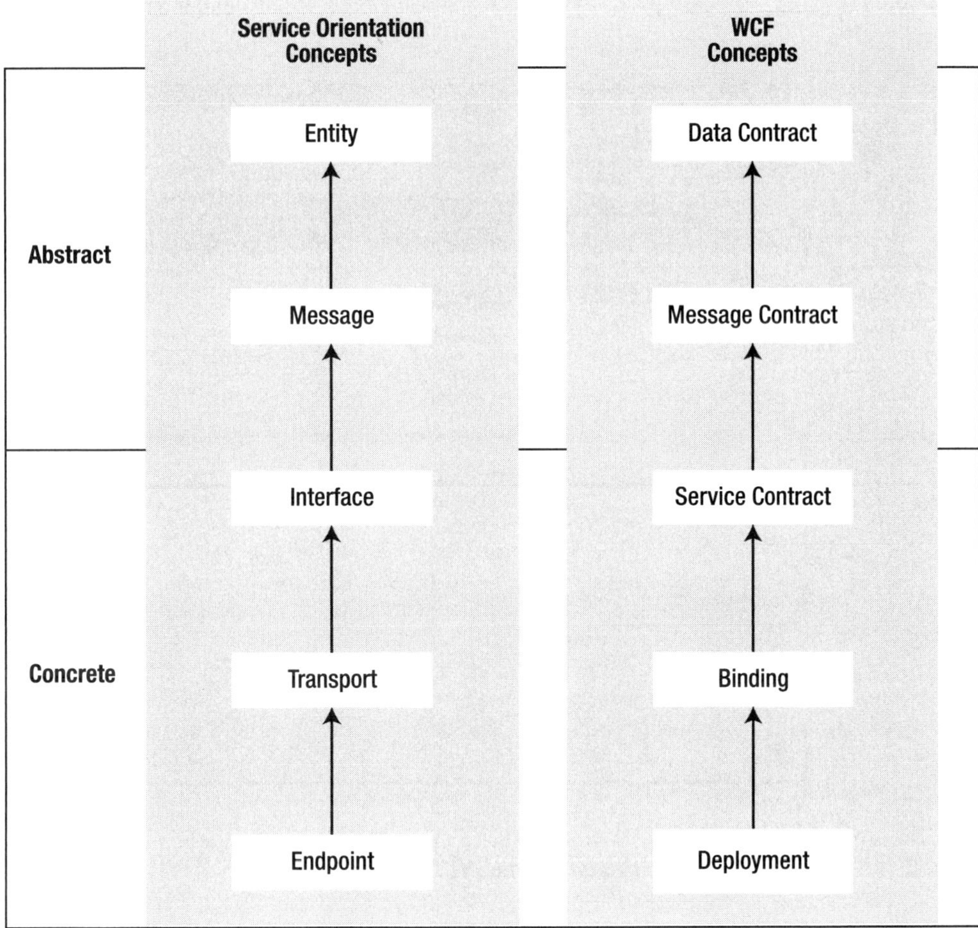

Figure 2-6. *WCF and service orientation mapping*

Support of Visual Studio 2005

WCF is a technology that comes with the .NET Framework 3.0. One of the advantages of using the .NET Framework is that you can use any of the languages supported by the CLR to build SOA applications. Any technology can be successful only if it has the required tools and designers to develop the components. Since the introduction of Visual Basic, Microsoft has always tried to simplify development by utilizing Visual Studio and the integrated development environment (IDE). WCF is actually one of the pillars for Windows Vista but can also run on Windows XP and Windows 2003 through the .NET Framework 3.0. Visual Studio 2005 supports WCF.

Figure 2-7 demonstrates that you get the required templates, IntelliSense in the configuration file, and the familiar IDE for creating WCF services. Developers who are already familiar with the Visual Studio IDE can leverage it to create service-oriented connected systems. You don't need to learn a new language for creating service-oriented applications. Languages such as C# and VB .NET, plus all the other CLR-compatible languages, have been extended to use the capabilities of the classes of WCF. Chapter 4 discusses the Visual Studio IDE and how WCF utilizes the IDE.

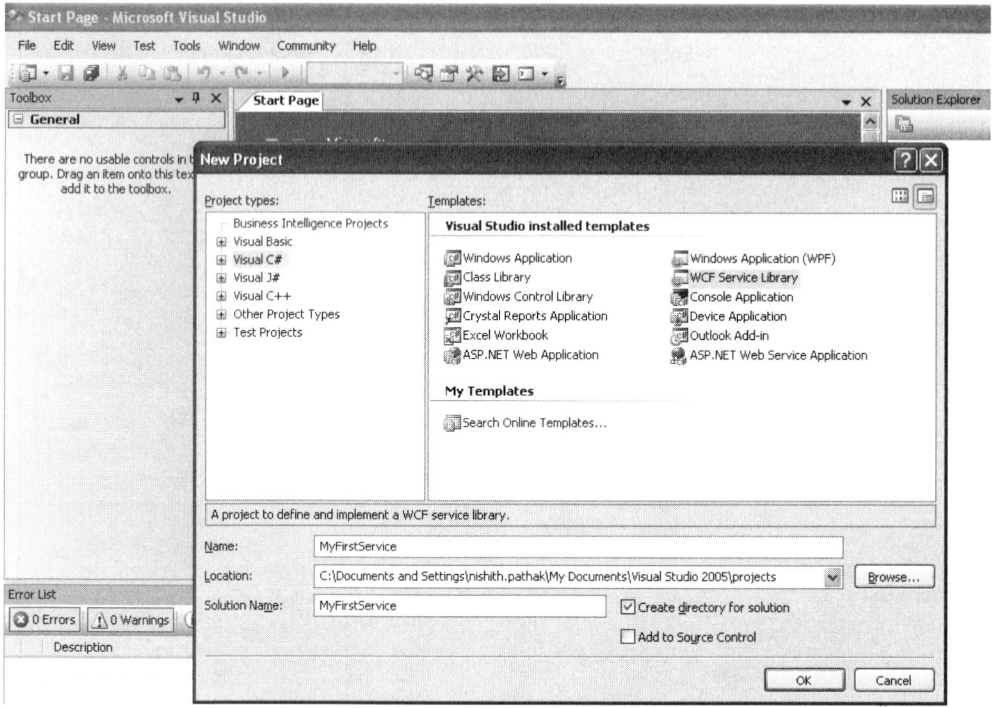

Figure 2-7. *Creating a WCF service in Visual Studio .NET 2005*

One Service, Multiple Endpoints

If you look at the current distributed technology stack, you will find that services are tightly coupled with the transport, the channels, the URLs, and the features the stack provides such as security and reliability. Service development is greatly affected by the transport you use. After defining the service, you have to specify some vital information such as what this service can do, how can it be accessed, and where it is available. These three are encapsulated in endpoints. An *endpoint* contains information that gives the path through which the service is available. One service can have multiple endpoints, which makes it flexible and interoperable for any application requirements. Each of these endpoints can differ in the address, binding requirements, or contract getting implemented.

WCF provides a unique way to create services independent of the transport being used. Figure 2-8 shows that the same service can be exposed with two different endpoints. Both of the endpoints have different binding requirements. For example, Endpoint 1 and Endpoint 2 have the transaction support but run on different transport protocols. In the future, if you need to have another client that has different binding requirements, all you need to do is create another endpoint in the configuration file. This enables you to serve the needs of two or more clients requiring the same business logic encapsulated in the service with different technical capabilities.

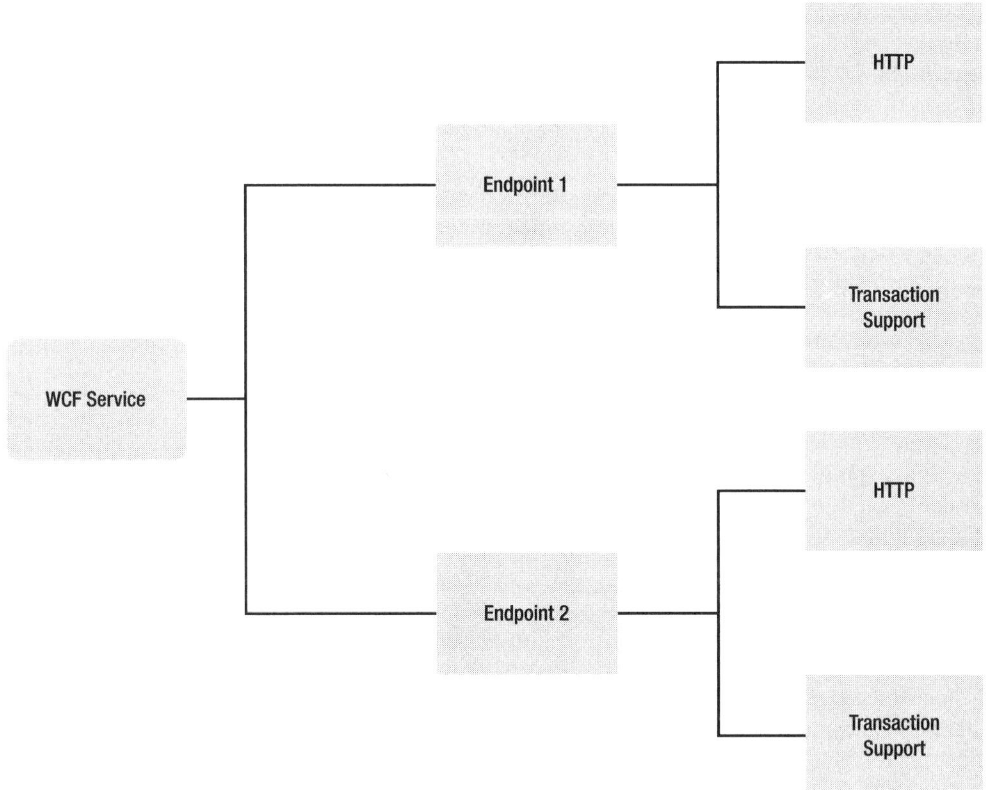

Figure 2-8. *One service with multiple endpoints*

Integration Technologies

In addition to extending the functionality of the .NET Framework and Visual Studio 2005, you can use WCF with BizTalk Server to provide both brokered and unbrokered application-to-application communication. Actually, BizTalk Server and WCF are complementary to each other. BizTalk Server provides business process orchestration, message transformation, business activity monitoring, and more, through designers and visual tools. WCF provides a unified framework for building secure and reliable transacted services. BizTalk Server is a key technology in and is responsible for orchestrating WCF services. In future versions of BizTalk Server, the orchestration process will use workflow foundation. BizTalk Server provides a WCF adapter that enables WFC services to be incorporated into business process orchestration. In future versions of BizTalk Server, the integration between these technologies will be even more seamless, with WCF providing the core messaging and web service capabilities of BizTalk Server and with WCF integrated in the native protocol of BizTalk Server.

Unifying Distributed Technologies

Many of the features in WCF have their deep roots in a number of technologies such as ASMX, Enterprise Services, .NET Remoting, MSMQ, and WSE. Though this book won't cover all these technologies, it's always good to take a sneak peek at each of these to get a better understanding of WCF.

ASMX

A web service is a component on the Web that is accessible through open standards such as SOAP and HTTP. Accessing a remote component is not a new concept. It was previously accomplished through RMI, CORBA, and DCOM. But these distributed components are based on proprietary standards or protocols. Earlier distributed technologies had two main problems:

- Interoperability
- Crossing firewalls

These proprietary standards cannot interoperate with each other because they have their own binary standards and protocols. Additionally, they send binary messages through a nonstandard port that results in creating "holes" in corporate firewalls. Web services deviate from all these issues by relying on web standards or protocols instead of relying on proprietary protocols. Web services are based on the notion of a *service* and transfer the data in *messages*.

A web service is a class that inherits from `System.Web.Services.WebService` and contains the method to be exposed with the `[WebMethod]` attribute over it. Listing 2-1 contains a class named `Employee` that has two public methods named `Gand so onustomer` and `DeleteCustomer`. The method name `Gand so onustomer` will be consumed only as web service methods because it has been decorated with the `[WebMethod]` attribute.

Listing 2-1. *Sample XML Web Service Class*

```
<%@ WebService Language="C#" Class="Order.Employee" %>
using System;
using System.Collections;
using System.ComponentModel;
using System.Data;
using System.Diagnostics;
using System.Web;
using System.Web.Services;

namespace Order
{
    public class Employee : WebService
    {
         [WebMethod()]
        public DataSet Gand so onustomer(int CustomerID)
        {
        // logic to retrieve customer
        }
```

```
        public DataSet DeleteCustomer(int CustomerID)
        {
        // logic to delete Orders of a customer
        }


    }
}
```

To access any remote components, you need a transport protocol, a message protocol, and the serialization mechanism for a client and server. In web services, the transport protocol is mainly HTTP, though it can be SMTP or TCP as well. As far as a message protocol is concerned, SOAP is the preferred and default message protocol. It also supports HTTP GET or HTTP POST. XML web services use XML serialization.

The following are the problems with ASMX:

- An ASMX page contains a complete set of information that describes how the data will be formatted, how to wrap the data in a SOAP header, and how to prepare it to be sent. However, it doesn't tell you how to deliver it over the transports and to use a specific type of security. All of those transport-oriented notions are missing from today's ASMX services, and this is something that WCF enhances quite significantly.

- Another limitation of ASMX is the tight coupling with the HTTP runtime and the dependence on IIS to host it. This problem is solved by WCF, which can be hosted by any Windows process that is able to host the .NET Framework 3.0.

- ASMX service is instantiated on a per-call basis, while WCF gives you flexibility by providing various instancing options such as Singleton, private session, per call. (We discuss these in detail in Chapter 4.)

- ASMX provides the way for interoperability but doesn't fulfill some of the basic requirements; for example, it does not provide or guarantee end-to-end security or reliable communication.

MSMQ

Distributed systems have been built for many years by using synchronous RPCs. This means the sender application must be online during each request while the receiver carries out the requested task. The receiver must be online for the sender to make requests, and the sender must be online to issue requests. In other words, both the sender and receiver need to be online to make the task operational. Some applications (especially ones supporting disconnected environments) need to communicate in an asynchronous manner. Asynchronous-based communication through messages has become one of the alternatives in distributed computing. In this communication model, the client begins the process by sending messages and then continues doing other work or even goes offline without waiting for the operation to complete. If the receiver is offline, the entire request from the sender gets stored in queues. Once the receiver is ready, it can consume the messages from the queue and do the necessary operations on it. The best advantage is that the sender and receiver do not need to be available at the same time. It also ensures the reliable delivery of messages in a loosely coupled environment.

Asynchronous-based communication requires a custom messaging infrastructure. Fortunately, many middleware systems such as IBM's MQSeries and Microsoft's MSMQ provide built-in powerful capabilities to address these issues. (These packaged software products provide transactional support, guaranteed delivery, and security.) Message queues are stores that hold application-specific messages. Applications can read, send, store, and delete the messages in queues.

MSMQ is a set of objects that allows you to perform queue messaging in Windows. You can use this technology to collect a series of messages, send them to the server for processing, and receive the results when they are finished. MSMQ essentially provides the infrastructure to develop highly available business-critical applications. `System.Messaging` is the .NET layer on top of MSMQ. It gives you the ability to build queued applications through .NET. One of the limitations in MSMQ is the ability to deal with corrupted messages. A message is referred to as corrupted when the message cannot get processed after several attempts. These corrupted message(s) block other messages in the queue. Since MSMQ does not support this feature, developers used to write a lot of code to deal with corrupted messages. Few features of MSMQ (such as security and searching on public queues) are tightly integrated with Active Directory. Another issue with MSMQ is that developers need to write MSMQ-specific plumbing code in client and service code especially while writing a complex listener code to listen these queues.

WSE

Web services have become the unvarying way for consuming the business logic across platforms. The core architecture of web services only formulates the way that a message gets formatted and how a web service can be defined in a standardized manner. This core architecture enables you to consume web services in an interoperable manner. As the business requirements that drive web services become more and more complex, developers require additional capabilities that current web services standards do not address. A few of those capabilities include the following:

- Security
- Routing
- Reliable messaging
- Transactions

Rather than providing these capabilities in a proprietary manner, it was necessary for the future of web services to provide these capabilities in an open way. Industry leaders such as Microsoft and IBM came together to provide these additional capabilities in a standardized manner and drafted some web service standards also known as the WS-* suite of protocols. This was done in order to create a standard infrastructure for building the next generation of web services. Some of the WS-* suite of protocols are HTTP, standards-based XML, SOAP, WS-Addressing, and Message Transmission Optimization Mechanism (MTOM). These protocols are merely the specifications and do not provide the implementation details. Microsoft has been generous enough to provide the class library on the top of the .NET Framework called WSE that encapsulates the implementations details and provides an easy-to-use API to consume these specifications. WSE is a runtime that is built on the .NET Framework and uses outbound and inbound message filters to intercept SOAP messages.

Tip Microsoft enhances WSE as new web service specifications come into the picture. To learn about the most recent updates on WSE, visit `http://msdn.microsoft.com/webservices/webservices/building/wse/default.aspx`.

WSE is an appealing technology in that it fundamentally helps accelerate the adoption of WS-* standards. WSE 3 is the latest version of WSE.

Enterprise Services

Every distributed component requires some basic services to work in a multiuser environment. In the early days of COM, developers spent a large amount of time creating an infrastructure to handle a large number of transactions, provide queuing infrastructure, and so on, for running the components. COM+ (also known as *component services*) provides an infrastructure that applications utilize to access services and capabilities beyond the scope of the developers who are actually building those applications. It also supports multitier architecture by providing the surrogate process to host the business objects. In many ways, COM+ is a combination of COM, DCOM, MTS, and MSMQ in a single product. This application infrastructure includes services such as transactions, resource management, security, and synchronization. By providing these services, it enables you to concentrate on building serviced components rather than worrying about the infrastructure required to run these business components. COM+ has two types of applications, namely, server applications and library applications. A *server application* is hosted by the COM+ surrogate process and supports all the services. Contrary to this, *library applications* are hosted by the client process, and certain COM+ services such as queued components and object pooling are not available to a library application. One of the many advantages of component services is that it allows you to select the appropriate services.

COM+ was initially for providing an infrastructure to COM components, but this does not mean it cannot be used from .NET. .NET components can also utilize COM+ services through the attributes and classes residing in the `System.EnterpriseServices` namespace. .NET Enterprise Services, which is the .NET layer on top of COM+, gives a powerful distributed component technology capability by providing the necessary service infrastructure to .NET assemblies. The classes in .NET that can be hosted by the COM+ application and use COM+ services are called *serviced components*. Any class in .NET that derives directly or indirectly from the `System.EnterpriseServices.ServicedComponent` class is called a *serviced component class*. Listing 2-2 illustrates these concepts for a fictitious `Account` class.

Listing 2-2. *Serviced Component for the* `Account` *Class*

```
using System.EnterpriseServices;
using System;

[Transaction(TransactionOption.Required)]
public class Account : ServicedComponent
```

```
{
   [AutoComplete]
   static void Main()
        {

        }
}
```

Enterprise Services, or COM+, is a component-oriented technology. It is used inside the service boundary and implements the complex business logic as with transactions spanning multiple objects and spanning multiple resources. However, Enterprise Services applications are tightly coupled with the infrastructure. Microsoft has always regarded Enterprise Services as the core technology for providing the infrastructure, but it also suffers heavily from interoperability.

How Do You Unify All These Technologies?

Most of these distributed technologies are based on the same concept. However, all of them provide specific services that are unique to the product. (That is, if you want to do queuing, you need to use MSMQ or `System.Messaging`; if you want to do transactions, you need to use `System.EnterpriseServices`; if you need to do security, you need to use WSE.) As a programmer, you are constantly forced to switch between these programming models.

Therefore, we need one distributed technology to gather the capabilities of the existing stack and provide a solution with a simple and flexible programming model. WCF does a great job of providing a unified programming model wherein you can compose all these different functionalities into your application without having to do a lot of context switching. Going forward, you have to just learn one programming model—WCF. If you want queuing, you just add an attribute to your WCF service contract that makes it queued. If you want to secure the communication with your WCF service, you just add the appropriate security attributes for authentication and privacy. If you are after transaction support, you just add the transaction attribute. This new programming paradigm should help you concentrate more on the business logic.

WCF provides a single programming model to leverage the features of any distributed technology in the stack, as shown in Figure 2-9. Though WCF takes the best features of all the distributed technology in the stack, the team developing WCF has not chosen to extend any of the existing distributed technologies; instead, the whole infrastructure has been revamped to support the predecessors and use the classes available in the .NET Framework 3.0. Developers now can select the features they need to incorporate into the component. (That is, the developer can choose to implement security and reliability without requiring the transaction support.)

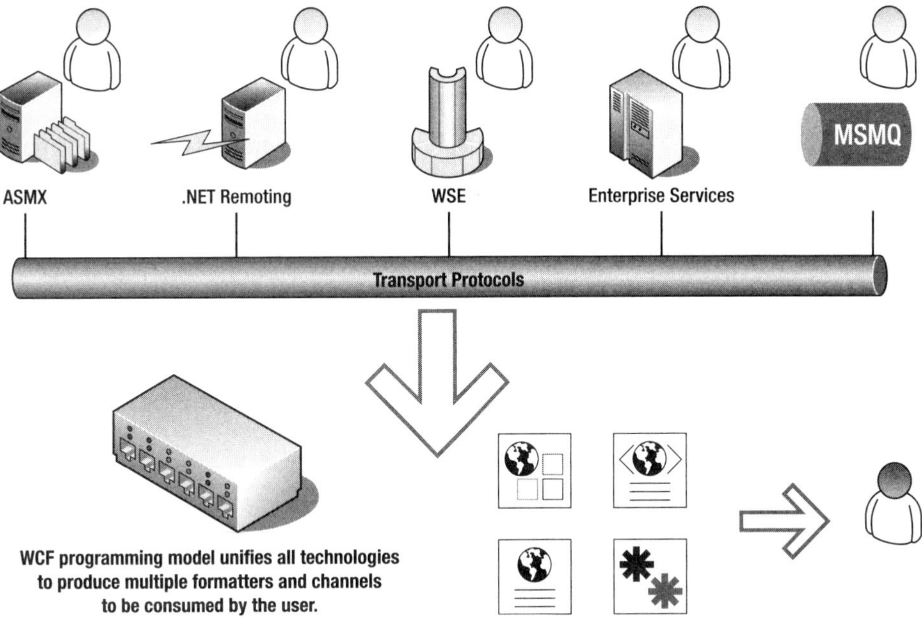

Figure 2-9. *Unification of existing technology*

Programming bugs are common in development environments. During testing, you can trap runtime errors by debugging the code. But finding bugs during the product environment is not as easy. You need the appropriate tools to help in instrumentation and in monitoring the health of an application. *Tracing* is a process to receive informative messages about the execution of a web application. In ASP.NET, tracing takes place through the methods available in the `Trace` class residing in the `Systems.Diagnostics` namespace. WCF extends the tracing capabilities of ASP.NET with lots of new features. WCF has also come up with end-to-end tracing through a trace viewer called `svcTraceViewer.exe` and also with message logging in the XML files.

■ **Note** Chapter 6 covers tracing in more detail.

WCF also has the queue management that is similar to queued components of COM+ and extends the API of MSMQ. With the queue management features of WCF, developers no longer need to write complex plumbing code of sending and receiving queues in the application. WCF comes with `NetProfileMsmqBinding` and other custom bindings to interact with queues. It also resolves the ability to handle corrupted message that was a nightmare for many MSMQ developers. Contrary to MSMQ, the queue management of WCF also supports application-to-application security and does not require Active Directory. WCF supports queue management through bindings, and you can decide the appropriate binding depending on the consuming application's requirements.

■ **Note** For more information about queue management, please refer to Chapter 8.

Writing a WCF application is similar to writing another application; you don't need to be concerned with the protocols or transport being used. Service endpoints that are the combination of address, binding, and contract (commonly known as the ABCs of WCF) can be specified in the configuration file that is separate from the service being developed. Endpoints are not a new concept. They were earlier defined in WSDL, but WCF extends this extensible model to other technologies such as Enterprise Services, thus giving a consistent model to its predecessors.

■ **Note** Chapter 3 covers the ABCs of WCF in more detail.

Services can now have multiple endpoints. These endpoints either can be defined in the code or can be defined in the configuration file. WCF can facilitate bindings changes without impacting the code using configuration files.

Summary

The world is now more connected since the introduction of the Web. A few basic needs of connected systems are security, transaction, and reliability along with interoperability in heterogeneous environments. As various networks bring the world more closely together than ever, you need to develop components that meet the needs of this connected environment.

Microsoft initiated its vision of connected systems through web services. However, being the first step toward developing connected systems, it has some vital pitfalls. WCF takes web services to the next level by providing developers with a highly productive framework for building secure, reliable, and interoperable applications and meeting today's demand of connected systems. WCF also integrates with the latest suite of WS-* protocols; when the latest protocols are released by WS-*, there will be service packs of WCF to implement them.

WCF provides a number of benefits that will make developers more productive, reduce the number of bugs, speed up application development, and simplify deployment. WCF helps achieve all those challenges using a unified programming model that provides for a unifying message style that is not only based on open standards but also is optimized for binary communication where applicable. WCF's unified programming model also provides for building secure, reliable, and interoperable applications. With that said, IT managers are understandably wary (since WCF is a new technology that requires a moderately steep learning curve). However, for most organizations, the benefits will far outweigh the negatives; and with WCF, you'll see great productivity gains for future development projects. We will explain how you do this in Chapter 3 by covering the unified programming models of WCF.

CHAPTER 3

Exploring the WCF Programming Model

Building connected systems on the Microsoft platform usually means using multiple technologies and as such different programming models. WCF comes with a unified programming model that makes your life as a developer much easier. Some of the benefits are as follows:

- Built-in support for a broad set of web service protocols
- Implicit use of service-oriented development principles
- A single API for building connected systems

As you read in Chapters 1 and 2, WCF combines and extends the features for connectivity that you find in the .NET Framework 1.0, 1.1, and 2.0. We are referring to technologies such as ASP.NET web services (ASMX), .NET Remoting, Enterprise Services, Web Services Enhancements, and the `System.Messaging` namespace. WCF is meant to provide an easier-to-understand and unified programming model compared to the previous set of technologies. It should make you more productive when creating connected systems. In addition, it provides superior ways to extend the application if the existing rich functionality doesn't fulfill your requirements.

This chapter covers the WCF programming model. It gives you some insight into the layered architecture of WCF. After reading this chapter, you should be familiar with the concepts of WCF and the programming model in particular. You will learn enough to create your first WCF-enabled application, and you will start the case-study application that we will show how to create throughout this book. Additionally, this chapter shows you where the extension points are inside WCF and explains when to use them.

The heart of WCF lives inside the `System.ServiceModel` namespace and the messaging system underneath it; we'll cover both in this book. This chapter won't go into the details of all the classes in the namespaces. (We will go through most of them throughout the next chapters.) This chapter will give you a basic understanding of the programming model and should give you a starting point to understand the more complex concepts of WCF.

To illustrate how to use WCF, we will present a case study of an imaginary company called QuickReturns Ltd. QuickReturns Ltd. is a stock-trading company that needs a connected system that requires functionality to trade stock on a stock exchange. Typical actors in the systems are Market Makers and Asset Managers. The appendix of this book describes the QuickReturns Ltd. case study. In this chapter, we will define the initial set of contracts and services that the QuickReturns Ltd. system offers.

After completing this chapter, you will have the following knowledge:

- You'll be familiar with the core architecture of WCF.
- You'll be familiar with all the terms that are used in WCF.
- You'll understand the unified programming model of WCF.
- You'll be able to start developing your first WCF-enabled application.
- You'll know in which areas WCF can be extended and when to do what.

Introducing the Technical Architecture

To be able to use WCF, you have to install certain Microsoft software on a supported Microsoft operating system. WCF is part of the .NET Framework 3.0 that comes with Windows Vista and, among others, contains the following technologies:

- Windows Communication Foundation (WCF)
- Windows Presentation Foundation (WPF)
- Windows Workflow Foundation (WF)
- Windows Card Services (WCS)

The .NET Framework supports the following operating systems:

- Windows XP Service Pack 2 and newer
- Windows Server 2003 Service Pack 1 and newer
- Windows Server 2003 Release 2
- Windows Vista
- Windows Server 2007

The .NET Framework 3.0 should also support revisions of the Windows platforms mentioned. The .NET Framework 3.0 is built on top of the .NET Framework 2.0 and in essence adds the aforementioned frameworks while the base frameworks stay the same. You can install the framework on any of the mentioned operating systems, and you can enable it easily in Windows Vista and Windows Server 2007.

To be able to develop connected systems with WCF, you also require a development environment. The recommended development environment for WCF is Visual Studio 2005. All versions of Visual Studio 2005, including Express Edition, are supported. Visual Studio 2005 also requires the .NET Framework 2.0, which Visual Studio 2005 will install if it's not already available.

■ **Note** The Windows software development kit (SDK) comes with a lot of sample code you can use to learn WCF and the other frameworks that are part of the .NET Framework 3.0. Refer to the .NET Framework 3.0 Developer Center on the Microsoft Developer Network at `http://msdn.microsoft.com/winfx/` to get the latest version. Refer to the appendix to get more details about the installation. Finally, refer to `http://www.netfx3.com` to get additional news, samples, and resources.

Introducing the Programming Approach

The programming model of WCF, and the programming models of the other frameworks that are part of the .NET Framework 3.0 in general, allows you to program in a few ways. In other words, you can accomplish your goals using any of the following approaches:

- You can use the object model programmatically.
- You can use configuration files.
- You can use declarative programming (attributes).

You will use all these approaches in most of your applications, and it is a great benefit for developers to be able to choose their preference. (That is, it is important to be able to make your application configurable for operations people, so you will not hard-code the URLs of your endpoints by using the object model.) The object model is the richest model in which you can basically accomplish everything you like. The WCF configuration model is built on top of the object model.

For now, it is good to remember you have three options and that you have to make sure you know the order of precedence in WCF (since you can override one model with the other). The order in which settings are applied is as follows:

1. Attributes are applied.
2. The configuration is applied.
3. The code runs.

In the following sections, we will show how to accomplish the same goals in different ways. We'll first cover what the "ABCs" of WCF are all about.

Learning the ABCs of WCF

What are the ABCs of WCF? This is a common question that is asked of WCF lovers. In short, ABC stands for address, binding, and contract:

- The *address* specifies where the messages can be sent (or where the service lives).
- The *binding* describes how to send the messages.
- The *contract* describes what the messages should contain.

Obviously, clients need to know the ABCs of a service to be able to use the service. An endpoint acts as a "gateway" to the outside world. Usually you can refer to these three items as the endpoint of a service defined in WCF. The Web Services Description Language (WSDL) is meant to describe service endpoints in a standardized way. A WSDL file describes what a service can do, how a service can be accessed, and where the service can be found.

Figure 3-1 illustrates all the components to consume WCF services using the programming model and to use and extend the messaging layer. In addition, you can see how the service model influences the messaging layer and which terms fit where. In this chapter, we'll concentrate on addresses, bindings, factories, listeners, channels, and messages on the messaging layer.

We'll address clients, services, endpoints, contracts, and behaviors on the service model side. Together, the address, binding, and contract are commonly referred to as an *endpoint*.

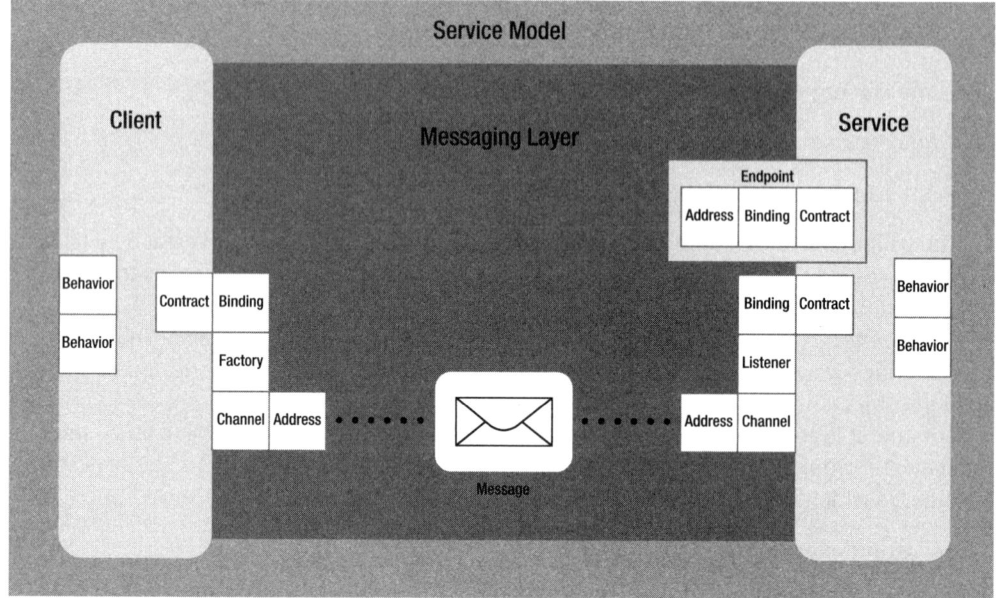

Figure 3-1. *The WCF programming model*

On the client side, you can see only one endpoint consisting of an address, binding, and contract. Think of the client as a piece inside your program that is able to communicate with a service, not your entire application. Commonly this is referred to as a *proxy* for that service. Of course, it is possible to have your client connect to multiple services by using multiple proxies with different endpoints (that is, connected to different services). The client side can have a specific behavior to do local configuration, such as concurrency, instancing, throttling, error handling, transaction control, security, and so on.

The service side can have multiple endpoints. A service just sits around and waits for messages to come in on its endpoints. And again on the service side, you see the same behaviors you can see on the client side that cover local configuration behaviors on the service or at the operation level.

You will learn more about behaviors, factories, listeners, and channels later in this chapter. We'll cover the ABCs of WCF in much greater detail now.

What Are Addresses?

Addressing a service is essential to being able to use a service. You need to have the address of a service to be able to send it a message. Addresses in WCF are URLs that define the protocol used, the machine where the service is running, and the path to the service. The port number is an optional field in the URL and depends on the protocol used. Table 3-1 lists the addressing specifications.

Table 3-1. *Addressing Specifications*

Address Section	Description
Transport scheme	This defines the transport protocol (or scheme).
Machinename	This specifies the fully qualified domain name of the machine.
Port	The port is an optional field and is specified as `:port`. Port 80 is the default for HTTP addresses.
Path	The path is the specific path to the service. You can define paths as names of directories separated by a forward slash. For example, `/Stock/GetQuote` is the path in the following address: `http://localhost:8080/Stock/GetQuote`.

So, the format of a service address is as follows:

```
scheme://<machinename>[:port]/path1/path2
```

As you can see, it is similar to a URL of a website. `scheme` can be any type of supported transport, `machinename` is the server name, `port` is the port where the service is listening, and `path` is essentially to differentiate services running on the same machine.

WCF supports several protocols, and each has its own particular addressing format. WS-Addressing is essential when WCF services use protocols other than HTTP. The foundation of a service is the SOAP protocol, which defines a basic message structure for simple (remote) object access containing an extensible envelope structure with a header and a body. In a SOAP message, endpoints are expressed as WS-Addressing endpoint reference constructs. With WS-Addressing you can also add specific headers inside the SOAP message that defines where message replies should go (if applicable in the used messaging exchange pattern).

Addressing HTTP

Services can be hosted in different ways, as you'll learn more about in Chapter 5. HTTP services can be either self-hosted or hosted on Internet Information Services (IIS). When addressing an HTTP service in a self-hosted scenario, you use the following format:

```
http://localhost:8080/QuickReturns/Exchange
```

When SSL is required, you can replace `http` with `https`. In a WCF configuration, you can set the HTTP address as follows:

```
<endpoint
    address="http://localhost:8080/QuickReturns/Exchange"
    bindingsSectionName="BasicHttpBinding"
    contract="IExchange" />
```

We'll cover the `bindingsSectionName` and `contract` attributes of the endpoint node in the following sections.

■ **Note** It is common to add versioning directives to the path of a service address. You can version the address like this: `http://localhost:8080/QuickReturns/Stock/v1/GetQuote`.

Addressing TCP

The TCP transport uses the `net.tcp:` scheme but otherwise follows the same rules as described for HTTP addresses. Here is an example:

```
net.tcp://localhost:8080/QuickReturns/Exchange
```

In a WCF configuration, you can set the `net.tcp` address as follows:

```
<endpoint
    address="net.tcp://localhost:8080/QuickReturns/Exchange"
    bindingsSectionName="NetTcpBinding"
    contract="IExchange" />
```

Addressing MSMQ

You can use the Microsoft Message Queue (MSMQ) transport in an asynchronous one-way (fire-and-forget) or duplex type of messaging pattern and use the MSMQ features of Windows. MSMQ has public and private queues. Public queues are usually available through Active Directory and can be accessed remotely whereas private queues are local queues that are available only on the local machine. MSMQ addresses use the `net.msmq` scheme and specify a machine name, queue type, and queue name. Port numbers don't have any meaning in the MSMQ address, so a sample MSMQ address is as follows:

```
net.msmq://localhost/private$/QuickReturnSettleTrade
```

In a WCF configuration, you can set the `net.msmq` address as follows:

```
<endpoint
    address=" net.msmq://localhost/private$/QuickReturnsSettleTrade"
    bindingsSectionName="NetMsmqBinding"
    contract="IExchange" />
```

Addressing Named Pipes

Named Pipes is a common way to provide a means to implement inter- or in-process communication. The Named Pipes transport in WCF supports only local communication and uses the `net.pipes` scheme. Port numbers don't have any meaning with the Named Pipes transport. This results in the following address format:

```
net.pipe://localhost/QuickReturns/Exchange
```

In a WCF configuration, you can set the `net.pipe` address as follows:

```
<endpoint
    address="net.pipe://localhost/QuickReturns/Exchange"
    bindingsSectionName="NetNamedPipeBinding"
    contract="IExchange" />
```

Base Addresses

WCF supports base addresses, which enables you to host multiple endpoints under the same base address and which shortcuts the duplication of the scheme, host, port, and root path in your configuration. To define two endpoints in a WCF configuration, you would add the following section to express QuickReturns Ltd.'s base address:

```
<host>
    <baseAddresses>
        <add baseAddress="http://localhost:8080/QuickReturns"/>
        <add baseAddress="net.tcp://localhost/QuickReturns"/>
    </baseAddresses>
</host>
```

This allows you to define the following endpoints:

```
<endpoint
    name="BasicHttpBinding"
    address="Exchange"
    bindingsSectionName="BasicHttpBinding"
    contract="IExchange" />

<endpoint
    name="NetNamedPipeBinding"
    address="Exchange"
    bindingsSectionName="NetNamedPipeBinding"
    contract="IExchange" />
```

What Are Bindings?

A *binding* defines how you can communicate with the service and as such has the biggest impact in the programming model of WCF. It is the primary extension point of the ABCs of WCF. The binding controls the following:

- The transport (HTTP, MSMQ, Named Pipes, TCP)
- The channels (one-way, duplex, request-reply)
- The encoding (XML, binary, MTOM…)
- The supported WS-* protocols (WS-Security, WS-Federation, WS-Reliability, WS-Transactions)

WCF provides a default set of bindings that should cover most of your requirements. If the default bindings don't cover your requirements, you can build your own binding by extending from `CustomBinding`.

Table 3-2 shows the features of each default binding that comes with WCF. As you can see, these features directly relate to the transport protocols, the encoding, and the WS-* protocols. The Configuration and Element columns relate to the configuration element in the application interoperability, the Transactions and Security Default Session columns relate to several of the WS-* protocols described in Chapters 1 and 2. The Duplex column specifies whether the binding supports the duplex messaging exchange pattern. As you can see, each transport we covered earlier has at least one associated predefined binding.

Table 3-2. *Predefined WCF Bindings*

Binding	Configuration	Security	Default Session	Transactions	Duplex
`basicHttpBinding`	Basic Profile 1.1	None	No		
`wsHttpBinding`	WS	Message	Optional	Yes	
`wsDualHttpBinding`	WS	Message	Yes	Yes	Yes
`wsFederationHttpBinding`	WS-Federation	Message	Yes	Yes	No
`netTcpBinding`	.NET	Transport	Optional	Yes	Yes
`netNamedPipeBinding`	.NET	Transport	Yes	Yes	Yes
`netMsmqBinding`	.NET	Transport	Yes	Yes	No
`netPeerTcpBinding`	Peer	Transport			Yes
`msmqIntegrationBinding`	MSMQ	Transport	Yes	Yes	

Remember, you can have multiple endpoints defined for a service so that your service supports any combination of these bindings.

WCF supports several transports on the Microsoft platform:

- HTTP(S)
- TCP
- Named Pipes
- MSMQ

Obviously, only HTTP(S) is truly an interoperable transport. When integration is required with different platforms, you can recognize interoperable bindings with the WS prefix. `BasicHttpBinding` is also an interoperable binding that maps very well on the pre-WCF service stacks such as ASMX. The bindings prefixed with `Net` are really Windows-centric, where it is expected that interoperability is not a requirement. So, you know up front what your requirements are and as such what transport fits best into your scenario. As mentioned, when you choose a binding, often you are choosing a transport as well. Table 3-3 lists the predefined WCF bindings and the transport(s) they support.

Table 3-3. *Predefined WCF Bindings Mapped on the Transports*

Binding	HTTP	HTTPS	TCP	MSMQ	Named Pipes
`BasicHttpBinding`	Yes	Yes	No	No	No
`WSHttpBinding`	Yes	Yes	Yes	No	No
`WSDualHttpBinding`	Yes	Yes	No	No	No
`WSFederationHttpBinding`	Yes	Yes	No	No	No

Binding	HTTP	HTTPS	TCP	MSMQ	Named Pipes
NetTcpBinding	No	No	Yes	No	No
NetNamedPipeBinding	No	No	No	No	Yes
NetMsmqBinding	No	No	No	Yes	No
NetPeerTcpBinding	No	No	Yes	No	No
MsmqIntegrationBinding	No	No	No	Yes	No

What Are Contracts?

One of the core principles of service orientation is explicit boundaries. When crossing boundaries in typical RPC technology, you will struggle with issues where the internals and externals are mixed up. The essence of *contracts* in service orientation is that you agree on what you expose to the outside in order to decide for yourself how you implement (and change) the inside. Service orientation draws a distinct line between the "external interface" and the "internal implementation." Contracts are not connected to the .NET type system but rather to an implementation of several standards by using the .NET type system. Contracts are the way service orientation achieves true interoperability between different platforms; see Chapter 13 for more details about this.

Contracts come in different flavors. A contract is a declaration of exposed behavior (the service contract), persistent data (the data contract), or message structure (the message contract). In the following sections, you will learn how to define and use each of these in the WCF programming model.

Messaging Exchange Patterns

WCF service contracts can express three message exchange patterns that can be used in your services. Note that bindings limit the message exchange patterns that are available.

Request-Reply

Request-reply is a two-way operation where each request correlates to a response. The client explicitly waits for a reply. Request-reply is the most common pattern in today's (ASMX) web services (and also RPC) world. In WCF, request-reply is the default pattern. Figure 3-2 illustrates the request-reply messaging exchange pattern.

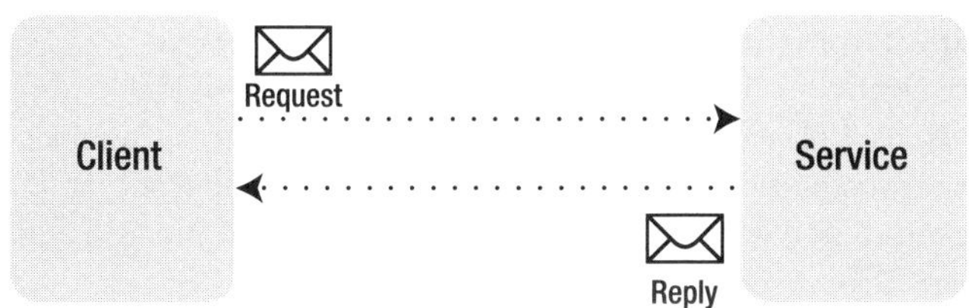

Figure 3-2. *Request-reply messaging exchange pattern*

One-Way

One-way is a "fire-and-forget" style of messaging, where the message is transmitted without waiting for a reply from the service. As you can see in Figure 3-3, the message is initiated on the client side and passed to the service side, but the client is not expecting a reply. This is similar to calling an asynchronous method (a delegate) with a void return type.

Figure 3-3. *One-way messaging exchange pattern*

Duplex

Duplex messaging is slightly more complex. A duplex channel is really a peer-to-peer connection, with both ends simultaneously acting as both a sender and a receiver (on different channels), as you can see in Figure 3-4. A duplex service defines two interfaces—one for each side of the wire. Please refer to Chapter 12 for more information about peer-to-peer (and duplex) messaging.

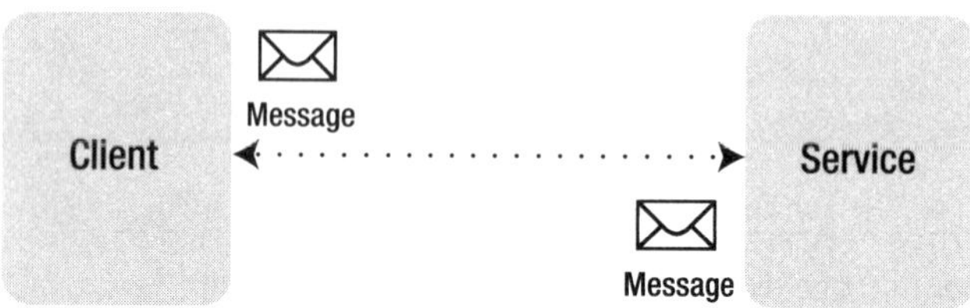

Figure 3-4. *Duplex messaging exchange pattern*

Service Contracts and Operations

The *service contract* expresses the "methods" that are exposed to the outside world. The service contract is also commonly referred to as the *service interface* or the *exposed behavior* of the service. It describes what you can expect from the service, and its policy describes what requirements the service has. Service contracts are implemented as .NET interfaces. The service interfaces are implemented as .NET classes implementing the .NET interfaces. To make the classes WCF service contracts, you must annotate the interface with the `[ServiceContract]` attribute. The operations need to be annotated with the `[OperationContract]` attribute. You can find the `ServiceContractAttribute` and `OperationContractAttribute` classes in the `System.ServiceModel` namespace, which you have to include with a `using` statement. Listing 3-1 shows the service contract defined as a .NET interface for QuickReturns Ltd., including two operation contracts.

Listing 3-1. `ServiceContract` *for the Trade Service*

```
using System.ServiceModel;
using QuickReturns.StockTrading.ExchangeService.DataContracts;

namespace QuickReturns.StockTrading.ExchangeService.Contracts
{
   [ServiceContract(Namespace = "http://QuickReturns")]
    interface ITradeService
    {
        [OperationContract()]
        Quote GetQuote(string ticker);

        [OperationContract()]
        void PublishQuote(Quote quote);
    }
}
```

This service is the exchange of the stock-trading application for QuickReturns Ltd. The contract of this service defines the interaction that is going on between the sellers and buyers on a stock market. Sellers offer their stocks by publishing quotes. A quote obviously defines the company the stock is for and what price the seller wants to have for it. Hence, the `PublishQuote` method is able to publish quotes by sellers on the trade service. The buyers, on the other hand, will query the trade service to get a quote on a specific type of stock for a specific company. Therefore, the `GetQuote` method is able to retrieve published quotes from the service. When the buyer finds an appropriate seller, the actual exchange of stocks can take place by a different service (which will be covered later in this book).

As you can see, the exchange service is marked with the `[ServiceContract]` attribute and currently has two operations, `GetQuote` and `PublishQuote`. These operations have the `[OperationContract]` attribute applied. WCF uses these attributes to determine which .NET methods it needs to invoke based on an incoming SOAP message. The attributes also determine the serialization WCF has to do for you. WCF serialization encompasses the mapping from SOAP messages to your .NET objects. In Listing 3-1, `Quote` is a custom .NET type where no mapping is defined yet. For the custom `Quote` object and any other custom object you want to pass between services and clients, you have to define data contracts. *Data contracts* control the mapping between SOAP messages and .NET objects. We'll cover data contracts in the next section.

To influence the service contract, the `[ServiceContract]` attribute has several parameters that have their own functions:

`CallbackContract`: Gets or sets the type of callback contract. This is useful when using the duplex messaging exchange pattern.

`ConfigurationName`: Defines the name as used in the configuration file to store the related configuration settings.

`Name`: Gets or sets the name for the `<portType>` element in WSDL. The default value is the name of the .NET interface.

Namespace: Gets or sets the namespace for the <portType> element in WSDL. The default value is the namespace of the .NET interface.

HasProtectionLevel: Defines a (read-only) value that indicates the protection level of the service. At the operation level, it is possible to define that the messages of the operation must be encrypted, signed, or both.

ProtectionLevel: Defines the protection level that the binding must support.

SessionMode: Gets or sets a value that defines whether the contract requires the WCF binding associated with the contract to use channel sessions. SessionMode is an enumeration with possible values of allowed, notallowed, and required. The default value is allowed.

The same is true for the [OperationContract] attribute. Several parameters are available to you:

Name: Specifies the name of the operation. The default is the name of the operation.

Action: Defines the (WS-Addressing) action of the request message.

AsyncPattern: Indicates that the operation is implemented asynchronously by using a Begin/End method pair.

IsInitiating: Defines a value that indicates whether the method implements an operation that can initiate a session on the server.

IsOneWay: Defines a value that indicates whether an operation returns a reply message.

IsTerminating: Defines a value that indicates whether the operation causes the server to close the session after the reply message is sent.

ProtectionLevel: Defines a value that indicates the protection level of the operation. You can define that the messages of the operation must be encrypted, signed, or both.

ReplyAction: Defines the value of the SOAP action for the reply message of the operation.

If you need full access to the message body and don't want to bother with serialization, another approach is using the Message object, as you can see in Listing 3-2.

Listing 3-2. ITradeServiceMessage *Interface Using the* Message *Object*

```
using System.ServiceModel;
using System.ServiceModel.Channels;

namespace QuickReturns.StockTrading.ExchangeService.Contracts
{
   [ServiceContract(Namespace = "http://QuickReturns")]
    interface ITradeServiceMessage
    {
        [OperationContract()]
        Message GetQuote(string ticker);
```

```
        [OperationContract()]
        void PublishQuote(Message quote);
    }
}
```

This way, you get access to the SOAP message directly, and WCF doesn't do any type-based serialization. As you can see, the code in Listing 3-2 differs from Listing 3-1. The `Quote` return type of the `GetQuote` method and the `Quote` parameter in the `PublishQuote` method are now replaced by the generic `Message` type. So instead of having the convenience of being able to access the properties of the type in an object-oriented way, you can now access the individual elements and attributes directly in the XML message. This can be useful in scenarios where the overhead that comes with serialization is too high.

■ **Note** During the course of this chapter and the book, you will read about the other requirements in the sample application; refer to the appendix and the accompanying sample code at `http://www.apress.com` to understand the application requirements and implementation. In this chapter, we'll use pieces of the sample application to explain the programming model.

Data Contracts

As discussed earlier, we are using a custom type called `Quote` for which you can define a data contract. WCF needs to know how to serialize your custom .NET types. You have two ways of letting WCF know how to do this. WCF knows implicit and explicit data contracts. Implicit data contracts are mappings of simple types in .NET. WCF has predefined mappings for all .NET simple types to their SOAP counterparts. So, you don't have to explicitly define data contracts for the .NET simple types you know in the `System` namespace including enums, delegates, and arrays or generics of the simple types in .NET.

Since you build up your types based on the simple types in .NET, or based on types that are themselves built up based on the simple types, you can also annotate your custom types with the `[Serializable]` attribute. This tells WCF to use implicit data contracts. If you use this way of serialization, you don't have to define a data contract. To influence the way you want the serialization to happen, you have to define an explicit data contract for your type. You can do this by defining a simple class with all the properties your type needs and annotating the class with the `[DataContract]` attribute. The `[DataContract]` attribute uses an opt-in model, where the .NET way of serializing in combination with formatters determines what gets serialized (public properties, private properties, and so on); therefore, you have to specifically annotate each property with the `[DataMember]` attribute. In Listing 3-3, we have defined a data contract for the `Quote` custom type in the stock-trading example.

Listing 3-3. *Data Contract for the Custom* `Quote` *Type*

```
using System;
using System.Runtime.Serialization;
```

```
namespace QuickReturns.StockTrading.ExchangeService.DataContracts
{
    [DataContract(Namespace=" http://QuickReturns")]
    public class Quote
    {
        [DataMember(Name="Ticker")]
        public string Ticker;

        [DataMember(Name="Bid")]
        public decimal Bid;

        [DataMember(Name="Ask")]
        public decimal Ask;

        [DataMember(Name="Publisher")]
        public string Publisher;

        [DataMember(Name="UpdateDateTime")]
        private DateTime UpdateDateTime;
    }
}
```

■ **Note** The `UpdateDateTime` field is private and attributed, so it will be serialized as part of the SOAP messages that WCF generates.

To influence the data contract, the `[DataContract]` attribute has several parameters that have their own functions:

`Name`: Defines the name for the data contract, which will also be the name in the XML schema (XSD, WSDL). The default value is the name you defined in .NET.

`Namespace`: Defines the namespace for the data contract. Use this property to specify a particular namespace if your type must return data that complies with a specific data contract or XML schema.

To influence the data members and to make versioning possible, you need to be aware of several parameters for the `[DataMember]` attribute:

`Name`: Defines the name for the data contract, which will also be the name in an XML schema (XSD, WSDL). The default value is the name you defined in .NET.

`Namespace`: Defines the namespace for the data contract. Use this property to specify a particular namespace if your type must return data that complies with a specific data contract or XML schema.

`IsRequired`: Gets or sets a value that instructs the serialization engine that the member must be present.

`Order`: Gets or sets the order of serialization and deserialization of a member. This can be important if clients rely on the order of the fields.

`EmitDefaultValue`: Gets or sets a value that specifies whether to generate a default value of null or 0 for a field or property being serialized.

Message Contracts

Sometimes you require more control over the SOAP envelope that WCF generates. For example, you may want to be able to map fields in your message to the SOAP headers instead of the SOAP body. This is when message contracts come into play. The `[MessageContract]` attribute allows you to map fields into either the SOAP body or the SOAP headers by means of the `[MessageBody]` and `[MessageHeader]` attributes, as shown in Listing 3-4.

Listing 3-4. `Quote` *as a* `MessageContract`

```
using System;
using System.ServiceModel;

namespace QuickReturns.StockTrading.ExchangeService.MessageContracts
{
    [MessageContract]
    public class QuoteMessage
    {
        [MessageBody]
        public string Ticker;

        [MessageBody]
        public decimal Bid;

        [MessageBody]
        public decimal Ask;

        [MessageHeader]
        public string Publisher;

        [MessageBody]
        private DateTime UpdateDateTime;
    }
}
```

In this example, the publisher has now moved from the SOAP body to the SOAP headers. Now you can use this message contract in an operation contract, just like you did with the data contract. So when you need direct control over the SOAP envelope, you can use message contracts to control how properties of your types map to the SOAP headers and SOAP body.

Looking at the WCF Layers "Inside"

WCF is a layered framework similar to the Open Systems Interactive (OSI) model. The service model layer is the layer you will use primarily to program against. The service model layer influences the layer underneath it, which is called the *messaging layer*. The messaging layer is the layer where all the actual transportation of messages across the channels on the network becomes reality. The reason for the separation is an architectural concept. It allows you to separate the actual messaging from the programming model, and this allows you to benefit just from the messaging layer (similar to what BizTalk Server does).

Figure 3-5 shows how the layering is organized. The messaging layer is the lower-level layer where you talk about transports, channels, protocols, and encoding. The service model layer is where you talk about behavior, contracts, and policy. Behaviors are the most important piece in the service model layer, whereas in the messaging layer channels are central.

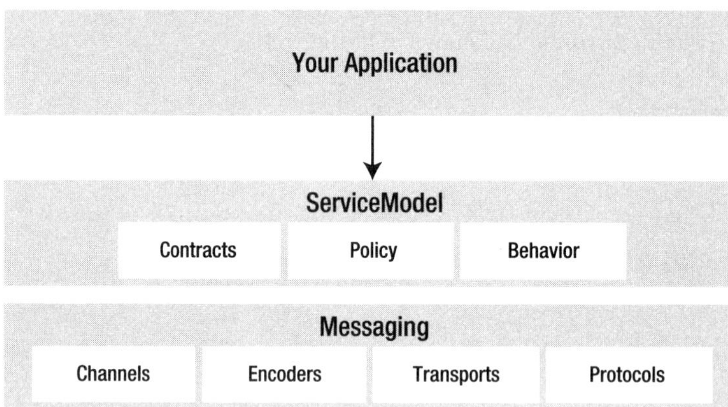

Figure 3-5. *WCF layers*

What Is the Messaging Layer?

The messaging layer is the layer where the actual communication on the wire is happening. This is the layer where the transports such as HTTP, MSMQ, TCP, and Named Pipes come into play. In addition to that, the encoding used for the messages and the format of the messages come into play. In other words, these are the protocols used inside the messages. Then, the protocols are implemented as channels; a *channel* allows you to clearly separate the combination of the transport and the messaging exchange pattern.

Channels

The address and binding together manifest themselves in the messaging layer of WCF. The address expresses where the message should go, and the binding is the model you use to manipulate the message. Going a bit lower into the stack of WCF, Figure 3-6 shows a layered description of the WCF messaging stack.

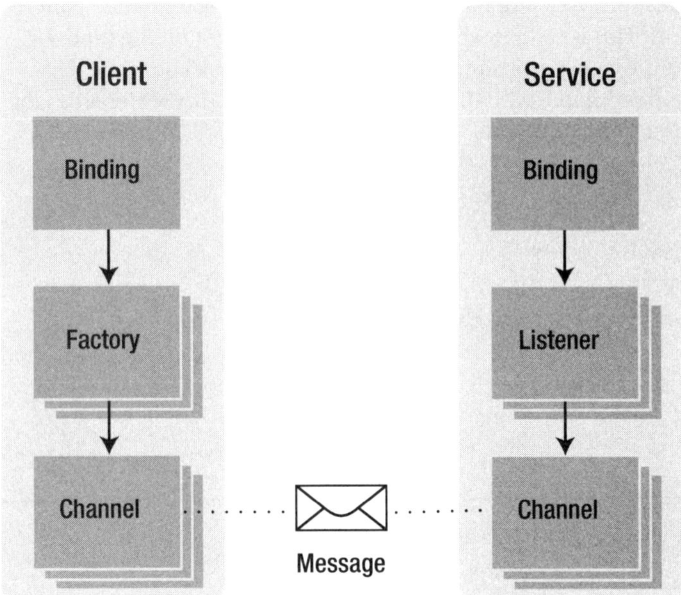

Figure 3-6. *WCF messaging stack*

The binding is the mechanism to control the channel stack. When you pick one of the predefined bindings mentioned earlier, you are picking, in essence, specific channels. Looking at the bottom of Figure 3-6, you can see the channels are responsible for transferring a message from the client side to the service side, and vice versa, depending on the messaging exchange pattern used. Obviously for this to work, the client side and the service side should be consistent to be able to exchange messages. In other words, they have to understand the messaging pattern, the transport, the protocols, and the encoding. On the client side, channels are created by factories to be able to talk *to* the service side across a specific channel or a set of channels. On the service side, listeners accept messages *from* channels.

Channels have input and output handlers that are responsible for consuming messages. Consuming messages can mean forwarding the messages across a certain transport or receiving messages across a certain transport through a specific messaging exchange pattern. The channel also applies security and performs validations. In the default WCF set of bindings, this results in support for the WS-* specifications. Channels can be connected to each other in a pipeline. Therefore, you don't have to rebuild security, reliability, or session state capabilities inside your channels for every transport. Bindings make it much easier to have the client side and the service side work together. The information about the binding is described by the policy in the metadata of the service, and as such you can rely on this information to align the information by means of imperative code or the more usual configuration. The metadata that is exposed based on the binding allows you to generate proxy code for use on the client side.

Shapes of Channels

Channels come in three shapes that correspond to the messaging exchange patterns described earlier. Channels are a way for WCF to separate these messaging exchange patterns from the transport. Given a transport, WCF implements only the messaging exchange patterns that are natural for the transport. This is so that when using the WCF programming model, you don't need to bother about the transports directly; rather, you can think about the messaging exchange pattern or channel shape. With the interfaces in Listing 3-5, WCF enables the three messaging exchange patterns in code.

Listing 3-5. *Channel Interfaces to Support the Different Shapes of Channels*

```
public interface IOutputChannel : IChannel {
    void Send(Message message);
}

public interface IInputChannel : IChannel {
    Message Receive();
}

public interface IDuplexChannel : IInputChannel, IOutputChannel { }

public interface IRequestChannel : IChannel {
    Message Request(Message message);
}

public interface IReplyChannel : IChannel {
    IRequestContext ReceiveRequest();
}

public interface IRequestContext : IDisposable {
    Message RequestMessage { get; }
    void Reply(Message message);
}
```

The `IOutputChannel` interface supports sending messages, and the `IInputChannel` interface supports receiving messages. Together these support the one-way messaging exchange pattern. `IInputChannel` and `IOutputChannel` are combined to create the `IDuplexChannel` interface, which supports the duplex messaging exchange pattern. The `IRequestChannel` interface supports sending requests, and the `IReplyChannel` interface supports receiving requests. Together they support the request-reply messaging exchange pattern. Finally, the `IRequestContext` interface allows you to receive multiple messages over the same channel. This improves concurrency and doesn't limit you from blocking the channel until the reply to a specific request is ready to be transmitted.

Channel Flavors

Channels come in three flavors:

- Transports
- Encoders
- Protocols

You now understand what these concepts encompass. A transport is really a way to talk to some source on the service side. As you know, WCF supports several transports and allows you to write your own to support other transports such as SMTP or FTP. On the encoding side, WCF supports several typical encoders that either are standards based such as Message Transmission Optimization Mechanism (MTOM) or are optimized for reading (binary) or readable (text). You could imagine other encoders that improve the size of the messages and minimize the data and as such the bandwidth used. Supported protocols in WCF are the most important WS-* standards. In this book, we'll cover several of them, specifically in Chapters 6, 7, 8, and 9.

What Is the Service Model Layer?

Whereas the messaging layer provides total control over the messages flowing around in your application, the service model layer is a higher-level abstraction layer that allows you to influence the messaging through object-oriented programming principles. This is really where the WCF team was able to reach its design goals. The service model layer offers an easy-to-use API with classes, methods, attributes, and configuration to build connected applications. Behaviors are the most important concept in this regard. You can apply multiple behaviors on the client and service sides. Behaviors don't influence the contract in any way; in other words, consumers of services don't know the details about the behavior of the service. Behaviors influence the conversion from messages to .NET types, instancing, throttling, concurrency, and error handling. Up until now in this book, we have covered the generic concepts of the entire API; the rest of this chapter is focused on the service model layer. This is the layer you will use the most.

Using ServiceHost and ChannelFactory

`ServiceHost` gives you access to the WCF hosting infrastructure on the server side whereas `ChannelFactory` gives you access to the WCF hosting infrastructure on the client side. The following sections cover the basics of `ServiceHost` and `ChannelFactory` from a programming model perspective.

In Chapter 4, you will learn about hosting web services in IIS. Chapter 5 covers the complete WCF hosting infrastructure and shows you the different options WCF offers in terms of hosting services in different types of applications and using services in different types of clients. In this chapter, we cover only self-hosting and console applications.

ServiceHost

`ServiceHost` is instantiated based on a particular service type you implemented and as such "hosts" your service. When a `ServiceHost` instance is available, you can do anything you like programmatically in regards to the ABCs and behavior (which we will cover later). So, Listing 3-6 and Listing 3-7 define and instantiate your first service in a specific service host that is initialized imperatively with an address, a binding, and a contract. We are using the basic examples given earlier, so we use a simple HTTP address and the `BasicHttpBinding` and `ITradeService` contracts you saw earlier.

Listing 3-6. `ServiceHost` *Instantiation Based on Imperative Calls*

```
using System;
using System.ServiceModel;
using QuickReturns.StockTrading.ExchangeService;
using QuickReturns.StockTrading.ExchangeService.Contracts;

namespace QuickReturns.StockTrading.ExchangeService.Hosts
{
    class Program
    {
        static void Main(string[] args)
        {
            Uri address = new Uri
                ("http://localhost:8080/QuickReturns/Exchange");
            Type serviceType = typeof(TradeService);
            BasicHttpBinding binding = new BasicHttpBinding();
            ServiceHost host = new ServiceHost(serviceType);
            host.AddServiceEndpoint(typeof(ITradeService), binding, address);
            host.Open();
            Console.WriteLine("Service started: Press Return to exit");
            Console.ReadLine();
        }
    }
}
```

Listing 3-7. `TradeService`

```
using System;
using System.Collections;
using System.ServiceModel;
using QuickReturns.StockTrading.ExchangeService.Contracts;
using QuickReturns.StockTrading.ExchangeService.DataContracts;

namespace QuickReturns.StockTrading.ExchangeService
{
    [ServiceBehavior(InstanceContextMode=InstanceContextMode.Single,
                    ReturnUnknownExceptionsAsFaults=true)]
    public class TradeService : ITradeService
    {
        private Hashtable tickers = new Hashtable();
        public Quote GetQuote(string ticker)
        {
            lock (tickers)
            {
```

```
                Quote quote = tickers[ticker] as Quote;
                if (quote == null)
                {
                    // Quote doesn't exist.
                    throw new Exception(
                        string.Format("No quotes found for ticker '{0}'",
                            ticker));
                }
                return quote;
            }
        }

        public void PublishQuote(Quote quote)
        {
            lock (tickers)
            {
                Quote storedQuote = tickers[quote.Ticker] as Quote;
                if (storedQuote == null)
                {
                    tickers.Add(quote.Ticker, quote);
                }
                else
                {
                    tickers[quote.Ticker] = quote;
                }
            }
        }
    }
}
```

As you can see, the implementation of the service is simple. It has one member variable (of type `Hashtable`) that is responsible for keeping the internal state of the service with the provided quotes in memory. In a more realistic scenario, this would of course be kept in some permanent state system (a back end based on a database). To be able to call into the service multiple times, you have to make sure the behavior of the service is a Singleton. Therefore, the `ServiceBehavior` attribute is applied with the `InstanceContextMode` property set to `InstanceContextMode.Single`. You will learn more about behaviors in the "Applying Behaviors" section. The `ReturnUnknownExceptionsAsFaults` property is able to track back the exception that can occur when a quote is requested for an unknown ticker to propagate to the client. For obvious reasons, by default WCF doesn't map .NET exceptions across the wire in SOAP faults.

In the "Introducing the Programming Approach" section, you learned the approaches you can take in programming WCF; you also learned that as soon as `ServiceHost` is there, any attributes and configuration have already been applied. In other words, Listing 3-8 shows the same thing in terms of the actual result, but the one with the configuration is much more maintainable.

Listing 3-8. `ServiceHost` *Instantiation Based on Configuration*

```
using System;
using System.ServiceModel;
using QuickReturns.StockTrading.ExchangeService;
using QuickReturns.StockTrading.ExchangeService.Contracts;

namespace QuickReturns.StockTrading.ExchangeService.Hosts
{
    class Program
    {
        static void Main(string[] args)
        {
            Type serviceType = typeof(TradeService);
            ServiceHost host = new ServiceHost(serviceType);
            host.Open();

            Console.WriteLine("Service started: Press Return to exit");
            Console.ReadLine();
        }
    }
}
```

Listing 3-9 provides the `App.config` file of the service. You can find the `TradeService` defined with its endpoints. Please note the `IMetadataExchange` endpoint. You specify this endpoint in order to allow consumers to retrieve the metadata (WSDL) of the service. If you want to use either `SvcUtil.exe` or Add Service Reference in Visual Studio, you need to enable the retrieval of metadata. The service is referring to a specific `behaviorConfiguration` called `serviceTypeBehaviors` that sets some service-wide settings too. The service-wide settings are as follows:

`serviceMetadata`: This allows you to set whether metadata may be retrieved for the service. You can set some additional attributes such as `ExternalMetadataLocation`, `HttpEnabled`, `HttpsEnabled`, `HttpGetUrl`, `HttpsGetUrl`, and `MetaDataExporter`. These are self-explanatory; please refer to the MSDN Help for more information.

`serviceDebug`: These settings allow you to express whether you want to leak specific service exception information and helpful HTML information pages for your services across the service boundary. This should be disabled in production scenarios but can be helpful during development. You can set some additional attributes such as `HttpHelpPageEnabled`, `HttpHelpPageUrl`, `HttpsHelpPageEnabled`, `HttpsHelpPageUrl`, and `IncludeExceptionDetailInFaults`. These are self-explanatory; please refer to the MSDN Help for more information.

We have set `httpGetEnabled` for the metadata and `httpHelpPageEnabled` and `includeExceptionDetailInFaults` because we need these in the remaining part of this section and the following section.

Listing 3-9. App.config

```
<?xml version="1.0" encoding="utf-8" ?>
<configuration>
<system.serviceModel>
   <services>
      <service name="QuickReturns.StockTrading.ExchangeService.TradeService"
               behaviorConfiguration="tradeServiceBehavior ">
          <host>
              <baseAddresses>
                 <add baseAddress="http://localhost:8080/QuickReturns"/>
              </baseAddresses>
          </host>
         <endpoint address="http://localhost:8080/QuickReturns/Exchange"
               binding="basicHttpBinding"
               contract="QuickReturns.StockTrading.ExchangeService.TradeService">
         </endpoint>
         <endpoint contract="IMetadataExchange"
                   binding="mexHttpBinding"
                   address="mex" />
      </service>
   </services>
   <serviceBehaviors>
        <behavior name="tradeServiceBehavior">
            <serviceMetadata httpGetEnabled="true"/>
            <serviceDebug httpHelpPageEnabled="true"
                includeExceptionDetailInFaults="true"/>
        </behavior>
  </serviceBehaviors>
</system.serviceModel>
</configuration>
```

When you take a closer look at ServiceHost at runtime, you can see that it falls into two pieces. The ServiceDescription is all about the endpoints and behaviors, and the second part is all about the runtime where you can find listeners, sites, and extensions. The ServiceDescription is built based on the configuration and can be changed with the imperative code you add. Figure 3-7 shows this graphically.

■ **Note** It is highly recommended you download and open the solution for this chapter to get a better understanding of the ServiceDescription. Look at it with the Visual Studio .NET debugger by using the Watches or QuickWatch window.

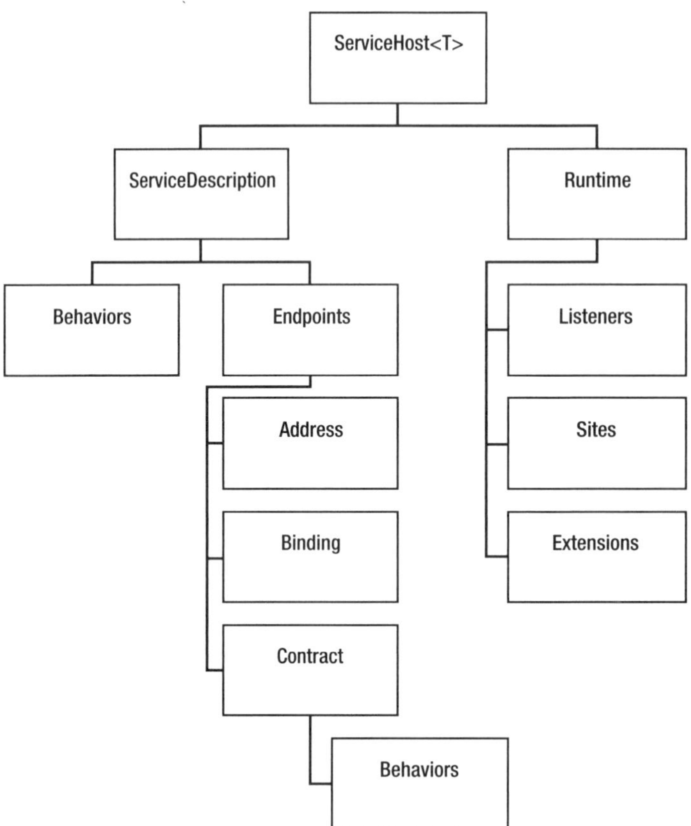

Figure 3-7. *Representation of the* `ServiceHost` *in memory*

We'll now explain what the `ServiceDescription` and runtime can do for you. The `ServiceHost` is always in a certain state (reflected by the `State` property of type `CommunicationState`). The possible states are `Created`, `Opening`, `Open`, `Closing`, `Closed`, and `Faulted`. When you start the `ServiceHost`, it activates the runtime and starts creating listeners and extensions. In the debugger, the `ServiceDescription` looks like Figure 3-8. As you can see, it shows you the same information as Figure 3-7.

A realistic scenario is that you subclass (extend) `ServiceHost` by hooking into the API and overriding the `OnInitialize` (and any other methods that are applicable in your scenario) to be able to abstract the logic to build up the description from external configuration or create a more suitable base class for your base library, project, department, or company to use. The `OnInitialize` method of the `ServiceHost` is a method suitable for doing this type of customization. Listing 3-10 shows you the same example as before, but now by subclassing `ServiceHost`.

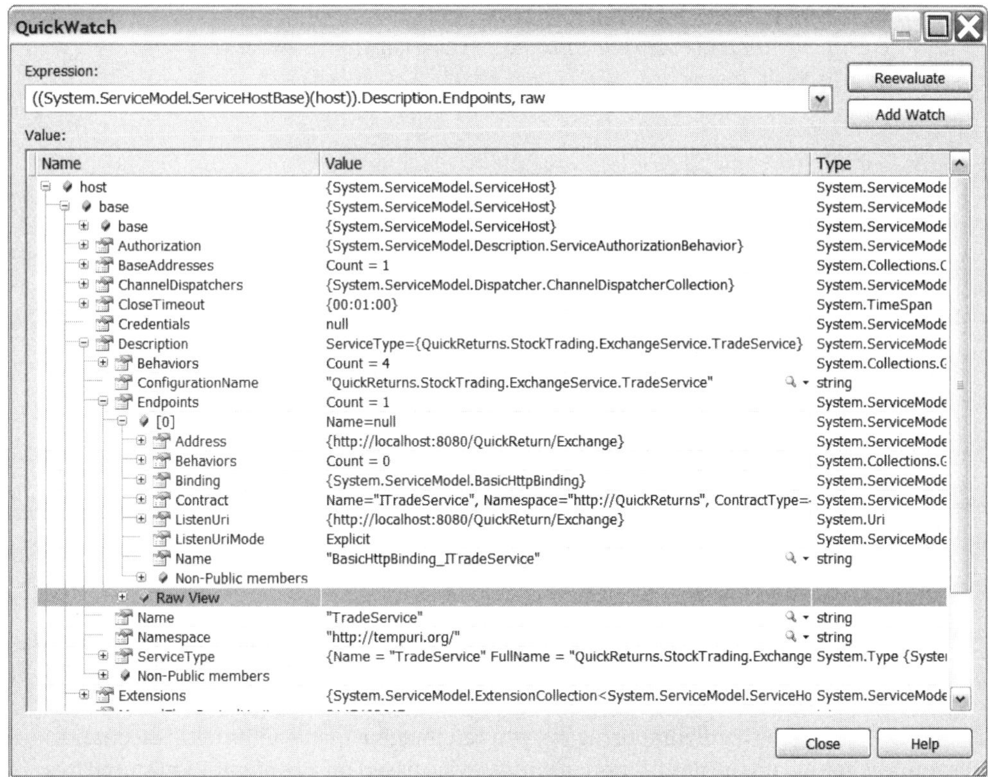

Figure 3-8. *QuickWatch window of the* `ServiceDescription` *in* `ServiceHost`

Listing 3-10. *Subclassed* `ServiceHost` *Instantiation Based on Imperative Calls*

```
using System;
using System.ServiceModel;
using QuickReturns.StockTrading.ExchangeService;
using QuickReturns.StockTrading.ExchangeService.Contracts;

namespace QuickReturns.StockTrading.ExchangeService.Hosts
{
   public class ExchangeServiceHost
   {
      static void Main(string[] args)
      {
         Uri baseAddress =
            new Uri("http://localhost:8080/QuickReturns");
         CustomServiceHost host =
            new CustomServiceHost(typeof(TradeService), baseAddress);
```

```
            host.Open();
            Console.WriteLine("Service started: Press Return to exit");
            Console.ReadLine();

        }
    }

    public class CustomServiceHost : ServiceHost
    {
        public CustomServiceHost(Type serviceType, params Uri[] baseAddresses)
            : base(serviceType, baseAddresses)
        {
        }

        protected override void OnInitialize()
        {
            BasicHttpBinding binding = new BasicHttpBinding();
            AddServiceEndpoint(typeof(ITradeService), binding, "Exchange");
        }
    }
}
```

Although this scenario is not really something you would do in a real application because you are hard-coding the configuration again, you can imagine the benefits of this scenario. An example is setting up the description of your service based on a configuration stored in a database.

Channel Factory

Just like `ServiceHost`, you instantiate `ChannelFactory` based on a specific service. There's a difference, though. The client knows only about the exposed contract of the service, not about its implementation. Therefore, in this case, the generic that is passed to `ChannelFactory` is the interface of the contract. In Listing 3-11, we have written a client that instantiates a `ChannelFactory` to open a channel to the service defined in the previous section about `ServiceHost`. Listing 3-12 shows the associated configuration files for use on the client side. To handle the third tenet (share the schema and not the class), it is best if you define the contract of the service separately and not create a separate assembly that you use on both the client side and the service side. This way, the service side can evolve without impacting the client side. Of course, the code uses the configuration best practice instead of the imperative code.

Listing 3-11. *The Client Code Using* `ChannelFactory`

```
using System;
using System.ServiceModel;
using System.ServiceModel.Channels;
using System.Runtime.Serialization;
```

```
namespace QuickReturns.StockTrading.ExchangeService.Clients
{
   [ServiceContract(Namespace = "http://QuickReturns")]
   interface ITradeService
   {
      [OperationContract()]
      Quote GetQuote(string ticker);

      [OperationContract()]
      void PublishQuote(Quote quote);
   }

   [DataContract(Namespace = "http://QuickReturns", Name = "Quote")]
   public class Quote
   {
      [DataMember(Name = "Ticker")]
      public string Ticker;

      [DataMember(Name = "Bid")]
      public decimal Bid;

      [DataMember(Name = "Ask")]
      public decimal Ask;

      [DataMember(Name = "Publisher")]
      public string Publisher;

      [DataMember(Name = "UpdateDateTime")]
      private DateTime UpdateDateTime;
   }

   class ExchangeServiceSimpleClient
   {
      static void Main(string[] args)
      {
         EndpointAddress address =
               new EndpointAddress
                 ("http://localhost:8080/QuickReturns/Exchange");
         BasicHttpBinding binding = new BasicHttpBinding();
         IChannelFactory<ITradeService> channelFactory =
new ChannelFactory<ITradeService>(binding);
         ITradeService proxy = channelFactory.CreateChannel(address);
```

```
            Quote msftQuote = new Quote();
            msftQuote.Ticker = "MSFT";
            msftQuote.Bid = 30.25M;
            msftQuote.Ask = 32.00M;
            msftQuote.Publisher = "PracticalWCF";

            Quote ibmQuote = new Quote();
            ibmQuote.Ticker = "IBM";
            ibmQuote.Bid = 80.50M;
            ibmQuote.Ask = 81.00M;
            ibmQuote.Publisher = "PracticalWCF";

            proxy.PublishQuote(msftQuote);
            proxy.PublishQuote(ibmQuote);

            Quote result = null;
            result = proxy.GetQuote("MSFT");
            Console.WriteLine("Ticker: {0} Ask: {1} Bid: {2}",
                result.Ticker, result.Ask, result.Bid);

            result = proxy.GetQuote("IBM");
            Console.WriteLine("Ticker: {0} Ask: {1} Bid: {2}",
                result.Ticker, result.Ask, result.Bid);

            try
            {
               result = proxy.GetQuote("ATT");
            }
            catch (Exception ex)
            {
               Console.WriteLine(ex.Message);
            }

            if (result == null)
            {
               Console.WriteLine("Ticker ATT not found!");
            }

            Console.WriteLine("Done! Press return to exit");
            Console.ReadLine();

        }
    }
}
```

Listing 3-12. *The* App.config *File for the Client Code*

```
<?xml version="1.0" encoding="utf-8" ?>
<configuration>
    <system.serviceModel>
        <client>
            <endpoint address="http://localhost:8080/QuickReturns/Exchange"
                binding="basicHttpBinding"
               contract="QuickReturns.StockTrading.ExchangeServiceClient.➥
                         ITradeService">
            </endpoint>
        </client>
    </system.serviceModel>
</configuration>
```

There is an easier way to consume services without using the ChannelFactory. You can generate the proxies using the SvcUtil.exe utility. The SvcUtil.exe utility retrieves the metadata (WSDL) of the service, and based on that it will generate the proxy classes that can be used to call the service. In addition, it will make sure the contracts are generated as interfaces as well. Therefore, you can leave out the service contract and data contract you saw in Listing 3-11. The following call to SvcUtil.exe generates a proxy class for use in your client (make sure your service is running):

```
svcutil.exe http://localhost:8080/QuickReturns
```

The utility will generate a proxy class based on the metadata of the service, which can be retrieved with the following URL:

```
http://localhost:8080/QuickReturns?WSDL
```

The utility will generate a proxy class for you (the file will be named TradeService.cs, and the configuration file is called Output.config). You can then simplify the client as shown in Listing 3-13. Listing 3-14 shows the generated Output.config configuration file.

Listing 3-13. *Simplified Client Code Using the Proxy Generated by* SvcUtil.exe

```
using System;
using quickReturns;

namespace QuickReturns.StockTrading.ExchangeService.Clients
{
   class ExchangeServiceClientProxy
   {
      static void Main(string[] args)
      {
         TradeServiceProxy proxy = new TradeServiceProxy();
```

```
            Quote msftQuote = new Quote();
            msftQuote.Ticker = "MSFT";
            msftQuote.Bid = 30.25M;
            msftQuote.Ask = 32.00M;
            msftQuote.Publisher = "PracticalWCF";

            Quote ibmQuote = new Quote();
            ibmQuote.Ticker = "IBM";
            ibmQuote.Bid = 80.50M;
            ibmQuote.Ask = 81.00M;
            ibmQuote.Publisher = "PracticalWCF";

            proxy.PublishQuote(msftQuote);
            proxy.PublishQuote(ibmQuote);

            Quote result = null;
            result = proxy.GetQuote("MSFT");
            Console.WriteLine("Ticker: {0} Ask: {1} Bid: {2}",
                result.Ticker, result.Ask, result.Bid);

            result = proxy.GetQuote("IBM");
            Console.WriteLine("Ticker: {0} Ask: {1} Bid: {2}",
                result.Ticker, result.Ask, result.Bid);

            try
            {
               result = proxy.GetQuote("ATT");
            }
            catch (Exception ex)
            {
               Console.WriteLine(ex.Message);
            }

            if (result == null)
            {
               Console.WriteLine("Ticker ATT not found!");
            }

            Console.WriteLine("Done! Press return to exit");
            Console.ReadLine();
        }
    }
}
```

Listing 3-14. `Output.config` *Generated by* `SvcUtil.exe`

```
<?xml version="1.0" encoding="utf-8"?>
<configuration>
    <system.serviceModel>
        <bindings>
            <basicHttpBinding>
                <binding name="basicHttpBinding"
                         closeTimeout="00:01:00"
                         openTimeout="00:01:00"
                         receiveTimeout="00:10:00"
                         sendTimeout="00:01:00"
                         allowCookies="false"
                         bypassProxyOnLocal="false"
                         hostNameComparisonMode="StrongWildcard"
                         maxBufferSize="65536"
                         maxBufferPoolSize="524288"
                         maxReceivedMessageSize="65536"
                         messageEncoding="Text"
                         textEncoding="utf-8"
                         transferMode="Buffered"
                         useDefaultWebProxy="true">
                <readerQuotas maxDepth="32"
                              maxStringContentLength="8192"
                              maxArrayLength="16384"
                              maxBytesPerRead="4096"
                              maxNameTableCharCount="16384" />
                <security mode="None">
                    <transport clientCredentialType="None"
                               proxyCredentialType="None"
                               realm="" />
                        <message clientCredentialType="UserName"
                                 algorithmSuite="Default" />
                </security>
                </binding>
            </basicHttpBinding>
        </bindings>
        <client>
            <endpoint address="http://localhost:8080/QuickReturns/Exchange"
                      binding="basicHttpBinding"
                      bindingConfiguration="basicHttpBinding"
                contract="ITradeService" name="basicHttpBinding" />
        </client>
    </system.serviceModel>
</configuration>
```

■Note With the code in the ServiceHost and ChannelFactory discussions, we have finalized the first bit of WCF code that actually compiles and runs. In the code that comes with this book, you can find the ExchangeService sample in the ExchangeService folder for Chapter 3 (c:\PracticalWCF\Chapter03\ExchangeService), complete with two flavors of clients that do some calls to publish and get quotes. The difference between the two clients (SimpleClient and SimpleClientWithProxy) is that the first is using ChannelFactory and the other is using a proxy generated with SvcUtil.exe. It is highly recommended you walk through this code with Visual Studio .NET in debug mode.

Service Description

The *service description* is an important concept when trying to understand WCF. The ABCs of WCF result in a service description as shown in Figure 3-7. In essence, the ServiceDescription is an in-memory representation of the environment where your service lives. It is either based on initialization code or based on a configuration file according to your wishes. Then, in later stages before starting your runtime, you have several options for modifying the service description through the WCF API. Please refer to the earlier ServiceHost discussion for details.

Service Runtime

The *service runtime* is an abstraction layer on top of the messaging layer. This layer is the bridge between your application code and the channels in the messaging layer. The messaging layer deals with transport, protocols, and so on, whereas the service runtime or the service model in general deals with the messages flowing through the messaging layer and conforming to a certain contracts. How they get to the other end of the wire is abstracted from the developer.

You see two similar concepts on the client and service side of the wire. Just like you learned about the factories and listeners in the channel layer, you will see a similar concept in the service runtime. The service runtime has typed proxies on the client side and dispatchers on the service side. Typed proxies and dispatchers are responsible for handing over messages from the service runtime to the messaging layer and the other way around. The typed proxy offers methods that are useful to your applications, and it transforms the method calls into WCF messages and hands them over to the messaging layer to transmit them to the service. The dispatcher is used on the service side to handle the messages coming in on the channels and is responsible for sending them over to your application code. Figure 3-9 shows this graphically.

As you can see in Figure 3-9, you have proxy operations and a proxy behavior on the client side that are responsible for influencing the channel layer. For every method in your service contract of your service, you have one proxy operation. The operations share one proxy behavior. The proxy behavior deals with all the messages flowing between the channel layer and your application. On the proxy behavior level, you can make interceptions to deal with parameter interception, serialization, formatting, the mapping to real methods, and so on. On the operation behavior level, you can perform such tasks as selecting channels, selecting operations (mapping methods), or inspecting messages.

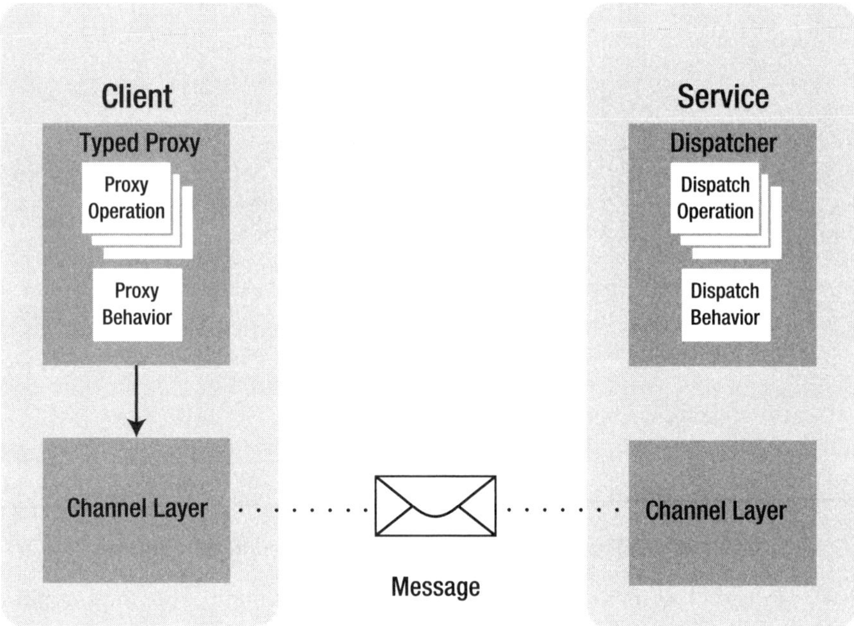

Figure 3-9. *The service model runtime*

On the service side, you'll see a similar concept. At the service level you can do more powerful tasks because the service side is richer in functionality. The dispatch behavior level allows you to perform tasks such as initializing channels, inspecting messages, handling exceptions, selecting operations, and handling concurrency. The dispatch operation level can handle tasks such as inspecting parameters, serializing, handling transactions, and invoking calls.

Applying Behaviors

Most of the details until now have addressed how the service looks from the outside and a little bit about how it works from the inside. A powerful concept you haven't read about a lot until now is behaviors. Influencing the internals of a service, behaviors are applied at the service level, operation level, contract level, and endpoint level. WCF comes with several behaviors out of the box, which we'll cover in this section.

With behaviors, it is possible to modify the runtime and eventually influence the internals of each type of concept where it applies (for example, endpoint, operation, contract, and service). From a programming model perspective, you can apply behaviors through configuration or by using the attributes available to you. Behaviors are something consumers of services have no direct notion of, and they are not expressed in the contract. So, they are all about concepts such as instancing lifetime, concurrency, and transactions.

The interface of behaviors is defined in such a way that it allows you to influence different levels of your service. The levels are validation, bindings, and two methods that do the actual work either on the client side or on the server side. Each behavior has the interface shown in

Listing 3-15, with one exception. The ServiceBehavior doesn't have the ApplyClientBehavior method because you can apply ServiceBehavior only on the service level.

Listing 3-15. *Generic* I...Behavior *Interface*

```
public interface I...Behavior
{
      void AddBindingParameters(ServiceEndpoint serviceEndpoint,
         BindingParameterCollection bindingParameters);
      void ApplyClientBehavior(ServiceEndpoint serviceEndpoint,
         ClientRuntime behavior);
      void ApplyDispatchBehavior(ServiceEndpoint serviceEndpoint,
         EndpointDispatcher endpointDispatcher, ...);
      void Validate(ServiceEndpoint serviceEndpoint);
}
```

The order in which the methods of the interface are called is as follows:

Validate: This is called when all the information is gathered to build the runtime.

AddBindingParameters: This method is called in the first step of building the runtime and before the underlying channel listener is constructed. This allows you to add the custom parameters expected by the underlying channel implementation.

ApplyClientBehavior/ApplyDispatchBehavior: The actual work takes place in these methods that apply either on the client or on the service side (depending on where you are).

■ **Note** Although the behavior interfaces look similar, there's no base IBehavior interface. In other words, to make them as intuitive as possible, they look similar. However, they have some minor differences. For example, the IServiceBehavior interface doesn't have the ApplyClientBehavior. In addition, the ApplyDispatchBehavior has some different parameters in certain interfaces. This is why we replaced the specific names of the behaviors with dots (...). Please refer to the MSDN Help to get more insight into all the behavior interfaces.

Service Behavior

You can define the [ServiceBehavior] attribute on the service implementation (class) level to specify service-wide execution behavior. In other words, you cannot apply this attribute to the interface (contract) level. This distinction is important. The behaviors in WCF have to do with the internals of the implementation, not with the service contract. Listing 3-16 shows the interface of the IServiceBehavior interface that the ServiceBehaviorAttribute implements.

Listing 3-16. `IServiceBehavior` *Interface*

```
public interface IServiceBehavior
{
      // Methods
      void AddBindingParameters(ServiceDescription description,
         ServiceHostBase serviceHostBase,
         Collection<ServiceEndpoint> endpoints,
         BindingParameterCollection parameters);
      void ApplyDispatchBehavior(ServiceDescription description,
         ServiceHostBase serviceHostBase);
      void Validate(ServiceDescription description,
         ServiceHostBase serviceHostBase);
}
```

As you can gather, the most important method on the `IServiceBehavior` interface is called `ApplyDispatchBehavior`, which comes with two parameters. The `ServiceDescription` is mainly provided to inspect the entire service description. However, in practice you could also modify it, although that is not typically what you do at this level. `Validate` is called in order for you to be able to validate the endpoint. WCF will automatically call it for you. The `ChannelDispatchers` collection that `ServiceHostBase` provides is obviously provided to inject code into the dispatcher pipeline and influence the dispatching behaviors. This is basically where the translation is made between the .NET objects and the actual sockets underneath the transport. Through the `AddBindingParameters` method and the provided `BindingParameterCollection`, you can pass information about the contract to the channel stack to implement concepts such as security and transactions. Therefore, you can probably imagine this is an important interception and extensibility point if you want to hook into the WCF programming model. This enables you to create even more powerful solutions than you get out of the box.

The default `[ServiceBehavior]` attribute already provides you with a lot of functionality that can be set through its properties (`Name`, `Namespace`, and `ConfigurationName` are omitted because they are common across WCF):

`AddressFilterMode` (`AddressFilterMode`): By default WCF will match messages to their destination endpoint, matching it with the WS-Addressing To header in the SOAP message. For example, setting `AddressFilterMode` to `AddressFilterMode.Prefix` will instruct WCF to match the endpoints on the start of the endpoint URI.

`AutomaticSessionShutdown` (`boolean`): Specifies whether to automatically close a session when a client closes an output session.

`ConcurrencyMode` (`ConcurrencyMode`): Specifies whether a service supports one thread, multiple threads, or reentrant calls. Valid values are `Reentrant`, `Single`, or `Multiple`. `Single` and `Multiple` correspond to single and multithreaded types of service, and the `Reentrant` service accepts calls that have the same thread context. It is particularly useful when a service calls another service, which subsequently calls back to the first service. In this case, if the first service is not reentrant, the sequence of calls results in a deadlock. The default is `percall` and is typically the best choice because it is best to keep your services stateless to provide scalability.

`IgnoreExtensionDataObject` (`boolean`): Specifies whether to send unknown serialization data onto the wire.

`IncludeExceptionDetailInFaults` (`boolean`): Specificies whether you want to leak specific service exception information across the service boundary. This is useful during debugging.

`InstanceContextMode` (`InstanceContextMode`): Gets or sets the value that indicates when new service objects are created. The default is `PerCall`; the other available values are `PerSession`, `Shareable`, and `Single`.

`MaxItemsInObjectGraph` (`int`): Specifies the maximum amount of items that are to be serialized as part of an object.

`ReleaseServiceInstanceOnTransactionComplete` (`boolean`): Gets or sets a value that specifies whether the service object is recycled when the current transaction completes.

`ReturnUnknownExceptionsAsFaults` (`boolean`): By default WCF doesn't provide the stack trace of issues occurring inside the service, because of the security risks involved. You should set this value only during development to troubleshoot a service; it specifies that unhandled exceptions are to be converted into a SOAP `Fault<string>` and sent as a fault message. In other words, this translates the world of .NET exceptions to SOAP faults. So, on the wire the details of exceptions can be read, which could potentially give too much detail of the internals of the service.

`TransactionAutoCompleteOnSessionClose` (`boolean`): Gets or sets a value that specifies whether pending transactions are completed when the current session closes.

`TransactionIsolationLevel` (`IsolationLevel`): Specifies the transaction isolation level. WCF relies on the .NET `System.Transactions` namespace to enable transactions.

`TransactionTimeout` (`Timespan/string`): Gets or sets the period within which a transaction must be completed before it times out (and rolls back).

`UseSynchronizationContext` (`boolean`): Gets or sets a value that specifies whether to use the current synchronization context to choose the thread of execution.

`ValidateMustUnderstand` (`boolean`): Gets or sets a value that specifies whether the system or the application enforces SOAP `MustUnderstand` header processing.

Contract Behavior

You can use the `IContractBehavior` interface to modify the dispatch behavior on the client or service level. `IContractBehavior` is an extension point you usually need only when you want to influence the dispatch behavior of WCF (see Listing 3-17).

Listing 3-17. `IContractBehavior` *Interface*

```
public interface IContractBehavior
{
      void AddBindingParameters(ContractDescription description,
         ServiceEndpoint endpoint,
         BindingParameterCollection parameters);
      void ApplyClientBehavior(ContractDescription description,
         ServiceEndpoint endpoint,
         ClientRuntime proxy);
      void ApplyDispatchBehavior(ContractDescription description,
         IEnumerable<ServiceEndpoint> endpoints,
         DispatchRuntime dispatch);
      void Validate(ContractDescription description,
         ServiceEndpoint endpoint);
}
```

When you implement the `IContractBehavior` interface in your client-side proxy or service, the `ApplyClientBehavior` and `ApplyDispatchBehavior` methods will be called when WCF is binding the proxies or dispatchers. Obviously, you can then influence the passed-in parameters. This is an extension point of the Service runtime.

■ **Tip** If you want to get a better understanding of what this interface can do for you, just implement it in your service and set a breakpoint in the body of your method. Then you can inspect the passed parameters and get a better understanding of what you can influence.

Channel Behavior

You can use the `IEndpointBehavior` interface to modify the channel behavior on the client or service side. `IEndpointBehavior` is an extension point that you usually need only when you want to influence the channel behavior of WCF (see Listing 3-18).

Listing 3-18. `IEndpointBehavior` *Interface*

```
public interface IEndpointBehavior
{
      void AddBindingParameters(ServiceEndpoint serviceEndpoint,
         BindingParameterCollection bindingParameters);
      void ApplyClientBehavior(ServiceEndpoint serviceEndpoint,
         ClientRuntime behavior);
      void ApplyDispatchBehavior(ServiceEndpoint serviceEndpoint,
         EndpointDispatcher endpointDispatcher);
      void Validate(ServiceEndpoint serviceEndpoint);
}
```

When you implement the `IEndpointBehavior` interface in your client-side proxy or service, the `ApplyClientBehavior` method will be called when WCF is applying behaviors at the channel level on the client side; the `ApplyDispatchBehavior` class does the same on the service side. Obviously, you can then influence the passed-in parameters. This is an extension point of the messaging layer.

Operation Behavior

You can apply the `[OperationBehavior]` attribute at the operation (method) level; it allows you to specify the specific operation behavior the method has during the execution of an operation. As with all behaviors, the `OperationBehavior` is internal to the service and has no influence on the contract.

Just like the `[ServiceBehavior]` attribute, the `[OperationBehavior]` attribute supports a few default properties:

`TransactionAutoComplete (boolean)`: Gets or sets a value that specifies whether the transaction in which the method executes is automatically committed if no unhandled exceptions occur.

`TransactionScopeRequired (boolean)`: Gets or sets a value that specifies whether a transaction scope is required in which the method executes. The transaction in which the method executes is automatically committed if no unhandled exceptions occur. The method will enlist in the transaction.

`Impersonation (boolean)`: Gets or sets a value that specifies whether the operation can impersonate the caller's identity.

`ReleaseInstanceMode (boolean)`: Gets or sets a value that specifies whether the service objects are recycled during the operation invocation process.

`AutoDisposeParameters (boolean)`: Determines whether the service runtime should dispose all input/output parameters once the operation is invoked.

Service Metadata Behavior

The `ServiceMetadataBehavior` is a specialized behavior that implements the `IServiceBehavior` interface. It intercepts requests for metadata of your service and makes it possible to enable or disable the publication of service metadata using an HTTP GET request (the HTML page shown in Figure 3-10).

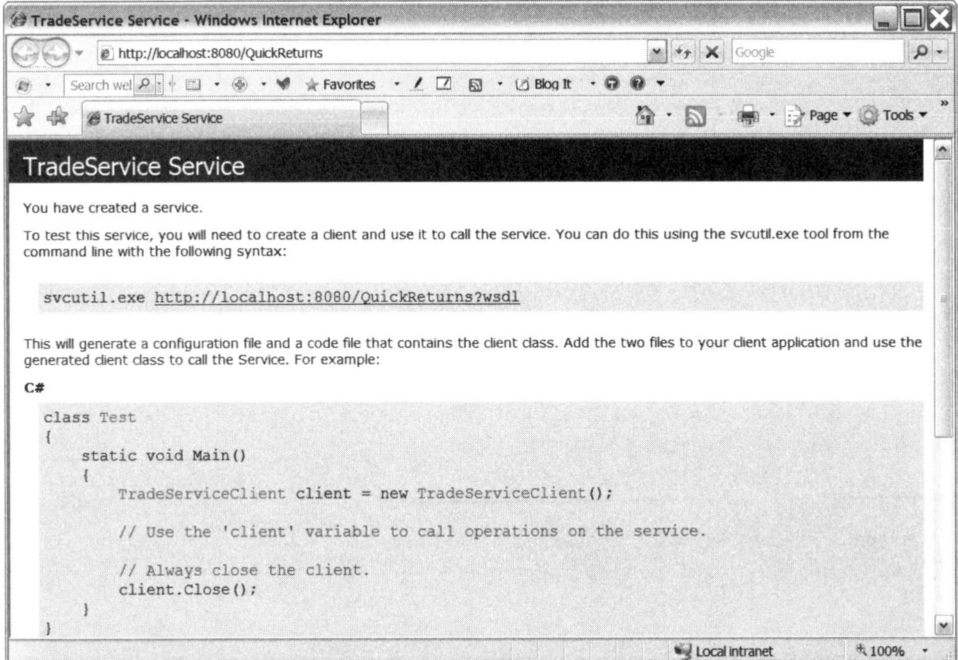

Figure 3-10. *The metadata page for the trade service*

In addition, it is possible to enable or disable the publication of this metadata through a WS-MetadataExchange (WS-MEX) request. If you know your consumers and handed them your metadata, it is a viable option not to allow others to retrieve the metadata. By default when adding a `baseAddress` to your service, just like we did in several of our samples, the `ServiceMetadataBehavior` is added automatically to the `Behaviors` collection. As expected, you can change this behavior either through configuration or by using imperative code. This way you can appropriately set the properties (`httpGetEnabled` and `httpHelpPageEnabled`) of the class. Of course, the best way to do this is by using a configuration file, as in the sample configuration file shown in Listing 3-19. You can retrieve the metadata (WSDL) by retrieving the base address appended with `?wsdl`. For example:

```
http://localhost:8080/QuickReturn?wsdl
```

Retrieving the base address in a browser results in Figure 3-10 being shown.

Listing 3-19. *Service Metadata in Configuration*

```
<?xml version="1.0" encoding="utf-8" ?>
<configuration>
<system.serviceModel>
   <services>
      <service name="QuickReturns.StockTrading.ExchangeService.TradeService"
               behaviorConfiguration="tradeServiceBehavior ">
         <host>
              <baseAddresses>
                  <add baseAddress="http://localhost:8080/QuickReturns"/>
              </baseAddresses>
         </host>
         <endpoint address="http://localhost:8080/QuickReturns/Exchange"
               binding="basicHttpBinding"
               contract="QuickReturns.StockTrading.ExchangeService.TradeService">
         </endpoint>
         <endpoint contract="IMetadataExchange"
                   binding="mexHttpBinding"
                   address="mex" />
      </service>
   </services>
   <serviceBehaviors>
        <behavior name="tradeServiceBehavior">
            <serviceMetadata httpGetEnabled="true"/>
            <serviceDebug httpHelpPageEnabled="true"
                includeExceptionDetailInFaults="true"/>
        </behavior>
   </serviceBehaviors>
</system.serviceModel>
</configuration>
```

Using the Configuration Tool

The .NET Framework 3.0 SDK comes with several utilities. One of the most useful utilities is the Microsoft Service Configuration Editor (SvcConfigEditor.exe), as shown in Figure 3-11. This utility enables you to open existing and create new WCF configuration files without editing XML files directly. With the tool, you can manage settings for both the client and the service. Additionally, it is possible to configure bindings, behaviors, extensions, host environments, and diagnostics.

■ **Tip** By default the configuration tool is installed in the Microsoft Windows SDK Bin folder (C:\Program Files\Microsoft SDKs\Windows\v6.0). It also comes with a help file in that same folder. When you use the configuration editor, we suggest you keep an eye on what the configuration editor is actually adding to your configuration file. It tends to add more information than you specify, and it is important you know what the configuration settings mean. So, always inspect the results in a text editor after you make changes with the configuration editor and try to understand what it did.

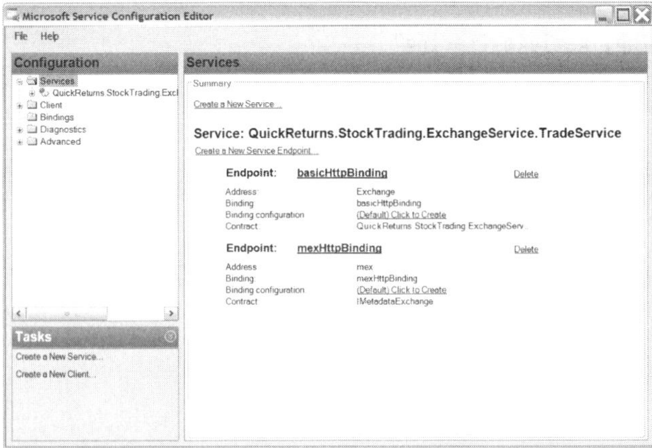

Figure 3-11. *Microsoft Service Configuration Editor*

Configuring Diagnostics

When you work with WCF, it is likely you will run into issues you don't understand completely. To investigate these issues, you will need to know what messages flow through your application and to trace them. Luckily, WCF provides integrated support for logging messages and tracing. You can configure diagnostics by using the Microsoft Service Configuration Editor or by manipulating the application configuration manually. Tracing works with listeners, similar to the Microsoft .NET Framework 2.0. Refer to Listing 3-20 for an example.

Listing 3-20. *Application Configuration with Tracing Enabled*

```
<?xml version="1.0" encoding="utf-8" ?>
<configuration>
<system.diagnostics>
    <sources>
        <source name="System.ServiceModel.MessageLogging"
                switchValue="Warning, ActivityTracing">
            <listeners>
                <add type="System.Diagnostics.DefaultTraceListener"
                     name="Default">
                    <filter type="" />
                </add>
                <add name="ServiceModelMessageLoggingListener">
                    <filter type="" />
                </add>
            </listeners>
        </source>
```

```
        <source name="System.ServiceModel"
                switchValue="Warning, ActivityTracing"
                propagateActivity="true">
            <listeners>
                <add type="System.Diagnostics.DefaultTraceListener"
                     name="Default">
                    <filter type="" />
                </add>
                <add name="ServiceModelTraceListener">
                    <filter type="" />
                </add>
            </listeners>
        </source>
    </sources>
    <sharedListeners>
        <add initializeData="C:\Temp\App_messages.svclog"
             type="System.Diagnostics.XmlWriterTraceListener, System, ➥
             Version=2.0.0.0, Culture=neutral, PublicKeyToken=b77a5c561934e089"
             name="ServiceModelMessageLoggingListener"
             traceOutputOptions="Timestamp">
            <filter type="" />
        </add>
        <add initializeData="C:\App_tracelog.svclog"
            type="System.Diagnostics.XmlWriterTraceListener, System, ➥
            Version=2.0.0.0, Culture=neutral, PublicKeyToken=b77a5c561934e089"
            name="ServiceModelTraceListener"
            traceOutputOptions="Timestamp">
            <filter type="" />
        </add>
    </sharedListeners>
</system.diagnostics>
<system.serviceModel>
<diagnostics>
    <messageLogging logEntireMessage="true"
                    logMalformedMessages="true"
                    logMessagesAtServiceLevel="true"
                    logMessagesAtTransportLevel="true" />
 </diagnostics>
<services>
  <service behaviorConfiguration="tradeServiceBehavior"
           name="QuickReturns.StockTrading.ExchangeService.TradeService">
    <endpoint address="Exchange"
              binding="basicHttpBinding"
              bindingConfiguration=""
              name="basicHttpBinding"
              contract="QuickReturns.StockTrading.ExchangeService. ➥
                        Contracts.ITradeService" />
```

```
    <endpoint address="mex"
              binding="mexHttpBinding"
              name="mexHttpBinding"
              contract="IMetadataExchange" />
    <host>
      <baseAddresses>
        <add baseAddress="http://localhost:8080/QuickReturns" />
      </baseAddresses>
    </host>
  </service>
</services>
  <behaviors>
    <serviceBehaviors>
      <behavior name="tradeServiceBehavior">
        <serviceMetadata httpGetEnabled="true"/>
        <serviceDebug httpHelpPageEnabled="true"
                      includeExceptionDetailInFaults="true"/>
      </behavior>
    </serviceBehaviors>
  </behaviors>
</system.serviceModel>
</configuration>
```

You can also edit the configuration file with the configuration tool's Diagnostics window, shown in Figure 3-12.

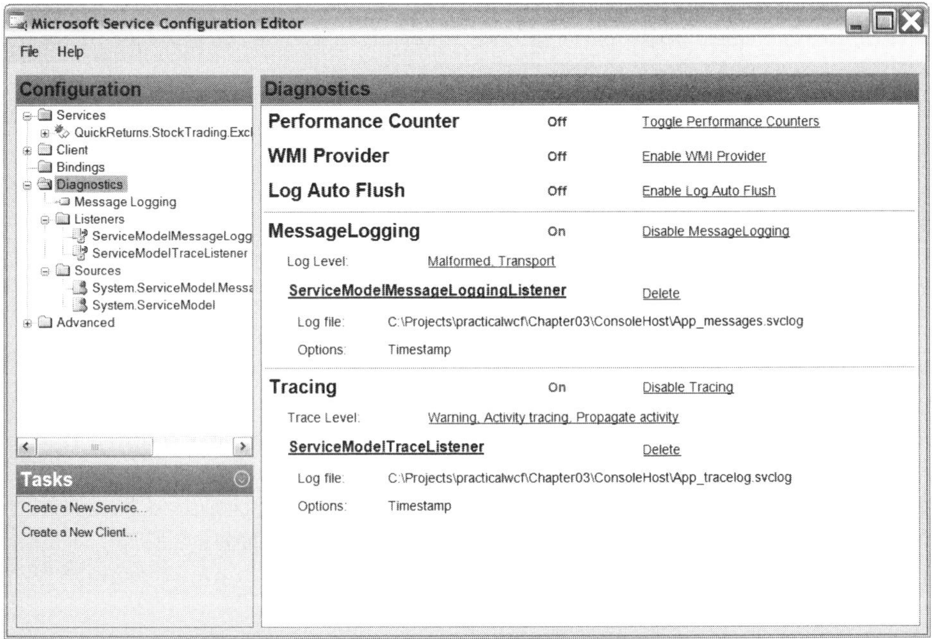

Figure 3-12. *Diagnostics window in the configuration tool*

In addition, the Windows SDK comes with a small utility that enables you to view the messages flowing through your application. The utility is called the Microsoft Service Trace Viewer (`SvcTraceViewer.exe`) and is in the same location as the configuration tool, as shown in Figure 3-13.

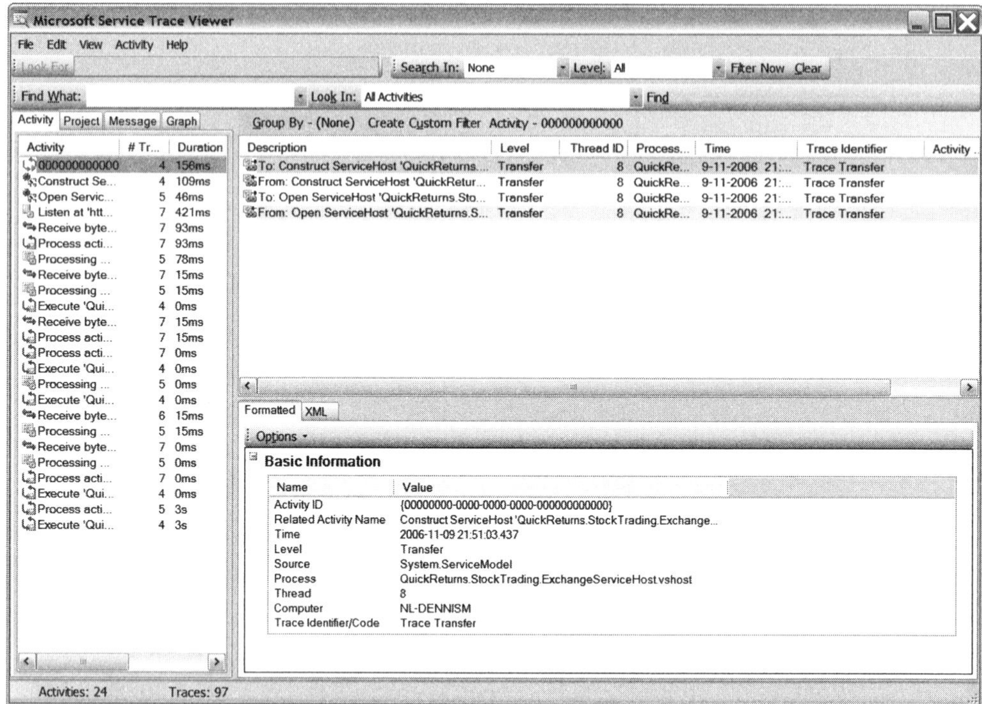

Figure 3-13. *Microsoft Service Trace Viewer*

The logging capabilities of WCF are extensive, and it is possible to enable a certain type of granularity as well. (In other words, it allows you to log full messages, just headers, malformed messages, messages at the service level or transport level, and so on, as shown in the second bold section of Listing 3-20.) You can then use the Service Trace Viewer to view the log files.

Tip By default, the Service Trace Viewer tool is installed in the Microsoft Windows SDK `Bin` folder (`C:\Program Files\Microsoft SDKs\Windows\v6.0`). It also comes with a compiled help file (CHM) in that same folder. We strongly suggest you run the sample application in this chapter and enable all or at least most of the tracing and diagnostics functionality in the configuration on both the client and service sides and then inspect the log files you are getting. This will enable you not only to understand the built-in capabilities around diagnostics but also to understand what is going on under the hood of the WCF programming model.

Configuring Instrumentation

Although any enterprise application needs instrumentation to satisfy operators, it is always useful if the platform also has instrumentation built in so you as an application developer don't have to be concerned about all the details of supporting instrumentation. Just like logging and tracing, you can enable performance counters and WMI from within the application configuration or the configuration tool for both the client side and the service side. You can also set the `performanceCountersEnabled` property to `ServiceOnly`. Listing 3-21 shows how you do this in an application configuration file.

Listing 3-21. *Application Configuration with Instrumentation Enabled*

```
<?xml version="1.0" encoding="utf-8"?>
<configuration>
   <system.serviceModel>
      <diagnostics wmiProviderEnabled="true" performanceCounters="All" />
      <client>
         <endpoint address="http://localhost:8080/QuickReturns/Exchange"
            binding="basicHttpBinding" bindingConfiguration=""
            contract="ITradeService" name="basicHttpBinding" />
      </client>
   </system.serviceModel>
</configuration>
```

In Figure 3-14, you see the Diagnostics window in the Microsoft Service Configuration Editor that you can use to enable performance counters and WMI events. This results in the marked changes in the configuration shown in Listing 3-21.

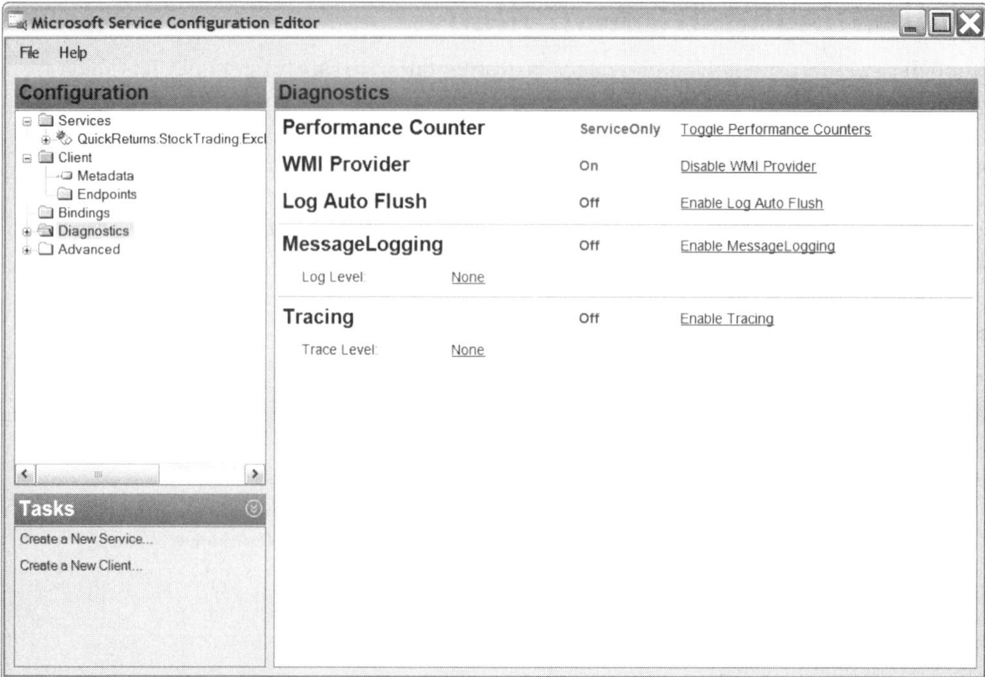

Figure 3-14. *Microsoft Service Configuration Editor with instrumentation enabled*

Summary

So now that you know how the unified programming model of WCF works and what its architecture is, you should be able to create your first WCF-enabled application. You should also be able to describe where the extension points are and be able to decide where you should extend in a particular scenario. We strongly suggest you continue with the next part of the book that builds on the foundation set in this chapter through the more advanced topics in the programming model around creating, consuming, and hosting services. However, make sure you have at least played around with the base services and client that comes in the accompanying code with the book.

P A R T 2

Programming with WCF

In Part 1, you investigated the basics of Service-Oriented Architecture and the building blocks of service-oriented computing (that is, SOAP, WSDL, UDDI, and so on). You also learned about the evolution of Microsoft offerings that provide a practical SOA platform to build services. You concentrated on the ASMX, WSE 1.0, WSE 2.0, and WSE 3.0 features initially. Then you learned about the unified programming model and how WCF provides the best tools to create secure, interoperable web services.

In this part, we'll discuss WCF technical features in detail. We'll concentrate on the programming aspects of WCF with the assistance of fictitious QuickReturns Ltd. stock market application. We'll initially guide you through installing WCF components. Then we'll walk you through creating services and hosting these services with WCF. We will discuss all the hosting options available in WCF in detail. Finally, we'll cover the management options available to manage WCF services to obtain the best return on investment for your application.

CHAPTER 4

Installing and Creating WCF Services

This chapter introduces how to implement WCF services. Much can be said about what constitutes a good service and a strong SOA architecture—Chapter 1 addresses those principles. Additionally, many have described web services and SOA as synonyms. We hope we've altered that perspective to clearly indicate that web services are an implementation model for SOA, just as message-oriented middleware and other loosely coupled technologies have provided in the past.

This chapter identifies the installation and configuration requirements of WCF and then presents a simplified set of examples for creating different types of contracts for services that are part of the QuickReturns Ltd. sample implementation. This chapter focuses primarily on the following:

- The requirements for WCF on the Windows XP, 2003, and Vista operating systems
- Creating WCF services and proxies using Visual Studio 2005 and .NET 3.0 Framework tools

To illustrate the simplified model, this chapter doesn't discuss the variations of how you can host the service. We'll explain that in more detail in later chapters.

WCF allows the abstraction and decoupling of a service's functionality from the actual transport protocols and physical characteristics of the communication interfaces. Prior chapters covered the ABCs of WCF, but here we'll focus on creating services. We will also more deeply dive into the technical aspects of the WCF programming model from this chapter onward.

Understanding the Requirements

We'll briefly cover the hardware and software requirements for both developing and running .NET 3.0 applications. It's important to note that Microsoft may change or update these requirements over time, so it's best to check Microsoft's website for the most up-to-date versions.

Hardware Requirements

Generally, the hardware requirements for running WCF as part of .NET 3.0 are simple. Running on top of .NET 2.0, the base level requirements are directly related to the .NET 2.0 runtime and .NET 2.0 SDK requirements.

Note The .NET runtime and the .NET SDK have different base requirements. Running the SDK, tools, utilities, and compilers requires additional resources. Given that most developers are leveraging Visual Studio .NET 2005 as their primary development environment (although not required), they should have as much memory, CPU, and disk space as they can afford.

At the time of this writing, Table 4-1 represents the minimum hardware requirements for the processor and RAM, and Table 4-2 represents the minimum hardware requirements for hard disk space.

Table 4-1. *Hardware Requirements: Processor and RAM*

Scenario	Processor Minimum	RAM Minimum
.NET Framework redistributable	400 megahertz (MHz)	96 megabytes (MB)
.NET Framework SDK	600MHz	128MB

Table 4-2. *Hardware Requirements: Hard Disk Space*

Scenario	Minimum
32-bit	280MB
64-bit	610MB

Note Microsoft publishes its requirements at `http://msdn2.microsoft.com/en-us/library/ms229070.aspx` and in the ReadMe file that is installed with the .NET SDK. You can find this in the `Program Files\Microsoft Visual Studio 8\SDK\v2.0` directory if it is installed as part of Visual Studio .NET.

Software Requirements

We'll now cover the software platform requirements for both developing and running .NET 3.0 applications. Note that although .NET 2.0 will run on Windows 2000 Service Pack 3, the .NET 3.0 bits, at the time of this writing, are not supported on any version of Windows 2000.

WCF is part of the .NET 3.0 Framework API that is fully integrated into the next major release of Windows—Windows Vista. Microsoft is also making the .NET 3.0 Framework backward compatible for certain versions of Windows, specifically Windows XP Service Pack 2 and Windows 2003 Service Pack 1.

At the time of this writing, the installation order is quite stringent. During research for this book, we've installed, deinstalled, reinstalled, and even wiped machines numerous times to get the beta and Community Technology Preview (CTP) components operating correctly. It's clear that machine virtualization is a blessing for this type of leading-edge work. Having discussed the "cleanliness" of the SDK installation process with the Microsoft program managers, we know they empathize with the development community and are looking to make the process as tight as possible.

■ **Note** The .NET 3.0 Framework is an additive set of class libraries, assemblies, and tools that runs on top of the .NET 2.0 Framework. Prior to being released to manufacturing, the working name was WinFX. The renaming has, as expected, caused confusion about the versioning, about what is included in each version, and about what installation packages are needed. However, with Vista, all the base components are distributed with the core operating system installation.

Appendix C contains detailed installation steps. The following are the component requirements to run and develop .NET 3.0 and WCF-based applications:

- Windows 2003 Service Pack 1, Windows XP Service Pack 2, Windows Vista
- The .NET Framework 2.0 redistributable package (x86/x64/I64), which is part of Vista (this is an add-on for Windows 2003 and XP Service Pack 2)
- The .NET 3.0 Framework components, which are part of Vista (these are add-ons for Windows 2003 and XP Service Pack 2)

The development environment requires a few extra tools and, as a general recommendation, should be equipped with a bit more resources for the hardware—specifically RAM, CPU, and disk space:

- Windows 2003 Service Pack 1, Windows XP Service Pack 2, or Windows Vista
- The .NET Framework 2.0 redistributable package (x86/x64/I64), which is part of Vista
- The .NET Framework 2.0 SDK (x86/x64/I64)
- The Microsoft Windows SDK—formerly known as Platform SDK
- The.NET Framework 3.0 runtime components (RTC), which are already included in Windows Vista
- *Recommended*: IIS installation—not required with Visual Studio 2005 development web server
- *Recommended*: Microsoft Visual Studio 2005 Express Edition (or "larger" version—Pro, Suite, and so on)
- *Recommended*: The .NET Framework 3.0 Development Tools for Visual Studio

Note that the .NET Framework 3.0 Development Tools for Visual Studio 2005 provide template support for .NET 3.0 projects and project items. They are not required, but they make working with WCF and .NET 3.0–based solutions and components inside Visual Studio 2005 a little bit easier because they add all the references and template code for you.

Note Developing WCF and .NET 3.0 Framework solutions requires only the .NET 2.0 Framework SDK. However, it is expected that most developers will use Visual Studio 2005. All versions of Visual Studio 2005 support the development of WCF (.NET 3.0) applications. You can find the .NET 2.0 runtime and SDK at `http://msdn.microsoft.com/netframework/downloads/updates/`. Currently, you can find all the .NET 3.0 components at `http://msdn.microsoft.com/windowsvista/downloads/products/`.

Installing the .NET 3.0 Development Components

This section lists the general steps for installing the .NET 3.0 (WCF) development components. (Appendix C lists the detailed installation steps for the required components.) This is the required installation order:

1. Install Visual Studio 2005 or .NET 2.0 SDK.
2. Install the .NET Framework 3.0 RTC.
3. Install the Windows SDK.
4. Install the .NET Framework 3.0 Development Tools (if using Visual Studio).

Tip At the time of this writing, Visual Studio 2005 has known compatibility issues with Vista. The Visual Studio 2005 team is working on a service pack to be available in 2007 to address these issues. Also note that for ASP.NET debugging, it's best to run Visual Studio 2005 from an elevated process.

WCF services can be hosted in any application process that loads the .NET 2.0 runtime, loads the appropriate .NET 3.0 Framework runtime components, and ultimately instantiates a `System.ServiceModel.ServiceHost` instance that listens on an endpoint for requests.

Note Chapter 5 provides greater detail about hosting, the various options available, the overall mechanics, and the nuances associated with the various hosting options.

This chapter focuses on getting up and running with WCF services and using the simplest of hosts—the ASP.NET development server and IIS. You can use IIS for both developing and deploying WCF services. Most of the mechanics of hosting WCF services inside ASP.NET are handled by an implementation of an `HttpHandler`. This handler is `System.ServiceModel.Activation.HttpHandler` and is mapped on a per-machine basis in the machine's `Web.config` file, which is located in the directory `%windir%\Microsoft.NET\Framework\v2.0.50727\CONFIG`.

IIS, WCF, AND THE HTTP API

Windows 2003, Windows XP Service Pack 2, and Windows Vista all provide the HTTP API to allow applications that create HTTP listeners to gain a series of advantages over the traditional Winsock mechanism that has been available in current and prior releases of Windows.

WCF is positioned to take full advantage of this capability, which for the most part sat dormant on the client platform. Check out the article "Http.sys in WinXP SP2: What It Means with Windows Communication Foundation" located at `http://www.dotnetjunkies.com/Tutorial/99DD7042-532D-4DB4-8625-1CD8BF422D64.dcik`.

■ **Note** All ASP.NET "resources" are mapped to types that implement the `IHttpHandler` interface as required by the ASP.NET hosting engine.

Within the `httpHandler` section of the machine's `Web.config`, the mapping appears as shown in Listing 4-1.

Listing 4-1. `*.svc` *Mapping for WCF Handler*

```
<add
   path="*.svc"
   verb="*"
   type="System.ServiceModel.Activation.HttpHandler, System.ServiceModel,
   Version=3.0.0.0, Culture=neutral, PublicKeyToken=b77a5c561934e089"
   validate="false" />
```

The `System.ServiceModel.Activation.HttpHandler` class is responsible for providing the `ServiceHost` environment inside the ASP.NET worker process for applications that are hosted on IIS. This handler, just as handlers provide for other extensions (`*.aspx`, `*.asmx`), is responsible for providing any runtime compilation of source code embedded inside the `*.svc` files, in addition to providing update detection of the same source code as is done for the other handler types.

Understanding Service Contracts

Service contracts, one of the Cs in the ABCs of WCF, are what are advertised to the consumers of your services. This advertisement generally takes place through a schema and a contract definition that supports a standardized method for publishing the service contract (along with data contracts). Today, that schema is either a Web Services Description Language (WSDL) contract or a WS-MetadataExchange (MEX) contract. These formats are industry-supported, open specifications. These specifications are located at the following locations:

WSDL: `http://www.w3.org/TR/wsdl`

MEX: `http://schemas.xmlsoap.org/ws/2004/09/mex/`

WSDL AND WS-METADATAEXCHANGE

WSDL is an XML Schema–based description of supported operations and messages for an endpoint.

MEX represents a message exchange protocol that allows the discovery of WSDL, WS-Policy, or XML Schema associated with a target namespace. More information is available at the following location: `http://specs.xmlsoap.org/ws/2004/09/mex/WS-MetadataExchange.pdf`.

Note For COM interop, a third type of contract exists—a typed contract. See Chapter 10 for more details.

The service is basically that, a *service*—something, perhaps a behavior, that takes place on behalf of another system. Services themselves can be a variety of types and generally fall into either informational or action oriented.

Platform and framework vendors have implemented the tools and libraries that can leverage these standardized contracts to provide a more seamless integration experience amongst the service provider and the consumers (sometimes referred to as *receivers* and *senders*). This is what WCF provides in its metadata model: the ability to both define and publish as well as consume these standardized schema definitions. It is possible, in WCF, to provide that support both programmatically at runtime and declaratively at design and configuration time.

WCF provides the standards and tools support primarily through `SvcUtil.exe`. This utility is the primary code and metadata interpretation tool. That, in combination with the WCF framework's ability to leverage reflection to interrogate types adorned with the appropriate attributes, makes generating and using the WCF framework less complicated than before. Figure 4-1 illustrates how service metadata is consumed by `SvcUtil.exe` for proxy generation; additionally, the same metadata is leveraged by the WCF framework for runtime interaction.

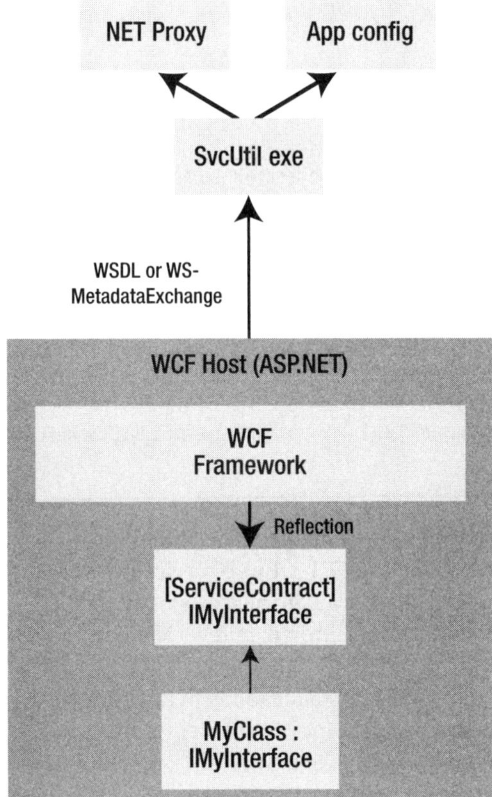

Figure 4-1. *Metadata publishing and client code generation*

Contract First or Code First?

There have been lots of discussions in SOA communities regarding best practices for either "code first" or "contract first" service development. We won't say one is better than the other. However, in a true "contract-first" paradigm, you'll spend all the up-front time generating the schema (WSDL) in XML that supports your service contract implementation. Frankly, we'd rather listen to someone scratch their nails on a blackboard than start with a whole bunch of XML. Although WCF can support a contract- and schema-driven starting point, for the most part you'll spend time adorning your types with attributes in a declarative model and allowing the WCF framework to generate the necessary schema and contract metadata.

The WCF programming model of "code first and then apply attributes to the interface" allows the WCF framework to do all the work of providing a standardized schema to publish to consumers of the service. This model works best in industries or organizations where you're the only provider of the service or where you're just working on internal solutions that require cross-application integration and you have full control over the interfaces.

.NET ATTRIBUTES BACKGROUND

.NET uses attributes throughout the framework. Attributes permeate many aspects of how your types are hosted by the .NET CLR. Things such as Code Access Security (CAS) and general assembly metadata all depend upon attributes that are part of the generated MSIL. This is one of the declarative aspects of .NET.

The ASP.NET 2.0 web service model relies as well on class- and method-level attributes that control how the .NET Framework manages the runtime support of web services through the request-reply cycle. For the most part, the declarative model remains the same when moving to WCF.

According to the WCF product team, this was somewhat intentional to help the migration and transition of both existing ASP.NET 2.0 web services and developers to the WCF model. That initial transition started with the introduction of Web Services Enhancements (WSE) from version 1.0 up through version 3.0. In fact, the transition from out-of-the-box ASP.NET 2.0 web services to WSE web services required no change from a coding perspective. All WSE required was the modification of the application (`Web.config`) file that the site was hosted on, in addition to a recompile to bind to the updated assemblies that were part of the WSE distributions.

WCF supports schema-first and contract-first development as well. This might sound like a new model in the .NET world, but it was possible under ASP.NET 1.1 web services as well; it just required some discipline to follow and implement. The paradigm also existed in the COM world; but again, discipline was required and tool support was limited, and we all need to get things done, right?

WCF offers the tools and framework support to provide the malleability of an implementation and definition that allows service architects to view what they implement from either the outside in or the inside out. The primary tool you'll use in WCF is `SvcUtil.exe`. We'll introduce how to use `SvcUtil.exe` in this chapter, but Chapter 5 covers it in more detail.

Service Design

WCF provides the complete decoupling at design time of the service from the actual ABCs of the service implementation. Why? This provides a greater level of flexibility in both choosing the implementation model today (which consists of both the service and the ABCs) and providing the greatest amount of flexibility and extensibility for supporting varied transports available today and in the future. In other words, you can write and maintain a single instance of your service code without regard for what the physical deployment model is.

Now, in the real world, you still need to consider what the service provides and what the overall performance is as it relates to marshaling objects across service boundaries and ultimately coupling physical nodes separated by a LAN, WAN, or the Internet. So, as good solution architects, you must never forget the "Eight Fallacies of Distributed Computing" by Peter Deutsch; see `http://today.java.net/jag/Fallacies.html` for more information.

In the ideal implementation, the service providers and service consumers will spend a significant amount of time collaborating from a business perspective. During that collaboration process, a service model will evolve to properly address many aspects of what the service contract will look like, including elements such as the following:

- Granularity
- Coupling

- Cohesion
- Security
- Performance
- Reliability
- Other "ilities" of architecture

To be clear, WCF doesn't address these aspects directly; that's up to the solution architect. WCF provides the base framework for implementing service contracts, in conjunction with the rest of the ABCs for a solid foundation of any SOA implementation.

Programming Model

So, Table 4-3 compares WCF's programming model to ASP.NET 2.0 web services and WSE.

Table 4-3. *Attribute Programming Model Comparison*

ASP.NET 2.0 Attribute	WCF Attribute	Comments
`[WebServiceAttribute]`	`[ServiceContractAttribute]`	Interface, class-level attribute
`[WebMethodAttribute]`	`[OperationContractAttribute]`	Method-level attribute
	`[DataContractAttribute]`	Class-level attribute
	`[DataMemberAttribute]`	Field, property, event-level attribute

You probably noticed the name change from web-oriented naming to more SOA nomenclature—*Service*, *Operation*, and *Data*. This was done intentionally to shift the architectural thinking from a web-only mentality to an "any transport" paradigm.

WSE 3.0 provides the ability for different transports in addition to supporting more complex message exchange patterns such as duplex channels (through the `ISoapDuplexChannel` interface). WCF now provides a much more simplistic model for implementation in addition to a fully extensible framework along with support for WS-* specifications such as WS-Transactions, WS-Reliability, and others.

"Hello, World"

Now, you'll see the simplest of examples (`Chapter04/Example01` in the downloadable code) in both ASP.NET 2.0 and WCF. This first sample is just to provide a minimal example of a service implementation. The example uses a "code first with attributes" model. To be clear, this is *not* a best practice—it's purely an example to show the similarities between ASP.NET 2.0 web services and WCF. The best practice is a contract-first model where you define the schema prior to coding the implementation. This removes the designer's bias toward any implementation details or restrictions.

■Note With some of the IIS-hosted samples, a set of scripts provides the IIS virtual directory creation and ASP.NET mapping, along with a script to remove the IIS virtual directory when done. The creation/removal scripts are in each example's directory and are named `CreateVirtualDirs.bat` and `DeleteVirtualDirs.bat`, respectively. You must be an administrator on the system from where these files are executed. Additionally, if you're on Vista, you must run from an elevated command prompt from the directory where these files exist.

Also, to ensure you focus on how the services are created, we will use only IIS as the hosting environment. (Chapter 5 discusses other WCF hosting options.)

ASP.NET 2.0 Web Service: "Hello, World"

Listing 4-2 shows `MyService.asmx`.

Listing 4-2. `MyService.asmx`

```
<%@ WebService Language="C#" Class="MyService" %>
using System.Web.Services;
[WebService]
public class MyService  : System.Web.Services.WebService
{
    [WebMethod]
    public string HelloWorld ( string yourName )
    {
        return "Hello, World to " + yourName;
    }
}
```

WCF Service: "Hello, World"

Listing 4-3 shows `MyService.svc`, and Listing 4-4 shows `Web.config`.

Listing 4-3. `MyService.svc`

```
<%@ ServiceHost Language="C#" Service="MyService" %>
using System.ServiceModel;
[ServiceContract]
public class MyService
{
    [OperationContract]
    public string HelloWorld ( string yourName )
    {
        return "Hello, World to " + yourName;
    }
}
```

Listing 4-4. `Web.config`

```
<?xml version="1.0"?>
<configuration>
  <system.serviceModel>
    <services>
      <service
      name="MyService"
      behaviorConfiguration="returnFaults">
        <endpoint
      contract="MyService"
      binding="wsHttpBinding"/>
      </service>
    </services>
    <behaviors>
    <serviceBehaviors>
      <behavior name="returnFaults">
        <serviceMetadata httpGetEnabled="true"/>
        <serviceDebug
          httpHelpPageEnabled="true"
          includeExceptionDetailInFaults="true"/>
      </behavior>
    </serviceBehaviors>
    </behaviors>
  </system.serviceModel>
</configuration>
```

Tip A best practice in WCF is to implement the service contract using an interface; then you implement the interface in a class and update the configuration file to point to the correct type.

From a coding and implementation perspective, the ASP.NET 2.0 web service and the WCF service aren't that different. The method bodies are identical. Deployment, under ASP.NET, is also nearly identical. When running from Visual Studio 2005, both can leverage the ASP.NET development server. Additionally, if running from IIS and the application mappings are correct, the deployment is identical between the ASP.NET 2.0 web services and WCF services.

The first obvious difference is that the WCF implementation requires a configuration (`Web.config`) file. The configuration file you see is one of the strengths of building services with WCF—you get almost complete control of the runtime characteristics of a service without forcing a change in the code. Configuration files are not required for WCF. However, given that this example is expected to be hosted by the ASP.NET runtime, a configuration file is required. In later chapters, we'll cover self-hosting and how to manage the WCF runtime characteristics through code.

"Hello, World" with Interfaces

A best practice in WCF is to define a contract up front, as an interface, and then provide the implementation of that interface in a concrete class. Why? This provides a clear abstraction of the contract from the implementation. The other aspect of this approach is a clear distinction of the service boundary (remember the "boundaries are explicit" SOA tenet) from the implementation. Although the service interface definition is in code, and not in metadata, it's a clear perimeter that permits some flexibility for exposing only what's necessary and that provides design-time and configuration-time flexibility.

WCF Service: "Hello, World"

The next example (Example02 in the downloadable code) follows the best practice of implementing the contract in a defined interface with the implementation provided for separately. The mapping, as you'll soon see, is managed through the framework either programmatically or through configuration options. Listing 4-5 shows `MyService.svc`.

Listing 4-5. `MyService.svc`

```
<%@ ServiceHost Language="C#" Service="MyService" %>
using System.ServiceModel;

[ServiceContract]
public interface IMyInterface
{
        [OperationContract]
        string HelloWorld ( string yourName );
}

public class MyService : IMyInterface
{
    public string HelloWorld( string yourName )
    {
        return "Hello, World to " + yourName;
    }
}
```

■ Note For Vista users, if you've run `CreateVirtualDirs.bat` (from an elevated prompt as required) and attempt to open the Visual Studio 2005 solution file with Visual Studio 2005, you will be presented with a message box indicating the site is configured with the wrong version of .NET. You can answer either Yes or No to this prompt. This is because of Visual Studio 2005 incompatibilities with the Vista RTM release. To validate the correct version mapped for the virtual site, you must use the IIS manager and ensure the site is mapped to an application pool configuration with ASP.NET 2.0. The `CreateVirtualDirs.bat` script handles this automatically.

The implementation now provides a clear contract definition, void of implementation details, that is attributed as required to provide the automatic generation of the metadata (either WSDL or MEX). This separation, in the same source file, can appear elsewhere. How the contract is implemented, and ultimately bound, is managed through a configuration file or programmatically. For this example, and probably what is destined to be the norm, we do it via configuration.

In the `Web.config` file for the WCF service, shown in Listing 4-6, the mapping between the type and the contract takes place through the `<services>` element inside the `<system.serviceModel>` section. Note the clear contract mapping to the implementation type, which is the interface definition.

Listing 4-6. `Web.config`

```
<?xml version="1.0"?>
<configuration>
  <system.serviceModel>
    <services>
      <service
      name="MyService"
      behaviorConfiguration="returnFaults">
        <endpoint
      contract="IMyInterface"
      binding="wsHttpBinding"/>
      </service>
    </services>
    <behaviors>
    <serviceBehaviors>
      <behavior name="returnFaults">
        <serviceMetadata httpGetEnabled="true"/>
        <serviceDebug
          httpHelpPageEnabled="true"
          includeExceptionDetailInFaults="true"/>
      </behavior>
    </serviceBehaviors>
    </behaviors>
  </system.serviceModel>
</configuration>
```

If you launch this service in the ASP.NET development server, you'll see something different from Figure 4-2 because the URL will differ by the IP port in use for the project. The ASP.NET development server dynamically chooses the IP port, unless you've overridden it. If you're using IIS, then the default port 80 is left off, and the URL appears as in Figure 4-2.

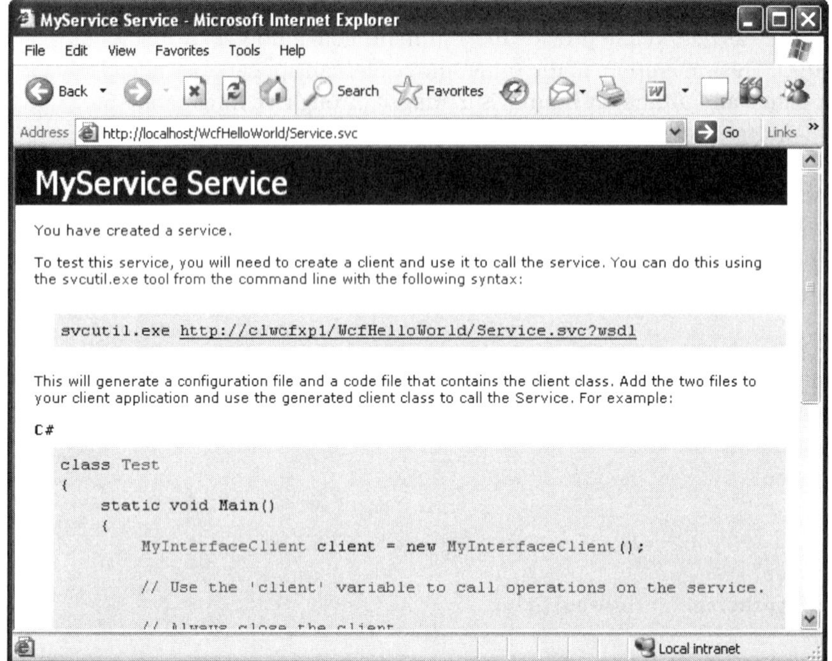

Figure 4-2. *Viewing the WCF "Hello, World" service*

The initial difference when consuming ASP.NET web services vs. WCF services is the use of different client proxy generation tools. You'll see that step in the following sections using two different methods: Visual Studio 2005 integration and the `SvcUtil.exe` utility.

Service Client Proxy

Now that you have a service, it's time to define a client for that service. So, add a C# console application, and place the implementation code in a separate file as part of the ASP.NET application. The following is part of the `Example03` sample code.

Proxy Generation: Using the Visual Studio 2005 Add-In

Similar to ASP.NET proxy creation, if you right-click the project in the IDE, you'll see three options for adding references. Select Add Service Reference, as shown in Figure 4-3.

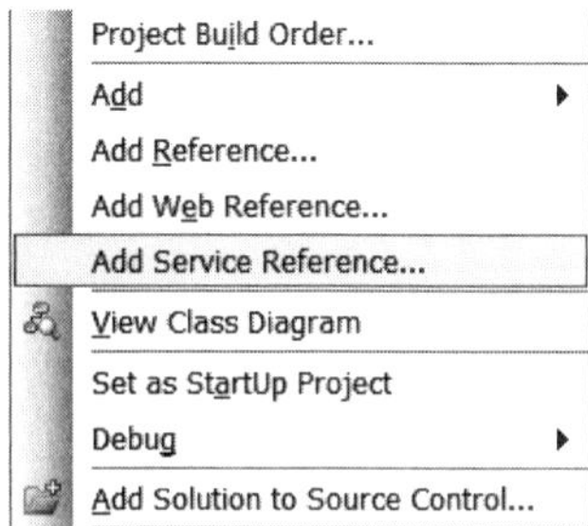

Figure 4-3. *Adding a reference to a WCF service*

This menu option is a wrapper around the `SvcUtil.exe` utility, actually spawning a process with the necessary parameters. Once you've selected the Add Service Reference option, you'll see the Add Service Reference dialog box, as shown in Figure 4-4.

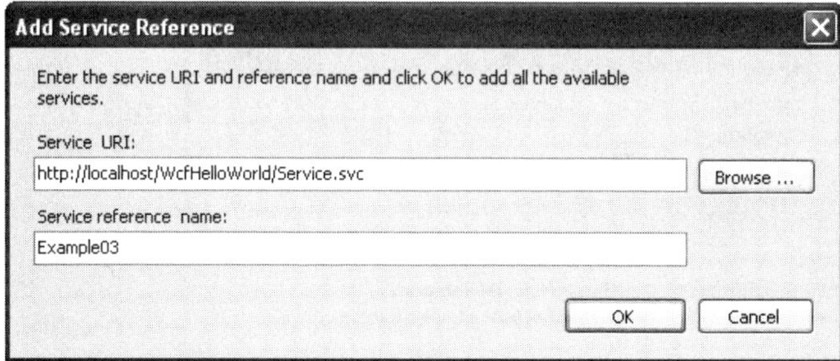

Figure 4-4. *Add Service Reference dialog box*

Click OK, and the add-in spawns `SvcUtil.exe`, generating (or modifying) the necessary proxy class and the required configuration file and adding the necessary references to the project. The project's references will now list the required WCF assemblies—`System.Runtime.Serialization` and `System.ServiceModel`. At this point, you're now ready to program your first service call into your service tier.

A brief explanation of the objects added to the project is necessary. During the `SvcUtil.exe` (Add Service Reference) call, the utility added the following items and references to the project automatically. Some are only to aid the Visual Studio integration; others are required for using the service directly through the proxy.

Service references: Within this folder two items were added. The first, a "map" file, provides support for the generation and regeneration of the proxy through the Visual Studio add-in. The second item—`Example03.cs`—represents the concrete proxy class implementation that leverages the namespace `System.ServiceModel` to provide a simple integration class.

Configuration: The second item is the `App.config` file. An `App.config` file (automatically renamed during the Visual Studio build process to `<assembly name>.config`) provides the runtime WCF configuration parameters. If you peer inside this file, you'll notice a tremendous amount of settings, many of which are either defaulted or redundant to the default settings. A general approach is to generate the file and then manage the file using the WCF `SvcConfigEditor.exe` editor utility. This utility is located in the Windows SDK `Bin` directory and accessible from within Visual Studio 2005 in the Tools menu as WCF SvcConfigEditor. Figure 4-5 shows the implementation of the tool.

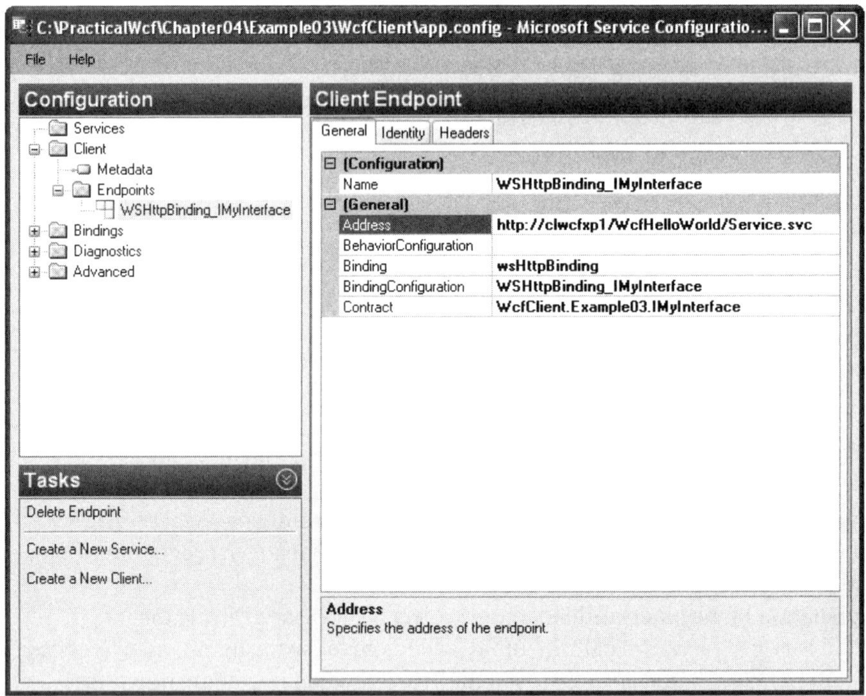

Figure 4-5. *Microsoft Service Configuration Editor*—`SvcConfigEditor.exe`

As you can see from the Microsoft Service Configuration Editor, you can manage a tremendous amount of detailed properties through the configuration tool. This is one of the greatest strengths of WCF—the ability to control many aspects of an implementation without impacting the core service implementation. That a service implementation doesn't need to change in order to migrate from an HTTP-based protocol to another message-oriented one is a core strength of WCF's metadata approach.

You'll see many parts are controllable through the runtime configuration; however, you need to define many aspects of a service implementation at the service contract level.

Proxy Generation: Using SvcUtil.exe

An alternative method is to leverage the `SvcUtil.exe` utility directly instead of the Visual Studio add-in. Again, the Visual Studio add-in calls `SvcUtil.exe`, with parameters, to generate the proxy when executed directly from within Visual Studio. You can see the command line and results of that command by viewing the Output window and setting the Show Output From drop-down list to Service Reference.

To generate the proxy manually, choose Start ➤ All Programs ➤ Microsoft Windows SDK ➤ CMD. This command prompt is useful because its path is set to the binary directory where the SDK tools and utilities are located.

We'll show how to use the `SvcUtil.exe` command-line tool to generate two outputs necessary for the example project: the client proxy source code file and the application configuration file. These files are then merged into the client project. The `SvcUtil.exe` can generate both. For this example, the following command (which should appear on a single line) produces both a proxy class and a configuration file:

```
svcutil /config:newConfig.config /out:"Example03.cs"
    /n:*,WcfClient.Example03
    "http://localhost/WcfHelloWorld/Service.svc?wsdl"
```

The command is fairly self-explanatory. The `/n` switch indicates in which namespace the generated proxy class should fall. The last parameter is the URL of the service endpoint where you can find schema information. Note that you can replace `?wsdl` with `?mex` because `SvcUtil.exe` supports both methods of discovery. Further help is available by executing `svcutil.exe /?` from the command prompt.

The next step is to take the output files `Example03.cs` and `newConfig.config` and merge them into the project. You can add the first file, `Example03.cs`, directly to the project by choosing Add Existing Item from the Project menu in Visual Studio 2005.

You need to add the second file as an application configuration (`App.config`) file in the project. If the project does not already have an `App.config` file, you can add one by again choosing Add Existing Item from the Project menu. If there is already an existing `App.config`, you need to merge the section `system.serviceModel`, ensuring you take all the appropriate child elements.

Client Code

The client code in `Example03`, shown in Listing 4-7, is a simple call through the proxy class. Here, you are leveraging a best practice of the `using` statement to ensure that the `Dispose()` method is called. The other option is to wrap it in a `try...finally` block, with a call to the object's `Dispose()` method inside the `finally` clause.

■ **Note** The `using` keyword is a shortcut method that expands in the generated MSIL to `try...finally` block. This has always been available to C# and is in VB .NET 2005.

Listing 4-7. `WcfClient program.cs`

```
using System;
namespace WcfClient
{
    class Program
    {
        static void Main( )
        {
            //using "block" as a shortcut for a try...finally block
            // with a call to the object Dispose() method in the finally block
            using( Example03.MyInterfaceClient proxy =
                new Example03.MyInterfaceClient() )
            {
               string result = proxy.HelloWorld( "Shawn" );
                Console.WriteLine( result );
                Console.WriteLine( "Press <enter> to exit..." );
                Console.ReadLine();
            }
        }
    }
}
```

Hosting on IIS

The previous examples are all included in the downloadable source code with an automated script for creating the virtual directory on IIS. This section shows you how to both create a .NET 3.0 WCF service and host it in IIS.

The first step to take is to create an empty solution file. This provides total control over the location of the file. If you bypass this step, Visual Studio 2005 creates the project where you want it to, but the solution file is put in your default location for your Visual Studio projects.

To generate an empty solution file that you'll add your projects to, from within Visual Studio select File ➤ New Project ➤ Other Project Types ➤ Visual Studio Solutions ➤ Blank Solution. Be sure to specify both the name and the location for the blank solution.

After creating the empty solution file, the next step is to add a .NET 3.0 (WCF) service web project. If you immediately add the project to the solution, the project files are created in the default `c:\inetpub\wwwroot` subdirectory. To gain a little more control, you can create the IIS virtual site before adding the project location to the solution file.

The next step is to just create a subdirectory where the solution file is located, as shown in Figure 4-6.

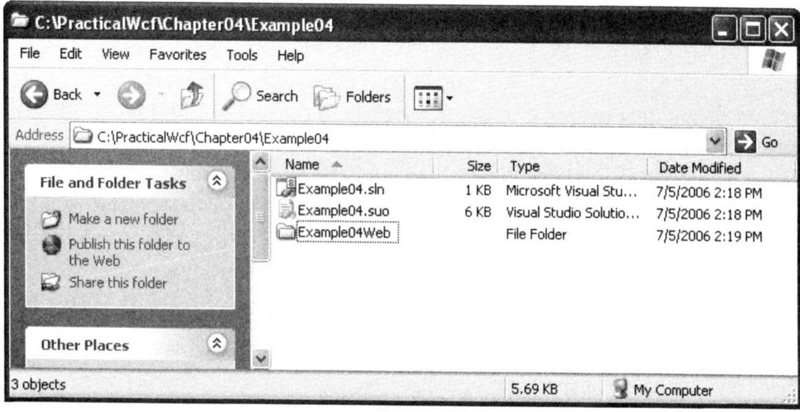

Figure 4-6. *Creating a subdirectory in solution folder*

Then, you need to create a mapping in IIS. You can navigate through IIS Manager; for simplicity, just right-click the folder, and select Properties.

Once the Properties dialog box appears, click the Web Sharing tab, as shown in Figure 4-7. Simply click the radio button Share This Folder, and the Edit Alias dialog appears. You can enable directory browsing to make it easier to view and click items in the website. Generally, this is a setting only for development.

Caution This setting allows users to browse all files on the site, just like Windows Explorer. Although it's a nice feature, be careful with it in production.

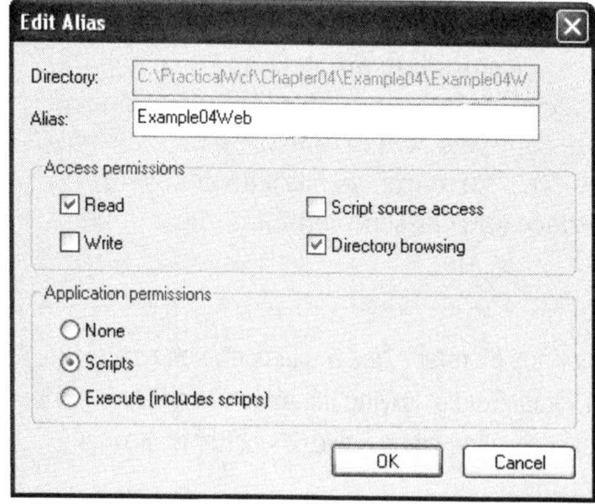

Figure 4-7. *Web Sharing tab's Edit Alias dialog box*

At this point, click OK several times to dismiss the dialog boxes. The site should now be available through the URL `http://localhost/Example04Web`. However, you still need to check the version of ASP.NET that is set for this site. If you have only .NET 2.0 installed—that is, .NET 1.1 was *never* installed—there should be nothing else to do; however, it doesn't hurt to just check.

So, launch IIS Manager (Start ➤ Control Panel ➤ Administrative Tools ➤ Internet Information Services). Once you see the Properties dialog box, click the ASP.NET tab, and then switch the version of ASP.NET using the drop-down list to the .NET 3.0–supported version, which is 2.0.50727 (the RTM version).

■ Tip If you don't see this icon, then either you have limited access on the machine or IIS is not installed. Please ensure IIS is installed and you have the appropriate permissions.

This example has one additional step—to provide access to resources known as *anonymous requests*. Anonymous requests are any requests that have no identity or Windows principals associated with the HTTP request.

Click the Directory Security tab, and then click Edit under the Anonymous Access and Authentication Control section of the dialog box. Ensure that the option Anonymous Access is enabled. This will allow the example to run without stepping into how to provide authentication credentials on the requests.

Dismiss all open dialog boxes by clicking the OK buttons. At this point, you now have a solution directory with a child project that has, or will have, all its resources (source code files and content) located in a directory of your choosing (that is, not in the default `c:\inetpub\wwwroot` directory).

Now you're ready to add the project to the solution you created earlier. In Visual Studio, select the solution in Solution Explorer, right-click, and then select Add ➤ New Web Site.

At this point, ensure you select the .NET 3.0/WCF service template, set HTTP as the location, use the URL that was set on the folder alias using web sharing in Windows Explorer, and set the language of your choice. Click OK, and the Visual Studio .NET 3.0 template system creates a project starting point for your service, giving you a complete project.

Notice that the project template leverages the special folder names for the application code and application data. In the prior example, the source code was hosted directly in the `*.svc` file. The project shown here, which is generated from the .NET 3.0 template, has a distinct source directory along with a `*.cs` file that contains the interface and class implementation.

■ Tip In the real world, it's best to separate the service interface (contract) and implementation types into their own assemblies (DLL), which translates to projects in Visual Studio. Having the structure as shown previously is a nice feature for ease of use, but from a physical separation perspective, it's better to provide distinct assemblies for the tiers.

If you look at the file system using Windows Explorer or using a command prompt and view the directory you started in, you'll see the same set of files listed under the project in Visual Studio Solution Explorer.

At this point, if you browse to the location http://localhost/example04Web/ using Internet Explorer, you'll see a directory listing (as long as the settings are like those in Figure 4-7).

If you click service.svc, you are then brought to the default help screen generated by System.ServiceModel.Activiation.HttpHandler for the *.svc extensions, as shown in Figure 4-2.

At this point, you follow the same steps in a client application, either generating a proxy class directly through the use of the SvcUtil.exe utility or right-clicking the project and generating the proxy through the Add Service Reference add-in feature, as shown previously.

The accompanying solution for this example has a complete console client that makes a call into the WCF service you just created.

ServiceContract Attribute

One of the valuable capabilities of WCF is getting control over how the WCF framework generates the metadata for the service contract. The examples presented so far have been the simplest forms, relying on the default settings and values that are generated by SvcUtil.exe (for the client) or at runtime by the framework.

When designing services, it's important to understand what is generated as metadata. You need an awareness of what the naming conventions are because they directly impact the generated service description metadata. This section helps you identify what capabilities exist in WCF for controlling how this metadata is created.

The ServiceContract attribute is the entry point into the definition of a service. In conjunction with binding and endpoint information (generally through configuration), it is this information that clients (service consumers) apply in order to exercise your service.

This represents the contract and not the behavior. To control the behavior, you need to leverage the behavior aspect of the WCF programming model. More specifically, apply the class-level attribute ServiceBehaviorAttribute and the required properties associated with your implementation. Chapter 3 provides more details on behaviors. Table 4-4 lists the properties that are part of the ServiceContractAttribute to control metadata generation and runtime capabilities support by WCF.

Table 4-4. ServiceContractAttribute *Properties*

Class Property	Description
CallBackContract	Designates the contract in duplex message exchange (two-way) pattern implementations.
Name	Controls the naming of the interface in the WSDL or metadata; allows overriding using the interface or class name in the generated metadata.
Namespace	Controls the namespace that is used in the WSDL or metadata from the default of tempuri.org.
SessionMode	Indicates whether this service requires bindings that can support sessions amongst more complex message exchange patterns. Used in conjunction with ServiceBehaviorAttribute that is applied on a class.

At the service contract level, you have a few options that give you a foundation to work upon for managing the emitted metadata. Since types are ultimately turned into XML to support the loosely coupled world of WCF services, you have two choices for serialization, described in Table 4-5.

Table 4-5. *Serialization Options*

Attribute Type	Description
`DataContractSerializer`	Default serialization class that handles serializable types in addition to contract types (data or message). Supports two modes: shared type and shared contract. The first is when both "types" exist on both sides of the channel—such as with .NET Remoting. The second type is a loosely coupled mode, where the only requirement is that types exist on both sides of the channel that can serialize/deserialize from the XML.
`XmlSerializer`	Serialization class that handles only serializable types. Use this class when you need greater control over the XML that is emitted from the WCF serialization process.

Let's take a look at a different example, one that's from the QuickReturns Ltd. company (`Example05`). Specifically, this section shows how to implement the exchange's service for `TradeSecurity`. (Please refer to Chapter 3 for background information on QuickReturns Ltd.)

The core requirement for `TradeSecurity` is a request-reply message exchange pattern. This pattern is a fairly simple but common interaction between service endpoints. The definition from the high-level view is the method requires a `Trade` schema, and on return, it provides an `Execution` schema. For the examples here, we'll just return a `decimal` in order to simplify the explanation.

You'll start by implementing the service contract using all the defaults. First, create an empty Visual Studio Solution. The Blank Solution template appears under Other Project Types ➤ Visual Studio Solutions after you choose File ➤ New Project.

Second, add a class library, or what's called a .NET 3.0/WCF service library to the project. Therefore, select the solution in Solution Explorer, and right-click. Then, choose Add ➤ New Project.

Once the Add New Project dialog box appears, ensure you select the .NET 3.0 grouping along with the .NET 3.0/WCF service library template. Also ensure you name your project `ExchangeService` along with validating the location of where the files are created.

■ **Tip** It's a best practice to separate your service library into a discrete compilation unit—a .NET assembly. This allows for greater specialization of the project team because you extend and integrate various parts of the system. Also, it allows for more loosely coupled versioning of system components. Obviously, if the system is simple, it's probably not necessary to take these control steps; however, it generally doesn't hurt to start out this way because when it grows beyond the "simple" system, you're better prepared.

At this point, Visual Studio adds the project, creating a source file that has a simple WCF implementation with the customary "Hello, World" method implementation. The template has embedded comments that provide some basic pointers on how to proceed with your implementation. Additionally, a commented code section provides the necessary steps on hosting the WCF service from your newly created WCF library in another project. The code provided in that commented section is for hosting outside ASP.NET. (Chapter 5 covers hosting options in depth.)

In addition to a sample implementation, the project references have been updated to make it easier to work with WCF applications.

Now in Solution Explorer, delete the generated `Class1.cs` file. Then right-click the project, and add a new item. Locate the .NET 3.0/WCF service item. Enter **TradeService** in the Name field, and click Add.

In the generated `TradeService.cs` file, replace the contents with Listing 4-8.

Listing 4-8. `TradeService.cs` *Implementation*

```
using System;
using System.ServiceModel;

namespace ExchangeService
{
    [ServiceContract(
        Namespace="http://PracticalWcf/Exchange/TradeService",
        Name="TradeService")
    ]
    public interface ITradeService
    {
        [OperationContract]
        decimal TradeSecurity( string ticker, int quantity );
    }
    public class TradeService : ITradeService
    {
        const decimal IBM_Price = 80.50m;
        const decimal MSFT_Price = 30.25m;
        public decimal TradeSecurity( string ticker, int quantity )
        {
            if( quantity < 1 )
                throw new ArgumentException(
                    "Invalid quantity", "quantity" );
            switch( ticker.ToLower() )
            {
                case "ibm":
                    return quantity * IBM_Price;
                case "msft":
                    return quantity * MSFT_Price;
                default:
                    throw new ArgumentException(
                        "SK security - only MSFT & IBM", "ticker" );
            }
        }
    }
}
```

Notice that the top of the file contains a reference to the `System.ServiceModel` namespace. This namespace contains the necessary types that provide attribute support for the contract declaration.

This implementation follows the best practice of separating the contract definition from the implementation. In the example, the `ServiceContract` attribute is applied to the `ITradeService` interface. Additionally, the single method signature within `ITradeService` has the `OperationContract` attribute. These attributes signal to the WCF runtime how to generate the metadata and WSDL necessary for discovering supported operations in addition to managing the actual runtime calls from clients.

The `TradeService` class simply implements `ITradeService`. How does the WCF runtime know what type to load in response to client requests? You'll see in a little bit how it takes place through configuration, specifically, how the ABCs are tied together.

Make sure it compiles before proceeding. If there are no errors, create a simple ASP.NET hosting project for this newly created .NET 3.0/WCF service library.

In Solution Explorer, add a new empty website—which is just a standard ASP.NET website to your solution. Do this either by right-clicking the solution and choosing Add New Web Site or by choosing File ➤ Add ➤ New Web Site from the Visual Studio menu.

Now, select the web project you just created in Solution Explorer, right-click, and choose to add a reference. Once the Add Reference dialog box opens, select the Projects tab, and choose the Exchange Service project from the list.

Now, right-click the project again, and add a `Web.config` (web configuration) file to the project if one does not already exist. Modify the contents of the `Web.config` file, ensuring the `<system.serviceModel>` section appears as a child to the `<configuration>` element, as shown in Listing 4-9.

Listing 4-9. *Website* `Web.config` *File (Partial)*

```
<?xml version="1.0"?>
<configuration>
  <system.serviceModel>
    <services>
      <service name="ExchangeService.TradeService"
               behaviorConfiguration="returnFaults">
        <endpoint contract="ExchangeService.ITradeService"
                  binding="wsHttpBinding"/>
      </service>
    </services>
    <behaviors>
      <serviceBehaviors>
        <behavior name="returnFaults">
          <serviceMetadata httpGetEnabled="true"/>
          <serviceDebug httpHelpPageEnabled="true"
                        includeExceptionDetailInFaults="true"/>
        </behavior>
      </serviceBehaviors>
    </behaviors>
  </system.serviceModel>
  <appSettings/>
  <connectionStrings/>
<system.web>
...
```

This configuration file contains a `system.serviceModel` section, in bold, that provides the necessary binding and contract information for the sample. The service element identifies the specific .NET type that is exposed through this service endpoint. The endpoint element identifies the specific contract that is bound to the service type listed. Since the example is using IIS activation, the `wsHttpBinding` is the binding used, which supports request-reply in addition to reliable, secure, and transactional message exchange.

Then, right-click again the web project, and add a .NET 3.0/WCF service. Modify the dialog box entries by specifying `TradeService.svc` as the name of the file and setting C# as the language.

Open the newly created `TradeService.svc` file, and replace the contents with this single line:

```
<%@ ServiceHost Language="C#" Service="ExchangeService.TradeService" %>
```

Note that the `Service` parameter is now set to a type that resides in the assembly generated from the exchange service project.

First, do a solution build (Build ➤ Build Solution). Now, right-click the web project, and choose View in Browser (you must have directory browsing enabled as in Figure 4-7). Once Internet Explorer opens and you see the directory listing, click the `TradeService.svc` file. At this point, the ASP.NET runtime will begin the compilation process, generating the required assemblies to service your request. After a few seconds (depending upon your machine configuration), you should see the standard help screen similar to what is shown in Figure 4-2.

You've now created a simple `TradeService` that leverages a best practice of separating the service implementation into its own assembly and referencing it from a web project. If you look at the accompanying solution, a simple client console project calls the service for a few securities.

If you enter the following into a browser (ensure the ASP.NET development server is running and the port for your site matches), you'll see the differences in the generated metadata for the namespace and name of the service:

```
http://localhost:8888/ExchangeWeb/TradeService.svc?wsdl
```

OperationContract Attribute

The `OperationContract` attribute, as with the `ServiceContract` attribute, provides for even greater control over the WSDL generation. Generally you'll accept most of the defaults, but for certain features, such as duplex messaging, you'll need to use options indicating the operation is one-way. Additionally, for session management, you'll be leveraging some of the options for overall service session management.

Table 4-6 describes the properties in the `OperationContract` attribute type.

Table 4-6. `OperationContractAttribute` *Properties*

Class Property	Description
`Action`	Controls the action on the request (input) message; the default is the contract namespace, contract name, and operation name. Use this in conjunction with * to indicate the operation can handle all unmatched operation requests—there can be only one of these, and it must take a message as a parameter.
`AsyncPattern`	Provides for the implementation of an asynchronous process on the server, client, or both tiers. This feature aids .NET clients in supporting operations with the efficiency of using a single client thread.
`IsInitiating`	Indicates that this operation is an initiation of a session; the default is `true`, so if you require session initiation, you need to set all operations to `false` except the initiation operation.
`IsOneWay`	Indicates that the operation returns nothing (`void`) or can't accept out parameters. The default is `false`; as a result, all operations without it return an empty message that is useful for capturing exceptions. If applying the value of `true` to an operation that is marked with a return type other than `void`, WCF doesn't throw a compiler error. Instead, it throws an `InvalidOperation` exception when the WCF framework inspects the `ServiceContract` types at runtime.
`IsTerminating`	Indicates this operation terminates the session and the channel should close.
`Name`	Overrides the operation name from the method name on the interface.
`ReplyAction`	Controls the action on the reply (output) message. Used in conjunction with the `Action` property.

The solution `Example06` has an updated version of the `ITradeService` service contract. In this version, the `OperationContract` properties have been explicitly set. You'll also notice that the `ServiceContract` attribute now has a new property indicating it supports sessions. Without the `ServiceContract.SessionMode` property being set to `SessionMode.Required`, the `OperationContract` properties of `IsInitiating` and `IsTerminating` would be illogical. This condition is not caught at compile time, only at reflection time.

Listing 4-10 is a snippet from `Example06`. Notice that some added properties have been set in both the `ServiceContract` and `OperationContract` attribute initialization.

Listing 4-10. `TradeService.cs` *with* `OperationContract` *Properties*

```
 [ServiceContract(
    Namespace = "http://PracticalWcf",
    Name = "TradeService",
    SessionMode = SessionMode.Required)
]
public interface ITradeService
{
    [OperationContract(
      Action="http://PracticalWcf/TradeSecurityNow",
      IsOneWay = false,
```

```
        IsTerminating = false,
        Name = "TradeSecurityNow"
        )]
    decimal TradeSecurity( string ticker, int quantity );
}
```

These changes provide control over the WSDL generated from the metadata on your service contract. If you take a brief "before" and "after" look, you'll see some of the changes.

If you open the URL that points to the WSDL for the definitions, you'll see the changes and added control. The URL to open is as follows (ensure your ASP.NET development server is running!):

```
http://localhost:8888/ExchangeWeb/TradeService.svc?wsdl=wsdl0
```

Note The generated URL by the .NET Framework may differ from the one shown here. To find the correct URL, look for the <wsdl:import...> element in the base URL.

Listing 4-11 is the generated WSDL before applying the `OperationContract` properties.

Listing 4-11. `TradeService.cs` *WSDL Before Property Changes*

```
<wsdl:input wsaw:Action="http://PracticalWcf/TradeService/TradeSecurity"
  message="tns:TradeService_TradeSecurityNow_InputMessage" />
```

Listing 4-12 shows the WSDL definition for a newly modified service contract.

Listing 4-12. `TradeService.cs` *WSDL after Property Changes*

```
<wsdl:input
    wsaw:Action="http://PracticalWcf/TradeSecurityNow"
    message="tns:TradeService_TradeSecurityNow_InputMessage"/>
```

Note the updated `Action` names for both the input and output messages. If you look inside the client proxy code generated as part of the project, you'll see the updated matching names for the new contract.

Caution Whenever an update to metadata occurs, ensure you regenerate the proxy. You can do this by selecting the "map" file in Solution Explorer for the service reference, right-clicking, and choosing Update Service Reference. This resubmits the call through `SvcUtil.exe` for the regeneration of the proxy type in your client project. This assumes you're working with Visual Studio integration.

Inside the client program, the only change required, other than updating the service reference through SvcUtil.exe, is to modify the method name on the proxy class from the following:

```
result = proxy.TradeSecurity( "MSFT", 2000 );
```

to the following:

```
result = proxy.TradeSecurityNow( "MSFT", 2000 );
```

The reason for this change is that the OperationContract.Name property is now set to TradeSecurityNow. As a result, when the call to SvcUtil.exe was made to regenerate the proxy, the new operation name instead of the old is used, which causes a break in the compile.

ServiceBehavior Attribute

So far, we've focused specifically on the contract definition. We've intentionally avoided any discussion of how a service behaves. Generally, service behavior is an implementation-dependant aspect of a solution. In addition to using ServiceBehavior, you also have an ability to apply behavior at the operation level with the OperationBehavior attribute (covered in the next section).

The ServiceBehavior attribute is applicable only at the class (implementation) level. Although the ServiceContract attribute was applicable at both the interface (contract) and the class levels, it is this distinction that is important. Behaviors in WCF are not part of the contract; they are implementation-specific aspects.

The capability exists to control service-wide behavior elements such as the following:

Concurrency: Controls threading behavior for an object and whether it supports reentrant calls. Valid only if the Instancing property is not PerCall.

Instancing: Controls new object creation and control object lifetime. The default is PerCall, which causes a new object on each method call. Generally, in session-oriented services, providing either PerSession or Shareable may provide better performance, albeit at the cost of concurrency management.

Throttling: Managed through configuration, when concurrency allows for multiple calls, to limit the number of concurrent calls, connections, total instances, and pending operations.

Transaction: Controls transaction aspects such as autocompletion, isolation level, and object recycling.

Session management: Provides automatic session shutdown or overrides default behavior.

Thread behavior: Forces the service thread to have affinity to the UI thread; this is helpful if the underlying service host is a WinForms application and updates to controls on that form may happen in the service implementation.

OperationBehavior Attribute

The other important behavior attribute is the `OperationBehavior` attribute. Although you have control over the service-wide behaviors using the `ServiceBehavior` attribute, you have more granular control at the operation level.

Again, these are implementation details applied at the class method level instead of the service interface. Operation aspects controllable through this attribute are as follows:

Transactional: Provides for autocompletion along with transaction flow and the required and supported options

Caller identity: When binding supports, provides the ability to execute under the caller's identity

Object recycling: Provides for overriding the `InstanceMode` mode of the `ServiceContractBehavior`

Understanding Data Contracts

Data contracts, in WCF, are the preferred method of abstracting your .NET types from the schema and XML serialized types. With WCF, you have choices for creating the metadata that is used to publish your service and how that impacts the runtime serialization of your .NET types into platform-agnostic schema types that are represented in XML.

The process is all hidden, if you choose, from the developer. Primitive types are easily mapped to leverage the default `DataContractSerializer`. Other types are controllable through the `DataContract` attribute capabilities. However, if you still want control, you can always leverage `XmlSerializer` to manage the serialization of your types into XML. So, in the following sections, we'll first walk you through some of the ways you can work with `XmlSerializer` before moving on to data contracts.

All the examples so far have leveraged the default `DataContractSerializer` type for XML serialization/deserialization. You'll take a brief look at levering `XmlSerializer` for managing the XML serialization process.

XML Serialization

WCF supports two primary means of XML serialization. For a majority of scenarios, the `DataContract` attribute and its corresponding `DataContractSerializer` type are the preferred means of providing this requirement. However, the secondary method, the `XmlSerializerFormat` attribute, provides finer control over the XML serialization process. Additionally, by providing your own implementation of `IXmlSerializable`, effectively overriding .NET default serialization, you can control serialization entirely.

We will stress that you can use the data contract capabilities most of the time when developing enterprise applications. This is especially true when you control, or at least influence, both sides of the wire. Even if you don't have influence on both sides of the wire, you probably can gain enough control to emit the XML as required by leveraging data contracts.

In Listing 4-13, the solution (`Example07`) has been expanded to include a concrete `Trade` class. This class represents the object (or message) that is presented to the exchange for requesting execution on a market order.

Listing 4-13. `TradeService` *Interface with* `Trade` *Parameter*

```
 [ServiceContract(
    Namespace = "http://PracticalWcf/Exchange/TradeService",
    Name = "TradeService",
    SessionMode = SessionMode.Required)
]
public interface ITradeService
{
    [OperationContract(
      IsOneWay = false,
      Name = "TradeSecurityAtMarket"
      )]
    decimal TradeSecurity( Trade trade );
}
```

The `TradeSecurity` interface is updated to take a `Trade` object and return a decimal result. Also recognize that the `Name` parameter on the operation is `TradeSecurityAtMarket`. We chose the name of the operation to override the default of `TradeSecurity` and provide a distinction of a market order vs. limit orders on the metadata.

The `Trade` class looks like Listing 4-14 (notice the absence of either a `Serializable` attribute or a `DataContract` attribute at the top of the class).

Listing 4-14. *First Few Lines of* `Trade` *Class*

```
namespace ExchangeService
{
    public class Trade
    {
        string _ticker;
        char _type;
        string _publisher;
        string _participant;
        decimal _quotedPrice;
        int _quantity;
        DateTime _tradeTime;
        decimal _executionAmount;


        /// <summary>
        /// Primary exchange security identifier
        /// </summary>
        public string Ticker
        {
            get { return _ticker; }
            set { _ticker = value; }
        }
```

If you launch the ASP.NET development server and view `TradeService.svc` in the browser, you'll see the error shown in Figure 4-8.

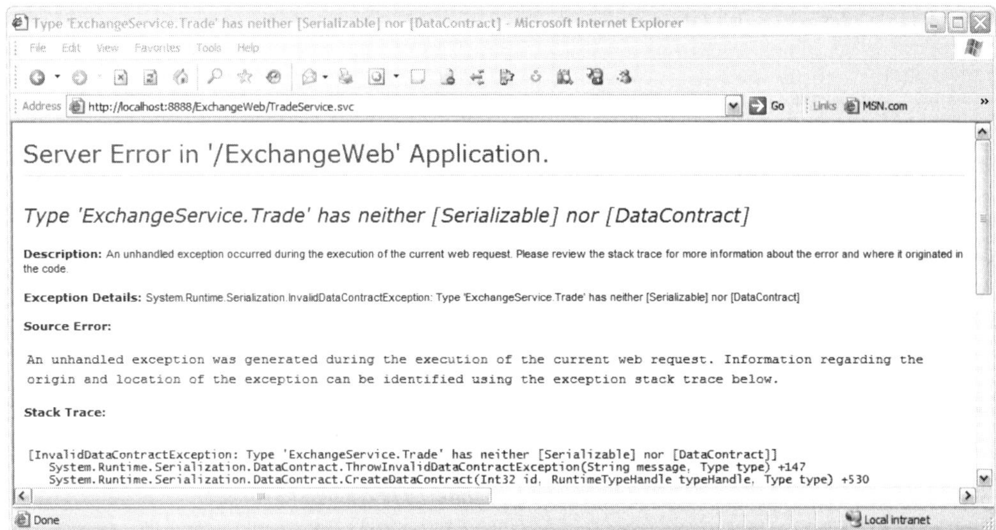

Figure 4-8. *Error page for nonserializable or missing data contract*

At this point, WCF doesn't know what to do. Therefore, let's apply the `Serializable` attribute to the `Trade` type and take a look at the generated schema, as shown in Listing 4-15.

Listing 4-15. `Trade` *Type with the* `Serializable` *Attribute*

```
namespace ExchangeService
{
    [Serializable]
    public class Trade
    {
        string _ticker;
        char _type;
        string _publisher;
...
```

To view the generated schema for the modified contract, first navigate to the following page: `http://localhost:8888/ExchangeWeb/TradeService.svc?wsdl`. Once at that page, if you locate the schema import, using the XPath `/wsdl:definitions/wsdl:import`, you'll see another reference to a schema. You need to load that schema as well. That location should be, depending upon your host and IP port, as follows: `http://localhost:8888/ExchangeWeb/TradeService.svc?wsdl=wsdl0`.

■ **Note** Again, you need to first open the base WSDL and search for the `<wsdl:import>` element, which will provide the correct location for the imported WSDL.

Notice the addition of the `wsdl0` parameter to the original WSDL request. Viewing that page, you should see something that contains XML and is similar to Listing 4-16.

Listing 4-16. `TradeService` *WSDL Definition*

```
<xsd:import
  schemaLocation="http://localhost:8888/ExchangeWeb/TradeService.svc?xsd=xsd2"
  namespace="http://schemas.datacontract.org/2004/07/ExchangeService" />
```

You need to go a little deeper, opening the `schemaLocation` URL from Listing 4-16 to get to the type's schema. If you browse to the `schemaLocation` from Listing 4-16, the code in Listing 4-17 appears.

Listing 4-17. *Trade Schema Contract-Only Serializable* (`Trade.cs`)

```
<?xml version="1.0" encoding="utf-8"?>
<xs:schema elementFormDefault="qualified"
  targetNamespace="http://schemas.datacontract.org/2004/07/ExchangeService"
  xmlns:xs="http://www.w3.org/2001/XMLSchema"
  xmlns:tns="http://schemas.datacontract.org/2004/07/ExchangeService"
  xmlns:ser="http://schemas.microsoft.com/2003/10/Serialization/">
  <xs:import
    schemaLocation="http://localhost:8888/ExchangeWeb/TradeService.svc?xsd=xsd1"
    namespace="http://schemas.microsoft.com/2003/10/Serialization/"/>
  <xs:complexType name="Trade">
    <xs:sequence>
      <xs:element name="_executionAmount" type="xs:decimal"/>
      <xs:element name="_participant" nillable="true" type="xs:string"/>
      <xs:element name="_publisher" nillable="true" type="xs:string"/>
      <xs:element name="_quantity" type="xs:int"/>
      <xs:element name="_quotedPrice" type="xs:decimal"/>
      <xs:element name="_ticker" nillable="true" type="xs:string"/>
      <xs:element name="_tradeTime" type="xs:dateTime"/>
      <xs:element name="_type" type="ser:char"/>
    </xs:sequence>
  </xs:complexType>
  <xs:element name="Trade" nillable="true" type="tns:Trade"/>
</xs:schema>
```

First, note the `targetNamespace` that was used. Since you didn't override the namespace using .NET XML serialization support, you get what `DataContractSerializer` defaults to—`http://schemas.data.coontract.org/2004/07/<serviceName>`. This is probably not desired. We'll get to this issue in a moment.

Second, the elements chosen by `DataContractSerializer` aren't the public properties but the fields (private or public) along with the underscore as part of the name; this is also an undesirable result. This is the default behavior, and fortunately you can control this by utilizing the XML serialization support that's part of the .NET Framework.

Finally, note the order of the elements—they're in alphabetical order, which is the default processing rule for `DataContractSerializer`.

Note This code is provided in the `Begin` folder as part of `Example07` on the Apress website (`http://www.apress.com`).

To control the WSDL generation, you need to switch from using `DataContractSerializer` to instead leveraging `XmlSerializer`; you can do this by decorating the service contract, at the interface level, with the `XmlSerializerFormat` attribute, as shown in Listing 4-18.

Listing 4-18. `TradeService` *with* `XmlSerializer` *Support (*`TradeService.cs`*)*

```
namespace ExchangeService
{
    [ServiceContract(
        Namespace = "http://PracticalWcf/Exchange/TradeService",
        Name = "TradeService",
        SessionMode = SessionMode.Required)
    ]
    [XmlSerializerFormat(
        Style = OperationFormatStyle.Document,
        Use = OperationFormatUse.Literal)]
    public interface ITradeService
    {
        [OperationContract(
          IsOneWay = false,
          Name = "TradeSecurityAtMarket"
          )]
        decimal TradeSecurity( Trade trade );
    }
```

Now, if you rerequest the imported namespace using the following URL, you'll see the schema updated with your `targetNamespace` attribute (check the schema import in the generated WSDL for the correct location):

```
http://localhost:8888/ExchangeWeb/TradeService.svc?xsd=xsd0
```

Note Again, we need to emphasize that to find the nested WSDL, you must search the base WSDL for the <wsdl:import> element and then the nested import of the type `schema` shown in this step.

Listing 4-19 shows the new schema.

Listing 4-19. *New Schema with* `XmlSerializer` *Support*

```
<?xml version="1.0" encoding="utf-8"?>
<xs:schema
    elementFormDefault="qualified"
    targetNamespace="http://PracticalWcf/Exchange/TradeService"
    xmlns:xs="http://www.w3.org/2001/XMLSchema"
    xmlns:tns="http://PracticalWcf/Exchange/TradeService">
  <xs:import
    schemaLocation="http://localhost:8888/ExchangeWeb/TradeService.svc?xsd=xsd1"
    namespace="http://microsoft.com/wsdl/types/"/>
  <xs:element name="TradeSecurityAtMarket">
    <xs:complexType>
      <xs:sequence>
        <xs:element minOccurs="0" maxOccurs="1" name="trade" type="tns:Trade"/>
      </xs:sequence>
    </xs:complexType>
  </xs:element>
  <xs:complexType name="Trade">
    <xs:sequence>
      <xs:element minOccurs="0" maxOccurs="1"
         name="Ticker" type="xs:string"/>
      <xs:element
         minOccurs="1" maxOccurs="1"
         name="Type" type="q1:char"
         xmlns:q1="http://microsoft.com/wsdl/types/"/>
      <xs:element
         minOccurs="0" maxOccurs="1"
         name="Publisher" type="xs:string"/>
      <xs:element
         minOccurs="0" maxOccurs="1"
         name="Participant" type="xs:string"/>
      <xs:element
         minOccurs="1" maxOccurs="1"
         name="QuotedPrice" type="xs:decimal"/>
      <xs:element
         minOccurs="1" maxOccurs="1"
         name="Quantity" type="xs:int"/>
      <xs:element
         minOccurs="1" maxOccurs="1"
         name="TradeTime" type="xs:dateTime"/>
      <xs:element
         minOccurs="1" maxOccurs="1"
         name="ExecutionAmount" type="xs:decimal"/>
    </xs:sequence>
  </xs:complexType>
```

```
  <xs:element name="TradeSecurityAtMarketResponse">
    <xs:complexType>
      <xs:sequence>
        <xs:element
          minOccurs="1" maxOccurs="1"
          name="TradeSecurityAtMarketResult" type="xs:decimal"/>
      </xs:sequence>
    </xs:complexType>
  </xs:element>
</xs:schema>
```

You now have a `targetNamespace` that reflects the namespace requirement; additionally, the elements within the `Trade` `complexType` are all the public property names and types. The `XmlSerializer` includes only the public properties or fields; additionally, they are serialized in the order presented in the class as requested through reflection.

Note This code is provided in the accompanying code as `Step1` in `Example07`.

It's possible to gain further control over the generated schema by continuing to leverage the capabilities of .NET XML serialization. If you want to modify or exclude public properties or fields and control the order and nullability, you can use the various attributes as described in the MSDN documentation under the topic "Attributes That Control XML Serialization." As a quick example just for fun, let's exclude the participant, modify the element name for `TradeTime`, and cause `Ticker` to be an attribute instead of an XML element. The example code now generates a schema, as shown in Listing 4-20.

Tip To get a full understanding of the capabilities of XML serialization in .NET, please refer to MSDN and search for *attributes that control XML serialization*.

Listing 4-20. *Trade Schema Using XML Serialization Control Attributes*

```
<xs:complexType name="Trade">
  <xs:sequence>
    <xs:element minOccurs="1" maxOccurs="1"
      name="Type" type="q1:char"
      xmlns:q1="http://microsoft.com/wsdl/types/"/>
    <xs:element minOccurs="0" maxOccurs="1"
      name="Publisher" type="xs:string"/>
    <xs:element minOccurs="1" maxOccurs="1"
      name="QuotedPrice" type="xs:decimal"/>
```

```
    <xs:element minOccurs="1" maxOccurs="1"
      name="Quantity" type="xs:int"/>
    <xs:element minOccurs="1" maxOccurs="1"
      name="ExecutionTime" type="xs:dateTime"/>
    <xs:element minOccurs="1" maxOccurs="1"
      name="ExecutionAmount" type="xs:decimal"/>
  </xs:sequence>
  <xs:attribute name="Ticker" type="xs:string"/>
</xs:complexType>
```

You'll notice now that the Ticker property appears as an XML Schema attribute instead of an element, the property TradeTime is now ExecutionTime, and the element Participant no longer appears in the schema.

■ **Note** The complete solution is provided in the accompanying code in the folder End as part of Example07.

So, with XmlSerialization support through the use of the XmlSerializer attribute on the service contract, it is possible to gain control over the XML Schema generation. Along with the ultimate extensibility by the implementation of the .NET interface IXmlSerializable on your .NET class, the capabilities to support just about any format required are present.

Data Contracts

Data contracts are the preferred means (because of their simplicity) for controlling what and how .NET type members are serialized to and from XML. Again, it's important to emphasize that one size does not fit all. Sometimes data contracts can't support the required schema generation. This happens most likely when you have no control over the schema and you must provide messages that match a published schema.

The first step in leveraging data contract capabilities in the WCF framework is to modify the Trade class by decorating it with the DataContract attribute, as shown in Listing 4-21.

Listing 4-21. Trade *Class with the* DataContract *Attribute*

```
using System;
using System.Runtime.Serialization;
namespace ExchangeService
{
    [DataContract(
        Namespace = "http://PracticalWcf/Exchange/Trade" )]
    public class Trade
```

If you rerequest the schema for the TradeService contract, you now have a Trade type that leverages DataContractFormatter support (DataContractFormatter is the default formatter type on the service contract if no Formatter attribute is present). The issue now is that you have no members of the trade that appear in the schema, as shown in Listing 4-22.

Listing 4-22. `Trade` *Class Schema with No Members*

```
<xs:complexType name="Trade">
  <xs:sequence/>
</xs:complexType>
<xs:element name="Trade" nillable="true" type="tns:Trade"/>
```

`DataContractSerializer`, by default, serializes only member fields or properties, either public or private, that are decorated with the `DataMember` attribute. This is in further support of the "boundaries are explicit" base tenet of SOA that the WCF team followed.

■ **Note** This example is part of the accompanying code in folder `Example08`.

So, once you have determined which `DataContract` members should be present on the service contract interface, you must adorn those members with the `DataMember` attribute, as shown in Listing 4-23.

Listing 4-23. `Trade` *with* `DataMember` *Attributes on Fields and Properties*

```
namespace ExchangeService
{
    [DataContract(
        Namespace = "http://PracticalWcf/Exchange/Trade" )]
    public class Trade
    {
        string _ticker;
        char _type;
        string _publisher;
        string _participant;

        [DataMember( Name = "QuotedPrice", IsRequired = false, Order = 1 )]
        internal double _quotedPrice;

        [DataMember( Name = "Quantity", IsRequired = true, Order = 0 )]
        private int _quantity;

        [DataMember( Name = "TradeTime", IsRequired = false, Order = 9 )]
        Nullable<DateTime> _tradeTime;

        double _executionAmount;
```

```
[DataMember(IsRequired = true, Order = 3)]
public string Ticker
{
    get { return _ticker; }
    set { _ticker = value; }
}

[DataMember(IsRequired = true, Order = 4)]
public char Type
{
    get { return _type; }
    set { _type = value; }
}

[DataMember(IsRequired = true, Order = 10)]
public string Publisher
{
    get { return _publisher; }
    set { _publisher = value; }
}

public string Participant
{
    get { return _participant; }
    set { _participant = value; }
}
```

Pay special attention to the mix of fields and properties that have the `DataMember` attribute. As stated, you can apply the `DataMember` attribute to either fields or properties. Additionally, these fields or properties' accessibility level can be either public or private. So, regardless of the accessibility level (public, private, internal), `DataContractSerializer` serializes those member fields or properties. We've also applied additional properties to several of the `DataMember` attributes (there are only three properties—a case for simplicity). These properties control the following:

- XML Schema optional support: `IsRequired`
- Physical order in the schema: `Order`
- Name of element: `Name`

Now, if you rerequest the schema for the `DataContract` type, you see the code in Listing 4-24.

Listing 4-24. `Trade` *Data Contract with* `DataMember` *Properties*

```
<xs:complexType name="Trade">
  <xs:sequence>
    <xs:element
        name="Quantity" type="xs:int"/>
```

```
    <xs:element
        minOccurs="0" name="QuotedPrice" type="xs:double"/>
    <xs:element
        name="Ticker" nillable="true" type="xs:string"/>
    <xs:element
        name="Type" type="ser:char"/>
    <xs:element
        minOccurs="0"
        name="TradeTime" nillable="true" type="xs:dateTime"/>
    <xs:element
        name="Publisher" nillable="true" type="xs:string"/>
  </xs:sequence>
</xs:complexType>
<xs:element name="Trade" nillable="true" type="tns:Trade"/>
```

You can see that the generated schema is produced that includes members marked with the DataMember attribute regardless of the accessibility level or whether it's a field or property. The primary reason for this method of processing data contracts is that the WCF team understands that many systems are developed by looking at predefined business classes—a code-first model. This gives designers and developers the flexibility for defining what should be included via a declarative model, without forcing developers down a significant refactoring path or back to design.

Another interesting aspect of DataMember is the Order property. The WCF framework (DataContractSerializer specifically) isn't as rigid as the XmlSeriaization framework in regard to specifying the order the elements appear. In fact, you can skip around (as shown in the example) and even duplicate Order values.

Message Contracts

Message contracts in WCF give you control over the SOAP message structure—both header and body content. You leverage the MessageContract attribute along with the MessageHeader, MessageBody, and Array variants of both (MessageHeaderArray and MessageBodyArray) to provide structure along with additional control over the content. With message contracts you can designate optional SOAP headers. With message body elements you can designate ProtectionLevel settings that provide WCF-enforced policies of signing and encrypting on those elements decorated with the ProtectionLevel property.

Message contracts work with either DataContractSerializer or XmlSerializer and provide you with additional control over the WSDL generation, specifically SOAP headers and body content. Additionally, message contracts provide support for SOAP header requirements designating specific endpoints for processing the message via the MessageHeader.Actor property. Additionally, the MessageHeader.Relay property indicates that the actor should continue to pass messages to the next endpoint after processing the request.

Message Contracts

In this section, we'll present a quick example of message contracts related to QuickReturns Ltd. Remember, three fields are required to be set to predefined values in the SOAP header. Why would you mandate headers in the SOAP request? One scenario that is common is for applying policies and rules based upon the content of the SOAP request. If you can promote or present some attribute of the request to the SOAP header, it's easily validated before any downstream code processes the request in your service implementation.

If you take a look at the `Trade` class in Listing 4-25 (part of the accompanying code in `Example09`), you can see that it has been updated with a specific namespace in addition to being decorated with the `DataMember` attribute with a mix of fields and properties. Additionally, the `Execution` class, shown in Listing 4-26, has been similarly decorated.

Listing 4-25. *Trade Data Contract (Partial)*

```
namespace ExchangeService
{
    [DataContract(
        Namespace = "http://PracticalWcf/Exchange/Trade" )]
    public class Trade
    {
        string _ticker;
        char _type;
        string _publisher;

        [DataMember(
            Name = "Participant", IsRequired = true, Order = 0 )]
        string _participant;

        [DataMember(
            Name = "QuotedPrice", IsRequired = false, Order = 1 )]
        internal double _quotedPrice;

        [DataMember(
            Name = "Quantity", IsRequired = true, Order = 1 )]
        private int _quantity;

        [DataMember(
            Name = "TradeTime", IsRequired = false, Order = 9 )]
        Nullable<DateTime> _tradeTime;

        double _executionAmount;

        /// <summary>
        /// Primary exchange security identifier
        /// </summary>
        [DataMember( IsRequired = true, Order = 3 )]
        public string Ticker
        {
            get { return _ticker; }
            set { _ticker = value; }
        }
```

Listing 4-26. *Execution Data Contract (Partial)*

```
namespace ExchangeService
{
    [DataContract(
        Namespace = "http://PracticalWcf/Exchange/Execution" )]
    public class Execution
    {
        [DataMember(Name= "SettleDate")]
        DateTime _settlementDate;

        [DataMember( Name = "Participant" )]
        string _participant;

        [DataMember( Name = "ExecutionAmount" )]
        double _executionAmount;

        [DataMember( Name = "TradeSubmitted" )]
        Trade _trade;
```

Message contracts allow the encapsulation of data contracts in addition to specifying what part of the message is in the message header and message body. So, for this example, we've added a single source code file that contains the definition of two additional classes: `TradeSecurityRequest` and `TradeSecurityResponse`. These classes are then decorated as required with the `MessageContract` attribute. Additionally, the members are then decorated with either the `MessageHeader` attribute or the `MessageBody` attribute, as shown in Listing 4-27.

Listing 4-27. *Messages—*`TradeSecurityRequest` *(Partial)*

```
 [MessageContract]
public class TradeSecurityRequest
{
    Trade _trade;
    string _particpant;
    string _publisher;
    string _ticker;

    [MessageHeader(MustUnderstand=true)]
    public string Participant
    {
        get
        {
            return _particpant;
        }
        set
        {
            _particpant = value;
        }
    }
```

```
    [MessageBody]
    public Trade TradeItem
    {
        get
        {
            return _trade;
        }
        set
        {
            _trade = value;
        }
    }
```

Looking at the MessageHeader attribute on Participant, the MustUnderstand property transfers the responsibility of enforcing this header on the SOAP request to the WCF framework. So, with a simple attribute and property value, we've now provided a simple validation. Listing 4-28 illustrates how to use the MessageContract and MessageBody attributes as applied to the TradeSecurityResponse message in this example.

Listing 4-28. TradeSecurityResponse *Message*

```
 [MessageContract]
public class TradeSecurityResponse
{
    [MessageBody]
    public Execution ExecutionReport;
}
```

The response message is simply an encapsulation of the execution data contract. We've simply encapsulated the data contracts and promoted certain fields or properties as header values.

If you take a look at the update TradeService implementation shown in Listing 4-29, you'll see several changes.

Listing 4-29. *Updated* TradeService *(Partial)*

```
[ServiceContract(
    Namespace = "http://PracticalWcf/Exchange",
    Name = "TradeService"
    )
]
public interface ITradeService
{
    [OperationContract(
    Action = "http://PracticalWcf/Exchange/TradeService/TradeSecurityAtMarket"
    )]
    [FaultContract( typeof( ArgumentException ) )]
    TradeSecurityResponse TradeSecurity( TradeSecurityRequest tradeRequest );
}
```

The first change is the explicit specification of the Action property of OperationContract. The second is the addition of the FaultContract attribute to the TradeSecurity method. And finally, the TradeSecurity interface itself, as defined in ITradeService, has been updated to take the respective message contracts from the classes defined in Messages.cs.

Specifically, the first change, the addition of Action, is for illustrative purposes only to show how you can control these values. The WCF framework would provide default WS-Addressing and SOAP headers as required based upon the ServiceContract namespace, name, and operation name.

The second change is the FaultContract attribute. So far, all the examples have had limited exception processing. However, it's important to note that .NET exceptions and SOAP exceptions are different. Therefore, the FaultContract capability of WCF provides a way to map, encapsulate, and override how faults are handled and reported. This is important because given the cross-platform capability of WCF, it would not be feasible to enforce knowledge of .NET types. Therefore, in this example, we've wrapped the TradeService implementation in a try...catch and provided a throw of FaultException in the catch block as follows:

```
throw new FaultException<ArgumentException>( ex );
```

The final change is the modification to the TradeSecurity operation. The signature has been updated to receive and respond with the corresponding TradeSecurityRequest and TradeSecurityResponse messages, respectively.

With the service contract change, the TradeSecurity implementation changes to match the interface signature. You now have direct and simple property-level access to the SOAP headers that the client of the service contract must present. Although we are using in our examples WCF-generated proxies and .NET clients, this requirement is a SOAP standard and regardless of the implementation technology—Java, C++, or some other SOAP framework—as long as they implement the specifications, you have enforcement of your MustUnderstand rule.

In Listing 4-30, we've provided the simple value validation of the three headers presented using .NET properties from the message contract.

Listing 4-30. TradeService *Header Check Implementation (Partial)*

```
public class TradeService : ITradeService
{
    const double IBM_Price = 80.50D;
    const double MSFT_Price = 30.25D;
    public TradeSecurityResponse TradeSecurity( TradeSecurityRequest trade )
    {
        try
        {
            //Embedded rules
            if( trade.Participant != "ABC" )
                throw new ArgumentException( "Particpant must be \"ABC\"" );

            if( trade.Publisher != "XYZ" )
                throw new ArgumentException( "Publisher must be \"XYZ\"" );

            if( trade.Ticker != "MSFT" )
                throw new ArgumentException( "Ticker must be \"MSFT\"" );
```

The completed solution provides for client-side trapping of the fault exceptions leveraging the WCF capabilities. On the client side, using WCF, apply the `FaultException` generic with the `ArgumentException` type to trap and process as required by the fault condition, as shown in Listing 4-31.

Listing 4-31. *Client* `program.cs` `Catch` *Block on Fault Exception (Partial)*

```
catch( FaultException<ArgumentException> ex )
{
     Console.WriteLine( "ArgumentException Occurred" );
     Console.WriteLine( "\tAction:\t" + ex.Action );
     Console.WriteLine( "\tName:\t" + ex.Code.Name );
     Console.WriteLine( "\tMessage:\t" + ex.Detail.Message );
}
```

The `FaultException` type provides access to the SOAP fault headers through simple properties, allowing exception handling or reporting as needed.

The service contract side of the channel is extensible by providing your own implementation of the `IErrorHandler` interface. This interface, when extended, is added to your own service contract implementations, or you can add it to the `DispatchBehavior.ErrorHandlers` collection, which can provide overriding how messages are transformed into objects and dispatched to methods.

Summary of Service Contracts

We'll now summarize some characteristics of the service contract capabilities and the types that are available for managing the generation of the schema and the serialization process.

DataContractSerializer

This is a summary of `DataContractSerializer`:

- Default serialization manager in WCF
- Works with the `DataContract`, `MessageContract`, `Serializable`, and `IXmlSerializable` types
- Default namespace is `http://schemas.data.coontract.org/2004/07/<serviceName>`
- Defaults to fields (public or private)
- Defaults to alpha sort

XmlSerialization (XmlSerializerFormat)

This is a summary of `XmlSerialization`:

- Works with the `Serializable` and `IXmlSerializable` types
- Controlled through .NET XML serialization rules—a host of XML attributes that provide an explicit override of default behavior

- Can control attribute vs. element—through the simple use of XML serialization attributes
- Can control order (but the `Order` property is rigid in .NET XML serialization)—again, through XML serialization attributes

DataContract

This is a summary of `DataContract`:

- Works with `DataContractSerializer`
- Includes only `DataMember` in serialization
- Overrides the `Name` or `Namespace` property—only two properties
- Default order is reflection based

DataMember

This is a summary of `DataMember`:

- Works with `DataContractSerializer` and `DataContract`
- Overrides `Name`, `IsRequired`, and `Order` only—only three properties
- `Order` property is not rigid

MessageContract

This is a summary of `MessageContract`:

- Works with the `DataContractSerializer` and `XmlSerializerFormat` attributes
- Provides control over SOAP message structure—header or body content
- Leverages the `MessageHeader`, `MessageBody`, `MessageHeaderArray`, and `MessageBodyArray` attributes for customization

Summary

In this chapter, we stepped through the initial installation and configuration of your first WCF services. We then provided background on service contracts, on data contracts, on different aspects of how WCF deals with serialization, and on important aspects of distributed computing.

We focused purely on the implementation details and not the actual hosting. The samples for this chapter all run either within IIS hosting or directly under the ASP.NET development server that comes with Visual Studio 2005.

So, the next chapter will cover the hosting options and the details associated with some of those options. What's important to take away from this chapter is the separation and decoupling of those who implement the service logic and those responsible for deployment and hosting. This provides solution designers with a framework that reduces bias based upon platform or implementation restrictions.

CHAPTER 5

Hosting and Consuming WCF Services

When your business relies on a service-oriented architecture, you need to make sure your services are robust. The most important driver behind the robustness of your application is where/how you host your service. You need to ask yourself several questions when thinking about hosting services: What are the availability requirements of my services? How am I going to manage and deploy my services? Do I need to support older versions of my services?

Learning how to cover these business requirements is essential to developing successful services. As you learned in Chapter 3, you have to host services on your own host. WCF doesn't come with its own host but instead comes with a class called `ServiceHost` that allows you to host WCF services in your own application easily. You don't have to think about any of the network transport specifics to be able to make sure your services are reachable. It's a matter of configuring your services' endpoints either programmatically or declaratively and calling the `Open` method of `ServiceHost`. All the generic functionality regarding bindings, channels, dispatchers, and listeners you learned about in Chapter 3 is baked into `ServiceHostBase` and `ServiceHost`. This means the responsibility of the application you use to host your service, the application where `ServiceHost` is running, is significantly less than you would expect up front.

This chapter is about which types of applications you can use to host `ServiceHost`. In addition, you will learn about the differences when you want to consume these services hosted in different applications.

After completing this chapter, you will have the following knowledge:

- The different hosting options available to you
- The advantages and disadvantages of each hosting option
- Guidance on when to choose each hosting option
- Architectural guidance on how Microsoft implemented the different hosting options and the extensibility points each option has

Exploring Your Hosting Options

On the Microsoft .NET platform, you have several types of managed Windows applications that you can create with Visual Studio .NET:

- WinForms applications
- Console applications
- Windows services
- Web applications (ASP.NET) hosted on Internet Information Services (IIS)
- WCF services inside IIS 7.0 and WAS on Windows Vista or Windows Server 2007

If you look through the project templates that come with Visual Studio 2005, you will find other options available at your disposal. For obvious reasons, we don't consider any of the other templates to be viable options to use in the services world. It is worth noting, however, that WCF doesn't block you from running your service in any other type of application as long as it provides you with a .NET application domain. If you don't know the concepts behind a .NET application domain, please refer to the "Understanding .NET Application Domains" sidebar. It all comes down to the requirements you have for your host. To summarize the options, think about the following three generic categories of hosts for your WCF services:

- Self-hosting in any managed .NET application
- Hosting in a Windows service
- Hosting in different versions of IIS

As you can imagine, all these have associated project templates in Visual Studio, as mentioned earlier in this section, and all of them have their own characteristics. To get a better understanding of which host is the best in each situation, you need to understand the requirements and the features hosts typically have. After you understand this, we will walk you through each hosting option individually.

UNDERSTANDING .NET APPLICATION DOMAINS

Assuming you understand the role of Windows processes and how to interact with them from managed code, you need to investigate the concept of a .NET application domain. To run your managed .NET code in a process, you create assemblies. These assemblies are not hosted directly within a Windows process. Instead, the common language runtime (CLR) isolates this managed code by creating separate logical partitions within a process called an *application domain*. A single process may contain multiple application domains, each of which is hosting distinct pieces of code encapsulated in assemblies. This subdivision of a traditional Windows process offers several benefits provided by the .NET Framework.

The main benefits are as follows:

- Application domains provide the operating system–neutral nature of the .NET platform by abstracting away the concept of an executable or library.
- Application domains can be controlled and (un)loaded as you want.
- Application domains provide isolation for an application or within a process where multiple application domains live. Application domains within a process are independent of each other and as such remain functional when one fails the other.

Hosting Environment Features

A .NET application requires a hosting Windows process. Inside that Windows process you can host multiple .NET application domains. An application domain is the means for the .NET CLR to isolate the managed code from Windows. The CLR automatically creates one default application domain in each worker process where it is initialized in a process. The default application domain is not unloaded until the process in which it runs shuts down. The CLR controls the shutdown of the default application domain. In most hosts, no code is running inside the default application domain. Instead, hosts (or *processes*) create a new application domain so the application domain can be closed independently of the process. In a lot of applications, it is desirable that the client-side code and server-side code execute in different application domains. Often these desires stem from reasons such as security and isolation.

The relationship between processes and application domains is similar to the relationship between applications and application domains and the WCF `ServiceHost`. As Figure 5-1 illustrates, every process has at least one application domain, and each application domain can host zero or more WCF `ServiceHost` instances. WCF requires at least an application domain hosted inside a Windows process.

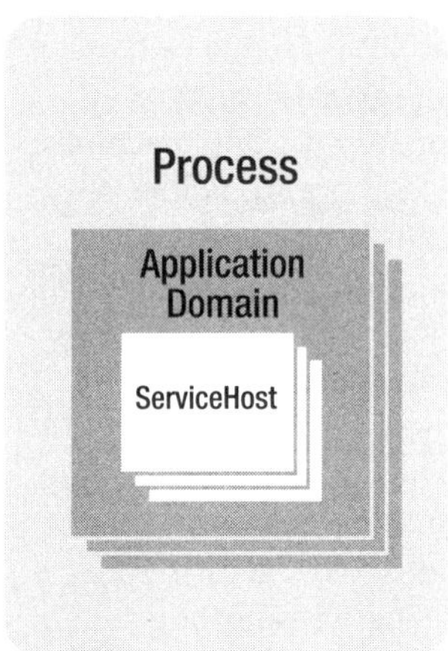

Figure 5-1. *Processes, application domains, and WCF* `ServiceHost` *relationship*

■ **Note** Although you can instantiate multiple instances of `ServiceHost`, it is easier to maintain one instance of `ServiceHost` per application domain. You can use multiple endpoints to expose multiple service interfaces in one host. More advanced hosts such as IIS and WAS do instantiate multiple instances of `ServiceHost` to provide isolation and different security contexts.

Therefore, the main responsibility of the host is to provide a Windows worker process and an application domain to the WCF `ServiceHost`. In addition, WCF relies on the security and configuration features provided by an application domain. A Windows process always runs under a default identity that WCF uses out of the box. However, WCF comes with features to impersonate users on several levels (which is covered in Chapter 7). If you don't use these features, then the Windows process that your service runs under provides the security context. As you know from previous chapters, by default WCF relies on the configuration features in the .NET Framework that are accessible through the application domain.

Some hosts come with additional features for managing applications running under them. Most notably, IIS comes with automatic process recycling, resource throttling, logging, health indicators, and other features.[1] You can learn more about these topics throughout the chapter.

Hosting Environment Requirements

Microsoft did a good job ensuring that you as a service developer don't have to care much about the hosting environment. `ServiceHost` abstracts all the technological difficulties away so you can focus on your service logic instead of the plumbing involved in hosting services. Based on your requirements, you have to choose a host. WCF is written primarily as a programming model, and one of the main design decisions for it is to be host agnostic. `ServiceHost` doesn't care where it is instantiated as long as it is running when you want your services to be reachable. In other words, it requires a process that runs a .NET application domain.

You need to consider certain requirements when choosing an application type (such as whether it's a console application, a WinForms application, and so on). You need to instantiate `ServiceHost` to provide you with the hosting environment where your services live. Typical .NET applications such as console and WinForms applications run on user desktop machines. These environments are not running all the time; hosting your services there is possible, but they're not typical enterprise-ready hosts. We consider enterprise-ready hosts to support a larger-scale service-oriented architecture, where services are exposing key business functionality on which multiple systems rely. These enterprise-ready hosts typically fulfill requirements such as high availability. As such, we don't consider console or WinForms applications to be enterprise-ready hosts.

Services usually run on servers and are managed and operated by operators. Usually the operators that manage servers don't like starting console applications or WinForms applications by hand when servers are rebooted. For your service applications to be ready to run in a data center, the only viable option for enterprise service-oriented scenarios is hosting your services either on IIS or as a Windows service.

Sometimes you'll require interprocess communication on a user's desktop machine. In this scenario, the service is active only when the user is using the application. Typical applications where you see interprocess communication requirements are console applications and WinForms applications. The applications are suitable to host these types of services.

To be able to determine which host is the most applicable host for your scenario, you should refer to your nonfunctional requirements. Typically, nonfunctional requirements state technical requirements for your application to ensure they meet the quality and maintainability of your application. For WCF applications, this comes down to the following topics:

Availability: When do you want to be able to reach your service?

Reliability: What happens when your service somehow breaks? How does this affect other consumers?

---

1. Different IIS versions have different manageability features that are supported by WCF. Most notably, IIS 5.1 on Windows XP comes with several limitations in the management user interface.

Manageability: Do you need easy access to information about what is happening on the host where WCF services live?

Versioning: Do you need to support older versions of the service? Do you know who is consuming your services?

Deployment: What is your deployment model? Are you installing through the Microsoft Installer process and Visual Studio deployment packages, or is xcopy sufficient?

State: Are your services stateless? Do you need sessions?

Based on these nonfunctional requirements, you can decide which host meets your needs. To help you with this choice, for the remaining part of this chapter you will look at the different hosting environments, including their advantages and disadvantages.

■ **Note** The WCF programming model is agnostic to where it is running, so switching to a different host later is always possible and doesn't mean you have to change your service implementation. Typically, you'll start with a self-hosted scenario in a console application to test-drive and prototype your services.

Self-Hosting Your Service

The most flexible and easiest way to host WCF services is by self-hosting. To be able to self-host your services, you have to meet two requirements. First, you need the WCF runtime; second, you need a managed .NET application in which you can host `ServiceHost`. It is your own responsibility to write the code that starts and stops the host.

The following are the advantages of self-hosting:

Is easy to use: With only a few lines of code you have your service running.

Is flexible: You can easily control the lifetime of your services through the `Open()` and `Close()` methods of `ServiceHost<T>`.

Is easy to debug: Debugging WCF services that are hosted in a self-hosted environment provides a familiar way of debugging, without having to attach to separate applications that activate your service.

Is easy to deploy: In general, deploying simple Windows applications is as easy as xcopy. You don't need any complex deployment scenarios on server farms, and the like, to deploy a simple Windows application that serves as a WCF `ServiceHost`.

Supports all bindings and transports: Self-hosting doesn't limit you to out-of-the-box bindings and transports whatsoever. On Windows XP and Windows Server 2003, IIS limits you to HTTP only.

The following are the disadvantages of self-hosting:

Limited availability: The service is reachable only when the application is running.

Limited features: Self-hosted applications have limited support for high availability, easy manageability, robustness, recoverability, versioning, and deployment scenarios. At least, out-of-the-box WCF doesn't provide these, so in a self-hosted scenario you have to implement these features yourself; IIS, for example, comes with several of these features by default.

In other words, you shouldn't consider self-hosting for enterprise scenarios. Self-hosting is suitable during the development or demonstration phases of your enterprise project. Another suitable example where you would self-host your services is when you want applications on a user desktop to communicate with each other or in a peer-to-peer scenario, as described in Chapter 12.

You saw several examples of self-hosting scenarios in Chapter 3. These examples all used simple console applications. To illustrate this better in a real-life scenario, this chapter presents a WinForms application that hosts a service that tracks published quotes for the Market Makers actors in the QuickReturns Ltd. case study.

For this scenario, you have two distinct WinForms applications. One is the Market Makers Manager application that Market Makers can use to publish quotes and trade their securities. The other is a separate WinForms application that tracks published quotes. It does that by exposing a service that implements the `ITradeTrackingService` contract, as described in Listing 5-1. The Market Makers Manager application calls this service when it successfully publishes a quote through the `TradeService`.

Listing 5-1. `ServiceContract` *for the Trade-Tracking Service*

```
using System.ServiceModel;
using QuickReturns.StockTrading.ExchangeService.DataContracts;

namespace QuickReturns.StockTrading.TradeTrackingService.Contracts
{
    [ServiceContract()]
    interface ITradeTrackingService
    {
        [OperationContract()]
        void PublishQuote(Quote quote);
    }
}
```

Hosting in Windows Services

Hosting a WCF service in a Windows service is a logical choice. Windows services shouldn't be confused with WCF services. They both use the word *service*, but they have different meanings. A *Windows service* is a process managed by the operating system. Windows comes with the Service Control Manager, which controls the services installed on the operating system. Windows uses services to support operating system features such as networking, USB, remote access, message queuing, and so on. You can use Visual Studio 2005 to create a Windows service using the Windows Service project template shown in Figure 5-2.

The Windows Service project template generates a project that contains two files: the `service1.cs` that contains the service implementation and the `program.cs` file that instantiates and essentially hosts the Windows service. To host your WCF service inside a Windows service, you merely need to implement the `Start()` and `Stop()` methods of the Windows service, as shown in Listing 5-2. Since the paradigm of starting Windows services is similar to starting your services inside WCF `ServiceHost`, you end up tying the lifetime of your WCF service to the lifetime of your Windows service.

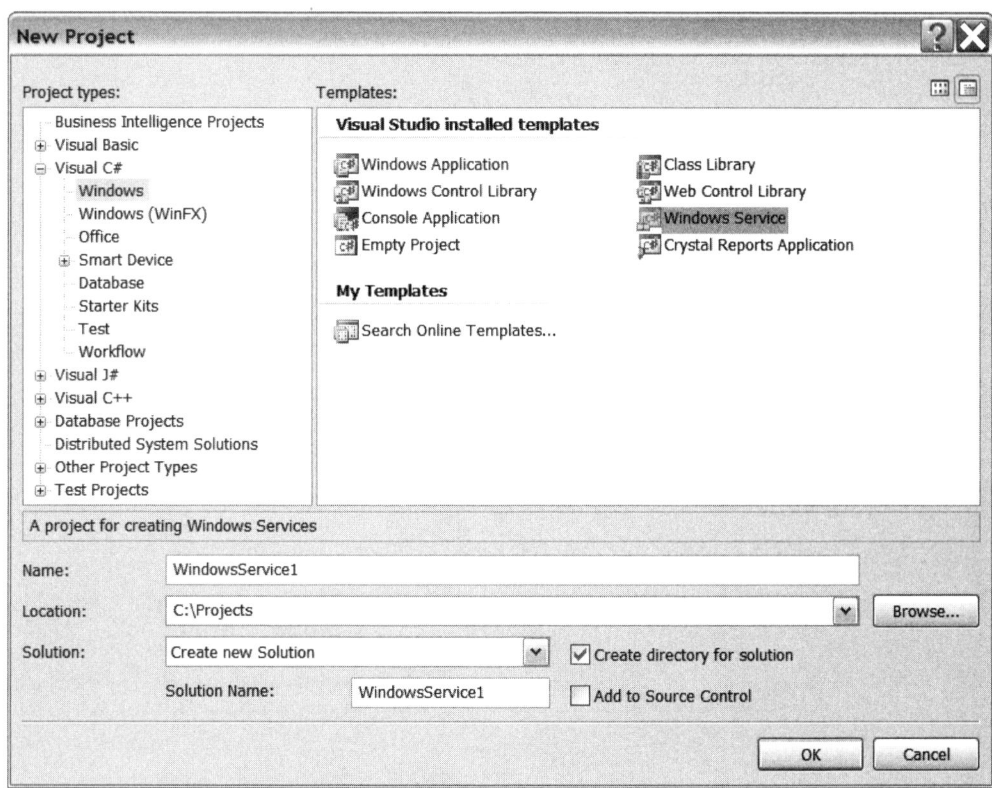

Figure 5-2. *Visual Studio 2005 Windows Service project template*

Listing 5-2. *Windows Service Hosting the WCF* `ServiceHost`

```
using System;
using System.ServiceModel;
using System.ServiceProcess;
using QuickReturns.StockTrading.ExchangeService;
```

```
namespace QuickReturns.StockTrading.ExchangeService.Hosts
{
    public partial class ExchangeWindowsService : ServiceBase
    {
        ServiceHost host;

        public ExchangeWindowsService()
        {
            InitializeComponent();
        }

        protected override void OnStart(string[] args)
        {
            Type serviceType = typeof(TradeService);
            host = new ServiceHost(serviceType);
            host.Open();
        }

        protected override void OnStop()
        {
            if(host != null)
               host.Close();
        }
    }
}
```

■ **Tip** If you want to debug your start-up (or shutdown) code, just insert the following line in your code: `System.Diagnostics.Debugger.Break();` (potentially surrounded by some logic to do this only in debug builds).

So, writing a Windows service that hosts your WCF service is pretty easy and comes with several benefits when compared to the self-hosting scenario from earlier in this chapter. On the other hand, writing a Windows service that hosts your WCF service also comes with some disadvantages that you need to understand.

The following are the advantages:

Automatic starting: The Windows Service Control Manager allows you to set the start-up type to automatic so that as soon as Windows boots, the service will be started, without an interactive login on the machine.

Recovery: The Windows Service Control Manager has built-in support to restart services when failures occur.

Security identity: The Windows Service Control Manager allows you to choose a specific security identity under which you want the service to run including built-in system or network service accounts.

Manageability: In general, Windows operators know a lot about the Service Control Manager and other management tools that can work with Windows service installation and configuration. This will improve the acceptance of Windows services in production environments; however, to make services maintainable, you would probably have to add some instrumentation and logging features.

Support for all bindings and transports: Self-hosting doesn't limit you in using any of the out-of-the-box bindings and transports whatsoever. On Windows XP and Windows Server 2003, IIS limits you to HTTP only.

The following are some of the disadvantages of Windows services:

Deployment: Services need to be installed with the .NET Framework `Installutil.exe` utility or through a custom action in an installer package.

Limited features: Windows services still have a limited set of out-of-the-box features to support high availability, easy manageability, versioning, and deployment scenarios. Essentially you have to cover these requirements yourself through custom code while, for example, IIS comes with several of these features by default. Windows services do add recoverability and some security features, but you still have to do some work yourself.

To be able to install a service in the Service Control Manager, you have to add an installer to the project. Visual Studio 2005 allows you to do this easily:

1. Open the Designer view of the Service class in your Windows service project.
2. Click the background of the designer to select the service itself, rather than any of its contents.
3. In the Properties window, click the Add Installer link in the gray area beneath the list of properties, as shown in Figure 5-3. By default, this adds a component class containing two installers to your project. The component is named ProjectInstaller, and the installers it contains are the installer for your service and the installer for the associated process of the service.

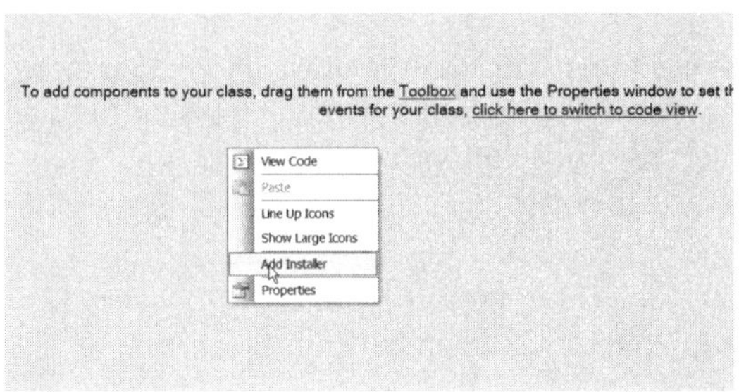

Figure 5-3. *The Add Installer function of a Windows service project*

4. Access the Designer view for ProjectInstaller, and click ServiceInstaller1.

5. In the Properties window, set the ServiceName property to **QuickReturns Exchange Service**.

6. Set the StartType property to **Automatic**, as shown in Figure 5-4.

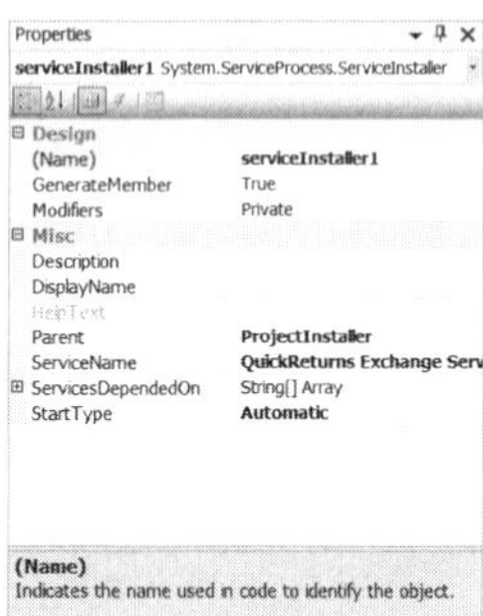

Figure 5-4. *The Properties window of QuickReturns Exchange Service*

7. Access the Designer view for ProjectInstaller, and click serviceProcessInstaller1.

8. In the Properties window, set the Account property to **Network Service**, as shown in Figure 5-5.

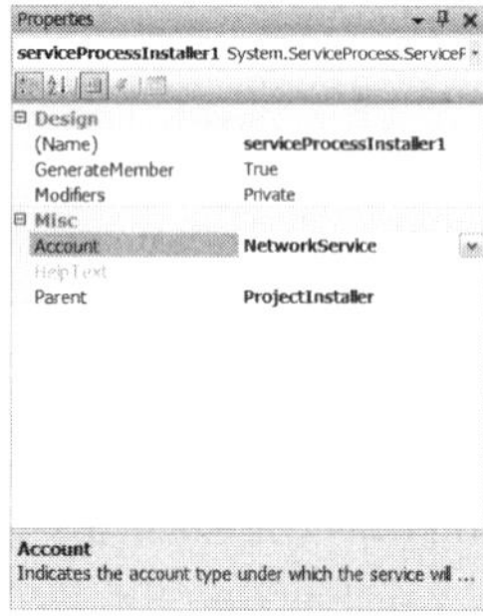

Figure 5-5. *The Properties window of QuickReturns Exchange Service*

To be able create a setup that can be used to install your Windows service, you need to add a Visual Studio setup and deployment project to the solution. The following steps describe how to add a setup and deployment project to your solution:

1. Select File ➤ Add ➤ New Project.

2. In the New Project dialog box, select the Other Project Types category, select Setup and Deployment, and then select Setup Project, as shown in Figure 5-6.

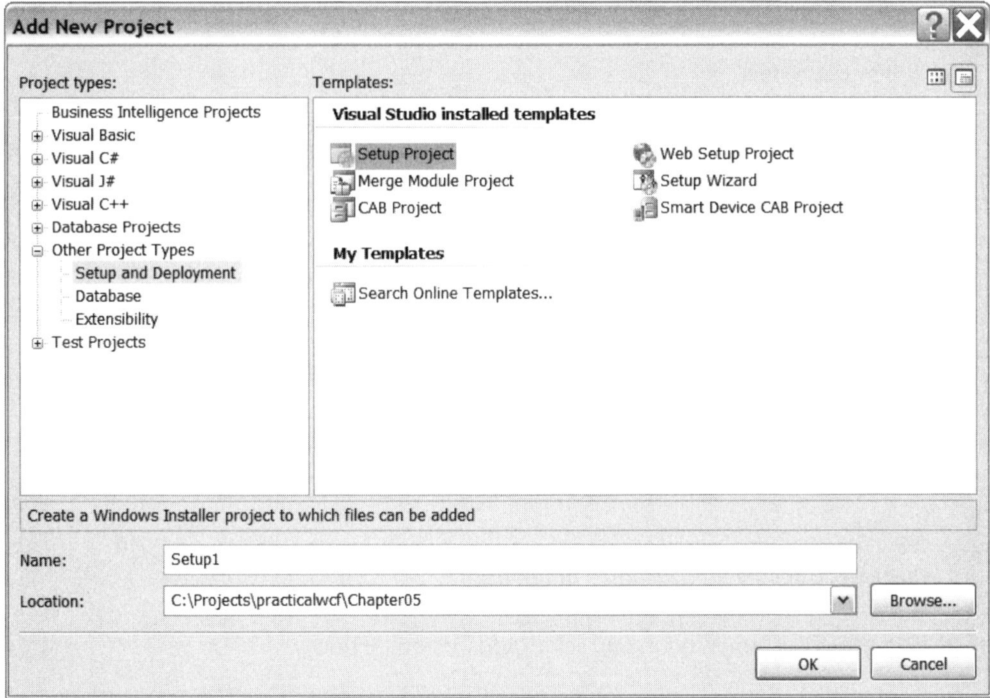

Figure 5-6. *Visual Studio 2005 setup project template*

3. In Solution Explorer, right-click the setup project, point to Add, then choose Project Output, as shown in Figure 5-7. The Add Project Output Group dialog box appears.

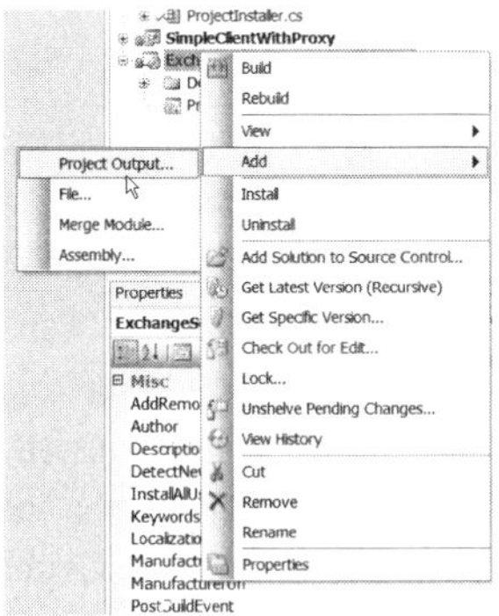

Figure 5-7. *Adding the Windows service project output*

4. Select the Windows service project.

5. From the list box, select Primary Output, and click OK.

This adds a project item for the primary output of your Windows service to the setup project. Now add a custom action to install the executable file. To add a custom action to the setup project, follow these steps:

1. In Solution Explorer, right-click the setup project, point to View, and then choose Custom Actions, as shown in Figure 5-8. The Custom Actions view appears.

Figure 5-8. *Opening the Custom Actions view*

2. Right-click Custom Actions, and select Add Custom Action.

3. Double-click the application folder in the list box to open it, select Primary Output from the Windows service project, and click OK. The primary output is added to all four nodes of the custom actions—Install, Commit, Rollback, and Uninstall.

4. Build the setup project.

When you compile the project, the output is a Microsoft Installer file (`.msi`) that you can use to install the service into the Windows Service Control Manager.

■ **Note** This chapter describes the basics of building Windows services and Windows service installers. Setting your Windows services to run under the unrestricted Localsystem account or the somewhat appropriate Network Service account is not always the best choice in terms of security best practices. Usually operators have the ability to choose the credentials during setup or adjust the security identity settings after installation through the Service Control Manager Management Console snap-in that can be accessed through Windows Computer Management. Please refer to Chapter 7 of this book, MSDN Help, or a book dedicated to .NET development for more details and best practices regarding developing Windows services.

Hosting Using Internet Information Services

Web service development on IIS has long been the domain of ASP.NET. When ASP.NET 1.0 was released, a web service framework was part of it. Microsoft leveraged the ASP.NET HTTP pipeline to make web services a reality on the Windows platform. Unfortunately, this tight coupling between ASP.NET and web services comes with several limitations in the service orientation world; the dependency on HTTP is the main culprit. Running the ASP.NET HTTP pipeline on a different host is hard and therefore is an uncommon scenario. Even then, ASP.NET web services (a.k.a. ASMX services) stay very web oriented in terms of deployment scenarios and configuration dependencies. Microsoft initially released several version of the Web Services Enhancements (WSE) to cover some of the limitations of ASP.NET web services, and especially to address the limitations in the implementation of the WS-* protocols. However, WSE was very dependent on the ASP.NET web service implementation.

As you learned in previous chapters, WCF services take a totally different approach to make service orientation a reality. The unified programming model of WCF is based on a strictly layered model to break the web-oriented paradigm and disconnect the service model and channel layer from the supported transports. This model allows WCF to support several different hosts of which IIS is the most important.

WCF was built to support Windows XP, Windows Server 2003, Windows Vista, and Windows Server 2007. Since IIS 5.1, which was released with Windows XP, a lot has changed. Still, Microsoft succeeded in supporting WCF on older versions. This was possible because of the features that the Microsoft .NET Framework and the CLR provide, which is what WCF is built on. In the following sections, you will learn the differences in the process models of the different IIS versions and the consequences for your WCF services.

Core IIS 5.1 and 6.0 Features

To be able to explain the differences, we first have to explain the core features of IIS. IIS has long been supporting multiple sites and multiple applications on one machine. To enable this, IIS introduced a common address model that is split into three main areas:

- Sites[2]
- Applications
- Virtual directories

Sites are bound to a particular scheme, network address, and port combination. IIS not only supports HTTP but also, depending on the version, FTP, NNTP, and SMTP. You can run multiple applications under the same site and under the same scheme, network, and port combination. A typical URI for an application is `http://localhost/MyApplication`. A virtual directory is simply a folder that is mapped to the network space of the site, which could be somewhere else on the file system. This way, you can keep the actual content or code of an application separate from the other applications that are part of the same site.

In IIS 6.0 Microsoft made some significant changes in the IIS process model. The IIS process model was split into application pools that can be shared among sites and applications, where each application runs in its own application domain. An *application pool* is a separate Windows worker process called `W3wp.exe` and is started only when it needs to start. In other words, IIS comes with an application activation model that allows IIS to start up an application pool when it receives a request for a particular application that is bound to that

2. IIS 5.1, released with Windows XP, supports only one site.

application pool. This enables IIS to host several thousands of applications on one server without keeping several thousand processes running. The activation architecture of IIS is an interesting model in the services world, as you will see in the "Windows Activation Services" section of this chapter.

Figure 5-9 shows the core IIS 6.0 architecture on the bottom of the HTTP protocol stack and on top of that at least four different processes:

`Lsass.exe`: Is responsible for the security features in IIS: the implementation of Windows Authentication and Secure Sockets Layer (SSL).

`Inetinfo.exe`: Is the process that hosts the non-HTTP services and the IIS Admin Service, including the Metabase.

`SvcHost.exe`: Is the process that can host operating system services; in the case of IIS, it hosts the web (HTTP) service.

`W3wp.exe`: Is a worker process. IIS can have multiple `W3wp.exe` processes, one for each application pool. To support web garden scenarios where one application is split in separate processes, you have multiple instances of the same worker process. This can provide additional scalability and performance benefits.

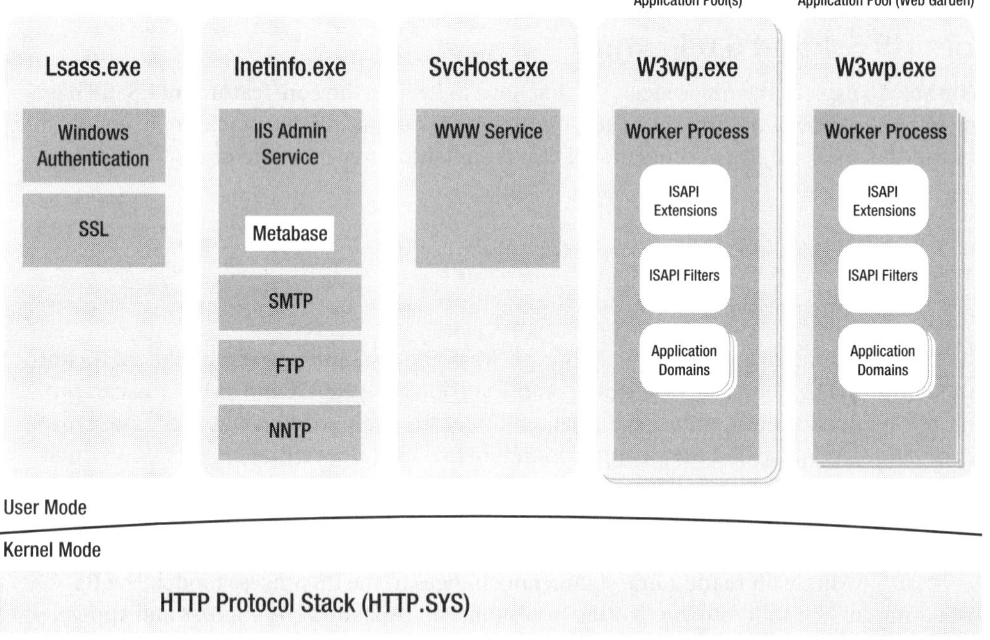

Figure 5-9. *IIS 6.0 core architecture*

■ **Note** We are describing the IIS 6.0 architecture here because that was the most widely used version of IIS before the release of WCF. In addition, WCF supports IIS 6.0, and the model closely resembles the implementation that was chosen with IIS 7.0 and Windows Activation Services, as you will learn in the remainder of this chapter. The main difference between IIS 5.1 and IIS 6.0 is the limitation in the amount of sites and application pools. IIS 5.1 supports only one site bound to one application pool.

Hosting WCF Services in IIS

To host a WCF Service in IIS, you need a new physical file with the `.svc` extension. The file associates a service with its implementation and is the means for IIS to create `ServiceHost` for you. IIS takes over the interaction between your service and `ServiceHost`; you no longer have to instantiate and start `ServiceHost` yourself. The first line of the `.svc` file contains a directive enclosed in the ASP.NET `<% Page %>` directive that tells the hosting environment to which service this file points. The service code can then reside inline as shown in Listing 5-3, in a separate assembly registered in the GAC, in an assembly that resides in the application's `Bin` folder, or in a C# file that resides under the application's `App_Code` folder. The most common scenario is to define endpoints in a configuration file. In IIS you have to define your endpoints in the `Web.config` file, as explained in the next section.

Listing 5-3 shows a sample `.svc` file based on the `TradeService` service you saw earlier. It has the service code defined inline. Listing 5-4 shows an example `.svc` file where the code resides in the `App_Code` folder.

Listing 5-3. `ExchangeServiceInline.svc` *File with Inline Code*

```
<%@ServiceHost Language="C#"
Service="QuickReturns.StockTrading.ExchangeService.TradeServiceInline" %>

using System;
using System.Collections;
using System.ServiceModel;
using QuickReturns.StockTrading.ExchangeService.Contracts;
using QuickReturns.StockTrading.ExchangeService.DataContracts;

namespace QuickReturns.StockTrading.ExchangeService
{
    [ServiceBehavior(InstanceContextMode=InstanceContextMode.Single,
                    IncludeExceptionDetailInFaults=true)]
    public class TradeServiceInline : ITradeService
    {
        public Quote GetQuote(string ticker)
        {
            ...
        }
```

```
        public void PublishQuote(Quote quote)
        {
            ...
        }
    }
}
```

Listing 5-4. ExchangeService.svc *File with External Code*

```
<% @ServiceHost language="C#"
Service=" QuickReturns.StockTrading.ExchangeService.TradeService"
CodeBehind="~/App_Code/TradeService.cs" %>
```

■ **Note** The sample code that comes with this book contains the TradeService service hosted inline and comes with its implementation in the App_Code folder to illustrate the concepts in this section. You can find it by opening the Chapter 5 solution file.

Configuring WCF Services in IIS

Hosting in IIS means you will have to set up the WCF configuration in the Web.config file of the application where you want to host your service. The service configuration in the Web.config file is similar to that of self-hosted services. Listing 5-5 shows an example of a Web.config file for the TradeService service.

Listing 5-5. Web.config *Used to Configure a Service Hosted in IIS*

```
<?xml version="1.0"?>
<configuration xmlns="http://schemas.microsoft.com/.NetConfiguration/v2.0">
   <system.serviceModel>
      <services>
         <service name="QuickReturns.StockTrading.ExchangeService.TradeService"
                  behaviorConfiguration="tradeServiceBehavior">
         <endpoint name="basicHttpBinding"
                   address=""
                   binding="basicHttpBinding"
                   contract="QuickReturns.StockTrading.ExchangeService.➥
                             Contracts.ITradeService"/>
         <endpoint name="mexHttpBinding"
                   contract="IMetadataExchange"
                   binding="mexHttpBinding"
                   address="mex" />
      </service>
```

```
    <service name="QuickReturns.StockTrading.ExchangeService.TradeServiceInline"
             behaviorConfiguration="tradeServiceBehavior">
          <endpoint name="basicHttpBinding"
                    address=""
                    binding="basicHttpBinding"
                    contract="QuickReturns.StockTrading.ExchangeService.➥
                              Contracts.ITradeService"/>
          <endpoint name="mexHttpbinding"
                    contract="IMetadataExchange"
                    binding="mexHttpBinding"
                    address="mex" />
       </service>
    </services>
    <behaviors>
       <serviceBehaviors>
          <behavior name="tradeServiceBehavior" >
             <serviceMetadata httpGetEnabled="true" />
          </behavior>
          <behavior name="returnFaults"
                    returnUnknownExceptionsAsFaults="true"/>
       </serviceBehaviors>
    </behaviors>
  </system.serviceModel>
</configuration>
```

Please note that the address attribute of the service is empty. The .svc file determines the *base* address of the service. You can, however, provide an additional string that would set the endpoint's address relative to the .svc file. For example, you can use http://localhost:8080/QuickReturns/Exchange.svc/**ExchangeService**.

The service name attribute specified in the config file functions as a lookup key for the corresponding ExchangeService.svc. It tells the hosting environment to which service this configuration belongs. The other attributes on the endpoint level are the same as explained previously.

In IIS, web configuration files can be nested in sites, applications, and virtual directories. WCF takes all the configuration files into account and merges services and their endpoints together. This means nested Web.config files are additive to each other, where the last file read in the bottom of the hierarchy takes precedence over files higher in the hierarchy.

Accessing ServiceHost in IIS

The default behavior of hosting your WCF services in IIS is that IIS controls the instantiation of ServiceHost. This limits you from having start-up and shutdown code before a message reaches your service. The advantage of no start-up and shutdown code is, of course, less code that potentially introduces errors. IIS provides you with an easier hosting environment, in terms of lines of code, than a console application. However, sometimes you need a way to circumvent this limitation. To do this and influence IIS in instantiating ServiceHost, you can build your own factory that creates your custom host. This way, you can access any of the events or override any of the methods you like.

To support custom ServiceHost activation, you should implement your own Factory that inherits from ServiceHostFactory, which is a factory class that can instantiate your custom host. That class is provided in order to hook up the events for ServiceHost; you can use this class and put the type as the Factory attribute in the .svc file, as shown in Listing 5-6. By overriding the CreateServiceHost method of the ServiceHostFactory class, you can perform similar tasks as you do in self-hosting scenarios, as you learned in Chapter 3. This enables you, among other things, to abstract the logic to build up the description from the external configuration or create a more suitable base class for your base library, project, department, or company to use.

Listing 5-7 shows the code of TradeServiceCustomHost and TradeServiceCustomHostFactory that creates the host.

Listing 5-6. .svc *File with a* CustomServiceHostFactory

```
<% @ServiceHost Language="C#" Debug="true"
   Service="QuickReturns.StockTrading.ExchangeService.TradeService"
   Factory="QuickReturns.StockTrading.ExchangeService.
TradeServiceCustomHostFactory" %>
```

Listing 5-7. TradeServiceCustomHostFactory *and* TradeServiceCustomHost

```
using System;
using System.ServiceModel;
using System.ServiceModel.Activation;

namespace QuickReturns.StockTrading.ExchangeService
{
   public class TradeServiceCustomHostFactory : ServiceHostFactory
   {
      protected override ServiceHost CreateServiceHost(
         Type serviceType, Uri[] baseAddresses)
      {
         TradeServiceCustomHost customServiceHost =
            new TradeServiceCustomHost(serviceType, baseAddresses);
         return customServiceHost;
      }
   }

   public class TradeServiceCustomHost : ServiceHost
   {
      public TradeServiceCustomHost(Type serviceType, params Uri[] baseAddresses)
         : base(serviceType, baseAddresses)
      {
      }
```

```
        protected override void ApplyConfiguration()
        {
            base.ApplyConfiguration();
        }
    }
}
```

Recycling

When you are hosting WCF services on IIS, the WCF services enjoy all the features of ASP.NET applications. You have to be aware of these features because they can cause unexpected behavior in the services world. One of the major features is application recycling, including application domain recycling and process recycling. Through the IIS Management Console, you can configure different rules when you want the recycling to happen. You can set certain thresholds on memory, on time, and on the amount of processed requests, as shown in Figure 5-10. When IIS recycles a worker process, all the application domains within the worker process will be recycled as well. Usually when critical files in an ASP.NET-based web application change, the application domain also recycles. This happens, for example, when changing the `Web.config` file or assemblies in the `Bin` folder.

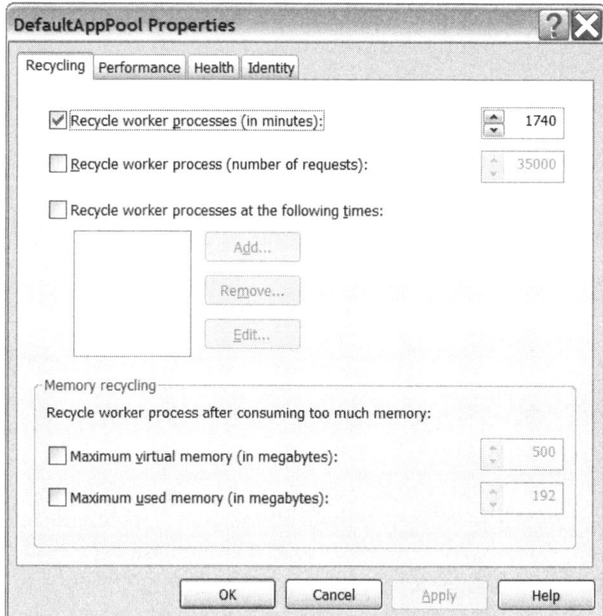

Figure 5-10. *Application pool recycling settings*

Note The process recycling described here covers recycling in Windows Server 2003. To enable process recycling in Windows XP and IIS 5.1, you can download the IIS 5.0 process recycling tool from the Microsoft website. The process recycle tool runs as a service on a computer running IIS 5.0 or 5.1.

After modifying an `.svc` file, the application domain is also recycled. The hosting environment will try to close all the WCF services' open connections gracefully in a timely manner. When services somehow don't close in time, they will be forced to abort. Through the `HostingEnvironmentSettings` configuration settings, you can influence the behavior of recycling, as you can see in Listing 5-8. The `idleTimeout` setting determines the amount of idle time in seconds for an application domain to be recycled. The `shutdowntimeout` setting determines the amount of time in seconds to gracefully shut down an application. After this timeout, it forces applications to shut down.

Listing 5-8. `Web.config` *with* `hostingenvironment` *Section for Recycling Settings*

```
<system.web>
    <hostingEnvironment idleTimeout="20"
                        shutdownTimeout="30"/>
</system.web>
```

When you are using WCF sessions, these recycling features are critical to understand. This is typically the case in the security and reliable messaging scenarios, as you will read in Chapters 6 and 8 of this book. By default, WCF stores session state in memory. This is a different implementation from ASP.NET session state and doesn't come with a configuration to switch over to persistent session state storage. However, in the security and reliable messaging scenarios you can, and should, benefit from the ASP.NET implementation. Using the ASP.NET compatibility features of WCF provides you with the SQL Server and state server implementations of ASP.NET session state to support enterprise-ready scenarios. In the next section, you will learn how to benefit from the WCF ASP.NET compatibility mode.

ASP.NET Compatibility Model

When hosting your WCF services in a load-balanced or even a web garden environment where subsequent requests in a session can be processed by different hosts or processes in the environment, you need out-of-process persistent storage for your session state. Out-of-the box WCF doesn't support persistent storage for session state. Instead, WCF stores all its session state in memory. When your WCF services are hosted in IIS, you can end up with recycling scenarios, as described in the previous section. Instead of building persistent storage for sessions all over again, WCF relies on the ASP.NET implementation for session state. This approach has one serious limitation: you limit your services to HTTP.

ASP.NET session state is not the only feature that is supported by the ASP.NET compatibility mode. It also supports features such as the HttpContext, globalization, and impersonation, just like you are used to with ASP.NET web services (ASMX). Refer to MSDN Help for the ASP.NET-specific features to enable out-of-process session state.

To see the limitation of the ASP.NET compatibility mode, you have to explicitly mark your services with the `AspNetCompatibilityRequirements` attribute, as shown in Listing 5-9.

Listing 5-9. `AspNetCompatiblityRequirements` *Attribute*

```
namespace QuickReturns.StockTrading.ExchangeService
{
    [ServiceBehavior(InstanceContextMode=InstanceContextMode.Single,
                    ReturnUnknownExceptionsAsFaults=true)]
```

```
    [AspNetCompatibilityRequirements(
     RequirementsMode=AspNetCompatibilityRequirementsMode.Allowed)]
    public class TradeService : ITradeService
    {
    ...
    }
}
```

The AspNetCompatibilityRequirementsMode attribute has the following allowed values:

NotAllowed: Indicates your services may *never* be run in the ASP.NET compatibility mode. You have to set this in scenarios where your service implementation doesn't work in ASP.NET compatibility mode, such as in scenarios where your services are not built for HTTP.

Allowed: Indicates your services *may* run in the ASP.NET compatibility mode. Pick this value only when you know your service may work in this mode.

Required: Indicates your service *must* run in the ASP.NET compatibility mode. Pick this value when your service requires persistent session storage.

When you choose the Required option, WCF will verify that all the supported endpoints for the services are HTTP endpoints and will throw an exception during ServiceHost initialization if they aren't. In addition to the AspNetCompatibilityRequirements attribute, you must set aspNetCompatibilityEnabled, as shown in Listing 5-10.

Listing 5-10. *Configuration with ASP.NET Compatibility Enabled*

```
<?xml version="1.0"?>
<configuration xmlns="http://schemas.microsoft.com/.NetConfiguration/v2.0">
   <system.serviceModel>
      <serviceHostingEnvironment aspNetCompatibilityEnabled="true"/>
      <services>
      ...
      </services>
      <behaviors>
      ...
      </behaviors>
  </system.serviceModel>
</configuration>
```

■ **Note** The sample code that comes with this book contains the TradeService service hosted in the ExchangeServiceInline.svc file that is configured to run in ASP.NET compatibility mode. You can find it by opening the Chapter 5 solution file.

Windows XP and IIS 5.1

IIS 5.0, which came as part of Windows 2000, split the process model of IIS and introduced worker processes. The primary reason for this change was to isolate applications so that IIS could host different applications that were less dependent on each other. IIS 5.0 was released with Windows 2000, and IIS 5.1 was released with Windows XP. WCF doesn't support hosting services on Windows 2000 with IIS 5.0; because of that, we will take a closer look at IIS 5.1 only. IIS 5.1 is supported but has a limitation of only one site, and each application runs in one worker process called `aspnet_wp.exe`. IIS 5.1 is a great version for developing ASP.NET websites and WCF services. It is not ready for enterprise use because it has connection limits and runs only on a client version of earlier Windows versions or Windows XP. In this chapter, we will talk about IIS 5.1

In Figure 5-11 you can see the process model of IIS 5.1. The architecture is split into two pieces. `W3svc.exe` on the left side hosts an HTTP listener, launches worker processes, and manages the configuration. The worker processes on the other side enable IIS 5.1 to host managed .NET applications, where `ASPNET_ISAPI.dll` is responsible for creating managed .NET application domains. Please note that on Windows XP the `W3svc.exe` Windows service is hosted in the `SvcHost.exe` process, together with the SMTP and FTP services.

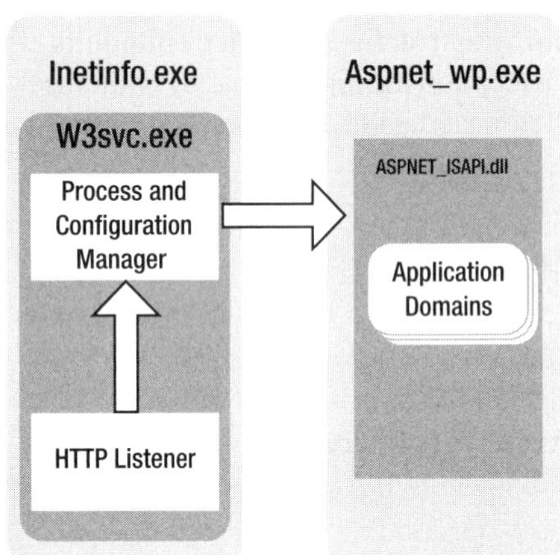

Figure 5-11. *IIS 5.1 process model architecture*

■Note You aren't required to have IIS to run ASP.NET and WCF services. For example, you can use the ASP.NET development web server that is provided with Visual Studio 2005. When Windows XP was released, Visual Studio didn't have this feature. You were required to work with IIS 5.1 to be able to develop web applications on Windows XP.

Windows Server 2003 and IIS 6.0

As of Windows Server 2003, Microsoft introduced the kernel mode HTTP stack called `HTTP.SYS`. `HTTP.SYS` is plugged into the IIS 6.0 architecture through `W3svc.exe`. `W3svc.exe` is a user mode component that bridges the kernel mode implementation of `HTTP.SYS` and connects this to the process and configuration management system that was already there in IIS 5.1. And as of IIS 6.0, the concept of application pools was more generalized. Although in IIS 5.1 only managed (ASP.NET) applications could be hosted in separate application pools, in IIS 6.0 all types of applications can be hosted in separate application pools. `ASPNET_ISAPI.dll` is still responsible for starting application domains in the managed ASP.NET world. Figure 5-12 illustrates the process model in IIS 6.0.

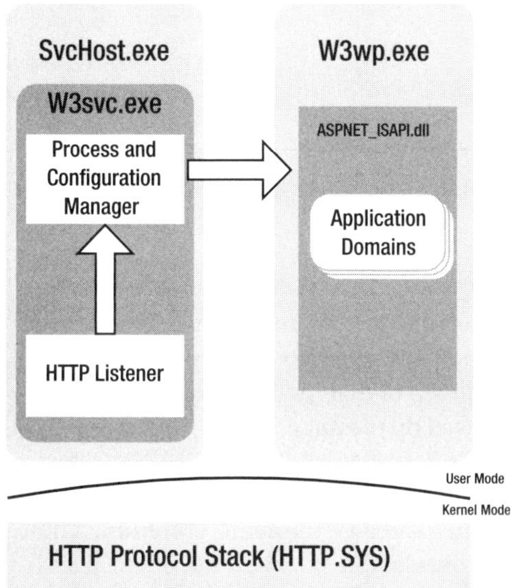

Figure 5-12. *IIS 6.0 process model architecture*

To host your services in IIS 6.0, please refer to Chapter 4.

Hosting in IIS 7.0

IIS 7.0 has established another big evolution in the web server world. As you can see in Figure 5-13, two big changes were made. First, now protocol-specific listener adapters support all four WCF transports, instead of only HTTP in IIS 6.0. In addition, a new operating system service is available called Windows Activation Services (WAS). Both `W3svc.exe` and WAS are running inside an operating system host called `SvcHost.exe`. To be able to use the power of the IIS 6.0 process model in conjunction with WCF, these changes were necessary. Why? you may ask. Well, WCF services also work in IIS 5.1 and IIS 6.0, so what benefits could you get by generalizing the process model and activation features in IIS? Simple—by generalizing the activation concept to make it protocol agnostic, instead of being bound to HTTP, you expand the activation features of the platform to basically all transports.

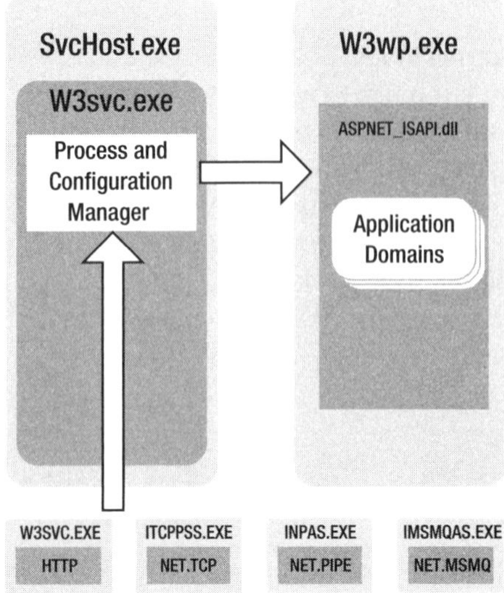

Figure 5-13. *IIS 7.0 process model architecture*

With the release of Windows Vista and Windows Server 2007, Microsoft moved the process management and configuration features of IIS and made this generally available inside the operating system. This enables any application built on top of that model to use the power of runtime activation and spawning worker processes based on messages coming in.

The protocol-specific listener adapters for HTTP, TCP/IP, Named Pipes, and MSMQ live inside their own process and are bridging the specific transports over to WAS. Listener adapters ask WAS to activate worker processes and then hand over the actual communication to the specific protocol handler inside these worker processes. So, WAS now has all the features that used to be part of `W3svc.exe`. By splitting this responsibility into separate processes, the three other transports also benefit from the process model and activation features that used to be built into IIS 6.0, but only for HTTP. To summarize, with IIS 7.0 you can host any WCF service across any transport that is provided out of the box inside IIS. In the next section, you will learn how WAS activation works and what you need to be aware of when you want to host your WCF services inside IIS 7.0 and WAS on Windows Vista or Windows Server 2007.

To host the `TradeService` that you have been using throughout this book inside IIS 7.0, all you have to do is configure IIS and place the `.svc` file created for IIS 6.0 in the site you will create. The following steps will enable you to configure IIS 7.0, WAS, and the .NET Framework 3.0 on Windows Server 2007 and get your `TradeService` running inside IIS 7.0:

1. Start the Server Manager (found in Administrative Tools).

2. Add the Web Server (IIS) role to the server.

3. Note that the web server installation automatically adds WAS.

4. On the Detailed Settings screen for IIS, select ASP.NET, and under Security select Basic and Windows Authentication. Keep the rest in its default settings.

5. This will install IIS and WAS.

6. By default, Windows Server 2007 comes without the .NET Framework 3.0 installed. To install .NET Framework 3.0, open the Add Features Wizard (Control Panel ➤ Programs ➤ Windows Features).

7. Click Add Features, and select .NET Framework 3.0 (if you want to experiment with the WCF MSMQ transport). Also select MSMQ.

Now you are all set to run your WCF services on IIS 7.0. The next step is to create an application in IIS in which to run your service. For this you need the Internet Information Services (IIS) Manager. You can find the IIS management tool in Administrative Tools in the Start menu. Then navigate to your server, then to your websites, and finally to the default website. Right-click the default website, and select Create Application, as illustrated in Figure 5-14.

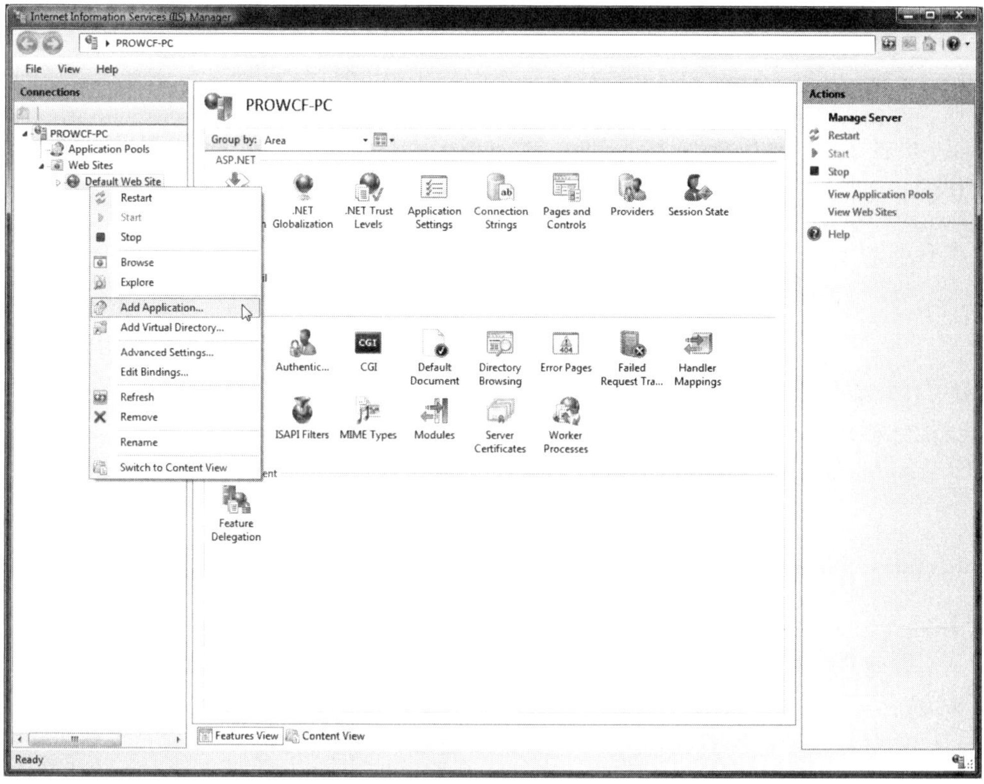

Figure 5-14. *Creating a new application in the Internet Information Services (IIS) Manager*

Now you need a folder on your local machine where you want to host your application's `.svc` files. As illustrated in Figure 5-15, you can give the application a name where the service can be reached (`http://localhost/<chosenname>`) and the folder where the files reside, and you can select the application pool.

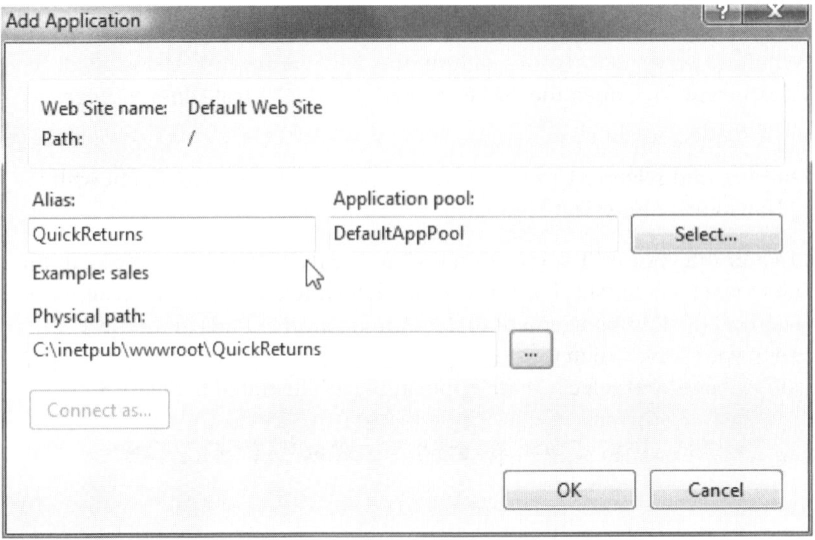

Figure 5-15. *Setting the properties for a new application in the Internet Information Services (IIS) Manager*

If you did everything correctly, your service is reachable through IIS 7.0. You can test this by navigating to your newly created application, for example: `http://localhost:8080/QuickReturns/Exchange.svc/ExchangeService`.

Windows Activation Services

WAS enables you to host any WCF service, supporting any transport inside the IIS model. WAS takes over creating worker processes and providing the configuration from the original `W3svc.exe` Windows service that you know from IIS 6.0 (and runs inside the `Inetinfo.exe` process). WAS and IIS now share the configuration store that defines sites, applications, application pools, and virtual directories. In this section, we'll walk you through the process of activation with WAS, as shown in Figure 5-16.

By default when no requests are being made to a newly booted server, Windows runs five services (if all the protocols are enabled). These are the following Windows services:

- WAS
- World Wide Web Publishing Service (hosting the listener adapter)
- `NET.TCP` listener adapter
- `NET.PIPE` listener adapter
- `NET.MSMQ` listener adapter

When the listener adapters start, they register themselves with WAS and receive the WAS/IIS configuration for their specific protocols. In this way, the listener adapters are aware of the sites and applications they should support. Each listener adapter then starts listening on the appropriate ports provided with the configuration so it can dispatch the requests coming in to the appropriate application.

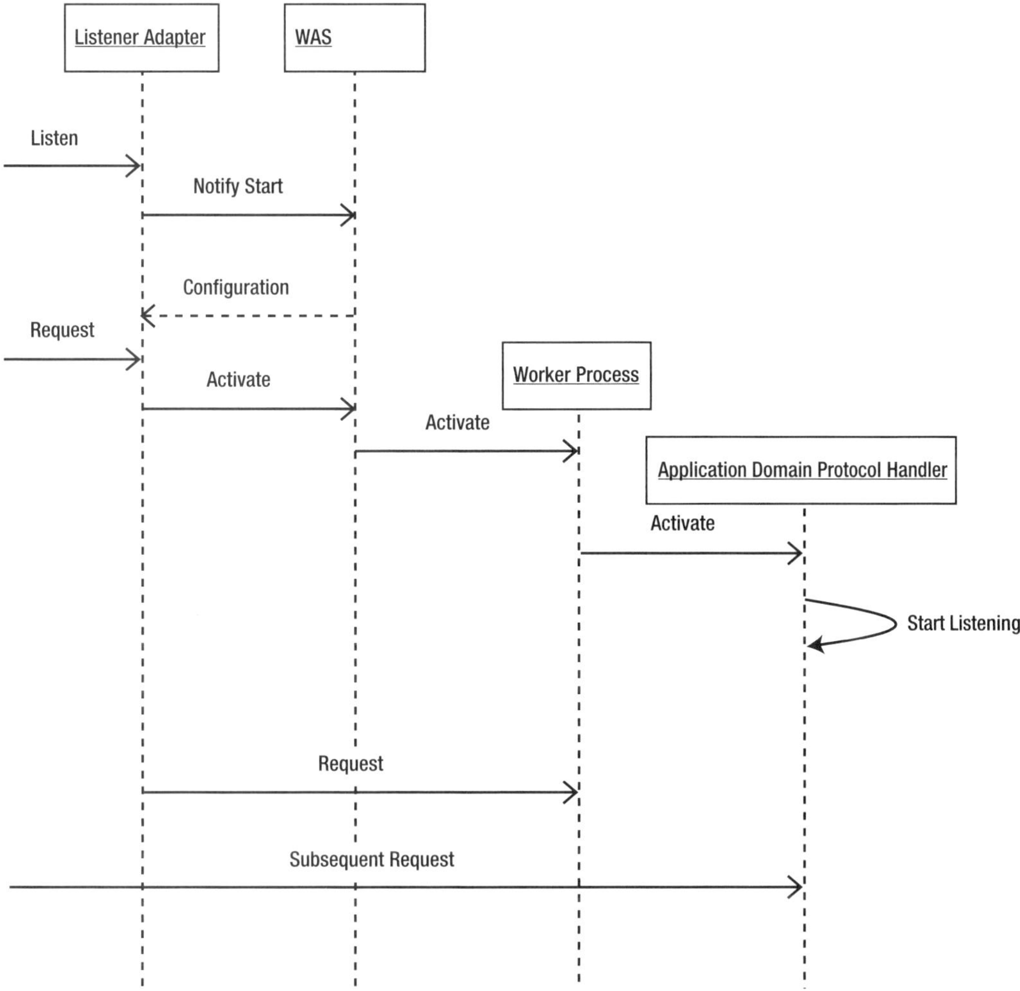

Figure 5-16. *Activation of worker processes with WAS for an HTTP request*

As soon as the first request comes in, the listener adapter will call WAS to activate the worker process, including a managed .NET application domain for the specific application for which the request is destined.

The request is then handed over to the so-called application domain protocol handler inside the worker process to handle the request and return the response to the client. It doesn't matter whether the request is a WCF service request, an ASP.NET request, or any other request for IIS 7.0. The activation process is created to enable worker processes to start when requests come in.

To start the WCF `ServiceHost` inside the application domain, the application domain protocol handler must call the static method called `EnsureServiceAvailable`. That method is protocol agnostic and activates the entire service including all endpoints and transports (not only the transport for the protocol handler that calls the method).

Note Inside the listener adapters and protocol handlers, some true magic is happening for HTTP and TCP in particular. Sockets are opened inside the listener adapters hosted in a separate process. Then when the first request comes in, the socket is actually handed over from the listener adapter to the application domain protocol handler to be able to handle the first request and any subsequent requests!

Hosting Options

In the previous section of this chapter, you learned the different options you have to host your services. In addition, you learned which business requirements (or nonfunctional requirements) can be covered by which hosting scenario. In general, you can apply a "Why not IIS?" approach. What do we mean by that? IIS provides the best match in terms of features, in particular in scenarios where your services are exposing key business functionality on which multiple systems rely. When you choose IIS and then have to choose between IIS 6.0 and IIS 7.0, you should obviously choose the latter because of the new activation features. In scenarios where you need interprocess communication, both WinForms and console applications are viable options. Windows services are essentially the only alternative to IIS and will typically be used when you are building a server product or when you need advanced control over the activation and lifetime of your services.

In the next section, we will go through the options you have to consume your services and what the hosting option means for the consumer side.

Consuming WCF Services

In the previous sections, you learned about the different hosting options you have. The chosen hosting scenario can have its influence on the consumer side. You can consume WCF services in several ways. If you are using WCF on the client side, you will be very productive because WCF comes with tools that can generate proxy classes to call WCF services. WCF provides the standards and tools support primarily through `SvcUtil.exe`. You'll use this as the primary metadata interpretation tool. That, in combination with the WCF Framework's ability to leverage reflection to interrogate types adorned with the appropriate attributes, makes the generation and use of the WCF Framework less complicated than with existing frameworks. In addition, Visual Studio 2005 comes with easy-to-use features to add service references to your projects and seamlessly generate proxy classes for you.

Essentially, you have the following options:

- Retrieve the WSDL from the service, and handcraft a proxy to call the service. This is a typical scenario when you don't have WCF on the client side. For this scenario, please refer to Chapter 13.
- Use the Add Service Reference features of Visual Studio 2005, and let it generate a proxy to use in your client.
- Use the `SvcUtil.exe` tool to generate proxy classes.

In the following sections, we will go through the latter two options: Visual Studio 2005 and SvcUtil.exe.

Service Proxies

A *service proxy* enables you to work with services in an object-oriented way. Proxy classes abstract the communication model used by the service so you as a client developer are not directly aware you are talking to a (remote) service. It is as if you are calling local code. The proxy class implements the service interface of the service and thus enables you to call methods on the service interface as if these are local methods. Proxies are generated for any custom type that is used in the service interface. Listing 5-11 contains pieces of a generated proxy for the TradeService service in the QuickReturns Ltd. sample. It illustrates that on the client side a Quote is available that maps to the Quote object on the server side, although they are distinct classes. The Quote object serializes according to the contract so that on the service side it can be serialized into the service-side version of the Quote data contract. In addition, you can see the GetQuote and PlaceQuote methods calling a base class that will eventually make the call across the service boundary via the configured transport.

Listing 5-11. *Sample Generated Proxy for the* TradeService *Service*

```
namespace SimpleClientWithProxy.ExchangeService
{
   [DataContract()]
   public partial class Quote : object, IExtensibleDataObject
   {
      // Left out the Quote Datamembers in printed code, see sample code
   }
}

[GeneratedCode("System.ServiceModel", "3.0.0.0")]
[ServiceContract()]
public interface ITradeService
{
   [
      OperationContract(Action = "http://tempuri.org/ITradeService/GetQuote",
         ReplyAction = "http://tempuri.org/ITradeService/GetQuoteResponse")]
   Quote GetQuote(string ticker);

   [
      OperationContract(Action = "http://tempuri.org/ITradeService/PublishQuote",
         ReplyAction = "http://tempuri.org/ITradeService/PublishQuoteResponse")]
   void PublishQuote(Quote quote);
}
```

```
[GeneratedCode("System.ServiceModel", "3.0.0.0")]
public interface ITradeServiceChannel : ITradeService, IClientChannel
{
}

[GeneratedCode("System.ServiceModel", "3.0.0.0")]
public partial class TradeServiceClient : ClientBase<ITradeService>, ITradeService
{
   // Left out some constructors in printed code, see sample code

   public SimpleClientWithProxy.ExchangeService.Quote
      GetQuote(string ticker)
   {
      return base.Channel.GetQuote(ticker);
   }

   public void PublishQuote(
      SimpleClientWithProxy.ExchangeService.Quote quote)
   {
      base.Channel.PublishQuote(quote);
   }
}
```

Using Visual Studio 2005

Similar to ASP.NET proxy creation, if you right-click the project from the IDE, you'll see three options for adding references, as shown in Figure 5-17.

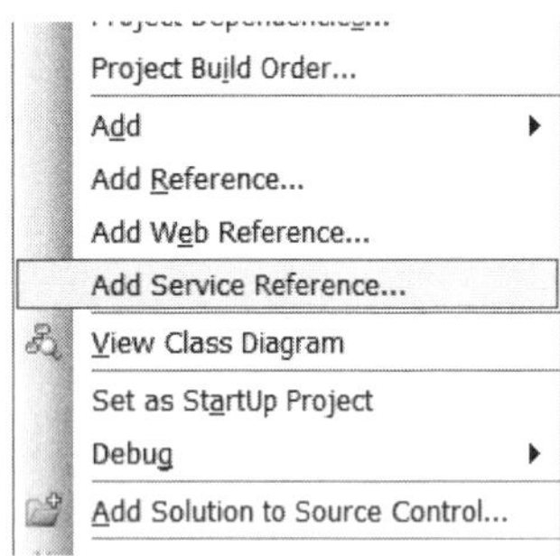

Figure 5-17. *Adding a reference to a WCF service*

The option you're looking for is Add Service Reference. This menu option is a wrapper around the `SvcUtil.exe` utility (which is explained in the next section), actually spawning a process with the necessary parameters. Once you've selected Add Service Reference, you'll see the dialog box shown in Figure 5-18.

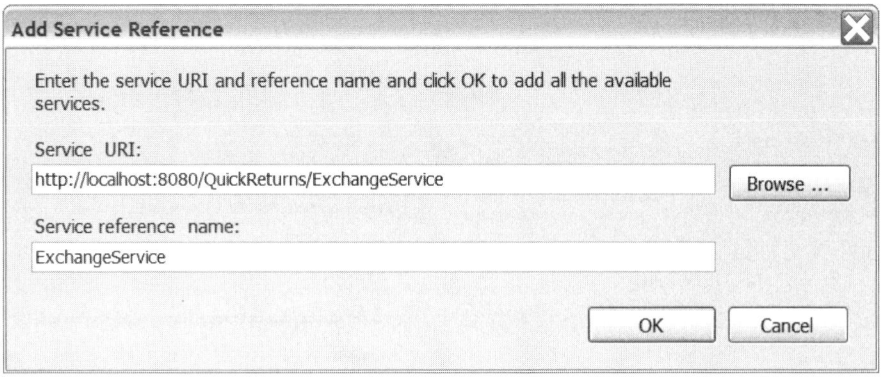

Figure 5-18. *Add Service Reference dialog box*

Once you've clicked OK in the dialog box, the add-in spawns `SvcUtil.exe`, generating the necessary proxy class and the required configuration file (or modifying it) and adding the necessary references to the project. The project's references will now list the WCF assemblies.

Note For this to work, you have to have the Windows `ServiceHost` running or change the URL to point to any of the services hosted in IIS (a URL pointing to any of the `.svc` files).

At this point, you're now ready to program your first service call in your service tier. The example solution file has been modified in the following ways to help you review the code:

- `Set Startup Projects` on the solution has multiple projects selected.
- The `ExchangeServiceIISHost` web project has `Use dynamic ports` set to false and a hard-coded setting for `Port Number`.

A brief explanation of the objects added to the project is necessary. During the `SvcUtil.exe` (Add Service Reference) call, we added the following items and references to the project automatically. Some are merely to aid the Visual Studio integration; others are required for the direct use of the service through the proxy.

Service references: Within this folder, we added two items. First, a "map" file provides support for the generation and regeneration of the proxy through the Visual Studio add-in. Second, `ExchangeService.cs` represents the concrete proxy class implementation that leverages the namespace `System.ServiceModel` to provide a simple integration class.

Configuration: The second item is the `App.config` file. An `App.config` file (automatically renamed during the Visual Studio build process to `<assembly name>.config`) provides the runtime WCF configuration parameters. What you will notice if you peek inside this file is a tremendous amount of settings, many of which are either defaulted or superfluous. A general approach is to generate the file and then manage the file using the WCF `SvcConfigEditor.exe` editor utility. This utility is located in the Windows SDK `Bin` directory. You can also find it in the Visual Studio 2005 Tools menu. Figure 5-19 shows the implementation of the tool.

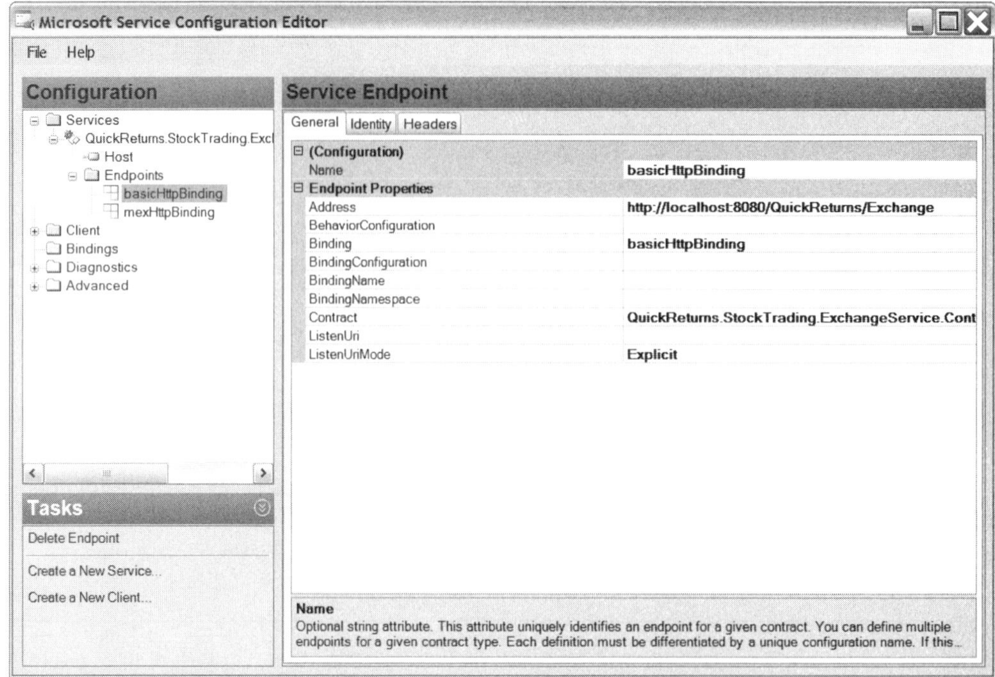

Figure 5-19. `SvcConfigEditor.exe`

As you can see from the `SvcConfigEditor.exe` screen in Figure 5-19, you can manage a tremendous amount of detailed properties through configuration. This is one of the greatest strengths of WCF—the ability to control many aspects of an implementation without impacting the core service implementation. The concept that a service implementation doesn't need to change in order to migrate from an HTTP-based protocol to another message-oriented one is an example. To get more information about the features of the tool, refer to Chapter 3 of this book or the MSDN help.

Command-Line Implementation

An alternative method is to leverage the `SvcUtil.exe` utility directly instead of the Visual Studio add-in. Again, the Visual Studio add-in calls the `SvcUtil.exe`, with parameters, to generate the proxy when executed directly from within Visual Studio. You can see the command line and results of that command by viewing the Output window and setting the Show output in the drop-down list to Service Reference.

To generate manually, choose the CMD window by selecting Start ➤ All Programs ➤ Microsoft Windows SDK ➤ CMD. This command prompt is useful because its path is set to the binary directory where the SDK tools and utilities are located.

You'll use the `SvcUtil.exe` command-line tool to generate two outputs that could be used in the `SimpleClientWithProxy` project. However, the sample code that comes with this chapter used the Add Service Reference method described in the previous section. The steps described here explain how to generate the same outputs as Add Service Reference. The output files it generates are the client proxy source code file and the application configuration file. These files are then merged into the client project. The SvcUtil.exe can generate both. For this example, the following command (it is all a single line despite what's shown here) produces both a proxy class and a configuration file:

```
svcutil /config:app.config /out:"ExchangeService.cs" /language:csharp /n:*,
SimpleClientWithProxy.ExchangeService "http://localhost/ExchangeService/➥
ExchangeService.svc"
```

■ **Caution** For this to work, you need a running version of the Windows ServiceHost, or you have to change the URL to point to any of the services hosted in IIS (a URL pointing to any of the .svc files discussed in this chapter). In addition, your service requires the metadataexchange endpoint, as described in Chapter 3. The code that comes with this chapter has the metadataexchange endpoint configured, but it is left out of the inline code in this chapter!

The command is fairly self-explanatory. The /n switch indicates under which namespace the generated proxy class should fall. The last parameter is the URL of the service endpoint where schema information can be found. Note that the ?wsdl can be replaced by ?mex because SvcUtil.exe supports both methods of discovery. Further help is available by executing svcutil.exe /? from the command prompt.

The next step is to take the output files ExchangeService.cs and App.config and merge them into the project. You can just add the first file, ExchangeService.cs, directly to the project by choosing Add Existing Item from the Project menu in Visual Studio 2005.

You need to add the second file as an application configuration (App.config) file to the project. If the project does not already have an App.config file, you can add it by again choosing Add Existing Item from the Project menu. If there is already an existing App.config, you need to merge the section system.serviceModel, ensuring you take all the appropriate child elements.

Summary

Now you know all about your alternatives in terms of hosting, you are able to build WCF applications and host them anywhere you like. In addition, you are now able to explain the benefits of hosting in the most recent environment available, IIS 7.0 on Windows Vista or Windows Server 2007 in combination with WAS. In the next chapter, you will learn about managing WCF services. Of course, IIS 7.0 comes with several manageability features, but to gain insight into WCF specifics that IIS 7.0 doesn't know about, the next chapter will dive into this important topic. More advanced management features are required and delivered by WCF.

CHAPTER 6

Managing WCF Services

Any new technology goes through numerous phases in its life cycle. The most exciting phase is the envisioning or evangelizing phase where you are exposed to snazzy marketing material and promises of higher productivity. Then the technology graduates to a phase of gradual implementation by the industry. It is correct to conclude that most people get caught up in the euphoria of technical features in these two phases. Senior managers (that is, CIOs and CTOs) of organizations are keen to deliver the "latest and greatest" technology to their shareholders. However, developers tend to focus their attention on implementing the technology. The development cycle for most of these new applications is much shorter when you compare it to the expected life span of the systems. All these systems need to be maintained efficiently to justify the return on investment (ROI) over a long period of time. Unfortunately, in most cases people tend to overlook the management and operation of new technology. Specifically, how do you continue to support the new system? What are the operational processes that can assist in managing each component? Often, these questions are not appropriately answered when trying to promote new technology.

In fact, organizations often spend millions of dollars building the most state-of-the-art technical solution but are reluctant to consider a substantial budget for operating and managing the new technology. We heard the best description of this dilemma described eloquently by a Microsoft speaker once—he compared operating and managing a new technology to raising a baby. The most exciting part for the parents is conceiving and giving birth to the baby. However, the difficult part of parenting starts after the baby is born. This is similar to the technology life cycle. A lot of emphasis is put on the conception and first implementation of a new technology. However, you achieve most of the effort and the value-added activity (the return to the business stakeholders) by carefully managing and monitoring the system. With the latest trend of outsourcing operational activities to overseas developer centers, the issue of managing the day-to-day operations of any technology is gaining more attention every day. Microsoft has recognized this industry trend and invested in WCF service management to address this issue.

You investigated the WCF architecture and learned how to create and host WCF services in the previous chapters. In this chapter, you will learn how to manage and monitor a WCF service. The objectives of this chapter are as follows:

- We will illustrate the WCF management tools available to developers so they can be more productive. We will discuss the value of building custom code, implementing logging and tracing, using performance counters, and using WMI objects.

- We will illustrate the value of message logging, tracing, WMI, and performance monitors to system administrators for monitoring their IT systems and maintaining them efficiently.

- We will explain the custom performance monitors that business users can work with to cater to different business activities.
- We will explain the custom performance counters and WMI tools available to senior management to monitor their ROI.

We'll first cover the business drivers for managing and monitoring WCF services.

Exploring the Business Drivers

You need to justify the business value of any IT investment before stakeholders approve the costs to implement it. Stakeholders expect several important features from any new IT investment. The typical questions they will ask are as follows:

- How do I track the new technology's performance? The business may need to produce statistics for ROI figures or be aware of salability issues. It may need to know whether the new solution will process 100,000 requests a day. Can you track and log these 100,000 requests and data mine to derive valuable business information?
- Can the system administrators monitor the activity? Most important, does it have the capability to let the system administrators know when the system fails? Is it an expensive exercise to manage these activities? How much extra effort is involved to build a separate IT system to monitor the new application?
- How extensible is the technology? Do you need to have a complete rewrite of code to modify simple business logic? Or is it a simple task through a configuration setting? What happens when the upgrades become available? Will the new technology be backward compatible?

The WCF service management tools address all these business drivers. WCF provides the user interface to the back-office system when it comes to the traceability of business activities. This can take place in many ways. You can utilize configuration files to create the plumbing for services and clients. WCF also makes deploying the services and clients easy. When the application is operational, you can use runtime tools to monitor its activity. You can use specific WCF performance counters (and custom-built ones) to track server activities. You can also use Windows Management Instrumentation (WMI) to monitor the application.

What happens if your service fails? Is there a way to trace the origin of the failure? You can utilize message logging and tracing to evaluate how each message is processed using WCF tools. These tools are also helpful when the system administrator tries to pinpoint a failure of the system. WCF also utilizes the event log to record errors and warnings for easier diagnosis of issues by a system administrator. The same tools can also assist developers in validating and debugging their code. The WCF tools provide a complete record of the service's activities, from UI screens to back-office systems. These tools and defined processes will assist an organization's senior management in addressing the proper governance and accountability for IT systems in their organizations.

You will learn how to utilize these tools throughout this chapter. Specifically, you will begin your journey by implementing a custom monitoring system built using an "interfaces" approach. We will demonstrate how you can manage WCF services by writing custom code similar to any other .NET application. You will purposely look at the current code required to manage an application in this manner so that you can contrast this with how the WCF tools alleviate this overhead. We hope you will appreciate the flexibility and the power of the tools, which can produce extensive tracing information by simply "flicking a switch." In addition, you will investigate configuration files, tracing and message logging activities, performance counters, and WMI objects in this chapter. However, we will not cover the Windows event log implementations. This is similar to any other .NET development application that communicates with the event log. You'll start your learning process with custom code now.

Building Custom Code to Monitor Activity

The most common implementation option among developers is to develop their own custom code for monitoring. Developers can utilize interfaces in C# or VB .NET to build monitoring classes to audit, trace, and manage their services. This was common with ASMX and other previous technologies because of the lack of tools available "out of the box" from the Windows platform. This method also delivers the flexibility to concentrate on the features the developer prefers to monitor. In this section, you'll investigate how you can utilize custom code building to implement some monitoring functionality in the QuickReturns Ltd. example. Specifically, you will create an `ITradeMonitor` interface that will act as a framework monitor to the `ExchangeService` service requests.

■ **Note** We have decided to use Chapter 4's `Example04` to build these monitoring examples, and we have decided to self-host the service. This is different from Chapter 4's implementation of the service being hosted as an IIS service. The design change is simply to facilitate the ease of creating sample code. The self-host concepts will facilitate IIS hosting without any major modifications (that is, you need to make some trivial changes such as creating a `Web.config` file as opposed to an `App.config` file). We have used Visual Studio 2005 as the IDE for these examples.

Here are the steps for implementing the code:

1. Open the Visual Studio 2005 IDE (Start ➤ Programs ➤ Microsoft Visual Studio 2005 ➤ Microsoft Visual Studio 2005).

2. Create a blank solution in Visual Studio 2005 (File ➤ New ➤ Project).

3. You will see the New Project dialog box. Select Other Project Types, then select Visual Studio Solutions, and finally choose Blank Solution. Name this solution `WCFManagement`, and point to your preferred directory (in this case we have chosen `C:\PracticalWcf\Chapter06`), as shown in Figure 6-1.

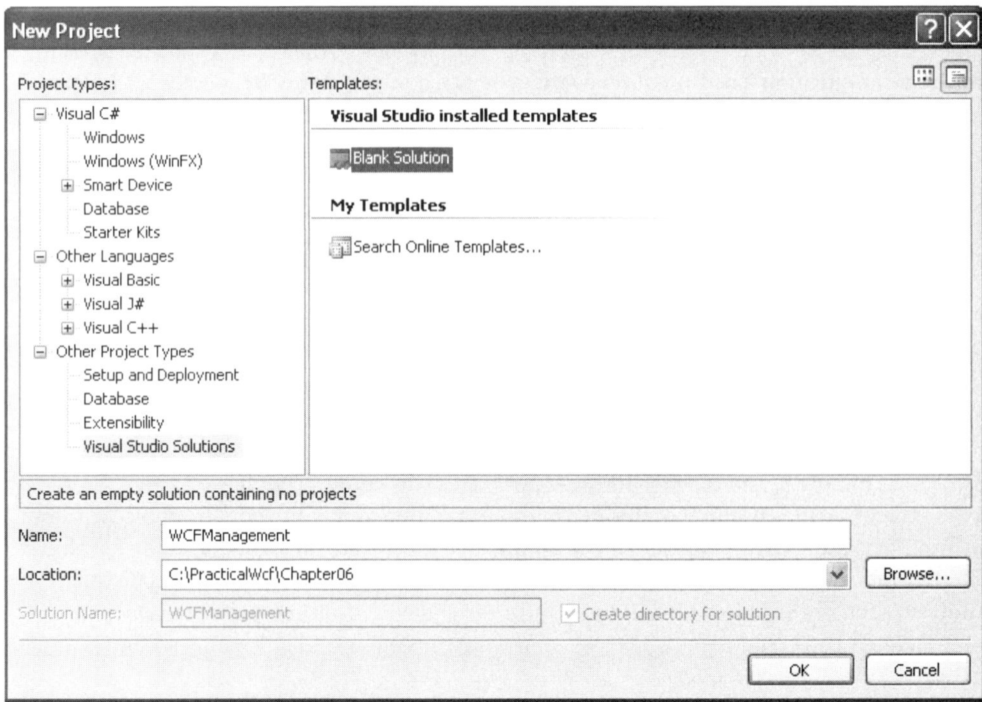

Figure 6-1. *Creating a blank solution file*

4. Add the `ExchangeService` project from Chapter 4's `Example04` folder. Now you need to make some changes to the code. Specifically, add a new C# file to the project by right-clicking ExchangeService and selecting Add ➤ New Item. When the Add New Item dialog box appears, name it `ITradeMonitor.cs`, as shown in Figure 6-2.

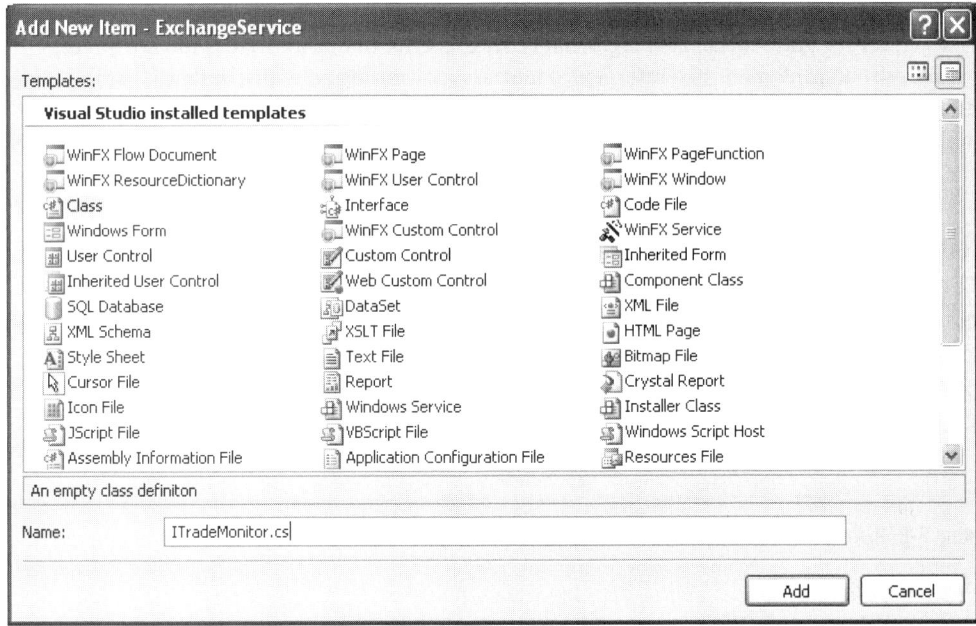

Figure 6-2. *Adding the* `ITradeMonitor` *class to* `ExchangeService`

Listing 6-1 illustrates the code in this class.

Listing 6-1. `ITradeService.cs`

```
Using System;
using System.Collections.Generic;
using System.ServiceModel;
using System.Text;

namespace ExchangeService
{
    [ServiceContract]
    public interface ITradeMonitor
    {
        [OperationContract]
        string StartMonitoring(string ticker);
        [OperationContract]
        string StopMonitoring(string ticker);
    }
}
```

The ITradeMonitor interface is simple. You are implementing two methods: StartMonitoring and StopMonitoring. What is the objective of this interface? You are forcing the classes that implement this interface to address monitoring activities that are "before" and "after" implementing the business logic. Therefore, alter TradeService.cs to implement this interface, as shown in Listing 6-2.

■ **Note** We are illustrating how to use custom-built interfaces as monitoring utilities in order to illustrate WCF managing and monitoring concepts. We have not implemented the best practices or any optimization required to run this in production environments. This is an exercise to illustrate the "pain" developers will encounter when implementing management logic. We will walk through the WCF tools available that can deliver far more efficient and productive outcomes with only a configuration file switch.

Listing 6-2. *Altering the* TradeService.cs *Code*

```
using System;
using System.ServiceModel;

namespace ExchangeService
{
    [ServiceContract(
        Namespace = "http://PracticalWcf/Exchange/TradeService",
        Name = "TradeService")
    ]
    public interface ITradeService
    {
        [OperationContract]
        double TradeSecurity(string ticker, int quantity);
    }
    public class TradeService : ITradeService, ITradeMonitor
    {
        //Same code as Example 4, Chapter 4

        public string StartMonitoring(string ticker)
        {
            lock (this)
            {
                // Start the monitoring process here. In other words, you can
                // configure this function to start a manual log file
                // or send information to the event log. For this example, we are
                // returning a string to indicate the monitoring has commenced.
                return "Monitoring has started for " + ticker;
            }
        }
```

```
        public string StopMonitoring(string ticker)
        {
            lock (this)
            {
                // End the monitoring process here.
                return "Monitoring has finished for " +ticker;
            }
        }
    }//end of TradeService Class
}//end of Namespace
```

In this code, you have implemented the ITradeMonitor interface in TradeService.cs and will display a message and the ticker name as the functionality of these methods. Traditionally, developers utilized this mechanism to create log files, implement auditing, and enable trace information. The WCF service is operational now, so let's try to host it (refer to Chapter 5 for detailed descriptions on various hosting options in WCF).

As mentioned, we will show how to utilize the self-hosting option for this example. Therefore, create a new console project (select File ➤ Add ➤ New Project ➤ Console Application) called TradeServiceHost, and add it to the WCFManagement solution. Rename the program.cs file to host.cs. You will need to add a reference to the ExchangeService project and add a reference to the System.ServiceModel namespace. Listing 6-3 illustrates the code for host.cs.

Listing 6-3. *Self-Hosting Code*

```
using System;
using System.Collections.Generic;
using System.ServiceModel;
using System.Text;

namespace ExchangeService
{
    public class Program
    {
        public static void Main(string[] args)
        {
            using (ServiceHost host = new ServiceHost(typeof(
                 TradeService),
                 new Uri[] { new Uri("http://localhost:8000/") }))
            {
                host.Open();
                Console.WriteLine("The WCF Management trading
                    service is available.");
                Console.ReadKey();
            }
        }
    }
}
```

In this code, you are creating a WCF self-hosted service on port 8000 on the localhost machine. You display a message indicating the service is functioning after you start the host with the host.Open() method. You also need to add the endpoints for ITradeService and ITradeMonitor. Both these endpoints will use wsHttpBinding as the preferred binding mechanism.

Next, you need to detail this information in the App.config file. You can add App.config by right-clicking the solution and choosing Add New Item. Listing 6-4 shows the code for App.config.

Listing 6-4. *Configuration File for* host.cs

```
<?xml version="1.0" encoding="utf-8" ?>
<configuration>
  <system.serviceModel>
      <services>
       <service name="ExchangeService.TradeService"
              behaviorConfiguration="returnFaults">
         <endpoint address="http://localhost:8000/TradeService"
              binding="basicHttpBinding"
          contract="ExchangeService.ITradeService" />
        <endpoint address=http://localhost:8000/TradeMonitor
          binding="wsHttpBinding"
          contract="ExchangeService.ITradeMonitor" />
       </service>
      </services>
      <behaviors>
       <serviceBehaviors>
        <behavior name="returnFaults">
          <serviceMetadata httpGetEnabled="true"/>
          <serviceDebug httpHelpPageEnabled="true"
              includeExceptionDetailInFaults="true"/>
        </behavior>
      </serviceBehaviors>
    </behaviors>
  </system.serviceModel>
</configuration>
```

Now you'll concentrate on the client that consumes these services. You will reuse the WCFSimpleClient project from Example04 from Chapter 4. You will alter the code to implement the ITradeMonitor interface and utilize the StartMonitoring and EndMonitoring code. You need to right-click the solution file and select the Add Project option to achieve this. You will also need to add references to System.SystemModel and System.Runtime.Serialiation. Listing 6-5 shows the client code.

Listing 6-5. *Client Code for the Trade Service*

```
ITradeService proxy = new System.ServiceModel.ChannelFactory
    <ITradeService>("TradeServiceConfiguration").CreateChannel();
ITradeMonitor monitor = new System.ServiceModel.ChannelFactory
    <ITradeMonitor>("TradeMonitorConfiguration").CreateChannel();
Console.WriteLine( "\nTrade IBM" );
    Console.WriteLine(monitor.StartMonitoring("IBM"));
double result = proxy.TradeSecurity( "IBM", 1000 );
Console.WriteLine( "Cost was " + result );
    Console.WriteLine(monitor.StopMonitoring("IBM"));
```

Finally, you need to add the configuration code for the client, as shown in Listing 6-6.

Listing 6-6. *Client Configuration Settings for the Trade Service*

```
<?xml version="1.0" encoding="utf-8"?>
<configuration>
  <system.serviceModel>
    <client>
      <endpoint name="TradeServiceConfiguration"
            address="http://localhost:8000/TradeService"
            binding="wsHttpBinding"
          contract="ExchangeService.ITradeService"/>
      <endpoint name="TradeMonitorConfiguration"
            address="http://localhost:8000/TradeMonitor"
            binding="wsHttpBinding"
          contract="ExchangeService.ITradeMonitor"/>
    </client>
  </system.serviceModel>
</configuration>
```

Now you are ready to test your new monitoring code, so right-click the solution file, and select Build All. Start the service, browse to the `Bin\debug` directory of the `TradeServiceHost` project, and double-click `TradeServiceHost.exe`. You should see the screen shown in Figure 6-3.

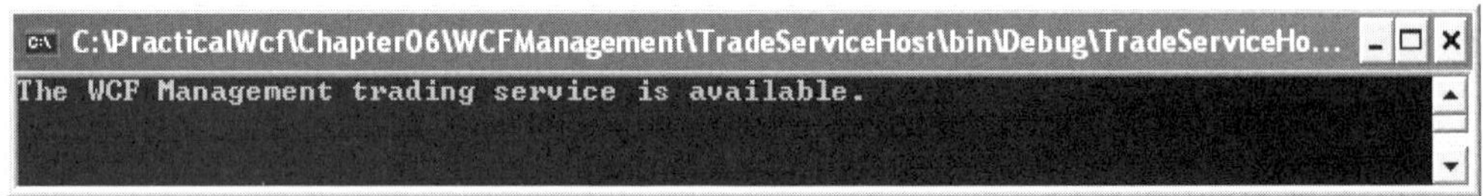

Figure 6-3. `TradeServiceHost` *running*

Let's execute the client now. Browse to the `Bin\debug` directory of the `WCFSimpleClient` project, and execute `WCFSimpleClient.exe`. You should see the screen shown in Figure 6-4.

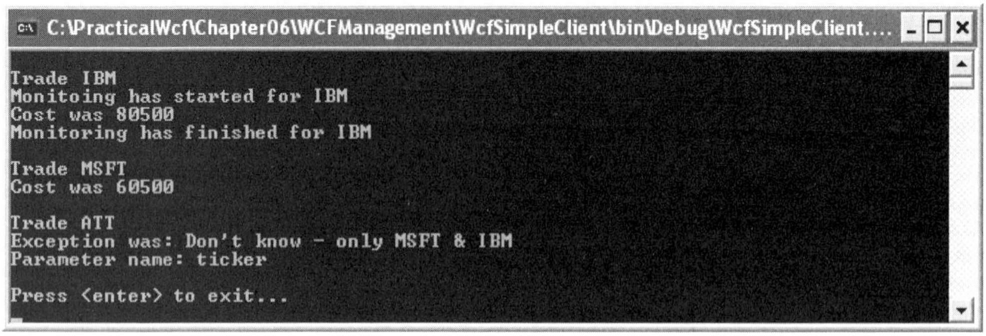

```
C:\PracticalWcf\Chapter06\WCFManagement\WcfSimpleClient\bin\Debug\WcfSimpleClient....
Trade IBM
Monitoing has started for IBM
Cost was 80500
Monitoring has finished for IBM

Trade MSFT
Cost was 60500

Trade ATT
Exception was: Don't know - only MSFT & IBM
Parameter name: ticker

Press <enter> to exit...
```

Figure 6-4. `TradeServiceClient` *running*

As you can probably gather, creating custom code to manage a web service is a tedious task. You should also not discount the developer effort that goes into creating these modules. You can use the same time and effort to solve more business problems (as opposed to building a custom framework that manages services). You probably are saying now, "There must be a better way to do these monitoring activities. There must be better tools to utilize my time and effort. What does WCF offer?"

We believe that one of the most appealing features about WCF is its management functionality. It is safe to say that with Microsoft service offerings, WinFx and WCF will have the greatest breath and depth when they address the management of services. The management is one of the key features that really sells WCF. Therefore, what do you have in WCF to assist you?

- Using configuration files
- Using tracing functionality
- Using message logging
- Using performance monitors—both built-in WCF counters and custom-made counters
- Implementing WMI

Using Configuration Files

You have already been exposed to the concept of using a configuration file in an application. Configuration files usually assist you in the form of `App.config` or `Web.config` files for WCF services. These are great tools to alter the behavior of programs without changing code. These runtime tools are extensively used in WCF. You can manage settings for WCF bindings, behaviors, services, and diagnostics without manually modifying the configuration files in a text editor. The executable used for this activity is `SvcConfigEditor.exe`. You can find it in the <Drive Name>:\Program Files\Microsoft SDKs\Windows\v6.0\Bin directory. The main features of this tool are as follows:

- You can create new configuration files for services and clients using a wizard approach. This process will guide you to choose binding, behavior, contract, and diagnostic settings.
- You can validate an existing configuration file against the standard `System.Configuration` schema.
- You can modify and manage configuration settings for services, executables, COM+ services, and web-hosted services.

You'll now investigate how you can use `SvcConfigEditor.exe` to improve the QuickReturns Ltd. example.

Configuration Editor: SvcConfigEditor.exe

Open the `App.config` file of the `WCFSimpleClient` project (refer to Listing 6-6). You are attempting to utilize `SvcConfigEditor.exe` to modify the content and add a new binding to the client. Here are the steps:

1. Navigate to `<Drive Name>:\Program Files\Microsoft SDKs\Windows\v6.0\Bin`, and open `SvcConfigEditor.exe`. You can also refer to the help file in the same directory.
2. Select File ➤ Open ➤ Config File, navigate to the directory of the `App.config` file for the `WCFSimpleClient` application, and open the file. Your screen should be similar to Figure 6-5.

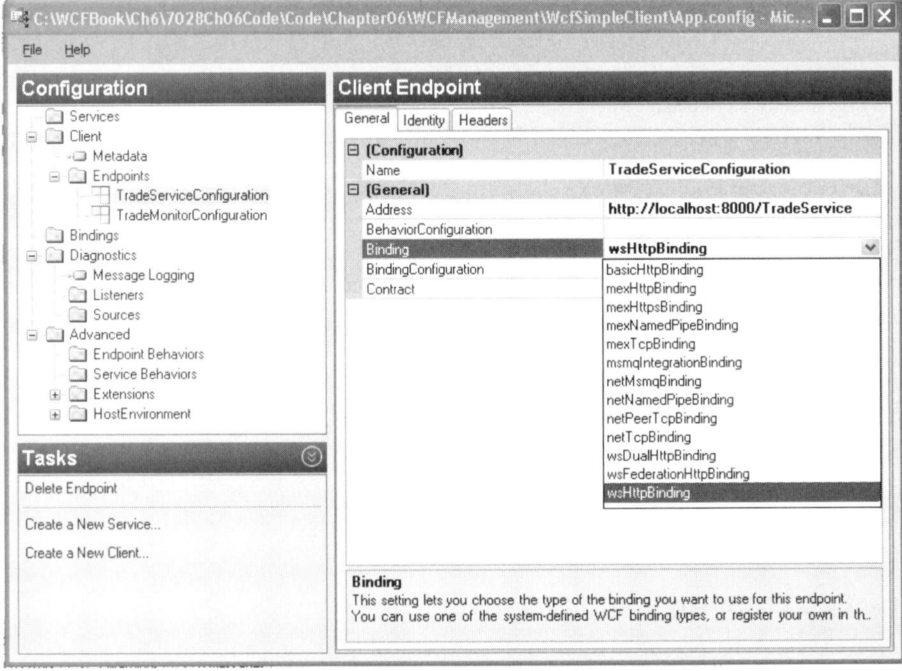

Figure 6-5. *Service Configuration Editor screen for the* `WCFSimpleClient App.config` *file*

You can view and modify every element of the configuration file using this graphical user interface. You can simply select the element you want to modify and type in the new value. For this example, let's change the `wsHTTPBinding` setting of the client to `basicHttpBinding`. Therefore, select the `Binding` element, and change the value to `basicHttpBinding` for the `TradeService` endpoint. Save the settings using File ➤ Save. You also need to change the binding settings for the `TradeServiceHost` `App.config` file for the same endpoint information and change `wsHttpBinding` to `basicHttpBinding`. Otherwise, an error will occur because of a binding mismatch. Now open the new configuration file, and view the changes in Visual Studio 2005. You can clearly view the changes in Listing 6-7 performed by `SvcConfigEditor.exe` and compare it to Listing 6-6.

Listing 6-7. `WCTSimpleClient` `App.config` *File After the Service Configuration Editor Change*

```
<?xml version="1.0" encoding="utf-8"?>
<configuration>
  <system.serviceModel>
    <client>
      <endpoint address=http://localhost:8000/TradeService
            binding="wsHttpBinding"
            bindingConfiguration=""
            contract="ExchangeService.ITradeService"
            name="TradeServiceConfiguration" />
      <endpoint address=http://localhost:8000/TradeMonitor
            binding="wsHttpBinding"
            contract="ExchangeService.ITradeMonitor"
            name="TradeMonitorConfiguration" />
    </client>
  </system.serviceModel>
</configuration>
```

The configuration file changes are quite trivial with WCF services (refer to Chapter 3 for more details). You will also utilize `SvcConfigEditor.exe` in the rest of the chapter to apply numerous configuration file changes to implement message logging, tracing, performance counters, and WMI providers. Now you'll concentrate on adding tracing and message logging capabilities to a WCF service.

Using Tracing and Message Logging Capabilities

Implementing tracing and implementing message logging capabilities are similar tasks in WCF. Therefore, we will cover them together. We'll first clarify what circumstances dictate message logging and then cover where you use tracing.

Message Logging

You can use *message logging* to monitor the activity of incoming and outgoing messages from a service. This will enable you to view and evaluate the message content that is received by the services. This is valuable in tracking malformed messages for system administrators and developers. The business users will also be interested in the content that describes the user's input requests that are derived through the message log. Several options are available for message logging in WCF.

Message logging can occur at two levels: the service level and the transport level. At the service level, messages get logged immediately, and at the transport level messages are logged when the WCF runtime calls the transport mechanism to transfer the messages. WCF messaging offers three switches to manage this activity. They are `logMessagesAtServiceLevel`, `logMalformedMessages`, and `logMessagesAtTransportLevel`, which are set in the `messageLogging` element. You can also utilize *filters* to set the boundaries for capturing messages.

At the service level, all messages are logged even if filters are defined. If they are defined, only the messages that agree with the filters are logged. This happens before the WCF runtime is called. The transport layer messages are ready to be encoded after reaching the WCF runtime. If the filters are defined, it will log only those messages that correspond to the filter. Otherwise, it will record all messages. You'll now learn how to activate message logging and define filters.

Caution You need to be careful with assigning read access to message logging and tracing. Traditionally, only system administrators should have the privileges to activate or deactivate these processes. This could be a security breach in your solution architecture.

Enabling Message Logging

The following are the steps for using `SvcConfigEditor.exe` to enable message logging.

Note We are using the `TradeServiceHost` project's `App.config` file to demonstrate message logging and tracing. It is important to note that production services should not be targeted to rigorous tracing and message logging. This will affect the productivity of the service, which primarily should facilitate the business processes, not tracing and message logging.

---

1. Open `SvcConfigEditor.exe`.
2. Open the `TradeServiceHost` project's `App.config` file (File ➤ Open).
3. Navigate to the Diagnostics window, and click the Enable Message Logging link. This action will add a `ServiceModelMessageLoggingListener` class to the project to enable message logging. You can also configure the extent of the logging (where the log is stored on disk). Your screen should look like Figure 6-6.

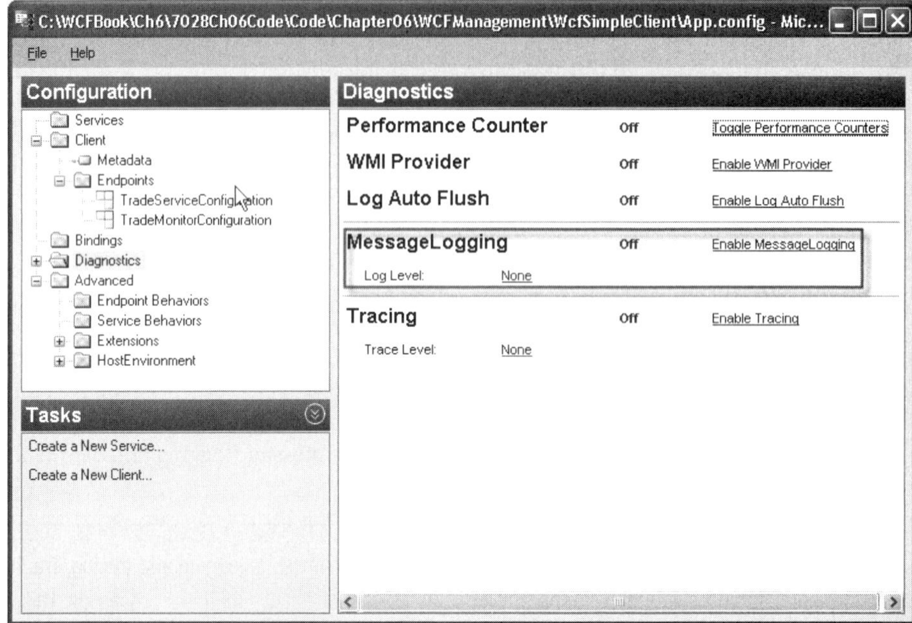

Figure 6-6. *Enabling message logging*

4. Save the file in the Service Configuration Editor. Build the solution, and run the server and the client. You should view the message log file in the specified location. It is interesting to revisit the `App.config` file to view the changes by enabling message logging, as shown in Listing 6-8.

Listing 6-8. *Additional Code in the* `TradeServiceHost App.config` *File*

```
...
  <system.diagnostics>
    <sources>
      <source name="System.ServiceModel.MessageLogging"
              switchValue="Warning, ActivityTracing">
        <listeners>
          <add type="System.Diagnostics.DefaultTraceListener"
                     name="Default">
            <filter type="" />
          </add>
          <add name="ServiceModelMessageLoggingListener">
            <filter type="" />
          </add>
        </listeners>
      </source>
    </sources>
```

```
    <sharedListeners>
      <add initializeData="
           C:\PracticalWcf\Chapter06\WCFManagement\\WcfSimpleClient\
           App_messages.svclog"
        type="System.Diagnostics.XmlWriterTraceListener, System,
            Version=2.0.0.0, Culture=neutral, PublicKeyToken=b77a5c561934e089"
        name="ServiceModelMessageLoggingListener"
              traceOutputOptions="Timestamp">
        <filter type="" />
      </add>
    </sharedListeners>
  </system.diagnostics>
  <system.serviceModel>
    <diagnostics>
      <messageLogging logMalformedMessages="true"
                logMessagesAtServiceLevel="false"
        logMessagesAtTransportLevel="true" />
    </diagnostics>
...
```

How do you add a filter to the message logger? You can just include XML tags that direct the WCF runtime to log the images that correspond to this namespace and ignore the others. Listing 6-9 details the modification to the `App.config` file. You need to add the `<filters>` section to the `<messageLogging>` section of the `App.config` file. How do you view these message log files? We will show how to use the `SvcTraceViewer.exe` utility for this (discussed in the next section).

Listing 6-9. *Adding a Filter to the Message Log*

```
<messageLogging logEntireMessage="true"
     logMalformedMessages="true" logMessagesAtServiceLevel="true"
     logMessagesAtTransportLevel="true" maxMessagesToLog="420">
     <filters>
        <add xmlns:soap="http://www.w3.org/2003/05/soap-envelope">
                        /soap:Envelope/soap:Headers
        </add>
     </filters>
</messageLogging>
```

Enabling Tracing

We'll now cover how to enable tracing. How does tracing differentiate from message logging? Tracing mechanisms act as the instrumentation for service messages and fault monitoring. It is similar to a Visual Studio debugger that helps you step through and step into code. Therefore, tracing is primarily a great tool to track the message flow of the application.

How do you enable tracing in WCF? Please follow steps 1 to 4 in the previous section. You need to click the Enable Tracing hyperlink to enable tracing, as in Figure 6-6. This will add a

`ServiceModelTraceListener` instance to the runtime. You configure the name and location for your trace file if you have specific requirements.

Then build the solution, and run the server and client. All the communication for initializing the host, the communication between the host and the client, and the destruction of the host instance will be recorded in this trace file. How will you be able to view this content? You can use `SvcTraceViewer.exe`.

Using SvcTraceViewer.exe

The `SvcTraceViewer.exe` utility will enable you to view both message log files and trace files. You can find it at `<Drive Name>:\Program Files\Microsoft SDKs\Windows\v6.0\Bin`. Open the trace file from the `TradeServiceHost` communications with the `WCFSimpleClient` console application. (Navigate to the correct directory, and select File ➤ Open to open the file.) You should see a screen similar to Figure 6-7.

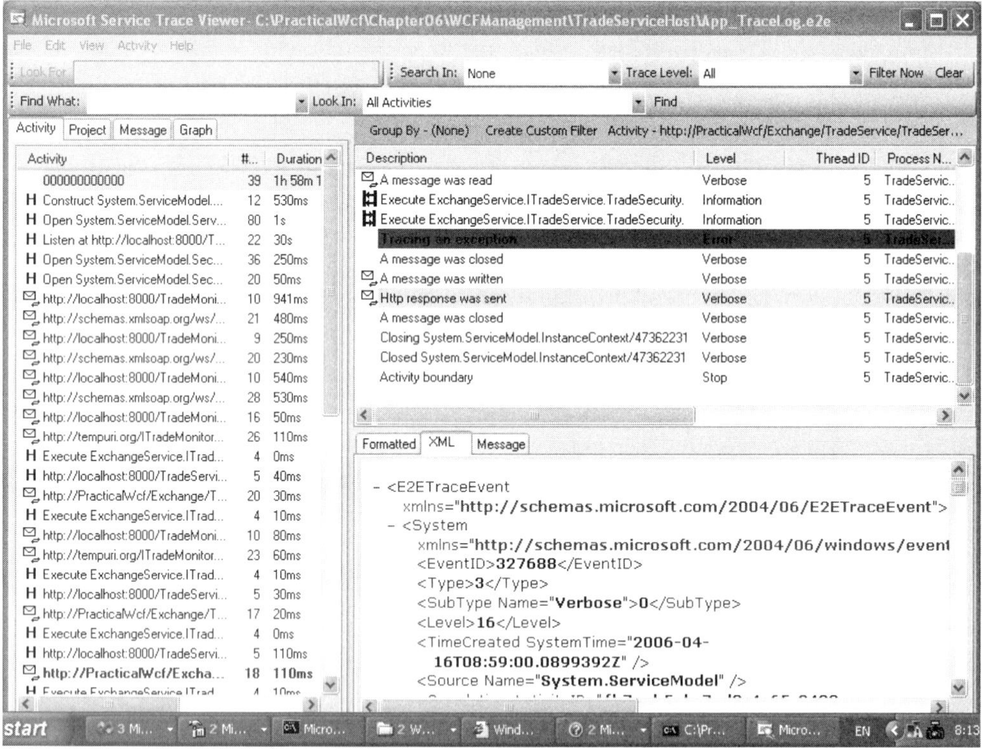

Figure 6-7. `SvcTraceViewer.exe` *reading the trace file*

This is a comprehensive implementation of the step-by-step process of the WCF service. It starts with the object creation at the top and records each interaction with the WCF runtime and the clients. It clearly details object activities, message sends, and all errors in the host's life cycle. You can view each of the XML messages in the bottom pane. It also records the duration of each activity. You can also get a graphical timeline representation by clicking the Graph tab. This is a comprehensive tool that adds a lot of value for developers and system administrators who are investigating tracing and message log files. Please refer to the SvcTraceViewer help file (in the same directory) for further information.

Utilizing WCF Performance Counters

WCF implements "out-of-the-box" performance counters to assist developers and system administrators in monitoring WCF services. You can use these performance counters for business uses to justify the costs, risks, and return on the investment of software systems. WCF performance counters address four major areas: AppDomain, ServiceHost, Endpoint, and Operation. All operation counters monitor activities on "calls per second" and "call duration" items. The following are some other important WCF counters; most of them are self-explanatory:

- Calls: Total Number of Calls
- CallsOutstanding
- CallsSucceeded
- CallsErrored
- CallsDuration

These are some security-related counters:

- SecurityCallsNotAuthenticated
- SecurityCallsNotAuthorized
- SecurityCallsTampered
- SecurityImpersonationsFailed

These are some important transaction and messaging performance counters:

- TxCommitted
- TxAborted
- TxInDoubt
- RMSessionsStarted
- RMSessionsCompleted
- RMSessionsFaulted
- RMMessagesDiscarded
- RMQPoisonedMessages
- RMBufferSize

Note Performance counters consume a lot of memory. Therefore, make sure you allocate substantial memory when you run performance counters. It is good practice to add the `<performanceCounters fileMappingSize="1000000" />` line to the `App.config` file to increase the memory size. This will replace the default size of 524,288 bytes.

Enabling Built-in WCF Performance Counters

Enabling WCF performance counters is a pretty straightforward process. The easiest way is to open the configuration file in `SvcConfigEditor.exe`. In the Diagnostics window in the Service Configuration Editor, you need to click only the Toggle Performance Counters link and save the file to enable WCF built-in counters in your code. This will enter the following line in the `App.config` file:

```
<diagnostics performanceCounters="All">
```

You'll now see some performance counters in action. Specifically, you will monitor the `TradeServiceHost` service activity using these counters. Here are the steps:

1. Open `App.config` of `TradeServiceHost` using the Service Configuration Editor, and change the diagnostic element to include performance counters. You can do this by checking the Enable Performance Counter box.

2. Build the `WCFManagement` solution. Run `TradeServiceHost` and the `WCFSimpleClient` module as the client. This will create the instances for the performance counters to track against.

3. Open Performance Monitor by selecting Start ➤ Control Panel ➤ Administrative Tools ➤ Performance or by entering **perfmon.exe** at the Start ➤ Run command. You should see Figure 6-8.

4. Click the + button to add a performance counter.

You will see the screen shown in Figure 6-9. You can clearly view the WCF-related counters under the Processor section. They are prefixed by *ServiceModel* text.

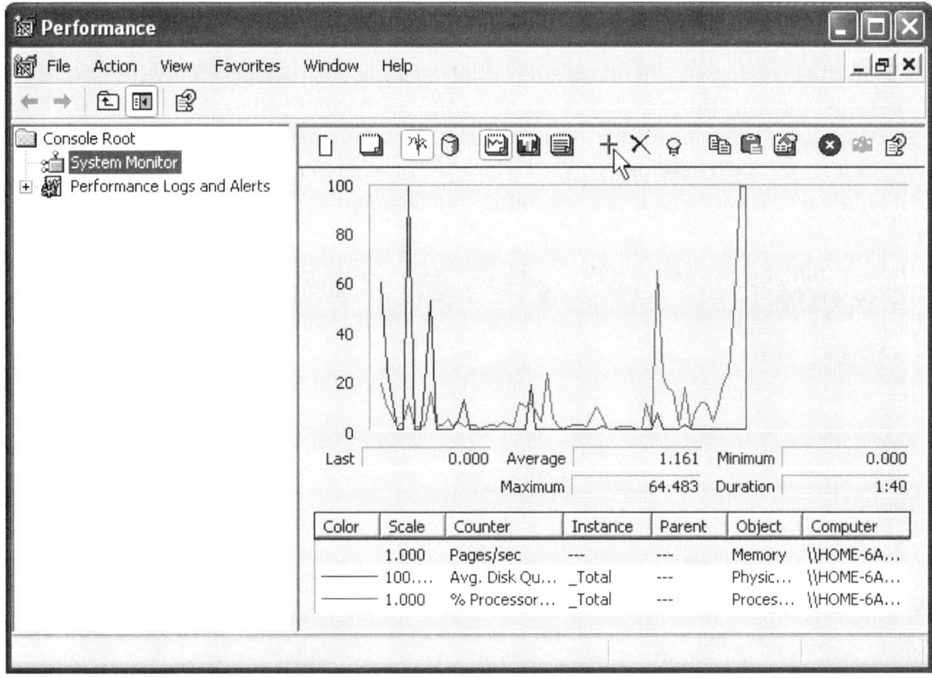

Figure 6-8. *Adding a performance counter*

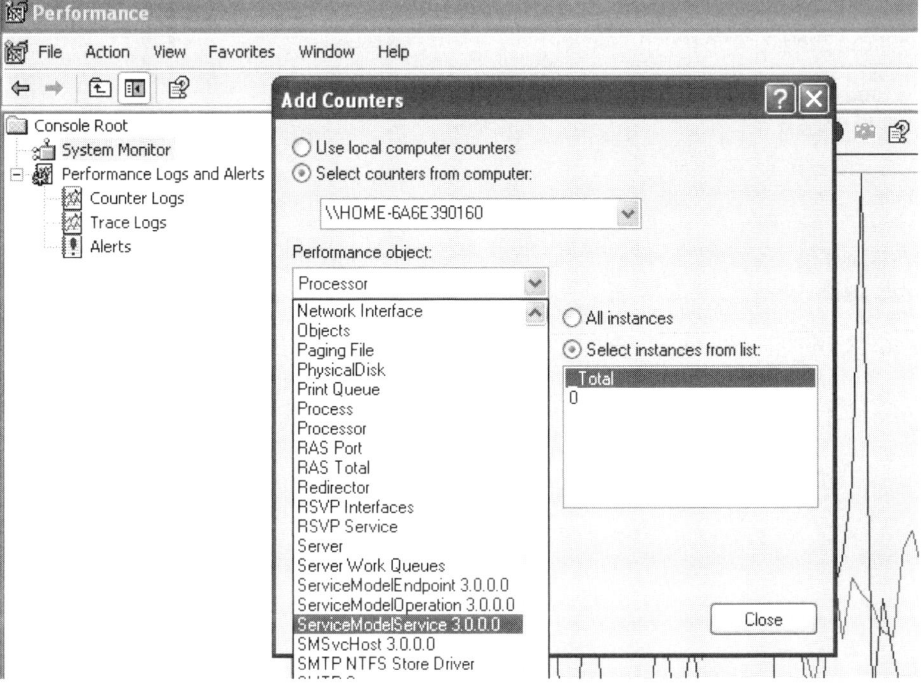

Figure 6-9. *Selecting WCF performance counters*

Please select the ServiceModelService 3.0.0.0 family of counters. This will select all the counters that are built in to the WCF `ServiceModel` namespace. You will see the screen shown in Figure 6-10 when you try to add one of these counters. You can pick any counter (such as Calls Total, Calls Faulted, and so on) from the list. This will instruct you to choose the WCF instances on the right side of the Add Counters dialog box. You are currently monitoring the `TradeServiceHost` service. Therefore, you can pick the TradeService HTTP (since you are using the HTTP binding variation) instance to monitor and click Add to include it in the graph.

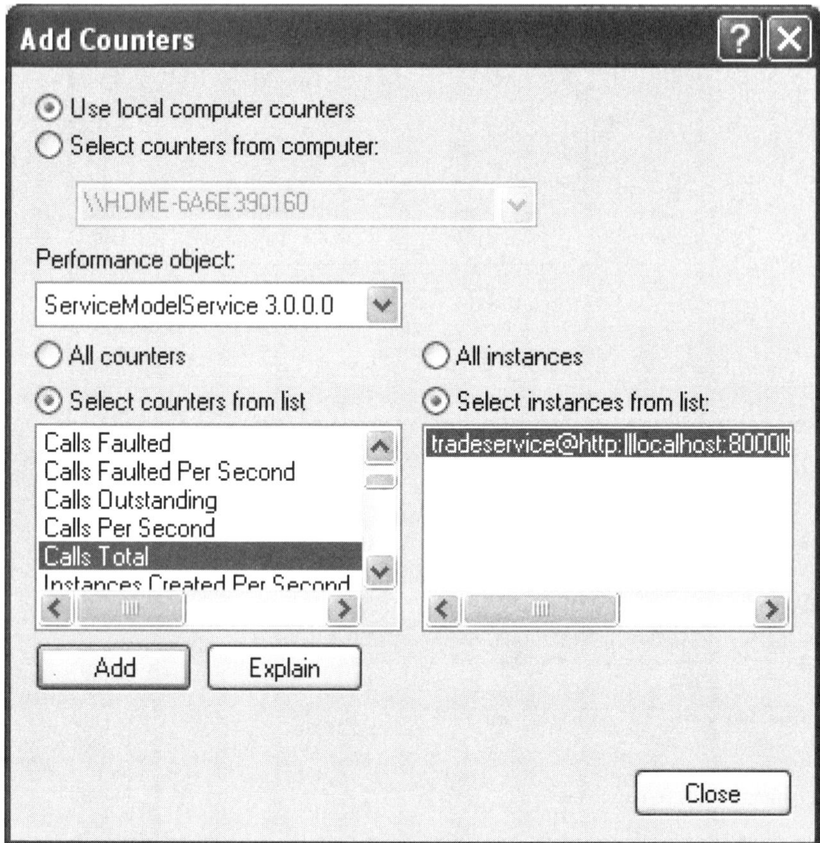

Figure 6-10. *Picking performance counters for the* `TradeServiceHost` *instance*

Figure 6-11 clearly illustrates the Calls: Total Number of Calls counters for both the `TradeService` and `TradeMonitor` services in the `WCFManagement` solution. These are built-in performance counters provided by Microsoft. However, you can build custom counters to address specific business needs.

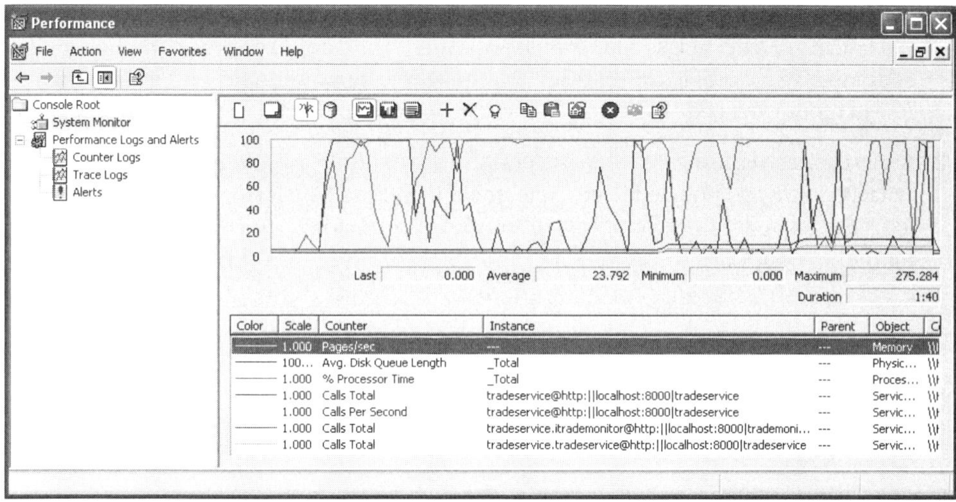

Figure 6-11. *Performance counters for* `TradeService` *and* `TradeMonitor`

Creating Custom Performance Counters

You can also create custom counters for WCF. This gives the flexibility to the system administrators to address specific technical needs of the system. This also assists the business users in monitoring "business information" by leveraging the Performance Monitor utility. The latter is appealing to the senior management of an organization because it gives them a set of tools to measure the success or failure of their IT systems.

QuickReturns Ltd. is a stock-brokering house that will have many stockbrokers dealing in multiple securities. How will management track the total value of the stockbrokers' daily trades? You can assume this stock-brokering firm has a particular interest in Microsoft stock. They may think this is "good buy" and want to keep a keen eye on the fluctuation of the stock price. How do you accommodate this scenario? Will you be able to utilize performance counters to address these business needs?

You will be addressing both these concerns utilizing performance counters. It is not a tedious task to implement custom performance counters in WCF. You will create a new console application called `TradingServicePerfMonHost` and use this project to create the performance counters. However, you will not create any new clients for this service. You will utilize the self-hosting method and invoke the service calls from the `main()` function. This is the same as having multiple clients trying to send requests to the host. The following are the steps. This design principle minimizes unnecessary code.

1. First you need to add a class to the ExchangeService project. You could have modified the TradeService.cs class. However, it is cleaner to add a new class and implement the code, and we want to leave TradeService.cs for you to experiment with. Please feel free to modify the code available on the Apress website (http://www.apress.com).

2. Right-click the ExchangeService project, and select Add ➤ New Item. Call this class TradePerfMon.cs. You need to add references to System.ServiceModel, System.Diagnostics, and System.Runtime.InteropServices. Listing 6-10 shows the code for the new class.

Listing 6-10. TradePerfMon.cs

```
using System;
using System.Collections.Generic;
using System.Diagnostics;
using System.Management;
using System.Management.Instrumentation;
using System.Runtime.InteropServices;
using System.ServiceModel;
using System.ServiceModel.Description;
using System.Text;
using System.Threading;

namespace ExchangeService
{
    [ServiceContract(
        Namespace = "http://PracticalWcf/Exchange/TradeService",
        Name = "TradeService")
    ]

    public interface ITradePerfMonService
    {
        [OperationContract]
        double TradeSecurity(string ticker, int quantity);
    }
    [ServiceBehavior(InstanceContextMode = InstanceContextMode.Single)]
    public class TradePerfMon : ITradePerfMonService
    {
       private double totalValue = 0;
       private double microsoftVolume = 0;
       private const string CounterCategoryName =
           "Trade Service PerfMon";
       private const string TotalCounterName = "Trade Total Value";
       private const string MicrosoftCounterName =
           "Microsoft Trade Volume";
```

```
        private PerformanceCounterCategory counterCategory = null;
        private PerformanceCounter totalCounter = null;
        private PerformanceCounter microsoftCounter = null;
        const double IBM_Price = 80.50D;
        const double MSFT_Price = 30.25D;

         public TradePerfMon()
         {
           if (PerformanceCounterCategory.Exists(CounterCategoryName))
           {
         PerformanceCounterCategory.Delete(CounterCategoryName);
            }

CounterCreationData totalCounter = new CounterCreationData
   (TotalCounterName, "Total Dollar value of Trade Service
   transactions.",PerformanceCounterType.NumberOfItemsHEX32);
 CounterCreationData microsoftCounter = new
   CounterCreationData(MicrosoftCounterName, "Total Microsoft
   securities being traded", PerformanceCounterType.NumberOfItemsHEX32);
 CounterCreationDataCollection counterCollection = new
   CounterCreationDataCollection(new CounterCreationData[]
   { totalCounter, microsoftCounter });
 this.counterCategory = PerformanceCounterCategory.Create(
   CounterCategoryName,"Trade Service PerfMon Counters",
   PerformanceCounterCategoryType.MultiInstance,counterCollection);
 totalValue = 0;
 microsoftVolume = 0;
         }
    }
}
```

In this code, first you initialize the variables to implement the Total Value counter and the Microsoft Volume counter. Then you create the foundations for the performance counters in the `TradePerfMon` constructor. You will first check whether the performance counter category (that is, `Trade Service PerfMon`) is available. If so, delete it because you will create it again. Then you create the Total Value counter and the Microsoft Volume counter and add them to the performance counter collection.

The next step is to initialize the counters. The following code illustrates this concept:

```
public void InitializeCounters(
  System.ServiceModel.Description.ServiceEndpointCollection endpoints)
{
    List<string> names = new List<string>();
    foreach (ServiceEndpoint endpoint in endpoints)
    {
        names.Add(string.Format("{0}@{1}",
          this.GetType().Name, endpoint.Address.ToString()));
    }
```

```
    while (true)
    {
        try
        {
            foreach (string name in names)
            {
                string condition = string.Format("SELECT * FROM
                  Service WHERE Name=\"{0}\"", name);
                SelectQuery query = new SelectQuery(condition);
                ManagementScope managementScope = new
                    ManagementScope(@"\\.\root\ServiceModel",
                   new ConnectionOptions());
                ManagementObjectSearcher searcher = new
                    ManagementObjectSearcher(managementScope, query);
                ManagementObjectCollection instances = searcher.Get();
                foreach (ManagementBaseObject instance in instances)
                {
                    PropertyData data = instance.Properties["
                       CounterInstanceName"];

                    this.totalCounter = new PerformanceCounter(
                        CounterCategoryName, TotalCounterName,
                        data.Value.ToString());
                    this.totalCounter.ReadOnly = false;
                    this.totalCounter.RawValue = 0;
                    this.microsoftCounter = new PerformanceCounter(
                        CounterCategoryName, MicrosoftCounterName,
                       data.Value.ToString());
                    this.microsoftCounter.ReadOnly = false;
                    this.microsoftCounter.RawValue = 0;

                    break;
                }
            }
            break;
         }
        catch(COMException)
        {

        }

    }
    Console.WriteLine("Counters initialized.");
}
```

In this code, you use a Windows Management Instrumentation Query Language (WQL) query to select the counters that are available to the runtime. Therefore, the query at runtime for `totalCounters` will be `SELECT * FROM Service WHERE Name= "tradeperfmon@http://localhost:8000/tradeperfmonservice`. This query is executed in the scope of the `root\ServiceModel` namespace to retrieve data about the `TradePerMon` service from WMI. From the data that is retrieved, the code extracts the value of the `CounterInstanceName` property. That property value provides the name by which the current instance of the service is identified within the Windows performance counter infrastructure. Then you initialize the `totalValue` and `microsoftCounter` counters.

The next step is to code the `TradeSecurity` function:

```
        public double TradeSecurity(string ticker, int quantity)
        {
            double result = 0;
            if (quantity < 1)
                throw new ArgumentException(
                    "Invalid quantity", "quantity");
            switch (ticker.ToLower())
            {
               case "ibm":
                        result = quantity * IBM_Price;
                        totalValue = +result;
                        if (this.totalCounter != null)
                            this.totalCounter.RawValue = (int)totalValue;
                        return result;
                case "msft":
                        result = quantity * IBM_Price;
                        totalValue = +result;
                        microsoftVolume = +quantity;
                        if (this.totalCounter != null)
                            this.totalCounter.RawValue = (int)totalValue;
                        if (this.microsoftCounter !=null)
                            this.microsoftCounter.RawValue = (int)microsoftVolume;
                        return result;
                default:
                    throw new ArgumentException(
                        "Don't know - only MSFT & IBM", "ticker");

            }
        }

    }
}
```

This is similar to the previous `TradeSecurity` function. The only difference is you add the logic to increment the `totalValue` field and the `microsoftVolume` field. Then it is used as the source for the counters.

The next step is to create a self-hosting application to invoke the `TradeSecurity` function so you can record values against the custom counters.

Create a new console project called TradingServicePerfMonHost (right-click the WCFManagement solution, and select Add ➤ New Project). You also need to add a reference to the System.ServiceModel namespace. Put the code in Listing 6-11 in the Program.cs file.

Listing 6-11. *Code for* Program.cs *File in* TradingServicePerfMonHost

```
using System;
using System.Collections.Generic;
using System.Messaging;
using System.ServiceModel;
using System.Text;

namespace ExchangeService
{
    public class Program
    {
        public static void Main(string[] args)
        {
            TradePerfMon trade = new TradePerfMon();
            using (ServiceHost host = new ServiceHost(typeof(
                TradePerfMon), new Uri[] { new Uri("
                     http://localhost:8000/TradePerfMonService") }))
            {
                host.Open();
                trade.InitializeCounters(host.Description.Endpoints);
                Console.WriteLine("The WCF Management trading
                      service is available.");
                for (int index = 1; index < 225; index++)
                {
                    Console.WriteLine("IBM - traded " + (index+100) +
                       " shares  for " + trade.TradeSecurity("IBM",
                       (index+100)) + " dollars" );
                    // you are deliberately increasing the total volume
                    of trades to view the difference in the
                   Perfomance Monitor)
                    Console.WriteLine("MSFT - tradedtrade " + index +
                      " shares for " + trade.TradeSecurity("MSFT",
                        index) + " dollars");
                    System.Threading.Thread.Sleep(1000);
                }

                Console.ReadKey();
            }
        }
    }
}
```

In this code, first you instantiate an object type of `TradePerfMon`. Then you create a host type of `TradePerfMon` and open the host. The configuration settings are read from the `App.config` file. Then you invoke the `IntializeCounters` function to initiate the counters. Then you utilize a loop to create a series of trades. This is deliberately done to view the custom performance counters in action. Please note that we have tweaked some variables (that is, the `index` variable in Listing 6-11) to differentiate the counters when they become available (for cosmetic changes—to view them as separate entities from each other).

The next step is to create the `App.config` file for the host application, as shown in Listing 6-12. Please ignore the `wmiProviderEnabled="true"` flag. We will discuss this in the next section. This is similar to the previous host application.

Listing 6-12. `App.config` *File for the Host Application*

```
<?xml version="1.0" encoding="utf-8" ?>
<configuration>
  <system.serviceModel>
    <diagnostics wmiProviderEnabled="true"
           performanceCounters="All">
      <messageLogging logEntireMessage="true"
           logMalformedMessages="true"
        logMessagesAtServiceLevel="true"
            logMessagesAtTransportLevel="true" />
    </diagnostics>
    <services>
      <service name="ExchangeService.TradePerfMon">
        <endpoint address=http://localhost:8000/TradePerfMonService
                binding="basicHttpBinding"
          contract="ExchangeService.ITradePerfMonService" />
      </service>
    </services>
  </system.serviceModel>
</configuration>
```

Now you'll build the `WCFManagement` solution and make the `TradeServicePerfMonHost` the start-up application:

1. Right-click the `WCFManagement` solution, and select Set As Startup Project. Compile the solution, and run the code. You should see a screen similar to Figure 6-12 to indicate that trading takes place in a loop structure.

2. Now you are ready to capture these custom counters in the Performance Monitor. How do you do it? Open Performance Monitor (select Start ➤ Run, and enter **perfmon.exe**), and click the Add button.

```
file:///C:/PracticalWcf/Chapter06/WCFManagement/TradingServicePerfMonHost/bin/Debug...
IBM - traded 132 shares  for 10626 dollars
MSFT - tradedtrade 32 shares for 2576 dollars
IBM - traded 133 shares  for 10706.5 dollars
MSFT - tradedtrade 33 shares for 2656.5 dollars
IBM - traded 134 shares  for 10787 dollars
MSFT - tradedtrade 34 shares for 2737 dollars
IBM - traded 135 shares  for 10867.5 dollars
MSFT - tradedtrade 35 shares for 2817.5 dollars
IBM - traded 136 shares  for 10948 dollars
MSFT - tradedtrade 36 shares for 2898 dollars
IBM - traded 137 shares  for 11028.5 dollars
MSFT - tradedtrade 37 shares for 2978.5 dollars
IBM - traded 138 shares  for 11109 dollars
MSFT - tradedtrade 38 shares for 3059 dollars
IBM - traded 139 shares  for 11189.5 dollars
MSFT - tradedtrade 39 shares for 3139.5 dollars
IBM - traded 140 shares  for 11270 dollars
MSFT - tradedtrade 40 shares for 3220 dollars
IBM - traded 141 shares  for 11350.5 dollars
MSFT - tradedtrade 41 shares for 3300.5 dollars
IBM - traded 142 shares  for 11431 dollars
MSFT - tradedtrade 42 shares for 3381 dollars
IBM - traded 143 shares  for 11511.5 dollars
MSFT - tradedtrade 43 shares for 3461.5 dollars
```

Figure 6-12. `TradeServicePerfMonHost` *application running*

3. You should view the new custom counter collection Trade Service PerfMon. You should view the two counters, Trade Total Value and Microsoft Trade Volume, under the collection. You should also see the existing instances of the host application. Your screen should be similar to Figure 6-13.

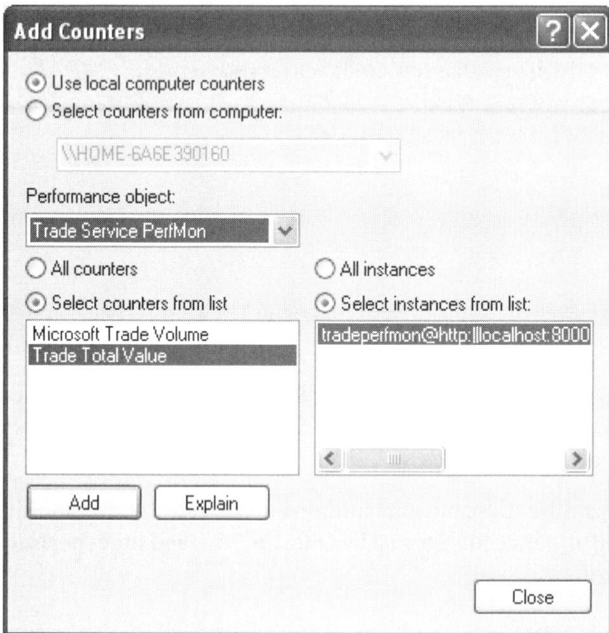

Figure 6-13. *Custom* `TradeService` *counters*

Select both of these counters, and investigate how the total value of the trades and Microsoft volumes of trading are doing. This information will be valuable for business users to make decisions about Microsoft volumes and the state of the business by analyzing the daily total turnover. Since you are using a loop to trade stocks, the values of both the total value and the Microsoft volumes are increasing steadily. Please note we are using two different scales for the total value and the Microsoft volume, since the total value will be far greater than the Microsoft volume amount, as shown in Figure 6-14.

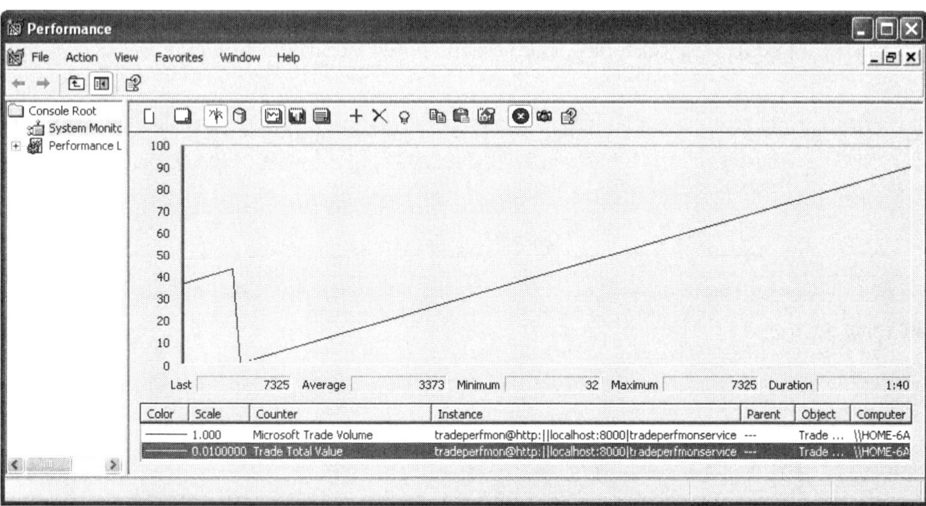

Figure 6-14. *Custom performance counters in action*

This is how you utilize Performance Monitor to manage your WCF service. Now you'll learn how you can use WMI to facilitate WCF management.

Using Windows Management Instrumentation

WMI is an "add-in" component to the Windows operating system that enables monitoring on a variety of object models. WMI was created as a web-based enterprise management (WBEM) tool that you can use to monitor and maintain complex enterprise applications over web browsers. You can invoke WMI from many technologies, such as C++, Visual Basic, C# (and any managed code implementation—J# or VB .NET), ODBC, and so on. It integrates seamlessly with the WCF programming model to monitor and manage WCF services also.

You can enable WMI with the flip of a switch in WCF. WCF services provide information to WMI at runtime. Therefore, you can use existing WMI tools to monitor and manipulate these services. You can use the WMI programming interfaces to construct custom network and business operation consoles for your WCF applications. It is easy to enable WMI monitoring in WCF services. All you have to do is to include the following line in the configuration file:

```
<diagnostics wmiProviderEnabled="true" >
```

This enables all the WMI objects for WCF. However, how can you view this information? You need to install WMI CIM Studio to view the WMI interactions. This is a free download available from Microsoft. It is an ActiveX component that plugs into Internet Explorer. Here are the steps to utilize WMI for WCF services:

1. Run `TradeServicePerfMonHost.exe` (since you need a live instance to monitor).
2. Open WMI CIM Studio (Start ➤ Programs ➤ WMI Tools ➤ WMI CIM Studio).
3. You will be asked to enter the starting point for the namespace in which you are interested. Enter **root\ServiceModel**. Your screen should be similar to Figure 6-15.

Figure 6-15. *Opening WMI CMI Studio with the correct namespace*

4. You will be asked to select your user details. Then you will be presented with a comprehensive view of every WMI interface that deals with WCF. You can monitor bindings, services, behaviors, contracts, and so on, from this interface. Therefore, can you monitor the `TradeService` instance with this interface? Yes, you can. You can get a list of all running services by clicking the instance icon, as shown in Figure 6-16.

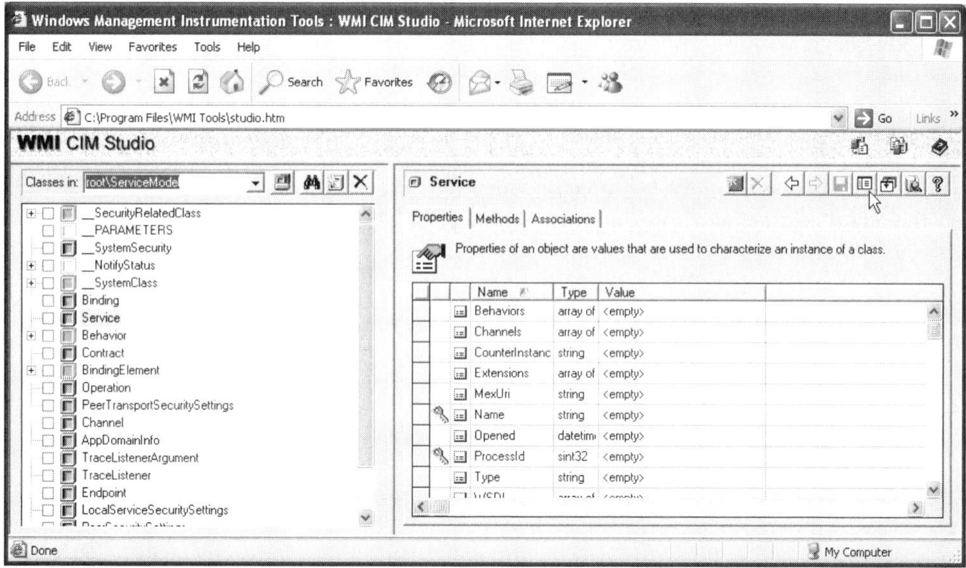

Figure 6-16. *Services in WMI CIM Studio*

When you click the instance icon, you will see a list of running WCF services. Please choose the `TradeService` instance. Your screen should be similar to Figure 6-17.

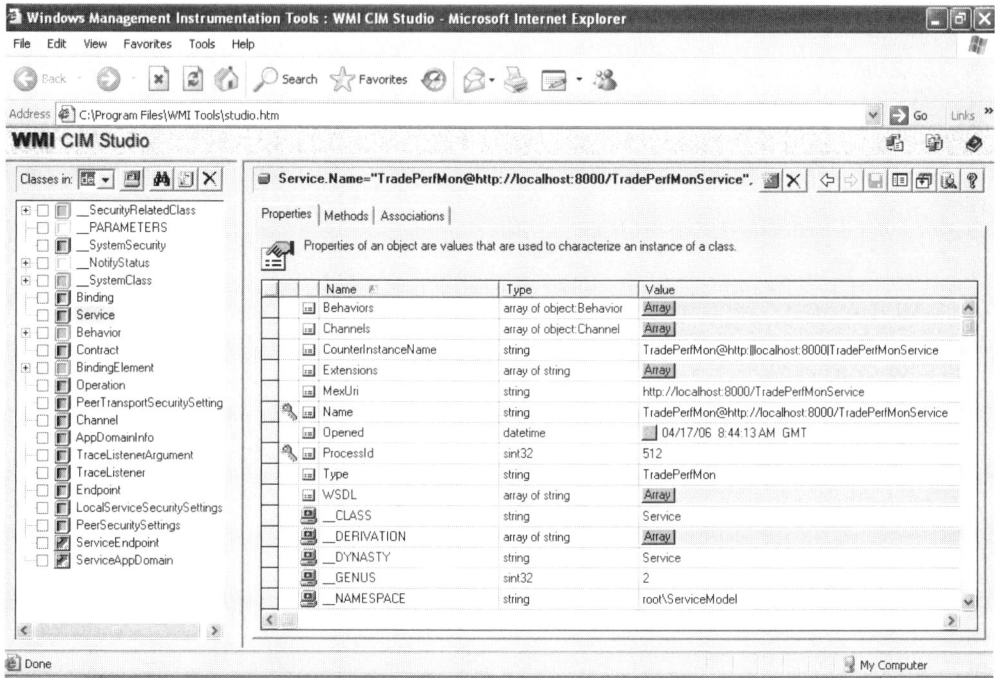

Figure 6-17. *Current running* `TradeService` *instances*

Therefore, you can navigate to each WMI element and query the WCF service in great detail. This is a great monitoring tool for system administrators and developers.

Summary

You have learned a lot about WCF management and monitoring in this chapter. We discussed that you can utilize the following methods to manage WCF services:

- Developers can use custom-built interface to monitor the service activity.
- Developers and system administrators can utilize message logging and tracing in WCF to track and debug the WCF service. They can use `SvcTraceViewer.exe` to view the message logs and trace data.
- Developers and system administrators can extensively use the `SvcConfigEditor.exe` tool to modify the configuration files.
- Business users, system administrators, and developers can use the "out-of-the-box" performance counters to monitor service activity. They can also build custom Performance Monitor counters to facilitate business needs.
- Developers and system administrators can use WMI CIM Studio to monitor WMI activity on WCF services.

Now you are familiar with how to manage and monitor web services. WCF security is one of the most intriguing and important topics in WCF. The next chapter will shed some light on this topic.

PART 3

■ ■ ■

Advanced Topics in WCF

You have investigated the WCF basics of creating services, evaluated the "out-of-the-box" hosting options, and learned how to consume them using clients. You have also learned about the management tools available in WCF to efficiently manage these WCF services. These features will assist you in creating simple WCF applications. However, the real-world SOA applications will have many other demanding features to implement.

These complex real-world web service implementations will address security issues (both client and service), reliable messaging, transactions, COM+ integration, data integration issues, and peer-to-peer communications. An enterprise can achieve the eventual "value proposition" by utilizing these advanced features of WCF. In this part, you will concentrate on these topics. In addition, you'll investigate the WCF interoperability options available to seamlessly communicate with non-Microsoft platforms in Chapter 13.

CHAPTER 7

Implementing WCF Security

Security is one of the fundamental features of any software platform. In fact, security requirements have grown exponentially in the past decade because of the increasing popularity of public networks. Securing a distributed enterprise (one that is physically scattered around the world) using a public network such as the Internet is a challenging task. Malicious hackers, identity fraudsters, and disgruntled employees cost organizations millions of dollars every year. So, how do you address these issues as a senior stakeholder of a company? What does WCF offer in the security space to combat these issues?

You can secure your enterprise in many ways. Initially, you need to secure an organization at the physical level. You need to ensure your server farms are behind locked doors and are carefully monitored for access. You should restrict the access to all resources as much as possible. One emerging option is to outsource server farms to reputable third parties, which set up stringent measures to limit physical access to server farms. These outsourced hardware facilities have strict access controls to prevent any unauthorized access to the servers. They are in most cases built underground and without any windows or external access points. When you are comfortable with the level of security with your hardware devices by using services such as these, you can turn your attention to software practices.

You can address security requirements for applications in many aspects of software development. Some of these aspects are the platform, the data, the hosts, and the communications between clients and services. In this chapter, we will discuss only platform-level security. Our main focus will be to show the mechanisms available to protect your messages between services and clients.

WCF is a distributed application platform based on SOAP. Basically, WCF addresses the communication between multiple nodes and multiple applications, and you utilize SOAP to achieve the communication in WCF. Bindings in WCF (that is, HTTP, TCP, MSMQ, and so on) provide you with different options to optimize SOAP messages depending on your business requirements. In this chapter, we will address messages traveling from one node to another through intermediaries (with firewalls) and messages traveling on public networks (the Internet). These scenarios introduce many security threats. We will discuss these threats in the next section. In a nutshell, this chapter discusses the following items to illustrate the WCF security concepts:

- Why do you need to be concerned about security in SOAP messages?
- What are the WCF security features that address these issues?
  - Credentials and claims
  - Transport-level security
  - Message-level security
  - Mixed mode (transport level and message level)
  - The federated security model in WCF
- Authorization
- Auditing
- Windows CardSpace (formally known as Infocard)

You'll start your journey by learning why you need to address WCF security. What are the business drivers behind addressing security on the latest Microsoft platform offerings? What value does WCF add to solve the security concerns of a CTO or CIO? The next section will answer these questions.

Introducing the Business Drivers

WCF is based on the communication mechanism between clients and services using messages. These messages are vulnerable on numerous fronts. An authorized party must create the client message to conform to a standard that the service can comprehend. In most cases, the messages need to be encrypted and signed to verify the authenticity of the sending party. The communication line between the client and the service needs to be secure. The receiver should also be able to decrypt the messages and verify the integrity of the sender. Therefore, security plays a major part in any enterprise architecture solution.

Here are some other examples of business drivers:

- You need to audit and track the communication between clients and services to prevent malicious acts. In the QuickReturns Ltd. example, an intruder can intercept the messages between the clients and the service. If they can use the valid client details to initiate trades on the market and withdraw funds from the client's account, this can have disastrous implications for QuickReturns Ltd. Therefore, how do you stop these malicious attacks? What is available in WCF to prevent these attacks?

- How can you guarantee the messages arrived from the client (that is, how do you implement nonrepudiation)? How do you know whether messages were intended for the correct service? Can the client sign the messages with the private key, and can the service verify the authenticity by utilizing a public key?

- Do you know whether a purchase order was submitted only once? What happens if a rogue intruder replays the same order to generate bogus orders for the service? What measures are in place to stop these attacks? If these attacks continue, how do you eradicate the threat before it escalates to a denial of service attack?

How can you address these security concerns? What does WCF offer to counter these issues? You'll take a closer look at what WCF has to offer in the next section.

Introducing the WCF Security Features

Microsoft has invested a lot of effort in guaranteeing the security in the Vista platform. Microsoft counterparts viewed its security as a weakness in the early 1990s. Since then, Microsoft has done a commendable job shrugging off that stigma. You may remember the initiative to ensure "secure code" and the "trusted access security" campaigns that Microsoft implemented to address this issue. Microsoft's objective was to educate developers so they will address security needs in the fundamental design.

Windows 2003 Server implemented security as "highest security turned on" by default. You had to downgrade the security privileges to obtain access to resources. WCF is also based on the "guilty until proven innocent" and "all user input is evil" concepts. Any distributed application is prone to many forms of malicious attacks by intruders. The modern distributed software architectures leverage public networks such as the Internet to send business-sensitive information. This information can be compromised at various locations (such as by packet sniffing on the wire, malicious systems administrators at routing destinations, and so on). Therefore, the security model for WCF needs to be comprehensive to handle all these threats. The core of WCF security is to address four important features:

Confidentiality: Is the information confidential between the sender and the receiver? This feature will ensure that "unauthorized" parties do not get the opportunity to view the message. You usually achieve this by utilizing encryption algorithms.

Integrity: This feature ensures that the receiver of the message gets the same information that the sender sends without any data tampering. You usually sign messages using digital signatures to achieve integrity.

Authentication: This is to verify who the sender is and who the receiver is. Are they known to the system or the application?

Authorization: At the authorization stage, you know who the sender or the receiver is. However, you also need to know whether they are authorized to perform the action they are requesting from the application.

These are the key features the WCF security model attempts to address. You achieve the physical implementation of addressing these issues by configuring bindings in WCF. WCF offers a rich set of binding to address these security issues. You also have the flexibility of extending or creating custom bindings to address specific security needs if necessary. In the next section, you'll investigate how to use bindings in WCF to implement security.

Security Features of Bindings

Bindings define one or more WS-* protocols that WCF supports. Every binding addresses two important aspects of messaging. These aspects are the encoding and transport of the message. *Encoding* defines the way messages are serialized. *Transport* defines the mechanisms that get the messages from the sender to the receiver. Let's look at the `BasicHttpBinding` binding as an example. It uses the WS-I Basic Profile XML encoding and HTTP for transport. This binding is designed to support interoperable scenarios with other platforms. Therefore, it does not implement security by default. (However, you can extend this binding to implement security by utilizing custom code.) You need to utilize `WsHttpBinding` or `WsDualHttpBinding` to implement security.

Note Please consult Chapter 3 for an extensive discussion of bindings. This chapter will concentrate only on the security implications and extensions of bindings. However, it is important to note that the binary-encoded bindings (that is, `Net*Binding`) require WCF on both the sender and the receiver ends because of optimization and performance reasons. `NetMsmqBinding` is used for asynchronous scenarios. `NetTcpBinding` and `NetNamedPipeBinding` support reliable sessions and transactions.

You can also build your custom binding by utilizing the `System.ServiceModel.Channels` namespace. You can define security features, encoding, and serialization options that are suitable to your requirements using the classes available in this namespace. Similarly, you can also utilize the `ProtectionLevel` binding property to enforce integrity and confidentiality. The options available for the `ProtectionLevel` property are as follows:

`None`: Only authenticate the binding.

`Sign`: Ensure integrity in the transmitted data.

`EncryptAndSign`: Ensure both confidentially and integrity.

Protection Levels

WCF security encrypts and signs the messages by default. This could lead to "overkill" in some instances. Therefore, you can implement integrity where confidentiality is not a requirement (such as when debugging code by developers). In such cases, WCF provides the facility to set the protection level on the message. The following application file snippet illustrates how to achieve this using configuration files; the messages are required to be signed only before they are sent:

```
<bindings>
  <wsHttpBinding>
    <binding name="test">
      <security mode="Message">
        <message defaultProtectionLevel="Sign"/>
      </security>
    </binding>
  </wsHttpBinding>
</bindings>
```

Message exchange patterns (MEPs) determine how the messages are sent from the sender to the receiver. How are these message patterns implemented in WCF? Can you implement security on all these bindings for one-way and request-reply patterns? WCF does implement security support for both the MEPs. However, duplex MEP is available only in `WsDuaHttpBinding`, `NetTcpBinding`, and `NetNamedPipeBinding`.

How do you present your rights to WCF runtime via bindings? What are the mechanisms available in WCF to pass on your requests to access resources? These questions are answered by implementing credentials and claims in WCF. The following section will discuss what these are.

Credentials and Claims

WCF security is based on credentials. What are these credentials? A *credential* is an XML-compatible entity that assists the Windows runtime in identifying a user. Credentials consist of one or more claims. A *claim* can be a username, a digital certificate, or a custom token that specifies the holder's right to access the application. This information will assist the Windows runtime in granting or denying access to the WCF application. The Windows runtime will verify the claims by the user. Therefore, if the user is using a certificate, the runtime will inspect the certificate information and verify whether the user is who they say they are. This is the authentication concept discussed earlier. When the user is authenticated, the certificate key could be used to decrypt the data. This will fulfill the integrity feature discussed earlier. This could be followed by an authorization check that will verify whether the user has access to the data and functions of the application. Therefore, we can summarize a set of claims into the user's complete access privileges in WCF.

There are several setup *claim sets* in WCF (that is, certificates, usernames, Kerberos tickets, and custom tokens). They are mapped to a standard internal claim set in WCF runtime. Therefore, the user can alternate between one claim and another (that is, between the username and the custom token pair) without any issues with the Windows runtime. After the first communication with the server, the user session will commonly use a *token* to present the claim set information without checking for authentication, authorization, and integrity for subsequent requests. This is designed to improve response times.

Note In WCF, the highest security level is activated by default. Therefore, the user needs to decrease the security levels if they want to accommodate security requirements. Also, the security model facilitates configuration-level changes without any code or runtime modifications (which is the same as reliable messaging, transaction support in WCF, and so on). Therefore, if you alter your MSMQ binding to replace with the `WSHttpBinding` binding, the application will seamlessly integrate with the same security context.

How do you extract claim information in WCF? How can you investigate the claim information using code? Let's examine this with the assistance of the QuickReturns Ltd. sample application.

Note You will reuse the Chapter 6 code in this example. The service and client functionality will be the same. Specifically, the server will expose a security trading service, and the client will make requests to trade securities. Please consult the code that accompanies this chapter to maximize your learning experience.

The most significant code changes will be in the ExchangeService class. You will modify the code to reflect the claims the client will make to gain access to the service. Here are the steps:

1. Open Visual Studio 2005 (select Start ➤ Programs ➤ MS Visual Studio 2005 ➤ Microsoft Visual Studio 2005).

2. Create a blank solution in Visual Studio 2005 (select File ➤ New ➤ Project).

3. Select Visual Studio Solutions ➤ Other Project Types, and choose Blank Solution. Name this solution WCFSecurity, and point to your preferred directory (C:\PracticalWcf\Chapter07 in this example).

4. Add the ExchangeService project from Chapter 6 (right-click the WCFSecurity solution, and select Add ➤ Existing Project). The next step is to make some changes to the TradeSecurity code. As shown in Listing 7-1, modify the code to gain access to claim information. The rest of the class is identical to the Chapter 6 code.

Listing 7-1. *Adding Claim Access Code to the* ExchangeService *Class*

```
public double TradeSecurity(string ticker, int quantity)
        {
            Console.WriteLine("Claim made at " + System.DateTime.Now.TimeOfDay);
            System.ServiceModel.OperationContext opx;
            opx = OperationContext.Current;
            if (opx != null)
            {
                System.IdentityModel.Policy.AuthorizationContext ctx =
                    opx.ServiceSecurityContext.AuthorizationContext;
                foreach (System.IdentityModel.Claims.ClaimSet cs in ctx.ClaimSets)
                {
                    Console.WriteLine("Claim Issued by : " + cs.Issuer);
                    foreach (System.IdentityModel.Claims.Claim claim in cs)
                    {
                        Console.WriteLine("Claim Type - " + claim.ClaimType);
                        Console.WriteLine("Claim Resource name - " +
            claim.Resource);
                        Console.WriteLine("Claim Right - " + claim.Right);
                    }
                }
            }
            if (quantity < 1)
                throw new ArgumentException(
                    "Invalid quantity", "quantity");
            switch (ticker.ToLower())
            {
                case "ibm":
                    return quantity * IBM_Price;
```

```
            case "msft":
                return quantity * MSFT_Price;
            default:
                throw new ArgumentException(
                    "Don't know - only MSFT & IBM", "ticker");
        }
    }
```

Initially you need to gain access to the authorization context, available from the current operation context by utilizing the `ServiceSecurityContext.AuthorizationContext` property. Then you go through all the `ClaimSets` the user is presenting to the service. These `ClaimSets` are comprised of individual claims. These are the claims that the client needs to present to the service to gain access to the QuickReturns Ltd. application. This claim information is printed on the console for you to read. You are printing only the `ClaimType`, `Resource` (the claim is for), and `Right` information for the purpose of this example. The next step is to create the host console application to host this newly modified `ExchangeService` class.

5. This example uses the self-hosting option. Create a new console project by right-clicking and selecting Solution ➤ Add ➤ New Project ➤ Console Application. Name it `ClaimHost`, and add it to the `WCFSecurity` solution. Rename the `program.cs` file to `host.cs`. You are creating a WCF self-hosted service on port 8000 on the `localhost` machine. You display a message to inform the service is functioning after you start the host with the `host.Open()` method. The code and the config file are identical to the Chapter 6 `TradeServiceHost` project. You will utilize the `WsHttpBinding` to communicate with the service endpoints. (Please refer to Listing 6-2 for the `host.cs` code and Listing 6-4 for the `App.config` file in Chapter 6 for the code.)

6. Let's concentrate on the client that consumes this service now. Create a new console project called `ClaimClient`, and add it to the `WCFSecurity` solution. The code for the client is identical to Listing 6-5 in Chapter 6. You will also use `WsHttpBinding` to bind with the service endpoint. The `App.config` file is also identical to Listing 6-5.

7. Build the solution to create executables for `ClaimHost` and `ClaimClient`.

Try to execute your application. Let's run the service first. Your screen should be similar to Figure 7-1.

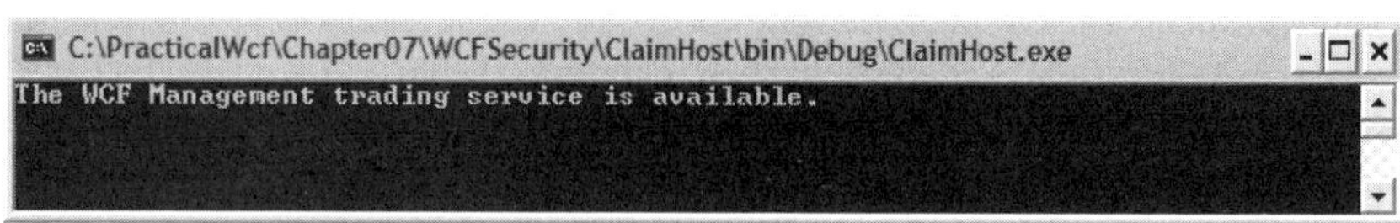

Figure 7-1. `ClaimHost` *application running*

The next step is to run the client. Let's navigate to the client's directory and execute the client. Your screen should look like Figure 7-2.

```
C:\PracticalWcf\Chapter07\WCFSecurity\ClaimClient\bin\Debug\ClaimClient.exe
Trade IBM
Cost was 80500

Trade MSFT
Cost was 60500

Trade ATT
Exception was: Don't know - only MSFT & IBM
Parameter name: ticker

Press <enter> to exit...
```

Figure 7-2. `ClaimClient` *application running*

You will notice while the client was running, the `ClaimHost` window recorded all the claims the client was presenting over `WsHttpBinding`. The screen will display the `Issuer` for the `ClaimSet` and the `ClaimType`, `Resource`, and `Right` information for each claim. Your screen should look like Figure 7-3.

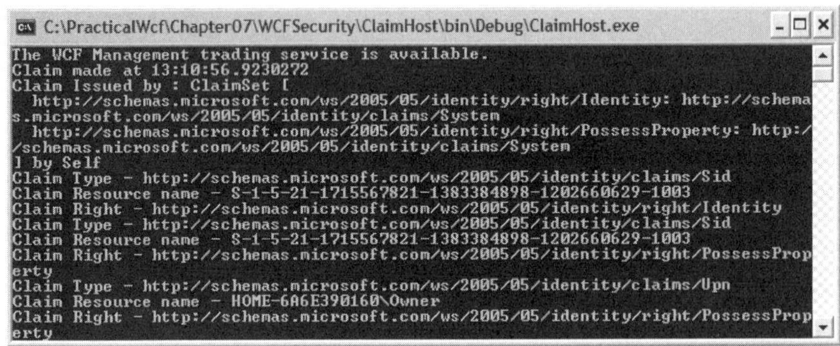

Figure 7-3. *Displaying claim information at the service host console*

This screen displays all the claim information to authenticate the client (the `ClaimClient` instance) to the service (`ClaimHost`). The issuer of the `ClaimSet` is `Self` in this scenario (that is, the services and the client are running on the same machine). Then you loop through all the claims one by one. You first display the `ClaimType`. Then you display the `Resource` that the claim is for, and finally, you display the `Right` for the resource.

You are familiar with the mechanisms the client utilizes to submit claims to WCF services. However, what are the options available to present these claims to the WCF runtime? The next section will answer this question.

Presenting Credentials and Claims to WCF

The user's credentials can be presented to the Windows runtime in one of two ways: by utilizing the transport level or by utilizing the message level. The *transport level* will provide the credentials as part of the message transport. This is similar to Secure Sockets Layer (SSL) communication. The transport-level protocols will verify the credentials with the Windows runtime and establish a secure session between the client and the service. However, there is no explicit security for the messages that travel utilizing the protected transport layer.

Unfortunately, the transport security also terminates at the destination SSL gateway. The messages will be exposed to malicious intruders as soon as the messages exit the destination's SSL gateway. This may not be the actual hosting web server. Many companies implement SSL accelerators on proxy servers in their DMZ. This leaves the message's subject open to possible hijacking in the network between their accelerators and their servers. However, this is a common and proven security feature that the industry has utilized successfully (provided the destination organization takes steps to secure the messages as soon as the messages enter their organization).

The second option is to implement credentials at the *message level*, where the credentials are embedded in the message. No credentials are transported at the transport layer. The message will not be exposed to malicious hackers until the receiver can decrypt the message using a special key known to the receiver. However, this method is slower than the transport-level credentials because of the extra encryptions with messages. The message size will also be larger than the transport-level messages. The first message between the sender and receiver initiates the authentication and authorization between the two entities. The subsequent messages will have an optimized token to replace the complete credential set to counter the slow response times. This mechanism will attempt to reduce the size limitation and increase the speed of the communication. The credentials of the service and client are specified in the binding information. You can have the following options as the credential types in WCF:

None: No security is provided via the transport level or messaging level. `BasicHttpBinding` uses this mode by default. The rest of the other bindings do not use it. (In other words, their security mode needs to be specified explicitly.)

Transport: This uses transport-level security (that is, SSL).

Message: This uses SOAP messages to provide authentication, authorization, integrity, and confidentiality. These SOAP messages are WS-Security compliant.

Mixed mode: This uses both transport-level and message-level security. Confidentiality and integrity are delivered by the transport layer. Authentication and authorization are provided by the message level.

Both: This is available only in the `NetMsmqBinding` binding. This provides authentication at both the message level and the transport level.

Binding Support for Credentials

Table 7-1 lists the most common bindings and whether they support transport, message, or mixed modes.

Table 7-1. *Binding Support for Credential Types*

Binding	Transport Mode?	Message Mode?	Mixed Mode?
`BasicHttpBinding`	Yes	Yes	Yes
`WsHttpBinding`	Yes	Yes	Yes
`WsDualHttpBinding`	No	Yes	No
`NetTcpBinding`	Yes	Yes	Yes

Table 7-1. *Continued*

Binding	Transport Mode?	Message Mode?	Mixed Mode?
NetNamedPipeBinding	Yes	No	No
NetMsmqBinding	Yes	Yes	No
MsmqIntegrationBinding	Yes	No	No

You are now familiar with bindings and the modes they support. How do you set this mode in code? You change the credentials by setting the binding credentials in the binding's `Mode` property, which you can find in the `Security` property of the binding. You can also set them using the `bindingCredentials` property of the `Binding` object. Figure 7-4 illustrates the security mode being set using a `WsHttpBinding` at the message level.

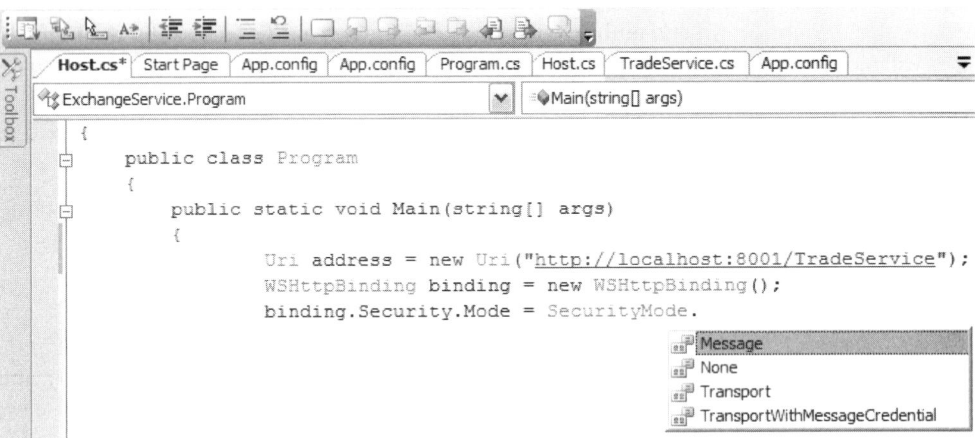

Figure 7-4. *Adding the security mode*

Please note that this `TradeService` instance is scheduled to run on port 8001. However, all the examples in this chapter will utilize port 8000 as the endpoint. In the next section, you'll look at these credential security levels in more detail with some sample code.

Transport-Level Security

Under the transport-level model, the credentials are applied at the transport level. Therefore, all the messages between the sender and the receiver are not visible to any intruders. They also work effectively on point-to-point scenarios. It is difficult to implement transport-level security when there are multiple routing mechanisms to multiple recipients. Multiple gateways will expose the messages to intruders when the message is transferred from one SSL provider to another. This feature will make the transport-level security unrealistic for non-point-to-point scenarios. However, you can use hardware accelerators to achieve quick response times under this model. Transport-level security is also considered for high throughput and faster response times because of this feature. Transport-level security provides mechanisms to authenticate both the service and the client so they adhere to confidentiality, integrity, and authorization.

CODE VERSUS CONFIGURATION FILES REGARDING SECURITY

One of the most flexible features in WCF is the ability to implement the same task by either coding explicitly or utilizing configuration files. It is helpful to use configuration files regarding WCF security. Configuration files give you the flexibility to alter the security features without recompiling the code. This is common when the security standards get superseded by the latest security offerings. However, for the purposes of the next example, you will use explicit code on the service side. The client is configured using application configuration files. This was intentionally done to illustrate the flexibility of the WCF security model.

Transport-level security (specifically, SSL) is a proven concept and has wide acceptance in the technical community. Also, SSL hardware accelerators will expedite the message transmission speed. However, SSL supports only a subset of claim types. They are Windows authentication, digest authentication, and certificates. SSL does not support the rich WS-Security or Security Access Markup Language (SAML) token claim types in WCF. SAML tokens are a key element to achieve distributed computing security on multiple platforms. WCF offers several transport credential types:

None: This is for anonymous clients. This setting specifies that the client does not need to present any credentials to the service. This is not recommended.

Basic: This specifies Windows basic authentication. This is implemented according to RFC 2617 (which is available at `http://www.rfc-editor.org`).

Digest: This specifies digest authentication between the service and the client.

Ntlm: This specifies NTLM authentication.

Windows: This specifies Windows Kerberos authentication.

Certificate: This performs client authentication using an X.509 certificate.

How do you implement transport-level security in WCF? In the following exercise, you will reuse the `TradeServiceHost` and `WcfSimpleClient` projects from Chapter 6. Specifically, you will add these two projects to the `WCFSecurity` solution. Here are the steps:

1. Add the `TradeServiceHost` project and the `WcfSimpleClient` project to the `WCFSecurity` solution (right-click the `WCFSecurity` solution, and select Add ➤ Existing Project).

2. You need to modify the code for the `host.cs` file in the `TradeServiceHost` project. Listing 7-2 shows the code.

Listing 7-2. *Code for* `host.cs` *File in the* `TradeServiceHost` *Project*

```
using System;
using System.Collections.Generic;
using System.ServiceModel;
using System.Text;
```

```
namespace ExchangeService
{
    public class Program
    {
        public static void Main(string[] args)
        {
                Uri address = new Uri("https://localhost:8000/TradeService");
                WSHttpBinding binding = new WSHttpBinding();
                binding.Security.Mode = SecurityMode.Transport;
                // The clients of the service do not need to be
                // authenticated - since we are running over SSL
                binding.Security.Transport.ClientCredentialType =
              HttpClientCredentialType.None;
                Type contract = typeof(ExchangeService.ITradeService);
                ServiceHost host = new ServiceHost(typeof(TradeService));
                host.Open();
                Console.WriteLine("The WCF Management trading
               service is available.");
                Console.ReadKey();
        }
    }
}
```

Initially you will create a new URI and `WsHttpBinding` for your endpoint. It is important to know that the URI is an HTTPS endpoint—not an HTTP endpoint. This is to utilize SSL as a transport credential provider. Then you set the binding security credential as `Transport`. You are not requesting the client to authenticate over SSL. Therefore, you utilize `HttpClientCredentialType.None`. Finally, you specify the contract and then activate the service. Now you'll work on the client code.

3. You are not altering any code with the `WcfSimpleClient` project's `program.cs` file. You are utilizing the `App.config` file of the project to enhance the security. Therefore, the `App.config` file of the `WcfSimpleClient` project should be similar to Listing 7-3. (Please note that you are altering code only for the `TradeService` functions. The `TradeServiceMonitoring` functions are not altered as a result of this exercise. The code is similar, so we won't reiterate the same concepts. Therefore, we have deleted the monitoring code from the sample code for this chapter.)

Listing 7-3. `App.config` *File for the* `WcfSimpleClient` *Project*

```
<?xml version="1.0" encoding="utf-8"?>
<configuration>
  <system.serviceModel>
    <client>
```

```
      <endpoint
        address="https://localhost:8000/TradeService"
        binding="wsHttpBinding"
        bindingConfiguration="TradeWsHttpBinding"
        contract="ExchangeService.ITradeService"
        name="TradeServiceConfiguration" />

    </client>

    <bindings>
      <wsHttpBinding>
        <binding name="TradeWsHttpBinding">
          <security mode="Transport">
            <transport clientCredentialType="None"/>
          </security>
        </binding>
      </wsHttpBinding>
    </bindings>
  </system.serviceModel>
</configuration>
```

This is similar to the Chapter 6 `TradeService` configuration file. However, you have altered the binding information to facilitate transport security. You have declared a new `TradeWsHttpBinding` section to detail the binding information. This section details that you are utilizing `Transport` as the security mode and you are not requiring the client to authenticate against the service.

4. Compile and build the `TradeServiceHost` and `WcfSimpleClient` projects. Navigate to the service, and start the service first. You will see an image similar to Figure 7-1. Then start the client, and you will be presented with Figure 7-2. You will also view the `ClaimSet` activity in the service console. (This looks like Figure 7-3. However, the claim data will be different because you are utilizing transport-level security.)

The next step is to examine what message-level security provides in WCF.

Message-Level Security

Message-level security relies on the message itself to secure the communication. The authentication, authorization, integrity, and confidentiality are met using the message data. It does not rely on the transport mechanism to provide any security for it. The message mode provides an end-to-end security context for the enterprise. This also works well with multiple hops and multiple recipients. Since you are not relying on the transport layer, you can expand the message headers to implement multiple security assertions. This is a great tool to build federation services. Persistence of message headers will enable you to utilize integrity and confidentiality checks. You can also have rich claim support (in SAML, Custom Tokens, WS-Trust, and so on) in message-level security. You can utilize multiple authentication mechanisms at different gateways. However, the downside is the message can get considerably larger because of additional header information. Therefore, the throughput will be slower than transport-level security. Message-level security also provides mechanisms to authenticate and authorize both services and clients. You can also implement message-level security as utilizing binding by explicit coding or configuration files. What are the message credential types available in WCF? They are as follows:

None: There is no message-level security with the client and the service. Therefore, the user is anonymous.

Windows: The client uses Windows credentials in SOAP messages to authenticate with the service.

Username: The client needs to be authenticated using the username credentials. However, WCF does not provide any encryption to protect the username credentials.

Certificate: The client needs to be authenticated using an X.509 certificate.

Infocard: The client is required to be authenticated using Windows CardSpace—formally known as Infocard. This is discussed later in the "Windows CardSpace" section.

You'll now learn how to implement message-level security in WCF. You will modify the `TradeServiceHost` service to utilize a certificate to authenticate the service to the Windows runtime. You will call this certificate `localhost`. You will also use another certificate called `WCFUser` to authenticate the client to the service. Therefore, when the message leaves the client, it will be protected until it gets to the service machine's Windows runtime. You will use explicit code (as opposed to configuration files) in both the client and the service for this exercise. Here are the steps:

1. The first step is to create two certificates for `localhost` and `WCFUser`. Let's use `makecert.exe` to create these certificates:

   ```
   makecert.exe -sr CurrentUser -ss My -a sha1 -n CN=localhost -sky
   exchange  -pe
   certmgr.exe -add -r CurrentUser -s My -c -n localhost -r CurrentUser -s
   TrustedPeople
   ```

   This command will make a certificate called `localhost` in the store location `CurrentUser` and use the store name `My`. Then the following command adds the newly created certificate to the `TrustedPeople` container. These steps will ensure that you have a valid service certificate. The client will also be based on the local machine for the purposes of this example. Therefore, the following command will create the `WCFUser` certificate for the client to authenticate against the server:

   ```
   makecert.exe -sr CurrentUser -ss My-a sha1 -n CN=WCFUser -sky
   exchange  -pe
   certmgr.exe -add -r CurrentUser -s My -c -n WCFUser -r CurrentUser -s
   TrustedPeople
   ```

You can verify that the certificate is created without any errors by invoking the MMC console for certificates by selecting Start ➤ Run and typing **certmgr.msc** and pressing Enter. (Or you can select Start ➤ Run and type **mmc**. Then press Enter, and select Add Certificates snap in if the view is not available.) Your screen should look like Figure 7-5.

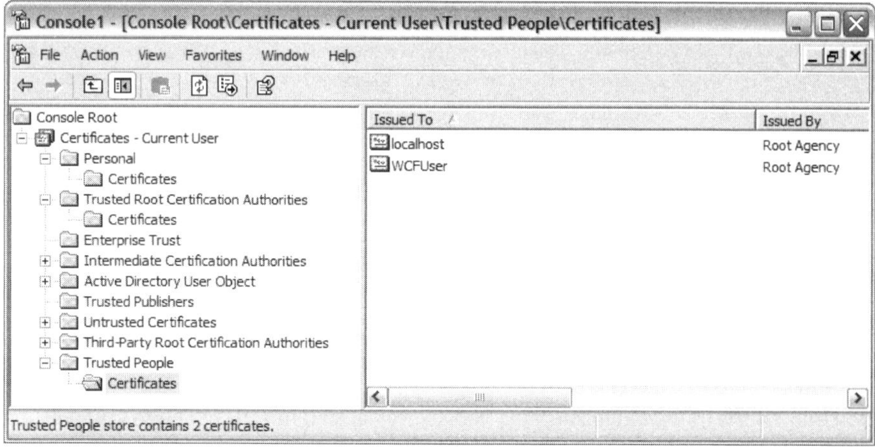

Figure 7-5. *Verifying certificates for the service and the client authentication*

Listing 7-4 shows the code for the `host.cs` file on `TradeServiceHost`.

Listing 7-4. `host.cs` *File of* `TradeServiceHost` *Project*

```
using System;
using System.Collections.Generic;
using System.ServiceModel;
using System.Text;
using System.Security.Cryptography.X509Certificates;

namespace ExchangeService
{
    public class Program
    {
        public static void Main(string[] args)
        {
                Uri address = new Uri("http://localhost:8001/TradeService");
                WSHttpBinding binding = new WSHttpBinding();
                // Set the security mode
                binding.Security.Mode = SecurityMode.Message;
                binding.Security.Message.ClientCredentialType =
                    MessageCredentialType.Certificate;
```

```
                Type contract = typeof(ExchangeService.ITradeService);
                ServiceHost host = new ServiceHost(typeof(TradeService));
                host.AddServiceEndpoint(contract, binding, address);
                //Set the service certificate.
                host.Credentials.ServiceCertificate.SetCertificate(
                    StoreLocation.CurrentUser,
                    StoreName.My,
                    X509FindType.FindBySubjectName,
                    "localhost");
                host.Open();
                Console.WriteLine("The WCF Management trading service
                 is available.");
                Console.ReadKey();
        }
    }
}
```

You need to import System.Security.Cryptography.X509Certificates into the code first. This is mandatory to utilize certificate-related functions. Then you will specify the client credential type as Certificate. Then you set the certificate for the service. You can use this certificate to authenticate against the Windows runtime to validate that the service has access to the business data. Therefore, even if an intruder hacks into the service, the intruder will not be able to access business information without the certificate information. You'll now see how the client is implemented.

2. Modify the program.cs file in the WcfSimpleClient project according to Listing 7-5.

Listing 7-5. *Client Code to Run* TradeServiceHost *Service*

```
using System;
using System.ServiceModel.Channels;
using System.ServiceModel;
using System.Security.Cryptography.X509Certificates;

namespace ExchangeService
{
    class Program
    {
        static void Main( string[] args )
        {
            EndpointAddress address =
                new EndpointAddress("http://localhost:8001/TradeService");
            WSHttpBinding binding = new WSHttpBinding();
            binding.Security.Mode = SecurityMode.Message;
            binding.Security.Message.ClientCredentialType =
                MessageCredentialType.Certificate;
```

```
            System.ServiceModel.ChannelFactory<ITradeService> cf =
                new ChannelFactory<ITradeService>(binding,address);
            cf.Credentials.ClientCertificate.SetCertificate(
                StoreLocation.CurrentUser,
                StoreName.My,
                X509FindType.FindBySubjectName,
                "WCFUser");
            cf.Credentials.ServiceCertificate.SetDefaultCertificate(
                StoreLocation.CurrentUser,
                StoreName.My,
                X509FindType.FindBySubjectName,
                "localhost");
            ITradeService proxy = cf.CreateChannel();

        //.... The rest of the code is unchanged.
        }
    }
}
```

The code is similar to service code. You will initially set the security mode as `Message`. Then you inform the runtime that the clients will be using certificates to authenticate themselves. Then you set the `WCFUser` certificate credentials. You use the `SetCertificate` method that specifies the `StoreLocation` and `StoreName` and ask the certificate to be found using the subject name. This certificate will give all the information a client will need to present to the server to authenticate. Then you try to set the server's certificate. Please remember the service needs to authenticate itself to the Windows runtime. This certificate information can be available only to a valid client. Therefore, you minimize the risk of an intruder getting access to the service by presenting a single compromised client certificate under this design (that is, the client needs to know both the client and server certificate information to gain access to the service).

3. The `App.config` file for both the service and the client is simple. They have to only define the endpoint of the `TradeService` since you have implemented the security settings in the code. Compile and build the service and the client. First run the service and then the client. You should view images that are similar to Figure 7-1, Figure 7-2, and Figure 7-3.

It is also beneficial to analyze the messages that travel between the service and the client. You will be able to view the encrypted message data using `SvcTraceView.exe`. (Please consult Chapter 6 to learn about `SvcTraceViewer.exe`, how to implement it, and its location.) This view will enable the user to analyze every message that transfers between the client and the service. This will enhance your knowledge regarding the "under-the-covers" WCF implementation to facilitate message-level security. (Figure 7-6 illustrates how the certificate claim set in the message header was understood by the server authentication system.) The next step is to learn about mixed mode security.

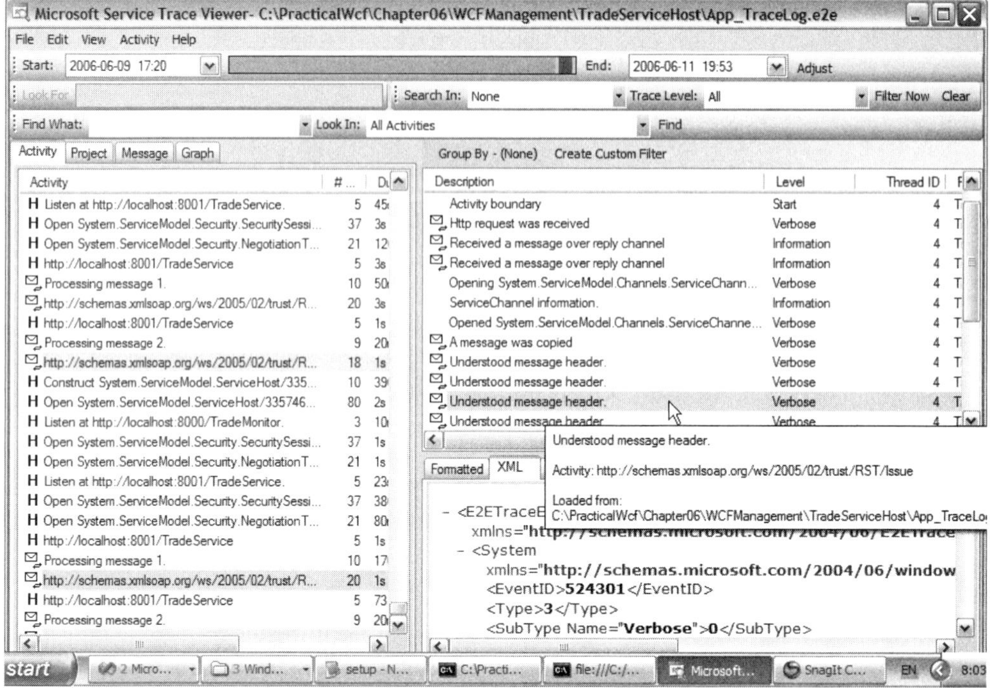

Figure 7-6. *Using* `SvcTraceView.exe` *to analyze message-level security*

Mixed Mode

Transport mode credentials are faster than message level. However, they have limited credential types (like no SAML tokens). The message-level security has a richer set of credentials. However, because of XML serialization and deserialization, they are slower than transport mode. Will it be possible to have a rich set of claims and at the same time be optimized to the wire? WCF does offer this flexibility, called *mixed mode*. Mixed mode offers the rich claims and federation advantages message-level offers. It supports multifactor authentication using rich credentials. You can also use custom tokens in mixed mode. Therefore, mixed mode offers a secure and fast option to transmit data between services and clients.

Mixed mode will perform the integrity and confidentiality at the transport level. The authentication and the authorization takes place at the message level. You can use the `TransportWithMessageCredential` property (refer to Figure 7-4) to specify mixed mode with the `binding.Security.Mode` setting. It is simple to implement mixed code. The service code will be similar to Listing 7-6.

Listing 7-6. *Implementing Mixed Mode in the Service*

```
using System;
using System.Collections.Generic;
using System.ServiceModel;
using System.Text;
using System.Security.Cryptography.X509Certificates;
```

```
namespace ExchangeService
{
    public class Program
    {
        public static void Main(string[] args)
        {
                Uri address = new Uri("https://localhost:8001/TradeService");
                WSHttpBinding binding = new WSHttpBinding();
                // Set the security mode
                binding.Security.Mode = SecurityMode.TransportWithMessageCredential;
                binding.Security.Message.ClientCredentialType =
                    MessageCredentialType.Certificate;

                Type contract = typeof(ExchangeService.ITradeService);
                ServiceHost host = new ServiceHost(typeof(TradeService));
                host.AddServiceEndpoint(contract, binding, address);
                // The rest of the code is the same
```

It is important to note that the URL is HTTPS. You are relying on SSL for integrity and confidentiality. Then you set the security mode to `TransportWithMessageCredential` and dictate that the client must authenticate using a certificate to gain access to the service. The `program.cs` file of the `WcfSimpleClient` will look like Listing 7-7.

Listing 7-7. *Client Code for Mixed Mode Security*

```
using System.Net
namespace ExchangeService
{
    class Program
    {
        static void Main( string[] args )
        {
            ServicePointManager.ServerCertificateValidationCallback =
                delegate(Object obj, X509Certificate certificate,
                X509Chain chain, SslPolicyErrors errors)
                { return true;
                    // Need to implement company specific validations
                };

            EndpointAddress address =
                new EndpointAddress("https://localhost:8001/TradeService");
            WSHttpBinding binding = new WSHttpBinding();
            binding.Security.Mode =
                SecurityMode.TransportWithMessageCredential;
            binding.Security.Message.ClientCredentialType =
                MessageCredentialType.Certificate;
```

```
System.ServiceModel.ChannelFactory<ITradeService> cf =
    new ChannelFactory<ITradeService>(binding,address);
cf.Credentials.ClientCertificate.SetCertificate(
    StoreLocation.CurrentUser,
    StoreName.My,
    X509FindType.FindByThumbprint,
    "43 5d 98 05 7b a1 73 87 66 ca 89 a1 ae 0e 3c 76 2c 12 2b 95");
```

You need to inform the client to initiate the SSL session with the service first. You do this by utilizing the `ServicePointManager.ServerCertificateValidationCallback` delegate. This delegate will initialize the SSL connection. The implementation of this delegate can be different from company to company. (That is, every organization will have a different matrix to validate their digital claims. Usually the code will check for a `CN=CompanyName` entry.) Therefore, you have returned `true` for the purpose of this example. Then you set the security mode and set the client certificate. This time you are using the `FindByThumbprint` function (as opposed to `FindByName`). You can derive the thumbprints from accessing the properties of the certificate. Build the server and client, and your output should be similar to Figures 7-1, 7-2, and 7-3.

Do you need to authenticate and authorize every time you send a SOAP message to the server? Doesn't this consume valuable resources to verify the identity of the sender when the sender has already established their identity using claims? Yes, you can counter this scenario in WCF. It is commonly referred to as *secure sessions*.

A secure session is established when the first call is made from the client to the server. The client will initially present the credentials to the service to authenticate. The service will create a special token that will be inserted into the SOAP header to keep track of the client's credentials. The subsequent requests from the client will present this special token to the service to gain access to the service. Please view Listing 7-7 in `SvcTraceViewer.exe`, and navigate through the messages between the client and the server. You will find this token information in the header of the SOAP message.

We have discussed security mainly on point-to-point client and service scenarios. However, large enterprises employ thousands of employees. Certificates are commonly used to authenticate these employees. Does this mean every employee needs to know all the other employees' certificate information to send a message to one of them? What happens when one enterprise merges with another enterprise? Does the enterprise A employee need to know all the enterprise B certificate details? You can use federated credentials to address this issue in WCF.

Federated Security Model in WCF

The concept of federated credentials is important in the modern age of distributed computing. It means you can delegate the "verification" of a claim to a third party. The third party will in return give you a key that you can use to communicate with a service. The third party (commonly referred to as the *broker* or *security token service*) has a trust relationship with the service. Therefore, whenever a client comes with a certified credential from the broker, the service will trust the client's credentials. Figure 7-7 explains this scenario further.

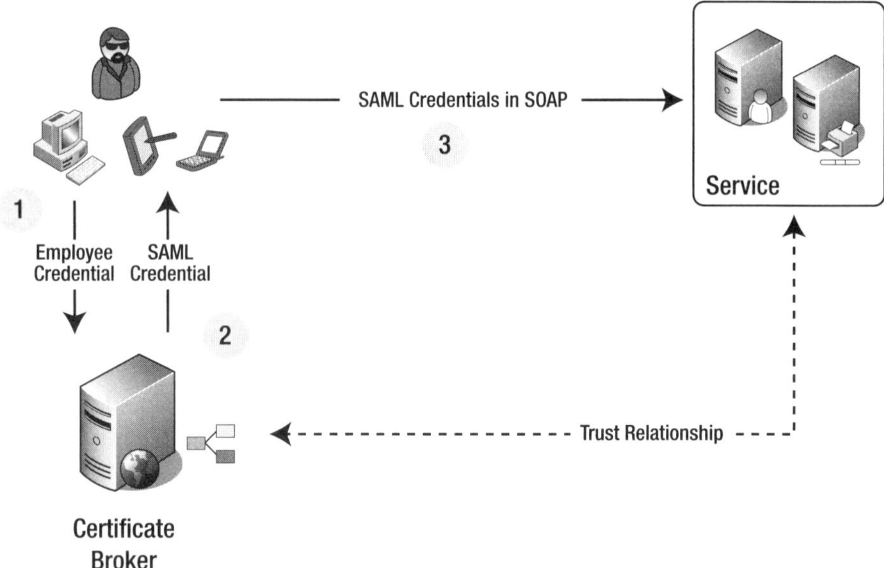

Figure 7-7. *Federated credentials in action*

You are assuming the client employee is using a certificate in this scenario. The employee may use multiple devices (such as a computer, PDA device, and so on) to make a request of a service that is part of an external enterprise. The employee will first liaise with the certificate broker by providing the employee certificate stating his intentions of consuming the service. The broker will analyze the certificate and confirm its authenticity. Then the broker will issue an SAML-based credential set to the user to communicate with the service. This SAML token is signed with the special key from the broker to validate the token. This key is known only to the service that the employee is attempting to consume.

The client uses the SAML token in the request SOAP message header to send a request to the service. The service will analyze the SAML token and verify it is from a known certificate broker to the service (that is, using the special key from the broker). The service will check the trust relationship between the service and the certificate broker and proceed with the client request.

Federated credentials play a key role in future security implementations. You can use the flexibility of proving one set of credentials to a user (that is, certificate by the client) and converting it to another set of credentials (an SAML token) in many scenarios to add value to the customers. You also have the flexibility of altering your internal security mechanisms. (That is, the client can provide a username password pair to replace the certificate.) However, your external implementation of the claims will not be changed. The broker will still create the same SAML token with the username-password pair. You do this by utilizing `WSFederationHttpBinding` in WCF. In the next section, you will investigate authorization.

Authorization in WCF

How can you authorize users in WCF? What is the difference between authentication and authorization in the first place? You should also take this opportunity to investigate some of the .NET Framework offerings to handle authentication and authorization. You'll first investigate the fundamentals of the .NET application security model.

■ **Note** The .NET Framework offers a rich set of APIs (based in the `IPrincipal` interface) to manage authentication and authorization. The objective is to create a specialized, static (once only) `Principal` object after the Active Directory authentication is approved. This `Principal` object will securely live on the client's desktop and attend authorization requests during the life span of the user session. The authorization and authentication are provided by different providers. This provider information is usually based in configuration files. The objective is to seamlessly transfer the user context from one authorization or authentication provider without any code changes. This is the best practice in the industry. It is important to note that WCF explicitly does not address authentication and authorization. What WCF does is evaluate claims and authenticate and authorize these claim sets utilizing .NET Framework to satisfy the security requirements.

IPrincipal Interface

The cornerstones of the .NET security models are the `IPrincipal` interfaces. The developers will build an object that extends `IPrincipal` (usually called `Principal`) to incorporate the authentication and authorization information regarding a specific user. So, what is the difference between authentication and authorization?

> *Authentication*: This is the process of identifying users. This is commonly performed by requesting a username-password pair or a certificate to verify the authenticity of the user. (Who is the user? Can you identify him as a manager in your system?)

> *Authorization*: Authorization happens after authentication. Authorization addresses the question, what does the user have access to after the authentication? Therefore, the user is already known to the Windows runtime, but what can the user access in the system? For example, does the user have delete access for a purchase order if the user logs in as a Manager role?

Authentication is mainly performed by API calls to Active Directory. Active Directory will return with a confirmation of the identity or deny the access to the system. The authorization details in most cases have to be explicitly coded. Authorization in .NET is based on roles. (For example, the SeniorManager role can delete the purchase orders as opposed to the Manager role, which is not entitled for the same privilege.) Therefore, before you delete a purchase order, you need to check whether the currently logged in user has the SeniorManager role attached to his profile. You do this by utilizing the `IsInRole` function. The code is similar to the following code. This code queries whether the currently logged in user has the SeniorManager role to proceed to delete the purchase order:

```
Using System;
Using System.Threading;
if (Thread.CurrentPrincipal.IsInRole("SeniorManager"))
{
    // Code to delete purchase order
}
```

You can also utilize .NET Framework security to force the runtime to authorize entities at the function level. The following code snippet will demand the permissions you need to check before the user can execute the function. This is an alternative to the `IsInRole` feature of .NET Framework.

```
using System.Security.Permissions;
...
[PrincipalPermission(SecurityAction.Demand, Role="SeniorManager")]
public bool DeletePurchaseorder()
{
    // Code to delete purchase order.
}
```

It is important to understand the basics of authentication and authorization to grasp the security concepts in WCF and the .NET Framework. You'll now learn how to implement authorization in WCF security. Here are the steps:

1. The first step is to add the authorization information to the `ExchangeService` module. You have not enforced any authorization check to the code until now. You have relied on the Windows authentication models to authenticate the user. As soon as the authentication is valid, the client has been able to extract the stock prices from the service. Let's tie authorization to the user's Windows credentials. Let's assume you are going to restrict the access to the `TradeService` function only to administrators for the purposes of this example. Therefore, any other user who is not part of the Administrator group will not be able to access the service. Code this logic into `ExchangeService`, as illustrated in Listing 7-8. The code explicitly instructs the .NET runtime to check whether the user has the Administrator role.

Listing 7-8. `ExchangeService` *Code to Include Authorization*

```
using System;
using System.ServiceModel;
using System.Security.Permissions;

namespace ExchangeService
{
```

```
// Same code as before

public class TradeService : ITradeService, ITradeMonitor
{
    const double IBM_Price = 80.50D;
    const double MSFT_Price = 30.25D;

    // Invokers must belong to the Administrator group.
    [PrincipalPermission(SecurityAction.Demand,
    Role = "Administrators")]
    public double TradeSecurity(string ticker, int quantity)
    {
        Console.WriteLine("Claim made at " + System.DateTime.Now.TimeOfDay);
        System.ServiceModel.OperationContext opx;
        opx = OperationContext.Current;
    // Same code as before
```

2. Now you'll create the service. Add a new project to the `WCFSecurity` solution by right-clicking the `WCFSecurity` solution and then selecting Add ➤ New Project. Call it `AuthAuditHost`. (Note that we will use the same project to illustrate auditing in the next section.) The code will be similar to Listing 7-9.

Listing 7-9. *Code for the* `host.cs` *File of the* `AuthAuditHost` *Project*

```
using System;
using System.ServiceModel;
using System.ServiceModel.Description;

namespace ExchangeService
{
    public class Program
    {
        public static void Main(string[] args)
        {
            Uri address = new Uri("http://localhost:8001/TradeService");
            WSHttpBinding binding = new WSHttpBinding();
            Type contract = typeof(ExchangeService.ITradeService);
            ServiceHost host = new ServiceHost(typeof(TradeService));
            host.AddServiceEndpoint(contract, binding, address);
            host.Open();
            Console.WriteLine("The WCF Management trading service is available.");
            Console.ReadKey();
        }
    }
}
```

3. Create the client now. Create a new console application called `AuthAuditClient`, and add it to the `WCFSecurity` solution. (Right-click the `WCFSecurity` solution, and select Add ➤ New Project.) The code will be similar to Listing 7-10. You have added some exception management code to address the exceptions that arise if the user does not have the Administrator role.

Listing 7-10. *Code for the* `program.cs` *File of the* `AuthAuditClient` *Project*

```
using System;
using System.ServiceModel.Channels;
using System.ServiceModel;

namespace ExchangeService
{
    class Program
    {
        static void Main( string[] args )
        {
            EndpointAddress address =
               new EndpointAddress("http://localhost:8001/TradeService");
            WSHttpBinding binding = new WSHttpBinding();
            System.ServiceModel.ChannelFactory<ITradeService> cf =
                new ChannelFactory<ITradeService>(binding, address);
            ITradeService proxy = cf.CreateChannel();

            Console.WriteLine("\nTrade IBM");
            try
            {
                double result = proxy.TradeSecurity("IBM", 1000);
                Console.WriteLine("Cost was " + result);
                Console.WriteLine("\nTrade MSFT");
                result = proxy.TradeSecurity("MSFT", 2000);
                Console.WriteLine("Cost was " + result);
            }
            catch (Exception ex)
            {
                Console.Write("Can not perform task. Error Message -
                " + ex.Message);
            }
            Console.WriteLine("\n\nPress <enter> to exit...");
            Console.ReadLine();
        }
    }
}
```

4. Now execute the service, and then run the application. Your screen should be similar to Figure 7-1. You are currently logged in as an user who is part of the Administrator group. Therefore, when you execute the client, you should get a screen that looks like Figure 7-8.

```
C:\PracticalWcf\Chapter07\WCFSecurity\AuthAuditClient\bin\Debug\AuthAuditClient.exe

Trade IBM
Cost was 80500

Trade MSFT
Cost was 60500

Press <enter> to exit...
```

Figure 7-8. `AuthAuditClient` *running under an Administrator account*

We'll now show how to run this client under a different account without administrator access. We have created a user account called `chris` without any administrator access. Use the following `runas` command to run the client:

```
runas /noprofile /user:local\chris AuthAuditClient.exe
```

This command will execute `AuthAuditClient.exe` as the `chris` account. You don't need to load the user profile in this case. Therefore, you use the `/noprofile` flag. You will be asked to enter the password for the `chris` account. When the password is validated, the client will run under the new account (`chris`). Your screen should look like Figure 7-9.

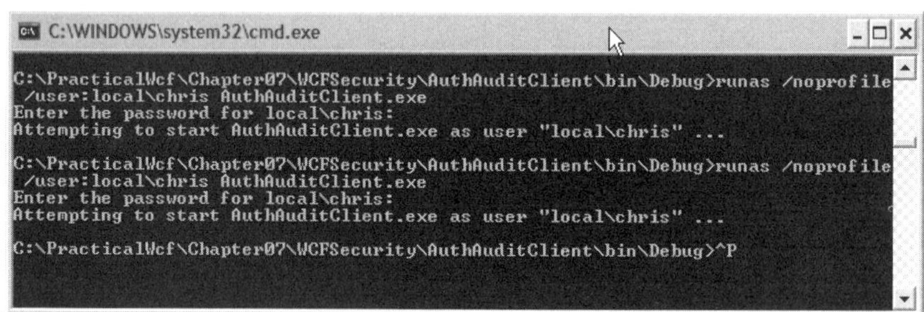

Figure 7-9. *Using the* `runas` *command to execute the client under a different account*

Since the `chris` account is not part of the Administrator group (and does not have a role to reflect it in his Windows profile), you should see the screen shown in Figure 7-10, which denies access to the service.

```
AuthAuditClient.exe (running as local\chris)
Trade IBM
Can not perform task. Error Message - Access is denied.
Press <enter> to exit...
```

Figure 7-10. *Access denied for users who do not have the correct roles*

Authorization Options for One-Way Communications

What happens when the message is only one-way? Is there a requirement to authorize the sender at the receiver's end? Does WCF support this functionality? WCF implements mechanisms that do not require any negotiation between the client and service. WCF supports a one-shot, or non-negotiated, security mode for this purpose. To support one-shot security mode, you will set the flag `negotiateServiceCredential="false"` at the message level. However, you need to provide the valid credentials to authenticate the request. This will ensure the message initiated from a trusted source even when the authorization is ignored at the service end. The following configuration snippet illustrates this feature:

```
<bindings>
  <wsHttpBinding>
    <binding name="test">
      <security mode="Message">
        <message negotiateServiceCredential="false"
               clientCredentialType="Certificate"/>
      </security>
    </binding>
  </wsHttpBinding>
</bindings>
<behaviors>
  <behavior name="credentialConfig">
    <clientCredentials>
      <!-- Other configuration not shown. -->
      <serviceCertificate storeLocation="CurrentUser" storeName="My"
      x509FindType="FindBySubjectDistinguishedName"
      findValue="localhost"/>
    </clientCredentials>
  </behavior>
</behaviors>
```

WCF also implements multiple membership providers to assist developers to integrate to Active Directory, LDAP, and custom directory structures. You can also create your own providers to suit specialized scenarios. WCF also ships with multiple role provider classes that will reduce developer effort.

You have investigated the WCF security model, authentication, and authorization in detail. Is there a way to track these security-related features and their impact? Does WCF offer any "auditing" mechanisms to trace and monitor security activities? You'll investigate this feature in the next section.

Auditing for Security Features in WCF

WCF has a rich set of utilities to address security auditing. It leverages the Event Viewer extensively to record any security-related events. You also have access to a rich set of APIs that will enable you to directly communicate with the Event Viewer. Let's examine how you can leverage Event Viewer now. You will enhance `AuthAuditHost` to record all the security events to the Event Viewer. Listing 7-11 shows the code for the modified `host.cs` file of `AuthAuditHost`.

Listing 7-11. *Enabling Auditing for the Service*

```
using System;
using System.ServiceModel;
using System.ServiceModel.Description;

namespace ExchangeService
{
    public class Program
    {
        public static void Main(string[] args)
        {
            Uri address = new Uri("http://localhost:8001/TradeService");
            WSHttpBinding binding = new WSHttpBinding();
            Type contract = typeof(ExchangeService.ITradeService);
            ServiceHost host = new ServiceHost(typeof(TradeService));
            host.AddServiceEndpoint(contract, binding, address);

            // Add Auditing to the service
            ServiceSecurityAuditBehavior auditProvider =
                host.Description.Behaviors.Find<ServiceSecurityAuditBehavior>();
            if (auditProvider == null)
            {
                auditProvider = new ServiceSecurityAuditBehavior();
            }
            auditProvider.AuditLogLocation = AuditLogLocation.Application;
            auditProvider.MessageAuthenticationAuditLevel =
                AuditLevel.SuccessOrFailure;
            auditProvider.ServiceAuthorizationAuditLevel =
                AuditLevel.SuccessOrFailure;
```

```
            host.Description.Behaviors.Add(auditProvider);
            host.Open();
            Console.WriteLine("The WCF Management trading service is available.");
            Console.ReadKey();
        }
    }
}
```

Auditing is available in WCF using `ServiceSecurityAuditBehavior` from the `System.ServiceModel.Description` namespace. First, you will check whether the audit provider is available in the current context. If it doesn't already exist, then you create an audit provider using the `ServiceSecurityAuditBehavior` class. Next, you specify the audit location. This can be either the application or the security log. Choose the application log for this example. Then you can specify the audit level. The available levels are `success`, `failure`, or both `success and failure`. For this example, you have chosen the `success and failure` option. You can set these levels utilizing the `MessageAuthenticationAuditLevel` and `ServiceAuthorizationAuditLevel` properties for the message. Therefore, all the auditing information regarding messages and server authorization will be recorded on the server's application log. Finally, you add the audit provider to the service.

Now run the service and then the client. Let's check whether the information is available in the event log. Choose Start ➤ My Computer ➤ Manage ➤ System Tools ➤ Event Viewer, or choose Start ➤ Run ➤ Eventvwr.exe. Look under the application log under the event log, as shown in Figure 7-11.

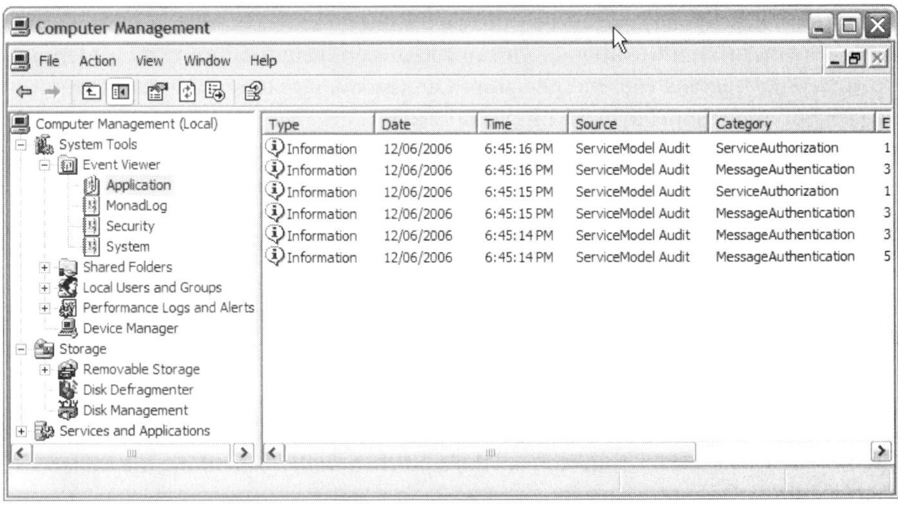

Figure 7-11. *Application log entries for the* `AuthAuditHost` *service*

Let's look at one log entry to verify the details. Your screen should be similar to Figure 7-12. This entry describes a successful authorization call made by the `AuthAuditClient` instance.

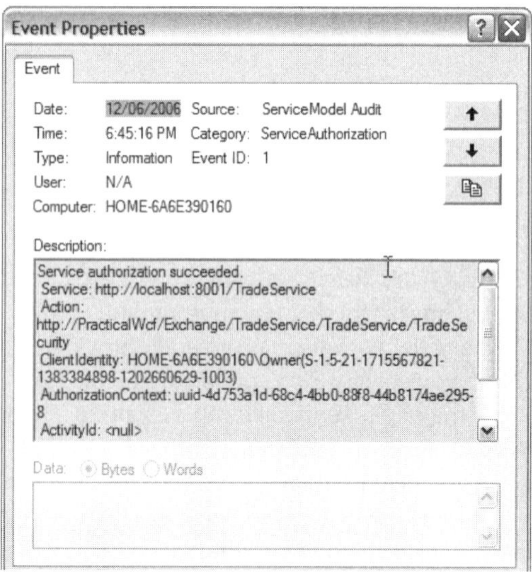

Figure 7-12. *Audit log entry that illustrates successful authorization by* `AuthAuditClient`

You are familiar with WCF authentication, authorization, and auditing concepts. However, how do you manage your identity in a distributed environment? Is it fair to conclude that the identities are all scattered over a public network such as the Internet? Some of our traces of information are stored in Amazon accounts. You might also have a .NET Passport identity to sign on to your Hotmail account. Are you also an avid buyer and seller on eBay? Is there a way you can leverage all these identities at once? Or can you present your "platinum" eBay identity to convince Amazon to upgrade your membership? Can you manage them centrally? Does WCF offer a programming model to make this vision reality?

Windows CardSpace

Windows CardSpace (formally known as Infocard) is a specialized metaidentity system that helps you manage multiple identities. Let's take an everyday example. You use your driver's license to prove you are a valid driver on the road. How do you prove this to a suspecting police officer who inquires about it? You show them a valid driver's license *card*. In addition, you use a card to prove to a bank teller (or an automatic teller machine) that you have the correct credentials to withdraw money. Basically, you use different physical cards to accommodate different situations. However, you need a mechanism to manage all the cards every day. A common practice in real life is to store all the cards in a wallet. Therefore, the wallet becomes your identity metasystem in everyday life.

You can use the same concept in distributed computing. The .NET Passport system has provided an e-mail and password to validate you. This is similar to the bank providing a card to withdraw cash. Similarly, your employees will give the administration digital signature that proves they are legitimate employees of the company. How do you store all these identities and extract them on demand to facilitate your needs? The answer lies in Windows CardSpace. Windows CardSpace is an identity metasystem that handles multiple identities for you.

What are cards, and how many types of cards does CardSpace support? A *card* is a digitally signed entity that illustrates the user's claims to a system. In general, two types of cards exist. The first one is the personal card. The user can issue these cards to herself. This is similar to picking an e-mail address and a password for a Passport account. The second type is the provider card. This is provided by a trusted third party. These cannot be issued by the user. This is similar to a bank card that is given to you by the bank.

How Does Windows CardSpace Work?

How does CardSpace work? You may remember that your bank card has a magnetic strip on the back of it. This stores your claims to the bank system. Windows CardSpace works the same. CardSpace converts your personal or provider cards to special tokens and validates their authenticity on demand. Different card types can use different tokens for this validations. Personal cards use SAML 1.1 token types by default. However, provider card tokens are subject to an organization's technology preferences.

■ Note It is important to note that CardSpace is based on the WS-Trust specification. Windows CardSpace can use SAML tokens to validate the user claims. However, it is not restricted to SAML tokens. It can use any custom token algorithm as long the server can validate the credentials. It is also important to understand that the Windows CardSpace is the Microsoft implementation of an identity metasystem. There are other identity metasystems based on other software platforms. Currently, CardSpace is available only on the Windows XP SP2, Windows Server 2003 SP1, and Windows Vista operating systems.

So, what is the difference between Passport and CardSpace? Microsoft .NET Passport is one identity system that enables access to multiple Microsoft resources. Passport's single identity system fits well into the metaidentity system of CardSpace. Microsoft has also indicated that a metaidentity system that supports multiple identities is more scalable than attempting to dominate the world with a single identity system (such as Passport). CardSpace is already supported by a Java toolkit from Ping Identity (a major player in the identity space). Therefore, you can utilize multiple identities on heterogeneous platforms to validate identities with CardSpace.

How do you know whether you have CardSpace available on your system? How can you set up cards that can be used by WCF for authentication purposes? You can verify the CardSpace availability by navigating to Start ➤ Control Panel. You should have an icon called Digital Identities. Your screen should be similar to Figure 7-13.

When you double-click the icon, you will see a wizard that will assist you in creating personal cards and exporting provider cards. This interface acts as a container for all your identity needs. Now you'll learn how to use CardSpace in WCF.

Figure 7-13. *Checking whether you have CardSpace available on your system*

Enabling Windows CardSpace in WCF

CardSpace is one of the client credential types in WCF. CardSpace is used as an authentication mechanism on the client side. The server receives a token that summarizes the claims in the personal or provider card. However, the service side must authenticate itself using an X.509 certificate to verify the authenticity. (In other words, since you rely on a foreign token, you need to make sure you have valid credentials at the server side to execute the service.) Therefore, the configuration file will be similar to Listing 7-12.

Listing 7-12. *Service Application Configuration File for CardSpace Support*

```
<?xml version="1.0" ?>
<configuration>
    <system.serviceModel>
    <services>
            <service type="ExchangeService.TradeService"
                <endpoint address="http://localhost:8000/TradeMonitor"
                    binding="wsFederationBinding"
                    bindingConfiguration="wsBinding"
                    contract="ExchangeService.ITradeMonitor">
                    <identity>
                        <certificateReference findValue="localhost"
                            storeLocation="LocalMachine"
                            storeName="TrustedPeople"
                            x509FindType="FindBySubjectName" />
                    </identity>
                </endpoint>
            </service>
        </services>
    </system.serviceModel>
```

```
    <wsHttpBinding>
        <binding configurationName="wsBinding">
            <security mode="Message">
                <message clientCredentialType="IssuedToken" />
            </security>
        </binding>
    </wsHttpBinding>
</configuration>
```

You will use the `localhost` certificate to authenticate the service to the server runtime. CardSpace also utilizes the message-level security. The client credential type you use to utilize CardSpace is called `IssuedToken`. The client configuration file is similar to the server configuration file. The client credential type will be `IssuedToken`, and you need to make sure you set the server certificate properly. When the service is built and running, you can execute the client instance. When the client instance runs for the first time, Figure 7-14 will appear. This is a confirmation request by the Windows CardSpace instance to proceed to choose a card to communicate with the service. You can navigate through the wizards and select the appropriate card to use.

Then you can select the CardSpace controller you prefer to use to communicate with the service. The Windows runtime will then create a special token that embeds the user's claims and sends it to the service to validate the claims. Figure 7-15 shows the dialog box that requests the user to select one of his cards to submit to the service.

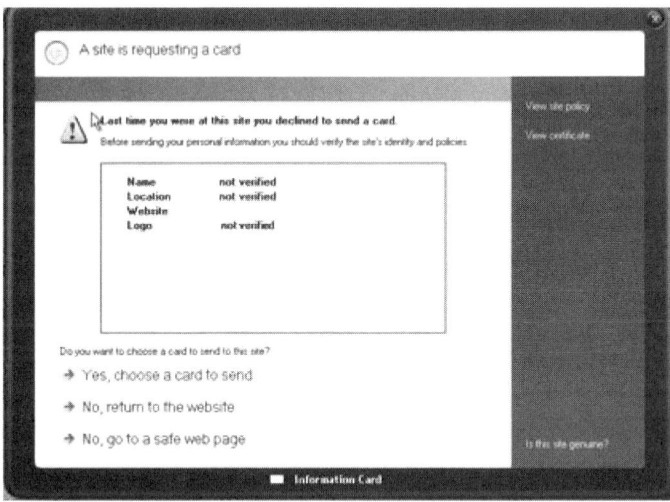

Figure 7-14. *Windows CardSpace request dialog box*

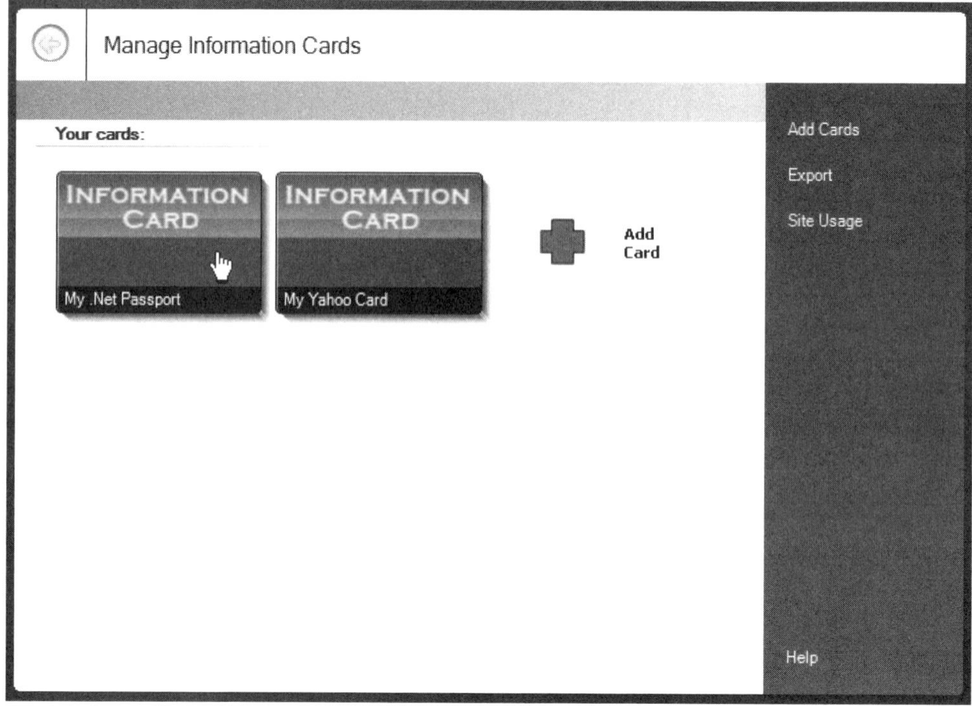

Figure 7-15. *Selecting a CardSpace card to authenticate against the service*

Summary

You learned the essentials of WCF security in this chapter. We discussed the following concepts in detail:

- WCF security is based on four important concepts: authentication, authorization, integrity, and confidentiality.
- You can utilize WCF security at the transport layer, message layer, or at both the transport and message layer (mixed). These are commonly referred to as *modes*.
- Transport-layer security depends on the transport (specifically, SSL) to protect the communication between the client and the service. This method is faster. However, the credential types supported in WCF are limited (in other words, no rich SAML tokens). The messages can also be vulnerable in the recipient's domain after the messages leave the SSL gateway.
- Message-level security is slower than transport mode. However, the developers can use a rich set of credentials. Message mode will guarantee the message will get to the receiver without being exposed at transport level. Therefore, it supports *n*-ton security.
- Mixed mode supports integrity and confidentiality at the transport layer. Authentication and authorization are achieved at the message layer.

- WCF also supports federated claims and Windows CardSpace. WCF uses CardSpace as a client credential type. Both personal cards and provider cards are supported.
- WCF also enables authorization at the Windows level and will support multiple membership providers as role providers. It also supports a comprehensive auditing and tracing API.

Now you are familiar with the security features of WCF. The next chapter discusses reliable messaging and how it is implemented in WCF. Reliable messaging is an important concept in distributed computing. It will enable reliable communication channels between multiple enterprises (on heterogeneous platforms) with failover mechanisms.

CHAPTER 8

Implementing Reliable Messaging and Queue-Based Communications

WCF helps you implement reliable communications over an infrastructure that might be unreliable. Application infrastructure is prone to failure. Network connectivity often breaks, services might not always be available, or messages get lost. WCF provides you with the functionality to overcome these limitations in the infrastructure.

You will learn in this chapter how to ensure reliable communication in a distributed environment where the application endpoints might be available only intermittently. Reliable messaging in WCF helps developers solve a number of challenges that have plagued them for many years. You will learn about the following in this chapter:

- The need for reliable messaging
- Challenges in implementing reliable messaging
- Reliable sessions
- Queuing support in WCF
- How to integrate with legacy applications using MSMQ

Let's consider our QuickReturns Ltd. scenario. Say you decide to sell a stock that has declared a loss. You put in your order to sell. However, the message never reaches the trading application, and the stock loses more value before you realize what has happened. This could potentially cost you thousands of dollars. Alternatively, say you put in a buy order, which may accidentally be sent multiple times. This can occur for a number of reasons, prime amongst them being the lack of an acknowledgment from the receiving end. You could end up buying stocks that you didn't really plan to buy. Further, say you want to apply the proceeds of the sale of one stock to buy a second stock. The message to buy goes through, but the sell message fails. This can cause a lot of problems in your portfolio.

You could also experience network-related issues. For example, say the network is clogged by buy/sell orders, and the router is overcome. Or say the wireless connection on your laptop blinks, and your order does not go through. Moreover, since the application is working over the Internet, the congestion is completely out of anyone's control and can result in messages being lost, causing you a real monetary loss. All of these scenarios are real and problematic and need to be addressed successfully to achieve reliability.

Reliable messaging helps overcome some of these issues since WCF also tracks the liveliness of the available resources. This helps both the reliability and the scalability aspects of your application. An additional piece of functionality that reliability offers you is a network adaptive rate of sending messages. In other words, WCF monitors the network congestion and will either speed up or slow down the rates at which messages flow across the network, thus providing a pseudo load-balancing functionality.

Let's dive into the implementation of reliable messaging in WCF.

The Need for Reliable Messaging

Why should you be excited about reliable messaging? It certainly does not seem at first to be cool, interesting, or even something to get mildly excited about.

Providing reliability to messages has been somewhat of a nightmare in distributed applications irrespective of the transport. A lot of issues are associated with it. For example, the servers or a network connection might not be available. Even worse, the connection itself might be disrupted for reasons that are not readily predictable. As the developer and architect, you must design around these issues. If you look at the concepts of SOA in general, a key requirement that really should be the fifth tenet of SOA is reliability. (Please refer to Chapter 1 for the four tenets of SOA.) It is of little value to have an architecture that does not provide reliability at its core for message communications.

Reliable messaging in the context of SOA guarantees that a message will actually be received at the destination. To do this, you need to ensure that a destination is available. In the SOA world, this option does not exist since you might not control the destination. In the scenario of reliable messaging, you need to compensate for the fact that messages may not arrive at the destination as intended because of unforeseen and unknown reasons. Hence, you need to hold on to the message until the destination is available and the entire message has in fact passed successfully. Finally, should something go wrong, you need to detect that an error has occurred, recover from it, and then resend the message, which will then be reprocessed. This has been extremely difficult to do in the past, and when a custom implementation has been delivered, it has been prohibitively expensive to implement and maintain.

Therefore, software industry leaders including Microsoft, IBM, BEA, and TIBCO created the WS-ReliableMessaging standard. This addresses the problem of being able to allow messages to be delivered reliably between applications despite failures within software components, networks, or systems. You accomplish this by standardizing on the SOAP and WSDL requirements to identify the application endpoints and bindings.

WCF allows for reliable messaging in a web service environment by facilitating that messages are delivered only once (in other words, no duplicates) and in order. However, since the standard for message queues is not in place across the industry, Microsoft decided to build this capability on top of MSMQ, which provides a buffer mechanism between the client and the service and in essence decouples them. However, reliable messaging can also be something of a misnomer since it does not provide for durability, unless you consider MSMQ as the container.

For example, if the server application is down for a period of time longer than the timeout defined in the client application, the message will indeed never be delivered. Or if you persist messages to a durable store—that is, you write these to the disk on the client side but no such strategy exists on the server side—there really is no reliability. Although the implementation does in fact take into account the requirements for reliability, at least for version 1 of WCF, there is no real support for durability. The WS-ReliableMessaging specification specifies only that the receiving endpoint is required to send an acknowledgment that the message has indeed been received.

Despite these limitations, in the scenario that both ends of the application—that is, the client endpoint and the server endpoint—are indeed up and running, reliable messaging offers you a host of advantages. The failures at the transport level are overcome, more often than not without writing a single line of additional code.

Challenges of Implementing Reliable Messaging

Implementing reliable messaging has multiple challenges. We'll broadly categorize them into communication issues and processing issues. More often than not, these are interrelated challenges that are nontrivial in nature to solve.

Communication Issues

Communication issues typically revolve around the physical transport. In a service-oriented world, the quality of the communication layer is often not within our control. The main communication issues are the following:

Network issues: The actual physical network is not available. So, what happens to your messages? Do you compensate for this? How do you compensate for this? The server is down or the router is struggling to cope with high levels of network congestion.

Connection drops: You send the message; however, the connection to the destination is lost before the message arrives at the destination. How do you detect the drop, and more important, how do you recover from this? In this scenario, say your machine has the network cable unplugged or the wireless card on the laptop momentarily blinks. Prior to WCF, the messages would be lost, unless of course you had envisioned this and written lots of code to overcome the scenario.

Lost messages: This is much like the load of laundry that loses one sock. You don't know what happened to your message. You sent it, the network was available, and your connection was stable, but for some reason the message didn't arrive at the destination. How do you prevent this situation?

Out-of-order messages: You put in a sell order for MSFT stock, the proceeds of which you want applied to the purchase of a really hot energy stock. Naturally the sell order needs to arrive before the purchase; otherwise, your account will not have the adequate funds to buy the energy stock. How do you go about avoiding this scenario?

Processing Issues

Processing issues have to do with the internal applications. When an error occurs, how is it handled internally by the application? Let's look at the main processing challenges:

Messages are lost when an error occurs: Your message was received at the location. However, before it actually enters the system, an error occurred, and the message vanished into the network. How do you prevent this? Take a sell order for MSFT, for example, which is received by the QuickReturns Ltd. application. Before the entire message was actually received, the network dropped some packets. Though you have sent the sell order and it has been received at the server, it never entered the sell application.

Interrelated messages are processed individually: You might have a set of messages that need to be processed as one transaction. However, these are treated as individual requests by your system. Once again, the order to sell for MSFT and the order to buy for the energy stock could be processed as a single transaction. Both the messages are related to each other and need to be processed as such.

Failure leads to an inconsistent state: The failure of the delivery of a message in some scenarios leads to an inconsistent state, whereby the client is actually expecting a response. However, since the service might be unavailable, this leads to the client continuing to wait until a timeout occurs.

Messages cannot be retired: Your sale of the marketing stock netted you more money than you expected, which you would like to apply toward the energy stock. So, you resubmit the buy order with a changed quantity. How do you handle this scenario?

The good news is that WCF enables you to overcome these challenges fairly easily with its built-in support for reliable messaging and reliable sessions. Moreover, providing this functionality is fairly straightforward and does not require the services of a highly skilled programmer or reams of code.

WCF makes adding reliability to the distributed application somewhat of a nonevent. This is especially true in an environment where both ends of the application are "likely" to be available, and it provides it at no extra cost or effort. The lack of a durable store for messages is a reality for version 1 of the WCF implementation. Durability can be provided using MSMQ. At the same time, it is important to keep in mind that the reliable messaging feature set in WCF is not a silver bullet, and it wasn't designed to be one. The reliable messaging feature set in the end is about as reliable or unreliable as the network available to it.

Reliable Sessions

WCF reliable messaging provides reliability between two given endpoints regardless of the number of intermediaries between the two. This also includes intermediaries that might use alternatives such as HTTP proxies and ones that use SOAP. A great benefit in WCF is the ability to switch from one transport mechanism to another using configuration settings. (For example, you start by using TCP with binary encoding and then change to reliable messaging over HTTP by modifying only the configuration files. It really is pretty much as simple as that.)

WCF provides reliability and resilience. This means the following:

Guaranteed delivery: Messages are guaranteed to be delivered once and only once. What this means is that your message will get to its destination without any chance of failure, vanishing into the ether, or duplications.

In-order delivery: The messages will be delivered in the same order as they were sent.

Resilience: WCF offers resilience to network outages, delivery destinations being unavailable, SOAP errors, and failures at the intermediaries. Features such as `AcknowledgementInterval`, `FlowControl`, and `InactivityTimeout` help the application be more aware of its environment.

Reliable sessions essentially support interactive communication between endpoints. The reliable session channel runs under a condition of low latency, and the exchange of messages are at fairly short intervals. Internally it handles the two main issues facing reliable messaging. These issues are lost or duplicated messages and messages arriving in an order different from the one in which they were sent. The reliable session provides SOAP messages with the functionality that is almost analogous to that provided by TCP in the TCP/IP stack to the IP packets. A TCP socket connection provides the infrastructure for once-only delivery of IP packets between nodes. However, there are significant differences between reliable messaging and the implementation of TCP.

The reliability provided by WCF reliable sessions is at the SOAP message level, rather than the packet level, which is arbitrarily defined. This once again is the implementation from the WS-ReliableMessaging standard, which is an interoperable industry-standard implementation. The reliability is provided in a transport-neutral manner and not just for TCP. Additionally, it is not tied to a particular transport session (that is, TCP session) but is for the lifetime of the session, which may or may not be over a single transport. Reliable sessions provide you with the means to use multiple transport sessions concurrently or sequentially without any fuss. Moreover, the reliability provided is for the end-to-end delivery rather than between two nodes of a transport. What this means is that when compared to TCP, which ensures reliability between only two ends of a connection, WCF reliability is end to end from a sender node to a receiver node irrespective of the number of intermediaries. Also, you must keep in mind that the reliable sessions can support out-of-order delivery (First In First Out, or FIFO, which really is that the messages should be processed in the order they arrive in rather than the logical order) should this be desired.

WCF provides you with a number of settings to implement fairly sophisticated means of applying network congestion detection, timeout intervals, retry counts, ordering, and so on. These are a lot more than just the simple retry events you are familiar with, and they help overcome issues by responding quicker to the loss of a message. (For further details on this, please refer to the WCF SDK documentation.)

Let's now dive into how you actually implement reliable sessions.

■ **Note** The code in this chapter is slightly different from the code in Chapter 7. The reasoning behind this is to reinforce the concepts within this chapter. For complete listings of the code, please refer to the solution files.

Enabling WCF Web Service with Reliable Sessions

Assume you have an interface implemented that is called `ITradeService`, as shown in Listing 8-1.

Listing 8-1. `ITradeService`

```
using System;
using System.Collections.Generic;
using System.ServiceModel;
using System.Text;

namespace QuickReturns
{
   [ServiceContract]
   public interface ITradeService

   {
      [OperationContract]
      string BeginTrade();
      ...
      void Buy();
      [OperationContract]
      void EndTrade();
   }
}
```

The `AddTrade` and `EndTrade` parameters that are provided for the `OperationContract` attribute ensure that any sequence of invocations to the operation begin with the method and complete with the `CompleteDeal()` method. The client application invokes `BeginTrade()` and then invokes `AddTrade()` twice. It has a `Buy()` method followed by an `EndTrade()` method. Let's now assume that one of the `AddTrade()` invocations never reached the service. In this case, the service would still operate in a valid manner, and the application would not miss `AddTrade()`. Similarly, consider the scenario where both the invocations have arrived at the destination. For whatever reason, one of them was delayed and arrived after `CompleteDeal()` was invoked. The execution sequence would still execute in a valid manner. However, this would not be in the sequence intended by the client. Overcoming these problems is a fairly simple task.

To begin, make the changes shown in Listing 8-2 to `ITradeService` in order to ensure that you do not have a scenario where messages could potentially be received out of order.

Listing 8-2. `ITradeService` *Changes*

```
[ServiceContract(SessionMode=SessionMode.Allowed)]
public interface ITradeService
```

This change will ensure that the messages are delivered in the order you intended. That is practically all you need to do to ensure that you avoid the scenario where messages are received out of order.

You now need to make the same change to the definition of `ITradeService` in the client, as shown in Listing 8-3.

Listing 8-3. *Modifying* `ITradeService`

```
<?xml version="1.0" encoding="utf-8" ?>
<configuration>
  <system.serviceModel>

    <client>
      <endpoint
          address="http://localhost/servicemodelsamples/service.svc"
          binding="wsHttpBinding"
          bindingConfiguration="Binding1"
          contract="Microsoft.ServiceModel.Samples.ICalculator" />
    </client>

    <!-- binding configuration - configures WSHttp binding for reliable sessions -->
    <bindings>
      <wsHttpBinding>
        <binding name="Binding1">
          <reliableSession enabled="true" />
        </binding>
      </wsHttpBinding>
    </bindings>

  </system.serviceModel>

</configuration>
```

You will now modify the `App.config` file of the host project to incorporate the implementation of the WS-ReliableMessaging standard as implemented in the Windows Communication Framework. You can do this by double-clicking the `App.config` file in the IDE or by simply opening it in Windows Notepad. Add the lines shown in Listing 8-4 to the file.

Listing 8-4. *Modifying the Service Host* `App.config`

```
<?xml version="1.0" encoding="utf-8" ?>
<configuration>
    <appSettings>
        <!-- use appSetting to configure base address provided by host -->
        <add key="baseAddress" value="http://localhost:8000/TradeService" />
    </appSettings>
    <system.serviceModel>
       <services>
            <service name="QuickReturns.TradeService">
                <endpoint address="" binding="wsHttpBinding"
                   contract="QuickReturns.ITradeService"/>
```

```
                <!-- Must have an HTTP base address for this -->
                <endpoint address="mex"
                    binding="mexHttpBinding"
                    contract="IMetadataExchange" />
            </service>
        </services>
        <!-- binding configuration - configures WSHttp binding
               for reliable sessions -->
            <bindings>
                <wsHttpBinding>
                    <binding name="Binding1">
                        <reliableSession enabled="true" />
                    </binding>
                </wsHttpBinding>
            </bindings>
    </system.serviceModel>
</configuration>
```

You will make similar changes to your client `App.config` file as well.

We recommend that you test this application using multiple machines. Put the server application on one machine and the client on the other. Ensure that you can invoke the service; once you have verified this, you can simulate problems. For example, remove the network cable from the server to simulate an intermittent connection, and try calling the service. If the executing thread blocks until the connection becomes available, then as soon as you plug the server back in, you will notice that the call will complete successfully. The magic of reliable sessions is in fact implemented by the `ReliableSessionBindingElement` class, which you will look at more in depth next.

MOVING LARGE VOLUMES OF DATA RELIABLY

Moving large amounts of data between endpoints is somewhat of a sticky situation. Assume that you have a requirement to move files that are 2GB in size between endpoints in your application. Under most circumstances, streaming offers you an ideal solution.

However, imagine that you are streaming this data across the wire and, because of a network outage, you lose the connection. Given that you have implemented reliable messaging in your solution, the message will be recovered. Here you have a small issue. When streaming data, the file is considered to be a single message. Let's assume you transferred 1GB prior to the outage. Therefore, the message will be resent from the beginning when the transmission resumes. You will be starting over, which is not only annoying but can be avoided.

The solution is to implement chunking instead of streaming in this scenario. With *chunking*, the sending application will divide the message into smaller files (for instance, 1,000 files of 2MB). The downside of this approach is that the throughput is likely to be lower than that of streaming because of the overhead of reliable messaging and the chunking taking place. When you need reliability while moving large files, use chunking. You should be aware that chunking per se is not a feature of WCF even though it can be implemented fairly easily. In the end, which threshold will trigger the switch from streaming to chunking is a decision you as an architect will make based upon the operational environment.

ReliableSessionBindingElement Class

The ReliableSessionBindingElement class provides the implementation of the reliable session and ordering mechanisms as defined in the WS-ReliableMessaging specification.

This is provided on all of the standard protocols, such as netTCPBinding, wsHttpBinding, and wsDualHttpBinding. The default values are false/off for the first two of these.

You can also provide reliable sessions for custom bindings quite easily. You would define the reliable session in the same manner as you did for Http in the previous section. Your code will look like Listing 8-5.

Listing 8-5. *Changing the Bindings*

```
<bindings>
    <customBinding>
        <binding configurationName="ReliabilityHTTP">
            <reliableSession/>
            <httpTransport/>
        </binding>
    </customBinding>
</bindings>
```

We discuss the actual implementation of custom bindings in greater detail in Chapter 3.

Some Pointers on Reliable Messaging

When using the functionality of reliable messaging, it is important to follow some basic principles to ensure the scalability of the application.

It is advisable to keep your network in mind, and this includes the transports, firewalls, proxies, and whatever else might be between the client application and the server application.

Internally in WCF, a transfer window is used to hold messages on the client as well as on the server in the event of either not being reachable. This is a volatile cache and is fully configurable. You can find the property in System.ServiceModel.Channels.ReliableSessionBindingElement.MaxTransferWindow; the value of this is in fact the number of messages that can be held within the transfer window. On the client side, this sets the number of messages held awaiting acknowledgments, while on the server it indicates the number of messages that can be buffered for the service in a given transfer window. By default, the value on this is eight messages; however, you can configure this size depending on the utilization, bandwidth, and latency of your network infrastructure.

For example, even if the sender keeps up with data rate, latency could be high if there are several intermediaries between the sender and receiver or an intermediary or network. Thus, the sender will have to wait for acknowledgments for the messages in its transfer window before accepting new messages to send on the wire. The smaller the buffer with high latency, the less effective the utilization of the network is. On the other hand, too high a transfer window size may impact the service because the service may have to catch up to the high rate of sends from the client.

Optimally you would like your network to have the lowest latency possible, but this is often not the case. The transfer window can actually help out here. Keep in mind that setting this value to 1, for example, might actually cause lost messages or dropped messages, thus defeating the entire purpose of reliable messaging. Buffering, when used correctly, will increase the concurrency of your application. If you are in doubt as to what you should set this value at, it is advisable to leave it at its default setting.

Note Before you decide to change any of the default settings, you should test and benchmark the different settings for your environment.

Should you decide on a nondefault value, you should configure it on both the client and the server. The correct value will in all likelihood require a measure of trial and error, as well as some degree of understanding of the network.

Another aspect to keep in mind is flow control, which is a mechanism to help the sender and receiver more or less keep pace with each other. Although the `TransferWindow` property does help in this regard, another tool is available to you, namely, the `FlowControlEnabled` property.

This is a piece of magic pulled off by the WCF team that actually can allow the client and service to either speed up or slow down, depending on how quickly each of them can produce and consume messages. It is recommended that you set this to true.

On the next logical level in concurrent applications, the response of the service is governed by the `MaxPendingChannels` property. This property sets the number of client sessions with which the service can do a handshake. It is possible that a service might not have enough channels available, and in this scenario, when a client attempts to establish a session, it will be refused. That is not something you want. At the same time, setting this value too high could have adverse effects as well. The default value for the `System.ServiceModel.Channels.ReliableSessionBindingElement.MaxPendingChannels` property is 4. What you should set it to depends on your infrastructure.

When hosting your application, it is important to take into account a few more points. Reliable sessions are stateful, and the state is maintained in the application domain. This means all messages that are part of a reliable session must be processed within the same application domain. This is a constraint in the event you are thinking of using a web farm or in any scenario where the number of servers is more than one. Additionally, when you are using dual HTTP channels, it is possible that each client might require more than two connects, which is the default. Duplex reliable connections in certain cases could require two connections each way. The fallout of this is that you could enter a potential deadlock situation using dual HTTP reliable sessions. This is easily overcome by setting the `MaxConnections` property to a suitably high number in your configuration files. This can be done quite easily by simply adding `<add name = "*" maxconnection = "nn" />` to the connection management element. Keep in mind that `nn` is the number of maximum connections you would like to set.

Message queuing is used primarily when you require true asynchronous messaging where the lifetimes of the client and the service might not overlap. And the second scenario is where you require reliability. In the real world, applications go down, and services are not always available, especially in scenarios where you face poor network infrastructures. WCF uses the underlying MSMQ technology to provide you with the means of leveraging the available technology to implement reliability, as you will see in the next section.

Reliable messaging, as you have seen, does not provide you with a silver bullet. In particular, the WS-ReliableMessaging standard–compliant implementation means you really do not have any durable storage for your messages. Using MSMQ, which is supported out of the box in WCF, allows you to overcome the infrastructure unreliability to a greater extent. Queuing enables you to effectively uncouple the transport for the messages from the actual processing of the message. Moreover, the reliability provided is really only as reliable as the underlying infrastructure in an environment where you do not have control over both endpoints of your application. Figure 8-1 shows conceptually what happens. Figure 8-1 describes using persistent stores to utilize the MSMQ communication between a WCF application and an MSMQ legacy application.

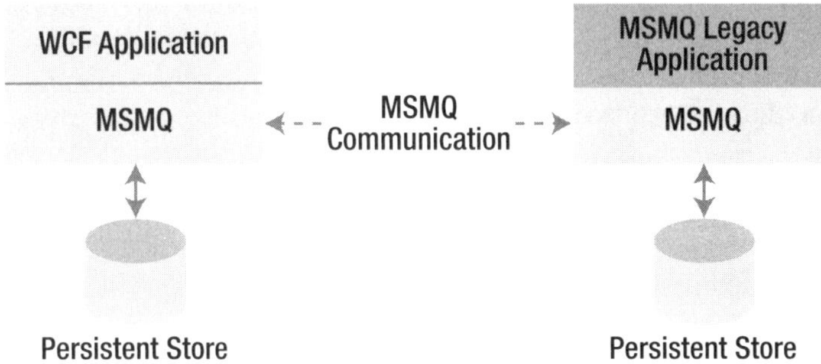

Figure 8-1. *Conceptual MSMQ usage with WCF*

Queuing in WCF

While designing distributed applications, selecting a transport is fairly important. Factors that you should consider include the requirements of the client and the service but, most important, whether you need a direct transport or a more isolated transport. In other words, unlike a direct transport such as HTTP or TCP where all the communication will fail if the network goes down, you want more resilience in the transport to overcome this issue. Typically, using a queued transport will overcome this scenario, since it is backed by a store (that is, a durability container).

Out of the box WCF provides the ability to use MSMQ, which is the Microsoft implementation of queued transports at the operating system level. Queues store messages from a sending application on behalf of a receiving application and later forward these messages to the receiving application. They ensure the reliable transfer of messages between queues. WCF provides support for queuing by using Microsoft Message Queuing (MSMQ) as a transport and enables the following features:

Loosely coupled applications: Sending applications and receiving applications are not dependent upon knowing whether the other is available. Moreover, both ends can send and receive messages without being dependent upon how quickly the messages are actually processed. This in effect also makes the overall application achieve higher levels of availability.

Failure isolation: The fact that loose coupling enables messages to be sent to the queue or received from the queue without actually needing the endpoints to be running adds a level of failure isolation. For example, let's look at the scenario where the server side of the application is unavailable and the client can continue to send messages to the queue. Once the server (receiver) is available, it will pick the messages up and process them.

Load leveling: Multiple instances of the server application are able to read from the same queue and help the application scale out to meet the additional load. Additionally, a high rate and volume of transactions are unlikely to overwhelm the receiver, since the messages will remain in the queue until processed by the receiving application at a rate completely independent of the client application.

Disconnected operations: As you have examined, reliability can suffer greatly in environments with unreliable network availability. Queues allow these operations to continue even when the endpoints are disconnected by providing a durable, albeit transient, message store. When the connection to the receiver application is established again, the queue will simply forward the messages to the receiver application for further processing.

It is also important to keep in mind that WCF uses MSMQ not only as the transport channel when communicating with WCF endpoints but also as a means of integrating with legacy applications. Legacy applications in this context are anything written prior to the release of WCF. These are applications that originally used MSMQ in order to provide a degree of reliability in the world before WCF.

In addition, queuing in WCF is not synonymous with MSMQ. MSMQ is supported out of the box in WCF (but is a feature of the Windows operating system), which makes its usage easy. If you wanted to implement your own version of queues, you could do that using the custom transport properties.

Durable storage, again, is not available out of the box with WCF since the WS-ReliableMessaging standard does not specify any rules about this. Durable storage, however, is possible using persistent queues, which are a feature of MSMQ and not WCF. This is a somewhat subtle but important distinction. The "reliable" aspect of reliable messaging really depends on how stable your network is. It is more about the actual transport than trying to ensure 100 percent delivery. It simply is not possible to achieve this without having control over both ends of the application infrastructure (sender and receiver), which in turn opens up an entirely different set of questions quite beyond the scope of this book. `NetMsmqBinding` offers you a solution, but be aware that it is not WS-ReliableMessaging compliant for the very reasons we have discussed.

Having stated that, you must also weigh the advantages offered by the NetMSMQ binding stack, including durable storage, transactional I/O, and reliable guaranteed delivery of messages. The trade-offs are that you lose interoperability as offered by a web service environment and are in essence operating on a Windows infrastructure only.

The NetMSMQ binding in WCF offers two distinct scenarios. One is where it is used as a transport channel between two WCF application endpoints, and the second scenario is where MSMQ is actually used to integrate with legacy applications that use MSMQ, also known as the *integration channel*. Hence, you could integrate a WCF receiver or client endpoint to your legacy application using MSMQ. This is possible since the queue channel in WCF is actually independent of MSMQ behavior and is in effect only abstracting it.

To get started with MSMQ, you first need to install it on your machine if you have not already done so.

Installing MSMQ

To install MSMQ, choose Add or Remove Programs from the Windows Control Panel to open the dialog box shown in Figure 8-2.

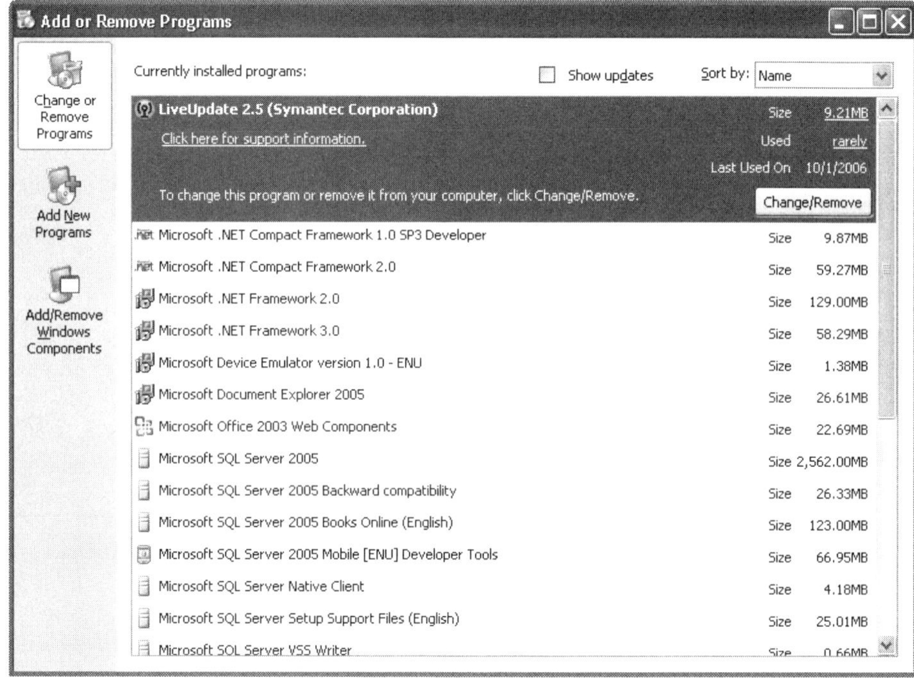

Figure 8-2. *Selecting Add or Remove Programs*

Click Add/Remove Windows Components, and then select Application Server in the Windows Components Wizard, as shown Figure 8-3, and click the Details button.

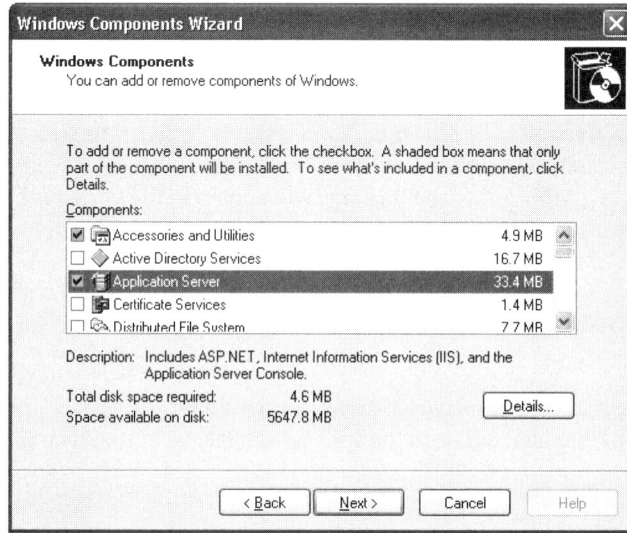

Figure 8-3. *Selecting Application Server*

If Message Queuing is not checked in the Application Server dialog box (as indicated in Figure 8-4), then check it and click the OK button. Then click the Next button in the Windows Components Wizard, and follow the instructions on the subsequent screens to install MSMQ.

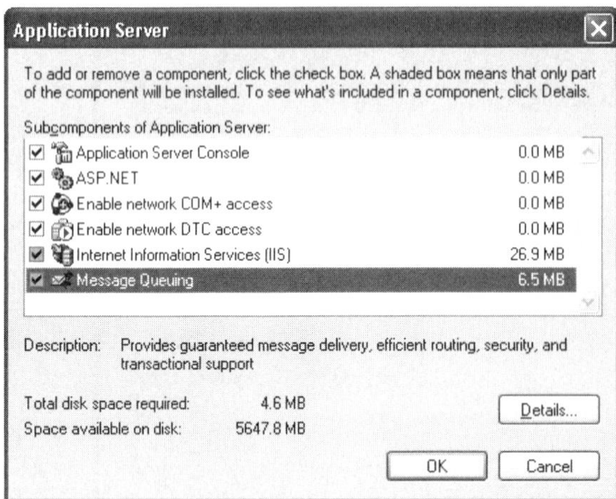

Figure 8-4. *Selecting Message Queuing*

Microsoft Message Queues in Windows Server 2007

WCF abstracts out MSMQ, though the behavior of MSMQ itself has remained the same, with the exception of MSMQ under Windows Server 2007. If you have worked with MSMQ in the past, you will recognize the familiar queue and the dead letter queue (DLQ). The *queue* is the active channel where MSMQ actually stores the messages that are relevant and that will be processed by the receiver application. The *dead letter queue* is where the messages end up if they have timed out or have become irrelevant.

Windows Server 2007 also introduces the concept of a *poison queue*. A poison message is one that has exceeded the number of retries. (In other words, say a receiver application is trying to process a message, but it encounters an error. In this scenario, the message queue will retry delivery until the timeout occurs. At this point, the message will end up in the DLQ. With WCF on Windows Server 2007, a message will continue its set of retry attempts, and once that is achieved, it will be put onto the poison queue.)

In WCF, poison message handling provides a way for the receiving application to deal with poison messages. The poison message handling is provided by the following properties in each of the available queued bindings:

`MaxImmediateRetries`: An integer value that indicates the maximum number of times to retry delivery of the message from the main queue to the application. The default value is 5.

`MaxRetryCycles`: An integer value that indicates the maximum number of retry cycles. A retry cycle consists of putting a message back into the application queue from the retry queue to attempt delivery again. The default value is Max Value or 2,147,483,647, which is the largest possible value for an int32.

`RetryCycleDelay`: The time delay between retry cycles attempting to deliver a message again. The default value is ten minutes. The retry cycle and the retry cycle delay together provide a mechanism to address the problem where a retry after a periodic delay fixes the problem.

`RejectAfterLastRetry`: A Boolean value that indicates what action to take for a message that has failed delivery after the maximum number of retries has been attempted. If true, the message is dropped, and a negative acknowledgment is returned to the sender. If false, the message is sent to the poison message queue. The default value is false. This is used when the receiving application cannot process the message after several attempts. If you set the value to false, the message is moved to the poison queue. A queued WCF service can then read the messages out of the poison queue for processing. A negative acknowledgment to the sender is as yet unsupported so will be ignored under MSMQ 3.0.

■ **Note** The poison message feature is supported only on Windows Server 2007 at the time of writing. Another major difference area in Vista is in the DLQ. Under the currently supported versions of Windows, there exists a single DLQ on a system-wide basis. However, with Vista you have the option of having DLQs on a per-application basis. Windows Server 2007 also introduces the concepts of the subqueue and transactional remote receives. The latter allows receiving applications to get the message in a transactional manner. MSMQ did not support this earlier, though the functionality could be implemented in a convoluted manner by using the peek method or by writing a custom dispatcher. Please refer to `http://msdn.microsoft.com/library/default.asp?url=/library/en-us/wcecomm5/html/wce50lrfmsmqqueuepeek.asp` for further documentation on the peek method because it is implemented currently in MSMQ. In Figure 8-5, you can see how a message is retried for a predefined number of times (in this case three times) and then sent on to the poison queue. You can implement your own logic for how you want to handle messages in the poison queue. Please refer to `http://msdn.microsoft.com/library/default.asp?url=/library/en-us/msmq/html/42fe2009-310b-42fa-a65e-6d395c15ada5.asp` for further details.

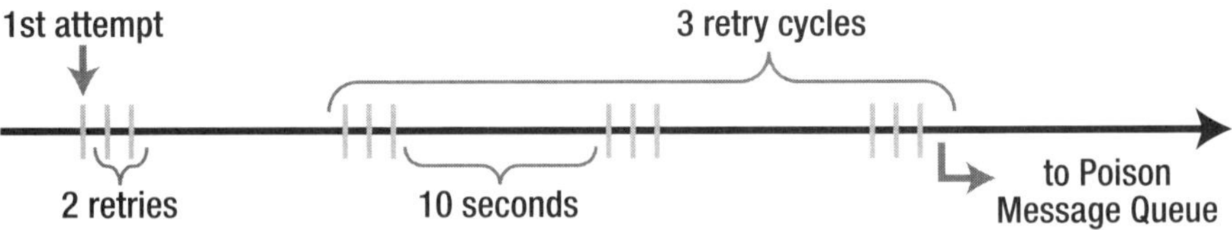

Figure 8-5. *Retries in queues*

As an MSMQ veteran, you will also miss the peek method that was available in previous MSMQ implementations. WCF does not support the peek method; however, MSMQ retains the behavior, which has nothing to do with WCF per se.

The requirement for application-wide queues in the past depended upon the usage of public queues. This in turn required Active Directory. Utilizing private queues was not an option, particularly when you needed to cross authentication boundaries. WCF no longer requires the public queues, since the behavior of the MSMQ channel is akin to that of the HTTP channel.

The channel stack, as you have seen in earlier chapters, is where WCF actually sends and receives its messages. The transport channels, as you know, are where the messages get exchanged between WCF endpoints, and the MSMQ transport channels, as you will see, are really no different from the HTTP transport channels.

Transport Channels

The MSMQ transport channel is really geared toward allowing two WCF endpoints to communicate with each other using MSMQ. The transport channel supports using SOAP within a message over MSMQ. You will typically use this when your network is inherently unreliable or you want to ensure that your messages are delivered irrespective of the infrastructure issues. In other words, use it when you are more concerned about transacted I/O and absolute guaranteed delivery rather than interoperability. You can accomplish this by using `NetMsmqBinding`, which is predefined in WCF.

Let's look at how you can use queuing in a WCF service as the transport channel. We'll use a self-hosted version of `TradeService` to illustrate the exchange of messages using the MSMQ transport and its failover.

■ **Note** Please keep in mind that the code snippets in the following listings are incomplete; you should refer to the code samples for the complete listings. You can find the complete listing under `\ProWCF\Chapter8\QueueMessaging`.

Begin by modifying `TradeService` as shown in Listing 8-6 to make it a self-hosted service. Then utilize `NetMsmqBinding`, and create the queues as required.

Listing 8-6. *Modifying* `TradeService` *for MSMQ*

```
using System;
using System.Configuration;
using System.Messaging;
using System.ServiceModel;

namespace QuickReturns
{
    // Define a service contract.
    [ServiceContract]
    public interface ITradeService
    {
        [OperationContract(IsOneWay=true)]
        void DoTrade(string BuyStock, string  SellStock, int Amount);

    }
```

```
// Service class which implements the service contract.
// Added code to write output to the console window
public class TradeService : ITradeService
{
    [OperationBehavior]
    public void DoTrade(string BuyStock, string SellStock, int Amount)
    {

        Console.WriteLine("Received Request to Sell Stock {0}
             with  the quantity of {1} from And Buy {2}",
             SellStock.ToString() , Amount.ToString(),
             BuyStock.ToString());
        Console.WriteLine();


    }

    // Host the service within this EXE console application.
    public static void Main()
    {
        // Get MSMQ queue name from app settings in configuration
        string queueName = ConfigurationManager.AppSettings["queueName"];

        // Create the transacted MSMQ queue if necessary.
        if (!MessageQueue.Exists(queueName))
            MessageQueue.Create(queueName, true);

        // Get the base address that is used to listen for
             WS-MetaDataExchange requests
        // This is useful to generate a proxy for the client
        string baseAddress = ConfigurationManager.AppSettings["baseAddress"];

        // Create a ServiceHost for the TradeService type.
        using (ServiceHost serviceHost = new ServiceHost(
              typeof(TradeService), new Uri(baseAddress)))
        {

                serviceHost.Open();

                Console.WriteLine("The Trade Service is online.");
                Console.WriteLine("Press <ENTER> to terminate service.");
                Console.WriteLine();
                Console.ReadLine();
                // Close the ServiceHost to shutdown the service.
                serviceHost.Close();
        }
    }

}
```

Notice that you add a reference to the `System.Messaging` namespace, which provides the support for MSMQ. You also add code to create a message, should one not exist. You create the host service like you did in Chapter 4.

Define the `App.config` file that specifies the service address and uses the standard `NetMsmqBinding` binding for `TradeService`. The code looks like Listing 8-7.

Listing 8-7. `TradeService NetMsmqBinding`

```
<?xml version="1.0" encoding="utf-8" ?>
<configuration xmlns="http://schemas.microsoft.com/.NetConfiguration/v2.0">
             <system.serviceModel>
                   <services>
             <service
               behaviorConfiguration="MyServiceTypeBehaviors"
                name="QuickReturns.TradeService">
               <endpoint address="net.msmq://localhost/private/TradeQueue"
                          binding="netMsmqBinding"
                          bindingConfiguration="DomainlessMsmqBinding"
                          contract="QuickReturns.ITradeService"
                          />
              <!-- Add the following endpoint.  -->
              <!-- Note: your service must have an http base
                         address to add this endpoint. -->
              <endpoint contract="IMetadataExchange" binding=
                         "mexHttpBinding" address="mex" />

            </service>
        </services>

        <bindings>
            <netMsmqBinding>
              <binding name="DomainlessMsmqBinding" >
              <security>
                <transport
                  msmqAuthenticationMode="None"
                  msmqProtectionLevel="None"/>
              </security>
              </binding>
            </netMsmqBinding>
        </bindings>
...
</configuration>
```

You then modify the client to be able to utilize the NetMSMQ bindings, as shown in Listing 8-8.

Listing 8-8. *Modifying the Client*

```
using System;
using System.Data;
using System.Messaging;
using System.Configuration;
using System.Web;
using System.Transactions;
namespace QuickReturns
{
    class Client
    {
        static void Main()
        {
            // Create a proxy for the client
            using (TradeServiceClient proxy = new TradeServiceClient())
            {
                //Create a transaction scope.
                using (TransactionScope scope = new TransactionScope
                     (TransactionScopeOption.Required))
                {

                    proxy.DoTrade("MSFT", "IBM", 60);
                    Console.WriteLine("Selling 60 stocks of IBM and Buying MSFT ");

                    proxy.DoTrade("ACN","ABN", 100);
                    Console.WriteLine("Selling 60 stocks of ABN and Buying ACN ");

                    // Complete the transaction.
                    scope.Complete();
...
}
```

As you have seen, you add a transaction scope around the DoTrade method in order to have the service utilize the NetMSMQ binding correctly. You will learn more about transactions in the next chapter. Now modify the App.config file for the client in order to use MSMQ, as per Listing 8-9.

Listing 8-9. *Modifying the Client* App.config

```
<?xml version="1.0" encoding="utf-8"?>
<configuration>
    <system.serviceModel>
        <bindings>
            <netMsmqBinding>
                <binding name="NetMsmqBinding_ITradeService" closeTimeout="00:01:00"
```

```
                openTimeout="00:01:00" receiveTimeout="00:10:00"
                      sendTimeout="00:01:00"
                deadLetterQueue="System" durable="true"
                       exactlyOnce="true"
                maxReceivedMessageSize="65536" maxRetryCycles="2"
                       receiveErrorHandling="Fault"
                receiveRetryCount="5" retryCycleDelay="00:30:00"
                       timeToLive="1.00:00:00"
                useSourceJournal="false" useMsmqTracing="false"
                       queueTransferProtocol="Native"
                maxBufferPoolSize="524288" useActiveDirectory="false">
                <readerQuotas maxDepth="32" maxStringContentLength=
                      "8192" maxArrayLength="16384"
                    maxBytesPerRead="4096" maxNameTableCharCount=
                        "16384" />
                <security mode="Transport">
                    <transport msmqAuthenticationMode="None"
                        msmqProtectionLevel="None" />
                    <message clientCredentialType="Windows" />
                </security>

            </binding>
        </netMsmqBinding>
    </bindings>
    <client>
        <endpoint address="net.msmq://localhost/private/
                    TradeQueue" binding="netMsmqBinding"
            bindingConfiguration="NetMsmqBinding_ITradeService"
                    contract="ITradeService"
            name="NetMsmqBinding_ITradeService" />
    </client>
  </system.serviceModel>
</configuration>
```

In this code, you set timeouts, the dead letter queue (should the message time out), the number of retries, and several related parameters. You also define that the client should use the netMSMQBinding elements.

Right-click the solution, and set the client, TradeService, as the start-up project. Run the application. Close TradeService, and let the client send messages. You can then browse the MSMQ queues in the Computer Management console and see the messages in the queue, as shown in Figure 8-6.

Start another version of TradeService, and you should be able to see the same messages being processed by the service.

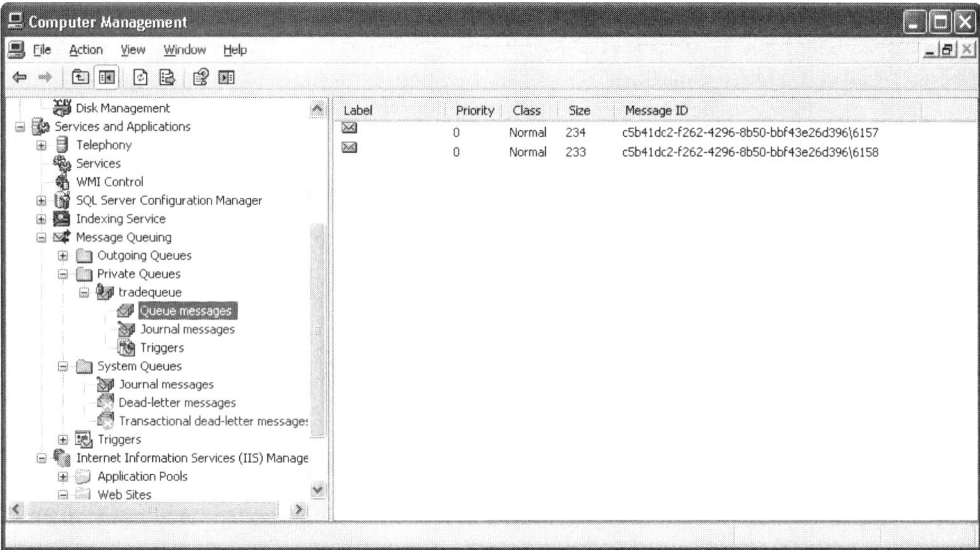

Figure 8-6. *Messages in* `TradeQueue`

The scenario here addresses the use of discrete transactions; however, in some cases, you would need to use batch processing. Typically when you will be dealing with back-end applications such as order-clearing systems, you would encounter this issue. For further thoughts on batch processing with queues, please refer to the "Batch Processing with Queues Using Sessions" sidebar.

BATCH PROCESSING WITH QUEUES USING SESSIONS

When messages are processed together or in a specified order, you can use a queue to group them to facilitate batch processing by a single receiving application. To understand this better, you'll now look at an example.

Say you are selling products online and want to process orders that consist of multiple line items. The client application stores each of these line items as messages in a queue to be processed by a back-end order-processing system implemented as a WCF service. In a farmed back-end order-processing system, if each line item message is processed by a different back-end server, the performance will suffer. In a non-farmed system with only a single back-end server, the server must process unrelated order line items as they come out of the queue. This complicates the business logic and degrades performance because the server switches between processing different orders.

For performance and for correctness, it is best to have a single back-end system to process all line items associated with an order. WCF provides the concept of a *session*, which allows a server to maintain state for a client over a series of interactions. You can use a session to group all the messages related to an order so that a single receiving application and the same service instance can process all the related messages.

The MSMQ transport channel at the sender places the body of the WCF message within the MSMQ message and sends it via the MSMQ transport. It is the job of the MSMQ transport channel stack at the receiver to unpack the WCF message from the MSMQ message and then to dispatch it as an invocation operation on the WCF service. The common theme in WCF is that the real work of messaging is in the channel, which abstracts out most of the complexities involved from the developer to make life simpler.

Implementing the MSMQ transport channel in WCF to integrate two WCF endpoints, as you have seen, is a straightforward task. Let's now look at the integration channel.

Integration Channels

Massive amounts of applications have already been deployed and will not be thrown away because of an emerging set of tools. We would prefer the world to become WCF compliant overnight, but the chances of that happening are slim.

WCF addresses this issue with a practical solution. The queuing channel within WCF offers the concept of integration channels, which should be used to communicate with the legacy applications that use MSMQ. The integration channel for queues in WCF continues to use the classic MSMQ messaging formats and is implemented via the `MsmqIntegrationBinding` binding.

What is occurring here is that the MSMQ message is mapped out to a WCF message and, once this has been achieved, invokes the WCF service. Alternatively, when you have a WCF application sending out a message, the reverse of the previous occurs. The properties of the WCF message are mapped back to those available in the legacy MSMQ message format, thus enabling the legacy application to consume the message.

The next section discusses the two scenarios in greater detail.

Integrating a WCF Client with an MSMQ Receiver

Leveraging existing investments in applications is a scenario that you will witness fairly often. Typically you will find that your key business processes are on opposite sides of the queue, and typically one of them will not be a WCF application.

In this scenario, the WCF client will hand the message to the integration channel, which will convert it to the MSMQ message format. Then the queue manager will store it in its local store. When the receiver MSMQ application becomes available, it will hand the message over to the queue manager for the receiver application and be consumed, as shown in Figure 8-7.

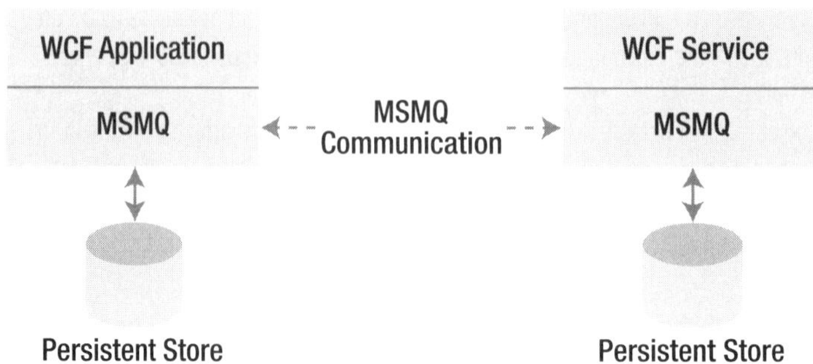

Figure 8-7. *Integrating with an MSMQ application*

You will now look at how you can integrate your WCF application to a legacy application using the MSMQ integration channel. Here are the steps (assuming you already have the message-receiving service up and running).

First, create an interface that defines the service contract for the WCF service that will send queued messages to the MSMQ receiver, as shown in Listing 8-10.

Listing 8-10. *MSMQ Receiver Interface*

```
 [ServiceContract]
interface ITradeService
{
    [OperationContract(IsOneWay = true)]
    void SubmitPurchaseOrder(MsmqMessage<BuyTrade> msg);
}
```

Second, create the configuration that specifies the use of the `IntegrationBinding` binding, as shown in Listing 8-11.

Listing 8-11. `IntegrationBinding` *Configuration*

```
<?xml version="1.0" encoding="utf-8" ?>
<configuration xmlns="http://schemas.microsoft.com/.NetConfiguration/v2.0">
    <system.serviceModel>

    <client>
        <endpoint  name="TradeServiceLegacy"
                address="msmq.formatname:DIRECT=OS:.\private$\LegacyQueue"
                binding="msmqIntegrationBinding"
                bindingConfiguration="TradeServiceBinding"
                contract="QuickReturns.ITradeService">
      </endpoint>
    </client>

    <bindings>
      <msmqIntegrationBinding>
        <binding name="TradeServiceBinding" >
          <security mode="None" />
        </binding>
      </msmqIntegrationBinding>
    </bindings>
  </system.serviceModel>
</configuration>
```

You can now perform a buy or a sell in a transacted manner using MSMQ. And that is it. It is quite easy to integrate an MSMQ application with a WCF application. Now that you have accomplished this, you'll see how you can integrate an MSMQ client with a WCF application.

Integrating an MSMQ Client with WCF Service

This scenario is commonly encountered when legacy applications need to interact with newer, more up-to-date applications. Traditionally this has been a nightmare scenario.

Legacy applications seldom have the flexibility to be able to be integrated with newer technologies. In a business scenario, when critical processes reside in two different technologies, this equates to a great deal of frustration. However, if your legacy application uses MSMQ for messaging, then you can rectify this situation easily with WCF. The sender can still continue sending messages as it always has, and no change is required to the client application. WCF can easily integrate and communicate with the legacy system. Figure 8-8 illustrates this scenario.

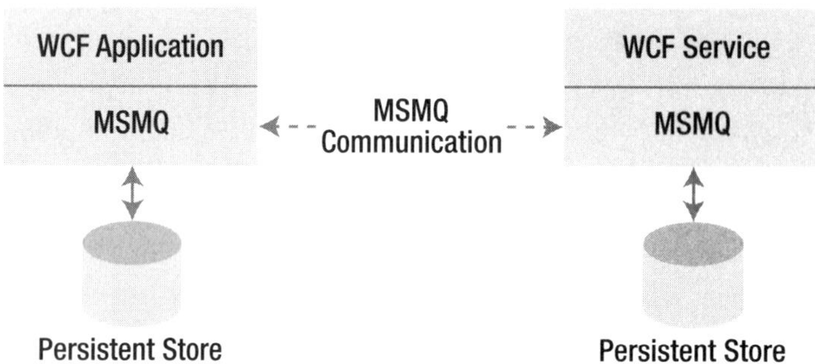

Figure 8-8. *Integrating with a WCF client*

The `msmqIntegrationBinding` binding also allows you to integrate with MSMQ clients fairly easily. Let's see how you can accomplish this.

Create an interface that defines the service contract for the WCF service that will receive queued messages from an MSMQ client, as shown in Listing 8-12.

Listing 8-12. `msmqIntegrationBinding`

```
// Define a service contract.
 [ServiceContract(Namespace = "http://QuickReturns")]
 [KnownType(typeof(SomeOrder))]
public interface ITradeProcessor
{
    [OperationContract(IsOneWay = true, Action = "*")]
    void SubmitSomeOrder(MsmqMessage<SomeOrder> msg);
}
```

Next implement the `IOrderProcessor` interface, and apply the `ServiceBehavior` attribute, as shown here:

```
// Service class which implements the service contract.
// Added code to write output to the console window
public class TradeProcessorService : ITradeProcessor
```

```
{
    [OperationBehavior(TransactionScopeRequired = true,
             TransactionAutoComplete = true)]
    public void SubmitSomeOrder(MsmqMessage<SomeOrder> somemsg)
    {
        SomeOrder so = (SomeOrder)somemsg.Body;
                    }
}
```

You will now create the configuration to use the integration binding, as shown in Listing 8-13.

Listing 8-13. *Configuration for Integration Binding*

```
<?xml version="1.0" encoding="utf-8" ?>
<configuration >
  <appSettings>
    <!-- use appSetting to configure MSMQ queue name -->
    <add key="orderQueueName" value=".\private$\ReceiveOrders" />
  </appSettings>
  <system.serviceModel>
    <services>
      <service
        name="QuickReturns.LegacyReceive" >
        <endpoint address="msmq.formatname:DIRECT=OS:.\private$\ReceiveOrders"
                                binding="msmqIntegrationBinding"
                  bindingConfiguration="OrderProcessorBinding"
                  contract="QuickReturnsLegacyReceive">
        </endpoint>
      </service>
    </services>

    <bindings>
      <msmqIntegrationBinding>
        <binding name="OrderProcessorBinding" >
          <security mode="None" />
        </binding>
      </msmqIntegrationBinding>
    </bindings>
</system.serviceModel>
```

What you have accomplished here is to define the service endpoints and let the application know to which method to bind the application. And you told it where the endpoint is actually located.

You will now create the service host, in this case using a console-based executable, as shown in Listing 8-14.

Listing 8-14. *Creating the Service Host*

```
// Host the service within this EXE console application.
public static void Main()
{
// Get MSMQ queue name from app settings in configuration
    string queueName = ConfigurationManager.AppSettings["LegacyQueue"];

// Create the transacted MSMQ queue if necessary.
    if (!MessageQueue.Exists(queueName))
        MessageQueue.Create(queueName, true);
    using (ServiceHost serviceHost = new ServiceHost(typeof(TradeService)))
    {
        serviceHost.Open();

// The service can now be accessed.
        Console.WriteLine("The service is ready.");
        Console.WriteLine("Press <ENTER> to terminate service.");
        Console.ReadLine();

// Close the ServiceHostBase to shutdown the service.
        serviceHost.Close();
    }
}
```

Start the host, and you are good to receive and process messages from an MSMQ client.

As you have seen, using queues with WCF is fairly easy. There is not a lot of complexity or code required to integrate legacy applications using the integration channel with WCF.

Some Pointers on Using MSMQ

As you have seen, MSMQ offers you the ability to provide a durable store for your messages and an easy way to integrate with other non-WCF applications that use MSMQ, but you should keep in mind a few pitfalls and pointers when using MSMQ:

- It is important to note that the durability of the messages depends on the durability of the queue. MSMQ queues have a property called `Durable`. This means that when set to true, every message received on the queue will be written to disk until processed. If this property is set to false, keep in mind that if the machine hosting the queue fails, all messages in the queue will be lost. By default, this is set to true. It does have some performance overhead; however, it is not recommended that you change this to anything else, since that would mean that end-to-end reliability could no longer be guaranteed. Of course, both the client and server ends need to have durability enabled to provide the reliability that you want.

- Disabling the DLQ is not recommended. If you are developing for MSMQ 4.0 or later, it is recommended that you configure one DLQ per application and use the poison message–handling capabilities. For more information, please refer to the MSMQ guide on MSDN.

- Again, in a web farm scenario, be aware that MSMQ 3.0 is not able to perform remote transacted reads. This is a limitation on MSMQ and not WCF.
- In general while using the MSMQ channels, please ensure complete familiarity with the base technology, since your issues are likely to be more with the MSMQ infrastructure rather than WCF.

Summary

In this chapter, you learned the following:

- Why you need reliable messaging
- How to use the reliable messaging options offered by WCF
- How to implement reliable messaging using reliable sessions
- What queuing channels are available in WCF
- How to use the MSMQ transport channel
- How to use the integration channel
- How to integrate with an MSMQ receiver application
- How to integrate your application with an MSMQ client

We recommend the Vista SDK and WCF documentation for further information about this topic. Please dive into the code listings that implement reliable messaging within the .NET Framework also. You'll find the API-level implementation of the subject discussed here, as well as guidance on best practices.

In Chapter 9, you will learn about support for transactions in WCF and how to implement transactions. Transactions are important in business dealings. Executing a set of processes as a transaction can ensure reliability and consistency of data.

CHAPTER 9

Using Transactions in WCF

Transactions are fundamental to applications in order to ensure consistent behavior for data. In addition, they are a fundamental building block for ensuring the implementation of atomic, consistent, independent, and durable (ACID) behavior in an application. In the QuickReturns Ltd. application, ACID behavior means that when you do make a trade, it is absolute. It will either be complete in its entirety or be rolled back, leaving no room for ambiguity. If you were to put in a buy order for a stock, you would definitely want to be sure that the trade were absolute, right? Without transactions, you would not be sure that the trade was indeed conducted, and you would have no means of verifying the validity without ambiguity. Having a transactional system ensures that trades are consistently applied and are final. After all, you want to be clear about whether a trade has actually occurred.

You need to ensure that the systems being built provide you with features such as recoverability. That is, if a service or machine fails, when it does come back, data is still available. Scalability is another area where transactions are critical, since it clearly earmarks the point at which resources are requested and released at the end of the transaction. This enables you to avoid deadlocks, whereby two or more threads are trying to acquire the same resources, causing the application to hang. Typically deadlocks are resolved by making one of the threads release its resources. Transactions are critical in this to ensure safe system state and to ensure that any data that was being applied is rolled back successfully. Finally, transactions are important to preserve data integrity. (In other words, when you perform the same query to your persistent data store, you want to receive the same result each time.) Transactions are the basis of ensuring this. These are key business drivers for transactional support in any enterprise application.

WCF provides rich support for transactions, and you will look at that support in detail in this chapter. Specifically, we will cover the following topics:

- The need for transactions
- The types of transactions in WCF
- How to define transactions in WCF
- How to use transactions with queues

This chapter builds on the concepts introduced in Chapter 8; it is important that you are familiar with those concepts, since they really do go hand in hand with each other.

What's a Transaction?

What is a transaction? Broadly speaking, a *transaction* is a mechanism to ensure that several operations succeed or fail as an atomic unit. In other words, it ensures that all operations succeed or all operations fail in the event that even one of the constituent components of the transaction encounters an error. Broadly speaking, transactions enforce the ACID rule popularized in database programming. WCF provides a simple centralized manner to support transactions within your applications. Prior to WCF, although there were mechanisms to support transactions (`Begin Transaction...End Transaction` in Visual Basic, for example), a single standard means of being able to support nondatabase transactions was not a trivial task to say the least. A transaction enables you to carry out a set of operations as a single execution unit whereby you achieve reliable results.

In the QuickReturns Ltd. scenario, you conduct trades on the stock exchange, and not knowing for sure whether a trade was successful could have disastrous results. Using the transaction mechanism, you achieve the following results:

Atomicity: The trades go through the system as single unit, thus achieving durability or aborting as a single unit, where nothing goes through in a rollback of the transaction.

Consistency: This guarantees that the transaction is a correct transformation in the system state. All orders that are part of a single transaction do so with the correct attributes (buy/sell, associated quantities/prices), and that behavior is repeatable identically time after time.

Isolation: This ensures that each transaction is independent and isolated from other transactions that could be occurring simultaneously in the system. The transactions do not have any impact on the behavior of any other transaction that might be occurring in the system. Looking at the trade system, it is more than likely that more than one user is using the system to trade at the same time. The isolation of the transactions ensures that the trades conducted by other users, or even multiple trades occurring at the same time from a single user, are treated as being distinct and separate from each other.

Durability: As the name suggests, this ensures that all data is committed to a nonvolatile resource such as a database, an XML file, or even a flat file. The data of the transaction must remain available even though the transaction has long since completed. For us, this provides a record for the trades provided. You can check when a particular trade was conducted and have the data available to you whenever you want it.

WCF implements the WS-Atomic protocol to enable transaction support. This enables you to build transactions that can interact with multiple endpoints inside WCF and with third-party systems such as web services.

A transaction has multiple discrete players involved in the process. These components interact with each other and are essential for any given transaction. If you consider Figure 9-1, you can see that any transaction has three essential components: the application, the persistent store, and the transaction manager.

Note Looking again at QuickReturns Ltd. from a business perspective, you might need transactions that span multiple business activities. For example, you might put in a sell order and then want to buy oil futures at a predefined price. Should you be unable to get your oil futures at the desired price, you might want to hold off on the sale itself. This scenario is referred to as a *compensating transaction*, whereby all discrete components of the flow are treated as a single transaction. The compensating transaction offers looser coupling than the atomic transaction protocol, with the trade-off that compensating transactions are inherently more difficult to code and maintain. WCF does not provide support for compensating transactions out of the box. In other words, should you need a compensating transaction, you would need to implement the code yourself, use a complementary product such as Windows Workflow Foundation, or utilize Microsoft Distributed Transaction Coordinator (MS DTC) to achieve this.

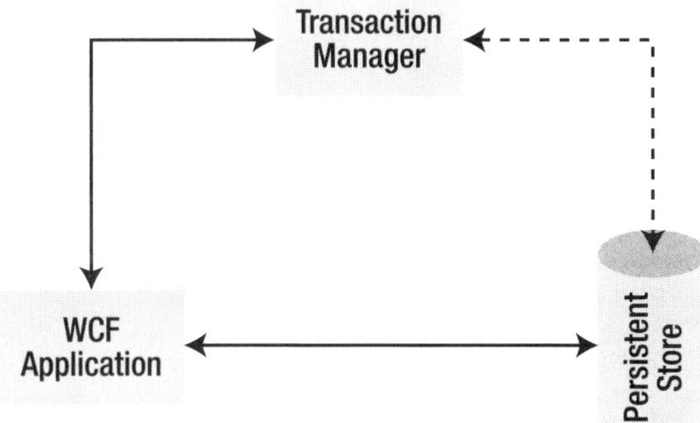

Figure 9-1. *Participants in a transaction*

KERNEL TRANSACTION COORDINATOR

The Kernel Transaction Coordinator is a feature of Windows Server 2007 that allows you to make the transaction available as a kernel object rather than a user object. The advantage of the Kernel Transaction Manager (KTM) is that it allows you to access system objects such as the file system or access files via transactions. You can leverage this in conjunction with WCF applications that need to read from files and write to files, for example, to provide transactional support where hitherto there was none.

It is important to keep in mind that the KTM is not part of WCF but rather the Windows Server 2007 family. You can find more information about the KTM and its usage at `http://msdn.microsoft.com/library/default.asp?url=/library/en-us/KTM/fs/transaction_managers.asp`.

The application imitates a transaction, which could be over any of the supported protocols, in essence to commit it to a persistent store such as SQL Server or Oracle or even a flat file. The coordination between the application and the persistent store to comply with the ACID rule for transactions takes place by the transaction manager in the background. This could be the Lightweight Transaction Manager (LTM), the MS DTC, or even a custom transaction manager. The role of the transaction manager is to enlist all parties in the transaction, preparing them for the transaction. This means ensuring that they are available and ready to participate in the transaction. (The persistent store is also referred to as a *resource manager* in some documentation.) Then you can commit, or you can roll back if the data is not persisted. The LTM is implemented by `System.Transactions` and provides an extremely fast means for transaction management for volatile data within the application domain. Figure 9-2 displays the transaction stack in .NET 3.0 including the kernel transaction manager, which will be available in Windows Server 2007. (See the "Kernel Transaction Coordinator" sidebar for more information.)

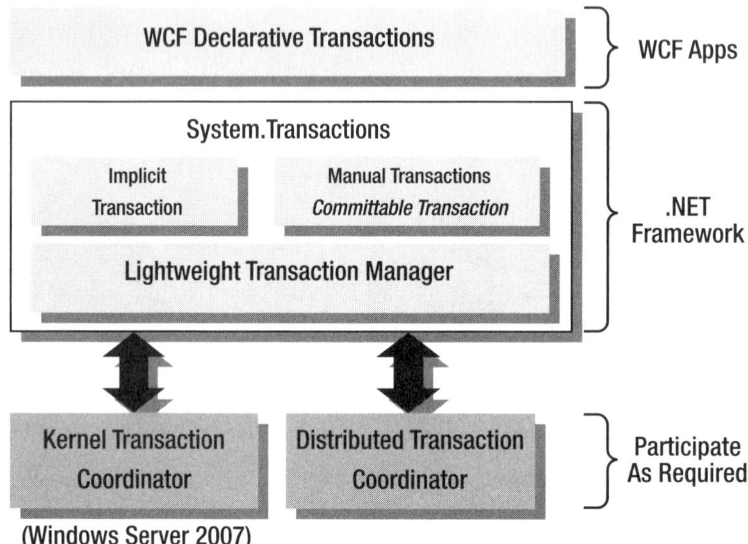

Figure 9-2. *Transactions in .NET 3.0*

Understanding the Types of Transactions in WCF

Implementing reliable messaging has multiple challenges. You could broadly categorize these challenges into communication issues and processing issues. More often than not, these are interrelated challenges that are nontrivial in nature to solve. In WCF, the transaction is implemented in `System.ServiceModel`, which easily enables you to configure `TimeOuts`, activation (Just in Time), and the behavior of the transaction in terms of functionality, contracts, and flow. The `System.Transactions` namespace allows you to implement your own transaction or use the `System.Transactions` namespace's `TransactionScope` class to use the implicit model within WCF.

The transactions themselves internally use a mechanism called *two-phase commit*. The two-phase commit protocol lets all the nodes involved in a distributed transaction participate in an atomic manner. During the course of the two-phase commit transaction protocol, the state of the transaction transitions multiple times. The two-phase commit protocol has three stages: active, phase 1, and phase 2. In the active stage, the transaction is created. The superior resource manager (the resource manager of the creator) will enlist the other resource managers, who will become active in the transaction. In phase 1 of the two-phase commit transaction, the creator has issued the commit command for the transaction, and the enlisted resource managers respond about whether they are prepared to commit. If the responses are prepared to commit, the transaction will move to phase 2. Otherwise, it will abort.

In phase 2 of the two-phase commit transaction, the superior resource manager will write a durable entry to an internal log and then issue the commit to the enlisted resource managers. Once this is done, the superior resource manager will begin sending the commit to the enlisted resource managers and, irrespective of any errors (network, resource unavailability, and so on), will continue until all enlisted resource managers have been sent a commit message. Then the superior resource manager will wait for the confirmation of the commit from the enlisted resource managers or for an error message. Alternatively, it will wait until a timeout occurs. Should all enlisted resource managers respond positively about the commit, the superior resource manager will erase the log entry, and the transaction will end. In the event of an error, the transaction will abort. Internally the `System.Transactions` namespace utilizes the two-phase commit protocol. Figure 9-3 explains this graphically.

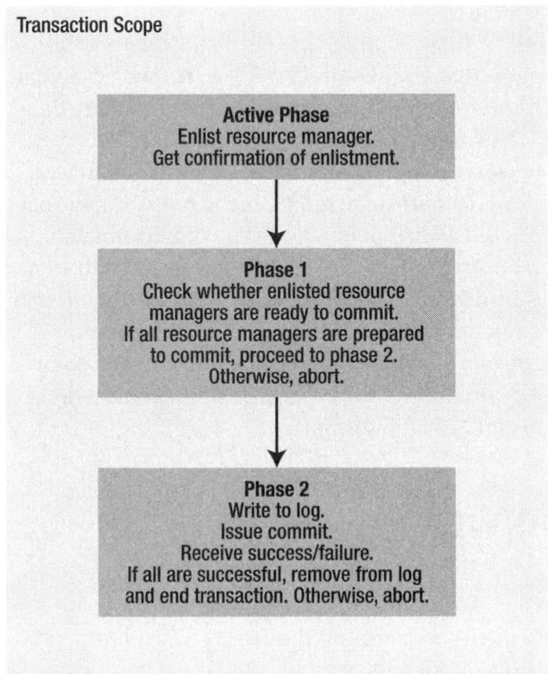

Figure 9-3. *The two-phase commit transaction*

MS DTC AND WCF

The MS DTC is designed to support transactions that span multiple Windows systems. Each of the machines participating in the transaction has local transaction managers that are enlisted by MS DTC for the transaction, and the initiating manager handles the coordination between the local managers on the remote systems. The transaction is executed as a single atomic transaction whereby MS DTC will commit to all participating machines in a single unit or roll back the transactions across all the participating machines. MS DTC transactions utilize the OLE transaction–compliant resource managers and explicitly control the duration and the scope of the transaction; they can be invoked from any application written in C or C++. You can interface with these applications through the interop interfaces in WCF, which we'll discuss in greater detail in Chapter 10.

For further details about MS DTC programming, please refer to the DTC Programmer's Reference at `http://msdn.microsoft.com/library/default.asp?url=/library/en-us/cossdk/html/c0f7d3dd-4da1-45df-8516-d0d2ec1b0ca6.asp`.

So in the QuickReturns Ltd. scenario, when the client invokes the trade, it will utilize its resource manager to enlist the trade service's resource manager. Then in phase 1 of the two-phase commit, it will get its confirmation to participate in the transaction, once the data has been marshaled to the trade service resource manager. And then in the second phase, the data would be committed as well as the transaction completed.

In addition to this, you can also use the MS DTC to implement transactions that span multiple Windows (XP/2003 or later) infrastructures. In the scenario where MS DTC is utilized to provide transactions, each of the machines and applications that participate within the transaction has its own local resource managers that cooperatively manage transactions that span multiple systems. *Distributed* transactions are in essence transactions that update data across two or more systems as a single unit. Distributed transactions are required and are difficult to implement in the absence of the MS DTC since the application's resource manager must detect and recover from a variety of failure scenarios, including the network infrastructure, local availability of resources in a distributed environment, and state management across multiple machines. We'll concentrate on `System.ServiceModel` primarily, though we will dive into the problem space of distributed transactions in the next section. For further details about MS DTC in the context of WCF, please refer to the "MS DTC and WCF" sidebar.

If you look at a scenario in the QuickReturns Ltd. application where you would at some point like to register the trade with the broker and the stock exchange as single transaction, you will begin to appreciate the requirements for MS DTC support.

Defining Transactions in WCF

WCF supports the WS-Atomic transaction protocol. Transactions in WCF have been defined with the `System.ServiceModel` namespace and feature three main components. These are the `ServiceBehavior` attribute, the `OperationBehavior` attribute, and the `TransactionFlow` attribute. You will look at each of these in a little more depth and examine what these achieve individually in the transaction in the following sections. You'll learn about their implications prior to jumping into the how-tos of implementing them.

Using the TransactionFlow Attribute

The `TransactionFlow` attribute specifies whether the service can be related to the external interactions and the level at which the incoming transaction is accepted. The only options available are `Allowed`, `NotAllowed`, and `Mandatory`. You set this in `App.config`, which essentially passes information about the transaction to the service, and will either slow down or speed up the rate of transactions depending upon the network conditions. Transaction flow is determined by the bindings and by default is disabled. Unless you explicitly utilize it, it will not be enabled, as you can see in Listing 9-1. The listing enables the transaction flow for the `ITradeService` interface.

Listing 9-1. *Enabling Transaction Flow*

```
<!-- binding configuration - configures WSHttp binding
     for Transactions sessions -->
<bindings>
    <wsHttpBinding>
        <binding name="ITradeService" transactionFlow="true">
            <reliableSession enabled="false" />
        </binding>
    </wsHttpBinding>
</bindings>
<behaviors>
      <serviceBehaviors>
          <behavior name="MyServiceTypeBehaviors" >
              <!-- Add the following element to your service
                     behavior configuration. -->
              <serviceMetadata httpGetEnabled="true"/>
              <serviceDebug httpHelpPageEnabled="true"
                   includeExceptionDetailInFaults="false"/>
             </behavior>
        </serviceBehaviors>
</behaviors>
```

Using the ServiceBehavior Attribute and the OperationBehavior Attribute

The `ServiceBehavior` attribute defines the behavior of the contract and the attributes of the transaction. In essence, this is how the transaction will behave under circumstances such as a failure in the network; it specifies whether resources should be released when a transaction completes, as well as concurrency in the transaction. The attributes of the `ServiceBehavior` attribute include the following:

`TransactionAutoCompleteOnSessionClose`: Specifies whether outstanding transactions are completed when the session closes and by default is false. For example, if in the trading service you were to shut the trading service down, this affects how the incoming sessions would behave. The default setting ensures that if an error occurs (when the service is shut down or unavailable or when there is a network error), then the transaction would abort and roll back to its original state. You can also set this to true, in which case the incoming session will degrade gracefully. In other words, it will shut down in a controlled fashion rather than just crash. Additionally, any uncompleted transaction is successfully completed. However, this is from the perspective of the client and can potentially lead to an inconsistent state, since the trade service will not be available though the client thinks that the transactions did commit correctly.

`ReleaseServiceInstanceOnTransactionComplete`: Specifies whether the underlying service instance is released when a transaction completes. The default value for this property is true. This means each instance will create a new transaction scope. Releasing the service instance is an internal action taken by the service and has no impact on sessions and/or instances established by clients. The transaction scope is the entire process of enlisting the various parties in a communication, exchanging the data, and then terminating the connection once the exchange of the data is completed. In the QuickReturns Ltd. example, the transaction scope would be establishing the client connectivity to the trade service and then passing the actual trade messages. Then, once the service has received the data, it includes terminating the specific connection created for the transaction. Managing transaction scope was quite a daunting task if it had to be done manually.

Within the `ReleaseServiceInstanceOnTransactionComplete` attribute, you have four primary ways of completing transactions:

- An operation marked with `TransactionAutoComplete` equal to true returns control to the initiator of the transaction.
- A service calls the `SetTransactionComplete`.
- A client closes a session associated with an active transaction that is still executing or there is a network error; in either of these scenarios, the result is a rollback if the `TransactionAutoComlete` is set to false.
- Alternatively, the transaction aborts, for any given reason. These can be set quite easily in the `OperationBehavior` attribute, as defined in Listing 9-2.

Listing 9-2. *Setting the* `OperationBehavior` *Attribute*

```
[OperationBehavior(TransactionScopeRequired=true,TransactionAutoComplete=true)]
void ITradeService.AddTrade(Trade trade)
```

Keep in mind that if this property is set to true, `ConcurrencyMode` must be set to `Single`, or else the service will throw invalid configuration exceptions.

The TransactionIsolationLevel property deals with how the data is to be versioned (or in other words, the isolation level to be applied). If TransactionScopeRequired is set to true and no transaction is flowed, then the TransactionIsolationLevel property takes one of the IsolationLevel values: ReadCommited where only nonvolatile data can be read or ReadUnCommited where even volatile data can be read. If this property is left blank, it will default to Unspecified. This specifies that the method accepts any isolation level for a transaction that flows into it and uses Serializable where each transaction is completely separate from any other transaction when you create a new transaction. Should you decide to change the default value on the calling application, please keep in mind that it must match the local values for the transaction to succeed. A mismatch in the values will cause the transaction to fail.

The TransactionTimeout property, just as the name suggests, sets the time period within which a new transaction created at the service must complete. If this time is reached and the transaction is still not completed, it aborts. The TimeSpan set in this property is used as the TransactionScope timeout for any operations that have TransactionScopeRequired set to true and that have established a new transaction. Although it is important to give your transactions adequate time to complete, setting this value too high or too low will have a serious impact on the performance of the application. Listing 9-3 shows how to implement the transaction isolation level, which in this case is set to ReadCommited.

Listing 9-3. *Setting the Transaction Isolation Level*

```
ServiceBehavior(TransactionIsolationLevel=
      System.Transactions.IsolationLevel.ReadCommited)]
    public class TradeService : ITradeService
```

The OperationBehavior attribute, as the name suggests, helps you configure the behavior of the transaction. By default this is set to false, which in turn means that if a transaction scope has not been defined, then the operation will occur outside the scope of the transaction.

Let's put this into context; as you saw in the previous chapter, you were not using transactions or defining the OperationBehavior attribute in the code. So, even though the trade service was receiving the messages reliably from the client application, there really was no guarantee that the data was actually persisted correctly. This is a scary scenario.

However, keep in mind that even when the OperationBehavior attribute is set to false and you do want a transaction scope, it is derived from the calling application. So, what happens if you have defined a TransactionScope on the client and none on the service? In this case, what occurs is that the transaction scope of the client would be utilized to create a transaction scope on the service, even though none was defined for the service. This is a boon for developers, who can now really decouple their application from the implementation of the service.

Now that you have gone through the dense and somewhat difficult theory and attributes of the transaction, you'll look at how to add transaction support to the WCF application.

■ **Note** We will continue to build upon the concepts covered in Chapter 8, since reliable messaging and transactions really do go hand in hand. As you have seen, having just reliable messaging or transactions independently does not allow you to offer the reliable and durable results or the solution you will want.

Defining Transactions in QuickReturns Ltd.

You'll now begin to modify the QuickReturns Ltd. application to use transactions. Open the `Chapter09\ReliableMessaging\QuickReturnsTransactional` solution.

We will assume that you are going to sell a stock and log the sale in a database. The two deals will be committed in a single transaction. You'll begin by modifying the client.

■ **Note** The `TradeServiceDB` database used in this example uses SQL Server Express, which is freely downloadable from `http://msdn.microsoft.com/vstudio/express/sql/download/default.aspx`. You must have this installed for the example to work. To install SQL Express, you need the executable. It is recommended that once the download begins, you select the Run option when prompted. Once the download completes, this will automatically launch the installation. It is recommended that you accept the default settings during the installation process. You can find complete details of the installation and additional components at the previously mentioned link. Also, keep in mind that if you have installed Visual Studio 2005 in a non-Express edition, SQL Server Express is installed by default. Please check your local installation to see whether SQL Server Express was already installed as part of your Visual Studio installation.

Begin by adding a reference to `System.Transactions` in the QuickReturns Ltd. solution. Open `program.cs` in the client application of `TradeService`, and modify it to look like the code in Listing 9-4. You begin with adding support for the transactions by referencing `System.Transactions`. Thereafter, you add a transaction endpoint in order to allow the client application to utilize transactions.

Listing 9-4. *Modifying the Client* `program.cs` *for Transactions*

```
using System;
using System.ServiceModel;
using System.Transactions;

namespace QuickReturns
{
    //The service contract is defined in generatedClient.cs,
          generated from the service by the svcutil tool.

    //Client implementation code.
    class Client
    {
        static void Main()
        {
            // Create a client using either wsat or oletx
                  endpoint configurations
            TradeServiceClient client = new TradeServiceClient(
                  "WSAtomicTransaction_endpoint");
```

```
            // In the event you decide to use the Ole transaction
                  endpoint, uncomment the line below and comment the line above
            // TradeServiceClient client = new
                  TradeServiceClient("OleTransactions_endpoint");

            // Start a transaction scope
            using (TransactionScope tx =
                        new TransactionScope(TransactionScopeOption.RequiresNew))
            {
                Console.WriteLine("Starting transaction");

                // Call the Add service operation
                //  - generatedClient will flow the required active transaction
                int qty;
                int price;
                int result;


                // Call the CalcValue service operation
                // - generatedClient will not flow the active transaction
                qty = 100;
                price = 15;
                result = client.CalcValue(qty, price);
                Console.WriteLine("  Sold ACN Quantity {0},
                   For$ {1} With a Total Value of ${2}",
                   qty, price, result);

                                // Complete the transaction scope
                Console.WriteLine("  Completing transaction");
                tx.Complete();
            }

            Console.WriteLine("Transaction Committed");

            // Closing the client gracefully closes the
                connection and cleans up resources
            client.Close();

            Console.WriteLine("Press <ENTER> to terminate client.");
            Console.ReadLine();
        }
    }
}
```

You will notice that the transaction scope is defined, which encapsulates the operations you want to handle in a single transaction.

You now modify the `App.config` file on the client project to reflect the usage of transactions, as shown in Listing 9-5. What you are doing here is enabling the transaction flow attribute.

Listing 9-5. *Modifying the Client* `App.config`

```
<system.serviceModel>
    <client>
       <endpoint name="TradeServiceConfiguration"
         address="http://localhost:8000/TradeService"
       binding="wsHttpBinding "
       bindingConfiguration="ReliableHttpBinding"
       contract="Client.ITradeService,Client"/>
    </client>
    <bindings>
        <wsHttpBinding>
            <binding name="ReliableHttpBinding" transactionFlow="true">
                <reliableSession enabled="true" ordered ="true"/>
            </binding>
        </wsHttpBinding>
    </bindings>
</system.serviceModel>
```

Now that this is done, modify the `ITradeService` interface in the client project. This will then reflect the changes that you will be making to `ITradeService` later. Listing 9-6 shows the changes.

Listing 9-6. *Modifying the Client* `ITradeService`

```
<configuration>
  <system.serviceModel>
    <bindings>
      <netTcpBinding>
        <binding name="transactionalOleTransactionsTcpBinding"
                 transactionFlow="true"
                 transactionProtocol="OleTransactions" />
      </netTcpBinding>
      <wsHttpBinding>
        <binding name="transactionalWsatHttpBinding"
                 transactionFlow="true" />
      </wsHttpBinding>
    </bindings>
    <client>
      <endpoint
        address="http://localhost:8000/QuickReturns/TradeService"
        binding="wsHttpBinding"
        bindingConfiguration="transactionalWsatHttpBinding"
        contract="ITradeService"
        name="WSAtomicTransaction_endpoint">
```

```
        <!--The username and the domain over here will have to be replaced
        by the identity under which the service will be running-->
         <!--identity>
              <userPrincipalName value="username@domain" />
         </identity-->
      </endpoint>
      <endpoint
        address="net.tcp://localhost:8008/QuickReturns/TradeService"
        binding="netTcpBinding"
        bindingConfiguration="transactionalOleTransactionsTcpBinding"
        contract="ITradeService"
        name="OleTransactions_endpoint">
        <!--The username and the domain over here will have to be replaced
        by the identity under which the service will be running -->
         <!--identity>
              <userPrincipalName value="username@domain" />
         </identity-->
      </endpoint>
    </client>
  </system.serviceModel>
</configuration>
```

Now that you have accomplished this, you can enhance the trade service so you can accomplish your goals. You will enhance the `CalculateTradeValue()` method in order to be able to accommodate the trade and log being handled in a single transaction.

Next you'll modify `ITradeService` of the QuickReturns Ltd. trade service in the same manner as you did for the client. Please refer to Listing 9-7 for details.

Listing 9-7. *Modifying* `ITradeService` *in the QuickReturns Ltd. Trade Service*

```
using System;
using System.ServiceModel;
using System.Transactions;
using System.Configuration;
using System.Data.SqlClient;
using System.Globalization;

namespace QuickReturns
{
    // Define a service contract.
    [ServiceContract(Namespace = "QuickReturns")]
    public interface ITradeService
    {
        [OperationContract]
        [TransactionFlow(TransactionFlowOption.Mandatory)]
        int CalculateTradeValue(int qty, int price);

    }
```

Once you have included the references to System.Transactions and in particular Sys.Data.SqlClient, you have laid the basis for supporting transactions, as well as supporting the logging database. So, now look at Listing 9-8, where you will set the transaction isolation level for the trade service.

Listing 9-8. *Setting the Transaction Isolation Level*

```
// Service class that implements the service contract.
 [ServiceBehavior(TransactionIsolationLevel =
      System.Transactions.IsolationLevel.Serializable)]
```

Now you'll set the transaction scope, which will encapsulate the operations you want to occur within the transaction, as shown in Listing 9-9.

Listing 9-9. *Setting the Transaction Scope*

```
public class TradeService : ITradeService
{

    [OperationBehavior(TransactionScopeRequired = true)]

     public int CalculateTradeValue(int qty, int price)
    {
        RecordToLog(String.Format(CultureInfo.CurrentCulture,
         "Recording  CAN Trade Value {0} with price {1}",
         qty,price ));
        return qty * price;
    }

    private static void RecordToLog(string recordText)
    {
        // Record the operations performed
        if (ConfigurationManager.AppSettings["usingSql"] == "true")
        {
            using (SqlConnection conn = new
            SqlConnection(ConfigurationManager.AppSettings
            ["connectionString"]))
            {
                conn.Open();
               // you are now going to log our trade to the Log Table.
                     By actually inserting the data into the table.
                SqlCommand cmdLog = new SqlCommand(
                   "INSERT into Log (Entry) Values (@Entry)",
                   conn);
                cmdLog.Parameters.AddWithValue("@Entry", recordText);
                cmdLog.ExecuteNonQuery();
                cmdLog.Dispose();
```

```
                Console.WriteLine("  Logging Trade to database:
                  {0}", recordText);

                conn.Close();
            }
        }
        else
            Console.WriteLine("  Noting row: {0}", recordText);
    }
}
```

Next you can modify the App.config file for the service host in order to ensure that all transactions are passed on to the QuickReturns Ltd. trade service. The console-based service host does not require any modifications, since the host service itself does not change. You will be calculating the trade value and returning this to the client, as well as logging the trade into the TradeService database. This is a simple database with a log table, which has an identity field and the log field. Both the transactions are occurring within a transaction scope and will fail or succeed as a single unit, as shown in Listing 9-10.

Listing 9-10. *Modifying the Host* App.config *File*

```
<?xml version="1.0" encoding="utf-8" ?>
<configuration>
  <appSettings>
    <!-- Sets connect to a database -->
    <add key="usingSql" value="true" />
    <!-- Sets the database connection string -->
    <add key="connectionString" value="DataSource=.\SQLEXPRESS;
            AttachDbFilename=
            |DataDirectory|\TradeServiceDb.mdf;Integrated Security=
            True;User Instance=True" />
</appSettings>
```

Now that you have established the database connectivity for the logging, you can modify the <Service> attributes. In Listing 9-11, you will be configuring the bindings of the service to use the WS-Atomic transaction protocol.

Listing 9-11. *Setting the* WSAtomicTransaction *Binding Configuration in* App.config

```
<system.serviceModel>
  <services>
    <service
        name="QuickReturns.TradeService"
        behaviorConfiguration="TradeServiceBehavior">
```

```
      <host>
        <baseAddresses>
          <add baseAddress="http://localhost:8000/QuickReturns/tradeservice" />
          <add baseAddress="net.tcp://localhost:8080/QuickReturns/tradeservice" />
        </baseAddresses>
      </host>

      <!-- specify wsHttpBinding with the WSAtomicTransacttional
             binding configuration -->
      <endpoint address=""
                binding="wsHttpBinding"
                bindingConfiguration="transactionalWsatHttpBinding"
                contract="QuickReturns.ITradeService"
                name="WSAtomicTransaction_endpoint" />

      <!-- specify netTcpBinding and an OleTransactions
             transactional binding configuration since that is
             what WCF uses internally-->
      <endpoint address=""
                binding="netTcpBinding"
                bindingConfiguration="transactionalOleTransactionsTcpBinding"
                contract="QuickReturns.ITradeService"
                name="OleTransactions_endpoint" />

        <!–specify the Metadata Exchange -->
      <endpoint address="mex"
                binding="mexHttpBinding"
                contract="IMetadataExchange"
                name="mex_endpoint"/>
    </service>
  </services>
```

In Listing 9-12, you will continue to modify `App.config` so that it utilizes the `transactionFlow` and sets it to true.

Listing 9-12. *Configuring Transaction Flow*

```
<!-- binding configuration - configures transaction flow  -->
<bindings>
  <netTcpBinding>
    <binding name="transactionalOleTransactionsTcpBinding
         " transactionFlow="true"  transactionProtocol=
         "OleTransactions"/>
  </netTcpBinding>
```

```
      <wsHttpBinding>
        <binding name="transactionalWsatHttpBinding" transactionFlow="true" />
      </wsHttpBinding>
    </bindings>

    <!--For debugging purposes -->
    <behaviors>
      <serviceBehaviors>
        <behavior name="TradeServiceBehavior" >
          <serviceMetadata httpGetEnabled="true" />
          <serviceDebug includeExceptionDetailInFaults="false" />
        </behavior>
      </serviceBehaviors>
    </behaviors>

  </system.serviceModel>
</configuration>
```

Finally, all you need to do is to enable the support for WS-Atomic transactions in WCF. To do this, you need to first open the .NET Framework command prompt. You can find this in the Microsoft .NET Framework SDK 3.0 program group, as shown in Figure 9-4.

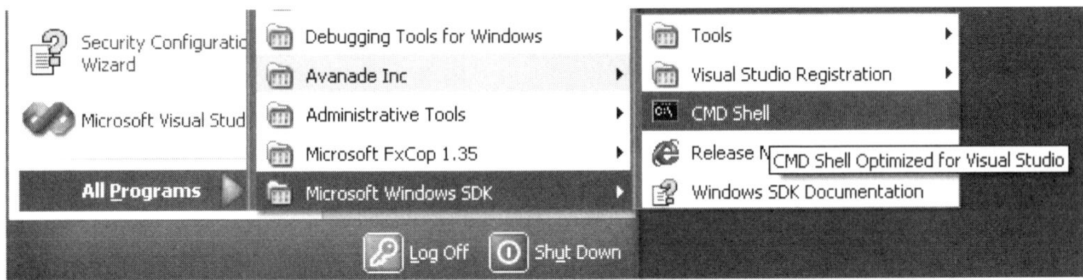

Figure 9-4. *Selecting the .NET command prompt*

At the command prompt, run `xws_reg -wsat+`, and press Enter, and you are done with configuring the transaction support for QuickReturns Ltd.

You can also register `WsatUI.dll` using `regasm.exe` to provide the Microsoft Management Console snap-in for WSAT configuration. Navigate to Control Panel ➤ Administrative Tools ➤ Component Services, and select Properties from My Computer, as shown in Figure 9-5.

To register `WsatUI.dll`, you need to run `regasm.exe /codebase WsatUI.dll` at the command prompt. You can then configure the parameters of the WS-Atomic transaction protocol from the user interface, as illustrated in Figure 9-6.

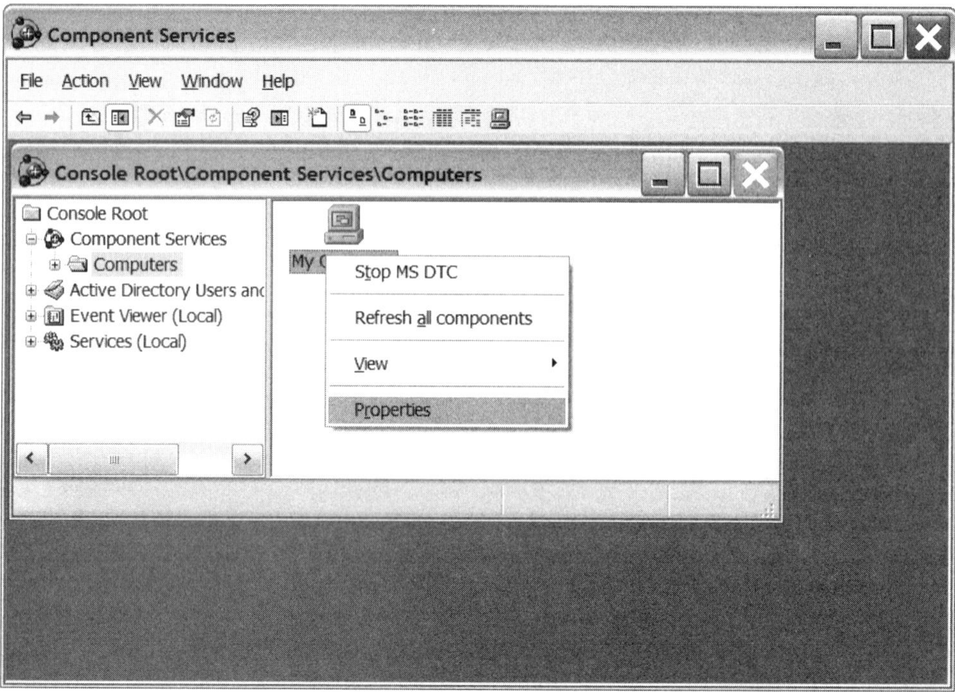

Figure 9-5. *Selecting the properties for My Computer in Component Services*

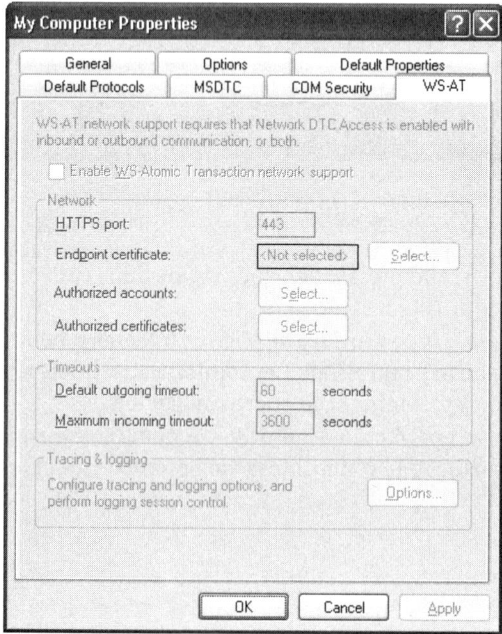

Figure 9-6. *The* `WsatUI.dll` *user interface*

When you run the application, you should see that the trades sent by the client show up in the TradeAuditService window and also that the committed trades show up in the window.

You have seen how to configure the application to use transactions in conjunction with reliable messaging. You will now learn how to make your queues utilize transactions easily.

Working with Transactions and Queues

In Chapter 8 you saw that MSMQ plays an important part in WCF and offers you a great deal of advantages in terms of reliability in scenarios that require integration with legacy applications as well as in scenarios where you require guaranteed delivery.

It is important to note that the queuing and dequeuing of messages between a client and the queue is implicitly transactional. In other words, the transfer of a message to and from a queue is transactional in nature; either the entire message will get on the queue or no part of it will be placed on the queue. This is comfortable for scenarios that require one-way messaging only. However, what if you require a series of operations under the sponsorship of a single transaction scope?

The scenario where you require multiple operations to occur as a single transaction in the context of MSMQ is often referred to as a *sessiongram*, while the single one-way operation is referred to as a *datagram*. In using sessiongram scenarios, what you are aiming for is for a group of operations to occur within the scope of a single transaction *exactly once and in order.* Open the `Chapter09\QueueMessaging` solution.

■ Note In reality, a transaction using message queues requires two transactions. The first transaction occurs between the application and the queue, and a second occurs between the queue and the receiver. If an error occurs in either one of these transactions, the transaction will abort. However, note that the messages sent under the transaction are discarded, while messages received by the queue remain in the queue until they are retried at a later time. Transactions using queues provide a level of isolation, inherent reliability, and security. However, for version 1.0 of WCF, they are not interoperable with heterogeneous systems that do not use MSMQ. Technically, you can use IBM MQSeries through the interop mechanism, which you will study in Chapters 10 and 13.

WCF makes programming MSMQ transaction scenarios a lot simpler than you would assume, as you will see, in how you configure the audit service and the client parts of your application.

Examine `QueueMessagingClient` shown in Listing 9-13. We have added support for transactions and are setting a transaction scope.

Listing 9-13. *QuickReturns Ltd.* `QueueMessagingClient`

```
using System;
using System.Transactions;

namespace QuickReturns
```

```
{
   class Client
   {
      public static void Main()
      {
         // Create a proxy for the client
         using (TradeServiceClient proxy = new TradeServiceClient())
         {
            //Create a transaction scope. This is the only line of
                code required to enable transactions in WCF
                using MSMQ
            using (TransactionScope scope = new
               TransactionScope(TransactionScopeOption.Required))
            {
               proxy.DoTrade("MSFT", "IBM", 60);
               Console.WriteLine("Beginning Transaction 1....");
                Console.WriteLine("Selling 1000 stocks of ACN and Buying IBM ");
                Console.WriteLine("Ending Transaction 1....");
                Console.WriteLine("");
                //Mark the beginning of the second transaction..
                Console.WriteLine("Beginning Transaction 2....");
               proxy.DoTrade("ACN", "ABN", 100);
               Console.WriteLine("Selling 100 stocks of ABN and Buying ACN ");
               Console.WriteLine("Beginning Transaction 2....");

               // Complete the transaction.
               scope.Complete();
            }

         }

         Console.WriteLine();
         Console.WriteLine("Press <ENTER> to terminate client.");
         Console.ReadLine();
      }
   }
}
```

MSMQ operations are by default one-way only, and to enable transactions on the service, you would require either a duplex or a request-response contract. In the current scenario, this is not possible. If you run your client only, you will see the console application shown in Figure 9-7. At this point, the messages have been put on the queue successfully, and you can rest assured that the queue will deliver the messages to the trade service when it does become available.

Even though the service is not running, the queue is able to pick up the messages and store these for when the service becomes available. You must keep in mind that the reliable and durable storage provided is in fact a feature of MSMQ and not WCF. The WS-ReliableMessaging standard does not make any assertion regarding message durability.

This means that should the machine crash, any messages that existed are lost. On the other hand, MSMQ, as a technology independent of WCF, provides you with a transport that is both reliable and durable. Messages that have persisted to the queue survive machine reboots and are lost only in the event of a catastrophic hardware failure. In the current scenario, you can benefit from this feature where the client has passed on the messages to MSMQ and the trade service is not available. To simulate a failure scenario, you could reboot the machine and then start `TradeService`, and the messages would be delivered successfully. MSMQ also provides you with the means of decoupling the transport from the application. By doing this, MSMQ can open up a whole new world of scenarios for integration. An application at the end of the queue may or may not be a WCF application or even a Windows-based application. The only requirement is that it is able to communicate with MSMQ. This decoupling of the transport from the application, as well as the availability of a durable store for the application, provides you the tools to build highly resilient enterprise applications without having to write code, since the Windows platform provides you with the functionality out of the box.

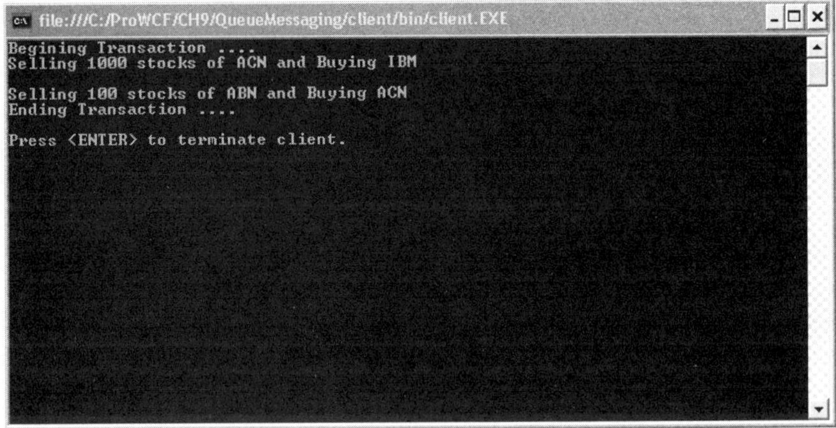

Figure 9-7. *The client placing messages on the queue*

Note WCF provides support for integrating with MSMQ out of the box. However, queues are possible even without MSMQ, and you could decide to write your own queue provider. Technically, it would be possible to interact with your queue provider if it provides an API that WCF understands. This, although technically possible, is extremely difficult to accomplish. Please refer to `http://msdn.microsoft.com/library/default.asp?url=/library/en-us/msmq/html/ff917e87-05d5-478f-9430-0f560675ece1.asp` for further details about the MSMQ provider. To get started with building custom queue providers, refer to `http://www.wsmq.com/`. WSMQ is an open source initiative to provide a web service–based message queue and will help you get started in writing your own queues.

When you do start an instance of the trade service, the messages are passed on to the service by the queue, as shown in Figure 9-8.

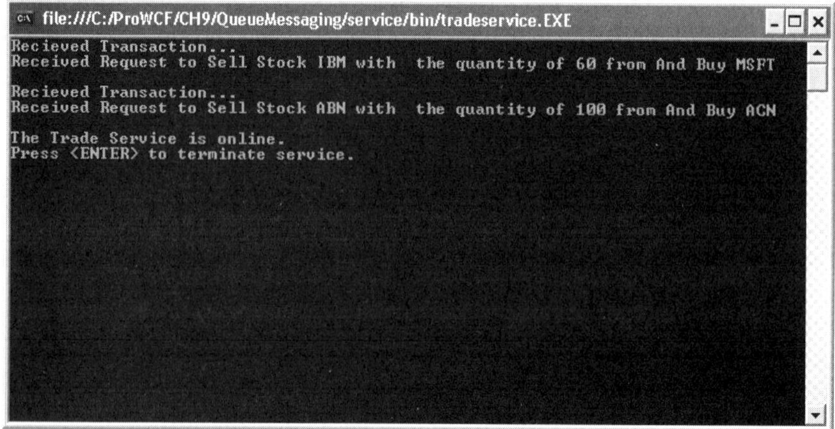

Figure 9-8. *Transactions received by the trade service*

A rule of thumb when using transactions with queues is the setting for `ExactlyOnce`; set this to true if you are using transacted queues and to false if using nontransacted queues. However, be aware that setting this to false can degrade reliability, and you should evaluate this on a case-by-case basis.

A WORD ABOUT DLQ AND POISON QUEUES

In Chapter 8 you learned about the dead letter queues (DLQs) and poison queue functionality. It is possible to use the functionality provided by the poison queue to ensure your transactions are retried multiple times at set intervals rather than failing after the first attempt. This feature will become available in Windows Server 2007 and will add to the powerful arsenal of tools available to you.

A message will generally become poisoned if the queue has tried to deliver it to the receiver but the number of retries has been exceeded. Although this can happen because of network outages and service unavailability amongst other reasons, you can configure the message to be retried after a set amount of time has elapsed, as well as configure the number of times the queue should retry. Once this number has been exceeded, the message will be placed in the DLQ.

The DLQ is configurable on a per-system or per-application basis in Windows Server 2007. In versions of Windows Server prior to Windows Server 2007, you have only one DLQ per system. Consequently, if multiple applications or multiple parts of an application are using MSMQ, all the messages that have exceeded their retry or timeout parameters will end up in this queue. Processing the messages from the DLQ then becomes a challenge, especially if you have discrete destinations based on message types. For example, if you take the QuickReturns Ltd. application, in an MSMQ scenario you might have trade messages, as well as messages related to the trader's accounts. You would need to write discrete code to interrogate the messages and route these to their appropriate destinations when building systems not based on MSMQ 4.0 or later.

The ability to configure per-application DLQs in Windows Server 2007 means that you can then have one DLQ for the trade service and another DLQ for the account service. Doing the latter will give you further flexibility for providing greater levels of resilience in your application. It is recommended that you study these features as they become available in MSMQ 4.0 on Windows Server 2007 and, as an architect, utilize the functionality available to you to increase the reliability of your applications.

Summary

In this chapter, you learned the following:

- The need for transactions to solve issues around deadlocks, ensuring repeatability and recoverability
- How transactions are supported by WCF with the WS-Atomic transaction protocol
- How to use transactions with your services and sessions using the various behavior attributes provided by WCF including the `ServiceBehavior` and `OperationBehavior` attributes
- How to use the MSMQ transport channel with transactions by incorporating support for transactions within your application

We recommend the Windows Server 2007 SDK and WCF documentation for further reading on this topic. Please dive into the code listings about implementing the `System.Transactions` namespace within the .NET Framework also.

Transactions are critical to your applications, and you must look at the requirements for transactions in conjunction with the scope of reliable messaging since these go hand in hand. It is safe to say that building an enterprise application without transactional support is a recipe for failure.

Looking ahead to Chapter 10, you will learn about how to integrate with legacy COM+ applications. Some of the topics that would be covered are aimed at not only the aspects around integration but also how to run COM+ services within WCF, as well as typed and early bound contracts with COM.

CHAPTER 10

Integrating with COM+

This chapter is about working with the past. That past is based upon component technology created by Microsoft to provide, at first, a desktop-oriented protocol for reusing application logic. That technology expanded into a distributed technology that helped better position Microsoft in the enterprise and provide a challenge to competing technologies.

Not without faults, numerous applications were developed based upon this component technology. As a result, we can't forget the amount of investment by enterprises in this technology. It would damage Microsoft's credibility and the marketability if Microsoft introduced a new technology that would force an enterprise to scrap its original investments. Therefore, Microsoft and the WCF team worked hard to provide an evolutionary, as opposed to revolutionary, approach for bridging the technological divide, never forgetting the famous quote "Those who cannot remember the past are condemned to repeat it."[1]

Introduced in 1993, Component Object Model (COM) was the basis for other emerging technologies from Microsoft such as Object Linking and Embedding (OLE), ActiveX, and Distributed COM (DCOM). COM was initially introduced to compete with Common Object Request Broker Architecture (CORBA), a language-independent and cross-platform distributed system technology. They did share some core principles, but they were not compatible. Concepts and techniques such as Interface Definition Language (IDL) are present in both technologies. But, binary interoperability didn't exist.

COM+, introduced in 1998, was more of ancillary technology that worked with COM but did not replace it. Key features of COM+ are transactional components, queued components, role-based security, and object pooling. COM+ 1.5 added features such as application pooling, SOAP services, services without components, and some other features.[2]

Today, COM+ 1.5 is a core part of the Windows platform. Even with the .NET base class library (BCL) COM interoperability still occurs. Runtime callable wrappers (RCW) are used throughout the .NET BCL—one prime example in .NET 2.0 is the web browser control, which is, as stated in the MSDN documentation, a managed wrapper for the web browser's ActiveX control. Additionally, serviced components use COM+ transactions.

---

1. Attributed to George Santayana, 19th-century philosopher

2. You can learn more in the topic "What's new in COM+ 1.5" on MSDN at `http://msdn.microsoft.com/library/en-us/cossdk/html/e7073ba5-6b19-4d94-8cc0-b4e16bb44afd.asp`.

Why Integrate with COM+?

Although the future of the Windows platform seems to be a managed world, COM+ will still be around. COM exists in the core Windows platform[3] but most important also in the billions of lines of code that independent software developers have written to produce solutions. A great number of solutions have been built on COM+ by enterprises that have also spent billions of their dollars. So, clearly WCF needs to work with legacy implementations in order to justify an investment in extending existing applications.

Few applications built today are completely stand-alone. In fact, the terms *application* and *solution* need a little definition. Generally, an *application* represents a stand-alone deployable set of components, functionality, and so on. A *solution*, however, represents a combination of applications coupled together (either tightly or loosely) to address numerous business-processing requirements.

So today, we need to build solutions. These solutions will most likely require integration with existing data and processes that exist in legacy technology, where some of that technology will be COM+. The other part of the enterprise solution demands that existing COM+ applications aren't going to be thrown away and rewritten in .NET and WCF. Since we're building all these new applications based upon .NET and they'll of course offer fantastic services that you'll just need to share, you'll need a way to provide legacy COM+ applications to call your services, just as any other application would. Fortunately, the WCF team has provided the core tools to facilitate both sides of the interoperability needs.

This chapter will walk you through how to consume COM+ application services from WCF clients. Additionally, you'll look at how legacy applications can use applications that expose WCF services built on .NET 3.0.

Running a COM+ Application As a WCF Service

Let's take a look at a scenario involving QuickReturns Ltd.'s `OldHorse` position-tracking system (or a custody system), as shown in Figure 10-1. `OldHorse` was built in the late 1990s using Visual Basic 6. Since other groups within QuickReturns Ltd. leverage `OldHorse`, the `OldHorse` development team provided COM interfaces allowing client applications to interoperate with `OldHorse` using COM+.

When an Asset Manager makes a trade, it's necessary that the trade information is posted to the custody system. Additionally, as you'll see later, it's necessary that the custody system checks with the Asset Manager's system for pricing and pending trade information.

3. In addition to the Win32 API that has gone legacy—but still exists and matures

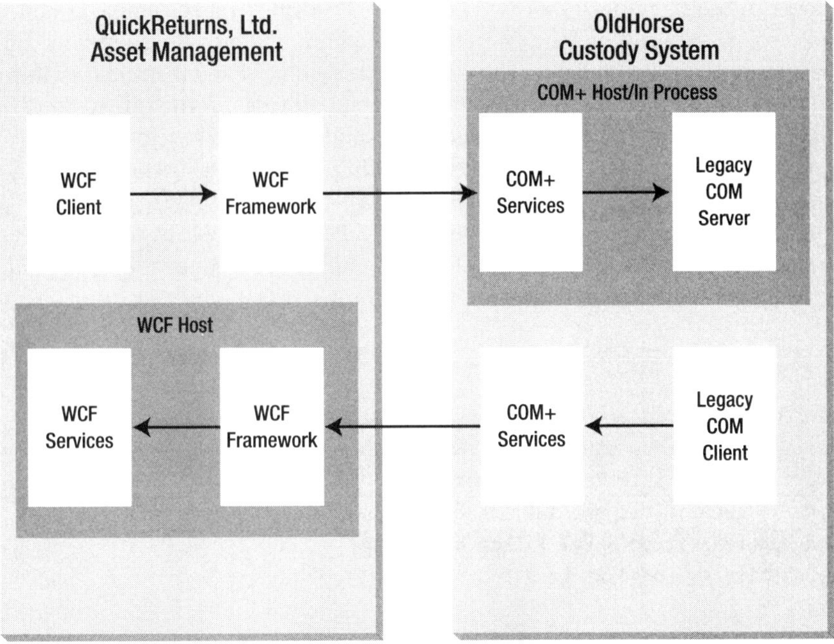

Figure 10-1. *QuickReturns Ltd.'s* `OldHorse` *system*

Visual Basic 6 COM+ Component Sample Setup

The example we'll use is a simple Visual Basic 6 COM (ActiveX DLL) component that exposes two interfaces. The complete solution is contained in the chapter sample code's `Visual Basic 6 Project` folder. The following code snippets are just the method signatures representing the Visual Basic 6 COM interface. This is an illustration of a Visual Basic 6 component and should not be viewed as a Visual Basic 6 best practice.

When looking at Visual Basic 6 COM components, you'll soon see that some issues relate to how the WCF interfaces leverage type library information in regard to COM+ application components. Visual Basic 6 COM packs both the component logic and the type library information inside the COM DLL; doing so adds some attributes that prevent some interfaces from being initially wrapped in WCF COM+ integration.

Prior to working through this example, set up a virtual directory in IIS called `VB6ComSample` that is set for ASP.NET 2.0 and has anonymous access enabled.

The PositionManagement interface shown in Listing 10-1 provides a set of simple methods that allow the retrieval of the position for a given ticker, in addition to providing a method for updating the persisted quantity associated with a ticker.[4] One element that is not shown is a constructor. COM+ objects don't offer a constructor. They can provide information in other ways, such as with an initialization method. Visual Basic 6 and COM offer several ways of providing static configuration information such as COM+ initialization strings on the configured component; however, that requires implementing IObjectConstructString in Visual Basic 6 and using the ConstructionEnable attribute in .NET. For the example code and to keep it simple, we're just showing method interfaces. The ability to provide a connection string on object construction is something that could be provided through COM+ initialization.

Listing 10-1. PositionManagement.cls

```
'Simple interface that allows a nominal change in the quantity of a position
'ticker: Ticker symbol of security
'quantity: Amount (+/-) to shift existing position
'Throws an error if quantity is not sufficient to support the change (overdrawn)
Public Function UpdatePosition(ByVal Ticker As String, _
        ByVal Quantity As Long) As Long
...
Public Function GetQuantity(ByVal Ticker As String) As Long
...
```

The second component is the Position component. This class represents mostly a data class with read/write properties. In addition, it has two methods; one provides a retrieval of a specific position for a ticker, and the other returns a concrete Position object for a specific ticker. Listing 10-2 shows the abbreviated class, and the full class is part of the chapter code in \OldHorsePositionTracking\VB6\PositionManagement.

Listing 10-2. *Visual Basic 6* Position *Class:* Position.cls

```
Public Property Let Quantity(ByVal vData As Long)
...
Public Property Get Quantity() As Long
...
Public Property Let Ticker(ByVal vData As String)
...
Public Property Get Ticker() As String
...
Public Function GetQuantity(ByVal Ticker As String) As Long
...
Public Function GetPosition(ByVal Ticker As String) As Position
...
```

4. Note these are simplified interfaces for example purposes only and do not represent a proper interface definition for a fully functional custody system.

One additional aspect of the `PositonManagement` class is that it's configured in Visual Basic 6 to be an MTS component with a Required transaction setting. This setting is reflected in the generated WCF service inside the configuration file and is handled automatically by the COM+ Integration Wizard, which makes a call to the `ComSvcConfig.exe` utility. This allows flow from a WCF client to your COM+ component, ultimately being managed by the Microsoft Distributed Transaction Coordinator (MSDTC).

Once the project is built to an ActiveX DLL, it is ready to be installed and configured as a COM+ application. Briefly, for a Visual Basic 6 COM component, you follow these steps to create the `OldHorse` COM+ application:[5]

1. From Administrative Tools, launch Component Services.[6] Then, expand the Component Services node until you are at the computer you want to configure for your COM+ application. In this example, it's the local machine, or My Computer. Select the COM+ Applications object in the console, right-click, and choose New Application, as shown in Figure 10-2.

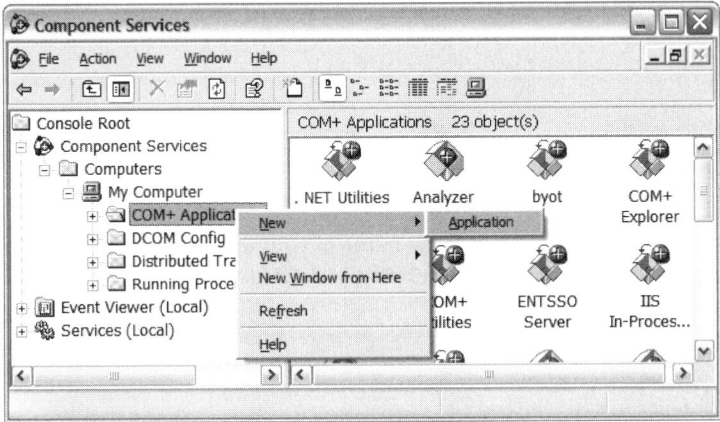

Figure 10-2. *Creating a new COM+ application*

5. We won't go into too much depth about how to create Visual Basic 6 COM+ applications. Note that these steps for COM+ applications are programmable through the COM Administration type library. However, .NET offers the `RegSvcs.exe` utility that provides a simple command-line interface for this.

6. You can also get to this Microsoft Management Console (MMC) via the dcomcnfg.exe command.

2. At this point you're presented with the COM+ Application Install Wizard. Click through the first page of the wizard. On the second page, click the Create an Empty Application button, as shown in Figure 10-3.

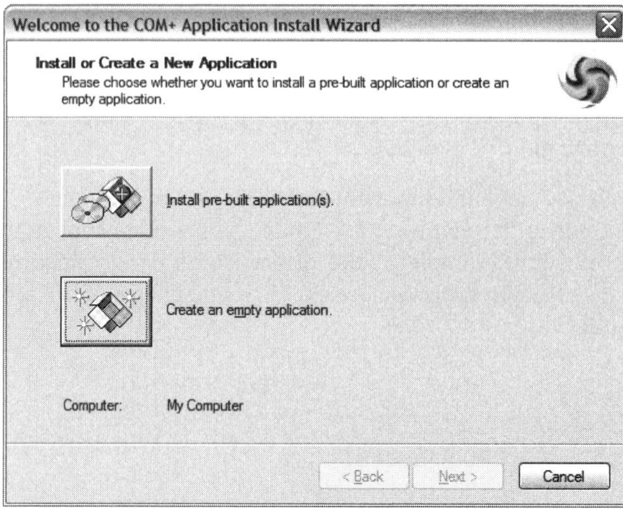

Figure 10-3. *Creating an empty COM+ application*

3. On the next page of the wizard, enter the name of your application, and ensure you select Library Application as the activation type (see Figure 10-4).

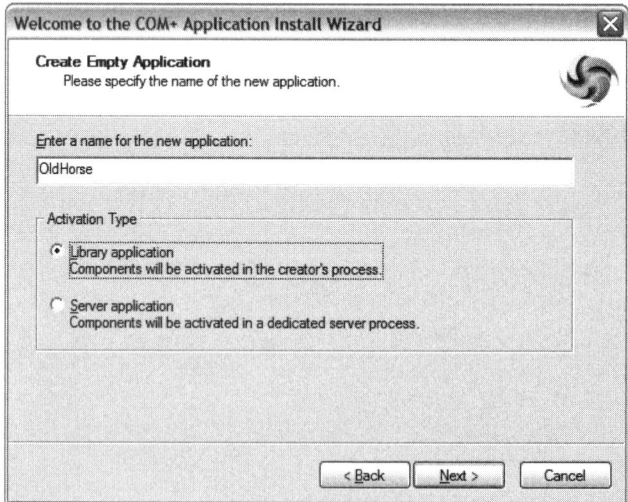

Figure 10-4. `OldHorse` *library activation*

4. Click through the last page of the wizard. At this point, you should now have a COM+ application defined in Component Services. However, this is an empty package and has no associated components.

5. The next step is to add your compiled ActiveX DLL into the package. Do that by first selecting the Components tree from within the `OldHorse` COM+ application. Right-click the Components folder under the `OldHorse` application, and then choose ➤ New ➤ Component, as shown in Figure 10-5.

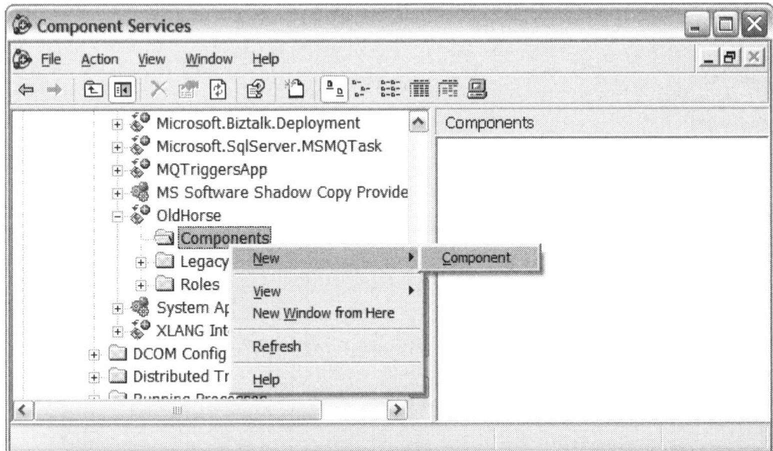

Figure 10-5. *Adding a new component to the* `OldHorse` *application*

6. This opens the COM+ Component Installation Wizard. Click Next in the wizard, and then choose Install New Component(s). Then, navigate to where your Visual Basic 6 COM component's DLL resides (if you have extracted the samples, it is located in the directory `\OldHorsePositionTracking\VB6\PositionManagement\bin`). Choose it, and then click Next until the wizard is dismissed.

At this point you should have a COM+ application with the components shown in Figure 10-6.

First, you'll see two components each with a single interface listed—the name manufactured by the Visual Basic 6 framework. Second, in the right pane, notice the Required transaction attribute. (You can see this view by clicking the detail view.) This attribute forces the activation of this component within a COM+ transaction—either a new transaction or an inherited transactional context from the caller.

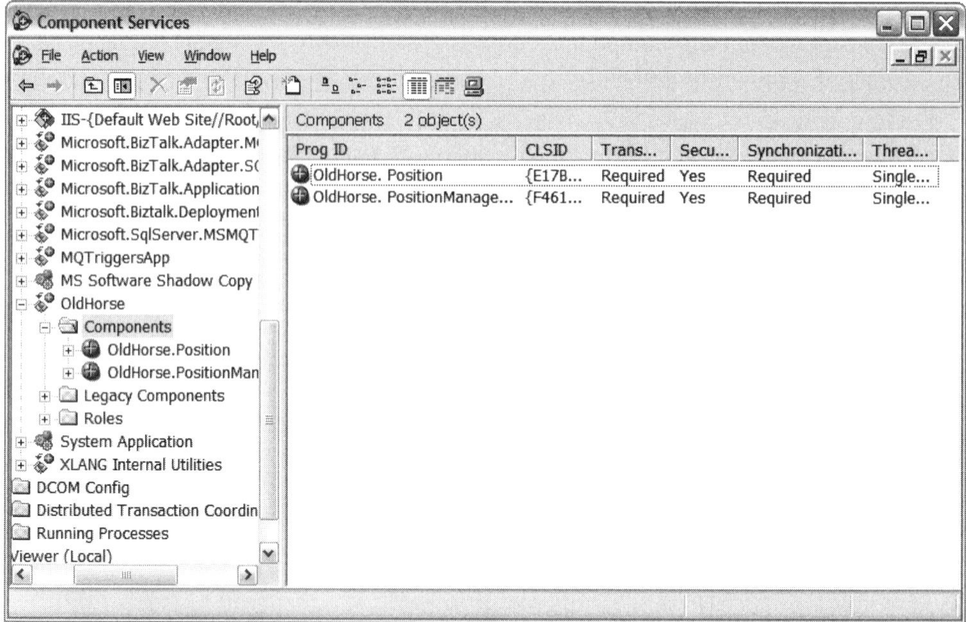

Figure 10-6. *Configured* `OldHorse` *COM+ application*

COM+ Application WCF Service Wrapper

Once a COM+ application is configured, you're ready to leverage WCF's utilities for creating the necessary resources for calling a COM+ component from a WCF client. The primary utility for this is the `ComSvcConfig.exe` utility. This is a command-line utility that is installed with the .NET 3.0 runtime. Additionally, the `SvcConfigEditor.exe` utility provides a graphical interface with some additional features that help hide the complexities of the command-line `ComSvcConfig.exe` utility. One suggestion is to get used to the `SvcConfigEditor.exe` utility; it facilitates the composition of proper configuration files for WCF with configuration-time validation of many elements.

Using SvcConfigEditor.exe Utility

Before you proceed, it's important to understand some caveats related to COM+ interoperability with WCF. There are restrictions as to what COM+ interfaces can be exposed as a web service through the COM+ Integration layer. Those restrictions are listed in the SDK, but some of them are as follows:

Interfaces that pass object references as parameters: This violates a core tenet of SOA in that passing a reference across a service boundary is expensive.

Interfaces that pass types that are not compatible with the .NET Framework COM interop conversions: This is a general incompatibility issue for types that won't serialize between the interoperability layers.

Interfaces for applications that have application pooling enabled when hosted by COM+: This causes multiple listeners on the same URI moniker issues because there will be more than one application pool attempting to reserve the service endpoint address.

Interfaces from managed components that have not been added to the global assembly cache (GAC): This is a general limitation of how COM+ hosts configured managed components. There are other means of using COM+ from managed applications (services without components[7]), but they are not supported with WCF COM+ integration.

The first item mentioned here is important because given that one of the core tenets of SOA is that boundaries are explicit, it would be expensive to share an interface pointer across the service boundary. Also, given that the default WCF service behavior `InstanceContext` mode is `PerCall`, this is something your SOA implementation should consider.

In addition to the previously listed limitations, you'll soon see some limitations with Visual Basic 6 components and, specifically, how Visual Basic 6 components are implemented.

At this point, you're ready to create a WCF interoperability layer around your COM+ components. Start by launching the `SvcConfigEditor.exe` utility, which is located in the Microsoft SDK's `Bin` directory. The easiest way is to launch the CMD shell shortcut that gets installed on your Start menu under the Microsoft Windows SDK program group or from within the Visual Studio 2005 Tools menu as WCF Service Configuration Editor.

Start with no configuration file, and have the utility generate the necessary parts; this will allow you to call the `OldHorse` component from a WCF client.

From the menu bar of `SvcConfigEditor.exe`, select File ➤ Integrate ➤ COM+ Application. At this point you should see a listing of all the COM+ applications, including `OldHorse`, that are present on the local machine, as shown in Figure 10-7.

If you expand the `OldHorse.PositionManagement` node until you are able to see the list of interfaces (which will list only one), then select the `_PositionManagement` interface, and click Next. At this point, you should see the page shown in Figure 10-8.

---

7. Services without components were introduced with COM+ 1.5. See `http://msdn2.microsoft.com/en-us/library/ms172373.aspx`.

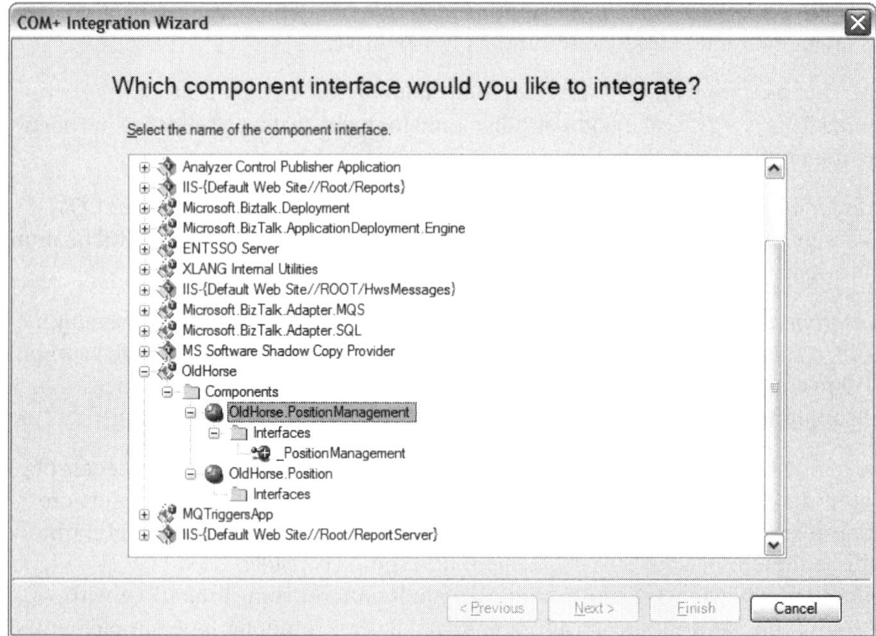

Figure 10-7. *COM+ Integration Wizard*

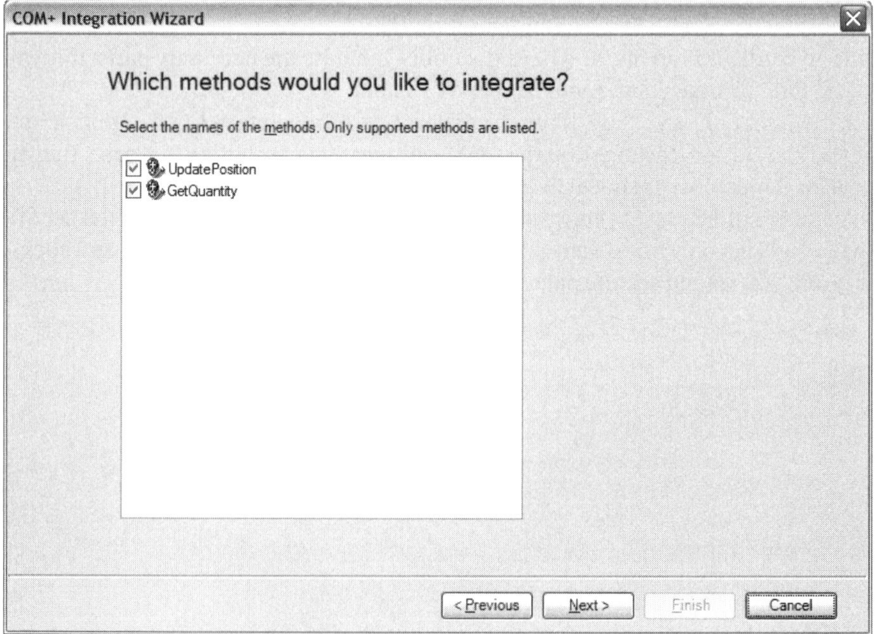

Figure 10-8. `_PositionManagement` *interface*

Keep all selected, and just click Next. This presents the Hosting Mode options. Choose the web hosting in-process mode, which allows per-message activation and hosting within the IIS/WAS worker process. The other hosting options are not available for library-activated (in-process) applications and are enabled when the activation type is Server Activated (out-of-process). Ensure that the Add MEX endpoint option is enabled. This allows clients to leverage WS-Metadata Exchange to query the interface for contract and service information.

The next page of the wizard lists the IIS virtual directories on the local machine. Make sure you choose an IIS virtual directory that is configured for .NET 2.0. For this example, we've preconfigured a virtual directory called `/localhost/VB6ComSample` (see Figure 10-9) that is configured for ASP.NET 2.0.

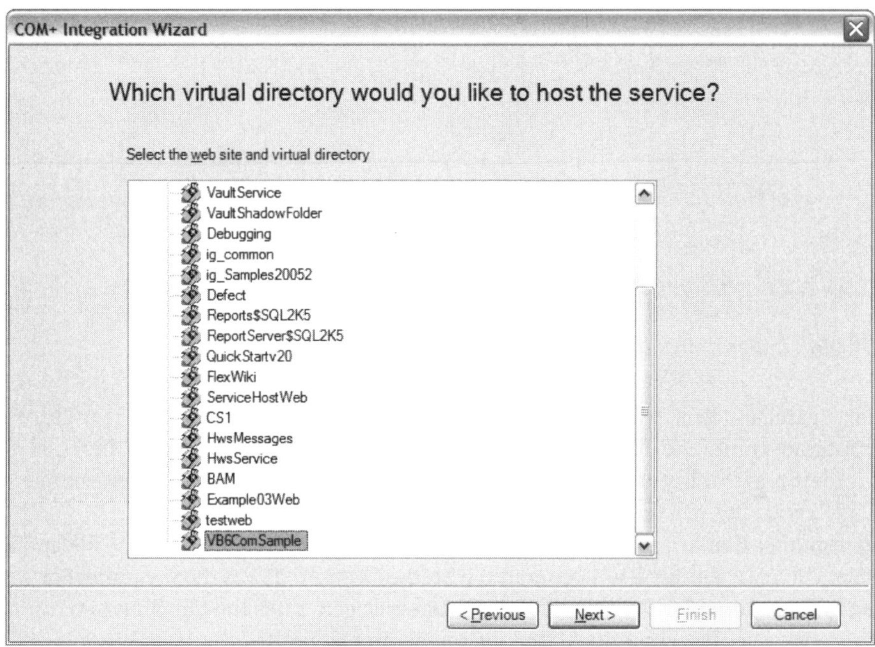

Figure 10-9. *Choosing an IIS virtual directory*

At that point, click Next, and you're presented with the summary of options shown in Figure 10-10.

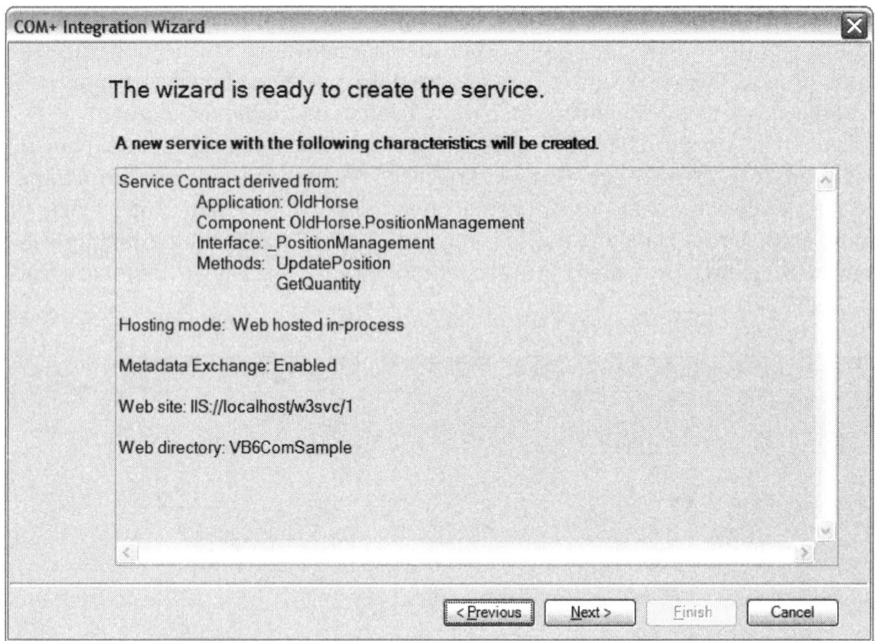

Figure 10-10. *COM+ integration summary page*

Click Next again, and `SvcConfigEditor.exe` makes a call to the `ComSvcConfig.exe` utility with the appropriate command-line options. This generates two files in the virtual directory. If the `SvcConfigEditor.exe` utility cannot find the `ComSvcConfig.exe` utility, you'll be presented with a message box asking you to specify where it can be located.[8]

The two resources that are generated provide the WCF wrapper service resource file and a `Web.config` file. The WCF service file is generated with the COM `ProgID` as the filename. For this example, the component `OldHorse.PositionManagement` generates the file `OldHorse.PositionManagement.svc`. The contents of that file appear in Listing 10-3.

Listing 10-3. `OldHorse.PositionManagement.svc`

```
<%@ServiceHost .ServiceModel.ComIntegration.
WasHostedComPlusFactory" WasHostedComP12Service=
"{f4612210-b755-4e17-87db-f82d9751d582},
{d3a08ae7-1857-409d-97aa-d86c0b366f5f}" %>
```

The SVC file contains a single line that points to the service factory that will provide the COM+ integration—`WasHostedComPlusFactory`. The second parameter, `WasHostedComP12Service`, provides two initialization parameters for the factory class. The first is the GUID for the COM interface as specified by the type library for the COM component. If you leverage a tool such as `OleView` (which comes with the Windows SDK), view the type library for `OldHorse`, and dump the

8. The `ComSvcConfig.exe` utility is located at `%SystemRoot%\Microsoft.NET\Framework\v3.0\Windows Communication Foundation`.

IDL, you'll see that the supplied GUID matches the UUID of the implementation class, which is `PositionManagement`.

The second parameter represents the COM+ application ID, which is visible by choosing the properties of the COM+ application from the Component Services management console. So, the combination of the application ID and the CLSID (`ProgID` reference from COM) is a direct pointer that allows the WCF COM+ integration runtime to locate, instantiate, and service the WCF client call.

If you check the properties of the `OldHorse.PositionManagement` component from within Component Services, you'll see that the CLSID GUID and application GUID both match the generated GUIDs in the `OldHorse.PositionManagement.svc` file, as shown in Figure 10-11.

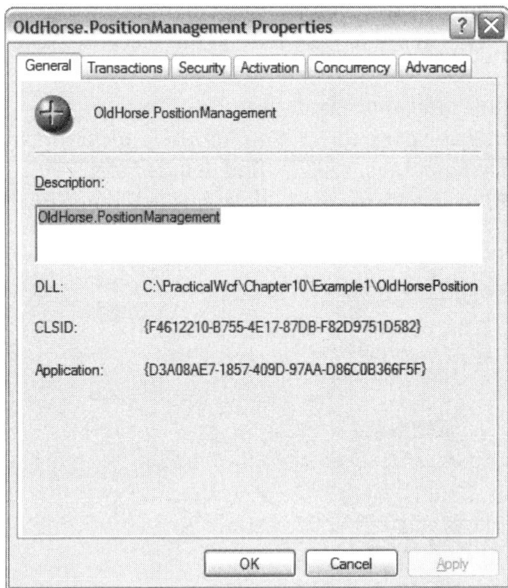

Figure 10-11. `OldHorse.PositionManagement` *properties*

Using ComSvcConfig.exe Utility

You can also use the stand-alone `ComSvcConfig.exe` utility to generate the required resource's COM+ application integration. The primary difference is it doesn't provide the up-front validation that the `SvcConfigEditor.exe` utility does for validating supported COM interfaces prior to generation. Instead, it provides that information as error messages at runtime.

Using the same COM+ application as an example, the following command generates the required resources for wrapping your COM+ application's `PositionManagement` interface in a WCF service and hosting inside IIS/WAS (all on a single line).

```
ComSvcConfig.exe /install /application:OldHorse
/contract:OldHorse.PositionManagement,_PositionManagement
/hosting:was /webdirectory:VB6ComSample /mex
```

In addition to the /install option listed here, there are two additional primary actions: /list and /uninstall. The /list option enumerates what WCF COM+ integration services currently exist on the local machine. The /uninstall option removes the application .svc file in addition to updating the Web.config (or application configuration) file, removing all references to the identified application and interface.

Client Proxy Generation

At this point, you're ready to create the client proxy for your WCF COM+ integration, using either the SvcUtil.exe utility or the Visual Studio 2005 Add Service Reference add-in, as described in Chapter 5. Before proceeding, ensure that the IIS website that you will be using has anonymous access enabled (accessed through the Directory Security tab in IIS Virtual Directory properties). A completed solution appears in the sample code in the \VB6ComClient directory.

In this section, you'll create a simple console application. Start Visual Studio 2005, and create a new Windows console project. Once you have done this, right-click the project (or select the Project menu), and choose Add Service Reference. You can find detailed steps for generating service proxies in Chapter 4. The URI to specify for the Add Service Reference dialog box looks like Figure 10-12.

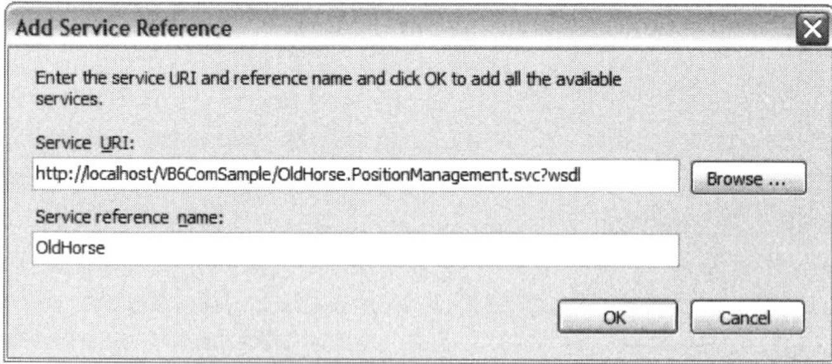

Figure 10-12. *Adding a service reference to a COM+ WCF wrapper*

Once you've generated the service reference, you can now provide the client code. Inside the Main method, the example code looks like Listing 10-4, which shows the completed client project's program.cs class file.

Listing 10-4. *WCF COM+ Integration Client*

```
namespace VB6ComClient
{
    class Program
    {
        static void Main( string[] args )
        {
            OldHorse._PositionManagementClient proxy =
               new VB6ComClient.OldHorse._PositionManagementClient();
```

```
            int q = proxy.GetQuantity( "MSFT" );
            Console.WriteLine( "We have " + q + " of MSFT" );
            q = proxy.UpdatePosition( "MSFT", 100 );
            Console.WriteLine( "We now have " + q + " of MSFT" );
            proxy.Close();
            proxy = null;
            Console.WriteLine("Press return to end..." );
            Console.ReadLine();

        }
    }
}
```

As shown in Listing 10-4, you simply instantiate a proxy type using the default constructor (which reads address, binding, and contract information from the configuration file). Using the `_PositionManagementClient` object (which was automatically generated from `SvcUtil.exe`), you then make a call to the methods exposed on the interface.

Consuming the `PositionManagement` interface from a WCF client is done just like with any other WCF-generated proxy type. In this model, the call is handed from the client over HTTP, which is then received by the IIS/`Http.sys` listener framework, and finally onto the WCF framework inside the `WasHostedComPlusFactory` type. The WCF framework does a runtime lookup of the COM+ information, instantiates the Visual Basic 6 COM component, and services the call.

One thing to note is that given the default service `InstanceContext` behavior is `PerCall`, the WCF COM+ integration framework will service each call with a new `PositionManagement` object. Therefore, if you require server-side state, you must modify the service behavior. Review Chapters 3 and 6 for details about service behavior.

Visual Basic 6 COM+ Hiding Interfaces

During the generation of the WCF COM+ integration components for your `OldHorse` Visual Basic 6 ActiveX DLL, the `Position` component, while visible in the component selection page as shown in Figure 10-7 earlier in the chapter, offered no visible interfaces for use with the WCF COM+ integration. This is because Visual Basic 6 generates hidden interfaces for the type library information that is bundled with the COM DLL for nonprimitive types. Generally, when using other COM+ languages, specifically C/C++, generating the type library information, a critical aspect of COM+ programming, is done using IDL and compiled into a type library (TLB) that is then used by the implementation programmer to ensure adherence to the *contract*. Any interfaces that have any hidden types as parameters or return values are not available in the WCF COM+ integration framework.

So, if you have an investment in Visual Basic 6 COM+ components, you may need to consider alternate methods of generation of type library information. Please see the sidebar "Visual Basic 6 COM and Contract-First Programming."

VISUAL BASIC 6 COM AND CONTRACT-FIRST PROGRAMMING

When COM was introduced, it provided a capable component architecture that permitted developers to leverage binary compatibility and reuse components across solutions. With this came the complexity of COM (reference tracking especially) and the language of COM itself. A core component of COM definitions are buried inside the type library for each COM component. C/C++ programmers are used to seeing IDL, which describes the COM interfaces of implementation components.

Visual Basic programmers are generally not accustomed to working with IDL. This is because Visual Basic 6 hides the inner workings of COM. However, it is possible to take a contract-first approach in working with Visual Basic 6 and COM.

Generally, you can find good references on the Internet, and the following link provides examples and shows how to provide a contract-first approach to Visual Basic 6 COM development: `http://msdn.microsoft.com/library/default.asp?url=/library/en-us/dncomg/html/msdn_vbscriptcom.asp`.

For the `OldHorse` Visual Basic 6 COM implementation, the reason the WCF COM+ Integration Wizard ignores the `Position` interface is because of the method `GetPosition` that returns a `Position` object. Visual Basic 6 has hidden the internally generated `_Position` (note the underscore) interface from consumers of the type library; therefore, it's not possible to create a type of `_Position` by a caller—generally that's up to the COM component.

Using `OleView.exe` (which comes with the Windows SDK), if you dump the IDL and inspect the `_Position` interface, you can see it's marked with a `hidden` attribute (see Listing 10-5).

Listing 10-5. `OldHorse` *Visual Basic 6 COM Position IDL*

```
    [
  odl,
  uuid(7E22753A-CD1B-4620-A952-E3CDFD456431),
  version(1.0),
  hidden,
  dual,
  nonextensible,
  oleautomation
]
interface _Position : IDispatch {
    [id(0x68030001), propput] HRESULT Quantity([in] long );
    [id(0x68030001), propget] HRESULT Quantity([out, retval] long* );
    [id(0x68030000), propput] HRESULT Ticker([in] BSTR );
    [id(0x68030000), propget] HRESULT Ticker([out, retval] BSTR* );
    [id(0x60030002)] HRESULT GetQuantity(
                    [in] BSTR Ticker,
                    [out, retval] long* );
    [id(0x60030003)] HRESULT GetPosition(
                    [in] BSTR Ticker,
                    [out, retval] _Position** );
};
```

USING OLEVIEW.EXE

OleView.exe is the COM/OLE viewer utility that helps you view COM interfaces and type libraries registered on a machine.

To view the OldHorse type library information, open OleView.exe, and then navigate into the Type Libraries folder. In that folder you should see the OldHorse (Ver 1.0) type library registration. Initially, in the right pane you'll see the type library information as stored in the registry under the HKCR\TypeLib\{GUID} where the GUID is the type library's UUID.

At this point, to view the IDL, double-click the entry OldHorse (Ver 1.0) in the left pane; this opens another window showing you the detailed interface information on the left pane along with the IDL in the right pane.

```
[
  uuid(E17BC5E8-0378-4775-88DE-BADB73C57F03),
  version(1.0)
]
coclass Position {
    [default] interface _Position;
};
```

Through the IDL you can see why the WCF COM+ Integration Wizard did not display this interface and how you use interface names when you are using the ComSvcConfig.exe utility. You don't actually use the class names as declared inside the Visual Basic 6 class files; you use the generated interface names that Visual Basic 6 provides (prefixed with an underscore, _).

So, again, if you require access to the Position object through the WCF service boundary, you have a couple of work-arounds (there may be more):

- Remediate Visual Basic 6 to leverage contract-first COM+ development (see the sidebar "Visual Basic 6 COM and Contract-First Programming").
- Provide a .NET wrapper that interacts directly with Visual Basic 6 COM components and exposes .NET types on the service boundary.

.NET Enterprise Services and COM+ Components

For another example, we've included a simple .NET 2.0 class library that represents the OldHorse2 COM+ application but written in .NET 2.0 using Enterprise Services and serviced components.

This solution file is located as part of the Chapter 10 projects:

```
OldHorsePositionTracking\DotNet\OldHorse2Sln
```

Prior to stepping through this example, set up a virtual directory inside IIS called DotNetComSample that is configured as ASP.NET 2.0 and has anonymous access enabled. The script CreateVirtualDirs.bat will create the IIS virtual directories and set the .NET runtime to 2.0 for the sites.

The solution also contains a couple of batch files (reg.bat and unreg.bat) that handle the GAC installation and COM+ application configuration. These batch files use the GacUtil.exe utility and the RegSvcs.exe utility that handles GAC and COM+ registration. As listed in the SDK requirements, a .NET component that is also a serviced component (COM+) must be registered in the GAC, which requires it to have a strong name.

The implementation of OldHorse2 is a mirror image of the Visual Basic 6 COM example, except it uses attributes from the Enterprise Services namespaces. Additionally, the Guid attribute is applied to ensure you leverage a consistent CLSID and APPID instead of relying on the framework to regenerate each time.

For the OldHorse2 project, Listing 10-6 shows the PositionManagement class. The code provides the sample simple interface as the Visual Basic 6 version along with Transaction attributes and AutoComplete attributes for transaction management.

Listing 10-6. OldHorse2 PositionManagement.cs

```
using System;
using System.EnterpriseServices;
using System.Runtime.InteropServices;

namespace OldHorse2
{

    [Guid( "3B26F4CA-E839-4ab6-86D4-AADB0A8AADA5" )]
    public interface IPositionManagement
    {
        long UpdatePosition( string ticker, long quantity );
        long GetQuantity( string ticker );
    }

    [Guid( "08F01AD6-F3EB-4f41-A73A-270AA942881A" )]
    [Transaction(TransactionOption.Required)]
    public class PositionManagement : ServicedComponent, IPositionManagement
    {
        public PositionManagement() {}

        #region IPositionManagement Members

        [AutoComplete]
        public long UpdatePosition( string ticker, long quantity )
        {
            IPosition pos = new Position();
            pos = pos.GetPosition( ticker );
            pos.Quantity += quantity;
            return pos.Quantity;
        }
```

```
        [AutoComplete]
        public long GetQuantity( string ticker )
        {
            IPosition pos = new Position();
            pos = pos.GetPosition( ticker );
            return pos.Quantity;
        }

        #endregion
    }
}
```

As you can see in the code in Listing 10-6, we've specifically provided the interface `IPositionManagement` that is implemented in the class `PositionManagement`, which also inherits from `ServicedComponent`. Additionally, the class has the `TransactionOption.Required` setting with each method having the `AutoComplete` attribute from Enterprise Services. This will ensure that each instance and call through the `PositionManagement` type takes place within a COM+ transaction.

In the same project, we've also defined the `Position` class. Listing 10-7 shows its contents. Notice that we've followed the same approach of providing a specific interface and corresponding implementation class.

Listing 10-7. `OldHorse2 Position.cs`

```
using System;
using System.Runtime.InteropServices;
using System.EnterpriseServices;

namespace OldHorse2
{
    [Guid( "D428B97A-13C8-4591-8AC3-5E8622A8C8BE" )]
    public interface IPosition
    {
        long Quantity
        { get; set; }

        string Ticker
        { get; set; }

        long GetQuantity( string ticker );
        IPosition GetPosition( string ticker );
    }
```

```
    [Guid( "02FD3A3B-CFCE-4298-8766-438C596002B4" )]
    public class Position : ServicedComponent, IPosition
    {
        ...
        #region IPosition Members
        public long Quantity
        ...
        public string Ticker
        ...
        public long GetQuantity( string ticker )
        ...
        public IPosition GetPosition( string ticker )
        ...
    }
}
```

Once the project is compiled to a managed assembly, it's necessary to register it in the GAC using the `GacUtil.exe` utility that comes with the .NET 2.0 Framework. The command to register is as follows:

```
gacutil /i bin\debug\OldHorse2.dll
```

Once it's registered in the GAC, you can then install it in COM+. .NET offers a useful command-line utility that does all the work for you. The following command creates the COM+ application along with registering the .NET assembly's components:

```
regsvcs bin\debug\OldHorse2.dll
```

You can attribute the assembly with Enterprise Services types that control the COM+ registration, shown in Listing 10-8; therefore, you don't have to build the application first and install the components through the wizard. If you want to script this outside of .NET or for non-.NET components, you could leverage the COM+ administrative interfaces for controlling COM+ applications.

Listing 10-8. `OldHorse2` *Assembly Attributes for COM+*

```
[assembly: ComVisible( true )]
[assembly: Guid( "c41f4ee8-3475-47b6-b381-5e7774e4287d" )]
[assembly: ApplicationName("OldHorse2")]
[assembly: ApplicationActivation(ActivationOption.Library)]
[assembly: ApplicationAccessControl(false)]
```

These commands are best executed from the Windows SDK command or Visual Studio 2005 command prompt—located under the Tools folder for the Windows SDK and Visual Studio 2005 by selecting Start ➤ All Programs. Additionally, the commands are contained in the batch files previously mentioned. Once registered, you should now see in Component Services the `OldHorse2` application, as shown in Figure 10-13.

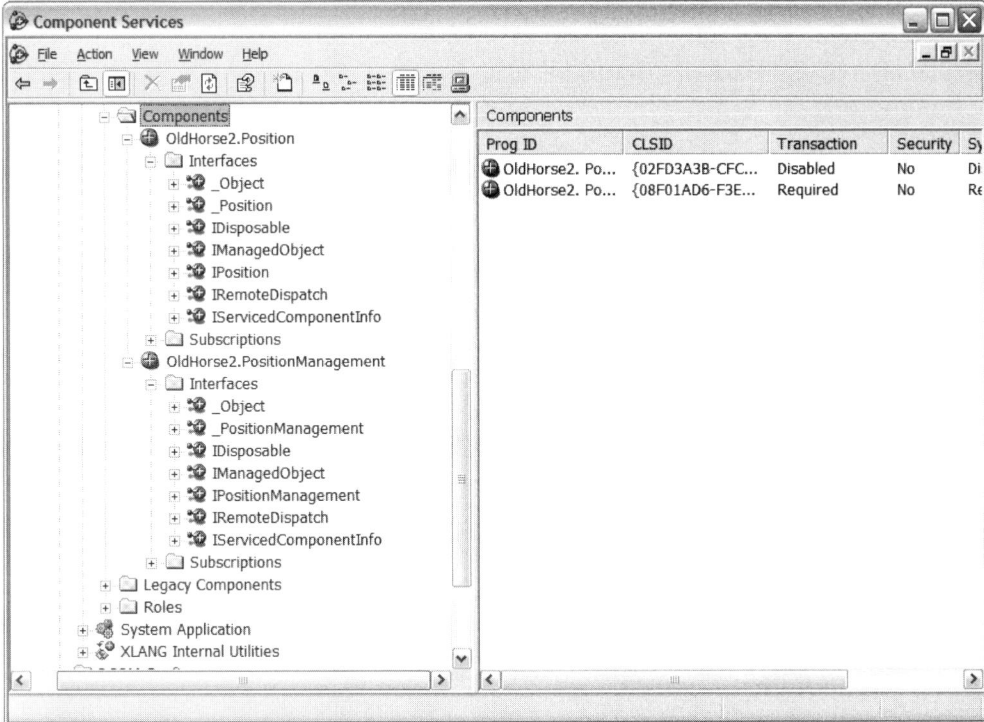

Figure 10-13. `OldHorse2` *.NET COM+ registration*

Now, using `OleView.exe` (from the Windows SDK), refer to the IDL that is generated by the .NET Framework. The full IDL files are located as part of the Chapter 10 code in the `\OldHorsePositionTracking` directory. Listing 10-9 shows the IDL listing.

Listing 10-9. `OldHorse2` *.NET IDL*

```
[
  odl,
  uuid(D428B97A-13C8-4591-8AC3-5E8622A8C8BE),
  version(1.0),
  dual,
  oleautomation,
  custom(0F21F359-AB84-41E8-9A78-36D110E6D2F9, OldHorse2.IPosition)

]
interface IPosition : IDispatch {
...
```

```
[
  odl,
  uuid(3B26F4CA-E839-4AB6-86D4-AADB0A8AADA5),
  version(1.0),
  dual,
  oleautomation,
  custom(0F21F359-AB84-41E8-9A78-36D110E6D2F9, OldHorse2.IPositionManagement)

]
interface IPositionManagement : IDispatch {
...
```

The code has been abbreviated here, but you can see that the declared interfaces `IPosition` and `IPositionManagement` both do not have the `hidden` attribute. Therefore, you should have a different experience when you run the WCF COM+ Integration Wizard, as shown in Figure 10-14.

Start the `SvcConfigEditor.exe` utility, and access the COM+ integration feature. You now see the `OldHorse2` application along with both the `IPosition` and `IPositionManagement` interfaces available for integration.

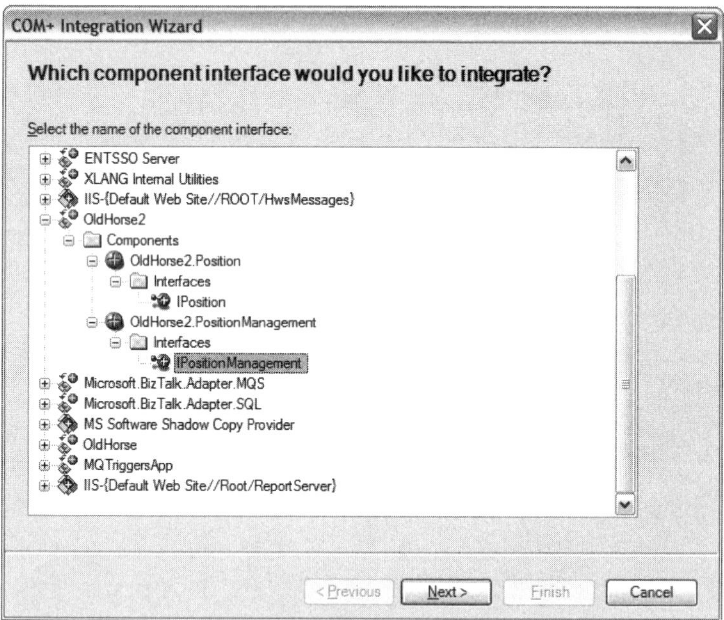

Figure 10-14. `OldHorse2` *WCF COM+ Integration Wizard*

Select the `IPositionManagement` interface, and click Next. You now see that both methods, as with the Visual Basic 6 COM component, appear (see Figure 10-15).

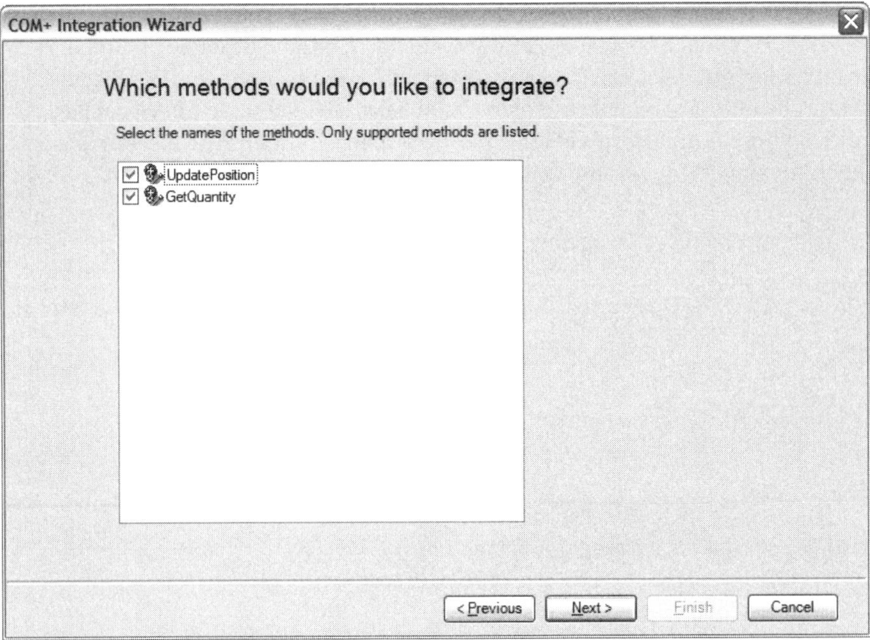

Figure 10-15. `OldHorse2.PositionManagement` *interface methods*

Click Next two times, and then click Finish. At this point you'll have two resources generated in the virtual directory root—a `Web.config` file along with the service host file called `OldHorse2.PositionManagement.svc`.

Client Proxy Generation

Once again, create a Visual Studio 2005 console application, and choose Add Service Reference to add to the project using the following URI shown in Figure 10-16.

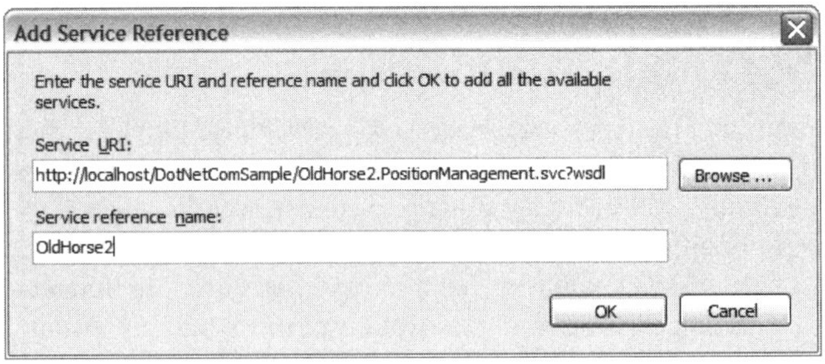

Add Service Reference

Enter the service URI and reference name and click OK to add all the available services.

Service URI:

http://localhost/DotNetComSample/OldHorse2.PositionManagement.svc?wsdl

Browse ...

Service reference name:

OldHorse2

OK Cancel

Figure 10-16. *Adding a service reference to the project*

In the completed solution, Listing 10-10 shows the code that performs the same call that the Visual Basic 6 COM client performed. The only difference is the type name no longer is prefixed with an underscore (_). This is because when authoring components in .NET, you have control over the interface names, where in Visual Basic 6 it's left up to the Visual Basic 6 framework, hidden from normal levels of control. Other than that, there's no discernable difference from the consumer side, as shown in Listing 10-10.

Listing 10-10. `OldHorse2` *Position Management Client*

```
namespace DotNetComClient
{
    class Program
    {
        static void Main( string[] args )
        {

            OldHorse2.PositionManagementClient();
            OldHorse2.PositionManagementClient proxy =
                new OldHorse2.PositionManagementClient();
            long q = proxy.GetQuantity("MSFT");
            Console.WriteLine( "We have " + q + " of MSFT" );
            q = proxy.UpdatePosition( "MSFT", 100 );
            Console.WriteLine( "We now have " + q + " of MSFT" );
            proxy.Close();
            proxy = null;
            Console.WriteLine( "Press return to end..." );
            Console.ReadLine();

        }
    }
}
```

Consuming WCF Services from COM+

Up to now, we've focused on solutions that need to leverage existing legacy application logic that is hosted in COM+. We've focused primarily on Visual Basic 6 given its distinct ability to hide some things that you need control over in order to fully leverage and reuse your application logic.

This section approaches the problem scenario from the perspective that these legacy solutions are not stagnant. In fact, it has been estimated that nearly 90 percent[9] of IT budgets are focused on maintaining and extending existing solutions—many of those built on Visual Basic 6 and other legacy technologies.

---

9. Erlikh, L. "Leveraging Legacy System Dollars for E-Business." (IEEE) IT Pro, May/June 2000. See also http://doi.ieeecomputersociety.org/10.1109/6294.846201 and http://www.cs.jyu.fi/~koskinen/smcosts.htm.

So, those applications aren't going away. In fact, they most likely will need to be extended to support new functionality or just change the way they interface with other applications.

For the examples in this chapter, you'll look at how you can make a WCF service look like a COM+ component. This allows your legacy clients that understand COM+ to work with your new .NET 3.0–based applications that expose service endpoints. Note that both the .NET 3.0 and .NET 2.0 runtimes are required when calling from any client. This is a requirement because the dynamic invocation framework is leveraged in process by the client process.

QuickReturns Ltd. Quote Service

The QuickReturns Ltd. system, built on .NET 2.0, provides a quote service using WCF. All parts of the QuickReturns Ltd. application leverage this service. Some of the `OldHorse` custody systems, however, require the ability to reuse this application logic, and they've chosen to use WCF COM integration capabilities. The new QuickReturns Ltd. quote service is hosted in ASP.NET and IIS and exposes its services using WCF.

Alternatively, we'll also discuss how you can leverage runtime registration of the COM interface through the use of the WSDL and MEX service monikers.

Typed Contract Service Moniker

We'll provide a quick walk-through for the first scenario, consuming a WCF service from COM clients. This example will provide both an automation client (VBScript) and an early binding client, Visual Basic 6. The Visual Studio 2005 solution file `QuickReturnsQuotes.sln` contains the website and proxy projects.

The first part of the solution is the `QuickReturnsQuotes` WCF service, which is hosted in IIS and ASP.NET. If you haven't already run the setup script, to set up this virtual directory in IIS, run the batch file `CreateVirtualDirs.bat`. The requirements are that IIS is installed along with .NET 2.0 and the .NET 3.0 runtime components.

Open the solution file `QuickReturnsQuotes.sln`. The solution file contains two projects. The first is the website that was just mapped using the scripts mentioned previously. If the project doesn't load, there's a problem with the script on your machine, and you'll have to map the site manually and reload the project. Ensure that you have IIS and .NET 2.0 installed and ASP.NET registered with IIS (use the `aspnet_regiis.exe` command in the `Framework` folder).

The second project represents the proxy that when compiled, with a strong name, will be registered both in the GAC and as a COM interface using the `RegSvcs.exe` utility that's part of the .NET 2.0 Framework.

This project has several extra member files along with both prebuild and postbuild event command lines:

`makeProxy.bat`: This is the batch file that calls `SvcUtil.exe` to generate the proxy stub source files; this file is part of the project prebuild steps.

`reg.bat`: This is the batch file that registers the assembly in the GAC and for COM interoperability; this file is part of the project post-build steps.

`unreg.bat`: This is the batch file that will remove the assembly from the GAC and from COM interoperability.

■ **Note** For the build steps and these batch files to work, Visual Studio 2005 must be installed in the default path. If you chose a different path or haven't installed Visual Studio 2005, you need to update the path to the utilities as required.

If you build the solution and all is successful, then you should have a GAC-installed assembly registered for COM interoperability and ready for use by COM clients. To verify, you can open Windows Explorer to the `C:\Windows\Assembly` path and see the assembly `TypedServiceProxy` listed, as shown in Figure 10-17.

C:\WINDOWS\assembly

File Edit View Favorites Tools Help

Back Search Folders Folder Sync

Address C:\WINDOWS\assembly Go

Assembly Name	Version	Cu...	Public Key Token	Proce...
System.Web.RegularExpressions	2.0.0.0		b03f5f7f11d50a3a	MSIL
System.Web.Services	1.0.50...		b03f5f7f11d50a3a	
System.Web.Services	2.0.0.0		b03f5f7f11d50a3a	MSIL
System.Windows.Forms	1.0.50...		b77a5c561934e089	
System.Windows.Forms	2.0.0.0		b77a5c561934e089	MSIL
System.Workflow.Activities	3.0.0.0		31bf3856ad364e35	MSIL
System.Workflow.ComponentModel	3.0.0.0		31bf3856ad364e35	MSIL
System.Workflow.Runtime	3.0.0.0		31bf3856ad364e35	MSIL
System.Xml	1.0.50...		b77a5c561934e089	
System.Xml	2.0.0.0		b77a5c561934e089	MSIL
TlbExpCode	1.0.50...		b03f5f7f11d50a3a	
TlbImpCode	1.0.50...		b03f5f7f11d50a3a	
TypedServiceProxy	1.0.0.0		3a958c403692ae2b	MSIL
UIAutomationClient	3.0.0.0		31bf3856ad364e35	MSIL
UIAutomationClientsideProviders	3.0.0.0		31bf3856ad364e35	MSIL
UIAutomationProvider	3.0.0.0		31bf3856ad364e35	MSIL
UIAutomationTypes	3.0.0.0		31bf3856ad364e35	MSIL
VBIDE	5.3.0.0		31bf3856ad364e35	MSIL
vjscor	1.0.50...		b03f5f7f11d50a3a	
vjscor	2.0.0.0		b03f5f7f11d50a3a	x86

1 object(s) selected My Computer

Figure 10-17. *QuickReturns Ltd. WCF proxy in the GAC*

■ **Note** If you haven't modified any of the project `Guid` attributes, then the next two steps are not required for this project to work. This would be a normal step in your solutions to validate the correct interface GUIDs.

The next step is to both verify the registration for COM and retrieve the interface ID that is stored in the registry. The best tool for this is `OleView.exe`, which comes with the Windows SDK. Start `OleView.exe`, and open the top-level node labeled Type Libraries. Scroll down until you find `TypedServiceProxy`, as shown in Figure 10-18.

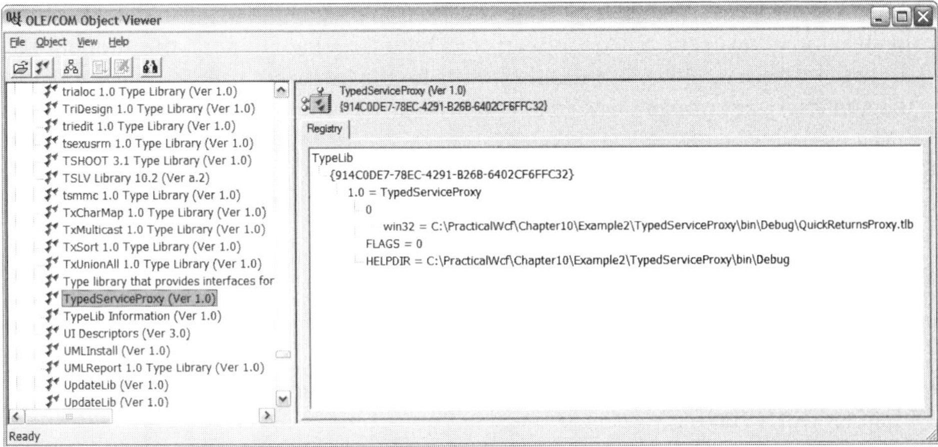

Figure 10-18. `TypedServiceProxy` *registered in COM*

The next step is you need to retrieve the interface ID (the GUID) for the `IQuoteService` interface. The `OleView.exe` utility can view the IDL for any COM registered classes. Double-click the item `TypedServiceProxy` in the list to open the ITypeLib Viewer, as shown in Figure 10-19.

ITypeLib Viewer

File View

TypedServiceProxy
- dispinterface IQuoteService
- interface IQuoteService
- dispinterface IQuoteServiceChai
- interface IQuoteServiceChannel
- coclass QuoteServiceProxy

```
// Generated .IDL file (by the OLE/COM Object Viewer)
//
// typelib filename: QuickReturnsProxy.tlb

[
  uuid(914C0DE7-78EC-4291-B26B-6402CF6FFC32),
  version(1.0),
  custom(90883F05-3D28-11D2-8F17-00A0C9A6186D, "TypedServiceProxy, Version=1.0.0.0,
Culture=neutral, PublicKeyToken=3a958c403692ae2b")

]
library TypedServiceProxy
{
    // TLib :     // TLib : mscorlib.dll : {BED7F4EA-1A96-11D2-8F08-00A0C9A6186D}
    importlib("mscorlib.tlb");
    // TLib : OLE Automation : {00020430-0000-0000-C000-000000000046}
    importlib("stdole2.tlb");

    // Forward declare all types defined in this typelib
    interface IQuoteService;
    interface IQuoteServiceChannel;

    [
      odl,
      uuid(058E1BEC-C44A-31FB-98C8-9FB223C46FAF),
      version(1.0),
      dual,
      oleautomation,
      custom(0F21F359-AB84-41E8-9A78-36D110E6D2F9, "IQuoteService")

    ]
    interface IQuoteService : IDispatch {
        [id(0x60020000)]
        HRESULT GetQuote(
                        [in] BSTR ticker,
                        [out, retval] double* pRetVal);
    };
```

Ready

Figure 10-19. *ITypeLib Viewer for* `TypedServiceProxy`

Find in the right pane of the viewer the IDL definition for the `IQuoteService` interface (which inherits from `IDispatch`—implying it supports automation as well as early bind COM clients). Now, just above it (like attributes in .NET) is a list of IDL attributes for this interface. We're looking for the universally unique identifier (UUID) just above it. For this component, its value is 058E1BEC-C44A-31FB-98C8-9FB223C46FAF.

Inside the project file TypedServiceProxy, you'll see a VBScript file that illustrates how to call from an automation client. Since this is an early bound client, it requires the interface ID to be part of the service moniker construction string for the GetObject call. The call sequence is into the quote service through COM and then through the WCF framework to the quote service .NET assembly hosted in IIS/ASP.NET.

Listing 10-11 is the source file for QuickReturnsScriptClient.vbs; note the wrap on some lines.

Listing 10-11. QuickReturnsScriptClient.vbs *Automation Client*

```
Option Explicit
Dim quoteProxy, moniker, result
moniker = "service:address=http://localhost/QuickReturnsQuotes/service.svc,
      binding=wsHttpBinding"
moniker = moniker + ", contract={058E1BEC-C44A-31FB-98C8-9FB223C46FAF}"
'... cut comments

Set quoteProxy = GetObject(moniker)
result = quoteProxy.GetQuote("MSFT")
WScript.Echo "MSFT's price is " + CStr(result)
```

The moniker string value used for the GetObject COM call provides the address endpoint URI in addition to the binding type, which is wsHttpBinding because we're hosting in IIS. The final parameter of the moniker is the contract type. Using this GUID, the WCF framework looks up the type library information to obtain the COM interface and instantiates the proxy on the client side. The proxy in turn leverages the .NET Framework 3.0 to construct a channel and message for the request through the service boundary. This is all done "automagically" by the WCF components, which must be installed on the client tier as well.

Typed Contract: Early Bound

Visual Basic 6 can use early binding. *Early binding* allows the lookup and discovery of the interfaces in your COM component at design time. So, at runtime the COM client is expecting that the same UUID of your interface is registered (via type library registration). The type library that needs to be registered and referenced is part of the reg.bat batch file in the TypedServiceProxy project—QuickReturnsProxy.tlb. COM interfaces are to be considered immutable. If they change, then the underlying IDL will change. Therefore, any changes to your interfaces in the base WCF service class will require a regeneration of the proxy and a regeneration of the type library for use by clients.

■Note If you open the Visual Basic 6 project, you may need to reset the project references back to the TypedServiceProxy on your machine. That's accessible from Project ➤ References from within the Visual Basic 6 IDE.

If you look at the Visual Basic 6 project TypedServiceVbClient, you can see that the project should have a reference to the TypedServiceProxy type library. In the button click event handler, you can now make references directly to the types inside the COM interface (see Listing 10-12; please note the line wrap).

Listing 10-12. *Early Bound Visual Basic 6 Client*

```
Private Sub Command1_Click()
    Dim obj As TypedServiceProxy.QuoteServiceClient
    Dim moniker, Ticker As String
    Dim price As Double

    moniker = "service:address=http://localhost/QuickReturnsQuotes/
service.svc, binding=wsHttpBinding"
    On Error GoTo ErrHandler

    Ticker = UCase(Trim(txtTicker.Text))
    Set obj = GetObject(moniker)
    price = obj.GetQuote(Ticker)
    MsgBox "Price is " & CStr(price)
    Exit Sub

ErrHandler:
    MsgBox Err.Number & " : " & Err.Description & " : " & Err.Source
End Sub
```

The obj object is declared to be of the interface proxy type. The moniker is then set to include only the address and the binding type. Since you're using just the default settings for the wsHttpBinding, you aren't required to supply a bindingConfiguration value. If you required overriding any of the default settings for the binding, you could supply an application configuration file with the name file.exe.config and place it in the program directory of the client. For this example, the filename would be TypedServiceVbClient.exe.config.

You then use the COM GetObject statement, which makes a call through the COM framework into the Service Control Manager (SCM, or affectionately known as "scum"), activating the COM registered WCF proxy type. Then as each method is called on the activated instance, the WCF framework is responsible for both transforming and marshaling the call from COM into the WCF framework and ultimately across the service boundary to the service class.

Dynamic Discovery

There are scenarios where registering the COM type library is not feasible. An example is Microsoft Excel spreadsheets that require dynamic discovery and invocation through COM locally to WCF services. For this, the WCF framework and the COM integration provide a dynamic model, or what's known as *late binding*.

What the WCF framework provides is the runtime construction of a proxy and COM interface for the COM client at object construction time. By first querying the service metadata, after being provided some initialization parameters, the WCF framework generates both a WCF proxy and a COM callable wrapper that the COM client interfaces with. You currently have two choices for the service monikers: WS-MetadataExchange (MEX) and WSDL. Given this is a nontyped model, it is callable only by clients that support automation (`IDispatch`) such as VBScript, Visual Basic 6, Excel, and so on.

Metadata Exchange Contract Service Moniker

WCF supports the WS-MetadataExchange protocol that provides the discovery of services in addition to policy and schema information. Please see Chapter 4 for more information. The WCF COM integration framework uses this to dynamically derive the service endpoint interfaces along with binding and service behavior.

Starting with the scripting sample from the project file in Listing 10-2, there's an additional VBScript file: `QuickReturnsScriptClientMex.vbs`. Listing 10-13 shows its contents (note the line wrap).

Listing 10-13. *QuickReturns Ltd. Script Using Mex Service Moniker*

```
Option Explicit
Dim quoteProxy, moniker, result

moniker="service:mexAddress=http://localhost/QuickReturnsQuotes/service.svc/mex, "
moniker=moniker + "address=http://localhost/QuickReturnsQuotes/service.svc,"
moniker=moniker + "contract=IQuoteService, "
moniker=moniker + "contractNamespace=http://PracticalWcf/QuoteService, "
moniker=moniker + "binding=WSHttpBinding_IQuoteService, "
moniker=moniker + "bindingNamespace=http://tempuri.org/"

Set quoteProxy = GetObject(moniker)
result = quoteProxy.GetQuote("MSFT")
WScript.Echo "MSFT's price is " + CStr(result) WSDL Contract Service Moniker
```

From the code in Listing 10-13, you don't have a local configuration file or a strongly typed object (in COM or .NET). Therefore, you must supply the "discovery" information to the `GetObject` call. One part is the URI for where the MEX metadata is found. The others are the URI of the service endpoint, binding, and contract information that will be mapped into the MEX response.

The `contract` and `contractNamespace` comes directly from the metadata binding information inside the <wsdl:binding> element from the metadata. This must match what the MEX response contains; otherwise, you'll receive a mismatch on the contract error. For this sample, this represents the <wsdl:binding> element that is visible if you request the WSDL for the service using the following URI:

```
http://localhost/QuickReturnsQuotes/service.svc?wsdl
```

WSDL Contract Service Moniker

Similar to how WCF works with the WS-MetadataExchange protocol to dynamically derive the COM and WCF interfaces and types, the service moniker can also work with a WSDL contract. Listing 10-14, contained in the file `QuickReturnsScriptClientWsdl.vbs`, illustrates how to make a call using the service moniker for WSDL.

Listing 10-14. *QuickReturns Ltd. Script Using WSDL Service Moniker*

```
Option Explicit
Dim quoteProxy, wsdl, moniker, result

wsdl = GetWsdlFromUrl ("http://localhost/QuickReturnsQuotes/service.svc?wsdl" )
moniker="service:wsdl=" & wsdl & ", "
moniker=moniker + "address=http://localhost/QuickReturnsQuotes/service.svc,"
moniker=moniker + "contract=IQuoteService, "
moniker=moniker + "contractNamespace=http://tempuri.org/, "
moniker=moniker + "binding=WSHttpBinding_IQuoteService, "
moniker=moniker + "bindingNamespace=http://tempuri.org/"
Set quoteProxy = GetObject(moniker)

result = quoteProxy.GetQuote("MSFT")
WScript.Echo "MSFT's price is " + CStr(result)

Function GetWsdlFromUrl( strUrl )
    Dim WinHttpReq, resp
    Set WinHttpReq = CreateObject("WinHttp.WinHttpRequest.5)
    resp = WinHttpReq.Open("GET", strUrl, False)
    WinHttpReq.Send()
    GetWsdlFromUrl = WinHttpReq.ResponseText
End Function
```

■ **Note** For the previous dynamic HTTP request for the WSDL to work, the correct version of the `WinHttp` services component needs to be referenced by the `CreateObject` call. On some installations, this may be `WinHttp.WinHttpRequest.5.1`. Please see `http://msdn.microsoft.com/library/en-us/winhttp/http/winhttp_start_page.asp` for more information.

The first statement after the variable declarations makes a call to the included function that invokes `GetWsdlFromUrl`. This VBScript function just makes an HTTP get call to the URI to retrieve the HTTP response, which for that URI is the WSDL document for the service interface.

The moniker initialization string is then composed of the WSDL response along with the remaining service moniker attributes. The WSDL string is an XML response that fully describes the `IQuoteService` interface exposed at the endpoint address. It's the same XML you would see if you opened the URL `http://localhost/QuickReturnsQuotes/service.svc?wsdl` directly from a browser.

Again, using the dynamic service moniker, the COM interface makes a call into the WCF framework to dynamically construct the types necessary to make a round-trip request into the WCF service that is hosted in IIS—all without the COM client knowing the underlying workings of how to work with WCF (other than the moniker construction). What the dynamic generation provides is the generation of a fully configured proxy that matches the service endpoints' advertised metadata including policy, security, and contract information.

Briefly, let's summarize what the high-level steps are required to consume a WCF service as a COM interface leveraging a typed contract service moniker:

1. Generate a proxy using the WCF `SvcUtil.exe` utility.
2. Create a project/solution in Visual Studio 2005 that contains the generated proxy class file.[10]
3. Add the attribute `ComVisible` to the solution; you can add this to the `AssemblyInfo.cs` file.
4. Provide a strong name for the assembly; this is optional but allows loading to the GAC to ensure a single version is loaded.
5. Register the assembly for COM using the `RegAsm` tool.
6. Install the assembly in the GAC; this is optional but ensures a single version is loaded.
7. Create an application configuration file for your client executable; for example, if the client is called `OldHorseClient.exe`, then the configuration file is `OldHorseClient.exe.config`. This is the standard .NET configuration file-naming requirement.
8. Use the `GetObject` statement in your COM environment (Visual Basic 6, scripting, and so on) with the service moniker to instantiate the WCF service interface.

Security Credentials with IChannelCredentials

In any modern IT infrastructure, security is paramount for interoperability amongst applications in a distributed solution. In our example, there are clear requirements for securing our services. The examples so far haven't demonstrated any way of securing our services, whether exposed to legacy COM+ clients or wrapping COM+ services with the WCF services.

Chapter 7 discussed WCF security in detail and covered both the declarative and programmatic means for securing services. Fortunately, the COM+ interoperability tier of WCF leverages the same base framework for supplying both transport and message security.

For the final steps in the COM+ integration, we'll show how to secure the WCF service that you are consuming from late-bound COM+ clients. A few additional steps are required to configure the IIS instance that hosts the `QuickReturnsQuotesSecure` website. Again, we've supplied a script, `CreateVirtualDirs.bat`, that configures IIS and sets the ASP.NET runtime to .NET 2.0, which is required for running .NET 3.0 services.

The first modification is to the service `Web.config`. Here you add the necessary security configuration elements to enable both transport-level and message-level security. Make the modification to the binding element that is associated with the endpoint, as shown in Listing 10-15.

---

10. This is not required, but it makes things easier.

ENABLING SSL ON IIS

Using transport security requires SSL; consequently, you need to enable the website to use SSL, which requires the presence of a server certificate.

To install a test certificate, you can leverage the IIS 6 Resource Kit (`SelfSSL.exe`).[11] Simply execute the following command:

```
selfssl /t
```

This installs a server certificate for use by IIS and places it in the Trusted Certificate list. WCF by default validates the certificate if you trust the issuer, so, for this example, it will fail without the `/t` switch.

Listing 10-15. *Security-Enabled* `Web.config`

```
<bindings>
  <wsHttpBinding>
    <binding name="Binding1">
     <security mode="TransportWithMessageCredential">
       <message clientCredentialType="UserName" />
     </security>
    </binding>
  </wsHttpBinding>
</bindings>
```

For this solution, we are using `wsHttpBinding`. To add transport and message security, you add the security element and set the mode to `TransportWithMessageCredential`. This mode provides both an SSL-based channel along with message-encoded authentication. Additionally, for the message element, you inform the WCF framework that you require `UserName` authentication. This informs WCF that the client embeds a username and password into the message, and this will pass over SSL.

The solution includes the project `TypedServiceProxySecure` class library that contains a set of batch files that dynamically generate the proxy file along with providing both GAC installation and COM+ registration. These steps are in the prebuild and post-build steps associated with the project.

Once you've configured your service to support the security model required, you can now update the late-bound VBScript client to make a call matching the security requirements of the service.

If you take the late-bound VBScript file `QuickReturnsScriptClientMex.vbs` and run it without specifying any credentials, you'll see an exception raised to the client indicating that the username is not provided, so you need to specify it in `ClientCredentials`.

Fortunately, COM+ integration makes that easy from the COM+ client. You just need to make a call to set the credentials on the channel. Listing 10-16 shows the updated VBScript that supports username and password authentication (watch the line wrap).

11. You can download the IIS 6 Resource Kit from the following URL: `http://www.microsoft.com/downloads/details.aspx?FamilyID=56fc92ee-a71a-4c73-b628-ade629c89499&DisplayLang=en`.

Listing 10-16. *Late-Bound VBScript with Security*

```
Option Explicit
Dim quoteProxy, moniker, result

moniker="service:mexAddress=http://xpshawnci/QuickReturnsQuotesSecure/"
moniker=moniker + "service.svc/mex, "
moniker=moniker + "address=https://xpshawnci/QuickReturnsQuotesSecure/service.svc, "
moniker=moniker + "contract=IQuoteService, "
moniker=moniker + "contractNamespace=http://tempuri.org/, "
moniker=moniker + "binding=WSHttpBinding_IQuoteService, "
moniker=moniker + "bindingNamespace=http://tempuri.org/"

Set quoteProxy = GetObject(moniker)
quoteProxy.ChannelCredentials.SetUserNameCredential "xpshawnci\soauser", "p@ssw0rd"

result = quoteProxy.GetQuote("MSFT")
WScript.Echo "MSFT's price is " + CStr(result)
```

The only modification you needed to make is adding the call, shown in bold. Here we made a call to the ChannelCredentials.SetUserNameCredential method, passing in the username and password of the principal. The WCF framework then generates a security token that is put into the message. On the receiving side, the server validates that token. If we supplied an invalid username or password, the error that the late-bound client receives is that the "security token could not be validated" message.

Internally, the SetUserNameCredential call creates a new ClientCredential object, setting the username and password, and adds it to an internal collection of security credentials that are associated to the channel.

Other methods of supplying credentials are part of the IChannelCredentials interface, implemented by the System.ServiceModel.ComIntegration.ChannelCredentials type. The IChannelCredentials interface supports other credential types such as Windows credentials (SetWindowsCredentials), certificate based (SetClientCertificateFromStore, SetClientCertificateFromStoreByName), and SetIssueToken for use with Security Token Service (STS) services.

Summary

This chapter focused on interoperability with COM, both from a consumer and service perspective. Although you might be lucky enough to forget the past, WCF hasn't left it all in the dust. The WCF framework provides a strong extensible starting point to help in the evolutionary model of moving solutions into the SOA age.

The next chapter focuses on working with data in and around WCF. All relevant services in some form have data associated with them. Without the data, you have fairly empty services. With WCF and SOA in general, careful consideration is required to understand not only the "how to" but also the implications of what happens to data as it crosses the explicit service boundaries.

CHAPTER 11

Working with Data

Data is the "Holy Grail" of an application. Almost every application needs to operate on data—whether it's creating, consuming, or processing data. Without data, almost all applications would be useless. You can use many patterns when designing applications to work with data. In the early days of DNA and client-server applications, a favorite approach was the *n*-tier approach where the application was divided into *n* tiers (the most common division was three tiers). In the *three-tier* approach, the first tier is the presentation tier, which handles all the presentation of the application (the user interface) and is essentially what the user interacts with. The next tier is the business layer, which contains all the business rules to which the application needs to adhere. The last tier is the data layer, which performs all the create, read, update, and delete (CRUD) functionality. The data layer usually connects to the required back-end data sources using one of many well-known mechanisms such as OLE DB, ODBC, and so on.

In the SOA world, however, data is transferred in the form of a "message" over the wire. You can think of the WCF as a messaging infrastructure because it can receive, process, and dispatch messages. In addition, it can also construct messages and dispatch and deliver them to a desired location. Often, the messages are represented as objects in memory and need to be converted to an appropriate format so they can be transmitted across the wire. The process of converting them is called *serialization* and is explained in the "XML Serialization" section. Similarly, on the other end of the wire, the process of converting the message to an object that can be represented in memory is called *deserialization*. This chapter introduces the concepts of data contracts in addition to the basics of serialization.

After completing this chapter, you will have the following knowledge:

- You'll know why you need serialization.
- You'll understand the serialization options available in WCF.
- You'll understand best practices for data connectivity.

Understanding the Data Transfer Architecture

At the heart of the message capabilities of WCF is the `Message` class. The WCF architecture and runtime are essentially two pillars—the channel stack and the service framework—and the `Message` class is the bridge between the two. The first pillar (the channel stack) on the "send side" converts a `Message` instance with some specified action to the act of either sending or receiving data. On the other hand, with the channel stack operating on the receiving side, it is responsible for the reverse—converting an action into some specific message.

Although there is no restriction on using the `Message` class and channel stack *directly*, it is not usually recommended because it is fairly expensive (time-wise) and complex. Also, there are runtime issues such as lack of metadata support, lack of strongly typed proxies, and so on. To overcome these restrictions, WCF has the second pillar—the framework that provides a relatively easy programming model for working with `Message` objects. This framework maps .NET types and services via service contracts and sends messages to operations that are .NET methods that are marked with the `[OperationContract]` attribute. The framework converts the incoming `Message` instances into the parameters on the server side. On the client side, it does the reverse and converts the return types to the outgoing `Message` instance.

Although the `Message` class is the most fundamental concept of WCF, it is usually not interacted with directly. You should use one of the other WCF service model constructs (such as data contracts, discussed later in the "Introducing Data Contracts" section), message contracts, and operation contracts (both introduced in Chapter 3) to describe the incoming and outgoing messages. You should use `Message` only when working with some advanced scenarios. We'll discuss all the aforementioned `Message` classes and WCF constructs a little later in this chapter in the "Introducing Message Contracts" section.

Regardless of which construct you use whenever the message contents are described using message contracts or parameters, the message contents need to be serialized to convert these between the .NET type to the relevant SOAP or binary representation. Before you examine each of the options available in WCF, you need to understand the serialization options available and the advantages and challenges of each of them.

Exploring the Serialization Options in WCF

Serialization is nothing but the process of converting the state of an object into a format that can be either persisted to disk or transmitted over the wire. On the flip side, deserialization is the process of converting an incoming stream, which is either read from disk or read over the wire to an object in memory. Collectively, this allows data to be stored and transmitted with relative ease.

This is all good, but why serialize in the first place? Serialization is a key aspect of any distributed technology, and .NET is no different. For example, in an ASP.NET application, you can use serialization to save the session state to the configured medium (that is, memory, state server, or database). One of the main problems that serialization solves for you is *interoperability* with other systems and platforms. Serialization is not a new concept, but it is an important one because without serialization, it would be difficult to support interoperability between various platforms. Since XML serialization converts the object or data structure at hand to an architecture-independent format, you do not encounter issues with different programming languages, operating systems, and hardware such as memory layout, byte ordering, or even that different platforms represent data structures differently.

The .NET Framework features two options for serializing objects—binary and XML serialization. The primary difference between the two is that binary serialization allows you to maintain type fidelity, whereas XML serialization does not. In other words, type fidelity allows for preserving the "complete state" of an object including any private members of the object. However, by default, XML serialization will serialize only the public fields and properties of the object. If, for example, you need to pass an object "by value" across either machine or domain boundaries, then you would need to use binary serialization. You can use binary serialization only when both the runtimes and platforms on either end of the stream are the same; this is because the platforms know how the type is represented internally in memory. If this is not the case, then the object would not be able to deserialize on the other end. XML serialization, as the name suggests, uses XML and as a result is a better choice for sharing data across different platforms or the Internet.

In .NET by default only primitive types (such as integers) are serializable, and there is no need for any additional steps to serialize these primitive types. Since the .NET runtime has no knowledge of complex types, these are not serialized by default, and the .NET runtime needs more information about how these types should be serialized. Because each operation in a WCF service needs to either consume or generate data, which is transmitted over the wire, in WCF it is important that every type is correctly serialized.

■ **Note** The ability to serialize an object can be enabled only when writing the code; in other words, serialization is a design-time feature. If this was not enabled at design time for an object, then that object cannot support serialization at runtime. The ability to serialize an object cannot be switched on at runtime in an ad hoc manner. Also note that *serializing* and *deserializing* are sometimes also known as *hydrating* and *dehydrating*.

WCF (being part of .NET 3.0) not only supports the serialization options available in .NET but also adds a few new ones. A data contract is the default option among all the following available options:

- `Serializable` attribute/`ISerializable` interface
- Data contracts
- XML serialization
- Message contracts
- Message class

Introducing Data Contracts

Data contracts are the "agreement" between a service and its consumer. At an abstract level, the contract defines how the data will be exchanged between the two and also defines what data is returned for each type (that is, serialized to XML). For a service and its consumer to communicate, they do not necessarily have to share the same types; they need to share only the data contracts. The default serialize engine in WCF is the data contract serializer, which is implemented as the `DataContractSerializer` class and is the recommended way to go for WCF. All .NET primitive types can be serialized without any other requirement. However, new complex types need to have an associated data contract defined before they can be serialized.

Data contracts are defined by applying the `[DataContract]` attribute to the type and can be applied to classes, structs, and enums. Just as each operation in a service needs to be decorated with the `[ServiceContract]` attribute, similarly every data member (such as fields, properties, and events) in the data contract needs to be decorated with the `[DataMember]` attribute. This indicates to the data contract serializer that this member needs to be serialized.

■ **Note** Unlike binary serialization that automatically includes all public and private members in a class and unlike XML serialization that automatically includes public members in a class, a data contract is designed with an "opt-in" model. This means the members of a class that are not explicitly marked with the `[DataMember]` attribute are not automatically serialized, regardless of their accessibility levels, and hence are *not* included in the data contract.

Some of the important aspects of data contracts and their implications in the WCF runtime are as follows:

- Member accessibility levels such as private, public, internal, and so on, do not affect the data contract. Members that are private in one context could end up being accessed publicly elsewhere after serialization.
- Static fields cannot be included in the data contract. As a result, if a `[DataMember]` attribute is applied to a static field, it will be ignored.
- All data members for a data contract need to be serialized and deserialized for the data contract to be valid.
- Every property should have the get and set accessors. This is important because the properties `get` and `set` are used during the serialization and deserialization process.
- There is no special process for generic types; they are treated the same as nongeneric types.
- The WCF runtime takes care of defining the underlying SOAP message and the serialization of the data. As long as the data types are serializable, WCF will handle the underlying message exchange.

For example, in the QuickReturns Ltd. trading application, look at the stock quote of a particular company. Figure 11-1 shows the data entities such as `Change`, price-to-earnings ratio (`PERatio`), average volume (`AvgVol`), `LastTrade`, and so on, that this quote will include.

As discussed earlier, to make this into a serializable type to allow you to transmit this data across to other applications, which may or may not be based on WCF, you need to apply the `[DataContract]` and `[DataMember]` attributes, as shown in Listing 11-1. Although this structure consists of mostly primitive data types, which can be serialized, you still need to explicitly mark them as part of the data contract so the runtime is aware of which members constitute the data members.

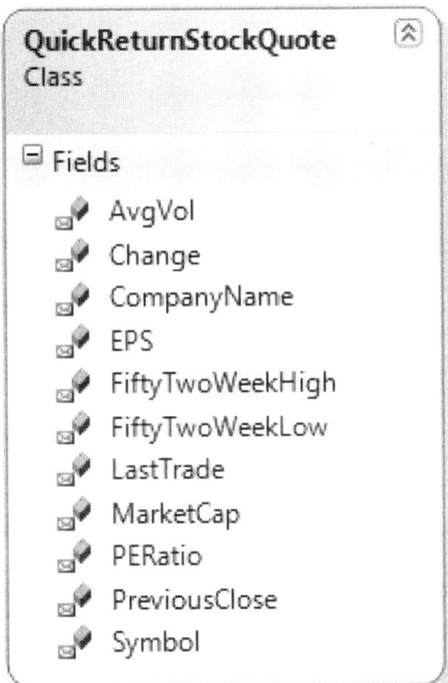

Figure 11-1. `QuickReturnStockQuote` *class*

Listing 11-1. `QuickReturnStockQuote` *Data Contract*

```
[DataContract]
public class QuickReturnStockQuote
{
    [DataMember]
    internal string Symbol;

    [DataMember]
    internal string CompanyName;

    [DataMember]
    internal decimal LastTrade;

    [DataMember]
    internal decimal Change;

    [DataMember]
    internal decimal PreviousClose;
```

```
    [DataMember]
    internal decimal AvgVol;

    [DataMember]
    internal double MarketCap;

    [DataMember]
    internal decimal PERatio;

    [DataMember]
    internal decimal EPS;

    [DataMember]
    internal decimal FiftyTwoWeekHigh;

    [DataMember]
    internal decimal FiftyTwoWeekLow;
}
```

Data Contract Names

Sometimes even though a consumer and a service might not share the same *type*, they can still pass data between each other as long as the data contracts are *equivalent* on both sides. This equivalence is based on a combination of the data contract and data member names. These data contract and data member names follow a few simple rules that you can use to map the different types in situations where they differ on either end. These data contract and member rules are as follows:

- The "fully qualified" data contract name consists of both the namespace and a name.
- Data members have only names (no namespaces).
- Namespaces, data contract, and member names are case-sensitive.

The default namespace for a data contract is in the form of a URI, which can be either absolute or relative. By default, the namespace is the same as the CLR namespace for that type and maps to `http://schemas.datacontract.org/2004/07/`*`Clr.Namespace`* with the correct CLR namespace. If required, you can change the default namespace in two ways. First, you can change the `Namespace` property of the `[DataContract]` attribute. Second, you can apply the `[ContractNamespace]` attribute to the relevant module or assembly.

A data contract's default name is the name for that type. You can use the `Name` property of the `[DataContract]` attribute to override the default name. Similar to the data contract, the default name for a data member is the name of that member (field or property). You can use the `Name` property on the `[DataMember]` attribute to override that default. Listing 11-2 shows an updated version of the data contract from Listing 11-1 with the default names overridden.

Listing 11-2. `QuickReturnStockQuote` *Data Contract with Names Specified*

```
[DataContract]
public class QuickReturnStockQuote
{
    [DataMember(Name = "TickerSymbol")]
    internal string Symbol;

    [DataMember]
    internal string CompanyName;

    [DataMember]
    internal decimal LastTrade;

    [DataMember]
    internal decimal Change;

    [DataMember]
    internal decimal PreviousClose;

    [DataMember(Name = "AverageVolume")]
    internal decimal AvgVol;

    [DataMember(Name = "MarketCapital")]
    internal double MarketCap;

    [DataMember(Name = "PriceEarningRatio")]
    internal decimal PERatio;

    [DataMember(Name = "EarningsPerShare")]
    internal decimal EPS;

    [DataMember(Name = "52WkHigh")]
    internal decimal FiftyTwoWeekHigh;

    [DataMember(Name = "52WkLow")]
    internal decimal FiftyTwoWeekLow;
}
```

Data Contract Equivalence

As stated earlier, both the client and service do not have to have the same type for them to be able to exchange data. However, they need to have the data contracts of both the types present on either end to be *equivalent*. Or in other words, they need to have the same namespace and names. Also, every data member on one side needs to have an equivalent on the other end.

Note In the case where both the sides have the same types but different data contracts (in other words, they are not equivalent), then the data contracts should not be given the same name and namespace. Doing so can lead to unexpected runtime exceptions.

If a data contract inherits from another data contract, then that data contract is treated as one data contract that includes all the types from the base. Also in accordance with the rules of object-oriented programming (OOP) when passing data contracts, a base class cannot be sent when the expected data contract is from a derived class. On the flip side, a data contract from the derived class can be sent when expecting data from the derived class but only if the receiving endpoint is aware of the derived type via the `[KnownType]` attribute. This attribute can be applied only to data contracts and not at the data member level and is discussed later in this chapter (in the "Introducing Data Contracts" section). As an example, the data contract for the `MyStockQuote` type shown in Listing 11-3 is the same as the one in Listing 11-2.

Listing 11-3. `MyStockQuote` *Data Contract*

```
[DataContract(Name="QuickReturnStockQuote")]
public class MyStockQuote
{
    internal string TickerSymbol;

    [DataMember(Name="CompanyName")]
    internal string Name;

    [DataMember]
    internal decimal LastTrade;

    [DataMember]
    internal decimal Change;

    [DataMember]
    internal decimal PreviousClose;

    [DataMember(Name = "AverageVolume")]
    internal decimal Volume;

    [DataMember(Name = "MarketCapital")]
    internal double MktCap;

    internal decimal PriceEarningRatio;

    [DataMember(Name = "EarningsPerShare")]
    internal decimal EPerS;
```

```
    [DataMember(Name = "52WkHigh")]
    internal decimal WeekHigh52;

    [DataMember(Name = "52WkLow")]
    internal decimal WeekLow52;
}
```

Another factor that affects the data equivalence is the order of members. Data contracts must have members in the same order. By default the order is alphabetical; however, you can change this using the `Order` property of the `[DataMember]` attribute. The sequences in which the ordering of elements occurs are as follows:

- The first in order is the data member of the base types if there is an inheritance hierarchy for the current data member type.
- Next are the data members of the current type in alphabetical order that *do not* have the `Order` property set in the `[DataMember]` attribute.
- Last are the data members that do have the `Order` property set in the `[DataMember]` attribute first; if more than one is set to the same `Order` property, then they appear alphabetically.

For example, the code in Listing 11-4 produces the same data equivalence.

Listing 11-4. *Coordinate Data Contract Equivalence*

```
[DataContract(Name = "QuickReturnStockQuote")]
public class MyStock1
{
    //Order is alphabetical (CompanyName, LastTrade, TickerSymbol)

    [DataMember]
    internal string CompanyName;

    [DataMember]
    internal decimal LastTrade;

    [DataMember]
    internal string TickerSymbol;
}

[DataContract(Name = "QuickReturnStockQuote")]
public class MyStock2
{
    //Even though the  TickerSymbol and LastTrade member orders have changed
    //the order is alphabetical (CompanyName, LastTrade, TickerSymbol)
    //and is equivalent to the preceding code.
```

```
    [DataMember]
    internal string CompanyName;

    [DataMember]
    internal string TickerSymbol;

    [DataMember]
    internal decimal LastTrade;
}

[DataContract(Name = "QuickReturnStockQuote")]
public class MyStock3
{
    //Order is according to the Order property (CompanyName, LastTrade,
    //TickerSymbol), equivalent to the preceding code.

    [DataMember(Order=1)]
    internal string CompanyName;

    [DataMember(Order=3)]
    internal string TickerSymbol;

    [DataMember(Order=2)]
    internal decimal LastTrade;
}

[DataContract(Name = "QuickReturnStockQuote")]
public class MyStock4 : MyStockBase
{
    //Order is alphabetical (CompanyName, LastTrade, TickerSymbol)
    //and includes all the data types from the current class and
    //the base class.

    [DataMember]
    internal decimal LastTrade;
}

[DataContract(Name = "QuickReturnStockQuote")]
public class MyStockBase
{
    [DataMember]
    internal string TickerSymbol;

    [DataMember]
    internal string CompanyName;
}
```

■ **Note** Primitive types and certain types, such as DateTime and XmlElement, are treated as primitive because they are always known to the .NET runtime. As a result, you do not need to add them via the [KnownType] attribute. The only exception to this is when using arrays of primitive types.

Sometimes both the endpoints involved will not be aware of the types and therefore warrant the use of the [KnownType] attribute. These situations are as follows:

- As stated earlier, the data type sent is inherited from the type that is being expected.
- The type sent is declared as an interface as opposed to a concrete implementation such as a class, structure, or enumeration. Since you cannot know in advance what type implements that interface, the [KnownType] attribute is required.
- The declared type that is being sent is declared of the type Object; because every type inherits from Object, the type cannot be known in advance.
- Some of the types, even though declared, might not fall in one of the previous three situations. For example, a HashTable internally stores the actual object using the Object type.

Listing 11-5 shows an example of how you can use the [KnownType] attribute when using a HashTable. The class QuickReturnPortfolio implements a HashTable, and because of the [KnownType] attribute, the runtime is aware that only the types QuickReturnStock and QuickReturnBond are stored in the HashTable.

Listing 11-5. *Data Contract Using* [KnownType] *Attribute*

```
[DataContract]
public class QuickReturnStock { }

[DataContract]
public class QuickReturnBond { }

[DataContract]
[KnownType(typeof(QuickReturnStock))]
[KnownType(typeof(QuickReturnPortfolio))]
public class QuickReturnPortfolio
{
    [DataMember]
    System.Collections.Hashtable thePortfolio;
}
```

Data Contract Versioning

Change is a fact of life, and in a service-oriented world you do not have the luxury of assuming that everyone will change their implementation as your solution evolves. Some consumers will still be using the old version of the contract; therefore, you need to be able to support them by versioning data contracts.

Broadly speaking, data contract changes fall into two categories—nonbreaking and breaking. *Nonbreaking* changes are when a consumer is able to communicate with a service using a newer version of a data contract, and vice versa. *Breaking* changes, on the other hand, do not allow this communication without changes to the consumer as well. Any change to a type that does not affect how an item is serialized and deserialized on the other end is a nonbreaking change. Listing 11-6 shows two versions of a class called `QuickReturnQuote`. Although the underlying type has changed between the two versions, the data contract is still the same because the `Name` property will be applied to the changing member to mask the internal name change.

Listing 11-6. *Coordinate Data Contract Equivalence*

```
//Version 1 of the QuickReturnQuote Class
[DataContract]
public class QuickReturnQuote
{
    [DataMember(Name = "TickerSymbol")]
    internal string Symbol;

     [DataMember]
    internal decimal LastTrade;

     [DataMember]
    internal decimal Change;
}

//Version 2 of the QuickReturnQuote Class
[DataContract]
public class QuickReturnQuote
{
    [DataMember]
    internal string TickerSymbol;

    [DataMember(Name="LastTrade")]
    internal decimal Value;

    [DataMember]
    internal decimal Change;
}
```

Table 11-1 summarizes the options available when changing a data contract and the impact that change has on the consumers, if any.

Table 11-1. *Data Contract Change and Its Impact*

Change	Impact of Change
Changing name or namespace	Breaking change
Changing order of data members	Breaking change
Renaming data members	Breaking change
Changing data contract	Breaking change
Adding data member	Nonbreaking change (in most cases)
Removing data member	Nonbreaking change (in most cases)

Changing contracts is a tricky situation no matter how careful you are. You can change the contracts in many ways—by adding, removing, or modifying—and you can cause many issues on either end of the wire. These can include the obvious issues where an exception will be thrown (and it would be easier to debug and fix) to the more interesting ones where the data may lack integrity and not make sense. Figure 11-2 shows a versioning decision tree that you can use to see the effect of any changes applied to the data contracts. The versioning decisions are depicted with blue diamonds, and the actions of those decisions are represented in rectangles. The arrows represent the direction of the flow. The green actions represent nonbreaking changes, and those in orange show breaking changes.

Let's take an example service and walk through the flowchart. When you need to modify your existing service and can do so by adding a new service, then the easiest way forward is to use service contract inheritance. This new type will be pointing to a new endpoint, which only the new consumers of this service will be aware of; the existing consumers will continue using the existing published version of the service. However, if this is not an option and you need to change the data contract, then (depending on the kind of change) this may or may not be easy. If you need to add more data, then, as you can see in Figure 11-2, the easiest option is adding new *optional* data members.

If adding new members is not an option and you need to change the service operation and its corresponding data contract, then, as shown in the decision tree, it is best to implement a new version of the data contract (depicted as "v.Next") within a new namespace and also pointing to a new endpoint. It is recommended that you incorporate a version number in the namespace. At this point if you choose, you can deprecate the old endpoint, and it is this action of deprecating that is breaking. If you are only deleting a service operation, you can keep the same data contract and just implement the "v.Next" version of the service and namespace pointing to a new endpoint.

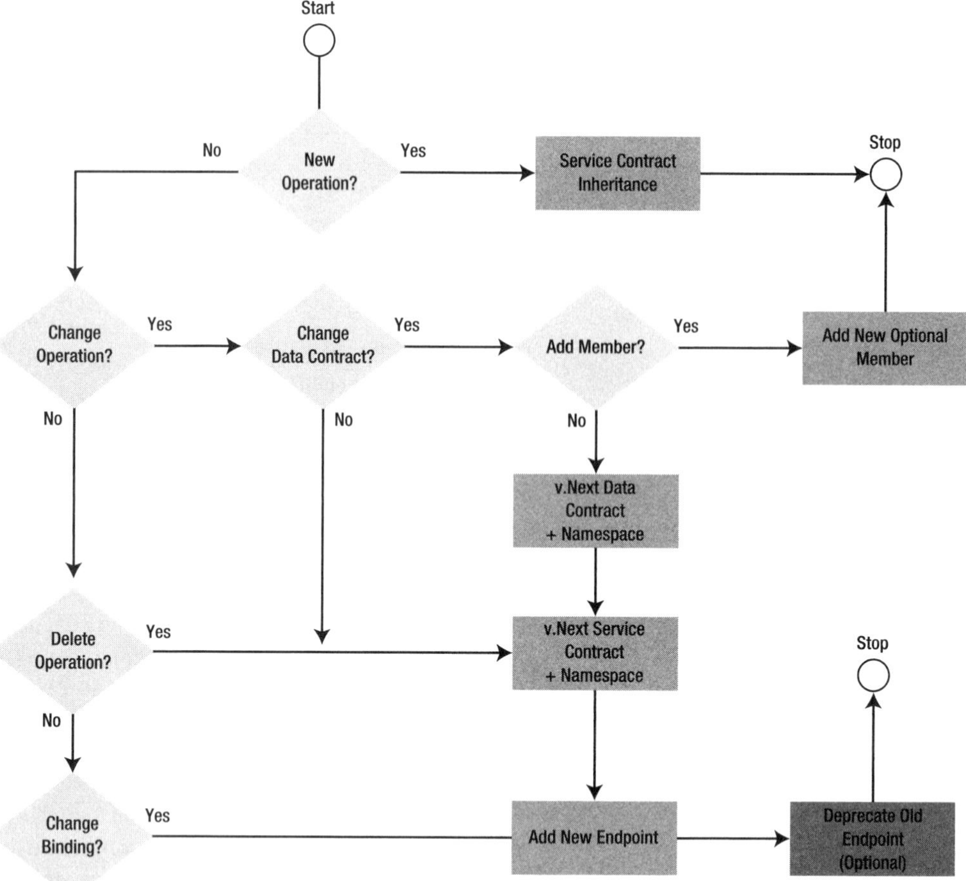

Figure 11-2. *Versioning decision tree*

Round-Tripping

As you have seen so far, versioning data contracts is fairly straightforward, and for the most part a data contract can evolve with the service in a nonbreaking fashion. But there is one feature called *round-tripping* where the type cannot be evolved. Round-tripping is when, for a data contract, data passes from a new version to an old version and back to a new version. Since round-tripping guarantees that no data is lost, enabling this makes the type forward-compatible with any changes supported by data contract versioning in the future.

For a type to take part in round-tripping, you need to implement the `IExtensibleDataObject` interface. This interface contains the property called `ExtensionData`, which is used to store any data from future versions of the data contract that might not be known to the current version. When the WCF runtime comes across any data that is not part of the original contract, that data is stored in this property and persisted. This property is essentially a "property bag" for the data and is not processed in any other fashion.

One caveat to using the round-tripping feature is that sometimes it may cause the WCF runtime to produce schema-invalid messages. Round-tripping should be disabled when strict schema compliance is a requirement, such as if a future version of a data contract adds new members. When serialized, these new members are stored in the ExtensionData property. Now, when this new data contract is serialized the next time, the ExtensionData property will be serialized instead of the content of that ExtensionData property (that is, the new members). This will result in a message with a schema in which the new members are not present.

If at some point in the future you do not like the support for unknown members and want to switch off round-tripping, you can do so quite easily. For example, you might have a requirement for strict schema compliance in the future. You can disable this feature by setting the IgnoreExtensionDataObject property in the [ServiceBehavior] attribute to true. Listing 11-7 shows how you can apply this at the service level. The class called Main implements a service defined by the interface IQuickReturnTraderChat.

Listing 11-7. *Sample Showing How to Ignore* ExtensionDataObject *at a Service Level*

```
[ServiceBehavior(InstanceContextMode =
      InstanceContextMode.Single,
      IgnoreExtensionDataObject=true)]
public partial class Main : Form, IQuickReturnTraderChat
{
    //Code removed for clarity
}
```

If you want to implement certain behaviors at an operation level as opposed to the service level, then use the [OperationBehavior] attribute instead of the [ServiceBehavior] attribute. However, the [OperationBehavior] attribute supports only a subset of features of the [ServiceBehavior] attribute.

■ **Note** The [ServiceBehavior] attribute specifies the internal execution behavior of a specific service and applies at the service-wide level, affecting all the operations within that service. You can use this attribute to enable most common features such as concurrency, exception details, automation session shutdown, transaction behavior, and so on, which otherwise would need to be manually implemented.

XML Serialization

As you have seen so far, the default option to serialize data types is the data contract serializer, which is implemented via the DataContractSerializer class. However, WCF also supports XmlSerializer. Although XmlSerializer supports fewer types compared to DataContractSerializer, it does provide better control over the resulting XML and also supports more of the XSD standard. Even though DataContractSerializer is the default option, sometimes using XmlSerializer is better:

- It's better if you are migrating an application from ASP.NET web services to WCF and want to reuse existing types instead of data contracts.
- It's better when more control over XML is required for it to adhere to some schema.
- It's better when services need to follow legacy SOAP encoding standards.

You also need to be aware of the underlying differences between the two platforms. Although the data contract serializer expects every member that needs to be serialized decorated with the `[DataMember]` attribute, `XmlSerializer`, on the other hand, serializes any public member. If you are not careful, this can lead to situations where data you were not expecting to be serialized is exposed, which can cause security and information disclosure issues.

■ **Note** The two serialization options (`DataContractSerializer` and `XmlSerializer`) serialize the same type to XML differently, which makes their interchange usage difficult because you might get runtime exceptions or behavior that might not be expected.

To use `XmlSerializer` instead of the data contract serializer, all you need to do is apply the `[XmlSerializerFormat]` attribute to the *service*. Listing 11-8 shows the `QuickReturnStockQuote` example discussed earlier in the chapter, implementing `XmlSerializer`. Note, in addition to the `required` attribute, the accessibility of the class members has changed to `public`. This is because, as we stated earlier, only public members will be serialized by `XmlSerializer`.

Listing 11-8. `QuickReturnStockQuote` *Using* `XmlSerializer`

```
[DataContract]
[XmlSerializerFormat]
public class QuickReturnStockQuote
{
    [DataMember(Name = "TickerSymbol")]
    public string Symbol;

    [DataMember]
    public string CompanyName;

    [DataMember]
    public decimal LastTrade;

    //Abbreviated for Clarity
}
```

You should be aware of the following rules when using `XmlSerializer`:

- The [XmlSerializer] attribute, when being used on methods or parameters, can be used only when the class is a typed message. This cannot be applied directly to a service operation's parameters or its return values. Do not worry if you are not aware of what a typed message or a [MessageContract] is; we'll define both in the "Introducing Message Contracts" section.
- This attribute takes precedence when applied to a typed message member when that message member has conflicting properties set. For example, the ElementName property on XmlSerializer overrides the Name property on the [MessageContract] attribute.
- Both the [SoapInclude] and [XmlInclude] attributes that are used to recognize a type when serializing or deserializing with SOAP are not supported; instead, use the [KnownType] attribute.
- When trying to do SOAP encoding, XmlSerializer does not support the [MessageHeaderArray] attribute, which is used to customize part of the SOAP header element.

Security

When switching from the data contract serializer to XmlSerializer, you need to take into account some security changes. Unlike the data contract serializer, XmlSerializer needs write access to the temp folder of the machine. And theoretically, another process could overwrite the temp assemblies that XmlSerializer created with other assemblies containing malicious code. Since XmlSerializer supports the loading of pregenerated serialized assemblies, it is recommended that you sign the WCF solution that uses XmlSerializer. If the solution is unsigned, then the possibility exists where a malicious program could place an assembly with the same name as the pregenerated assembly in the application folder or GAC and load it.

■ **Note** We have been primarily discussing XML serialization so far, but .NET also supports another called *binary serialization*. This allows an object in memory to be converted into a byte of streams, which—in addition to persisting to disk—allows you to marshal by value. *Marshal by value* is when objects are passed between application domains via parameters or return values. The objects need to have the flexibility to be serialized to allow them to do that. The binary serialization, although it is efficient and produces compact code, works only with the .NET platform and is not portable across platforms.

Introducing Message Contracts

When using data contracts, usually your concentration is on the data structure and the serialization aspects of those structures and not so much on the *SOAP message*, which carries the "payload" between the service and the consumer. In other words, the data contracts control the format of the SOAP message. However, if you are in a situation where you want an equal amount of control over both the structure and the content of the message because of operational reasons, then you need to use message contracts as opposed to data contracts. When using message contracts, you can use a *data type* as either the parameter to a service call or the return value from a call. And it is this data type that is precisely serialized to the SOAP message, defining the precise schema for the message. Another way to put it is a message contract is nothing but a mapping for a data type and the SOAP envelope that is created.

Applying the `[MessageContract]` attribute to a type defines its message contract. Those type members that need to be part of the SOAP header need to have the `[MessageHeader]` attribute applied, and those that will be part of the SOAP body need to have the `[MessageBodyMember]` attribute applied to them. You can apply both the `[MessageHeader]` attribute and the `[MessageBodyMember]` attribute to all members of a type irrespective of their accessibility levels.

Similar to the data contracts, you can use the `Name` and `Namespace` properties on the `[MessageHeader]` and `[MessageBodyMember]` attributes. If the namespace is not changed, the default is the same namespace of the service contract. Listing 11-9 shows the earlier example of `QuickReturnStockQuote` from Listing 11-2, which implements a message contract instead of a data contract. This allows you to precisely control the schema of the message when `QuickReturnStockQuote` is the data type.

Listing 11-9. `QuickReturnStockQuote` *Implementing a Message Contract*

```
[MessageContract]
public class QuickReturnStockQuote
{
    [MessageHeader(Name="TickerSymbol")]
    internal string Symbol;

    [MessageHeader]
    internal string CompanyName;

    [MessageBodyMember]
    internal decimal LastTrade;

    [MessageBodyMember]
    internal decimal Change;

    [MessageBodyMember]
    internal decimal PreviousClose;

    [MessageBodyMember(Name = "AverageVolume")]
    internal decimal AvgVol;

    [MessageBodyMember(Name = "MarketCapital")]
    internal double MarketCap;

    [MessageBodyMember(Name = "PriceEarningRatio")]
    internal decimal PERatio;
```

```
    [MessageBodyMember(Name = "EarningsPerShare")]
    internal decimal EPS;

    [MessageBodyMember(Name = "52WkHigh")]
    internal decimal FiftyTwoWeekHigh;

    [MessageBodyMember(Name = "52WkLow")]
    internal decimal FiftyTwoWeekLow;
}
```

Listing 11-10 shows the SOAP representation of `QuickReturnStockQuote`.

Listing 11-10. *SOAP Message Representation of* `QuickReturnStockQuote`

```
<soap:Envelope>
    <soap:Header>
        <TickerSymbol>MSFT</TickerSymbol>
        <CompanyName>Microsoft</CompanyName>
    </soap:Header>
    <soap:Body>
        <LastTrade>29.24</LastTrade>
        <Change>0.02</Change>
        <PreviousClose>29.17</PreviousClose>
        <AverageVolume>59.31</AverageVolume>
        <MarketCapital>287.44</MarketCapital>
        <PriceEarningRatio>24.37</PriceEarningRatio>
        <EarningsPerShare>1.20</EarningsPerShare>
        <_52WkHigh>29.40</_52WkHigh>
        <_52WkLow>21.45</_52WkLow>
    </soap:Body>
</soap:Envelope>
```

Fine-Tuning SOAP

As we have stated, a message contract is all about fine-tuning the various aspects of a SOAP envelope, empowering you with the ability to integrate with other platforms and also those that have a special interoperability need. In this section, you will see what options you have to customize the SOAP envelope; we'll cover aspects such as SOAP wrappers, element order, SOAP actions, SOAP header attributes, and so on.

You can also control the wrapping of the SOAP body parts. The default behavior is to have the body parts in a wrapper element when serialized. More than one body part should not be wrapped because it is not compliant with WS-I Basic Profile (version 1.1). The only situation where you would do this is for interoperability in some specific scenarios to another system that expects this format. You can control the name and the namespace of the wrapper element by setting the `WrapperName` and `WrapperNamespace` properties in the `[MessageContract]` attribute.

The default order of elements is alphabetical; however, both the `[MessageHeader]` and `[MessageBodyMember]` attributes support the `Order` property, which can be used to set the specific ordering of elements the same as in a data contract. The only difference when compared to the data contract is the inheritance scenario. Unlike the data contract, in a message contract the base type's members are not sorted before the child type's members.

If you need to implement a SOAP action, then you need to define that with the service operation of the service contract through the [OperationContract] attribute. To specify the SOAP action, you need to set the Action and ReplyAction properties on the [OperationContract] attribute when defining the service operation. The SOAP specification allows the three attributes listed in Table 11-2 in the header. By default, these headers are not emitted, but they can be set via the Actor, MustUnderstand, and Relay properties on the [MessageHeader] attribute, respectively. Note, if you have the property MustUnderstand set to true and you have a new version of the message contract, then you will get an exception at runtime because there is an extra header in the SOAP message that is "not understood."

Table 11-2. *Valid SOAP Header Attributes*

Value	Description
Actor (version 1.1)/Role (version 1.2)	Header's target URI
MustUnderstand	Specifies whether the node processing the header must understand it or not
Relay	Specifies whether the header can be relayed downstream to other nodes

At times a service might be required to support legacy XML. This is especially true in integration and interop situations where the platforms might differ between the consumer and the service. If required, you can enable the legacy XML encoding by setting the Use property on the [XmlSerializerFormat] attribute to Encoded, as shown in Listing 11-11. However, this is not recommended for two reasons. First, arrays are not supported, and second, it's because *object references* are preserved within the message body.

Listing 11-11. QuickReturnStockQuote *Using Legacy SOAP Encoding*

```
[XmlSerializerFormat(Use=OperationFormatUse.Encoded)]
public class QuickReturnStockQuote
{
    [DataMember(Name = "TickerSymbol")]
    public string Symbol;

    [DataMember]
    public string CompanyName;

    [DataMember]
    public decimal LastTrade;

    //Abbreviated for Clarity
}
```

The only time a message type can inherit from another type is when the base type also has a message contract. Also when inheriting, the message headers are a collection of all the headers in the inheritance hierarchy. Similarly, all the body parts are also consolidated in the inheritance hierarchy and are ordered first by the `Order` property specified in the `[MessageBodyMember]` attribute (if any) and then alphabetically. If the same name for either the header or the body part is repeated in the inheritance hierarchy, then the member that is lowest in the hierarchy is used to store the information.

Note If required, the WCF runtime allows you to use your own serializer by inheriting the `XmlObjectSerializer` class and overriding the `WriteStartObject`, `WriteObjectContent`, and `WriteEndObject` members.

You also need to consider the legacy XML support. If there is a requirement by your service to produce WSDL for interop scenarios, you need to treat this with care. WSDL and message contract support is tricky because WSDL supports only a subset of the message contract features. As a result, when generating WSDL, all the features from a message contract will not get reflected because of the lack of this support. You should consider these points when working with WSDL:

- WSDL does not have the notion of an array of headers and will show only one header as opposed to the array.
- Similar to the previous point, protection-level information is not fully supported and may be missing.
- The class name of the message contract type will be the message type generated in the WSDL.
- If many operations in a service contract use the same message contract across those operations, then the WSDL that is generated for that service contract will contain multiple message types even though at the end of the day they are the same type. These multiple messages are made unique in the WSDL by appending a numeral at the end such as 2, 3, and so on. As a result, the message types created when importing such a WSDL are identical except for their names.

Security

You have three options to make a message secure when using message contracts. Depending on which of the three options you choose, different parts of a SOAP message are digitally signed and encrypted. The options you have are to secure the entire SOAP message, to secure only the header of the SOAP message, or to secure only the body of the SOAP message (that is, the payload). To enable the option you choose, set the `ProtectionLevel` property on either the `[MessageHeader]` attribute or the `[MessageBodyMember]` attribute. Although for each header the protection level is determined individually, the body's security level is determined collectively with the highest level being applied across all body parts. For these security options to work, the bindings and behaviors need to be set up correctly (for example, attempting to sign without providing the correct credentials); otherwise, you will get an exception. Table 11-3 summarizes the possible values of this property.

Table 11-3. `ProtectionLevel` *Property Values*

Value	Description
`None`	No encryption or digital signature (this is also the default option)
`Sign`	Digital signature only
`EncyrptAndSign`	Both digitally signs and encrypts

Performance

Since every message header and body part is serialized independent of each other, the same namespace will be repeatedly declared for each of the same. It is recommended you consolidate these multiple headers and body parts into a single header or body part to reduce the size of the message on the wire and improve performance. For example, you can rewrite the original Listing 11-8 that showed `QuickReturnStockQuote` implemented as a message contract as shown in Listing 11-12.

Listing 11-12. `QuickReturnStockQuote` *Implemented for Optimal Performance*

```
[MessageContract]
public class QuickReturnStockQuote
{
    [MessageHeader(Name="TickerSymbol")]
    internal string Symbol;

    [MessageHeader]
    internal string CompanyName;

    [MessageBodyMember]
    internal StockDetails StockInformation;
}

[DataContract]
public class StockDetails {
    [DataMember]
    internal decimal LastTrade;

    [DataMember]
    internal decimal Change;

    [DataMember]
    internal decimal PreviousClose;
```

```
    [DataMember(Name = "AverageVolume")]
    internal decimal AvgVol;

    [DataMember(Name = "MarketCapital")]
    internal double MarketCap;

    [DataMember(Name = "PriceEarningRatio")]
    internal decimal PERatio;

    [DataMember(Name = "EarningsPerShare")]
    internal decimal EPS;

    [DataMember(Name = "52WkHigh")]
    internal decimal FiftyTwoWeekHigh;

    [DataMember(Name = "52WkLow")]
    internal decimal FiftyTwoWeekLow;
}
```

Using the Message Class

Up until now you have been looking at the various serialization techniques and data transfer architectures available to use as part of WCF. Understanding this basic foundation and how data transfers within WCF is key. In looking at data transfers, it is important to understand the core foundation of WCF—the `Message` class.

As stated earlier, the `Message` class is one of the two pillars of WCF and serves as a general-purpose container of data for all communication between a service and the consumers of that service. However, you should use it only in a few specific scenarios. For example, you should use it if you need either an alternative way of handling an incoming message or an alternative way of creating the outgoing message (say, saving the message to disk). The `Message` class is closely aligned to the SOAP protocol and contains a header and body. The `Message` class is defined in the `System.ServiceModel.Channels` namespace, and you create a simple message by calling the `CreateMessage` static method on the factory. Listing 11-13 shows a sample operation contract using `Message`.

Listing 11-13. `Message` *Class in Operations*

```
[ServiceContract()]
public interface IQuickReturnStock
{
    [OperationContract]
    System.ServiceModel.Channels.Message GetCurrentTicker();

    [OperationContract]
    void SetTickerSymbol(System.ServiceModel.Channels.Message data);
}
```

When you use the Message class in an operation, you should be aware of the following rules:

- The operation cannot have any out or ref parameters.
- You cannot have more than one input parameter, and that input parameter can be only type Message.
- The return type can be only Message or void.

Listing 11-14 shows an example of creating a simple message using an object. At the simplest level, the CreateMessage overloaded method takes objects and uses the default data contract serializer for serialization. There is also an overloaded version of CreateMessage, which takes XmlObjectSerializer as the serializer instead of using the default one.

Listing 11-14. *Creating Messages from Objects*

```
public class MyMessageService : IQuickReturnStock
{
    private Message IQuickReturnStock.GetCurrentTicker()
    {
        QuickReturnStockMessage stock = new QuickReturnStockMessage();
        stock.ticker = "MSFT";
        stock.companyName = "Microsoft Inc";
        MessageVersion ver =
            OperationContext.Current.IncomingMessageVersion();
        return Message.CreateMessage(ver,"GetDataResponse",stock);
    }

    //Abbreviated for clarity
}

[DataContract]
public class QuickReturnStockMessage
{
     [DataMember] public string ticker;
     [DataMember] public string companyName;
}
```

Similar to how the message in Listing 11-14 was created using objects, you could have created the same message using XML readers instead. A few scenarios where this would make more sense than using objects would be when reading from a file system, using an XmlDictionaryWriter object, creating fault messages (using CreateFault method), and so on.

When writing messages, you can do so using primarily three different methods. First is the WriteBodyContents method, which writes the body contents of the message to a given XML writer. Second is the WriteBody method, which writes the body content as well but also encloses the appropriate wrapper elements (such as <soap:body>). Third is the WriteMessage method, which writes out the entire message including the wrapping SOAP envelope and headers. Note if SOAP is turned off, all three methods produce the same result of writing out the message body contents.

When reading messages, the primary way to do so is via the GetReaderAtBodyContents method, which returns an XmlDictionaryReader object. Alternatively, if you require a type-safe way to access the message, then use the GetBody method, which allows access to the message body as a *typed object*. In addition, the Message class has properties such as Headers, Properties, Version, IsFault, IsEmpty, and so on, that represent access to other parts of the message such as message header, message properties, SOAP, WS-Addressing, and so on, that you might need.

Filtering

WCF has a concept of a filtering mechanism, which you can use to examine parts of messages and match them and then make some operational decision at runtime. This filtering mechanism is implemented as a set of classes and is designed to be fast with each filter implemented specifically for a certain kind of message matching. The filtering takes place after a message has been received and sits in the stack when the message is being dispatched to the relevant application. At this level, the filtering system can interact with all other WCF subsystems such as routing, security, event handling, and so on. An example is if there is a queue, then based on the priority of the message it can be moved to the front of the queue for processing.

Filtering is typically used when you need to route the message to different modules within a system depending on the content of the message. Two of the more common scenarios for this are routing and demultiplexing. In the first scenario, routing, the listener running at an endpoint filters for a specific action, and only matching actions get to the endpoint. In the second scenario of demultiplexing, various listeners are on the wire, and only those with the "filtered" endpoint address reach the intended endpoint.

Filters

Internally the filtering mechanism consists of a filter and a filter table. The filters implemented via an abstract MessageFilter class make a boolean decision based on the configured conditions. These filters are used in a filter table instead of being tested individually, and each filter has an associated table with the filter data. The filter table implements the IMessageFilterTable interface and is created by calling the generic CreateFilterTable<FilterData> method on the abstract MessageFilter class. The Match method on the MessageFilter class determines whether an incoming message satisfies a particular filter.

This method returns a true if a match was found based on the specified criteria. Once a filter is created, the criteria used cannot be changed because there is no implementation in the filter to detect this change. The only way to work around this is to delete the existing filter and create a new one with the updated criteria. WCF out of the box has a few concrete implementations of the abstract MessageFilter class, as shown in Table 11-4.

Table 11-4. *Concrete MessageFilter Implementations in WCF*

Classes	Description
XPathMessageFilter	Uses an XPath expression to specify the criteria
MatchAllMessageFilter	Matches all messages
MatchNoneMessageFilter	Matches none of the messages

Table 11-4. *Continued*

Classes	Description
`ActionMessageFilter`	Tests whether the message action matches a given set of actions
`EndpointAddressMessageFilter`	Tests whether the message is valid for a given addresses
`PrefixEndpointAddressMessageFilter`	Similar to `EndpointAddressMessageFilter`, except matches a prefix of the URI

Filter Tables

Internally the filter table is similar to a `HashTable` and is a key-value pair where the filter is the key and some metadata in the value. This metadata can contain any relevant information needed such as the type of the filter data, the actions to take for a matching message, and so on. Filter tables have methods that return both single matching and multiple matching records. Note, these records are not ordered in any sequence. The `MessageFilterTable` class is the most generic implementation of the `IMessageFilter` interface in WCF and can store any type of filter.

You can assign filter priorities using a number; the higher the number, the higher priority the filter has. You can assign the same priority to more than one type of filter at the same time. The same filter type can have more than one priority at the same time. You can match these filters in a top-down fashion, starting with the highest-priority filter. Once a matching filter is found at a certain priority, the WCF runtime does not examine any filters of that type with a lower priority.

■ **Note** If you want, you can also send attachments with WCF using Direct Internet Message Encapsulation (DIME). If you want to be WSE compliant, then you should use DIME's successor called Message Transmission Optimization Mechanism (MTOM). For more details, refer to Chapter 13.

Best Practices for Versioning

Versioning, in the context of data contracts, is all about schema validation because the entity that is consumed and used at the end of the schema itself. It is the changes to this schema you need to version. Versioning for data contracts can be divided into two groups—one that requires schema validation and a second that does not. The first group where schema validation is required is quite rare in today's enterprise environment, and many systems can handle the fact that certain elements are extra and not defined in a schema.

With Schema Validation

Data contracts should be considered *immutable* when schema validation is required "both ways" (that is, new to old, and vice versa). You should create a new data contract whenever a new version is required, because this will generate a new schema. This new data contract should also incorporate the relevant name, namespace, and updated service type information. In most cases, changes to data contracts in these circumstances need to be rippled across to every layer in the solution. This means if a data contract is part of another data contract and if the child data contract is updated, even though the parent is not, then the parent data contract would need to be versioned as well.

It is quite common that in a heterogeneous environment you do not have control over the incoming messages, though usually you do have some degree of control on the outgoing messages. If there is a requirement that the messages that are generated (that is, the outgoing messages) need to *strictly comply* with a schema, then you would need to turn off the round-tripping feature. Round-tripping is when the original incoming message, which you have no control over, has extra information that does not comply with your schema. This extra information is stored and then returned with the outgoing message. When this happens, if the outgoing message needs to be compliant with a schema, it won't be. You have two options to switch off round-tripping. One option is not to implement `IExtensibleDataObject`, and the second is to set the `IngoreExtensionDataObject` property to true on the `[ServiceBehavior]` attribute.

Without Schema Validation

When schema validation is not required, the guidelines for versioning are as follows:

- Type inheritance should not be used to version data contracts; instead, either create a new type or change the data contract on an existing type.
- Always implement the interface `IExtensibleDataObject` to support round-tripping.
- Do not change the name or namespace for the data contract because the versions for that data contract evolve. If the underlying type changes, then make appropriate changes to keep the data contract the same, for example, by using the `Name` property.
- Similar to the data contract point earlier, do not change any names or namespaces for the data members. If the underlying data member (such as field, property, event, and so on) changes, preserve the data member by using the `Name` property. Also, changing either the type or the order of any of the data member is not allowed because in most cases doing so will also cause the data contract to change.
- When there is a new version containing new data members, they should always follow these rules:
    - For the new member, the `IsRequired` property should be set to false (the default value).
    - A callback method using the `[OnDeserializing]` attribute should be provided in cases where a default value of `null` or `zero` for a data member is not acceptable. This should provide the default value that will be acceptable by the data member.
    - In the "old" version of the data contract, the `Order` property should not be set. Any new members added in subsequent versions should have their `Order` property set to that version. For example, version 2 of the data contract should have the `Order` property set to 2, version 3 to 3, and so on. The order of all the newly added members should be *after* the existing members; you can use the `Order` property to ensure this.

- Data members should not be removed even if the IsRequired property is set to false.
- The IsRequired property cannot be changed between versions.
- The EmitDefaultValue property cannot be changed for the required data members (that is, have the IsRequired property set to true) between versions.
- When creating a new version, do not create a branched version hierarchy.
- Enumerations are just like any other data members, and the same practices for reordering, adding, removing, and so on, apply as stated previously.

Putting It All Together: Quote Client Sample Application

We have introduced many different concepts in this chapter. In the following sections, we will show how to create a sample application that illustrates the concepts that we have discussed in this chapter. This sample consists of a service and a client. The service called QuickReturnQuoteService is quite straightforward and exposes two operations called GetPortfolio and GetQuote. The data contract for the service is exposed via a class called StockQuote. The first operation, GetPortfolio, accepts an array of stock tickers, which makes up the portfolio and returns an array of type StockQuote, which contains the details of each of the stocks in the portfolio. Similarly, GetQuote accepts one ticker and returns the type StockQuote.

Creating the Service

As mentioned, the service is quite simple and exposes the interface called IQuickReturnQuoteService. Listing 11-15 shows this interface. The service also has two endpoints—one over HTTP and the other a MEX endpoint. In this example, the service resides in a folder called wcf, which is part of inetpub and resides at C:\inetpub\wwwroot\wcf.

Listing 11-15. IQuickReturnQuoteService *Interface*

```
[ServiceContract]
public interface IQuickReturnQuoteService
{
    [OperationContract]
    StockQuote[] GetPortfolio(string[] portfolioTickers);

    [OperationContract]
    StockQuote GetQuote(string ticker);
}
```

The QuoteService class shown in Listing 11-16 is the concrete implementation for the IQuickReturnQuoteService interface for the service.

Listing 11-16. `QuoteService` *Concrete Implementation*

```
public class QuoteService : IQuickReturnQuoteService
{
    public StockQuote[] GetPortfolio(string[] portfolioTickers)
    {

        ArrayList tickers = new ArrayList();

        foreach (string stockTicker in portfolioTickers)
        {
            StockQuote stockQuote = new StockQuote(stockTicker);
            tickers.Add(stockQuote);
        }

        return (StockQuote[])tickers.ToArray(typeof(StockQuote));
    }

    public StockQuote GetQuote(string ticker)
    {
        StockQuote quote = new StockQuote(ticker);

        return quote;
    }
}
```

You can access the two endpoints exposed by the service via the `http://localhost/wcf/QuickReturnQuoteService.svc` and `http://localhost/wcf/QuickReturnQuoteService.svc/mex` URLs. Listing 11-17 and Listing 11-18 show the `.svc` file and the `Web.config` files. Note for a production system, it is recommended you switch off the debug options; this is enabled only for development purposes.

Listing 11-17. `QuickReturnQuoteService.svc` *File*

```
<%@ServiceHost language=c# Debug="true" Service="QuickReturn.QuoteService" %>
```

Listing 11-18. `Web.config`

```
<?xml version="1.0"?>
<configuration>
    <system.serviceModel>
        <services>
            <service name="QuickReturn.QuoteService"
                behaviorConfiguration="QuoteServiceBehavior">
                <endpoint  address=""
                    binding="wsHttpBinding"
                    contract="QuickReturn.IQuickReturnQuoteService"
                />
```

```
                <endpoint  address="mex"
                    binding="mexHttpBinding"
                    contract="IMetadataExchange"
                />
            </service>
        </services>

        <behaviors>
            <serviceBehaviors>
                <behavior name="QuoteServiceBehavior">
                    <serviceMetadata httpGetEnabled="true"/>
                    <serviceDebug
                        includeExceptionDetailInFaults="true"/>
                </behavior>
            </serviceBehaviors>
        </behaviors>
    </system.serviceModel>
</configuration>
```

The data contract is implemented via the `StockQuote` class, as shown in Listing 11-19. To show some of the versioning concepts, we have two versions of the data contract. Version 1 is simple and consists of just three data members: `LastTrade`, `CompanyName`, and `TickerSymbol`. Version 2 of the data contracts, which is shown in Listing 11-19, adds data members. Since we are not hooking into a stock exchange, to simulate this feed the constructor takes a few ticker symbols and randomly generates a number from 10 to 100 for the stock price. Note that we have abbreviated Listing 11-19 for clarity.

Listing 11-19. *Version 2 of the* `StockQuote` *Data Contract*

```
[DataContract]
public class StockQuote
{
    //Constructor - simulates the changes when connected to an exchange
    public StockQuote(string ticker)
    {
        Random rnd = new Random();
        int deltaTrade = rnd.Next(100);

        switch (ticker)
        {
            case "MSFT":
                symbol = ticker;
                companyName = "Microsoft";
                lastTrade = 35.0M + deltaTrade;
                break;
```

```
            case "IBM":
                symbol = ticker;
                companyName = "IBM";
                lastTrade = 34.0M + deltaTrade;
                break;
            case "INTU":
                symbol = ticker;
                companyName = "Intuit";
                lastTrade = 33.0M + deltaTrade;
                break;
            case "GOOG":
                symbol = ticker;
                companyName = "Google";
                lastTrade = 32.0M + deltaTrade;
                break;
        }
    }

    private string symbol;
    [DataMember(Name = "TickerSymbol")]
    public string Symbol  { ... }

    private string companyName;
    [DataMember]
    public string CompanyName { ... }

    private decimal lastTrade;
    [DataMember]
    public decimal LastTrade { ... }

    private decimal change;
    [DataMember]
    public decimal Change { ... }

    private decimal previousClose;
    [DataMember]
    public decimal PreviousClose { ... }

    private decimal avgVol;
    [DataMember(Name = "AverageVolume")]
    public decimal AvgVol { ... }

    private double marketCap;
    [DataMember(Name = "MarketCapital")]
    public double MarketCap { ... }
```

```
    private decimal peRatio;
    [DataMember(Name = "PriceEarningRatio")]
    public decimal PERatio { ... }

    private decimal eps;
    [DataMember(Name = "EarningsPerShare")]
    public decimal EPS { ... }

    private decimal fiftyTwoWeekHigh;
    [DataMember(Name = "52WkHigh")]
    public decimal FiftyTwoWeekHigh { ... }

    private decimal fiftyTwoWeekLow;
    [DataMember(Name = "52WkLow")]
    public decimal FiftyTwoWeekLow { ... }
}
```

Creating the Client

The client is a simple Windows form application that contains a DataGridView. There are two buttons each for invoking the `GetPortfolio` or `GetQuote` operation on the service. The data contract returned by the service is bound to this DataGridView. The client consumes both versions of the service, simulating a real-world situation where some consumers of the service would be using the newer version while others might still be using the old version of the service. This simulation can be done in two ways. The first way is to create two different client projects. The second is to create two different proxies. We chose the second way and have generated two proxies for the service. Each proxy is in a different code file called `QuoteService1.cs` and `QuoteService2.cs`. The first file, `QuoteService1.cs`, is used for version 1 of the service, and `QuoteService2.cs` is the proxy for version 2. If you download the sample application from the book's website, you can include *only* one of these files in the solution at any time.

We used the `SvsUtil.exe` tool to generate both the proxy and the service configuration for the service. The service configuration is saved in the `App.config` file for the client. Listing 11-20 shows the command line to use the `SvsUtil.exe` tool. Note that this assumes the service lives at `http://localhost/wcf`.

Listing 11-20. *Command Line to Generate Service Proxy*

```
svcutil /language:c# /config:App.config
        http://localhost/wcf/QuickReturnQuoteService.svc?wsdl
```

Listing 11-21 shows the `App.config` file that is automatically created by the `SvcUtil.exe` tool. Note, this tool adds many of the defaults such as service timeouts, buffer pool sizes, and so on. Depending on your operational requirements in a production environment, you might want to either handcraft these settings or modify the configuration file that the `SvcUtil.exe` tool generated.

Listing 11-21. `App.config` *Generated by* `SvcUtil.exe`

```
<?xml version="1.0" encoding="utf-8"?>
<configuration>
    <system.serviceModel>
        <bindings>
            <wsHttpBinding>
                <binding name="WSHttpBinding_IQuickReturnQuoteService"
                           closeTimeout="00:01:00"
                    openTimeout="00:01:00" receiveTimeout="00:10:00"
                           sendTimeout="00:01:00"
                    bypassProxyOnLocal="false" transactionFlow="false"
                           hostNameComparisonMode="StrongWildcard"
                    maxBufferPoolSize="524288" maxReceivedMessageSize="65536"
                    messageEncoding="Text" textEncoding="utf-8"
                           useDefaultWebProxy="true"
                    allowCookies="false">
                    <readerQuotas maxDepth="32" maxStringContentLength=
                           "8192" maxArrayLength="16384"
                        maxBytesPerRead="4096"
                        maxNameTableCharCount="16384" />
                    <reliableSession ordered="true" inactivityTimeout=
                        "00:10:00"
                        enabled="false" />
                    <security mode="Message">
                        <transport clientCredentialType="Windows"
                             proxyCredentialType="None"
                            realm="" />
                        <message clientCredentialType="Windows"
                            negotiateServiceCredential="true"
                              algorithmSuite="Default"
                              establishSecurityContext="true" />
                    </security>
                </binding>
            </wsHttpBinding>
        </bindings>
        <client>
            <endpoint address="http://localhost/wcf/
                    QuickReturnQuoteService.svc"
                binding="wsHttpBinding"
                    bindingConfiguration=
                    "WSHttpBinding_IQuickReturnQuoteService"
                contract="IQuickReturnQuoteService"
                     name="WSHttpBinding_IQuickReturnQuoteService">
```

```
                <identity>
                    <servicePrincipalName value=
                          "host/AmitBahree-PC " />
                </identity>
            </endpoint>
        </client>
    </system.serviceModel>
</configuration>
```

The code for the client where the service is invoked is fairly straightforward, as shown in Listing 11-22. Because you do not have any persistence storage, the tickers are hard-coded and the service is then invoked. The result from the service is bound to the data grid on the form.

Listing 11-22. *Calling the Service and Binding Data Contract to the Grid*

```
private void buttonGetPortfolio_Click(object sender, EventArgs e)
{
    this.Cursor = Cursors.WaitCursor;

    //We hard-code an array of a few stocks that we want the service
    //to return. In the real world, this would be retrieved
    //from some persistent store
    string[] stocks = { "INTU", "MSFT", "GOOG", "IBM" };

    //Invoke the Service
    StockQuote[] portfolio = theService.GetPortfolio(stocks);

    //Bind the data contract returned by the service to the grid.
    BindData(ref dataGridView, portfolio);
}

private void BindData(ref DataGridView dataGrid, object data)
{
    BindingSource bindingSource = new BindingSource();
    bindingSource.DataSource = data;

    dataGrid.DataSource = bindingSource;
    dataGrid.Columns["ExtensionData"].Visible = false;
}
```

As stated earlier, the client consumes two versions of the service. When you talk to the simpler version 1 of the service, you can see the result for both the `GetPortfolio` and `GetStock` operations in Figure 11-3 and Figure 11-4, respectively. Only three elements are known by the client—`LastTrade`, `CompanyName`, and `TickerSymbol`. To implement this old version, include the `QuoteService1.cs` file in the solution.

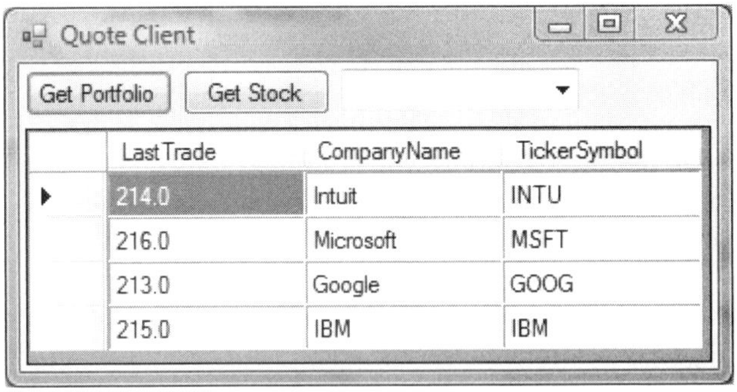

Figure 11-3. *Sample portfolio using version 1 of the service*

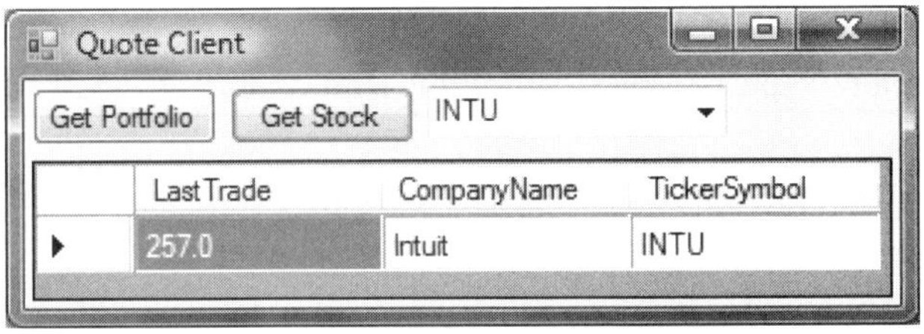

Figure 11-4. *Sample quote using version 1 of the service*

On the other hand, if the client is aware of the updated service and wants to consume version 2, then as you can see in Figure 11-5 and Figure 11-6 there are more data members returned by each of the operations. To implement this new version, include the `QuoteService2.cs` file in the solution instead of `QuoteService1.cs`.

Also note that no elements on the service end have changed in the sample—only the client elements have been changing to simulate a client that either consumes the old version or consumes the new version of the service.

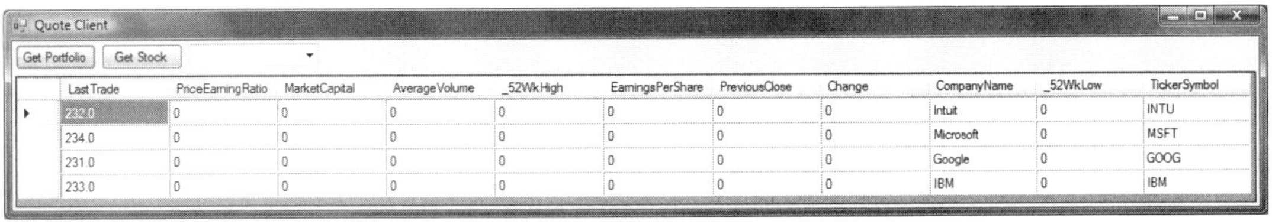

Figure 11-5. *Sample portfolio using version 2 of the service*

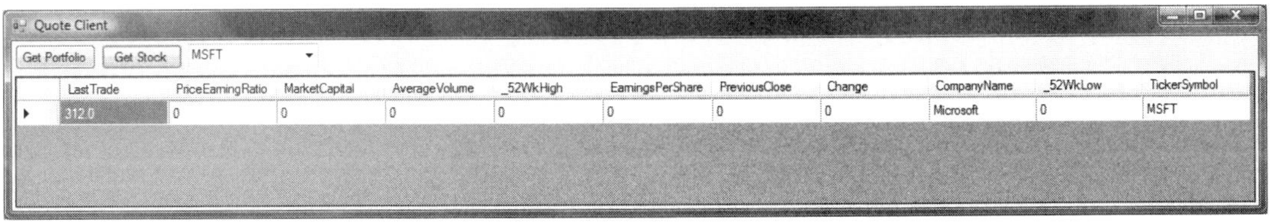

Figure 11-6. *Sample quote using version 2 of the service*

Summary

In conclusion, for any data to be passed to or from a service, first it needs to be serialized. Although both .NET and ASP.NET in general support serialization, WCF truly extends this concept and makes it easy to implement. Of the various options you examined, data contracts are the default and one of the most flexible serialization engines designed with change and versioning in mind. The WCF runtime flexibility allows you to switch to legacy support when required.

The ability to map your business components to data members in a natural OOP paradigm is a powerful feature. This makes the development, testing, and maintenance of data contracts along with versioning intuitive and easier. You also examined the powerful ability to filter the messages based on one or more criteria, allowing you to support scenarios, which earlier would require a lot of effort.

Today's needs demand application components that are available across the organization. The need for collaboration, online or offline, is the mandate for all companies. The next chapter will cover the aspects of developing peer-to-peer computing with WCF.

CHAPTER 12

Developing Peer-to-Peer Applications with WCF

In this chapter, we will dive into the concepts of peer-to-peer computing (also known as P2P). We will cover what P2P means, the advantages that it brings you, and the challenges that you'll face when working with P2P. We will also cover what a typical development environment looks like when writing P2P applications. We will explore some of the options provided by Microsoft in enabling P2P, both in the context of WCF and in Windows in general.

Introducing Peer-to-Peer Computing

Peer-to-peer computing is a term that has gained a lot of popularity in recent times. Today, organizations and businesses are increasingly depending on collaboration between individuals and groups to perform essential tasks. As a result, collaboration has become more essential at an individual level because these applications form more ad hoc online groups for business, entertainment, and cultural purposes.

Peer-to-peer computing essentially is a set of networked computers that rely on the computing power and bandwidth of the individual computers on the network as opposed to the traditional approach of relying on a smaller number of more powerful server computers on the network. A computer connected to a P2P network is called a *node* or *peer*. The nodes in a P2P network usually are connected on an ad hoc basis, and the real power in a P2P network lies in these nodes. The peers are responsible for uploading and downloading data among themselves without the need for a server.

Two types of P2P networks exist: a pure network and a hybrid network. A *pure* P2P network has no concept of a client or a server; it has only nodes, which act in the capacity of both a server and a client as needed. A *hybrid* P2P network, on the other hand, has a central server that keeps track of the various peers on the network. This server responds to requests from the peers for information only and does not store any data. The peers are responsible for hosting the information. For example, in a file-sharing P2P application, the files are stored by the peer, and the server is aware only of what files are stored at what peer.

In the real world, pure P2P solutions that implement only peering protocols and do not rely on the concept of clients and server are rare. Most P2P solutions rely on some nonpeer elements in the solution such as Domain Name System (DNS, used to translate computer hostnames to IP addresses). Some of the P2P solutions also have the notion of a *superpeer*, where other peers are connected to this superpeer in a star-like fashion. Over time, these superpeers could also be used as local servers. The networks in P2P applications are also called *meshes* (or sometimes a *mesh network*), akin to a wire mesh. Each node in a mesh at a minimum has bidirectional communication capability with its neighbors. A *cloud* is a mesh network with a specific address scope. These scopes are closely related to IPv6 scopes, and the peers in a cloud are those that can communicate within the same IPv6 scope.

Why Use P2P?

Usually, the nodes, or peers, in a P2P network are ordinary computers that most people use in their day-to-day life at home or work. Often these computers are on a home Internet connection (such as dial-up or broadband), and on average most of them are available only for a relatively short period of time in a day. Setting up a P2P network is relatively easy, and you do not need to have a technical background in computer science or be an ubergeek. As a result, P2P is popular and has a wide adoption rate among all categories of users.

One of the guiding principles for P2P solutions is that all nodes provide resources to the group such as processing power, bandwidth, storage, and so on. Therefore, when the overall demand increases with the addition of more nodes, so does the capacity. This is significantly different from a traditional client-server model, where adding more clients would slow everyone because more clients are competing for the same set of resources on the server. In addition, the distributed, ad hoc nature of the P2P network increases the resilience of the overall system by eliminating single points of failures by distributing data over multiple peers. Because of this, data can be shared effectively, and a network can be scaled up at a relatively low cost. By its nature, a P2P solution allows support for ad hoc and disconnected networks.

■ **Note** Although most users might have come across P2P applications that are used for sharing files, possibly using the likes of Gnutella, Kazaa, Napster, BitTorent, and so on, P2P applications are used across many problem domains and industries such as telephony and video, gaming, data replication, anonymity (such as Publius, Freenet, and so on), instant messaging, distributed computing (such as Distributed.net), and so on.

Broadly speaking, P2P solutions can fall into one of the following solution domains:

Real-time communication: P2P enables services such as serverless instant messaging and real-time game play. You can use instant messaging with voice and video today, but most implementations require the use of a server to function. If you are in an isolated network environment (such as those defined by many enterprises), then you would not be able to use most instant messaging solutions; but with serverless instant messaging, you could overcome these boundaries. Similarly, the real-time gaming networks are more aligned toward the enthusiastic gamer, allowing them to go head to head with other gamers. However, if you are not a hard-core gamer or if you want to set up an ad hoc game that can communicate in a variety of networking situations, without P2P networking this would be a significant challenge in today's environment.

Collaboration: P2P allows you to share files, workspaces, and experiences with others. Sharing workspaces allows a user to create an ad hoc workspace that can be populated with content and tools that can be used for solving a common goal. These can also provide collaborative functionality such as message boards; sharing files becomes just another aspect of this workspace. A P2P network allows one to share files in an easy and user-friendly way. Sharing your experiences with others in near real-time is a new opportunity using P2P networks. With the wide availability of wireless networks, it is becoming easier for people to share their day-to-day experiences in a more real-time fashion such as a music concert, snowfall whilst on a holiday, and so on. Similarly, using Groove (which is part of Microsoft Office 2007), a team does not need to be physically in the same office or even country, but they can still work in a secure environment in a virtual office or workspace. This allows them to share and synchronize files, manage projects, host discussion threads, schedule meetings, share text in real-time, and so on.

Content distribution: P2P allows for the easy distribution of content. This content could be software updates, text, audio, video, and so on. If you want to distribute a large amount of audio and video today, you need fairly big bandwidth requirements that can handle the volume. But when using a P2P, only a small number of peers would need to get the data from the centralized servers, and then they will propagate the content out on the mesh to the next closest peer that would want the content. Similarly, product updates, say, within an organization can be propagated quickly to everyone. For example, many enterprises use this model to distribute leadership content, patches, software updates, policy updates, and so on, throughout the organization. Many of the open source and Linux implementations also use this model to distribute their builds.

Distributed processing: P2P computing allows one to distribute computing tasks among various peers on the network and aggregate the results later. A large task usually is broken into smaller chunks that the peers can handle. Once each peer is finished with their task, they send the results to a central aggregation point. The peers can be configured to process these tasks only when it is idle if need be, so they do not use the resources of the machine when it is being used. One of the pioneers of this was the SETI@home project (run by the University of California). The SETI@home project brought this concept to the general public to the extent of sparking off contests between peers to see who could process more data in a given unit of time. Some of these contests effectively became bragging rights and showed off either that they had very powerful machines that could crunch more data or that they had more peers connected that collectively did more work.

The Challenges of P2P

P2P challenges can broadly be categorized in two segments: technical and legal. The technical aspects might cover topics such as difficult and complex to build, how one should achieve universal connectivity, and so on. The legal controversy is based on sharing music and movies originally made popular by file-sharing networks such as Napster. P2P networks, like most networks, can also be open to attacks. More specifically, some of the attacks are specifically designed for P2P networks such as poison attacks, polluting attacks, defection attacks, denial of service, and so on. We will cover these challenges and their possible solutions when we explore a typical P2P application stack in the next section.

■ **Note** *Poison attacks* are attacks where the contents are different from the description of that content. *Polluting attacks* are those where invalid chunks are added to an otherwise valid file. *Defection attacks* are those where users or software use the network without contributing resources to the network.

P2P faces many other challenges other than the immediate technical implementation details. Currently, there are no standards defined, which means interoperability between different P2P meshes is something that is difficult to achieve. Firewalls are becoming increasingly sophisticated, and although a P2P network can be based purely on IP, there are still many symmetric NAT firewalls out there. This might give the impression that these NATed addresses will cause the P2P mesh to not reach all endpoints. However, this rarely causes any issues and for the majority of the solutions is not a concern. Management and diagnostics are still issues. Because of the nondeterministic flow in a network, trying to diagnose a bug, for example, becomes a daunting task. Also, if you need to manage a P2P network and apply something like a distributed policy, then that also becomes a challenge. For example, many enterprises do not have control because of not being able to apply a distributed policy and because, indirectly, of the accountability. In many situations, this is not acceptable because of various regulatory, legal, and compliance requirements. This also makes it difficult to isolate and locate individual users who can cause security concerns (again because of the lack of user accountability).

On the legal challenges front, there is a perception because of the media coverage that all P2P is illegal and bad. And anonymous P2P networks allow one to share content easily, whether legal or not, so that does not help the cause. Although various companies and entities such as RIAA, Movie Studios, and so on, are fighting the battle in the courts, there is a lot of confusion to the end user. This is partly because the laws are different from country to country, and there is a lot of gray area and interpretation. For example, RIAA has gone after a few thousand users in the United States and is also looking to target some of those in the United Kingdom and other countries. However, certain countries such as France had legalized P2P at one time and later changed the local laws without absolute clarification. All this has led to more blurred distinction between what is legal and what is not.

■ **Note** We have kept the legal perception of P2P intentionally vague in this section. Since the local laws change so much based on the jurisdiction, it is not possible to cover all the situations here. The important part to remember is that the legal issues have nothing to do with the technology; rather, P2P is one specific implementation of the technology.

P2P Development Life Cycle

When developing and deploying P2P applications, you face three primary issues: how to achieve end-to-end connectivity; how to provide a common foundation consisting of various state data, identity management, and so on, for peers to use when exchanging state; and how to deploy and scale the solution in a secure manner. Each of these is an important piece of the puzzle to enable the P2P solution to work.

End-to-end connectivity: Because of the loose and disparate nature of a mesh, from a development and debugging perspective, ensuring that the various peers can seamlessly connect to each other is a challenge. Furthermore, complicating this is the fact that the peers connecting to the mesh might be using one or more communication technologies. Because of the nature of P2P applications, this also needs to support communication over various networks.

Common foundation: This is the "administrative" functionality that every P2P application needs in order to manage the various peers on the mesh. This includes identity management, contact management, node discovery, node naming, secure session management, multipeer communication, and so on.

Secure and scalable deployment: This is the ability to build on protocols specifically engineered for large-scale deployment, and it provides built-in security.

How Are Nodes Identified?

On a mesh, each node needs to be identified by a unique ID usually called a *peer ID* or *mesh ID*. To resolve these peer IDs to their corresponding Internet address, the Peer Name Resolution Protocol (PNRP) is used instead of DNS. Each peer node irrespective of type (such as computer, user, group, device, service, and so on) can have its own peer ID. This list of IDs is distributed among the peers using a multilevel cache and referral system that allows name resolution to scale to billions of IDs while requiring minimal resources on each node.

An *endpoint* is defined as a combination of a peer ID, port number, and communication protocol. Using an endpoint, data can be sent between nodes in two ways. One of these is for a peer to directly send the data to another peer. And the other is for a peer to send the data to all the other peers on the same mesh; this is also known as *flooding*. A flooded message could arrive at the same peer multiple times via different routes on the mesh.

Installing the Windows P2P Networking Stack

Windows P2P networking stack is not installed on Windows XP by default. If you are running Windows XP with Service Pack 2, then perform the following steps to install the P2P networking stack:

1. Click Start ➤ Control Panel ➤ Add/Remove Programs.
2. Click Add/Remove Components.
3. In Components, click Networking Services, and then select Details.
4. Select the Peer-to-Peer check box, and then select OK.
5. Click Next, and follow the instructions on the screen.

If you are running Windows XP with SP1, then you will need install the Windows Advanced Networking Pack for Windows XP, which is a free download available at `http://tinyurl.com/6ze98`.

If you are running Windows Vista, then this is already installed; however, you might have to enable the firewall exceptions. To do so, follow these steps:

1. Click Start ➤ Control Panel ➤ Security.
2. Under Windows Firewall, select Allow a Program Through Windows Firewall.
3. Click the Exceptions tab.
4. Check Windows Peer to Peer Collaboration Foundation.
5. Click OK.

Windows P2P Networking

Microsoft introduced the Windows peer-to-peer networking stack as a developer platform in Windows XP SP1. This stack is not installed by default; to install it on Windows XP (with SP2), you need to select the Peer-to-Peer option as part of the Networking Services within the Windows components that are available via the Add/Remove Programs option in the Control Panel. If you have only Windows XP SP1, then you need to install the Advanced Networking Pack to get the peer-to-peer networking stack.

Figure 12-1 shows the architecture for P2P networking as defined by Microsoft. The significant components that make up this stack are graphing, grouping, Name Service Provider (NSP), PNRP, and the identity manager. It is worth pointing out that this stack is *unmanaged code* with only a subset of the functionality exposed via WCF.

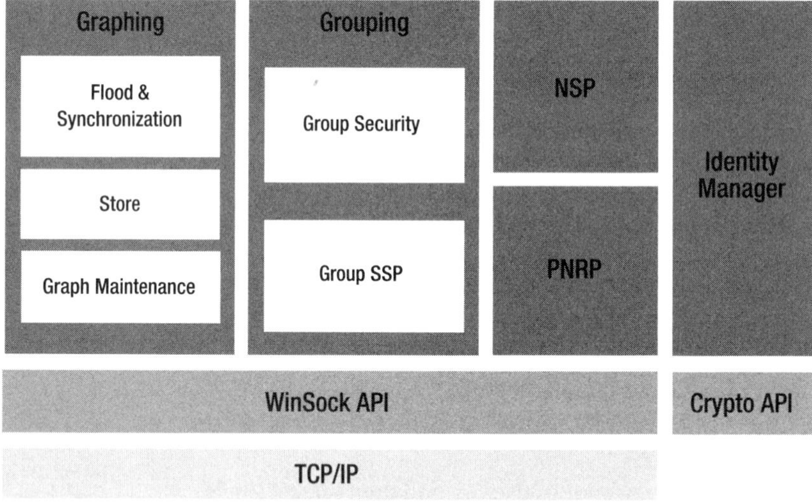

Figure 12-1. *Windows PNRP, graphing, grouping, and identity manager networking architecture*

Identity Management

P2P solutions usually do not use DNS because of the transient nature of the mesh. In theory, using Dynamic DNS is an option, but in actuality few DNS servers on the Internet support this in the real world. This raises an interesting question about how to resolve peer names to their network addresses (including ports, protocols, and so on). To allow this, Windows P2P networking is using PNRP. Some of the key attributes of PNRP that make it ideal for resolving names are as follows:

Name resolution is distributed and serverless: Each peer on the mesh caches a portion of the list of names on the mesh and further refers to other peers. Although this is not a true serverless environment, because there is a root node that is used to initiate the process, this node is not used for name resolutions.

Use IDs and not names: IDs identify peers instead of names. Since IDs are numbers, there are no language or locale issues.

Use multiple IDs: Since every service on the mesh can have its own identifier, the same node might end up having more than one ID.

Scale to large number of IDs: Because the list of IDs can grow to a large number, a multilevel cache and referral system is implemented between the peers that does not need significant resources.

Peer Names

Peer names can be registered either as secured or as unsecured. Unsecured names are recommended for use in a private network only, because the names are strings and can easily be spoofed. However, secured names need to be registered and are protected with a certificate and digital signature.

A PNRP ID is 256 bits long; the high-order 128 bits are a hash of the peer name assigned to the endpoint, and the lower 128 bits of the PNRP ID are an autogenerated number used for service location. The format for the peer name is *Authority.Classifier*. When using a secured network, the *Authority* is a secure hash (using Secure Hash Algorithm, SHA) of the public key of the peer name in hex. When using an unsecured network, the *Authority* is the single character 0 (zero). The *Classifier* is a Unicode string up to 150 characters long that identifies the application. The autogenerated number, used by the lower 128 bits, uniquely identifies different instances using the classifier participating in the same mesh. The combination of 256 bit mesh ID and the service location allow multiple PNPR IDs to be registered from a single computer.

PNRP Name Resolution

When a peer wants to resolve the peer name, it constructs the peer ID as discussed earlier and tries to find that entry in its cache for the ID. If a match is found, then it sends a PNRP request message to the peer and waits for a response. This approach ensures that the target peer node, with which another peer is trying to communicate, is active in the cloud. If no match is found, then an iterative process is used with the target peer that informs the sender of the peer that is the closest match to the ID that is trying to be resolved. It is up to the original sender at this stage to send the same request to the matching peer as the one to which it was pointing. If that new peer the sender was pointed to is also not the correct one, then that in turn will return the next closest matching peer to the sender, and so on.

When a PNRP request message is forwarded, both the nodes that are forwarded to and the responses received are cached. This prevents the situation where things could get into an endless loop. The name records have built-in security because of the public-private key pair. NSP is a mechanism by which you can access an arbitrary name provider; in the Windows P2P network stack, this provider interface is PNRP.

Graphing

A *graph* is a collection of peer nodes where one node may communicate to another using the neighbor's peer connections. A peer graph is built on the concept of flooding, which makes it possible to send data to all peers connected to that specific graph. To be able to handle deltas in this data, the flooding protocol sends these changes in data to all the peers. This is achieved by associating a unique GUID to each peer, which has an increasing version number or sequence number, and is further qualified by an age or a status. A synchronous process in a graph ensures that peers have the same set of data. The graphs themselves are insecure, and the P2P stack's architecture provides pluggable modules that provide security. These modules can define various aspects both at the connection and at the message level such as authentication, confidentiality, integrity, and so on.

Grouping

Grouping is nothing but a combination of graphing, PNRP, and the peer grouping "security provider" from Microsoft. This security provider provides management of the credentials of the members that are part of the group and supports the secure publication of records. Every group is identified by a unique ID that is used by peers on the network for identification. For groups, the PNRP secure names are used as IDs. Every peer has a set of two credentials—the first of which is to prove ownership to a peer's identity, a unique peer name, and credentials. The second set of credentials proves that a peer is a member of a group. For secure groups, participation is restricted to a known set of peers. Information is spread through the groups using records. A *record* consists of many pieces of information such as the peer's validity, data for record validity when challenged, a time stamp for validation, and the actual payload containing the record information. Security is a combination of the following:

- Peer name
- Group membership certificates
- Roles
- Secure publishing
- Security policies
- Secure connections

How Does a P2P Mesh Work?

As stated earlier, a mesh network is nothing but a P2P network and is responsible for routing data between nodes. A mesh network also allows for continuous connection, and if there are any blocked paths, they can be reconfigured in a hopping manner, from peer to peer, until a connection is established. This property makes them *self-healing*, allowing them to continue to operate even when a peer drops out. All peers in a mesh propagate the same mesh name, which gives new peers joining the mesh visibility into other nodes that are on the mesh. Figure 12-2 shows a sample mesh network with multiple peers connected.

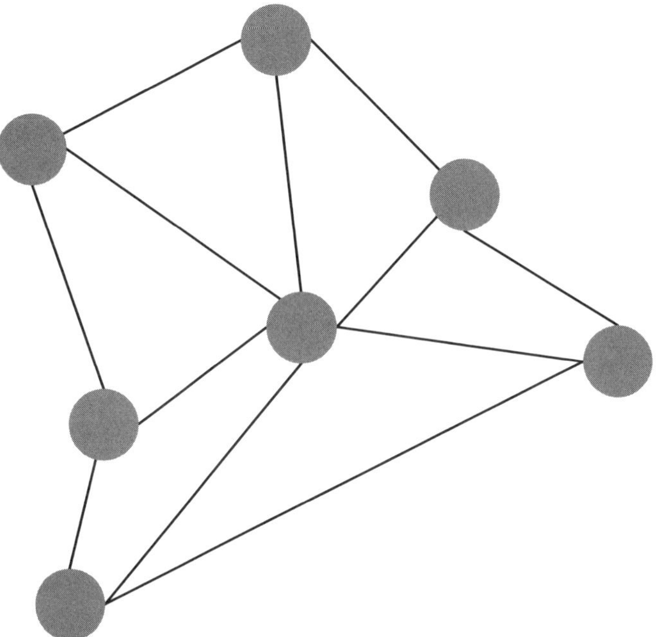

Figure 12-2. *Mesh network*

Mesh Flavors

Broadly speaking, two types of mesh networks are available, namely, the grouping and peer channel. Each of these options has their respective service models. Grouping is primarily used by the Data Replication service and is available in Windows XP (with SP2). The various peers, in the mesh, exchange messages by replicating records containing the data. Peer channel, on the other hand, is primarily a message-based service and is available in WCF. The peers in the mesh share data by building *synchronous* services. Both meshes have built-in security; grouping is implemented via a password and grouped certificates that are managed by the mesh. Peer channel security is also implemented via a password (to join the mesh) and individual certificates that are managed directly by the applications in the mesh. Both types of meshes support PNRP for node discovery; however, only peer channel supports a developer-supplied model such as web service. While a grouping mesh implementation is unmanaged and accessed via the Win32 API library, the peer channel is part of WCF, which is managed code.

The connection types between the peers in a mesh can also be of two topology types: full or partial. In full topology, each peer is connected to every other peer on the mesh. In partial topology, a peer is connected only to a handful of other peers—most likely those with which it exchanges the most data and has affinity. The example in Figure 12-2 shows a partial mesh because every peer is not connected to every other peer on the network. It is rare to come across a full topology mesh because it is not practical to operate in that mode. If there are N nodes in a full topology mesh, then each node is connected to $N - 1$ nodes at the same time. In other words, if there are 1,000 nodes in a mesh, each of the 1,000 nodes has a connection open to 999 other nodes at the same time. This would lead to a situation where the mesh would soon start running out of resources as more nodes joined the network.

Three types of P2P applications exist: one-to-one, one-to-many, and many-to-many. Figure 12-3 shows the normal flow of a P2P application. When one peer in a mesh wants to communicate with another, the steps are to find the other peer, send an invitation, and create a session between the two.

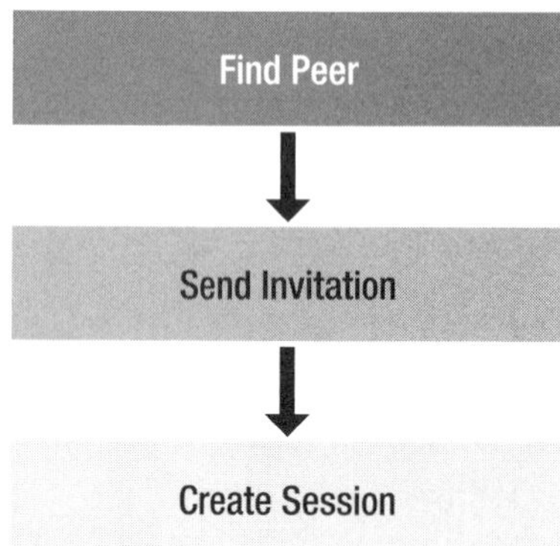

Figure 12-3. *P2P application flow*

Let's examine each of the previous steps in a little more detail:

1. *Find peer*: Essentially to "talk" to some other peer, the first task you need to do is find it. You have two ways to go about this. The first is to find other peers on the LAN you are part of. The other is to find peer or peer groups using PNRP. If you are finding other peers on the LAN, you should use the People Near Me feature and integrate that into your application. People Near Me uses WS-Discovery to find users who are signed in. People Near Me is out of the scope of this book, but at a high level it is collaboration with people located nearby. There are many requirements for this to work, such as people discovery, application discovery, metadata discovery, security, invitation, and so on. When using PNPR, on the other hand, it is a serverless name resolution that can be either on the local network or over the Internet.

2. *Send invitation*: Invitations are real-time and can go to People Near Me or peers over the Internet, via either a user message or some application data such as mesh name, endpoint, and so on. A listener at the other end detects this incoming invitation request and launches the appropriate application.

3. *Join mesh*: The last step to establish a session is to specify the mesh name and credentials (if applicable) that one is intending to join.

Figure 12-4 shows the scenario where you have peers that are part of a mesh and are trying to communicate with each other.

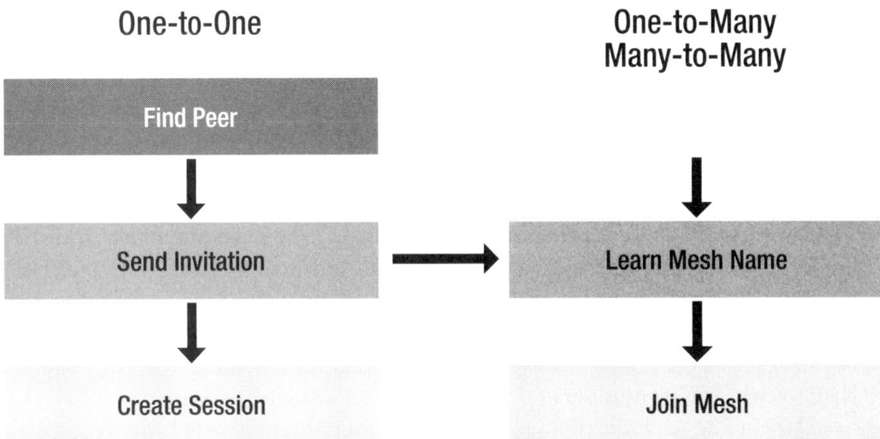

Figure 12-4. *P2P one-to-many application flow*

What Is Peer Channel?

The P2P networking stack that we have been discussing so far is unmanaged code, and a developer needs to use C++ to be using it to its full potential. This stack is part of Windows XP and will be improved as part of Windows Vista and Longhorn Server. Microsoft also has a managed code implementation for a subset of the functionality that is exposed by the P2P networking stack, called *peer channel*, and is released as part of WCF. Since peer channel is a managed stack, you can use any .NET language, which makes implementing P2P applications easier and more productive when compared to unmanaged code.

A typical channel in WCF has two participants, a client and a server, but a peer channel can have any number of participants. A message that is sent by one participant will be received by all other participants on the channel. However, certain mechanisms in peer channel allow you to send a message to only part of the mesh, instead of the whole mesh. To resolve the addresses of a node in a peer channel mesh, you can use either PNRP or a custom resolver. When a node is resolved, that target node can either accept or decline the connection. If the connection is accepted by the target node, it sends it a welcome message that among other things will contain the list of other nodes that are part of the mesh. If the connection is refused, then the existing node sends the prospective node a refusal message containing the reason and a list of the addresses of the other nodes in the mesh.

In WCF, a node that will be part of a mesh is defined via the `PeerNode` class in your application. The endpoint address for that node is defined via the `PeerNodeAddress` class (which internally implements the `EndpointAddress` class). The number of neighbors of each node dictate the overall structure of a peer channel mesh that is actively maintained, resulting in an evenly distributed mesh. For example, a node in the mesh tried to maintain from two to seven connections to its neighbors. Although an ideal state for the node is to have three connections, it will accept up to seven connections. Once a node has reached that threshold, it will start refusing any new connections. If a node loses all its neighbors, it will enter a maintenance cycle where it tries to acquire new neighbors to get to its optimum state of three connections. Also note, you cannot change or configure either the thresholds or the underlying mesh because the peer channel owns and maintains this.

The peer channel also tries to improve efficiency by limiting communication within the mesh by keeping repetitive messages passed to a minimum. When a node sends a message to the mesh, it sends it to the neighbors to which it is connected. These neighbors in turn inspect the message and then forward it to their neighbors, but they do not forward it to the neighbor from whom they got the message to start. In addition, a connection to a neighbor might be terminated if it keeps trying to resend a message that has been processed previously. Internally each node keeps an idempotent local cache of the WS-Addressing message ID and the ID of the neighbor that delivered that message. This allows an optimized mesh network that does not waste resources with repeating data.

A node can send messages to a subset of the mesh by assigning a hop count to the message. A *hop count* keeps a count of the number of nodes to which a message has been forwarded. This count is expressed as an integer within the message header and is decremented with each hop until it reaches a value of zero, after which it is not forwarded.

■ **Note** NetShell is available only when you have the P2P networking option installed in Windows XP. Although NetShell is installed by default on Windows Vista, you need to allow that as an exception in the firewall for it to work.

QuickReturnTraderChat Sample

To get a better understanding of how everything comes together using the peer channel, let us start with a simple application called `QuickReturnTraderChat`. We have a few traders spread across a stock exchange who need the ability to chat with each other. The exchange, being a secure environment, does not allow any access to IM clients and wants to use the `QuickReturnTraderChat` to talk to each other. This application allows more than one trader to broadcast a message to the other traders, similar to an IRC channel. You will first look at the nonsecure version of this sample and then later update that to make it secure so no one else can eavesdrop on the conversation.

The application is simple and is implemented as a Windows application containing one form. For clarity, we will not show the Windows form boilerplate code so you can concentrate on the peer channel aspects. You can always get the latest version of the complete source code from this book's website.

Message Interface

A peer channel service contract is just a WCF service contract with one requirement that the `OperationContract` attribute is set up as one-way, as shown in Listing 12-1. The interface is called `IQuickReturnTraderChat` and has only one operation called `Say`, which accepts two parameters: user and message.

Listing 12-1. `IQuickReturnTraderChat` *Service Contract*

```
[ServiceContract()]
public interface IQuickReturnTraderChat
{
    [OperationContract(IsOneWay = true)]
    void Say(string user, string message);
}
```

Service Configuration

Listing 12-2 shows the service side of the configuration. This application listens at the `net.p2p//QuickReturnTraderChat` address. Being a P2P application, the binding is set to `netPeerTcpBinding`, and the contract for the endpoint is set to `QuickReturnTraderChat.IQuickReturnTraderChat`, which follows the *Namespace.Interface* format. The binding configuration is intentionally kept separate (shown later in Listing 12-3).

Listing 12-2. *Service Configuration*

```
<service name="QuickReturnTraderChat.Main">
    <host>
        <baseAddresses>
            <add baseAddress="net.p2p://QuickReturnTraderChat"/>
        </baseAddresses>
    </host>

    <endpoint
        name="QuickTraderChat"
        address=""
        binding="netPeerTcpBinding"
        bindingConfiguration="BindingUnsecure"
        contract="QuickReturnTraderChat.IQuickReturnTraderChat"
      />
</service>
```

Binding Configuration File

As we stated earlier, a P2P application's binding is set to `netPeerTcpBinding` and the resolver mode to `Pnrp` (see Listing 12-3). Since this application is not secure, we have the security mode switched off by setting this to `None`.

Listing 12-3. *Binding Configuration*

```
<bindings>
    <netPeerTcpBinding>
        <binding  name="BindingUnsecure">
            <security mode="None"/>
            <resolver mode="Pnrp"/>
        </binding>
    </netPeerTcpBinding>
</bindings>
```

Main Application

The main application, as shown in Figure 12-5, consists of a Windows form that has two textboxes, one for the message being sent (called `textBoxMessage`) and the other to show the conversation (called `textBoxChat`). The form also contains one Send button (called `buttonSend`).

Figure 12-5. `QuickReturnTraderChat` *application*

The class implementing the Windows form is called `Main` and is implemented as shown in Listing 12-4. This form inherits from the .NET `Form` class and also implements the `IQuickReturnTraderChat` interface that was defined earlier. Since this is a WCF service, the class is decorated with the `ServiceBehavior` attribute and the `InstanceContextMode` controlling when a new service object should be created. In our case, we want this to behave as a Singleton; as a result, the `InstanceContextMode` is set to `Single`.

Listing 12-4. *Service Host Class Definition*

```
[ServiceBehavior(InstanceContextMode = InstanceContextMode.Single)]
public partial class Main : Form, IQuickReturnTraderChat
{
}
```

The class Main implements, as shown in Listing 12-5, two methods called StartService and StopService, which start and stop the service host. The class Main also has a few member variables exposing the Channel, ServiceHost, and ChannelFactory.

Listing 12-5. *Service Host Implementation*

```
IQuickReturnTraderChat channel;
ServiceHost host = null;
ChannelFactory<IQuickReturnTraderChat> channelFactory = null;
string userID = "";
private void StartService()
{
    //Instantiate new ServiceHost
    host = new ServiceHost(this);

     //Open ServiceHost
    host.Open();

    //Create a ChannelFactory and load the configuration setting
    channelFactory = new ChannelFactory<IQuickReturnTraderChat>
                                    ("QuickTraderChatEndpoint");
    channel = channelFactory.CreateChannel();

    //Lets others know that someone new has joined
    channel.Say("Admin", "*** New User " + userID + " Joined ****" +
                                              Environment.NewLine);
}
private void StopService()
{
     if (host != null)
     {
          channel.Say("Admin", "*** User " + userID + " Leaving ****" +
                                           Environment.NewLine);

          if (host.State != CommunicationState.Closed)
          {
               channelFactory.Close();
               host.Close();
          }
     }
}
```

IQuickReturnTraderChat Implementation (the Receiver)

You have both the service side and the receiver side of things in the same class. Listing 12-6 shows the configuration for the receiver, which is quite similar to the sender configuration and uses the same binding.

Listing 12-6. *Receiver Configuration*

```
<client>
    <endpoint
        name="QuickTraderChatEndpoint"
        address="net.p2p://QuickReturnTraderChat"
        binding="netPeerTcpBinding"
        bindingConfiguration="BindingUnsecure"
        contract="QuickReturnTraderChat.IQuickReturnTraderChat"
</client>
```

The receiver here is fairly simple because all it does is echo out the message to the chat textbox on the Windows form, as shown in Listing 12-7.

Listing 12-7. *Receiver Implementation*

```
void IQuickReturnTraderChat.Say(string user, string message)
{
    textBoxChat.Text += user + " says: " + message;
}
```

Invoking the Service

The service is invoked in the Click event of the Send button, as shown in Listing 12-8. The second line is where you invoke the service. As you might recall, the channel is of type `IQuickReturnTraderChat` and is defined in the class `Main` (shown in Listing 12-4 earlier in this chapter).

Listing 12-8. *Service Invocation*

```
private void buttonSend_Click(object sender, EventArgs e)
{
    string temp = textBoxMessage.Text + Environment.NewLine;

    //Invoke the Service
    channel.Say(userID, temp);

    textBoxMessage.Clear();
}
```

As you can see, creating a P2P application with WCF is fairly trivial, and you do not need to do anything with the Windows P2P networking stack. Although we have kept the application `QuickReturnTraderChat` fairly simple to show you how to implement a P2P application, if you need to do some more advanced tasks such as cloud management, detecting and repairing network splits, and so on, then you will need to use the P2P networking stack and C++. At the time of writing this, Microsoft does not have any .NET wrappers for the P2P stack, and you would need to interop to unmanaged code.

P2P Security

Security in a P2P network is an interesting challenge. When securing a P2P network, there are two points of interest from an application point of view. First, only authorized users get on the network. Second, the message you received originated from a known and trusted source, and the message itself has not been tampered with during transmission. The first option is relatively simple to achieve: when a new application or user logs onto the mesh, they are challenged to authenticate before they are allowed to join the mesh. The second aspect is a little more difficult because you are not directly connected to another peer in the mesh. However, with WCF this is relatively straightforward because the `PeerSecuritySettings` class is exposed via the `Security` property part of the `NetPeerTcpBinding` class.

So, how does it all come together with WCF? For `OutputChannels`, which reside on the sender, each message that is sent is signed using a certificate, and all messages, before being sent to an application, are validated for this credential. The certificate that is needed is provided by using the `PeerCredential.Certificate` property. The validation stated earlier can be implemented via an instance of the `X509CertificateValidator` class, which is provided as part of `PeerCredential.MessageSenderAuthentication`. When the message arrives on the other end, peer channel ensures the validity of the message before forwarding it up the chain to the application.

Peer Channel Security

As mentioned earlier, you specify the security settings for peer channel using the property called `Security`, which is available on `NetPeerTcpBinding`. This property operates like any other standard binding in WCF. You can apply four types of security at this level, and they are exposed via the `Mode` property; the underlying class is in the `PeerSecuritySettings` class. These four options for security are as follows:

`None`: No security is required.

`Transport`: No message security is implemented; only neighbor-to-neighbor security is required.

`Message`: Only message authentication is required when communicating over an open channel.

`TransportWithMessageCredential`: This is essentially a combination of `Transport` and `Message`, defined previously. This would require that the message be secure and that authentication is required over secure neighbor-to-neighbor channels.

Note If the security is enabled on the binding and is set to `Message` or `TransportWithMessageCredential`, then all messages that pass through both on the outbound and on the inbound need to be secured using `X.509Certificate`.

Peer channel provides two ways to authenticate two peers, which are configured using the `PeerTransportSecurityElement.CredentialType` property. This is either `Password` or `Certificate`. When this is set to `Password`, then every peer needs a password to connect. The owner of the mesh is responsible for setting the password initially and communicating the same to peers who you would allow to join the mesh. On the other hand, when this is set to `Certificate`, then authentication is based on `X509Certificate`.

When an application initiates a peer channel instance, an instance of the peer channel transport manager is started. The transport manager resolves the endpoint address of the requested peers and the mesh. PNRP acts as the default resolver for this; however, you can choose to implement a custom resolver as well. Once the address is resolved, the transport manager initiates a connection request to each of the peers.

Password-Based Authentication

When using the password-based authentication, the steps to initiate a connection are the same with the transport manager. The main difference is that when a peer initiates a connection request, the link between the two peers is over a SSL connection. Also, as the first step after initiating connection between the two peers, the initiator peer will send a custom handshake message that authenticates the password. If the responder peer is satisfied with this, it accepts the connection and sends a similar response to the originating peer. If the initiator peer is satisfied with this, the connection is established; if not, the connection is abandoned. This aforementioned handshake needs to contain some metadata for it to function. First, the certificate with the secure connection can be established, and second the password for the handshake can be established. The class `PeerCredential` is exposed as the `Peer` property on the `ChannelFactory.Credentials` property. This is demonstrated in the secure version of the chat sample that was discussed earlier in this chapter. This secure version is called `QuickReturnSecureTraderChat`, and you'll see it a little later in the "QuickReturnSecureTraderChat Sample" section.

Certificate-Based Authentication

When using the certificate-based authentication mode, the application has control of the authentication process as compared to the WCF runtime. There is no custom handshake involved; instead, the transport manager, after receiving the certificate, passes that on to the application to authenticate. To get this functionality, the application needs to provide a couple of certificates. The first certificate establishes the SSL connection and the identity between the peers. And, the second certificate provides a concrete implementation by the application for the `X509CertificateValidator` abstract class. Note, this is also demonstrated in the secure version of the chat sample a little later in the chapter.

Message Security

If you are interested in securing the message itself to ensure that it has not been tampered with during transmission, then you need to use the `Message` security option. Effectively, when this is requested, the peer channel on every outbound message includes a signature and, vice versa, on every inbound message validates the signature. The signature is validated against the same certificate (without the specific private keys, of course). The signatures added to the message are compatible with all the peers on the mesh.

■ **Note** How can peer channel verify signatures that are application specific? Well, it can verify signatures that are specific to the application because it provides a "hook" that allows you to participate in its signature verification routine. This hook is in a concrete implementation of the abstract `X509CertificateValidator` class. This allows you to have any criteria for the pass or fail validation.

QuickReturnSecureTraderChat Sample

The `QuickReturnSecureTraderChat` application essentially is the same as the `QuickReturnTraderChat` sample discussed earlier in the chapter with the exception that this one uses security. For the sake of simplicity, we implemented this as a separate solution. In the real world, you would probably read the security information via a configuration setting and based on that either enable or disable the security options.

You can set security, as discussed earlier, using either a password or an X.509 certificate. For this sample, we will use a password, but you will see how easy it is to change this to use a certificate.

Service Configuration

Listing 12-9 shows the service side of the configuration, which is similar to the service configuration used in the earlier example. Although the address and the namespace have been updated, the real configuration change is using a different binding depicted by the `bindingConfiguration` parameter.

Listing 12-9. *Service Configuration*

```
<service name="QuickReturnSecureTraderChat.Main">
    <host>
        <baseAddresses>
            <add baseAddress="net.p2p://QuickReturnSecureTraderChat"/>
        </baseAddresses>
    </host>

    <endpoint
        name="QuickTraderChatSecurePasswordEndPoint"
        address=""
        binding="netPeerTcpBinding"
        bindingConfiguration="BindingSecurePassword"
        contract="QuickReturnSecureTraderChat.IQuickReturnTraderChat"
        />
</service>
```

Binding Configuration

The updated binding configuration used both by the host and by the client in this example is called BindingSecurePassword. The main difference between this and the previous example is the addition of the security details, as shown in Listing 12-10. As you can see, we have the security mode set to Transport and the type to Password.

Listing 12-10. *Secure Binding Configuration*

```
<binding  name="BindingSecurePassword">
    <security mode="Transport">
        <transport credentialType="Password"/>
    </security>

    <resolver mode="Pnrp"/>
</binding>
```

Main Application

The main application is the same as shown in Figure 12-5. The only difference between this and the earlier example is the addition of a new member variable to hold the password, which is read from the App.config file.

■ **Note** It is not recommended to save the password in App.config in clear text because then anyone can open it and read the password. It is recommended to save the password in an encrypted storage or possibly accept the password from the user at runtime. To hold the password in memory, use the SecureString class, which was introduced in .NET 2.0.

Listing 12-11 shows the updated member variable used by the solution. The channel is of the type IQuickReturnTraderChat, which as you know is the contract implemented by the service. The members host and channelFactory are the service host and the channel factory, respectively. And the two string variables store the user and password that are read from the App.config file using ConfigurationManager.AppSettings in the constructor for the class Main.

Listing 12-11. *Member Variable List*

```
IQuickReturnTraderChat channel;
ServiceHost host = null;
ChannelFactory<IQuickReturnTraderChat> channelFactory = null;
string userID = "";
string password = null;
```

The StartService method in the class Main has been updated slightly, as shown in Listing 12-12. This now uses a different endpoint configuration file and sets the password for both the host and the channel. The StopService method remains the same as earlier and is not listed again here. As you can see in the listing, the password for both the host and the `ChannelFactory` is set via the `Credentials.Peer.MeshPassword` property. The binding configuration has been updated and is read from `QuickTraderChatSecurePasswordEndPoint`.

Listing 12-12. *Service Host Implementation*

```
private void StartService()
{
    //Instantiate new ServiceHost
    host = new ServiceHost(this);

    //Set the password
    host.Credentials.Peer.MeshPassword = password;

    //Open ServiceHost
    host.Open();

    //Create a ChannelFactory and load the configuration setting
    channelFactory = new ChannelFactory<IQuickReturnTraderChat>
                        ("QuickTraderChatSecurePasswordEndPoint");

    //Set the password for the ChannelFactory
    channelFactory.Credentials.Peer.MeshPassword = password;

    //Create the Channel
    channel = channelFactory.CreateChannel();

    //Lets others know that someone new has joined
    channel.Say("Admin", "*** New User " + userID +
                                " Joined ****" + Environment.NewLine);
}
```

One interesting behavior with the security is that if you have a set of peers listening on the same endpoint but with different passwords, then they will be isolated from each other. For example, say you have four users called User1, User2, User3, and User4. Say User1 and User2 are chatting and connected to the mesh using "password1." If User3 and User4 start chatting with another password, say "password2," then even though all four users are on the mesh and listening on the same endpoint, the messages between User1 and User2 cannot be seen by Users3 and User4, and vice versa.

Tip To use an X.509 certificate instead of a password to secure a mesh, set the transport `credentialType` in the binding to `Certificate`, and set the `Credentials.Peer.Certificate` property to the certificate on both the host and the client.

Working with NetShell

NetShell, also known as `netsh`, is an indispensable command-line utility for both administrators and developers. Although `netsh` is primarily aimed at administrators because it allows them to administer network services, it is equally useful to a developer. To start `netsh`, open a command prompt, and type **netsh**.

■ **Note** NetShell is available only when you have P2P networking option installed in Windows XP. Although NetShell is installed by default on Windows Vista, you need to allow that as an exception in the firewall for it to work.

The commands in `netsh` work with the concept of a "context" that determines the networking aspect within which you want to operate and accumulates various possible commands in that context. In most situations, you would switch to some context for the specific operation in which you are interested. Contexts can have subcontexts, which in turn can have further subcontexts, forming a tree-like hierarchy. Figure 12-6 shows how we switch the context to P2P ➤ PNRP ➤ Cloud.

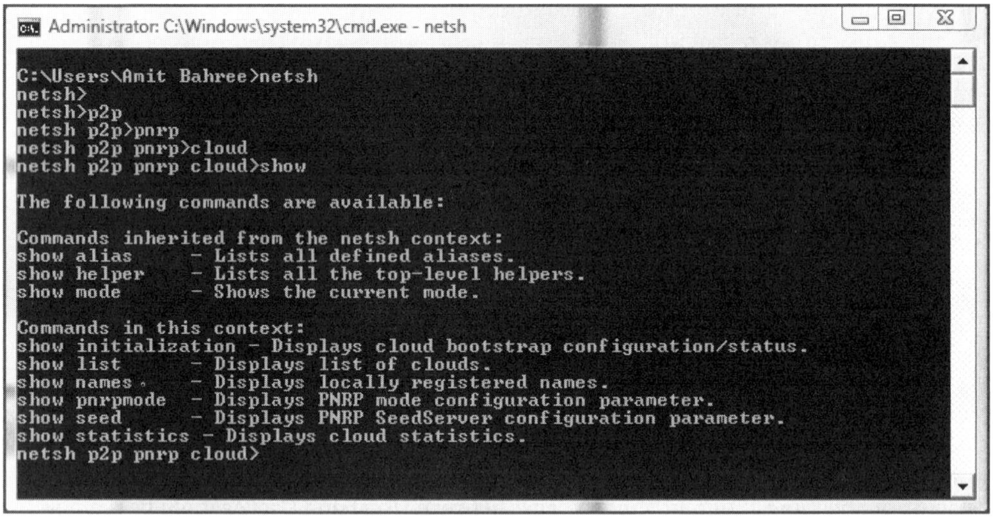

```
Administrator: C:\Windows\system32\cmd.exe - netsh

C:\Users\Amit Bahree>netsh
netsh>
netsh>p2p
netsh p2p>pnrp
netsh p2p pnrp>cloud
netsh p2p pnrp cloud>show

The following commands are available:

Commands inherited from the netsh context:
show alias     - Lists all defined aliases.
show helper    - Lists all the top-level helpers.
show mode      - Shows the current mode.

Commands in this context:
show initialization - Displays cloud bootstrap configuration/status.
show list      - Displays list of clouds.
show names     - Displays locally registered names.
show pnrpmode  - Displays PNRP mode configuration parameter.
show seed      - Displays PNRP SeedServer configuration parameter.
show statistics - Displays cloud statistics.
netsh p2p pnrp cloud>
```

Figure 12-6. `netsh` *context*

The commands you enter in `netsh` factor into the context on which you are working. For example, the command `show` entered (as shown in Figure 12-6) knows the context is `cloud` within a PNRP network and shows the commands for that context. You can switch from one context to another at any time.

Listing Clouds

If you want to see the clouds to which you are currently connected, then you will use the show list command, as shown in Figure 12-7. In this example, you can see two clouds, where one of those clouds was synchronizing, which later you can see has finished synchronizing.

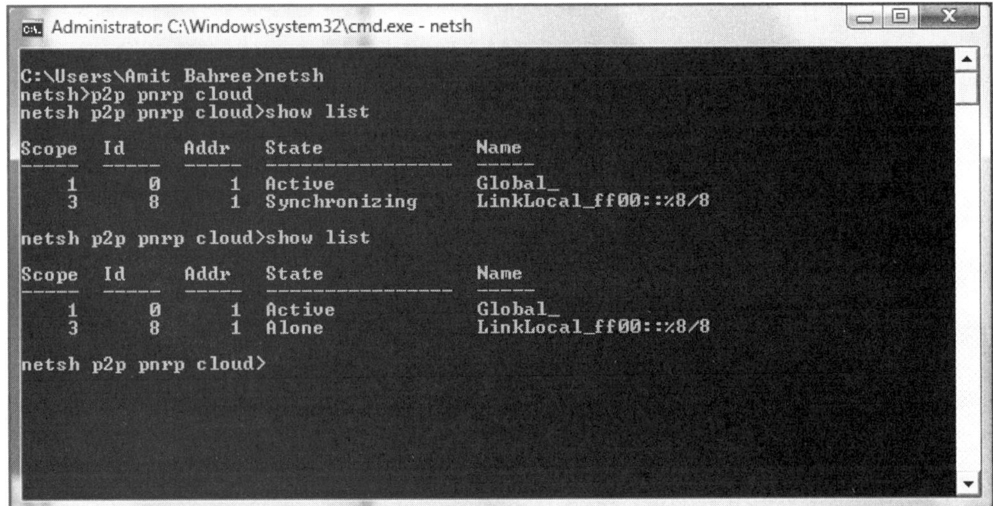

Figure 12-7. *Listing of clouds*

To see the configuration and status of the cloud, you use show initialization (or the short form show init). If a computer is connected to the Internet, then it is part of the global cloud called Global_. If a cloud is connected to one or two LANs, then individual clouds are available for each network adapter (or link). In Listing 12-13, you can see two clouds called Global_ and LinkLocal_ff00::%8/8.

Listing 12-13. *Cloud Listing*

```
Scope  Id     Addr   State             Name
-----  -----  -----  ----------------  -----
    1      0      1  Active            Global_
Synchronize server:    pnrpv2.ipv6.microsoft.com;pnrpv21.ipv6.microsoft.com
Use Server:            Used
Use SSDP:              No addresses
Use Persisted cache:   No addresses
Cloud Configured Mode:      Auto
Cloud Operational Mode:      Full Participant

Scope  Id     Addr   State             Name
-----  -----  -----  ----------------  -----
    3      8      1  Alone             LinkLocal_ff00::%8/8
```

```
Synchronize server:
Use Server:             Disabled
Use SSDP:               No addresses
Use Persisted cache:    No addresses
Cloud Configured Mode:       Auto
Cloud Operational Mode:       Full Participant
```

Scope, as the name suggests, represents the scope of the cloud and essentially shows the PNRPCLOUDINFO data structure that is part of the P2P SDK. The following list defines each of the columns in the previous data:

Scope: This is the scope of the cloud and can be one of the four values shown in Table 12-1 (in the next section).

Id: This represents the unique identifier for that cloud.

State: This represents the state of the cloud and is represented by the PNRP_CLOUD_STATE structure in the SDK. This can be one of the seven values shown in Table 12-2 (in the next section).

Synchronize Server: This represents the seed server used.

Use Server: If a caching server was used to load the current state of the cloud, then this displays the DNS name of that server.

Use SSDP: Simple Service Discovery Protocol (SSDP) is the protocol used to locate nearby nodes. You can use this to identify neighboring nodes if a seed server is not available.

Use Persisted cache: This represents any previous cached entries loaded.

Clouds Scopes

The scope of a cloud can be one of the four values shown in Table 12-1.

Table 12-1. *Cloud Scope Values*

Value	Description
0	The cloud can be in any scope (represented by PNRP_SCOPE_ANY).
1	The cloud is a global scope (represented by PNRP _GLOBAL_ SCOPE).
2	The cloud is a site-local scope (represented by PNRP_SITE_LOCAL_SCOPE).
3	The cloud is a link local scope (represented by PNRP_LINK_LOCAL_SCOPE).

The state of a cloud can be one of the seven values shown in Table 12-2.

Table 12-2. *Cloud State Values*

Value	Description
Virtual	The cloud is not yet initialized.
Synchronizing	The cloud is in the process of being initialized but is not active yet.
Active	The cloud is active.
Dead	The cloud has lost its connection to the network but was initialized.
Active	The cloud is active.
Disabled	The cloud is disabled in the registry.
No Net	The cloud has lost its connection to the network but was active.
Alone	The cloud is in stand-alone mode.

Listing Peers in a Cloud

To see the locally registered nodes in a cloud, use the command `show names` in `netsh`. In Listing 12-14, you can have two peers identified by `P2P Name` connected to the cloud. Note the exact list of peers you see will of course be different from the ones shown here. If you have the `QuickReturnTraderChat` application running from earlier in the chapter, then you should see that.

Listing 12-14. *Peer Listing*

```
P2P Name:       0.quickreturntraderchat
Identity:       2460f44f457b670116f55709f3e6324dd12ad70e.PnrpProtocolV2
Comment:        a?????????
PNRP ID:        cf284a913c76d8289f16c4fefbe18b7a.5bcca4c6a1090f379d15b0f12fc89b08
State:          OK
IP Addresses:   192.168.1.73:11989 tcp
                [2001:0000:4136:e37a:2847:1735:a83d:dc55]:11989 tcp

P2P Name:       0.78873591048
Identity:       2460f44f457b670116f55709f3e6324dd12ad70e.PnrpProtocolV2
Comment:        Local Machine Id
PNRP ID:        ad1d55aa343d35df9d118343e3c3de09.7700660055004400f956
ced74b6beb3cState:          OK
```

The following list defines each of the columns in the previous data:

`P2P Name`: This is the name of the peer connected to the cloud. The first peer in Listing 12-14, called `0.quickreturntraderchat`, is the `QuickReturnTraderChat` application discussed earlier in the chapter.

`Identity`: As the name suggests, this represents the identities. Note that the identities of both peers are the same. This is because these peers are unsecure and the default identity is used for them.

`PNRP ID`: This represents the corresponding 256-bit PNRP ID.

`IP Addresses`: This represents the endpoints (including the ports) associated with this peer.

Cloud Statistics

To see the cloud statistics, enter the command `show statistics` (or the abbreviated `show stat` will also work) in `netsh`. This will display the statistics for all the active clouds. For example, Listing 12-15 lists statistics for the `global` cloud. Although most of the entries are self-explanatory, the `IP Addresses` column is a list of the addresses that is used to connect to the cloud.

Listing 12-15. *Statistics*

```
IP Addresses:              [2001:0000:4136:e37a:2847:1735:a83d:dc55]:3540

Number of cache entries:      34
Estimated cloud size:         142
Number of registered names:   3
Throttled resolves:           0
Throttled solicits:           0
Throttled floods:             0
Throttled repairs:            0
```

There are more commands within the `cloud` context; we discussed only the more important ones to give you a basic understanding. We encourage you to use the documentation and SDK to explore other commands in `netsh`.

Working with Peers

To switch to the peer context from within PNRP, just type `peer` in `netsh`. The peer's context, as the name suggests, allows you to work with peers and gives you the ability to add, delete, and enumerate entries, among other things. We will not be covering all the commands—just a couple of the more interesting ones. As you know, before one peer can talk to another peer, it needs to resolve that peer. To do this with `netsh`, you use the `resolve` command—passing it the peer name. In this example, if you try to resolve the peer `0.quickreturntraderchat`, you get the result shown in Listing 12-16.

Listing 12-16. *Peer Resolution*

```
netsh p2p pnrp peer>resolve 0.quickreturntraderchat
Resolve started...
Found:
        Comment:    aD????????
        Addresses:  [fe80:0000:0000:0000:79ae:4fe7:e034:eac7]%8:28365
        Extended payload (binary):
        Comment:    aD????????
        Addresses:  [fe80:0000:0000:0000:79ae:4fe7:e034:eac7]%8:28136
```

```
        Extended payload (binary):
        Comment:    aD????????
        Addresses:  169.254.2.2:28365
                    192.168.1.73:28365
                    [2001:0000:4136:e37a:2847:1735:a83d:dc55]%0:28365
        Extended payload (binary):
```

We have two instances of `QuickReturnTraderChat` running, which you can see in the previous example. We also have two network cards, one of which is connected to the Internet and the other of which is on an internal network. The first network adapter (which is connected to the Internet connection) has the IP address of 192.168.1.73 (this is NATed of course), and the local only is 169.254.2.2. Both are listening on port 28365.

The other command of interest is `traceroute`, which resolved a peer with path tracing. If the name is registered, then the result is quite similar to the `resolve` command used earlier, as shown in Listing 12-17.

Listing 12-17. *Known Peer Traceroute*

```
netsh p2p pnrp peer>traceroute 0.quickreturntraderchat Global_
Resolve started...
Found:
        Addresses:  169.254.2.2:28365 tcp
                    192.168.1.73:28365 tcp
                    [2001:0000:4136:e37a:2847:1735:a83d:dc55]%0:28365
tcp
        Extended payload (string):
        Extended payload (binary):
Resolve Path:
[2001:0000:4136:e37a:2847:1735:a83d:dc55]:3540, (0), (0)
       Accepted
[2001:0000:4136:e37a:2847:1735:a83d:dc55]:3540, (0), (0)
       Accepted Final Inquire
```

However, on the other hand, if the peer is not registered, then you see more interesting behavior, as shown in Listing 12-18. Note an invalid name (`0.quickreturntraderchat`*`wedontkow`*) was provided to mimic this behavior. Also, the listing has been abbreviated for clarity. The exact number of hops would vary on the size of your cloud.

Listing 12-18. *Unknown Peer Traceroute*

```
netsh p2p pnrp peer>traceroute 0.quickreturntraderchatwedontkow Global_
Resolve started...
Not Found.
Resolve Path:
[2001:0000:4136:e37a:2847:1735:a83d:dc55]:3540, (0), (0)
       Accepted
[2001:0000:4136:e37e:140b:26c5:affa:3034]:3540, (8), (31)
       Rejected (Dead end)
```

```
[2001:0000:4136:e37e:244b:1e65:abdb:f294]:3540, (7), (140)
       Rejected (Dead end)
[2001:0000:4136:e37e:1c75:1b9a:bef2:f5a3]:3540, (4), (312)
       Accepted Suspicious
[2001:0000:4136:e37e:0c31:07f8:5351:cf06]:3540, (4), (2000)
       Rejected (Unreachable)
[2001:0000:4136:e37e:1c75:1b9a:bef2:f5a3]:3540, (4), (125)
       Rejected (Dead end)
[2001:0000:4136:e37a:384f:1905:bde1:91be]:3540, (4), (297)
       Rejected (Dead end)
[2001:0000:4136:e378:1cb4:2170:a795:ebd9]:3540, (3), (78)
       Rejected (Dead end)
 [2001:0000:4136:e37a:0c25:34ef:e7ef:9e09]:3540, (2), (203)
       Accepted
```

SOA with P2P

As stated earlier, one of the biggest challenges with the SOA approach is knowing how to deploy services. For example, when designing a solution, should you take the more traditional *n*-tier (DNA) approach with a middle tier, should the services be implemented in a more distributed approach where each service is a completely independent entity on the network, or should the approach be somewhere between those two extremes? Although SOA does not impose any technologies, platforms, and protocols, traditionally we treat the various entities involved, such as the service provider, consumer, service broker, and so on, as separate from each other. A better approach would be to treat these roles as different aspects for the services as opposed to explicit boundaries.

Instead of implementing a service on a server, if that service is implemented in every node of a network (such as a peer), then all the requirements of the server such as availability, scalability, and so on, can shift from one particular server to a function on the entire network. Hence, as the number of services on the network increases, the capabilities of the network increase proportionally, thus overall making it more scalable and robust. Also, unlike a traditional approach, in the P2P world, there is nothing to deploy other than the peer itself.

This is not to undermine the challenges that the services in a P2P environment face in an enterprise where there will be a disparate set of technologies and products on numerous runtimes. These will require different authentication and authorization approaches, and in many cases it would not be practical, because every service must also carry the weight of the network functionality that a peer provides in a P2P implementation. Also, operation requirements such as reliability, management, and so on, will have difficulty standardizing because of the disparate technologies. Lastly, there would be a significant overhead on the development team to ensure every service peer can deal with all the process, reliability, management, and so on, every time a new service is built.

If an enterprise can use a single runtime environment that provides a standardized implementation and uses a common set of libraries such as WCF, that would help eliminate many of these challenges. The caveat is that all the services need to adhere to this standard. Another option is to be more creative and implement “smart” networking intermediaries that will take ownership on areas of control such as security, reliability, operational management, and so on, when delegated to by the services. This frees the service endpoints to consume and provide services.

Effectively, we are trying to combine the best of how a centralized and a decentralized system would work. It is quite clear that there are many synergies between an SOA implementation and a P2P implementation. Today, the SOA implementations have concentrated a lot on web services, which in turn rely heavily on the central computing paradigm. Similarly, most P2P implementations today have concentrated more on their resilient paradigm. It is likely you will see a combination where both the peer and the web services rely on a common set for service description and invocation probably based on WSDL and SOAP. Figure 12-8 shows a high-level view of this convergence of web- and peer-based service orientation.

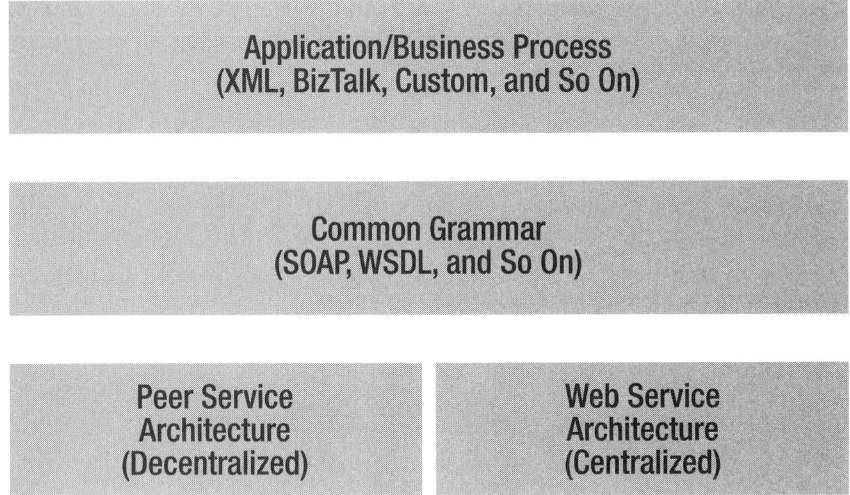

Figure 12-8. *Web+peer service orientation*

FUTURE DIRECTION

The future of P2P is interesting, and the trend would be the convergence of grid and P2P computing. Today these two technology stacks might seem quite different, but there is a lot of commonality overlap between the two. Some of the problems of P2P are peer discovery and topology formation, effective resource utilization, and standardization of APIs and interfaces.

Some of the enhancements that Microsoft is working on for P2P networking increase the mesh capabilities to provide support services such as replicated data, distributed agreements, and voting. Another fundamental shift is the ability to guarantee the loss of data. Today, P2P algorithms by design are built around this idea that data loss is a fact of life and partial failure is acceptable. However, the algorithms are being enhanced to support better real-time integration with Quality of Service (QoS) guarantees. QoS will help bandwidth-intensive applications such as Voice over IP (VOIP) or media streaming. There are also enhancements to add support for subgroups and routing controls within those.

Summary

To summarize, P2P is about PCs communicating directly with each other without going through a centralized server. Every node in a P2P network needs to carry the responsibility of both a server and a client. It is quite common to find a centralized server that is similar to a central registry and helps the nodes to find other nodes. This is a lightweight server and usually does not participate in the communication between the nodes. Successful P2P implementations such as instant messaging and file sharing that include thousands to millions of peers have proved that P2P networks are quite reliable and secure. Also, you learned that building P2P solutions with WCF and peer channel is relatively simple but powerful and easy to implement, debug, and deploy, which will enable further adoption by both developers and users.

The next chapter will introduce interoperability with other SOA implementations and will cover some of the "gotchas" of using J2EE, MTOM, and WS-ReliableMessaging, among others, in a cross-platform implementation.

CHAPTER 13

Implementing SOA Interoperability

How do you achieve the "connected systems" ideology that facilitates intelligent, stand-alone systems communicating with each other using a universal language? Is it practical to assume that one technology will dominate the market? Would that technology promote its proprietary standard as the default communication model? This is highly unlikely and defeats the core of SOA principals. Therefore, how will services on heterogeneous platforms communicate with each other? What interoperability options are available to an enterprise? How will WCF communicate with these non-Microsoft SOA offerings?

The objective of this chapter is to educate you about non-Microsoft SOA offerings and illustrate how they achieve interoperability between each other. We'll focus primarily on what products are available and where they stand in comparison to implementing solid interoperable stacks. We will not be able to dive into deep technical issues with each alternative SOA implementation. This chapter will merely introduce non-Microsoft offerings to increase your awareness. We will also discuss some practical issues regarding the interoperability of binary data, existing and emerging standards, and other competing technologies.

We'll conclude the chapter by discussing some of the key standards in the WS-* specifications that provide a solid enterprise-ready stack. These standards provide the foundation for rationalization in an enterprise of why WS-* and SOA are so critical for the future of integrated architectures. These standards will assist solution architects in identifying the critical success factors needed for investing in these technologies. We will specifically address Message Transmission Optimization Mechanism (MTOM) and WS-ReliableMessaging, as well as their vendor implementations. We will initiate the discussion by discussing the interoperability options available in Java.

Achieving Java/J2EE Interoperability

It is safe to assume that any enterprise in the world consists of multiple software platforms, and the stakeholders of the enterprise have made significant investments in existing solutions based on COM, COM+, and other non-Microsoft technologies. The WCF team has provided a comprehensive integration model to work alongside, around, and within existing COM+ solutions. In Chapter 10, we focused on how WCF can work with existing COM+ applications from both a client and a service. This chapter focuses on Java/J2EE (and other technology) interoperability capabilities and issues.

The tack for cross-platform interoperability is to work primarily with the standards as published by industry-supported and industry-controlled committees. However, each vendor has the tendency to implement its "interpretation" of the standard. To achieve a neutral perspective, the WCF team generated many compatibility tests for a subset of the different vendor implementations. In addition to internal testing, Microsoft created the WCF Interoperability Plug-Fest[1]program to work with stack vendors to achieve greater compliance and compatibility.

One of the more notable participants in the Plug-Fest program and offering general WCF interoperability has been Sun. The Sun web services team worked alongside the WCF team on several occasions and has publicly released an open source framework focused primarily on interoperability with WCF. Started as Project Tango,[2] it has evolved into Web Services Interoperability Technology[3] (WSIT), which is available today in open source form. The main capabilities and standards provided in WSIT are as follows:

- Bootstrapping communication (WS-MetaDataExchange)
- Securing communication (WS-SecurityPolicy, WS-Security, and WS-Trust)
- Optimizing communication (MTOM and WS-SecureConversation)
- Enabling reliability (WS-ReliableMessaging)
- Enabling atomic transactions (WS-Coordination and WS-AtomicTransactions)

Another major participant in the WCF/.NET interoperability process is the Axis project from the Apache Software Foundation.[4] It's a major participant in that the WCF team has worked with Axis on its own, ensuring WCF compliance with the WS-* standards by leveraging Axis. Additionally, the Axis team reports that it too has done interoperability testing for the Axis2 1.0 release from May 2006.

Non-Microsoft SOA Platforms

We briefly discussed Sun as a commercial product vendor that has resources focused on .NET and WCF interoperability. Sun is not alone in that commitment. We cannot cover in this short chapter what every vendor or open source team has produced in support of WS-* and WCF/.NET interoperability. However, we'll focus on a few key vendors that have openly supported and worked with .NET interoperability issues. Table 13-1 lists the leading vendors and their support of the WS-* standards within their products.[5]

---

1. You can find documents and background for the WCF Interoperability Plug-Fest program at `http://www.mssoapinterop.org/ilab/`.
2. You can find Harold Carr's blog entry about Project Tango at `http://weblogs.java.net/blog/haroldcarr/archive/2006/02/an_overview_of_1.html`.
3. You can find the WSIT home page at `http://java.sun.com/webservices/interop/index.jsp`.
4. You can find the Apache Axis2 home page at `http://ws.apache.org/axis2/`.
5. Apache is listed as a vendor even though it is an open source foundation supported by community members.

Table 13-1. *Vendor Implementation of WS-* Standards*

Vendor/Product	MTOM?	WS-Security?	WS-ReliableMessaging?
Microsoft	Yes	Yes	Yes
IBM	No	Yes	Yes
BEA	Yes	Yes	Yes
Sun	Yes	Yes	No
Apache	Yes	Yes	Yes
Tibco	No	Yes	No
gSOAP	Yes	Yes	No

One of the earliest interoperability efforts was to implement the WS-I Basic Profile. What is the WS-I Basic Profile? You'll dive into that topic now.

Interoperability with WS-I Basic Profile

In the beginning stages of the industry's implementation of the standards, people recognized that many of the stacks had been built upon an inconsistent foundation of technologies. Some vendors had chosen different versions of WSDL or SOAP as examples. Even how SOAP faults were returned by each implementation had been done differently in each implementation. So, getting interoperability amongst different implementations was a substantial challenge. In many instances, it was impossible without a significant amount of custom coding. Given the amount of coding required, it precluded the need for a vendor implementation and threw the whole "build vs. buy" question heavily in favor of in-house development when interoperability was required.

The early vendor SOA frameworks did not conform to common open standards (in other words, they were vendor specific). This was mostly because of both customer and market demands. However, this was a major obstacle to achieve "true" interoperability between multiple vendors.

The major industry participants combined resources forming the Web Services Interoperability (WS-I) Organization to facilitate and move web service standards forward in a non-proprietary and open manner. WS-I consists of a mix of products, services, and most important, user corporations—the primary focus of why we as solution architects exist. Currently, approximately 90 organizations are participating, with nearly 30 percent comprised of user corporations.[6] We'll discuss the core components of the Basic Profile in the next section.

Core Components

In April 2004, WS-I released Basic Profile 1.0.[7] This set of specifications laid the groundwork for vendors and customers to begin from a sound base. The specification represents the first generation of interoperable web service specifications. The importance of the Basic Profile cannot be minimized because with the initial release, many product companies and open source groups recognized that the market will no longer allow stand-alone proprietary interoperability stacks.

---

6. This is based upon WS-I.org information as of June 12, 2006.

7. You can find the WS-I Basic Profile 1.0 home page at `http://www.ws-i.org/Profiles/BasicProfile-1.0.html`.

The Basic Profile 1.0 specification is built upon a consistent set of foundation specifications that together form the core of it:[8]

- SOAP 1.1
- WSDL 1.1
- UDDI 2.0
- XML 1.0 (Second Edition)
- XML Schema Part 1: Structures
- XML Schema Part 2: Datatypes
- RFC 2246: The Transport Layer Security Protocol Version 1.0
- RFC 2459: Internet X.509 Public Key Infrastructure Certificate and CRL Profile
- RFC 2616: HyperText Transfer Protocol 1.1
- RFC 2818: HTTP over TLS
- RFC 2965: HTTP State Management Mechanism
- The Secure Sockets Layer Protocol Version 3.0

Given the agreement amongst the participants, interoperability at the basic level was now a greater possibility. In April 2006, the WS-I committee updated the Basic Profile to version 1.1 with some updates and some corrections to published errata. We want to emphasize that interoperability is not a guarantee that vendors will adhere to specifications. Given the complex nature of the WS-* specifications, small variations in how each framework interprets the specification generally lead to incompatibilities. This is why Microsoft has worked with other vendors to validate WCF with the major competitors that also happen to be members of the WS-I organization. We'll now discuss the Basic Profile implementation by Microsoft starting with ASP.NET.

ASP.NET Support of Basic Profile

Since ASP.NET 1.0/1.1 was a shipping product prior to the official specification release (it was still a "draft" in 2002), it didn't offer official support for Basic Profile 1.0; however, it was possible by following simple guidelines[9] to implement it. With ASP.NET 2.0, you enable support for Basic Profile 1.1 by applying the `WebServiceBinding` attribute to your service class, as shown in Listing 13-1.

Listing 13-1. *Enabling Basic Profile in ASP.NET 2.0*

```
[WebService(Namespace = "http://tempuri.org/")]
[WebServiceBinding(ConformsTo = WsiProfiles.BasicProfile1_1)]
public class WebService : System.Web.Services.WebService {…}
```

8. You can find IBM Developer Works at `http://www-128.ibm.com/developerworks/webservices/library/ws-basicprof.html`.

9. You can find WS-I Basic Profile 1.1 at `http://www.ws-i.org/Profiles/BasicProfile-1.1.html`.

Microsoft Web Service Extensions

During the evolution of web services, Microsoft provided an add-on framework to the core .NET runtime (both 1.1 and 2.0) in support of the evolving web service standards. With .NET 1.1 Microsoft released version 1.0 and 2.0 of Web Services Enhancements (WSE). With the release of .NET 2.0, Microsoft updated WSE to version 3.0.

WSE 2.0 offered no direct validation of producing services that were guaranteed to be Basic Profile compliant. Because ASP.NET 3.0 added the `WebServiceBinding` attribute to provide validation of conformance to Basic Profile 1.1, WSE 3.0 inherited that capability.

Additionally, the Microsoft Patterns and Practices team published a reference application[10] demonstrating how to build services that conform to WS-I Basic Profile along with an implementation guidance document.[11]

Windows Communication Foundation Basic Profile Support

WCF enables WS-I Basic Profile 1.1 through the `BasicHttpBinding` class. So, with WCF, writing base-level interoperable services that confirm to WS-I Basic Profile is as easy as leveraging the `BasicHttpBinding` class through code, as shown in Listing 13-2.

Listing 13-2. *Applying Basic Profile in Code*

```
Uri baseAddress = new Uri( "http://localhost:8080/MyService" );
//Instantiate new ServiceHost
myServiceHost = new ServiceHost( typeof( MyService ), baseAddress );
//the following for programmatic addition of Basic Profile 1.1
BasicHttpBinding binding = new BasicHttpBinding();
myServiceHost.AddServiceEndpoint(
    typeof( IMyInterface,
    binding,
    baseAddress);
```

In Listing 13-2, we just add the `BasicHttpBinding` instance to the `ServiceHost` instance's endpoints. Again, the power of WCF is that you can also enable the same capability for Basic Profile 1.1 support declaratively through configuration, as shown in Listing 13-3.

Listing 13-3. *Applying Basic Profile Through Configuration*

```
<bindings>
    <basicHttpBinding>
        <binding name="WebServiceSoap"
         ...
        </binding>
</bindings>
```

10. `http://msdn.microsoft.com/library/en-us/dnsvcinter/html/WSI-BP_MSDN_LandingPage.asp`

11. You can find the Microsoft WS-I Basic Security Profile sample application at `http://www.gotdotnet.com/codegallery/codegallery.aspx?id=0fecd2c7-b2b1-4d85-bd66-9d07a6ecbd86`.

Using the declarative, configuration-driven model allows the distinct abstraction of both the service and the client of the service (given both sides are WCF) from the transport and the messy details of the available bindings. Abstraction is critical to the WCF programming model and is what sets the tools and framework apart from the competing stacks such as Axis2. Although other stacks provide tools and a configuration-driven approach, the WCF/Visual Studio combination enables rapid development with generally a first working model without requiring you to learn additional object models or implementation patterns.

As the WS-* specifications advance requirements for greater control over security, reliable messaging, and atomic transactions, WCF allows, when using the declarative model, direct support without recoding the service or client implementation. So, with the declarative method, you can update the application configuration file as shown in Listing 13-4.

Listing 13-4. *Applying* `WSHttpBinding` *in Configuration*

```
<bindings>
    <wsHttpBinding>
        <binding name="... "
         ...
        </binding>
    </wsHttpBinding>
</bindings>
```

Through the `wsHttpBinding` configuration element you can now support additional levels of reliability and security that are demanded for both internal and external services for enterprise solutions.

Implementing Basic Profile ensures you of seamless integration with other services from non-Microsoft platforms. However, one of the most common issues of transferring information is sending attachments to another non-Microsoft platform. This is a necessity today with substantial binary files, graphics files, and product files (such as Acrobat PDF files) being exchanged between multiple platforms. Therefore, how do you send these binary data over WCF services? What mechanisms are available in WCF to achieve this?

Sending Binary Data Over Web Services

Generally, when you look at most types of services, they utilize short, succinct messages that contain primarily text. The one-way and two-way message exchange patterns that are the most common simply pass a few parameters. The parameters are generally primitives and possibly get another primitive or more complex type back. WCF, along with most web service frameworks, has been optimized for these patterns.

However, since the inception of messaging technologies (such as MQSeries/WebSphere MQ and other message-oriented middleware), solutions have required some type of large object transfer between tiers or potentially binary data. Many times in the past while the bulk of the solution focused on the short message exchange patterns, the large objects were sent out of band, potentially using FTP with PGP or other convoluted solutions. Existing systems leverage data formats that are usable cross platform in their existing forms. Image data (GIF, JPEG, and TIF) is an example of this type of data. Also, the prevalence of PDF files is another example of a data format that transgresses platforms easily.

Base64 Encoding

One method that can be leveraged is embedding the binary data as a Base64-encoded stream. This is a simple method, which is directly supported by the `xs:base64Binary` XML schema type. However, it has some significant drawbacks. The first is the additional overhead with the encoding/decoding of the binary data, which adds processing cost. The other potentially more significant issue is that the Base64 algorithm can increase the payload size by approximately 33 percent.[12]

Although effective, the overall issues related to size can impact the performance of services. Given the response is generally buffered prior to transmission, large objects will consume memory resources in addition to the CPU overhead of encoding. Also, given the direct embedding of the binary resource inside the XML document, this impacts the performance of XML parsers that are now required to buffer or read past the embedded data in order to obtain other elements and values.

SOAP with Attachments (SwA)

An alternative to embedding binary data inside the XML document was published in December 2000.[13] This specification was built upon the Multipurpose Internet Mail Extensions (MIME) specifications. A similar specification, WS-Attachments, follows the same pattern, leveraging MIME at its core. Both, as you'll soon see, have been superseded and have minimal industry support.

MIME provides a way to transfer the binary data alongside the core SOAP response inside a MIME message. Listing 13-5 shows a stub of a MIME message.

Listing 13-5. *SwA Message Sample*

```
MIME-Version: 1.0
Content-Type: Multipart/Related; boundary=MIME_boundary; type=text/xml;
        start="<claim061400a.xml@claiming-it.com>"
Content-Description: This is the optional message description.

--MIME_boundary
Content-Type: text/xml; charset=UTF-8
Content-Transfer-Encoding: 8bit
Content-ID: <claim061400a.xml@claiming-it.com>

<?xml version='1.0' ?>
<SOAP-ENV:Envelope
xmlns:SOAP-ENV="http://schemas.xmlsoap.org/soap/envelope/">
<SOAP-ENV:Body>
..
<theSignedForm href="cid:claim061400a.tiff@claiming-it.com"/>
..
```

12. You can find scenarios, patterns, and implementation guidance for WSE 3.0 at `http://msdn.microsoft.com/webservices/default.aspx?pull=/library/en-us/dnpag2/html/wssp.asp`.

13. You can find MIME, Section 6.8, Base64 Content-Transfer-Encoding, at `http://www.ietf.org/rfc/rfc2045.txt`.

```
</SOAP-ENV:Body>
</SOAP-ENV:Envelope>

--MIME_boundary
Content-Type: image/tiff
Content-Transfer-Encoding: binary
Content-ID: <claim061400a.tiff@claiming-it.com>

...binary TIFF image...
--MIME_boundary--
```

As shown in Listing 13-5, the section in bold is the body of the SOAP response. That response body contains an element called `theSignedForm` with a relative reference of `cid:....` The `cid` represents the `Content-ID` that is present within the MIME message. What SwA does provide is a way to optimize access to the XML body without forcing parsers and readers to consume the binary data until absolutely necessary.

SwA has several issues. One primary issue is that the URI reference outside the SOAP body bypasses any message-level security. To alleviate this, it's necessary to provide transport-level encryption or security such as SSL or S/MIME. However, these URI references could be outside the MIME message itself and not be required to be relative to the current message.

Direct Internet Message Encapsulation (DIME)

When Microsoft shipped WSE 1.0 for .NET 1.1, it provided a method for passing attachments in a SOAP message but outside the SOAP envelope. As a result of its presence as an attachment, it falls outside the capabilities of SOAP security and consequently requires transmission or transport-level security such as SSL. While only Microsoft submitted it to the Internet Engineering Task Force, both IBM and Microsoft authored it. Because of a variety of reasons, it didn't gain industry backing.

Direct Internet Message Encapsulation (DIME) leveraged fixed field size, and bytes are ordered according to network byte order, or *big-endian*. This works well for Windows and most Unix variants but requires additional overhead on platforms that don't conform to the same sequencing methods. DIME also supported chunking of a message, which is splitting a message over multiple DIME records.

The WSE 2.0 programming model requires developers to manipulate the SOAP response by adding attachments programmatically. Listing 13-6 is a snippet of WSE 2.0 code that adds the file attachment, along with its content type (`image/jpeg`) directly to the SOAP response.

Listing 13-6. *Using DIME in WSE 2.0*

```
[WebMethod]
public void GetFile(string fileName)
{
   SoapContext respContext = ResponseSoapContext.Current;
   DimeAttachment dimeAttach = new DimeAttachment("image/jpeg",
        TypeFormat.MediaType, fileName);
   respContext.Attachments.Add(dimeAttach);
}
```

As you can see in Listing 13-6, the implementation details are not abstracted from the service implementation. The service developer is now forced to understand the implications and requirements of transferring binary or large objects through the service tier. A more natural method signature would be just to return the binary data as a stream or an array of bytes.

Microsoft realized the transitional status of DIME, and when WSE 3.0 (for .NET 2.0) was released, Microsoft terminated the support of DIME. The technology that replaced it is called Message Transmission Optimization Mechanism (MTOM). Listing 13-7 is a similar interface but implemented with MTOM-expected support as part of WSE 3.0.

Listing 13-7. *Using MTOM in WSE 3.0*

```
[WebMethod]
public byte[] GetFile(string fileName)
{
    byte[] response;
    String filePath = AppDomain.CurrentDomain.BaseDirectory +
          @"App_Data\" + fileName;
    response = File.ReadAllBytes(filePath);
    return response;
}
```

As you'll soon see, the transition from the WSE 3.0 implementation of MTOM to the WCF implementation of MTOM is nearly seamless given the more natural way of implementing service interfaces without implementation-dependant details. Also, the WSE 3.0 MTOM is wire-level compatible with WCF's initial release.

Message Transmission Optimization Mechanism (MTOM)

With the limitations of the attachment-oriented approaches, industry participants developed a new specification that alleviated many of the issues of past specifications while ensuring compatibility with the emerging WS-* standards. Along with MTOM, XML-binary Optimization Packaging (XOP) is managed by the WCF encoding class `MtomMessageEncodingBindingElement`. This is controlled by setting the `messageEncoding` attribute on the binding with alternatives of `Text` or `Binary`. Listing 13-8 is an example of an application configuration that establishes through the declarative model that MTOM encoding should be used.

Listing 13-8. *Using MTOM Through Configuration*

```
<system.serviceModel>
    <services>
      <service name="MtomSvc.MtomSample">
        <endpoint binding="wsHttpBinding"
               contract="MtomSvc.IMtomSample"
               bindingConfiguration="MyBinding"/>
      </service>
    </services>
```

```
    <bindings>
      <wsHttpBinding>
        <binding name="MyBinding" messageEncoding="Mtom" />
      </wsHttpBinding>
    </bindings>
</system.serviceModel>
```

In the configuration file shown in Listing 13-8, we've applied the `Mtom` value to the `messageEncoding` attribute for the default settings of `wsHttpBinding`. This now tells the WCF framework that it should apply MTOM (with XOP) on the messages during normal channel processing inside the `WSHttpBinding` instance. The optimization of the content is then based upon how the XOP implementation is applied within `WSHttpBinding` by using the internal class `System.ServiceModel.Channels.MtomMessageEncoder`. What traverses the wire, across the chosen transport, is a series of MIME message consisting of a SOAP request and for the final response from the server a binary stream (marked as `Content-Type: application/octet-stream`).

In the Chapter 13 sample code, `MtomTest` provides a WCF client and server using configuration, and `WSHttpBinding` does its message exchange, leveraging the MTOM capabilities of WCF. The sample code contains a single service method that returns an array of bytes, as shown in Listing 13-9.

Listing 13-9. *WCF* `GetFile` *Service Contract*

```
namespace MtomSvc
{
    [ServiceContract()]
    public interface IMtomSample
    {
        [OperationContract(
             ProtectionLevel=System.Net.Security.ProtectionLevel.None)]
        byte[] GetFile( string fileName );
    }

    public class MtomSample : IMtomSample
    {
        public byte[] GetFile( string fileName )
        {
            byte[] result = File.ReadAllBytes(
                Path.Combine(
                      AppDomain.CurrentDomain.BaseDirectory, fileName) );

            return result;
        }
    }
```

We've taken the same method signature as illustrated in the WSE 3 example (Listing 13-7) that leveraged MTOM, and we defined an interface and provided an implementation in a concrete class. We've also applied an `OperationContract` property of `ProtectionLevel.None` to the operation so the only protection is authentication (the alternatives being `Sign` and `EncryptAndSign`).

Tip Check the requirements for running the samples on the MSDN site at `http://windowssdk.msdn.microsoft.com/en-us/library/ms751525.aspx`. Many of the samples from the SDK, including this book's code, have certain requirements for security and when running in workgroup mode.

The service class just reads the filename passed on the request into an array of bytes and then returns that to the caller. The `MtomTest` client application displays the results in a text box or, for the image request, converts it into an image and updates the Image control.

You'll now look at what occurs during the request and reply from the client. Figure 13-1 illustrates the calling sequence from client to server over the life of the request. This will illustrate the initial key exchange (and subsequent token generation) between the client and services. This also illustrates how the token is utilized to invoke a `GetFile()` command at the service.

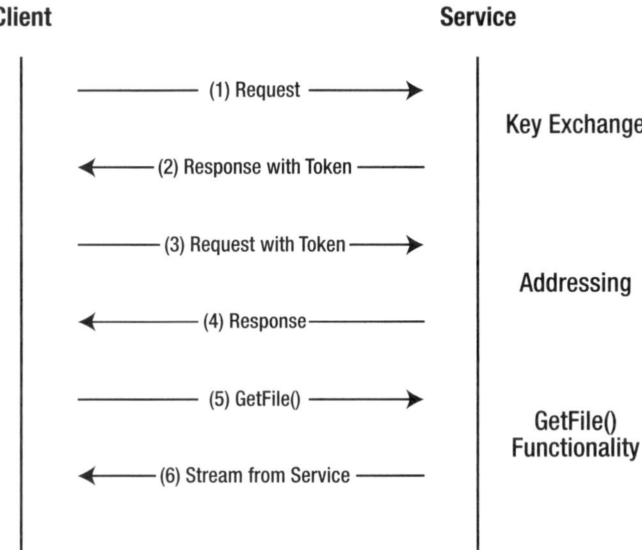

Figure 13-1. *MTOM message exchange*

The `MtomTest` sample directory contains several Ethereal[14] capture logs along with a series of text files taken from the MIME parts of the requests. Those text files are labeled `1.txt` through `6.txt`—they match Figure 13-1, with each odd-numbered file representing the request coming from the client and each even-numbered file representing the response from the server.

The first two request-reply pairs represent the key exchange as part of the WS-Security implementation within WCF. This is primarily for establishing a token exchange that will be used later for message signing. The third and fourth requests illustrate the token being used to inquire about endpoints. This objective of this call is to illustrate how the token is utilized by the client to communicate with the server. The following code snippet illustrates the binary token that is used to pass on credentials to the service:

---

14. You can find the W3C's Soap with Attachments at `http://www.w3.org/TR/SOAP-attachments`.

```
<s:Body>
<t:RequestSecurityTokenResponse Context="uuid-af1f0d7a-6fd7-4c06-9ce0-
7a5acb18669f-2" xmlns:t="http://schemas.xmlsoap.org/ws/2005/02/trust"
xmlns:u="http://docs.oasis-open.org/wss/2004/01/oasis-200401-
wss-wssecurity-utility-1.0.xsd">
<t:BinaryExchange ValueType="http://schemas.microsoft.com/net/2004/07/
secext/WS-SPNego">TlRMTVNTUAADAAAAGAAYAHgAAAAYABgAkAAAA
BAAEABIAAAAEAAQAF
gAAAAQABAAaAAAABAAEACoAAAANYKY4gUBKAoAAAAPQwBMAFcAQw
BGAFgAUAAxAGMAaQBjAG8AcgBpAGEAcwBDAEwAVwBDAEYAWABQAD
EA5OLHzcQEcZYAAAAAAAAAAAAAAAAAAAAAsz6BrLvbKI9JA2UWtQEQolh
SFoU9HXfUOvvvDPQuWoNlKxIgckKTwQ==
</t:BinaryExchange>
</t:RequestSecurityTokenResponse>
</s:Body>
```

The fifth request is the actual SOAP request using an action of `http://tempuri.org/IMtomSample/GetFile`. The body of the SOAP request contains an unencrypted request value inside the SOAP body:

```
<fileName>LogoText.JPG</fileName>
```

If you look at the file `6.txt`, you'll see a MIME message consisting of two parts. The first part is the SOAP envelope representing the `GetFileResponse` message, as shown in Listing 13-10. Inside that element is an `xop:Include` element that points to the second part of the MIME message.

Listing 13-10. `GetFileResult` *with XOP Reference*

```
<GetFileResult>
    <xop:Include
     href="cid:http%3A%2F%2Ftempuri.org%2F1%2F632858870617208016"
     xmlns:xop="http://www.w3.org/2004/08/xop/include"/>
</GetFileResult>
```

The second part of the MIME message is the raw binary stream as read initially from the file system into the `byte[]`. If you look in the file `6.txt`, you can see the MIME content header for the binary stream, as shown in Listing 13-11.

Listing 13-11. *Binary Content Part of MIME Message*

```
--uuid:c336b34f-7c2b-4ca6-9534-141723adcf4c+id=9
Content-ID: <http://tempuri.org/1/632858870617208016>
Content-Transfer-Encoding: binary
Content-Type: application/octet-stream

ÿØÿà JFIF  ` `  ÿÛ C \\ \           (binary data)
```

The `Content-ID` in this part of the MIME message is not HTML encoded, while in the SOAP response part (Listing 13-10) it is. The other aspect is that the encoding type is `binary` and marked as an `octet-stream`. What follows the customary set of two CR/LF (0x0D, 0x0A) is the raw binary data directly from the byte[]. The content length matches the original file size (you can examine this with the Ethereal logs) without any compression or modification.

The exchange used in Listing 13-10 doesn't apply any message level to either the request or the reply. If you update the OperationContract attribute's ProtectionLevel property to EncryptAndSign, you get message-level encryption on both the SOAP envelope and the binary data that is contained in the second part of the MIME message. The capture results with EncryptAndSign for the final response are contained in the file 6-WithEncryptAndSign.txt.

MTOM Industry Acceptance

The W3C published the MTOM specification in January 2005.[15] Since that time, several other key vendors have signed on to ship products that contain support for MTOM. Microsoft had been one of the first to support it with Visual Studio 2005 and WSE 3.0. Microsoft continues that support up through WCF.

At the time of this writing, many of the non-Microsoft frameworks have either indicated an intention to support MTOM in future versions of their application server software or have shipped early adopter (EA) code.

If you look at the Java technology stack, some competing technologies provide the foundation for web services. As a result, how you enable MTOM support in the Java environment varies by what choice you make with regard to the primary application server and development tools.

Sun's Tango project, along with its NetBeans tools and frameworks, provides a similar model to Microsoft. Both provide a metadata-driven approach and tools to abstract and simplify developing web services based upon the emerging standards.

Apache's Axis2 Support of MTOM

You'll now look at how Axis2 1.0 provides support for MTOM. Axis2 1.0 was released as an early adopter version in May 2006.[16] The Axis2 project was a major rewrite from the initial Axis web services project. Axis2 leverages a pipeline handler model for message handling (similar to Axis) with an extensibility model that allows both the community and enterprises to extend Axis2.

The Axis2 project has more of a code generation model with the use of tools to facilitate developing web services. Additionally, Axis2 uses the Axis Object Model Element (AXIOM OMElement) that becomes the primary message that is passed through the participants in a distributed architecture. The Axis2 project also has an Eclipse[17] plug-in wizard for helping generate code either from WSDL or from Java classes (WSDL2Java or Java2WSDL).[18]

So, using the MtomTest sample, you can first generate the WSDL using the SvcUtil.exe utility as provided with WCF using the following command line (after starting the WCFHost project):

```
svcutil /t:metadata http://localhost:8080/ FileService
```

---

15. You can find the Ethereal network protocol analyzer at http://www.ethereal.com/.

16. You can find MTOM and XOP at http://www.w3.org/TR/soap12-mtom/ and at http://www.w3.org/TR/xop10/.

17. You can find the Axis2 project at http://ws.apache.org/axis2/.

18. You can find the Eclipse IDE at http://www.eclipse.org.

This creates three output files representing the base WSDL with the two imports. Using this WSDL, you can now create the Java classes for consuming the `MtomTest` web service, as shown in Figure 13-2.

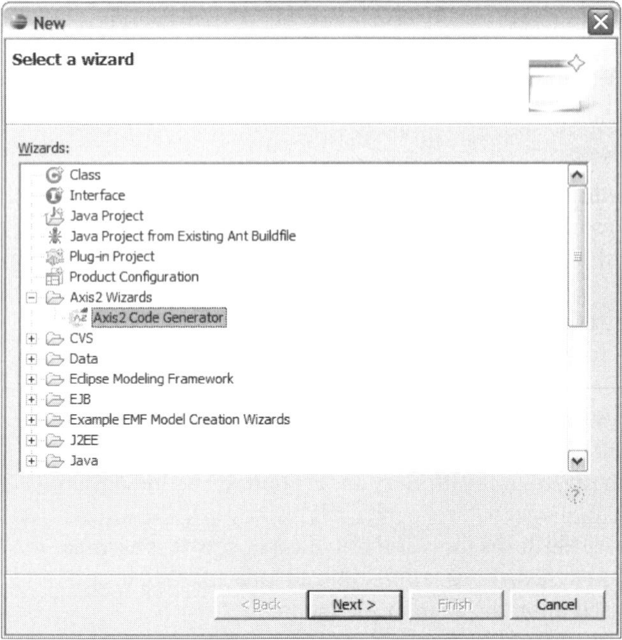

Figure 13-2. *Accessing Axis2 Code Generator from Eclipse*

The wizard lists the Axis2 Code Generator that's accessed from the New menu option. We won't cover in too much detail the capabilities of Code Generator. The next step is to choose either to generate a Java class from a WSDL or to generate a Java class to a WSDL. We will choose to generate a WSDL to a Java class (the Generate Java Source Code from a WSDL File option), as shown in Figure 13-3.

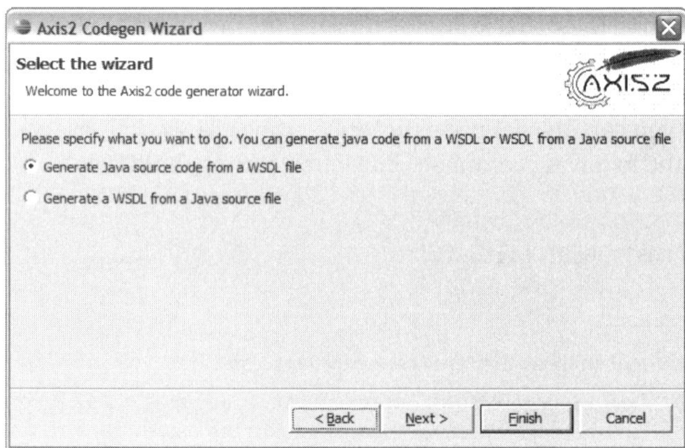

Figure 13-3. *Generating Java code from WSDL*

Click Next, and you will then be prompted to choose the input WSDL file. This will be the file you created using the `SvcUtil.exe` utility. Then click Next again, and you will see the choices for code generation, as shown in Figure 13-4.

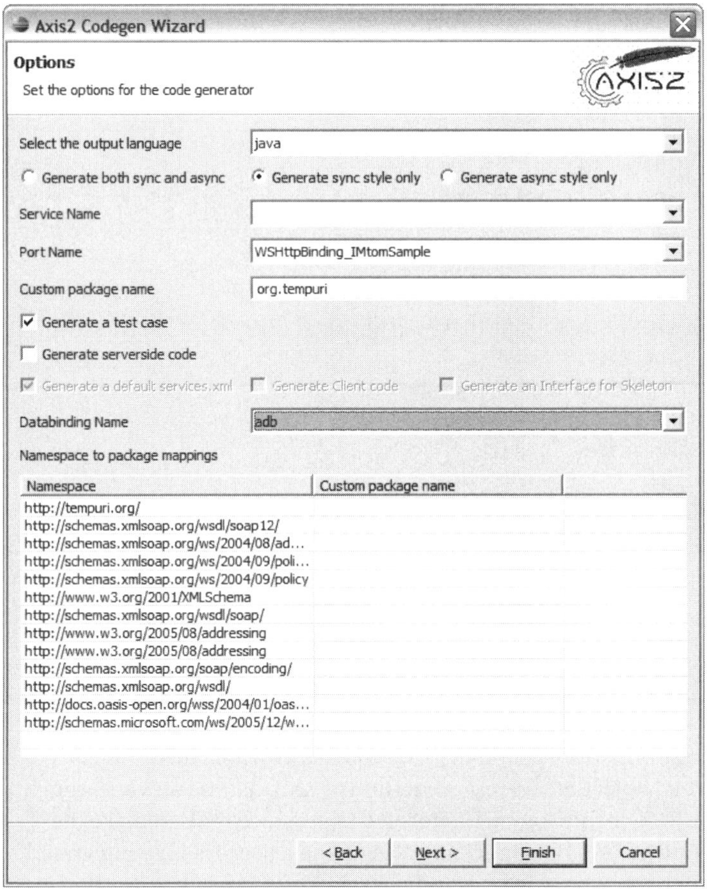

Figure 13-4. *Axis2 code generation options*

Enter the service name in the Service Name box shown in Figure 13-5. For this example, we'll just generate the client-side proxy along with a test case class that will demonstrate the calling paradigm provided by the Axis2 framework. We've just enabled synchronous calling and enabled the generation of a test case. The next page of the wizard asks for the output directory. Although the Finish button is enabled, you must specify a directory, or the wizard will complete without an error but won't produce any results. We've included the generated code as part of the chapter sample code; it's in the `MtomTest\Java` directory, and the WSDL used is in the `MtomTest\Wsdl` directory. Please note the `WSDL2Java`-generated class is called `FileServiceTest`.

Listing 13-12 shows the test case–generated code directly from the `WSDL2Java` wizard.

Listing 13-12. *Axis2* `WSDL2Java`*-Generated Code*

```
public class FileServiceTest extends junit.framework.TestCase {
    public void testGetFile() throws java.lang.Exception {
        org.tempuri. FileServiceStubstub = new org.tempuri.FileServiceStub ();
        org.apache.axiom.om.OMElement param4 =
                    (org.apache.axiom.om.OMElement)
                          getTestObject(org.apache.axiom.om.OMElement.class);

        // todo Fill in the param4 here
        assertNotNull(stub.GetFile(param4));
    }

    //Create an OMElement and provide it as the test object
    public org.apache.axiom.om.OMElement getTestObject(java.lang.Object dummy) {
     org.apache.axiom.om.OMFactory factory =
          org.apache.axiom.om.OMAbstractFactory.getOMFactory();
     org.apache.axiom.om.OMNamespace defNamespace =
          factory.createOMNamespace("", null);

     return org.apache.axiom.om.OMAbstractFactory.getOMFactory()
           .createOMElement("test", defNamespace);
    }
}
```

As you can see in the code, the main interaction from the developer perspective is navigating the `OMElement`, which is a hierarchical object model representing an XML InfoSet.[19]

Compare the coding approach presented by Axis2 and AXIOM to the experience presented by WCF. The .NET Framework from its initial inception has provided methods to develop against a strongly typed object model representation of XML data as well as through hierarchical navigation using XML technologies. Microsoft has provided tools to make the serialization and representation of XML data more seamless using a user-friendly integrated development environment (in other words, Visual Studio 2005). The key result is that you can do more with less coding, leaving the intricacies of working with XML to the framework.

Sun Microsystems' Support of MTOM

Sun, the creator of Java, has worked with Microsoft on WCF interoperability testing, as mentioned previously. The WSIT project, as of this writing, is in early adaptor form and source code only.[20] However, given the marketing from Sun's team and the demonstration at the JavaOne 2006 conference, it is clear Sun is committed to a viable and working framework.

---

19. You can find the Axis2 Eclipse plug-in at `http://ws.apache.org/axis2/tools/1_0/eclipse/wsdl2java-plugin.html`.

20. You can find an AXIOM tutorial at `http://ws.apache.org/axis2/1_0/OMTutorial.html#OM`.

WSIT relies on two foundational Java technologies: JAX-WS[21] and JAXB.[22] The combination of these technologies provides a similar development experience to the WCF model. Both rely on attributes and metadata for web service definition, and along with JAXB, they provide a strongly typed development experience that increases developer productivity.

Sun's NetBeans project, which is an open source stepchild of the Java community, provides a development environment that additionally alleviates the requirements that developers understand hand-coding to a new API or understand navigating an object graph. The NetBeans WSIT module,[23] as shown in Figure 13-5, hides the intricacies of the framework requirements.

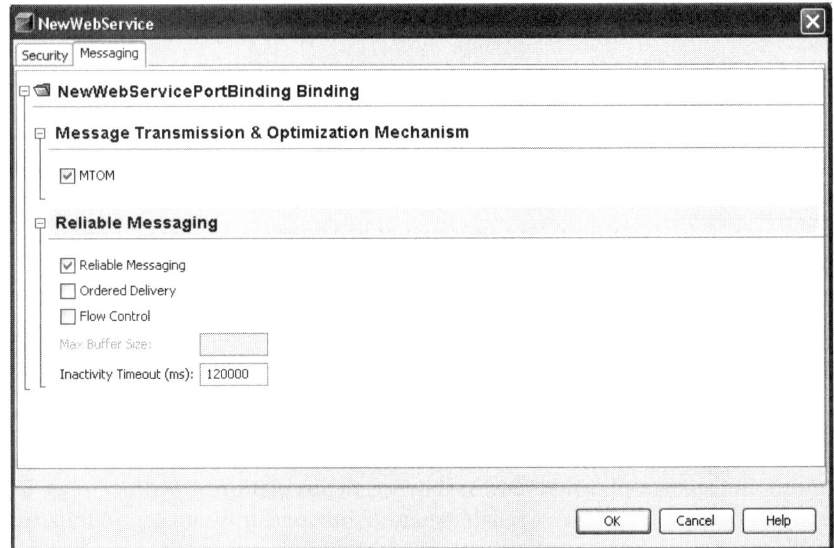

Figure 13-5. *NetBeans WSIT module*

Before moving on, we'll make a few important observations regarding the state of the Java community and the vendor support of a consistent approach to working with web services and the emerging standards: JBoss, acquired by Red Hat in 2006, has stated that it will no longer work with the Axis project and will proceed with the development of its own SOAP stack.[24] At the time of this writing, JBoss supports only 30 percent of the MTOM specification.[25] Additionally, neither IBM nor BEA has published or shipped a product that supports MTOM, although both companies were part of the W3C specification committee. Marketing and news releases indicate they are expected to ship products by 2007.

These are the options available to transfer binary data between Microsoft and non-Microsoft SOA offerings. We'll now discuss how WS-ReliableMessaging is used in non-Microsoft SOA offerings.

---

21. You can find GlassFish Project Tango/WSIT information at `https://wsit.dev.java.net/`.

22. `http://jax-ws.dev.java.net/`

23. `http://jaxb.dev.java.net/`

24. `http://websvc.netbeans.org/wsit/`

25. `http://wiki.jboss.org/wiki/Wiki.jsp?page=WebServiceStacks`

Using WS-ReliableMessaging

Solutions are questionable without reliability. If a system is either unavailable or loses requests for processing, the users of that system will eventually demand explanations. For example, if you're buying a book on Amazon and you get through the order process, think you've purchased the book, and then wait weeks for its pending arrival, how many times do you think you'll shop at Amazon again before investigating alternative services?

The situation is even worse if you're booking a trade that could be worth a considerable amount of money and the message to the clearance system gets lost. If you have a trader who just purchased 100,000 shares of Microsoft (MSFT), what happens if that ticket never makes it to the back-office system?

Since the inception of web services, their attraction for loosely coupled platform interoperability has been amazing. Web services represent a neutral technology that no one vendor owns or controls at the expense of both competitors and clients. Vendors can't hold clients to a single platform. However, web services have one significant drawback that we view as critical for the further acceptance of web services in the enterprise. This limitation has held back web services as the enabling glue for tying applications together in a loosely coupled manner. That limitation is reliability.

What is reliability? Well, the analogy of buying a book on Amazon or losing a trade while being handed off between systems certainly sounds familiar. The foundation of web services, for many implementations, has been HTTP. SOAP over HTTP is generally considered the default mechanism for web services. However, HTTP doesn't guarantee reliability when dealing with duplication, ordering, or system outages.

The WS-ReliableMessaging[26] (WS-RM) specification was created to address the needs of reliability for solutions that span applications across heterogeneous platforms. With WS-RM, it is possible to interact across applications in a reliable manner but, to clarify, not with durability.

The WS-RM specification addresses reliability from within a session or more specifically a service exchange between a client and a server. What WS-RM provides is a guarantee through delivery assurance that a message sent is received. That leaves the implementation, not the WS-RM specification, to fulfill the delivery assurance or raise a SOAP fault.

The key delivery assurances that can be provided by each WS-RM implementation are as follows:

`AtMostOnce`: Delivered without duplication but does not deal with lost messages

`AtLeastOnce`: Delivered once, or more; otherwise, if not delivered, raises a fault

`ExactlyOnce`: Delivered only once; otherwise fault

`InOrder`: Delivered in sequence sent; does not address duplication or dropped messages

---

■ **Note** The current WCF implementation supports `ExactlyOnce` with the `InOrder` capability optional. This is enabled by applying the `reliableSession` element in configuration or in code for a custom binding or on a binding that supports reliable sessions (such as `WSHttp`, `WSDual`, or `NetTcp`).

---

26. `http://wiki.jboss.org/wiki/Wiki.jsp?page=JBossWSSpecStatus`

Durability of the message once it has been sent or system availability is not part of the WS-RM specification or currently available in WCF.[27] A suggestion on how to approach the durability and system availability aspect, which is out of the scope of the WS-RM specification, has been to leverage MSMQ in conjunction with reliable sessions, but that doesn't address the cross-platform issues. However, by using gateway technologies such as Host Integration Server (HIS) or other MSMQ to IBM MQSeries bridges, it is possible. But again, the limitations on the stack from each vendor on each side of the channel come into play. So, unless you have an extensible stack and you're prepared to develop customized bindings on the receiving end, the current shipping limitation is WCF in conjunction with MSMQ.

Network availability is addressed by dealing with timeouts on acknowledgments. Inactivity timeout settings, when exceeded without acknowledgment, will result in failure. Therefore, if a session is interrupted by an unreliable network connection, the WCF stack and any WS-RM implementation that supports `AtLeastOnce` or `ExactlyOne` will raise a fault.

WS-ReliableMessaging Example

You'll now look at the `WsReliableMessaging` sample that's part of the Chapter 13 downloadable samples. Using the MTOM sample as a base, we've modified the bindings to indicate that we require reliable sessions on the service interface. Using the WCF Service Configuration Editor (`SvcConfigEditor.exe`) that's part of the Windows SDK (select Tools ➤ WCF SvcConfigEditor in Visual Studio), you can modify the `App.config` file for the `WcfHost` application in the sample, as shown in Figure 13-6.

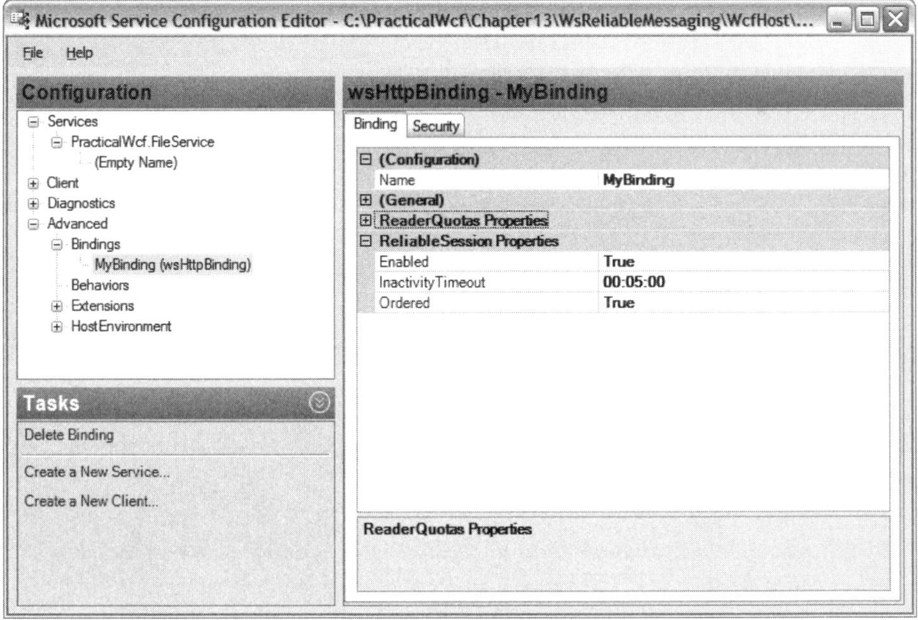

Figure 13-6. *Enabling WS-ReliableMessaging on* `WcfHost`

27. `http://specs.xmlsoap.org/ws/2005/02/rm/`

This configuration translates to the application configuration file shown in Listing 13-13.

Listing 13-13. *WS-ReliableMessaging Enabled via Configuration*

```
<system.serviceModel>
  <services>
    <service name="PracticalWcf.FileService">
      <endpoint
        binding="wsHttpBinding"
        bindingConfiguration="MyBinding"
        contract="PracticalWcf.IFileService" />
    </service>
  </services>
  <bindings>
    <wsHttpBinding>
      <binding
        name="MyBinding"
        messageEncoding="Mtom">
        <reliableSession
          inactivityTimeout="00:05:00"
          enabled="true" />
        <security>
          <message
            clientCredentialType="Windows"
            negotiateServiceCredential="true"
            establishSecurityContext="true" />
        </security>
      </binding>
    </wsHttpBinding>
  </bindings>
</system.serviceModel>
```

RELIABLE MESSAGING AND WS-SECURITY

The WS-ReliableMessaging specification "strongly recommends" securing reliable scenarios. The following is part of section 5 of the specification located at `http://specs.xmlsoap.org/ws/2005/02/rm/ws-reliablemessaging.pdf`:

> *It is strongly recommended that the communication between services be secured using the mechanisms described in WS-Security. In order to properly secure messages, the body and all relevant headers need to be included in the signature....*

The specification goes on to clarify the suggestion based upon sequencing and in the end to alleviate message replay concerns. Given the "strong" suggestions from the committee and the significant IBM representation on the committee as part of the WCF architects, it's no surprise the requirement exists with WCF.

The reliableSession element shown in Listing 13-13 enables WS-ReliableMessaging on all the service interface interactions that leverage WSHttpBinding. Note that the establishSecurityContext attribute is set to true (the default) for the binding. At this time, WCF requires a combination of WS-Security with reliable sessions. If you set the establishSecurityContext attribute to false, when starting the host, you will receive a System.InvalidOperation exception with the message “{"Cannot establish reliable session without secure conversation. Enable secure conversation."}.”

Keeping with the WCF core ability to support both a declarative and a programmatic-driven implementation, it is also possible via code to enable reliable sessions, as shown in Listing 13-14.

Listing 13-14. *WS-ReliableMessaging Using Code*

```
WSHttpBinding binding =
    new WSHttpBinding( SecurityMode.Message, true );

myServiceHost.AddServiceEndpoint(
    typeof( IFileService),
    binding,
    baseAddress);
```

The code in Listing 13-14 uses the WSHttpBinding constructor override that accepts a SecurityMode value along with a Boolean value that enables reliable sessions on the binding. An alternate override is to specify a configuration name, which allows a mix of a programmatic-driven approach and a configuration-driven approach to development.

If you examine the HTTP traffic for the service exchange, you now see an overall increase (doubling) of the request-reply between the client and server for the same service interface call. What is happening is that with each request, additional acknowledgment messages are indicating success on each message. These additional messages are the delivery assurance mechanism as part of WS-ReliableMessaging. An example of one of these messages is contained in the \Capture directory as the file Ack.txt. This message contains the CreateSequenceResponse as a reply to an initial CreateSequence initiation that establishes the reliable session. The full Ethereal capture is present in the file wsrm.log in the \Capture directory. You can find full details of the exchange of messages in section 2.4 of the WS-ReliableMessaging specification.[28]

Platform Support of WS-ReliableMessaging

Industry and platform support of WS-ReliableMessaging is a critical aspect of overall web service adoption in the enterprise. Prior to web services, applications were coupled using varied means, with some being file based and many using queued messaging technologies such as MQSeries or Tibco. Most of the time, the coupling was tighter than ideal.

As web services became more prevalent, the desire to connect systems both within an enterprise and outside the firewall has been a critical success factor to the technologies' overall adoption. However, the reliability of the underlying protocol, primarily HTTP, has left it for low-value and low-risk scenarios.

---

28. You can find Shy Cohen's blog about demystifying reliable messaging at http://blogs.msdn.com/shycohen/archive/2006/02/20/535717.aspx.

With WS-ReliableMessaging, you now have a means, theoretically, to connect these heterogeneous systems using orthogonal approaches that aren't incompatible "on the wire." Now, when dealing with varied application architects and organizations, you can converse in a language that is consistent across implementations. You can discuss the web service contract and not the details of how you plan to converse. You can publish your metadata on your services or consume the metadata of the partners you need to interact with, all using a common language.

The differences between each implementation, however, are stark at the time of this writing. IBM, for example, has indicated only a "statement of direction" in its 6.1 release of WebSphere Application Server,[29] with a target date of "early 2007." JBoss (now part of Red Hat) has not provided any support in its JBossWS 1.0 as of this writing. Also, given JBoss's stated direction away from Axis and that Red Hat has dropped its application server in favor of JBoss, it's not clear what target it has.[30] BEA Systems' WebLogic application server has no publicly announced support or a timeframe for it.

The two most notable implementations are the Sun Tango/WSIT project, previously mentioned, and Axis2. Both teams, along with the WCF teams, are working on platform interoperability tests to ensure that at shipping time (or close to it) there will be viable frameworks that support interoperability with WCF.

Summary

One of the key objectives of SOA is to obtain interoperability between heterogeneous platforms. WCF achieves this objective by implementing common standards that are endorsed by competitive vendors. IBM, Sun, BEA, and the Tibco products comply with WCF by implementing WSIT standards. These are available today as open source offerings. WCF also complies with Basic Profile to be compatible with the early web service offerings.

Some of these WSIT standards include bootstrapping communication (WS-MetaDataExchange), securing communication (WS-SecurityPolicy, WS-Security, and WS-Trust), optimizing communication (MTOM and WS-SecureConversation), enabling reliability (WS-ReliableMessaging), and enabling atomic transactions (WS-Coordination and WS-AtomicTransactions). MTOM also helps developers transfer binary attachments from one platform to another (that is, from Microsoft WCF to Apache Axis2). WS-ReliableMessaging implemented by WCF offers "guaranteed delivery" similar to traditional Tibco or MQSeries offerings. Therefore, WCF offers a wide variety of interoperability options to integrate with non-Microsoft platforms through these various WS-* standards to achieve service-oriented computing.

---

29. `http://specs.xmlsoap.org/ws/2005/02/rm/ws-reliablemessaging.pdf`

30. You can find the IBM WebSphere 6.1 software announcement from April 11, 2006, at `http://www-306.ibm.com/common/ssi/rep_ca/6/897/ENUS206-076/ENUS206-076.PDF`.

31. Get the status of the JBoss WS specification at `http://wiki.jboss.org/wiki/Wiki.jsp?page=JBossWSSpecStatus`

PART 4

Appendixes

APPENDIX A

QuickReturns Ltd.

QuickReturns Ltd. is the sample company we use throughout this book to explain the concepts of the Windows Communication Foundation. This appendix contains the high-level architecture that we created.

The following is a simplified model of an equity trading market and participants. We have combined some of the roles in order to simplify the perspective. This model is not meant to replicate the real interorganizational structure; it's just a basic representation for demonstration needs.

The following are the primary participants along with a general description of what services they provide or expect from other participants:

Asset Manager: This is an individual providing portfolio management and issuing trades to buy or sell stock through a market. Asset Managers make decisions about what specific securities to buy or sell in order to establish a portfolio that meets their client's needs.

Market Maker: This is an individual providing execution and market-making activities on a set of stocks listed on an exchange. Market Makers provide orderly market monitoring by maintaining two-sided displayed quotes, ensuring the quote is not inverted in the spread. They provide liquidity needs for investors. They clear and settle transactions through the Depository.

Exchange: This is an entity that provides an organized forum for Market Makers to publish market prices on listed securities. The Exchange provides execution services and systems that match, capture, record, and track security transactions amongst market participants.

Depository/Securities Processing System: This is an entity that keeps track of open positions for all market participants on the listed securities. Generally, each participant would have their own securities-processing system or subscribe to a corresponding service from another participant. However, for this example, the model is simplified, and the Depository provides all the necessary needs.

Market Overview

Figure A-1 shows an overview of how the example stock-trading market works.

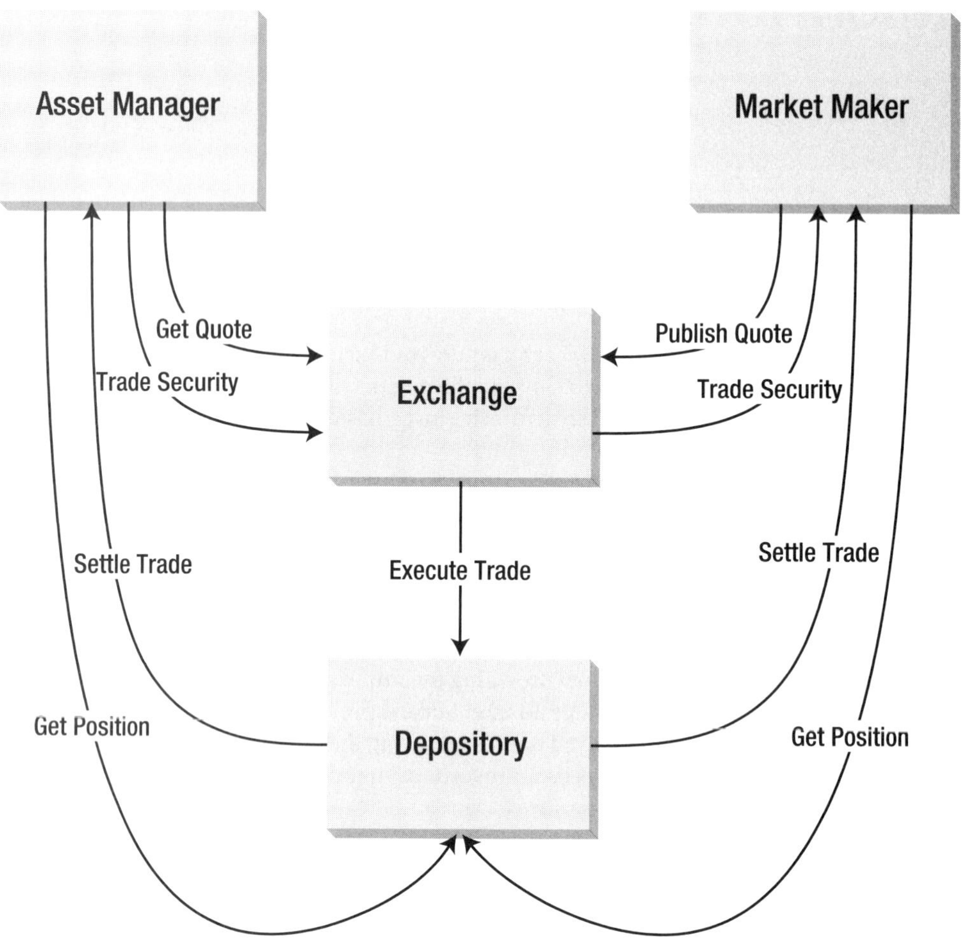

Figure A-1. *Market overview*

Services and Collaboration

The following sections list each entity with the primary service they publish along with the primary consumers of that service (in parenthesis).

Asset Manager

The following are the specifics of the Asset Manager.

Settle Trade (Depository)

This is where a participant is notified by the Depository that a trade has settled; this includes the settlement details.

```
public void SettleTrade ( Settlement settlement );
```

Market Maker

The following are the specifics of the Market Maker.

Trade Security (Exchange)

This is where a participant is notified that another participant has "hit" either a bid or an asking price on a listed security based upon the published quote.

```
public Execution TradeSecurity ( Trade trade );
```

Settle Trade (Depository)

This is where a participant is notified by the Depository that a trade has settled; this includes the settlement details.

```
public void SettleTrade ( Settlement settlement );
```

Exchange

The following are the specifics of the Exchange.

Publish Quote (Market Maker)

This is the process where a Market Maker announces what their bid is and asks for a particular security.

```
public void PublishQuote ( Quote quote );
```

Get Quote (Asset Manager)

This is where an exchange provides the announced bid. We use this to inquire about the listed securities by the participants.

```
public Quote GetQuote ( String ticker );
```

Trade Security (Asset Manager)

This is where a participant chooses to buy or sell, based upon an asking or bid quote, respectively, as published on the Exchange.

```
public Execution TradeSecurity ( Trade trade );
```

Depository

The following are the specifics of the Depository.

Execute Trade (Exchange)

This is when a trade occurs on an Exchange, and the Depository is notified in order to update appropriate positions, both cash and security, and provide notification to the respective participants through settlement reporting.

```
public void ExecuteTrade ( Execution execution );
```

Get Position (Asset Manager, Market Maker)

This is where a participant requests the position on either a security position or a cash position. Positions can be reported in either positive (long) or negative (short) numbers, but fractional shares are not allowed.

```
public Position GetPosition ( String ticker );
```

Data Contracts

The following are the data contracts in the application.

Quote

A *quote* represents what the "market" is for a given listed security. Table A-1 shows the quote data contract.

Table A-1. *Quote Data Contract*

Field	Format	Description
Ticker	String	Primary exchange security identifier
Bid	Decimal	The price at which the publisher is willing to buy the security
Ask	Decimal	The price at which the publisher is willing to sell the security
Publisher	String	Identifier of publisher
Update Time	DateTime	Update time in GMT for the published quote

Trade

A *trade* represents a commitment to buy or sell a set quantity of shares for a specific listed security by a specific publisher. Table A-2 shows the trade data contract.

Table A-2. *Trade Data Contract*

Field	Format	Description
Ticker	String	Primary exchange security identifier
Type	Character	B or S for Buy or Sell
Publisher	String	Identifier of publisher
Participant	String	Identifier of participant
Quoted price	Decimal	Price from original quote corresponding to either the bid price or the ask price when the trade is a sell or buy type, respectively
Quantity	Integer	Quantity of shares as part of the trade
Trade Time	DateTime	Time stamp in GMT of when the trade was requested using the exchange's clock as the master

Execution

An *execution* represents a committed exchange of a security amongst market participants at a set price and quantity. An execution is generally provided as a result of a trade and to the Depository for position tracking. Table A-3 shows the execution data contract.

Table A-3. *Execution Data Contract*

Field	Format	Description
Trade	Trade Type	The corresponding trade
Settlement Date	DateTime	The expected settlement date

Settlement

A *settlement* represents the final update, cash, and position, at settlement time (T+1 in our model), on an executed trade between market participants. Table A-4 shows the settlement data contract.

Table A-4. *Settlement Data Contract*

Field	Format	Description
Execution	Execution Type	The corresponding execution type
Status	Enum	Indicator of settlement status: Cleared, Failed, DK (do not know)

Position

A *position* represents a long or short (+/–) quantity that is registered in a specific market participant's account at the Depository. Positions are impacted by execution reports. Table A-5 shows the position data contract.

Table A-5. *Position Data Contract*

Field	Format	Description
Ticker	String	Primary exchange security identifier
Participant	String	Identifier of participant
Quantity	Integer	Quantity of shares on an account for the market participant
Unsettled Quantity	Integer	Summary quantity of any unsettled trades
Unsettled Trades	Execution []	List of unsettled trades encapsulated in execution type array

APPENDIX B

History of Microsoft Web Service Implementations

Microsoft web services have evolved over the years from the initial release with .NET 1.0 to the release of WCF today. Figure B-1 shows how the framework has evolved and, at a high level, the features that were added with each iteration.

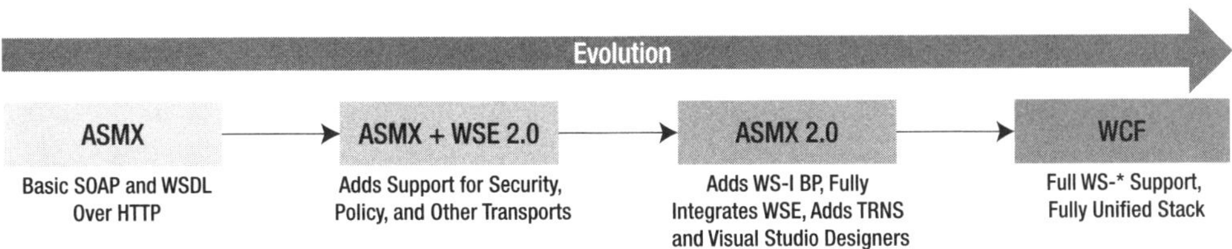

Figure B-1. *Evolution of web services in .NET*

When .NET Framework 1.*x* was released, it was the first runtime implementation from Microsoft that provided rich web service support out of the box for developers. Even today it provides the easiest way to code, debug, and deploy web services in the industry. To support web services natively, the .NET runtime also has to support all the underlying protocols and infrastructure required such as XML, HTTP, XSD, SOAP, and so on, out of the box. Version 1.*x* of the .NET Framework introduced web services as part of ASP.NET pages. Although web services were the catalyst, the .NET runtime provides the ease of development so developers can build efficient, secure, and reliable web services. Visual Studio .NET provides a robust environment that allows you to easily create, deploy, and maintain applications developed using XML web services.

ASMX Pages

ASP.NET was designed to provide a web service infrastructure and programming model that allows developers to create, deploy, and maintain web services without the need to understand SOAP, WSDL, and so on. ASP.NET accomplished this goal through the introduction of XML web services, which is built on top of ASP.NET and the .NET Framework. Developers can easily create web services by creating files with `.asmx` extensions (for example, `Customers.asmx`) and deploying them as part of a web application. Like ASPX files, ASMX files are intercepted by an

ISAPI extension (aspnet_isapi.dll) and processed in a separate ASP.NET worker process. The ASMX file must either reference a .NET class or contain the class itself. The only mandatory entry in the ASMX file is the WebService directive, which specifies the class and the language. Listing B-1 shows an example of the directive where the class being used is Customers.

Listing B-1. WebService *Directive in an* .asmx *File*

```
<% WebService Language="c#" Class="Customers" Codebehind="Customers.cs" %>
```

You can set the default XML namespace for the web service by applying the WebService attribute to the class implementing the web service; in addition, you should change the default namespace from http://tempuri.org to something unique. Methods of this class do not have the ability to process web service requests. To make the methods available through a web service, you need to apply a WebMethod attribute to the public method. Once these methods are decorated with the WebMethod attribute, they are called *web methods* and can communicate over the wire. This class can also optionally derive from the WebService class, which allows the web service to gain access to the common ASP.NET objects such as User, Context, Session, Application, and so on. Listing B-2 shows a sample containing two public methods; one is a web service, and the other is not because we have the WebMethod attribute on only one method.

Listing B-2. *Defining Web Service Methods*

```
<%@ WebService Language="C#" Class="Util" %>
using System.Web.Services;
using System;
[WebService(Namespace="http://www.quickreturn.com/")]
public class CalculateReturn: WebService
{
    [WebMethod]
    public int Multiply(int a, int b)
    {
        return a * b;
    }
    public int Add(int a, int b)
    {
        return a + b;
    }
}
```

Web Services Enhancements (WSE)

Web Services Enhancements (WSE, pronounced as "wizzy") is a set of .NET class libraries; WSE is an add-on to the .NET Framework and provides support for several WS-* specifications, such as WS-Security, WS-Routing, DIME, WS-Attachments, and so on. WSE is installed as a set of .NET assemblies. These are implemented as filters that integrate with ASP.NET web services. Clients that consume these web services can expand and interrogate the SOAP message headers using WSE.

WSE provides its functionality by writing headers to outbound SOAP messages and reading headers from inbound SOAP messages. In some cases, it might also need to transform the SOAP message body (such as for encrypt/decrypt as per the WS-Security specification if security is enabled). The functionality is encapsulated as a set of filters, one each for outbound and inbound messages. As shown in Figure B-2, all messages are intercepted by these filters.

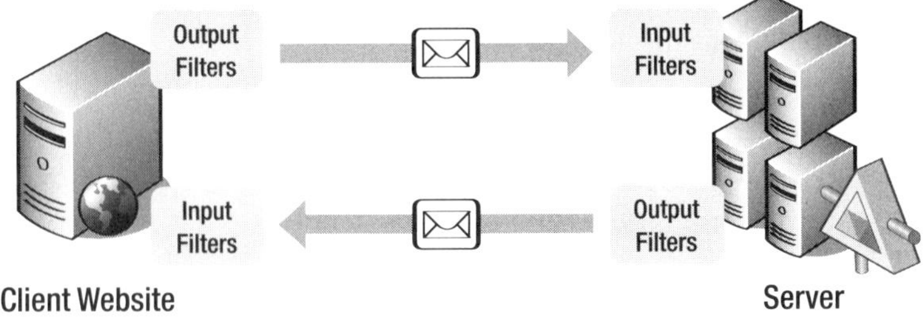

Figure B-2. *WSE input/output filters*

You can access the WSE filter chain via the `Pipeline` class and integrate it with the ASP.NET web service runtime. New proxy base classes called `WebServicesClientProtocol` expose the new inbound and outbound filters. This new base class extends the default base class (`SoapHttpClientProtocol`). This new proxy ensures that the filters have a chance to process the SOAP message when a client invokes a remote web service call.

The `WebServicesClientProtocol` proxy class is implemented using two new classes called `SoapWebRequest` and `SoapWebResponse`. The `SoapWebRequest` implementation is quite straightforward; it parses the incoming request stream for the SOAP message using the `SoapEnvelope` class and passes the request through the chain of output filters, where each filter gets a chance to process the headers and modify them as needed. The behavior of each filter in turn is controlled via the `SoapContext` class. Figure B-3 shows the interaction between the various objects.

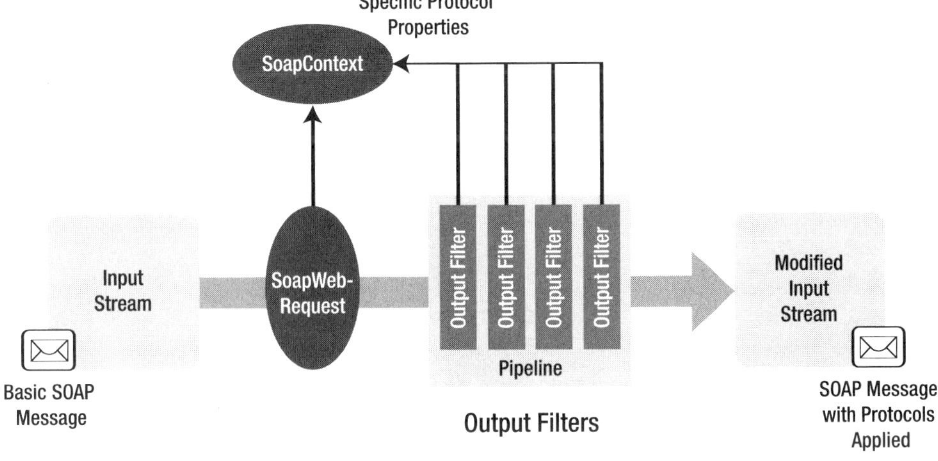

Figure B-3. `SoapWebRequest` *processing an output filter*

On the other hand, the behavior of `SoapWebResponse` is just the opposite of `SoapWebRequest`. `SoapWebResponse` parses a response stream for the SOAP message through each filter where the filter can examine and modify the data as needed. Figure B-4 shows the interaction between the various components.

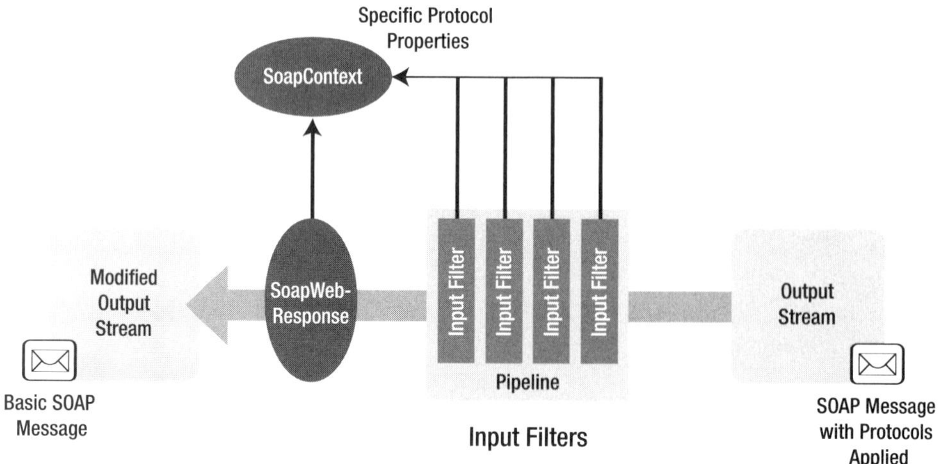

Figure B-4. `SoapWebResponse` *processing an output filter*

WSE filters are exposed to ASP.NET web services through a SOAP extension via `Microsoft.Web.Services.WebServicesExtension` on the server. This class copies the inbound or outbound messages to a temporary memory stream, allowing the filters to modify the headers as needed before serialization/deserialization. Figure B-5 shows the integration with ASP.NET.

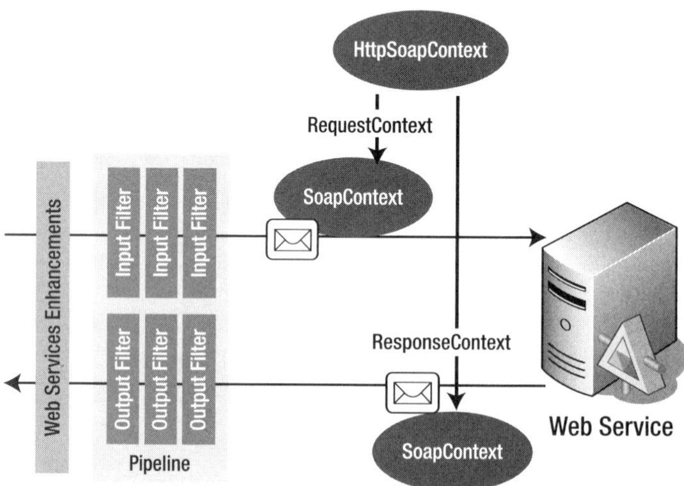

Figure B-5. *WSE integrating with ASP.NET*

Tip To make ASP.NET web services compatible with WCF services, you can embrace Basic Profiling (BP) conformance, use SOAP 1.1, and keep interoperable schemas as simple as possible. Try avoiding RPC/encoded, because it is not BP compliant. Also try avoiding SOAP extensions because they are harder to migrate.

WSE 1.0

WSE 1.0 replaced the Microsoft Web Services Development Kit (WSDK) and provided support for WS-Security, WS-Routing, WS-Attachments, and DIME specifications for the .NET Framework. The support came only from Microsoft and not from OASIS because OASIS was still ratifying the specification and because other vendors had yet to add support in their respective implementations. With this release, developers now could support various security features such as digital signatures, encryption, message routing capabilities, and the ability to include message attachments that are not serialized in XML.

WSE 2.0

WSE 2.0 is a different assembly and namespace from WSE 1.0. The new assembly name is `Microsoft.Web.Services2` instead of `Microsoft.Web.Services`. The name of the WSE 2.0 configuration element is `<microsoft.web.services2>`, and the WSE 2.0 root namespace is `microsoft.web.services2`. Although WSE 2.0 tries to maintain compatibility with the older version, it introduces some noncompatible and breaking changes because it is a major revision from version 1.0 and it keeps up with the rapidly moving web service standards. If there are two different versions of WSE implementations on either end of a web service call, a SOAP fault will always be returned as the two implement different versions of the specification. WSE 1.0 implements WS-Routing and WS-Security, while the new WSE 2.0 implements WS-Addressing and the new OASIS WS-Security standard. To make the transition as easy as possible from WSE 1.0 to 2.0, Microsoft supports side-by-side deployment of both versions. One caveat to this, however, is that any given web service cannot use both WSE 1.0 and 2.0 at the same time—it can be configured to use only one or the other. Consumers of the web service can use either version, though. A few other areas that have changed are as follows:

- Messaging enhancements
- WSDL support
- Security enhancements
- WS-Trust and WS-SecureConversation support
- Next-hop routing

Messaging Enhancements

WSE extends the basic web service functionality of ASP.NET (via the `SoapExtension` framework) and adds features such as security. The catch to this is that the solution is then tied to using only HTTP as the transport protocol when using ASP.NET web services. WSE, however, provides lower-level APIs (via `SoapSender` and `SoapReceiver`) that are transport neutral.

WSDL Support

WSE 2.0 adds complete support both for generating and for consuming WSDL. It can automatically generate WSDL definitions of endpoints when requested. It also has a new command-line tool called `WseWsdl2.exe` that can generate proxy classes from WSDL definitions and that currently supports HTTP and TCP.

Security Enhancements

WSE 2.0 adds support for the OASIS WS-Security standard, which affects only the message format and not the overall functionality. This adds a role-based authentication model for restricted access and is implemented via the `IPrincipal` interface along with the `IsInRole` method for authentication-specific user roles. WSE 2.0 also improves the security token and has a new Security Setting tool that helps create a policy file describing the security requirements of the application.

Support for WS-Trust and WS-SecureConversation

WSE 2.0 also adds support for WS-Trust and WS-SecureConversation, which define how to derive a session token that can be used over multiple operations and hence make the process more efficient and scalable.

Next-Hop Routing

WSE 2.0 supports a next-hop routing model where routing decisions are made on a node-to-node basis without requiring an explicit routing path in the header. Because of this all, WS-Routing functionality has been replaced by a new routing model based on WS-Addressing headers.

WSE 3.0

Unlike WSE 1.0 and 2.0, whose main objective was to provide a practical and usable implementation of the emerging WS-* security specifications, the strongest emphasis in WSE 3.0 is the simplification of message-level security and the implementation of interoperability. Broadly, the WSE 3.0 had the following design goals:

- Providing a way to build secure web services easily
- Simplifying the building of SOA solutions
- Future proofing and adding interoperability

Policy and Turnkey Security Profiles

In WSE 2.0 there was no correlation between the code written to secure a message and the declarative policy in place. In WSE 3.0, however, both the declarative and imperative programming models have been provided to secure the message. This is achieved either by using a `Policy` attribute or by using the `SetPolicy` method on the client-generated proxy class. Listing B-3 shows an example of how to set the policy to `QuickReturnsServerPolicy`.

Listing B-3. *Setting the Policy*

```
[WebService(Namespace = "http://quickreturns.com/samples")]
[Policy("QuickReturnsServerPolicy")]
public class WSSecurityUsernameService : System.Web.Services.WebService
{
   [WebMethod]
   public List<StockQuote> StockQuoteRequest([XmlArray(),
       XmlArrayItem("Symbol"] string[] symbols)
   {
      // Business logic here...
   }
}
```

Table B-1 lists the turnkey security profiles that over time have become standard in many implementations. For most situations, you would pick one of these policies and devote your time to implementing your business logic.

Table B-1. *Turnkey Security Profiles*

Turnkey Security Profile	Description
UsernameOverTransport	The client is identified against an external store such as Active Directory, SQL Server, or ADAM. The message is secured at the transport level through SSL.
UsernameForCertificate	The client is identified against an external store such as Active Directory, SQL Server, or ADAM. The message is secured via an X.509 server certificate.
AnonymousForCertificate	The client is anonymous, and anyone can access the server. The message is secured via an X.509 server certificate.
MutualCertificate10 and 11	X.509 certificates are exchanged between the client and server in order to secure the data exchange between them.
Kerberos	Kerberos is a way to securely communicate identity across an insecure network and is supported by Windows domains. Kerberos tickets are used for authentication and message protection. Kerberos also supports features such as impersonation and delegation in order to execute the service on behalf of the user.

■ **Note** WSE 3.0 does not support WS-SecurityPolicy because the specification has changed since WSE 2.0. WSE 3.0 also does not implement WS-MEX for metadata exchange.

Hosting ASMX Web Services Without IIS

In WSE 3.0, ASMX web services can be hosted outside IIS and can be in hosted in any type of process called via TCP such as console applications, Windows services, COM+ components, WinForms, and so on. More custom transports such as UDP, MSMQ, and SMTP have also been published.

Using MTOM

Message Transport Optimization Mechanism (MTOM) enables you to send large amounts of binary data *efficiently* in a SOAP message. MTOM is W3C standardized and replaces DIME and WS-Attachments as the mechanism for sending large amounts of data. One advantage of MTOM is that it composes messages in the context of a security policy, so both the data and the SOAP message are secure. You also get reduced wire size with MTOM because binary characters are sent as MIME attachments over the wire.

Future Proofing

One of the main features of WSE 3.0 is to provide a path to WCF to facilitate the ability to build service-oriented applications based on web services. WSE 3.0 offers wire-level compatibility with WCF and can run side by side with WCF.

■ **Note** WSE 3.0 is wire-level compatible with WCF when using HTTP as the transport protocol along with corresponding turnkey security profiles. This compatibility and interoperability is not guaranteed when using any other transport protocol.

SOA and .NET v2.0

WSE 3.0 runs only with .NET 2.0 (because it extended ASP.NET 2.0 web services), integrates into Visual Studio 2005, and is supported by Microsoft. WSE 3.0 also ensures interoperability with WCF services when using the turnkey security profiles, ensuring that the investment you make today is still usable with Windows Vista.

Sample XML Schema

Listing B-4 shows an example of a schema describing a country, and Listing B-5 shows a sample XML document implementing that schema.

Listing B-4. *Simple Schema Sample*

```
<xs:schema
 xmlns:xs="http://www.w3.org/2001/XMLSchema">
 <xs:element name="country">
  <xs:complexType>
   <xs:sequence>
```

```
    <xs:element name="name" type="xs:string"/>
    <xs:element name="population" type="xs:decimal"/>
   </xs:sequence>
  </xs:complexType>
 </xs:element>
</xs:schema>
```

Listing B-5. *Sample XML Document Conforming to Previous Schema*

```
<country
 xmlns:xsi="http://www.w3.org/2001/XMLSchema-instance"
 xsi:noNamespaceSchemaLocation="country.xsd">
 <name>France</name>
 <population>69.5</population>
</country>
```

Sample Complex Schema

In Listing B-6, Address is defined as a complex type, with five elements and one attribute declared. As a result, any instance of type Address must consist of these five elements (that is, name, street, city, state, and zip) and one attribute (that is, country). In addition, complex types can be nested and also define occurrence constraints in the schema.

Listing B-6. *Sample Complex Type Schema*

```
<xsd:complexType name="Address" >
  <xsd:sequence>
    <xsd:element name="name"   type="xsd:string"/>
    <xsd:element name="street" type="xsd:string"/>
    <xsd:element name="city"   type="xsd:string"/>
    <xsd:element name="state"  type="xsd:string"/>
    <xsd:element name="zip"    type="xsd:decimal"/>
  </xsd:sequence>
  <xsd:attribute name="country" type="xsd:NMTOKEN" fixed="US"/>
</xsd:complexType>
```

SOAP Message Example

To illustrate what SOAP messages look like, we'll show an example of a web service used by an online retailer that accepts a unique product identifier and returns details about the product such as the name, description, price, and availability. Listing B-7 shows an example of such a service called GetProductDetails that accepts one parameter called ProductID. The Envelope namespace will always point to http://schemas.xmlsoap.org/soap/envelope, as described in the specification.

Listing B-7. *Sample SOAP Request Message from a Client*

```
<soap:Envelope xmlns:soap="http://schemas.xmlsoap.org/soap/envelope/">
  <soap:Body>
    <getProductDetails xmlns="http://www.quickreturns.com/ws">
      <productID>5820948</productID>
    </getProductDetails>
  </soap:Body>
</soap:Envelope>
```

The response from the service also has the same structure of an envelope with the two headers. Listing B-8 shows an example of what the response of the previous `GetProductDetails` will contain. In this example, the service sends some additional attributes such as `Product Name`, `Description`, `Price`, and a Boolean stating whether the product is in stock.

Listing B-8. *Sample Response SOAP Message from a Server*

```
<soap:Envelope xmlns:soap="http://schemas.xmlsoap.org/soap/envelope/">
  <soap:Body>
    <getProductDetailsResponse xmlns="http://www.quickreturns.com/ws">
      <getProductDetailsResult>
        <productName>Wireless Keyboard</productName>
        <productID>123321</productID>
        <description>RF Wireless Keyboard, available in Black</description>
        <price>96.50</price>
        <inStock>true</inStock>
      </getProductDetailsResult>
    </getProductDetailsResponse>
  </soap:Body>
</soap:Envelope>
```

Summary

This appendix gave you a high-level overview of the history of the Microsoft web service stack. We covered several evolutions from plain SOAP to ASMX to WSE.

APPENDIX C

WCF and .NET Framework Installation Steps

This appendix shows how to install the necessary components for supporting a .NET 3.0 Framework development environment. Several steps are required, but if you follow the steps presented in this appendix, the setup and configuration will be trouble free. (Chapter 4 details the base installation and system requirements.)

Installing Internet Information Services

Although not required for WCF development or hosting, IIS is one of the hosting options, and some of the book examples leverage IIS for hosting.

You can install IIS on both Windows XP and Windows 2003 by selecting Start ➤ Control Panel ➤ Add or Remove Programs. This opens the Add or Remove Programs dialog box.

Once the Add or Remove Programs dialog box appears, click Add/Remove Windows Components. At this point, slight differences between Windows 2003 and Windows XP exist.

Windows 2003

On Windows 2003, you add or modify ASP.NET support by using the Application Server configuration component. Once the Windows Component Wizard appears, select Application Server in the list, and click the Details button on the lower right. This installation is IIS 6.0.

This displays the Application Server Component dialog box. Ensure that the ASP.NET checkbox is selected. If it's not selected, you need to enable it and click through the wizard. You'll need the installation media if you are doing this for the first time. As usual, the installation wizard may prompt you for the location of the installation files.

Note Selecting ASP.NET in the Application Server Components dialog box automatically selects the necessary IIS components on both Windows 2003 and Windows XP.

Windows XP

Windows XP doesn't support ASP.NET from an initial base installation perspective because it's not part of the operating system installation process. Installing IIS and ASP.NET is handled a bit differently. Here are the instructions. After choosing Add/Remove Windows Components, the Windows Component Wizard appears. Scroll down to the Internet Information Services (IIS) option if it's not visible. Ensure that the checkbox is enabled.

■ **Note** Selecting IIS in the dialog box selects all the default options to support IIS and subsequently ASP.NET.

Once done, click OK, and then click through the rest of the wizard. You'll need the installation media if the bits have not been configured before. The installation wizard may prompt you for the location of the installation files.

Installing Visual Studio 2005 or the .NET 2.0 SDK

The installation steps for Windows XP and Windows 2003 from this point forward are identical.

.NET 3.0 (the distribution components that contain WCF) is built for .NET 2.0; however, the version of the common language runtime (CLR) that comes with Windows 2003 is .NET Framework 1.1. Also, for Windows XP, the base installation has no version of .NET. So, some prerequisites need to be in place before you're ready to start developing.

Visual Studio 2005 provides developers with an integrated development environment (IDE) that is capable of producing WCF services and additional projects; it also provides the developer with a productive environment where development time is significantly reduced. The additional .NET Framework 3.0 Development Tools for Visual Studio 2005 project templates provide the base generation of the required components and references for creating .NET 3.0 (WCF) applications and components.

Although Visual Studio 2005 is not required, it is recommended as the primary development environment for all .NET 2.0 and .NET 3.0 applications. As a reminder, the .NET 3.0 components and supporting .NET Framework 3.0 development tools for Visual Studio 2005 are supported on all versions of Visual Studio 2005, including Visual Studio 2005 Express, which is available for free from the Microsoft Visual Studio site.[1]

.NET 2.0 SDK

The .NET 2.0 SDK gives you all the necessary tools, utilities, documentation, and samples to get you started developing. The primary missing part is an IDE that's tailored for .NET development. Although the SDK provides a debugger, it's not at the level of what Visual Studio 2005 can offer; it lacks many of the capabilities for stepping through code and easily establishing simple and more complex breakpoints.

---

1. `http://msdn.microsoft.com/vstudio/express/default.aspx`

.NET 2.0 Runtime Installation

The SDK relies on the redistributable package for the processor architecture you have. If you haven't installed the .NET 2.0 runtime, the SDK installation informs you of the missing dependencies and exits. Other than accepting the licensing agreement, the runtime installation is straightforward. Then, if everything goes right, you'll see the Setup Complete dialog box to confirm a successful installation. Once the runtime is installed, the SDK installation is then run.

■ **Note** The runtime actually provides the compilers for VB .NET, C#, and Jscript; this provides support for the runtime compilation of source into .NET assemblies. You'll see with the SDK installation the added compilers for VC++ and J#, which are not provided with the runtime.

.NET 2.0 SDK Installation

The SDK is also available from the same download location as the runtime components. The runtime components are utilized to execute .NET 2.0 code. However, if you are curious about what the .NET Framework 2.0 offers, you need to install the 2.0 SDK. There are no additional fees, other than the operating system license.

Once again, the SDK installation is fairly straightforward, with only a few options that you can control. Again, you'll see the obligatory licensing dialog box. Once past that, you get to choose what part of the SDK you require. For testing, you can leave the defaults; however, the only required option is the Tools and Debugger option, because this provides the necessary compilers for turning source code into .NET assemblies (Microsoft Intermediate Language and metadata) that the runtime can leverage in the CLR.

After selecting the options, you can choose the target location. If you're resource starved (you have limited disk space), have multiple disks, or just need to take more control of the location, you can alter the location; however, we've chosen the default (that is, `c:\Program Files\Microsoft.NET\SDK`). If everything goes OK, you now have an environment that supports creating .NET assemblies along with hosting ASP.NET applications inside ASP.NET. At this point, you can skip to the "Registering ASP.NET" section later in the chapter.

■ **Note** The .NET 2.0 SDK installation interestingly installs many of its tools to the `C:\Program Files\Microsoft Visual Studio 8` directory in addition to the `C:\Program Files\Microsoft.NET\SDK\v2.0` directory. There's a good document on all the SDK tools located in the `Bin` directory for the SDK named `C:\Program Files\Microsoft.NET\SDK\v2.0\Bin\StartTools.htm`.

Visual Studio 2005

Given the relatively low cost of Visual Studio Express 2005 ("free forever"),[2] most developers are likely to leverage Visual Studio 2005 for .NET 3.0 development. Although not required, it does provide a well-integrated and productive environment to facilitate the development of .NET 3.0, WCF, ASP.NET, and .NET applications.

■ **Note** For this book, we've created all the samples, code, and development with Visual Studio 2005 Professional or Team Suite.

Installing Visual Studio 2005 is fairly straightforward. For the most part, accepting the default options provides all the necessary components for developing .NET 3.0 and WCF applications and supporting .NET Windows and web applications.

If you're installing from the DVD and have autorun enabled for the device, the Visual Studio 2005 Setup screen automatically appears. If not, browse to the installation directory (`<drive or unc>\vs\`), and launch `autorun.exe`.

Click Install Visual Studio 2005, and then you'll see a series of questions about reporting your setup experiences to Microsoft and the obligatory licensing screen and product key. On this screen, you are informed of any Visual Studio 2005 dependencies that are missing; the Visual Studio 2005 Smart Installer will detect and download these missing components as required, making installation far easier than it has been in the past.

After clicking Next, you can choose the default or full set of features to install; both provide the necessary components needed. If you choose Default or Full, the next step is to just click Install; however, if you decide to customize the installation, the Next button appears, and you're required to select or deselect options as you require.

When customizing the installation, ensure you've chosen a programming language that you are working with (C# or VB .NET); to provide ASP.NET web project support and the ASP.NET development server (ASP.NET outside of IIS), select Visual Web Developer. This feature adds all the project template support as required.

■ **Note** The Default option installs Crystal Reports, Microsoft SQL Server 2005 Express, and other options; it does not install the .NET 2.0 Quick Start applications that are a great set of examples of .NET-related technologies. So, if you have SQL running already or you would like to explore the examples, ensure you select Custom and deselect the other options as required.

---

2. `http://msdn.microsoft.com/vstudio/express/`

At this point, clicking Install starts the installation process. Depending upon your machine's resources (CPU, disk speed, and so on), installation can take some time. At completion, the Success screen appears; clicking Finish returns you to the Visual Studio Setup dialog box where you can choose to install the MSDN documentation.

The next section shows how to validate the ASP.NET part of the installation.

■ **Note** If you choose to not install the product documentation during the platform SDK installation, you are prompted during the .NET Framework 3.0 Development Tools for Visual Studio 2005 installation that you are missing documentation. It is also recommended that you check for service releases to gain access to the latest patches for Visual Studio 2005.

Registering ASP.NET

If you installed IIS *before* installing either Visual Studio 2005 or the .NET 2.0 SDK (or .NET 2.0 runtime), then you have an environment that is ready to support ASP.NET 2.0 applications hosted within IIS.

To verify that ASP.NET 2.0 is registered correctly on the development or runtime machine, you can perform a couple of steps. The verification steps are identical for both Windows XP and Windows 2003.

First, from Administrative Tools (Start ➤ Control Panel ➤ Administrative Tools), double-click Internet Information Services. This opens the Internet Information Services Management Console. Expand the local computer until you can see Default Web Site and all the folders below it. Click it once to select. Choose File ➤ Properties from the main menu; alternatively, right-click, and choose Properties.

At this point, the Default Web Site Properties dialog box appears. The appearance of an ASP.NET tab in this dialog box indicates a successful .NET 2.0 runtime installation. That tab, if you select it, allows you to configure features related to .NET 2.0. Additionally, it allows you to switch the version of ASP.NET on each virtual path. Figure C-1 shows the dialog box for the root website that has its ASP.NET version set to the RTM version of .NET 2.0.

■ **Note** The ASP.NET Version drop-down box lists all the versions of .NET that are installed; however, the only version of ASP.NET 2.0 and .NET 2.0 that .NET 3.0 (and consequently WCF) supports is .NET 2.0.

While you're developing WCF applications hosted in IIS, you'll get used to seeing this dialog box. You'll need to set this every time if you have mixed installs of .NET such as an earlier version of the .NET Framework (we have both 1.1 and 2.0 installed, with 1.1 as the root version).

If you don't see the ASP.NET tab, there's an issue with the ASP.NET 2.0 registration. At this point, please review the sidebar "ASP.NET Registration Issues."

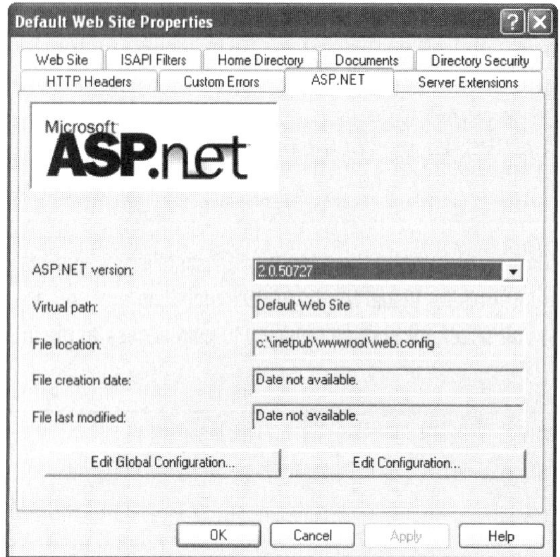

Figure C-1. *ASP.NET Website Configuration dialog box*

ASP.NET REGISTRATION ISSUES

Generally, it's a little bit easier to configure a development environment if you have IIS installed prior to installing Visual Studio or the SDK. If you've already installed Visual Studio or the .NET 2.0 SDK on your development environment or machine before installing IIS, you'll be missing the ASP.NET application configuration mappings that are managed within the IIS administration console.

Fortunately, a utility that comes with the .NET runtime can fix the problem. This utility is installed with the .NET runtime, and a specific version matches the particular version for each runtime. Specifically, there's one for 1.0, 1.1, and 2.0; for our needs, make sure it's the 2.0 version.

You must be an administrator on the machine where you run this utility. Open a command prompt by selecting Start ➤ Run, and enter **cmd** in the text box. Then click OK. Change to the .NET 2.0 Runtime directory using the following command:

```
cd %windir%\Microsoft.NET\Framework\v2.0.50727
```

The last directory name (v.2.0.50727) could change to reflect the latest .NET 2.0 version build number.

At this point, if you don't get any errors, you should be in the runtime directory. In that directory is a utility named `aspnet_regiis.exe`. All the command-line options for the utility are available by just running the utility. But for our needs, we'll show how to install using the `-i` switch. So, at the command prompt, enter the following command:

```
aspnet_regiis.exe -i <enter>
```

You'll see a bunch of messages indicating the installation. If you get any errors, you'll need to consult the documentation. It is important to note that this will upgrade the root website and all the virtual directories. If you are running this command on a web server with virtual directories, you will need to ensure that you are not going to break any existing applications by upgrading them to the 2.0 framework.

Installing .NET Framework 3.0 Runtime Components for XP and Windows 2003

The .NET 3.0 Framework RTC is an add-on for Windows XP and Windows 2003. The .NET 3.0 components are part of the Vista operating system and are included in the base installation. However, for Windows XP and Windows 2003, they are an additional installation that provides the managed API for the following:

- Windows Presentation Framework (WPF)
- Windows Workflow Foundation (WF[3])
- Windows Communication Foundation (WCF)

The managed APIs are .NET assemblies that abstract the base Win32 API and provide a more consistent way for working with base services of the operating system. They remove the need for having to use the Platform Invoke (PInvoke) capability as in previous .NET Frameworks.

The .NET 3.0 components are distributed either through an intelligent installer that downloads a “stub” user interface and leverages Background Intelligent Transfer (BITS) or as a large, single installation file. This stub user interface downloads in real time (during the installation) the necessary components required for a full install of .NET 3.0 from the Microsoft website.

The other option is to get the full install, which is a better option if installing multiple times or there are restrictions on accessing the Internet from workstations or servers that require the components.

Again, the .NET 3.0 RTC is the necessary managed .NET assemblies that are required at runtime (on users’ workstations or servers) that any application built to leverage .NET 3.0 must find at runtime.

Installing .NET 3.0 RTC

Installing the .NET 3.0 RTC is a straightforward process. Once you have access either to the full installer or to the Smart Installer, just launch and accept the license agreement. You can choose to also send a log of the setup to Microsoft for any post-installation analysis. Microsoft’s plan is to compile the results and then improve the setup experience and correct or provide support for any exceptions or errors.

During the installation, the Setup dialog box will minimize to the taskbar, and the status will appear in taskbar “bubble” dialog boxes. If you want, you can click the taskbar icon and view the installation progress at any time. Minimizing the dialog box just hides the installation dialog box, and the taskbar icon continues with the installation. Figure C-2 illustrates this taskbar icon.

After completing the .NET 3.0 RTC setup, you’ll be notified that it’s done. Click the bubble, and dismiss the dialog box. At this point, the machine has an environment that is ready to run applications based upon the .NET 3.0 managed APIs (WPF, WCF, and WF). Note that the only production requirements for running .NET 3.0 applications are the .NET 2.0 runtime and the .NET 3.0 RTC.

3. It’s WF, not WWF. They couldn’t use WWF because that was taken by the World Wildlife Foundation, which had successfully sued the World Wrestling Foundation, forcing the wrestling folks to change to WWE.

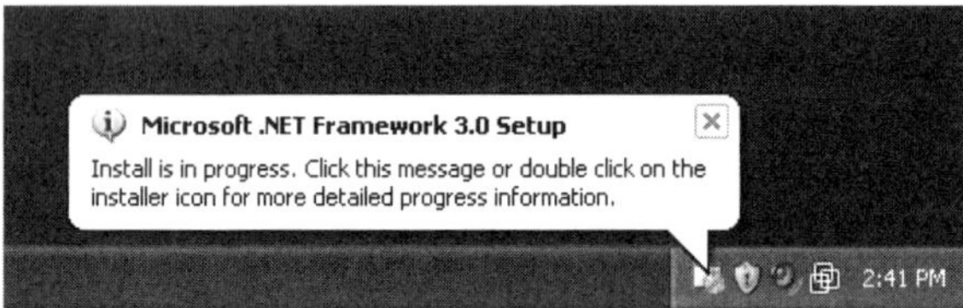

Figure C-2. *.NET 3.0 runtime components setup taskbar status bubble*

Installing Microsoft Windows SDK for Windows Vista

.NET 3.0, WPF, and WCF are considered to be the next-generation managed APIs provided by Microsoft for the Windows operating system. Microsoft has bundled additional tools, utilities, and documentation in the Microsoft Platform SDK package for Windows. With the release of the .NET 3.0 managed APIs, it is now known as the Microsoft Windows SDK.

The Microsoft Windows SDK contains a great set of technology examples that span the Win32 API, covering most aspects of the Windows platform in addition to the new set of .NET 3.0 managed APIs. Tools, samples, and documentation are provided in the Platform SDK, and although not a requirement, they facilitate developers working with .NET 3.0 applications. In addition to the Platform SDK, the debugging tools for Windows, PowerShell,[4] and other tools are installed.

Installing Windows SDK for All Platforms

The Windows SDK is installed either from a CD/DVD, from an ISO image, or from the Windows SDK installation website using the web installation method for Windows XP, Windows 2003, and Windows Vista.

If using an ISO image, you can mount the ISO image using a tool that can create a virtual CD/DVD drive and then follow the same CD/DVD installation steps.[5] The CD/DVD installation steps leverage autorun; or once the CD/DVD or ISO image is mounted (inserted), just double-click `Setup.exe` that is located in the root of the drive.

You can run the web installation method by accessing the web installer located on the Microsoft Downloads site. That location is currently `http://www.microsoft.com/downloads/details.aspx?FamilyId=A55B6B43-E24F-4EA3-A93E-40C0EC4F68E5&displaylang=en`, but it may change in future releases.

4. Check out `http://www.microsoft.com/technet/scriptcenter/hubs/msh.mspx` for good resources on the PowerShell.

5. One of the best tools that many developers leverage is Daemon Tools, located at `http://www.daemon-tools.cc/dtcc/download.php?mode=ViewCategory&catid=5`. Many have stuck with the 3.47 release because the 4.x release of Daemon Tools includes some additional ad-supported software that helps defray the costs for the developer (this is free stuff).

WINDOWS SDK INSTALLATION COMPONENTS

The Windows SDK contains a "chained" installation setup program. What happens during the installation is that the master `Setup.exe` file calls a series of Microsoft installation packages. These packages are present in the `Setup` directory of the image. The current collection of installation packages includes the following:

- Windows SDK
- MSDN Document Explorer
- Windows Debugging Tools
- .NET Compact Framework
- PowerShell, .NET-enabled command shell

It's important to note that the only required package is the Windows SDK, which is required for the tools and utilities that support WCF development. The MSDN Document Explorer is required if you install the associated documentation for the SDK.

During installation, there have been some issues with some of the subpackages failing because of unexpected prior installations (betas, prior releases, and so on). To work around those issues, it is possible to execute the MSI for the Windows SDK directly or for any of the subpackages you require. In fact, during the prolonged CTP and beta releases of WCF and .NET 3.0/WinFx, numerous issues were reported on the installation packages, which should be expected during the beta periods. Most of the issues we've encountered have been dutifully corrected by the SDK team.

After launching the Setup Wizard, you're presented with the welcome screen and licensing agreements. Then after accepting the license agreement, you're presented with the directories to which you want to install. Generally accepting the default directories makes things a bit easier to find when moving from machine to machine. Change it if you're resource starved or want the samples put somewhere else. After that, click through to the option screen, and ensure you select the .NET 3.0 tools or other options you require.

When the option screen is selected, select the suboptions related to the documentation, samples, and tools. The documentation and samples are provided in the .NET 3.0 or Win32 legacy version. For our needs, the .NET 3.0 set is what you require. Ensure that the option to install the tools for .NET 3.0 is selected.

Again, these parts are not required for WCF development. The SDK components provide helpful development tools, documentation, and samples that facilitate the development of WCF and .NET 3.0, as well as Win32-based applications.

Once the options are selected, click Next to proceed with the installation. During the installation, the Setup Wizard will provide feedback about what parts are being installed.

At the completion of the installation, if there were no errors, the Installation Complete screen will appear. If any installation errors occur, the left panel displays the specific failure information. At that point, it is possible to bypass some parts of the installation by running the subparts of the SDK directly. That is unless that part was the failing item. Please see the sidebar "Windows SDK Installation Components" for more information.

Installing .NET Framework 3.0 Development Tools

The .NET Framework 3.0 Development Tools provide the necessary template and add-in support for creating and managing projects that target the .NET 3.0 managed API extensions. These are supported only with Visual Studio 2005.

The installation is again straightforward with few options available. Launch the installer package, which you obtain directly from Microsoft. If you've installed the Visual Studio documentation, you'll jump right into the installation process.

After clicking through the welcome screen, you're prompted for the obligatory licensing agreement. Choose to accept or exit the installation; if you exit now, then you won't have project and add-in support inside Visual Studio 2005.

If you've decided not to install the Visual Studio 2005 documentation, you'll be presented with a message box or two indicating such, as shown in Figure C-3.

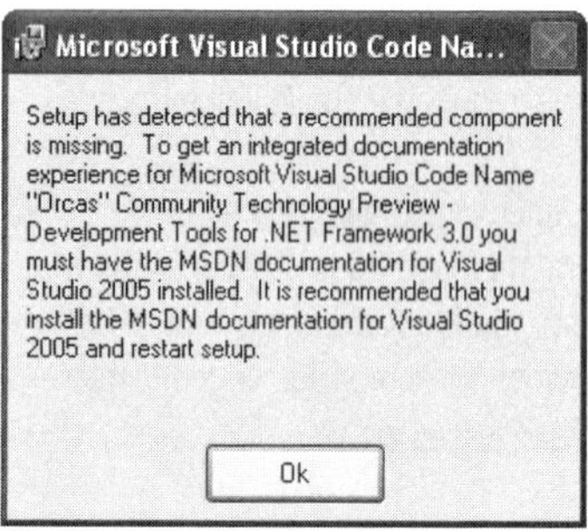

Figure C-3. *.NET 3.0 Visual Studio extensions warning of no documentation*

Regardless of whether the documentation is missing, you can still develop .NET 3.0 applications; you just lose the support of the integrated documentation within Visual Studio (or, more precisely, the MSDN local documentation).

During the installation, if you've installed the documentation, the MSDN collection merge will take place. That process can be time-consuming and depends upon the resources available on your machine (CPU, RAM, and so on).

Once the installation completes, you should verify whether the installation is complete. First, launch Visual Studio (Start ➤ All Programs ➤ Microsoft Visual Studio 2005 ➤ Microsoft Visual Studio 2005). Start a new project (File ➤ New ➤ Project), and confirm the existence of the .NET 3.0 templates. Figure C-4 shows the templates for C# and Windows (.NET 3.0).

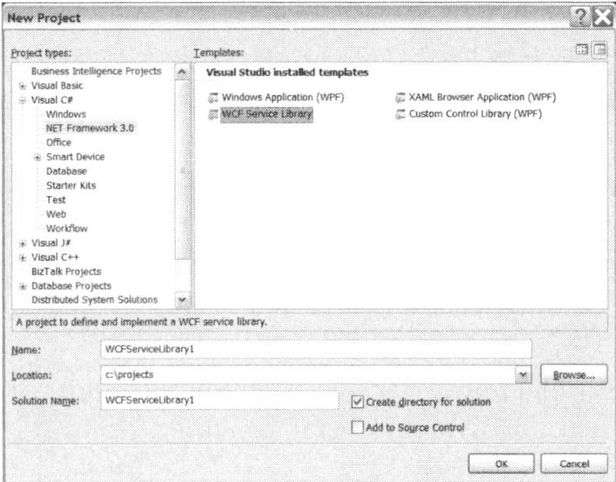

Figure C-4. *.NET 3.0 templates in Visual Studio*

In Figure C-4, the template WCF service library is a WCF template for creating a class library based upon WCF. The other templates are all related to WPF.

The next template to check is the website WCF service project templates. Start the new Web Site dialog box by choosing File ➤ New Web Site. If you see the project type WCF Service under Visual Studio Installed Templates, you have a good .NET 3.0 installation.

You use the WCF Service template to create the base "site" for an ASP.NET-hosted WCF service. The Location option at the bottom of the dialog box (File System ➤ HTTP ➤ FTP) determines how the development project is generated. If you're choosing File System, Visual Studio will leverage the Visual Studio development web server for your development and debugging needs. This is a great feature if you're limited to one installation of IIS on your machine.[6]

Making Windows Firewall Changes

All versions of Windows since Windows XP SP2 provide a built-in firewall. Additionally, depending upon your installation, you may have your own firewall software provided by a third party such as BlackICE or Symantec.

The following sections walk you through how to modify the Windows Firewall so you can host services or duplex clients on the machine being configured. This modification is required for IIS to listen on the network for external clients requesting services. If you'll be using only the ASP.NET development server as part of Visual Studio and not allowing external clients to access your services, you don't need to make firewall changes.

6. We've consulted for several clients that had hard restrictions on not installing IIS on workstations; getting IIS installed required significant effort and communication with the appropriate technology support groups to finally, begrudgingly, get it installed. This will reap major benefits in the future.

■ **Note** If you will be developing 100 percent on a local machine and not providing access to services' or clients' hosting services on your machine, you can skip modifying the Windows Firewall settings. Windows allows any localhost requests without going through the firewall.

Firewall Primer

Firewalls provide administrative control over Internet Protocol (IP)–level communications amongst network-connected computers. That communication is leveraging either Transmission Control Protocol (TCP) or User Datagram Protocol (UDP).

Firewall software (or hardware) provides a way to manage the IP ports and type of traffic (TCP/UDP) that is permitted to pass through these ports. Entry-level firewalls, such as the one provided with Windows, provide nonstateful packet inspection. To put it simply, they can provide either blocked or unblocked access from network-based computers, based upon their source address or network (scope setting) to the machine that is being configured.

Stateful packet inspection firewalls provide for tracking of packets amongst network machines over time (that's the state) and dives beyond the IP header into the application layer of the "conversation." This allows for greater rule-based restrictions and security. However, with that stateful inspection, there's significant overhead in the processing power required to manage the state and in providing the same or similar latency times that come with nonstateful firewalls.

Given the processing overhead associated with firewall software, if performance is a key requirement, you need to consider the impact a firewall (and the type of firewall) will have on the overall application architecture.

WCF Requirements

WCF is all about communication. Communication can occur between programs on the same system or different systems. However, it is generally between two or more network-based computers that are either present on the same LAN (same subnet) or located across a WAN or the Internet.

Depending upon the protocol and transport choices (the binding part of the ABCs of WCF), you'll need to think through, and perhaps diagnose, issues related to firewall restrictions. These firewalls may be Windows based, or they could be network appliances, such as Check Point or Pix from CISCO. Regardless, you need to be aware of the base-level network and port requirements of the binding choices that are made at deployment time in order to communicate with the network support groups so they can administer the changes necessary in the network topology to support your distributed WCF-based applications.

For our needs here, we'll focus on the built-in firewall that comes with Windows XP SP2 and later versions of Windows.

IIS Hosting and Activation

The Web has a default protocol, Hypertext Transport Protocol (HTTP), that runs on IP port 80 using TCP as the transport and session layer protocol.[7] That's the "default" port if not overridden in requests. IIS by default listens on port 80 for non-SSL traffic.

So, if you choose to host your WCF Services inside IIS, you need to ensure that port 80 is open as required in the firewall. You simply do that by accessing the Windows Firewall settings. To access the Windows Firewall configuration wizard, access it through the Control Panel (Start ➤ Control Panel ➤ Windows Firewall). At that point, you'll see the Windows Firewall configuration. Ensure that the firewall is set to Off (not recommended unless troubleshooting) or, if set to On, that the Don't Allow Exceptions option is not checked.

If the Don't Allow Exceptions option is enabled, the firewall restrictions are absolute. The policy for the Windows Firewall in this scenario is to not allow *any* unsolicited inbound requests to any services hosted on this machine. So, for our needs, if you require any requests from off the machine to access services listening on this machine, you need to modify the Exception list.

One quick but not recommended way is to completely turn off exceptions. We recommend that option only when troubleshooting issues related to network communication failures and to confirm it's the Windows Firewall that is the issue. The recommended approach is to disable the setting Don't Allow Exceptions and edit the Programs and Services list.

Now, with the Windows Firewall permitting exceptions, you can add the necessary ports to the Exception list. Next, click the Exceptions tab at the top of the Windows Firewall configuration wizard. Then click the Add Port button.

We don't use Add Program because that is designed for use only with client-type applications and not servers. Since we'll be opening ports required for IIS, we just want to open the default port 80. So, after clicking Add Port, enter the details as shown in Figure C-5.

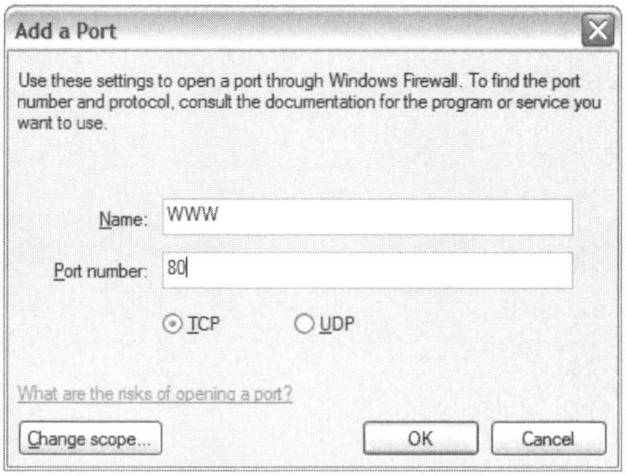

Figure C-5. *Adding port 80 rule*

7. For more information about the seven layers of the OSI model, see `http://en.wikipedia.org/wiki/OSI_model`.

The Name field is an arbitrary value that allows you to easily identify the rule name in the Exception list. We've chosen WWW for World Wide Web. The port number is the critical value. Since IIS uses port 80 over TCP as its default, we've used 80 and ensured TCP is selected as the type of protocol. For now, you don't need to modify the scope of the request because the rule we've just entered will allow any computer to access port 80, which IIS is listening on.

You're now ready to host a WCF service inside IIS. Again, if you're developing locally using only either IIS or the ASP.NET development server that comes with Visual Studio, you can skip the Windows Firewall configuration changes. We want to stress the base comprehension needed for understanding how the network, specifically IP, works for troubleshooting and configuring WCF solutions.

Summary

This appendix detailed the installation process for WCF components and infrastructure. You investigated initially how to install IIS. Then you went through the installation process of Visual Studio 2005. (We used Visual Studio 2005 as our IDE for WCF applications.) Then you investigated the installation process for .NET 3.0 and Windows SDK to create an environment to execute WCF-compliant code.

Index

B

C

Q

eBookshop

ASP Today

Apress®
THE EXPERT'S VOICE™